Jewish Culture and Identity in the Soviet Union

Jewish Culture and Identity in the Soviet Union

Edited by Yaacov Ro'i
and Avi Beker

New York University Press
New York and London

Copyright © 1991 by New York University
All rights reserved

Library of Congress Cataloging-in-Publication Data
Jewish culture and identity in the Soviet Union / edited by Yaacov
  Ro'i and Avi Beker.
    p.   cm.
  Includes a portion of the papers presented at a conference held at
Bar Ilan Univ., Ramat Gan, Dec. 1986 on the occasion of the 10th
anniversary of the Moscow Cultural Symposium on Jewish Activists.
  Includes bibliographical references.
  ISBN 978-0-8147-7432-8
  1. Jews—Soviet Union—History—1917- 2. Jews—Soviet Union—
Intellectual life. 3. Jews—Soviet Union—Identity. 4. Soviet
Union—Ethnic relations. I. Ro'i, Yaacov. II. Beker, Avi.
DS135.R92J463 1990
947'.004924—dc20   90-5483
                       CIP

New York University Press books are printed on acid-free paper,
and their binding materials are chosen for strength and durability.

Contents

Preface ix

Foreword *Martin Gilbert* xiii

Introduction *Edgar M. Bronfman* xvii

Contributors xix

I. The Historical Perspective

1. The Evolution of Jewish Culture and Identity in the Soviet Union *Zvi Gitelman* 3

II. The Revival of Jewish Identity

2. The Jewish National Movement in the Soviet Union: A Profile *Yossi Goldstein* 27

3. The Impact of Ideological Changes in the USSR on Different Generations of the Soviet Jewish Intelligentsia *Ludmilla Tsigelman* 42

4. Jewish Samizdat at the End of the Forties: Fragments from Margarita Aliger's Poem *Your Victory* *Isai Averbukh* 73

5. Jewish Samizdat and the Rise of Jewish National Consciousness *Stefani Hoffman* 88

6. The Role of the Synagogue and Religion in the Jewish National Awakening *Yaacov Ro'i* 112

7. The Struggle for the Study of Hebrew *Vera Yedidya* 136

8. Nehama Lifshitz: Symbol of the Jewish National Awakening
   Yaacov Ro'i   168

III. Jewish Themes and Motives in Officially Published Literature

9. Twenty-five Years of *Sovetish heymland:* Impressions and Criticism
   Chone Shmeruk   191

10. The Role of Officially Published Russian Literature in the Reawakening of Jewish National Consciousness (1953–1970)
    Shimon Markish   208

IV. Personal Testimonies

11. Background to the Present Jewish Cultural Movement in the Soviet Union   *Benjamin Fain*   235

12. A Brief Survey of the History of Hebrew Teaching in the USSR
    Mark Drachinsky   246

13. Jewish Samizdat   *Alexander Voronel*   255

14. The Moscow Symposium: Ten Years Later   *Eliahu Essas*   262

15. Soviet Jewish Culture Today: A Personal Israeli Account
    Erez Biton   266

V. Regime Policy

16. Jewish Culture in the USSR Today
    Lukasz Hirszowicz   273

17. Soviet Government Policy Toward the Exterritorial National Minorities: Comparison Between the Jews and the Germans
    Benjamin Pinkus   290

18. The Soviet Regime and Anti-Zionism: An Analysis
    Jonathan Frankel   310

19. The Right to Jewish Culture in the Soviet Union
    Stephen J. Roth   355

20. Notes on the Culture of the Non-Ashkenazi Jewish Communities Under Soviet Rule   *Michael Zand*   378

21. Superpower Relations and Jewish Identity in the Soviet Union   *Avi Beker*   445

Index   463

Preface

It was only after the submission of this entire compilation of essays and testimonies to the publisher that *perestroika* and *glasnost* entered effectively into the realm of Jewish life and culture in the Soviet Union. Unfortunately, it has not been feasible to incorporate these changes in the text of this volume. We feel and hope, however, that they have in no way impaired its findings and significance, although some of the statements made in one or two of the chapters may no longer be relevant.

In 1989 and more so in early 1990, we have witnessed revolutionary changes on both major fronts of Soviet Jewish rights: *aliya* and cultural activities. In 1989, 71,509 Jews emigrated from the Soviet Union (the highest number ever), and 11,994 of them settled in Israel (the largest number who have gone there since 1979). The trend of *aliya* in 1990 continues to be upward particularly because of American restrictions on immigration and the growing fears of anti-Semitism in the Soviet Union. This time the revival of Judaism in the Soviet Union is overshadowed by an unprecedented, panic-driven emigration-*aliya* movement at a rate of about 6,000 a month (in the first three months of 1990). There are already well over half a million persons who have registered for emigration with the Israeli consular mission in Moscow. Soviet officials have publicly rejected Arab pressure against *aliya*, stating that they will not renege on the principle of freedom of emigration.

The most powerful driving force motivating emigration amongst Soviet Jews is their collective and virtually universal perception that there is a massive resurgence of popular anti-Semitism. Though the government-sponsored media are actively condemning anti-Semitism, as are many liberal politicians and intellectuals, many Jews are frightened and wish to leave before things get worse. In a country where anti-Semitism is endemic, and where, until recently, it was orchestrated by state-sponsored organs, it is understandable why so many Jews fear that if Gorbachev is overthrown, the Soviet Union could revert to the days of the "Black Hundreds" and pogroms. Lacking any tradition of self-defence, Soviet Jews are particularly apprehensive of popular, "street" anti-Semitism and violent anti-Jewish pogroms in the event of a total collapse of the social order. It is characteristic that those who are leaving the Soviet Union today are mostly assimilated Jews without any experience of Jewish activism or a Jewish cultural background.

While the State of Israel will have to invest huge amounts of human and financial resources in order to absorb this *aliya,* there must be a parallel effort to strengthen Jewish life within the Soviet Union. The most dramatic development in this field was the first Congress of Jewish Communities and Organizations in the Soviet Union, which took place in Moscow in December 1989. Eight hundred participants, including one hundred Jewish and Israeli observers from overseas, attended the five-day conference at the Moscow Cinema Center. The delegates represented 204 Jewish organizations from seventy-seven cities from the Western Ukraine to the Far East, from Siberia to Transcaucasia. This first nationwide Jewish congress since 1918, created the Va'ad (committee)—the Confederation of Jewish Communities and Organizations in the USSR.

At the beginning of 1989 the Jewish cultural movement was still in its embryonic stage and basically unorganized. By the end of 1989 thousands of Jews all over the Soviet Union were flocking to Hebrew courses and Jewish cultural functions. Adults are enrolling together with their children, in Jewish educational frameworks primarily with a view to making *aliya.* Now in early 1990 about three hundred Jewish cultural and community groups are functioning in the Soviet Union. The authorities do not interfere with their activities although official recognition has not been granted to most of them. Several Jewish periodicals are being published in Moscow, Leningrad, and other cities. One interesting phenomenon is that this resurrection of Jewish life in the USSR is chaotic, competitive, and fragmented, representing diverse attempts to establish counterparts to almost every trend and religious and political view in the Jewish world. After so many years of Soviet-Communist education, young Jews can suddenly become consciously Jewish and even Zionist.

Aliya and Jewish culture are not necessarily mutually contradictory, as is sometimes thought. The two processes can move forward simultaneously and nourish each other, particularly when Jews are faced with the rise of anti-Semitism. The maintenance of various forms of Jewish life are crucial not only for the preservation of Jewish identity but also to help provide Jews with the ideological backbone to withstand anti-Semitism.

The chapters in this volume are in part the result of a research project undertaken by the Center for Research and Documentation on East European Jewry at the Hebrew University, Jerusalem, and in part papers presented at a conference on Soviet Jewish Culture and Identity held at Bar-Ilan University, Ramat Gan, in December 1986 on the occasion of the tenth anniversary of the Moscow Cultural Symposium of Jewish Activists.

The editors wish to express their thanks both to the center and to those organizations under whose auspices the conference took place: the World Jewish Congress, the Public Council for Soviet Jewry, and Bar-Ilan University.

The personal testimonies we have included have, on the whole, been left as they were presented at the Bar-Ilan conference. It is hoped that they will provide a more personal touch, which, if not representative of all the trends among Soviet Jewish activists, will give some idea of the wealth and variety of Jewish cultural activity in the Soviet Union in the 1970s and early 1980s. At the same time, the reader should bear in mind that despite the wide range of cultural activity described in this volume, the sum total of the Jewish cultural activity of the Soviet Jewish population in the post–World War II period has been minimal. Nonetheless, as this volume aims to show, Jews did succeed in maintaining a certain level of Jewish identity under the oppressive and discriminatory conditions of the pre-*perestroika* era.

At the time of writing it seems that the opportunities for Jewish cultural activity inside the Soviet Union are almost unbounded. And this is of critical importance even as the gates of emigration open. Without knowledge and appreciation of their tradition and culture Soviet Jews will continue seeking to assimilate, whether inside the Soviet Union or in the West. Even assuming that between half a million and a million Jews leave—large numbers—probably the majority of Soviet Jews will remain, at least for the near future. For those who remain there is a desperate need to revitalize Jewish life, in both its religious and cultural forms as widely, and as deeply, as possible.

Yaacov Ro'i
Avi Beker

Foreword
Martin Gilbert

The history of the Jews of the Soviet Union during the seven decades that followed the Bolshevik Revolution of 1917 has not been one that was conducive in any way to the flourishing, or even to the survival, of Jewish culture. In the very cities, towns, and regions which before 1917 had seen a flourishing of Jewish culture in all its aspects, the years following the Revolution brought severe repression. The widespread closing of synagogues and Jewish communal institutions made the public maintenance of Jewishness almost impossible, and even its practice extremely difficult. The proliferation of Jewish cultural, literary, and educational establishments, which had been so marked a feature of the prerevolutionary years, was destroyed within a decade. The Jewish newspapers, which had wide circulations in Yiddish, Russian, and Hebrew, ceased to exist. Even the Jewish theatrical tradition, which had reached a high point in czarist Russia, was brought to an end.

In the four decades that followed the Bolshevik Revolution of 1917, persecution went parallel with suppression. The murder of the great actor and director of the Moscow Yiddish State Theater, Solomon Mikhoels, in Minsk in 1948 was the tip of a cruel iceberg. By the time of the Jewish national revival of the 1960s, those who turned to their Jewish roots, to the Hebrew language, and to the inspiration of Jewish history had to do so with almost no guidance, no literature, no libraries, no institutions, and above all, in the teeth of severe official disapproval. How far off, today, seems the labor camp sentence on the twenty-three-year-old Jewish nurse, Ruth Aleksandrovich from Riga, charged with distributing six copies of a small,

Martin Gilbert's most recent book is *The Second World War*.

privately prepared brochure "For the Return of Soviet Jews to their Homeland," and fifteen copies of a second brochure, "Your Native Tongue," on the Hebrew language. Ruth Aleksandrovich told the court that she had advocated the learning of Hebrew in order to fill the gap created by the lack of Jewish schools in the Soviet Union.

Secretly prepared and clandestinely circulated brochures and tapes were symptomatic not only of the creation of Hebrew teaching circles, but also of the powerful impetus to emigration to Israel which was to lead in the decade beginning in 1970 to the arrival in Israel of more than 160,000 Soviet Jews. In fact, the rate of emigration soon far exceeded the numbers of those who had any contact with the Jewish cultural and linguistic renaissance. It is an irony of the situation that those relatively few Jewish activists who were refused their exit visas during that decade became the central figures in the teaching and promoting of Jewish values. It was through such circles as those of Ilya Essas and the brothers Aleksandr and Michael Kholmianskii, of Mark Niepomnashchii of Odessa, of Leonid Kelbert, the producer of Jewish plays in Leningrad, and of Hebrew teachers such as Gennadii Feldman in Minsk, that the spreading of Jewish culture became an integral part of the Jewish national and thus emigration movement; with these efforts came harassment, arrest, and imprisonment. Thus it was that Yosef Begun served three separate terms. It was perhaps more through this persecution than any other single factor that Western Jewry and the Israeli public became aware of the scale of the struggle and of the need to support it.

All those mentioned in the above paragraph now live in Israel. Jewish cultural activity has therefore been a victim of the very forces which served to liberate several hundreds of thousands of Soviet Jews. Even as I write these words, the pioneer Jewish historical urban geographer, Michael Beizer, trapped for many years in Leningrad, is now an advanced student at the Hebrew University, while Daniel Romanovskii, who collected important testimonies regarding the Holocaust in the region of Vitebsk while struggling to obtain his exit visa, is now in Jerusalem preparing a catalog of his testimonies under the auspices of Yad Vashem. We have now, therefore, to devise the means of continuing and indeed enhancing the work done by these refusenik pioneers in helping to raise Jewish consciousness throughout the Soviet Union.

These words were written nearly two years ago. Now, with the gates of emigration so suddenly and so widely opened, the need for Jewish cultural activity inside the Soviet Union is all the greater, and its possibilities—as of the opening months of 1990—considerable.

The fact that so many hundreds of Jews can now contemplate leaving, makes it imperative that they should know as much as possible of their heritage and their history. To leave is good; to leave as Jews is even better; and to leave for Israel is best of all.

Without knowledge, however, the attraction of the Jewish state is even less than the attraction of a Jewish life. Each must be cultivated by the efforts of Western Jews in spreading the message of Judaism in both its religious and secular aspects as widely, and as deeply, as possible, while time remains.

Introduction
Edgar M. Bronfman

What has happened in the Soviet Union in the brief span of time since Gorbachev's ascension is remarkable. General Secretary Gorbachev has prescribed profound changes in the Soviet Union's behavior as a nation both internally and internationally and this change calls for an energetic and imaginative Western response. The West has rightfully called for evidence of a real change and true movement. We should encourage further progress now through serious, sustained, and detailed engagement. Mr. Gorbachev's reform efforts face serious problems. The Soviet public wants improved economic conditions as proof that *perestroika* works. Yet the bureaucracy, both military and civilian, is replete with skepticism and even hostility. What Gorbachev is trying to do—as Nikita Khrushchev did thirty years ago—is to reach out to the people over the heads of the bureaucracy. The West's approach should be on two levels:

First, on the practical level, Western businesses, investors, foundations, and financial institutions, working with their governments, should broaden contacts with their Soviet counterparts to show that we are ready to welcome them into the modern economic reality and discuss with them in practical ways what is involved and what needs to be done to implement this.

Second, there is the political level. The U.S. government and other governments should respond to Gorbachev's endeavors to turn his back on seventy years of Soviet history and economic theory. His rejection of the idea that the Soviet Union can prosper without the rest of the world

Edgar M. Bronfman is president of the World Jewish Congress.

deserves a serious, respectful political response. It is in the United States's interest to prevent even a partial reversal of *perestroika*.

World Jewry has to think about how to acknowledge the significant changes that have affected Soviet Jewish life. We must acknowledge the positive response to our demands that have been made by the Soviet authorities under the leadership of Mikhail Gorbachev. There has been a sharp and continuing rise in the numbers of Jews permitted to emigrate, the backlog of long-time refuseniks has been largely eliminated, the Prisoners of Zion have all been freed, and more objective criteria have been laid down to define state secrets, the knowledge of which may still delay emigration.

Equally important are the new opportunities to practice the Jewish faith and study Jewish culture that the Soviet regime has recently made possible. The law against teaching Hebrew is no longer being enforced, and Jewish religious instruction and cultural expression are now being permitted de facto. This new development offers a great window of opportunity that Jews in the Diaspora and in Israel must take advantage of now, for no one can tell how long the window will remain open.

No matter how wide the gates open, large numbers of Jews in the Soviet Union are likely to remain there. If we do not want to lose them as Jews, we must teach them to be Jews. And if we want to create in them the desire to emigrate to Israel, they must have an understanding and appreciation of the meaning of Israel in the history of the Jewish people.

To carry out this task, Jews in the West must establish direct contact with the Jews of the Soviet Union. We must send rabbis and teachers to the Soviet Union from everywhere in the Diaspora and from Israel. We must send books and other Jewish educational materials. We must have "twin" Jewish communities in the West and Israel with communities in the Soviet Union.

This volume reviews the history of the struggle of Soviet Jewry to remain Jewish despite three generations of cultural and religious famine. Today the Jewish world has an opportunity that is rare in the history of our people—to create from a population estimated at two million or more, that has been without meaningful contact with Judaism for most of the past seventy years, a new Jewish community that understands and appreciates its heritage.

Contributors

Isai Averbukh was born in the USSR in 1943. He received his master's degree in world history and literature from the University of Odessa and has published poetry and articles in Russian and Hebrew. He was an active Zionist in the USSR and was involved in the underground distribution of Jewish literature there. He immigrated to Israel in 1971, and today he is involved in research on Soviet Jewry.

Avi Beker received his doctorate in political science from the Graduate Center of the City University of New York. He currently teaches at Bar-Ilan University and is the executive director of the World Jewish Congress in Israel. He was a member of the Israeli delegation to the United Nations from 1977 to 1982 and has published articles on international security and organization, disarmament, and Israel's foreign policy. He is the author of two books: *Disarmament without Order: The Politics of Disarmament at the United Nations* (1985) and *The United Nations and Israel: From Recognition to Reprehension* (1988).

Erez Biton was born in Oran, Algeria, in 1942 and immigrated to Israel in 1948. He is a social worker, psychologist, poet, and editor of the literary magazine *Apirion*.

Mark Drachinsky was born in Tbilisi, Georgia, in the Soviet Union and formerly taught Hebrew clandestinely in Moscow. In 1985, he immigrated to Israel and currently lives in Jerusalem. Mr. Drachinsky is a poet.

Eliahu Essas was born in Vilnius, USSR, in 1946. He received his M.A. in mathematics and began his Ph.D. studies in the Soviet Academy of

Sciences. He was a refusenik, denied exit visas from the USSR, for thirteen years. During that period he taught Hebrew and was instrumental in Jewish religious revival. He went to Israel in 1986.

Benjamin Fain was born in Kiev and studied physics at the Gorky University. He has published many articles and is the author of four books. He is considered one of the leading figures in the awakening of Jewish culture in the Soviet Union. He was one of the founders of the Movement for Jewish Culture. He immigrated to Israel in 1977 and now works in the Physics Department of Tel Aviv University.

Jonathan Frankel is Professor of history at the Hebrew University in Jerusalem in the Department of Russian Studies and at the Institute of Contemporary Jewry. He is the author of *Prophecy and Politics: Socialism, Nationalism, and the Russian Jews, 1862–1917* and is coeditor of *Studies of Contemporary Jewry: An Annual.*

Zvi Gitelman is Professor of Political Science at the University of Michigan. He is the author or coauthor of five books, the most recent of which is entitled A *Century of Ambivalence: The Jews of Russia and the Soviet Union, 1881 to the Present.*

Yossi Goldstein is Senior Lecturer in the Department of Jewish History, Haifa University and the Open University. He is the author of many articles and has written a book on the Zionist movement in Russia. He has now also completed a biography of Ehad Haam.

Lukasz Hirszowicz has held academic posts in Poland and England. He currently is head of the Soviet and East European Department in the Institute of Jewish Affairs in London and is the editor of *Soviet Jewish Affairs.* He is the author of *The Third Reich and the Arab East* and several articles on problems of Polish and Soviet Jewry.

Stefani Hoffman is the editor of *The Soviet Union and the Middle East,* a monthly publication of the Mayrock Center for Soviet Research of the Hebrew University. She has translated several books about Soviet Jewry.

Shimon Markish was born in Baku, the USSR, in 1931. He graduated from Moscow University in 1954 and immigrated to Switzerland via Hungary. He is Senior Lecturer in the Department of Humanities at the University of Geneva. He is an expert on Russian Jewish culture and has written two books: *Erasmus Jews* (1978) and *Le cas Grossman* (1983).

Benjamin Pinkus is Professor of History, Ben Gurion University. He was born in Warsaw in 1933 and immigrated to Israel in 1950. He received his master's degree from the Hebrew University and his doctorate from the University of Paris. He has published many books, his most recent entitled *The Jews of the Soviet Union: A History of a National Minority*.

Yaacov Ro'i is Associate Professor of Russian History at Tel Aviv University. Among his books are *Soviet Decision Making in Practice: The USSR and Israel, 1947–1954* and *The USSR and the Muslim World*. He has also written many articles on Soviet Middle Eastern policy, especially regarding Soviet-Israeli relations and Soviet policy on nationalities.

Stephen J. Roth is Director of the Institute of Jewish Affairs in London and Chairman of the Zionist Federation in Great Britain. An international lawyer specializing in legal issues affecting Soviet Jewry, Dr. Roth is also Chairman of the Helsinki Monitoring Committee of the International Council for Soviet Jewry.

Chone Shmeruk is Professor of Yiddish literature at the Hebrew University in Jerusalem. He has written extensively on Soviet Yiddish literature and edited a book entitled *A Shpigl oyf a Shteyn*, published in 1964 and reissued in 1987 in Jerusalem.

Ludmilla Tsigelman was born in Kiev. She acquired her Ph.D. in philosophy and worked in the Department of Philosophy at the University of Kiev and at the Institute for Scientific Information. She is now a researcher at the Center for the Study and Documentation of East European Jewry, at the Hebrew University, Jerusalem.

Alexander Voronel was born in September 1931 in Leningrad and is a physicist and a writer. He was the founder of a samizdat magazine entitled

Jews in the USSR, which was published in Moscow between 1972 and 1980 and explored the history, culture, and current situation of the Jews in the USSR.

Vera Yedidya was born in the USSR. She studied journalism at the University of Lvov. In 1972, she went to Israel and continued her studies at the Hebrew University and was a research assistant at the Department of Contemporary Jewry.

Michael Zand is Professor of Persian and Tadzhik literature at the Hebrew University of Jerusalem. He is the author of about 230 publications in various fields of Iranian philology, Judeo-Iranian studies, and studies of non-Ashkenazi Jewish communities of the Soviet Union.

I
THE HISTORICAL PERSPECTIVE

1
The Evolution of Jewish Culture and Identity in the Soviet Union
Zvi Gitelman

The symbiotic relationship between national culture and identity is obvious: a national culture cannot develop or even exist if there are very few people who identify with it and are prepared to live their lives within it. Yet, national identity, while not completely dependent on the existence and vitality of a national culture, is likely to be reduced to minimal and passive form in the absence of a national culture. For this reason, it was assumed by many both inside and outside the Soviet Union that the decline of an active, visible Jewish culture would inevitably lead to a weakening of both individual and group Jewish identity. Indeed, this has happened at various times during the nearly seven decades of the Soviet period, but there have been unexpected reversals of this tendency, making for distinctly nonlinear trends in both Jewish culture and Jewish identity. To some extent, these result from the twists and turns in Soviet policy. But to an equal extent, they are the consequence of Jewish reactions, not only to changes in official policy, but to changing conditions within and without the USSR and shifts in Jewish self-perceptions. Western social scientists and Marxist theoreticians shared an assumption, at least until the 1960s, that the dominant trend in developing and developed societies would be toward ethnic assimilation ("the merger of nations" in Marxist terms). To the delight of some, the consternation of others, and the surprise of many, ethnic consciousness and ethnic tensions survive in developed countries as different in their political and economic systems as the United States and the USSR, Canada and Yugoslavia, Belgium and Czechoslovakia, to cite but a few examples. Neither planned social engineering in the socialist states, nor the massive social changes flowing from economic development in the capitalist ones, have consigned ethnic identity and assertiveness to the garbage heap of history. Some Western analysts now view ethnicity not simply as an individual attribute, but as a potent resource that can be mobilized even in the most developed society to obtain important political, economic, and social goals.[1] Soviet leaders, including Leonid Brezhnev, have admitted that while "the unity of Soviet nations is now closer than ever, this does not mean, of course, that all questions of nationality relations have been solved."[2] The 1986 Party Program admits that "the complete unity of nations" in the USSR is a matter for the "remote historical future."[3] Soviet scholars are far more explicit than politicians in admitting that nationality integration "occurs slowly" and "proceeds at a different pace among different peoples," influenced "in considerable measure by subjective factors, although fundamentally it is unquestionably an objective factor."[4] One of the pioneers of empirical research on Soviet nationalities, L. M. Drobizheva, asserts that "the growth of national self-awareness among the people of the USSR is an objective, lawful process."[5]

Initial expectations of rapid integration and assimilation have been confounded because many held overly deterministic views of the consequences of economic development. The erroneous assumption was made that similar economic substructures produce similar social consequences. The subjective element even in "modern" people was underestimated, and the erroneous assumption was made that trends which seem to appear at the beginning of a historical epoch can be projected in linear fashion to its conclusion. Undoubtedly, the degree and nature of national self-consciousness and its survival vary widely among ethnic groups. Therefore, any analysis of Jewish identity and culture must address the specific conditions of that group, so different from most Soviet nationalities. The latter usually have their own territory which also includes the symbols of national sovereignty, and a full complement of institutions operating in their own language, whereas the Jews have none of these.

In analyzing culture and identity, it is useful, especially in the case of the Jews, to distinguish between two types of culture and two types of identity, the two sets paralleling each other. One can distinguish between active and passive culture, on the one hand, and between active and passive identity, on the other. Active culture involves the creation and consumption of cultural artifacts—publications, belles lettres, fine arts, scholarship, cinema, distinctive clothing, foods, the celebration of holidays with attendant symbols—and social interaction designed around cultural artifacts and interests. Passive culture encompasses patterns of thought and behavior which are not necessarily consciously ethnic, nor are they immediately perceived as such by others. But those patterns are derived from or are typical of the ethnic group. Thus, the most visible social characteristics of a group may come to define it as a distinct ethnic group, even though it may look more like a social one.

Similarly, active ethnic identity implies a positive, conscious affirmation of the identity and seeing it as desirable, something to be proud of and to show to others. This can take the form of publicly practicing the religion associated with the ethnic group, in those cases where there is a strong congruence between ethnicity and religion (Jews, Central Asian Muslims, Lithuanian Catholics, Georgians and Armenians, just to cite Soviet examples); or of speaking the ethnic language in public, reading and writing in that language; wearing certain clothes; attending cultural events; choosing schools on the basis of ethnicity and language, and the like. Passive identity is something which is accepted as a fact of life, and the affect toward it can be neutrality, ambivalence, or even hostility. Passive identity is conferred by genetics, history, accident of birth or, in the Soviet case, by the state itself requiring the nominal ethnic identification of all its citizens. State-imposed ethnic identification is probably the most important factor in creating a situation of almost total acculturation with nearly no assimilation among Soviet Jews. That is, almost all Soviet Jews have adopted, to a considerable extent, a culture which was not originally their own—in most cases, Russian, Georgian, or Tadzhik/Uzbek—but very few Jews who are not the offspring of interethnic marriages are assimilated, that is, have exchanged their original ethnic identity for another. Whatever they may desire, and however they may regard themselves, Jews who are identified as such on their internal passports are reminded on the many occasions upon which they have to produce them that in the eyes of the state, and, effectively, in the eyes of society as well, they are considered Jews. Thus, while the Soviet system has largely discouraged active Jewish identification, it remains paradoxically insistent on maintaining passive Jewish identity. That identity is reinforced by the anti-Semitism which permeates certain sectors of Soviet society.

The logical question, which has been asked many times, is, if the aim of the system is truly the amalgamation (*sliianie*) of the nationalities, why insist on the maintenance of at least passive identity through the internal passport system? Few doubt that Jews and many others, especially extraterritorial, or ex-territorial, minorities, would welcome the chance to change their official identities. Especially in view of a declining Slavic birth rate compared to that of the Central Asians, such opportunities could only increase the proportion of Slavs by increasing the number of people identifying themselves as Russian, and it would hasten the consolidation of many ethnic groups, a process already observable in the Caucasus, Karelia, the Volga region, and Siberia. I have not seen a satisfactory explanation for the maintenance of the current system in Soviet sources, except for the vague assertions that the current era is characterized by *sblizhenie* (drawing closer or rapprochement) of nations, and not their fusion or amalgamation *(sliianie)*. Perhaps the answer may lie in Leninist political culture. Control has always been a key value in that culture, going back to prerevolutionary days when Lenin parted ways with the Mensheviks over the issue of whether a smaller, more centralized, and hence controllable, party was to be preferred to a larger, but looser, one. When confronted with the choice between achieving genuine support for the system at the price of relaxing monopolistic control, as in reformist Czechoslovakia in 1968 or Poland in 1979–80, Soviet politicians chose control and coerced obedience over support and spontaneous backing.

Abolishing the identity requirement on the passports would diminish state control and permit spontaneous changing of ethnic identity. On a practical level, the absence of state-controlled ethnic identification would mean that some aspects of nationality policy would have to be abandoned. For example, at the present time, there is a kind of quota system which assigns "local cadres" preeminence in the non-Russian republics in Party and state posts, in admission to higher education, and in upper echelons of industry and agriculture. At the same time, the tremendous number of personnel changes made under Gorbachev have revealed quite clearly that the central government and Party will continue to be dominated by Slavs, and in particular by Russians, and perhaps to a greater extent than in any previous administration. Gorbachev has replaced more than half of the approximately eighty-five ministers in the central government. Not a single new appointee is a Central Asian or other non-European; the only Caucasian is Shevardnadze, the foreign minister. Almost all the rest are Slavs, and all but a handful of them are Russians. Clearly, "this is not accidental." Similar patterns are observable among the hundred or so (out of 159) *obkom* (regional Party committee) first secretaries who have been changed since

March 1985, the new heads of Central Committee departments and the other central institutions where wholesale personnel changes have been made. This policy of having members of the ethnic majority in the provinces dominate the state and Party apparatuses there while enhancing Russian control of the central organs could not be accomplished without the passport system.

Could the passport requirement be lifted selectively? After all, Soviet scholars have pointed out that some nationalities are way ahead of others on the road to *sliianie*, so could there not be some nationalities whose ethnic category could be eliminated and they could then choose to identify with some larger and unassimilated group? This has happened for certain small and diminishing peoples, so that the number of officially recognized nationalities has declined over the years. This has not happened to the Jews (perhaps with the exception of the Krymchaks), probably because they are too numerous and they present certain special problems from the official point of view and thus have to be easily located and identified. Moreover, granting Jews the right to assimilate officially might well arouse demands for similar treatment for other nonterritorial, disadvantaged groups such as Germans and Poles. Therefore, it is highly likely that official Jewish identity will be maintained for the foreseeable future.

This is of great importance for the preservation of Jewish identity, and indirectly, of Jewish culture. In the absence of recognized Jewish institutions—and there is no reason to believe that Jewish schools, for example, will be permitted in the near future—there are probably two main factors preserving even minimal Jewish identity in the Soviet Union—official identification and anti-Semitism. As Drobizheva remarks, "The distinctive feature of the sociopolitical situation in which a national community finds itself determines how clearly people perceive their national identity."[6] The Jews have a very distinct "sociopolitical situation" which defines their belonging to a group just as sharply, if not more so, than a common language, territory, or any of the other attributes normally associated with ethnic groups. They are no longer as much a community of *faith* as they are one of *fate*. Illusions about shedding their distinctive characteristics and identity were dispelled for many Soviet Jews first by the Nazis and later by the anti-Semitism of the Stalin period, never fully repudiated. Several Soviet researchers have remarked on the fact that the more educated strata are likely to have more links to their ethnic groups than others. It is precisely more educated people who are more aware of membership in a community of fate. "It is no accident that a common historical destiny is more often mentioned as an attribute that links a person to his people, and in particular, people from among the more educated strata of the population."[7] Since Jews remain the nationality with the highest levels of education in the Soviet population, and since their historical fate is so singular, consciousness of history alone represents a powerful force for national identity. This remains true even though much of Jewish history is obscured from the Soviet citizen by a policy of excluding it from curricula and even scholarship. The historical fate of the Jews is transmitted within the family and through a kind of folklore—more recently, by small groups who make an active effort to uncover it. There is enormous interest in whether this or that historical figure was a Jew, in the contributions Jews have made to civilization, and in the situation of Jews in various lands, in both the past and the present. This curiosity derives not merely from a thirst for historical knowledge, but from a need to locate oneself within a group, its achievements, and its fate. It is as if the individual's own status, at least in his own eyes, will be defined by the accomplishments of others who carry the same label. "If Einstein was a Jew, and I am a Jew, it does not quite follow that I am an Einstein, but. . . ."

For most Soviet Jews, passive Jewish identity is associated with passive involvement with Jewish culture. For a minority, passive identity turns into active identity, which, in turn, leads to attempts to live actively as cultural Jews, whether defined religiously, linguistically, artistically, or in other ways. The patterns may be represented by the following scheme:

$$\text{Passive identity} \xrightarrow{\text{(major tendency)}} \text{Passive culture}$$
$$\searrow$$
$$\text{(minor tendency) Active Identity} \longrightarrow \text{Active Culture}$$

Active culture is developed by minorities, but the size of those minorities, and the ratio between active and passive identity vary with the fluctuations in Soviet conditions: in times of great pressure, such as 1948–53, the proportion of active identifiers, and the amount of overt cultural activity, decline. In times of relative relaxation, such as the mid-1970s, active identity and culture grow, especially if external forces feed them. Moreover, the *kinds* of activity vary with surrounding conditions as well. Obviously, when emigration to Israel is a viable and realistic option, the number of active Zionists increases. When emigration appears to be unrealistic in the short run, other forms of Jewish activism, including religious study and practice, and/or Hebraic and Judaic studies, become more prominent. In other words, it is probably useless to think in terms of linear trends. Rather, both Soviet policy and the reactions of Soviet Jews are more dynamic and flexible than we often assume. This means that the possibilities of Jewish identity and cultural activity are more varied than commonly believed.

Confusion and inconsistency mark the early evolution of the Bolshevik attitude toward Jewish identity and, to a lesser extent, the culture that would accompany it. Before the Revolution, Lenin and Stalin—as well as most other socialists, whether Menshevik or Bolshevik—argued vehemently that Jews did not constitute a nation. Lenin began with the argument that since the Jews lacked a territory they could not be a nation. Stalin, in his 1913 essay on the national question, elaborated on this argument by postulating a definition of a nation, which included common language, territory, economy, and "psychology" among its criteria, and showing that the Jews did not meet these criteria. These positions were elaborated in the course of the polemic with the Bund; as such, they were motivated by the political needs of the moment as much as by conceptualization designed to set a long-term policy. Stalin fulminated against the growing cultural activity of the Bund which he characterized as follows:

The maintenance of everything Jewish, the preservation of all the national peculiarities of the Jews, even those that are patently noxious to the proletariat, the isolation of the Jews from everything non-Jewish, even the establishment of special hospitals, that is the level to which the Bund has sunk.[8]

The recommended course of action for the Jews, whom Lenin acknowledged to be "oppressed and persecuted" more than any other nationality, was assimilation. Since Jews were not a nation and were in any case assimilating in more progressive societies, as in Western Europe, they should reject the "spirit of the ghetto" and assimilate into a liberated humanity which will no longer persecute them.

The dogmatic assertion that Jews are not a nation ran up against the realities of a distinct Jewish identity, both in their own eyes and in that of others, as well as a highly visible and unique culture. Without making any concessions in their theoretical writings, the Bolsheviks pragmatically labeled the Jews a "nationality" and evolved specific policies toward them after 1917. A Commissariat for Jewish Affairs was established in the government, and Jewish Sections were created in the very Bolshevik party which had so vigorously rejected the Bund's demand to represent the interests of the Jewish workers within the Russian Social Democratic Labor party, at that point including Bolshevik, Menshevik, and Bundist constituencies. These were temporary concessions—the Jewish Commissariat was abolished in 1924 and the Jewish Sections in 1930—but the status of Jews as a nationality was never rescinded. When the internal passport system was introduced, Jews, like all others, were identified by nationality on their documents.

Jewish Communists agreed with their comrades of other nationalities that traditional Jewish culture—encompassing Judaism, Hebrew language and literature, and a full complement of social, economic, and cultural institutions, as well as political movements—would have to be abolished because it was feudal and bourgeois in nature. Therefore, vigorous and sometimes violent campaigns were launched against religion, Hebrew, and the Zionist and other Jewish political movements. The institutions of the prerevolutionary period—whether political parties or orphanages, schools or literary journals—were either abolished, driven underground, or taken over by the Communist authorities who reshaped their character in line with their own ideology. These tasks having been largely accomplished by the mid-1920s, many Communists assumed that nature could now take its course and the Jewish nationality would disappear by attrition. Younger generations, neither committed to rejected values and institutions nor barred from entry into the society around them, would assimilate happily into their surroundings. Other Party activists, especially those who had come to the Jewish Sections from the Jewish socialist parties, rejected immediate assimilation. They proposed that while assimilation remained the ultimate goal and solution to the "Jewish problem," there was an intermediate stage which would see the reconstruction of Jewish culture on a secular, socialist foundation. In line with the policy of *korenizatsiia* ("rooting" socialism among the Soviet nationalities by presenting it in their respective languages and national forms), activists of the Jewish Sections pushed for the establishment of Yiddish schools, newspapers, journals, theaters, and even courts and trade union cells, so that the message of socialism could be conveyed through the medium of Yiddish, the language of the Jewish working class. Indeed, the activity of the Sections was expanded beyond cultural affairs to include the economic rehabilitation of the ruined segments of the Jewish population, whether by settling them in agricultural colonies, providing assistance to artisans, or drawing them into the expanding industries. Tremendous energy and funds, as well as considerable manpower, were invested in constructing a network of well over a thousand elementary schools, dozens of newspapers, several theaters, and numerous journals, all of which were designed to be "socialist in content and Yiddish in form." By 1933, almost half of all Jewish children in school in Belorussia and the Ukraine, areas of the former Pale, were attending a Yiddish school. Local and even regional soviets operated in Yiddish; agricultural colonies were founded in Belorussia, the Ukraine, the Crimea, and Birobidzhan. While the stated purpose of the colonies was to "productivize" parts of the Jewish population, some saw them as a means of preserving Jewish identity and culture, since acculturation to Russian or Ukrainian would not be as likely as in the cities.[9]

The attempt to create a new type of Jewish culture, along with a new Jewish identity, ultimately failed for several reasons. True to its word, the Party clung to assimilation as the ultimate *desideratum*. It was hard to generate enthusiasm for an effort which was explicitly designated as temporary. As it turned out, massive Party support for the new culture lasted only about a decade. By the mid-1930s the campaign had run its course. In line with the shift from NEP (the New Economic Policy of 1921–27) to modernization through collectivization and industrialization, resources were diverted from promoting different forms in culture toward strengthening the common commitment to the Stalinist program. The demands of content superseded those of form. Especially in the period of the purges, it became risky to identify too closely with nationality cultures, for that exposed one to charges of "petty bourgeois nationalism."

A second obstacle to the success of the new culture was that form without content had limited appeal. Since the content of Jewish culture was so heavily religious in nature or origin, and that had to be expunged for ideological reasons, not much was left that the Soviet Jew could recognize as distinctly Jewish. There were some who urged the elimination, or at least reduction, of words and phrases of Hebrew origin in Yiddish, and the orthography was reformed to widen the gap between Hebrew and Yiddish forms, moving Soviet Yiddish away from the language of the "class enemy." As noted, institutions of the prerevolutionary period were also driven out of existence or distorted beyond recognition. Yiddish itself, especially in its

"Bolshevized" form, was insufficient to hold the loyalty of the Jews, and it certainly would not attract the younger generation. According to the 1926 census, there were 1,888,000 Jews whose mother tongue was Yiddish. Yet, in the late 1920s the total circulation of the three main Yiddish dailies was only 32,000, so that their total readership was probably no greater than 120,000 (assuming four readers per paper). A survey taken in 1928 found that Yiddish readers read mostly the Yiddish classics, followed by translations of the European classics, and, running a poor third, the new Yiddish literature of the Soviet period.

The curricula of the Yiddish schools reflected the narrowly constrained conception of the new culture. As one Jewish Communist pointed out, "The very concept of 'Jewish history' is excluded from the school. Any general course in the history of the class struggle may include elements describing the struggle of Jewish artisans against the Jewish or any other bourgeoisie."[10] Only the history of the Jews in Russia was touched on, in any case, because Soviet dogma contends that Jews living in different lands have no connection with each other. Moreover, the Yiddish schools naturally educated their pupils more explicitly against Judaism than schools operating in other languages, where all religions were attacked more evenhandedly. Religious parents therefore preferred to send their children to schools which they saw as "less anti-Semitic" than the Yiddish ones!

A third general problem with Yiddish culture was its practicability. Higher education was practically all in Russian, as were the great majority of secondary schools. Therefore, when a graduate of a Yiddish school wished to continue his education, he had to relearn all his subjects in Russian in order to compete successfully in the entrance examinations. Parents were reluctant to send their children to schools which would handicap them in their future education. Therefore, activists of the Jewish Sections would pressure the parents to send their children to the Yiddish school. A leading Jewish Communist commented that "gross distortions occurred in some cities where people who do not need Yiddish schools were forced—by use of terror—to attend them."[11]

A more general weakness of the new Yiddish culture was its perceived inferiority vis-à-vis Russian culture. Before 1917, when Jews had little opportunity to educate themselves in Russian culture and to be accepted into Russian society, Yiddish held its own. But now that the doors were opened wide to both general society and Russian culture, many Jews eagerly abandoned the Yiddish culture, which they associated with the *shtetl* (small

Jewish town) and a way of life they had been taught to regard as backward, and embraced the Russian language and culture, and to a lesser extent, Belorussian and Ukrainian cultures. Of the 18,000 Jewish Party members in 1927 who gave Yiddish as their mother tongue, only about 2,000 belonged to Party cells operating in Yiddish. Jewish workers resisted encouragement to read Yiddish newspapers and conduct trade union activities in Yiddish. "The Jewish worker does not want to read a [Yiddish] newspaper. He will break his teeth, he will not understand a word, but give him Russian. A Jewish comrade begins to speak in Yiddish at a workers' meeting—they don't want to listen. And when she finishes, they translate her [speech] even though you can't find a non-Jew here for love or money."[12] The resistance to Yiddish and desire for Russian stemmed from the conviction that Russian was a "higher" culture and that, in any case, it was the key to upward mobility. "A meeting of the transport workers. One comrade, a porter, takes the floor and comes out categorically against any work in Yiddish. When challenged, he answered: The matter is quite simple. . . . For many years I have carried hundreds of poods on my back day in and day out. Now I want to learn some Russian and become an office worker."[13]

These aspirations were accelerated by the economic transformations of the 1920s. Rapid and massive industrialization, and the urbanization that accompanied it, attracted enormous numbers of Jews, especially younger ones, away from the *shtetl* and into the cities. As they changed their residences and their vocations, they also changed their language, their clothing, their social associations, and their values. Jews, like others, were caught up in the heroic effort to rapidly transform the country from a backward one to the world's first industrial socialist state. To many, traditional Jewish culture appeared quaint and irrelevant, if not downright reactionary. The attempts to substitute a modernized Yiddish culture for it appeared artificial, unnecessary, and irrelevant. Thus, both forms of Jewish culture were weakened in the 1930s by secular economic and social changes. They were further weakened by Stalinist policies which considerably increased the risks attendant upon involvement not only with traditional culture, but even with Soviet Yiddish culture.

The corollary of these changes for Jewish identity was a parallel decline in both traditional identity and the one the Jewish Sections tried to create. This was, after all, the age of "internationalism." As people of different nationalities cooperated in socialist construction, as they streamed to the cities from their native villages and moved from one republic to another to work on the new construction sites, old ways of life faded into irrelevance. Jews came into friendly contact with members of other nationalities, rates of interethnic marriage rose steeply, and linguistic acculturation facilitated "friendship of the peoples." Probably at no other time in Soviet history was there as much Jewish acculturation as in the 1930s. To the extent that people changed their names, married non-Jews, and moved to areas remote from Jewish culture and population, there was probably a fair amount of assimilation—in the literal sense—as well. Many Soviet Jews lost their active Jewish identities and cultures at this time, and some even managed to abandon their passive identity.

Between 1939 and 1944 at least passive identity was forced back on them since it was so crucial to the invading Nazis and their allies to identify Jews. The degree of acculturation and identity with the Jewish people became irrelevant. Of course, many perceived Jewish identity as an unwelcome burden more than ever, but they could not shuck it off. On the other hand, the influx of over a million unassimilated and even unacculturated Jews from the Baltic and other annexed areas, made it possible to infuse Jewish identity with positive content. Many Soviet Jews have testified to the role these "freshly baked" Soviet citizens played in reconnecting them to world Jewry, teaching them about Jewish culture, religion, languages, and political ideas such as Zionism. For most Soviet Jews, however, the war braked the movement toward assimilation, now almost impossible, but the intensive acculturation of earlier decades left them suspended between a national consciousness they did not know what to do with, and an assimilationist solution they could no longer achieve.

In 1948 the closing of nearly all Jewish cultural institutions and the purge of leading Yiddish cultural figures left forced acculturation as the only option for Soviet Jews. Ironically, at the very same time, the "anticosmopolitan" campaign emphasized that assimilation was not possible in the land of Lenin. The founding of the State of Israel, and initial Soviet support of it, created hope among some Soviet Jews that emigration to the Jewish state would release them from the painful dilemma of acculturation without assimilation. But the very explicit condemnation of Zionism which went along with recognition of Israel left no doubt that *aliya* (the emigration of Jews to Israel) was not to be an option. So Jews who desired to live in a Jewish state or those who would have been content with Jewish culture in the USSR were denied these choices; those identified as Jews against their will and who saw nothing positive in this identification, were prevented from abandoning it.

The decade of partial de-Stalinization (1953–64) saw a token revival of Yiddish culture and a withdrawal from the more egregious and life-threatening forms of official anti-Semitism. Soviet Yiddish culture, though officially revived, was limited to vestigial organs, such as *Sovetish heymland*, and some amateur theaters. Since Yiddish schools were not reopened, nor was any other form of Jewish education permitted, it was clear that the authorities did not intend Jewish culture to have a future in the USSR. Aware of this, nationally minded Jews looked more and more toward emigration to Israel as the only realistic means of satisfying their desire for a meaningful Jewish life, but they were in a minority. The majority were reconciled to living in the USSR, which, in any case, seemed the only realistic option. As the discrimination of the Stalinist period eased somewhat, they concentrated their efforts on educational and vocational achievements. Their cultural life was by now almost exclusively non-Jewish, with two kinds of exceptions. First, the life-styles of most Jews could still be distinguished from that of their neighbors by their social characteristics. They differed in the pattern of their leisure activities, the extraordinarily high levels of education of the group, their urbanity, concentration in the largest metropolitan centers, prominence in artistic and scientific life, diminishing presence in official life, a certain kind of humor, and, among a particular subgroup, a tendency to relative nonconformity. In other words, being Jewish was now defined, informally and unofficially, by *social* characteristics, not by "culture" in the narrow sense of the word. Jews and non-Jews ascribed certain characteristics to Jews, and that was sufficient to define them as a group apart.[14] As Drobizheva puts it, "in the orientation of individuals, the place of an ethnically colored traditional culture is replaced by their professional culture, even in secondary forms symbolizing traditional culture."[15] Alexander Voronel has also pointed to the importance of professional identity for Soviet Jews. They "have no choice but to see themselves through the eyes of others. They have no resources for self-knowledge."[16] Once again, Drobizheva, summing up the findings of empirical research among several Soviet nationalities observed: "the 'grounds' for national identification change, but people continue to identify themselves with some national group, and as their general competence and knowledge grows, they do so even more freely. . . . Thus, the objective base of national self-awareness does not disappear, it simply changes. Indeed, the foundations for its continued growth expand."[17]

The second exception to full acculturation into non-Jewish culture were the most recent arrivals, the older and middle generations of the "Zapadniki," those who had been Baltic, Polish, Romanian, and Czechoslovak citizens before the war. Some continued to use Yiddish, and even Hebrew, in certain settings; practically all maintained some Jewish customs and traditions, whether ritual or culinary in nature. The first spontaneously organized Yiddish performing groups of the 1960s were in the Baltic. It is not by chance that the cautious, but increasingly visible and activist, movement to learn about Israel and to immigrate there also began in the Baltic. People from that region served as the mentors of Jews from the Soviet heartland who, quite independently, had begun to think along similar lines (parallel tendencies among Georgian Jews seemed to stem largely from their own religious and traditional resources and were not directly inspired, at least at the beginning, by what was happening in the Baltic and the heartland).

The June 1967 Arab-Israeli war did not create the reborn Zionist movement in the Soviet Union, but it was a powerful catalyst to its emergence into the open and to its geographical and numerical expansion. As in other Jewish communities, the war made people realize how personally catastrophic an Israeli defeat—loudly predicted by the Soviet media—would be. The unexpected Israeli victory evoked feelings of pride and relief. The unique consequence of the war for Soviet Jews was the realization that the Soviet government unequivocally supported those who declared their intention to destroy Israel. "Until June 1967 Soviet Jews had illusions about coexistence with the regime, despite the fact that it wanted to spiritually destroy the Jews. But suddenly they realized that the Soviet government identifies itself with those who wish to destroy the Jewish state, the sole hope left for the Jewish people. Russia spat on the Jewish people, 'and then we knew that we would never be able to live under such a regime.' "[18] Intensive anti-Zionist propaganda aroused curiosity about Zionism, and the Leningrad trial of late 1970 brought to the attention of great numbers of Soviet Jews the existence of young Zionists prepared to undertake drastic action in order to achieve their goals. The Zionist idea gained many adherents, and when the Soviets began to permit mass emigration in 1971, large-scale immigration to Israel began. By the mid-1970s the emigration movement had changed its character and direction considerably. Alongside those who held to the original aims, came tens of thousands of Jews who left their native country for reasons other than purely Zionist or even Jewish ones. Most of the latter emigrated to North America.

The consequence of these developments for culture was the growth of a "counterculture" which emphasized Hebrew, not Yiddish; Israel, not the USSR; and knowledge of Jewish history and culture in the broadest sense, not in the painfully restricted conceptions of the *Evsektsii* (Jewish sections of the Communist party). Though concentrated in the largest cities and in the Baltic, and forced to operate in very difficult conditions, this culture attracted thousands of people, and managed to exploit the available local resources as well as to gain access to Jewish cultural resources brought from abroad. For the first time in decades, Jewish identity came to mean for many identification with Israel, the Hebrew language, and the worldwide Jewish people. Thus, it was filled with substantive contemporary content. While the majority of Soviet Jews remained with their passive identity and socially defined culture, a significant minority, highly visible within and without the USSR, had moved to active identity and culture.

The prominent solution of the 1970s to the dilemmas of Jewish identity and culture was, then, emigration. But after over a quarter of a million Jews had left, the emigration option was successively narrowed until, by the mid-1980s, it was practically closed. Naturally, this depressed the number of new requests for invitations from abroad and especially discouraged many of the non-Zionist potential émigrés, except for those who had close relatives abroad. A hard core of Zionist-motivated people continues the struggle, but the new situation has apparently produced new directions in Jewish identity and culture, showing, once again, that these are dynamic and responsive to changing conditions.

One should distinguish between official and unofficial Jewish culture in the Soviet Union today. Official culture, that which is initiated, sponsored, or merely approved by the authorities, includes three main types of expression: (1) academic and literary culture; (2) amateur, but state-aided, culture, mainly of theatrical and musical varieties; and (3) officially sanctioned religious institutions and practices.

The first type is largely an elite culture, where the audience is not many times greater than the producers. The second type appeals to the greatest numbers, but places the least demands upon its audiences. The third type, though ideologically unpalatable to the authorities, is tolerated because it appeals only to a small, elderly, and nonthreatening group, while serving public relations purposes much more effectively than either of the other two. However, it should be emphasized that there are unintended—and, from the authorities' point of view, undesirable—consequences of permitting these forms of cultural expression. Officially sanctioned academic and literary works are relatively available and not risky to possess, and have sometimes spurred people to explore Jewish culture to a far greater extent than intended by the authorities. A Hebrew-Russian dictionary, for example, published in 1963, is a highly prized item among Zionists. Books on Israel are sources of information for those same people, despite the obvious negative slant that they have.[19] Musical and theatrical programs often give people at least a vague sense that there is something more to Jewish identity than a line on an internal passport. And as practically the only visible Jewish institution in the country, the synagogue serves a far broader constituency than its prime audience. People of all ages use the synagogue as a place to meet, whether to socialize, exchange information about Jewish matters, or simply strengthen their own identities and commitment by interaction with other, like-minded Jews. For the newly religious, the synagogue can serve important practical functions.

In the 1980s there seems to be a slight increase in officially sanctioned academic work on Judaica. Soviet sources make it clear that the older generation of librarians, curators and scholars is giving way to a small group of younger people, most of them apparently the students of their predecessors. Thus, it might well be that the authorities are not permitting a significant expansion in the Judaica field, but simply meeting current needs as dictated by biological processes. In any case, young scholars such as Shimon Iakirson, Igor Voevutskii, Aleksandra Aikhenvald, and Emmanuelis Zingeris—all in their late twenties or thirties—are publishing works on modern Hebrew grammar, Yiddish literature, Jewish philosophy, and bibliography. An issue of *Sovetish heymland* (no. 7, 1986), celebrating twenty-five years of the journal's appearance, presented thirty-one writers and artists born after 1945. Three of them are graduates of the special course for Yiddish writers at the literary institute named for Maksim Gorky. Their average age is thirty-four to thirty-five, and only three earn their living in Yiddish publications. The rest are teachers, translators, engineers, academics, physicians, and the like. There is even an army major among them. Six were born in areas annexed after 1939. Another six are from the Ukraine, five from Moscow, and two from Birobidzhan. Some come from families heavily involved in Yiddish culture, while others come from acculturated environments.[20]

Interviews with directors of Yiddish ensembles in Moscow, Vilnius, Kaunas, and Birobidzhan have brought to light a debate about whether theater must be presented only in Yiddish, or whether it is desirable to introduce Russian dialogue and commentary. Those based in Moscow, addressing more acculturated audiences, are in favor of introducing Russian, while the Baltic area directors are not. There does not seem to be much chance for the development of a Jewish culture in Russian, parallel to Anglo-Jewish culture, for example, whatever the outcome of this discussion.

Recent years have not seen synagogue closings. The visit to the United States of Konstantin Kharchev, chairman of the Council for Religious Affairs, signals a new sensitivity to the public relations dimensions of religious matters, and it is unlikely that there will be a frontal assault on recognized religious institutions. Increasingly, the token clergy, strategically placed in visible positions, will be graduates of the Budapest Jewish Theological Seminary where the level of study is necessarily low. The most that can be expected from the "official" clergy and associated institutions is that they will not interfere with "unofficial" religiosity and deny use of the few facilities left to the genuinely religious.

In sum, official culture in the 1980s seems designed to maintain the status quo, and that largely in order to buttress Soviet claims in the international arena. This is, of course, more palatable than the antireligious campaigns of 1957–64, or the annihilation of official culture in the last period of Stalin's life. Though a resurgence of Yiddish culture is highly unlikely, the existence of a cadre of cultural activists and of religious officials and institutions helps keep Jewish knowledge and consciousness alive, probably to a greater extent than the authorities would like—but that is a price they are willing to pay in order to "buy insurance" against embarrassment in international arenas.

There are direct parallels in unofficial culture to the modes of official culture. These emerged in the past two decades and have continued into the 1980s. Already in the samizdat of the 1960s there were gropings for scholarship and serious thought on Jewish matters. There is now a small academic culture of Judaica, produced and consumed by people whose professional interests lie elsewhere. There are amateur ethnographers, photographers who take pictures of former and present Jewish sites and monuments, people who do library research on Jewish subjects—a kind of activity that has parallels in Poland and elsewhere in Eastern Europe today. Young people, especially, learn Hebrew and Yiddish songs; Jewish stories and novels are read; liturgy is explored; and there is even interest in Jewish cuisine. The main difference between these endeavors and those of official culture, aside from the obvious difference of forum, is that the former is motivated primarily by a quest for self-discovery, for filling formal identity with cultural content, whereas the latter may be motivated largely—though perhaps not exclusively—by intellectual curiosity. Clearly, the study of Hebrew—for which there are only a few sanctioned opportunities—is directly linked to the hope for *aliya,* though there are those who do not see it explicitly in this way. The number of Hebrew students is not static, nor is their intensity uniform, but at the present writing there seem to be about 1,000 people involved in Moscow, and smaller numbers elsewhere. Many have underscored the remarkable facility in Hebrew that many Soviet Jews have acquired. Such facility is unlikely to be gained by people whose sole motivation is intellectual. Perhaps the lack of books, teachers, and other resources is compensated for by the powerful motivation to acquire a tool which will open the way not only to daily life in Israel but to the centuries-old treasure of mainstream Jewish culture. It is ironic that Hebrew captivates so many in the USSR at a time when it is out of vogue in many Jewish circles in the West.

Finally, the religious revival in the USSR has drawn much attention in the 1980s. It has not been possible to examine this phenomenon systematically, for obvious reasons, but it might be suggested that it stems from two or perhaps three sources. First, already in the 1960s and 1970s some of those who had acquired Jewish national consciousness and who were delving into culture, realized that, historically, Jewish culture is intimately tied to religion, and that all nonreligious forms were derivative of the Jewish religion. If one were determined to go back to the source itself, one would have to confront religion. Second, the spread of Judaism in recent years may be linked to the closing down of emigration. Energies that were once devoted to demonstrations, sit-ins, signing petitions, and jumping through the many bureaucratic hoops involved in the emigration process were turned to study and the exchange of ideas and information. It is as if Jews who could not emigrate out of the country began their "internal emigration" in a more profound and searching way than simply dropping out of the mainstream. If Jewish life could not be lived in Israel, at least for the moment it could be constructed in an alternative community within the Soviet Union. With great ingenuity and devotion, the necessities of a halakhic way of life were created or acquired. The gathering of some of the newly religious, most of them under forty years old, in classes and in summer resort areas symbolizes the sense of an integrated community, able to stand apart from Soviet life and create, at least partially, its own mode of living. For this group, numbering perhaps less than a thousand in the entire country, Jewish identity has become a religious-national identity. And third, there are indications that in the USSR as a whole, especially among the younger generation intelligentsia, there is a certain growing religiosity which derives some of its strength from the identification or association of religion with nationalism. This atmosphere or trend probably also affects the Jews.

It must be emphasized that all modes of culture and identity described above taken together encompass probably a minority of Soviet Jewry. They do not, for the most part, pertain to the non-Ashkenazic Jews whose Jewish identity and culture continue to derive largely from tradition rooted in religion. Living in the more traditional societies of Central Asia and the Caucasus, these Jews, like their Muslim and Christian neighbors, have primordial identities firm enough not to have been uprooted by Soviet power. Like their neighbors, too, their mores are rooted in religion and have survived the erosion of their theological foundations.

The majority of European Jews also have identities and cultures other than the categories described above. They are what Ted Friedgut has called the "silent majority,"[21] those whose identities and culture are passive and who are making their ways through Soviet society, as best they can, as *"riadovye sovetskie liudi"* (ordinary Soviet citizens), to use a favored Soviet phrase. Many of them are the parents of young Zionists and religious people, and they look uncomprehendingly on the activities of their children. Like Lenin, many of them believe that assimilation would be the true solution to their personal and collective "Jewish problem." Larissa Bogoraz, widow of the recently deceased political prisoner Anatolii Marchenko, wrote years ago: "Who am I now? . . . Unfortunately, I do not feel like a Jew. I understand that I have an unquestionable genetic tie with Jewry. . . . A more profound, or more general common bond is lacking, such as community of language, culture, history, tradition. . . . By all these characterizations, I am Russian. . . . And nevertheless, no, I am not Russian. I am a stranger today in this land."[22]

Some part of the "silent majority" is not indifferent to its Jewish identity but regards it as a burden. They see themselves as "invalids of the fifth category" (the fifth paragraph in the passport lists nationality). Jewish identity is for them a mark of Cain, difficult to erase and labeling them forever as pariahs. Neither official policies nor social realities seem likely to change quickly enough in this decade to change this perception.

The Jewish culture of the "silent majority" is at most a matter of a few inherited habits, a *shteyger* culture, to borrow a Yiddish term. There are patterns of everyday life and the social characteristics mentioned earlier that continue to mark Jews off as a distinct social, if not ethnic, group. But as educational levels of Jews decline owing to restrictive policies and new policies and new policies in higher education generally, and as Jews move further away from the religious and customary sources of their distinctive styles of life and values owing to the passage of the generations, acculturation, and intermarriage, the distinctiveness of Jews as a group will recede. Recently it has been noted that the "smart Jewish kids" in the United States are being displaced by Asian-Americans, whether in the Westinghouse science talent search, in the universities, or in the laboratories. This may happen in the Soviet Union as well, as "their" Asians come into their own, and as Jews become more like other Europeans. But just as predictions of irreversible Jewish assimilation have proved wrong, so it would be foolhardy to predict the future of Jewish culture and identity in the USSR. Erik Erikson reminds us that "In history, identifications and identities are bound to shift with changing technologies, cultures, and political systems."[23] Those shifts can be influenced to some extent even in as closed a society as the Soviet Union, and it will be the responsibility of Soviet Jews and their concerned brethren to move those shifts in desired directions.

Notes

1. See, for example, Nathan Glazer and Daniel Moynihan, eds., *Ethnicity: Theory and Experience* (Cambridge: Harvard University Press, 1975); D. Handelman, "The Organization of Ethnicity," *Ethnic Groups* no. 1, 1977; Jeffrey Ross et al., *The Mobilization of Collective Identity* (Washington, D.C.: University Press of America, 1980); Joseph Rothschild, *Ethnopolitics* (New York: Columbia University Press, 1981).
2. Brezhnev's report to the 26th Party Congress, *Pravda*, February 24, 1981.
3. *Pravda*, October 26, 1985.
4. M. I. Kulichenko, "Socioeconomic Foundations of Mutual Influence and En-

richment of National Culture in Conditions of Developed Socialism," *Voprosy istorii* no. 5, 1977, transl. in *Soviet Law and Government*, Summer 1978, p. 82. See also Kulichenko et al., *Osnovnye napravleniia izucheniia natsional'nykh otnoshenji v SSSR* (Moscow: Nauka, 1979).
5. L. M. Drobizheva, "Natsional'noe samosoznanie: baza formirovaniia i sotsial'no-kulturnye stimuly razvitiia," *Sovetskaia etnografiia* no. 5, 1985, transl. in *Soviet Law and Government*, Summer 1986, p. 51.
6. Ibid., p. 55.
7. Ibid., p. 68.
8. Joseph Stalin, *Marxism and the National Question* (New York: International Publishers, n.d.), p. 42.
9. For details on the attempts to create a secular, socialist, Yiddish culture, see Zvi Gitelman, *Jewish Nationality and Soviet Politics* (Princeton: Princeton University Press, 1972), chapter 6.
10. Y. Dardak, "Undzere dergraikhungen far 15 yor oktiabr afn gebit fun folkbildung," *Tsum XV yortog fun der oktiabr revoliutisie—sotsial ekonomisher zamlbukh* (Minsk: M.P.V., 1932), p. 173.
11. M. Kiper, "Oifgabn in der kultur-oifkler arbet," *Shtern*, June 28, 1927.
12. *Der veker*, February 16, 1923.
13. *Der emes*, April 6, 1924.
14. An American Jewish friend, born in Germany into a highly assimilated family, who is not a practicing Jew, says he "used to be a German," and "whether I have become an American" is a question as yet unresolved. He defines his identity as a Jew as follows: "For me, being a Jew means . . . to assume a cross, to incur an obligation (dear me, how German that sounds!), not to allow myself to be homogenized, to learn to think freely, sharply, dialectically and ironically, to maintain my humanity and to display it openly in this world." Needless to say, this is a highly subjective and unorthodox definition. But it points up the fact that people assign whatever meaning and content to Jewishness they please.
15. Drobizheva, op. cit., p. 65.
16. "The Social Pre-Conditions of the National Awakening of the Jews in the USSR," in A. Voronel and Victor Yakhot, *I Am a Jew: Essay on Jewish Identity in the Soviet Union* (New York: Academic Committee on Soviet Jewry and Anti-Defamation League, 1973), p. 31. See also, by the same editors, *Jewishness Rediscovered: Jewish Identity in the Soviet Union* (New York: Academic Committee on Soviet Jewry and Anti-Defamation League, 1974).
17. Drobizheva, op cit., pp. 68–69.
18. David Giladi, summarizing statements by Soviet immigrants to Israel at the Twenty-Eighth World Zionist Congress, in *Haaretz*, January 25, 1972.
19. Two recent examples are V. V. Benovolenskii, ed., *Gosudarstvo Izrail': spravochnik* (Moscow: Nauka, 1986) and L. I. Dadiani, *Kritika ideologii i politiki sotsial-sionizma* (Moscow: Mysl, 1986). The former contains a considerable amount of data on the economy, demography, and cultural life of Israel, while the latter deals with socialist-Zionist ideology and Israeli socialist parties, though in a highly selective and tendentious way.

20. For *Sovetish heymland* and the younger generation of Yiddish writers, see Chone Shmeruk, "Twenty-Five Years of *Sovetish heymland*," in this volume.
21. Theodore Friedgut, "Soviet Jewry: The Silent Majority," *Soviet Jewish Affairs*, vol. 10, no. 2, May 1980, pp. 3–19.
22. "Do I feel I belong to the Jewish People?" in Voronel and Yakhot, *I Am a Jew*, pp. 63–64.
23. Erik Erikson, "Identity, Psychosocial," in David L. Sills, ed., *International Encyclopedia of the Social Sciences* (New York: Macmillan, 1968), vol. 7, p. 61.

II
THE REVIVAL OF JEWISH IDENTITY

2

The Jewish National Movement in the Soviet Union: A Profile

Yossi Goldstein

The new patterns of Jewish national activity in the Soviet Union, which have evolved since the 1950s, accord with the unique situation in which Soviet Jewry found itself after the Second World War.[1] The following essay seeks to present a social portrait of the activists in the Jewish national movement and to explain their motivation for becoming active, the nature of their activity, and the Soviet reaction to it. Our discussion will cover the period from the opening of the gates to emigration in late 1968 until the Yom Kippur War (October 1973). The subjects covered and the conclusions drawn are mainly valid for this period; they are not applicable to later years, when circumstances and conditions altered, although Jewish national activity continued then as well. In the period under discussion, new political circumstances, connected with the Soviet Union's situation and standing as a world power, in particular with détente and the Soviet Union's bilateral relations with the United States, together with internal changes in the Soviet Union relating to the authorities' attitude toward the national minorities, generated this Jewish national activity, which differed substantively from later activity of this kind.[2]

Since what follows will focus on the activists in the Jewish national movement, our first problem is to define who is an "activist," even though such a definition is necessarily somewhat arbitrary. Is an *aliya* "activist" someone who carried out a certain number of activities as a member of the national movement, or who sent a number of petitions to the authorities? Does the term refer to someone who staged a hunger strike for several days in the offices of the Communist party in Moscow, or to someone who regularly visited a center of activity in Riga, Moscow, or Leningrad? As it seems that the term has no agreed, "objective" definition, we have for the purposes of our study chosen two criteria for defining an "activist." First, an "activist" is a person who emigrated from the Soviet Union to Israel. Second, he is someone who has been defined as an "activist" by his colleagues in the Soviet Union, Israel, or elsewhere, by the communications media, or by the Soviet authorities. Indeed, the sources used for our study are materials published in the West, including interviews given by "activists" in the late 1960s and the 1970s in Israel and elsewhere,[3] and a survey conducted in 1973–74 which examined the sociological characteristics of the "activists."[4] (That survey defined an activist as a person who had been termed one by at least five *olim* (immigrants to Israel) from the Soviet Union.)

Our sources show that the activists in the period under discussion had various socioeconomic and cultural indicators in common: most of them were at the peak of their activity in their late twenties to late thirties.[5] They were from the large and central cities in the Soviet Union,[6] and the majority had higher education.[7] About half of this group of activists grew up in the RSFSR, a quarter was from the Ukraine and Belorussia, while the remainder were from the territories annexed to the Soviet Union after World War II.[8] Prior to engaging in national activity their material situation had been generally "good."[9] As one of them put it: "The majority of the activists are relatively successful."[10]

A comparison between a group of activists in the Jewish national movement and the general Jewish urban population in the Soviet Union reveals that the activists had higher average educational and economic levels than the rest of the Jewish population, whose level of education was in any case higher than that of any other nationality.[11] The findings also show that two-thirds of these activists were married and had small families.

These data raise several questions: What motivated these people, who enjoyed material and social advantages (with the exception of political influence), to become active in the national movement? What led the Jewish activist to disavow his Soviet identity? What caused people in their mid-thirties, with families, who were more or less economically established, to make the decision to participate in the Jewish national movement, a step which almost always meant the loss of the benefits the Soviet government accords to persons in this class, and entailed a risk to their livelihood? The *aliya* activists' Jewish orientation, which might have been thought to be the prime motive for their activity, does not seem to provide the key in answering these questions. It emerges, in fact, that even though the activists' parents generally maintained an attachment to Judaism,[12] most of the activists had received no Jewish education and observed no religious customs whatsoever. Although one-quarter termed themselves "religious," only about 3 percent were punctiliously observant.[13] About half of them attended synagogue on Jewish festivals, though this was often more out of national than religious considerations.

The activists in the Jewish national movement had what may be termed a "secular" attitude toward Jewishness. For them, Jewish national identity for the most part did not include identification with traditional Jewish religious values. The majority of the activists, it emerges, adopted, whether knowingly or not, means of identification which differed from those of the general Jewish population and which set them apart in their Jewish nationalism.

The *aliya* activists were registered as Jews in their birth certificates. In the 1970 population census, nine out of every ten of them identified themselves, and usually their spouse and children as well, as members of the Jewish nationality.[14] Another means of identification used by the activists to distinguish themselves from the rest of the population in that census was the question of language. About two-thirds of them declared a "Jewish language" to be their mother tongue, with only one-third giving Russian. Given the fact that 95 percent of all the activists and their parents spoke Russian amongst themselves, the declaration of the Jewish language as their mother tongue was an obviously demonstrative act.

The activists' participation in ceremonies, festivities, and other public events relating to the Jewish holidays was one of their chief activities, serving as a means to demonstrate their national uniqueness (and also perhaps providing them with an opportunity to express a protest against the uniformity of the Soviet environment). To light Hanukkah candles, to eat unleavened bread on the Passover, to participate demonstratively in the Simhat Torah festivities—was a way of asserting their Jewish national identity.[15] In contrast, as we have noted, only a very small percentage of the activists observed everyday religious customs—activity that was usually conducted in private—such as laying phylacteries or maintaining *kashrut* (Jewish dietary laws).[16]

Another possible source of the activists' awakening could be sought in an expertise in Jewish culture, history, and literature. A systematic study of this sphere could indicate to what extent the activists' national orientation rested on a cognitive value base. However, it emerges that the level of knowledge of most of the activists in Jewish history, religion, and culture was quite poor. Their acquaintance with these subjects was mostly cursory, and some of them actually professed complete ignorance of them.[17]

We can conclude from the above that even though the majority of activists in the Jewish national movement in the Soviet Union had been connected with a religious way of life in the fairly recent past, nonetheless the immediate motivation for their actions must be sought in their own personal experiences and relationship to historical events or emotionally charged collective happenings.

Indeed, certain events in the annals of the Jewish people in the modern era left a deep impression on the activists. The most shattering of these was the Holocaust. Despite the fact that they were too young to actually remember the events themselves, a great many of them experienced an intensified national awareness and a heightened sense of solidarity with the Jewish people after learning about the Holocaust, whether from memoirs, the testimony of survivors, or memorial day ceremonies.[18] Approximately one-quarter of all the activists stated that learning about the Holocaust and its results had been a central factor in arousing them to national activity on the personal and collective planes alike, and had been largely instrumental in shaping their national consciousness. The lesson most of them learned from the Holocaust was the necessity of developing a national consciousness and of creating frameworks for collective national activism.[19]

The establishment of the State of Israel was another of the crucial events that moved and impressed Soviet Jews in the late 1940s and early 1950s.[20] Evidence of this may be seen in the atmosphere that surrounded the arrival of Israel's first minister to the Soviet Union, Golda Meir (then Meyerson), and, later, in the excitement generated by the visits of Israeli diplomats and other delegations to the Soviet Union's large cities.[21] However, because of the relatively young age of the activists, they did not stress Israel's establishment or its attendant events (including the War of Independence) as having motivated them to become active; rather, they looked upon the Jewish state as a given fact and, after the Holocaust, listed the Six-Day War as the main event which led them to become active in the Jewish national movement. The anxiety that gripped most of the Jewish people in the weeks before the June 1967 war, and the reaction of joy and enthusiasm that followed it, were shared by the activists.[22] Thus, information about the Holocaust, events connected with Israel, such as the War of Independence, the existence and activity of the Israeli legation in Moscow, meeting with official Israeli delegations that visited Moscow,[23] the Sinai Campaign,[24] and other events in the Arab-Israeli conflict, culminating in the Six-Day War, instilled in many activists an intense sense of alienation from Soviet society and its regime,[25] and directly or indirectly forged national feelings and a desire for a collective activity.

No less influential than the events which affected the entire Jewish people were the activists' individual experiences as Jews. They were particularly affected by the encounter with anti-Semitism, which many of them experienced as children[26] and which took many forms: difficulties in being accepted to institutions of higher learning,[27] discrimination during studies, problems in finding work,[28] in becoming established in jobs, and in promotion.[29] These, along with manifestations of hatred and intolerance in the surrounding society, also led to the formation of Jewish national consciousness and to a desire on the part of the individual activists to create frameworks for collective action. This discrimination did not necessarily prevent a large proportion of the activists from doing well—some of them, as noted above, were quite successful professionally and lived reasonably well—but many of them, particularly in the Ukraine, Belorussia, and the "annexed territories," felt they were being discriminated against, by institutions as well as by individuals, because of their Jewishness.[30] The considerable socioeconomic price of the Jewish existence in the Soviet Union was a major component in their decision to become active.

Yet another factor in the sphere of personal experience which led Soviet Jews to participate in the Jewish national movement and reinforced their feeling that such activity ought to be intensified, was the actual persecution —arrest, trial, and imprisonment—to which they and their families were subjected. About half of all the activists or members of the families had been arrested on various charges at some point in their lives. Most of the detainees were tried and imprisoned, many of them for periods of twenty years or more.[31] According to many of the activists, the personal discrimination and anti-Semitism they encountered, along with the arrests and trials they underwent, were significant factors in their decision to become active in the Jewish national movement.[32]

These findings help explain why these people became active in the Jewish national movement in the Soviet Union. They were not, as we have seen, motivated by a traditional Jewish way of life or by their knowledge of

Jewish history, religion, or culture, nor by their belief in the Zionist solution but rather by collective experiences undergone by the entire Jewish people, such as the Holocaust and the Six-Day War, together with their own personal experiences in Soviet society. These experiences assumed a value-laden cognitive and emotional significance which developed in the activists an awareness of their anomalous situation in the society around them and led them to endeavor to better their own future and that of their children.

The culmination of the process was the formation of a highly developed national awareness, which set the activists apart from other Jews. It is central to our analysis to stress that the activists in the movement were pushed out of the Soviet Union rather than pulled toward settling in Israel.[33]

Generally, not much time elapsed between the formation of the activist's national consciousness and identification, and the commencement of his actual activity in the national movement which amounted to giving expression to his identification. This was generally possible despite the objective difficulties posed by the Soviet regime.

The activists' endeavors in the national movement may be divided into three general categories:

1. Individual activity which did not involve public contact with other activists or with the authorities.
2. Collective activity within the Jewish community.
3. Public protest.

One widespread type of individual activity which involved no contact with other activists or with the authorities was listening to Israeli broadcasts. Despite the Soviets' jamming of these broadcasts and despite other reception difficulties, most of the activists listened to Israeli radio stations, particularly after the Six-Day War.[34] A different type of activity consisted of reading about Jewish subjects, chiefly post-1948 Jewish history and literature and other illegally circulated samizdat, that is, unofficial, uncensored, literature.[35] Collecting various souvenirs from Israel was yet another form of individual activity. In addition, most of the activists maintained postal ties of some sort with Israel, particularly after the Six-Day War.[36]

Among the activities falling under the rubric of collective activity within the Jewish community were meetings with representatives from Israel, such as embassy staff or tourists (until the Six-Day War), and members of

Israeli delegations to international conferences held in the Soviet Union, and with Jewish tourists arriving from the West.[37] Another widespread activity after the 1967 war was meetings with foreign correspondents, through whom various messages to the West were conveyed.[38] A different kind of public activity which demonstrated the participants' national feelings was attending festivities bearing saliently national characteristics, such as Israel's Independence Day, the festival of Hanukkah, or memorial assemblies for the victims of the Holocaust.[39]

Also in this category was the study of the Hebrew language, in which over two-thirds of the activists engaged at various levels of proficiency;[40] the holding of farewell parties in private homes for Jews who were about to leave the Soviet Union, and accompanying them to the train station or the airport;[41] listening to the radio in groups; and relaying general information about their activities or about Israel that was passed from person to person.

These two types of activities—those that were carried out in private and those that assumed a more public form—were not unique to the activists, but were engaged in also by a large percentage of the nonactivist Jews who settled in Israel, or even by Jews who had no thought of emigrating to Israel.

What made the members of the national movement distinctive was their public protest activity against the Soviet establishment. The protests, staged under the slogan of the right to *aliya* and as demonstrations of solidarity with Israel, took the form of sit-in strikes, hunger strikes, and organized demonstrations. Over half of the activists took part in such protests.[42]

Another form of protest was the sending of petitions to the supreme institutions of the Soviet Union and to various international bodies. Most of the activists took part in drawing up petitions and in getting other activists to sign them.[43] Jewish activists also engaged in public protests against the anti-Semitism manifested by the authorities or in their immediate environment.[44]

About 50 percent assisted in the publication of the underground samizdat press.[45] Since the authorities published virtually no books on Jewish subjects, the activists filled the vacuum by various means, which, because illegal, assumed an underground nature. Because of the difficulties involved in obtaining the material, which reached the activists through Jewish tourists from the West, journalists, and others, it was often typed or mimeographed by local Jews in order to allow as wide a circulation as possible.[46]

Insults of various sorts were the most frequent form of reaction by representatives of the Soviet government to this nationalist activity.[47] Persecution in the legal-judicial sphere was also common. As noted above, quite a few of the activists underwent the agonies of arrest, interrogation by the KGB, trial and imprisonment, or exile. According to the activists' testimony, arrest and interrogation were sometimes accompanied by severe psychological torture and by physical beatings.[48] Less frequent forms of harassment by the authorities were fines or actions such as cutting off the activists' telephones. Activists who attended synagogue worship were harassed by attacks and by disturbances during prayer.

The children of some of the activists also suffered because of their parents' desire to emigrate to Israel. We know of a number of instances in which children were expelled from school or from youth movements because of this, or were socially ostracized by their peers.

The authorities' reactions sometimes preceded but more often followed public activity in the Jewish national movement. The sharpest, and at the same time, most characteristic reaction, which generally came after the activist had made known his desire to emigrate, was directed against the activist in his professional capacity. A number of activists were dismissed from their jobs. Some of these joined the ranks of the unemployed, while others were accepted to lower-ranking jobs, either in the same place of work or quite often in a different, less qualified profession, that paid less well (sometimes as much as 40 percent less) than their previous employment.[49] The activist's spouse might also be fired or demoted although this was less common.[50] Those who suffered most from dismissals were persons working in government ministries, universities, and other institutions of higher education, and in industry or the technological professions.[51]

Activists were also deprived of any political standing in the Party or the Komsomol to the point of being expelled.[52] By contrast, the activist experienced no significant changes in his immediate surroundings in the wake of his desire to settle in Israel. The activist's Jewish and non-Jewish friends generally evinced a tolerant attitude toward him, and sometimes even one of positive sympathy.[53]

We have seen, then, that the profile of the movement's activists in the period 1968–73 differed from that of the average Jewish population in the large cities. The *aliya* activists generally had higher education and enjoyed greater material and social advantages than did other Jews. We have also seen that the activists in the Jewish national movement may be said to have had a "secular orientation" vis-à-vis their Jewishness, manifested chiefly in the Jewish-national identity which they adopted and which was generally unrelated to identification with traditional Jewish-religious values.

The immediate reasons for the activists' national awakening stemmed not, as noted, from their experience of a Jewish-religious way of life, but from their reactions to historical events such as the Holocaust and the Six-Day War, and from their personal experiences in Soviet society—including various manifestations of anti-Semitism—which left their mark on the activists and intensified their awareness of their anomalous situation within that society. It was these factors which drove them to participate in Jewish national activity.

What distinguished the activists in the Jewish national movement was their *public* protest against the Soviet establishment. This activity took various forms, such as the sending of petitions, participation in demonstrations, and similar acts which underscored their desire to leave the Soviet Union. In many instances, their activity brought in its wake aggressive Soviet reprisals, including arrest, exile, and even mental and physical torture.

Nevertheless, the activists had a powerful desire to leave, and many of them refused to be deterred until they attained their objective.

Notes

I wish to thank Yaacov Ro'i and Mordechai Altshuler for their helpful comments.

1. On the special situation of the Jews in the Soviet Union since 1917, and particularly after the First World War, see Lionel Kochan, ed., *The Jews in Soviet Russia Since 1917* (London and New York: Oxford University Press, 1978), 3d edition.
2. On the change in attitude, cf. Lukasz Hirszowicz, "The Soviet-Jewish Problem: Internal and International Developments," in ibid., pp. 366–409; and Z. Alexander, "The Soviet Union's *Aliya* Policy (1968–1978), " *Behinot,* 8–9 (Heb.; 1978–1979), pp. 51–71.
3. The "interviews" include (1) actual interviews conducted from 1972–79, which are preserved in the Center for Research and Documentation of East European Jewry at the Hebrew University of Jerusalem (henceforth CRD) and (2) biographical and autobiographical literature published since the end of the 1960s; see below.
4. This survey, conducted by the Center for Research and Documentation of East European Jewry, among 300 *aliya* activists who settled in Israel, consisted of

105 questions relating to their activities in the Soviet Union. The material, written up under the title "The Sociological Characteristics of the 'Aliya' Activists in the Soviet Union: Awakening or Continuity" (henceforth "Sociological Characteristics") has not been published in whole or in part.
5. "Sociological Characteristics," p. 6. The breakdown is as follows: 20.8 percent were "youngsters" aged up to 28; 46.5 percent were "mature" persons aged 29 to 42; and 32.7 percent were "old-timers" aged over 42. In reaction to his father's joining the Jewish national struggle, Yasha Kazakov said: "It is not only we of the younger generation who have experienced a national awakening. Father has shown that even people from the Stalin period, who received their education then, have found their way back to their people and their country." *Yediot aharonot,* March 4, 1970.
6. "Sociological Characteristics" p. 6. One of the main reasons for the concentration of activists in the large cities—where the majority of the Jews resided— was, according to activists such as David Drabkin of Moscow (interview in *Ma'ariv,* March 19, 1971) or Mikhail Shepshelovits of Riga (*Ma'ariv,* November 24, 1972), and others, the need for the moral backing of fellow activists and the mutual support of like-minded friends. The term "large cities" refers, among others, to cities such as Vilnius or Riga which are important Jewish centers.
7. One-third of all the activists were engineers, one-quarter were "scientific workers," one-fifth were members of the "free professions" (doctors, teachers, lawyers, chartered accountants, etc.), while the rest were "white collar" workers.
8. In percentages: 47.8 percent were from the major cities—Moscow, Leningrad, etc.; 25.1 percent of the group were from various places in the former Pale of Settlement; and one-quarter (25.4 percent) were from the "annexed territories."
9. Before they became active in the movement, 40 percent of them earned 100 rubles or less monthly; 32.3 percent earned between 100 rubles and 150 rubles monthly; and the remaining quarter earned over 150 rubles per month. The average gross income of the Soviet urban earner was 66 rubles in 1968 and 78 in 1973.
10. Testimony of Anatolii Dekatov, *Observer,* November 22, 1970; *Ma'ariv,* November 23, 1970.
11. Ze'ev Katz, "The Kremlin and the Jews: Past Stands and Future Possibilities," *Bitfutsot bagola,* (Heb.; Winter 1972), p. 103. Katz's data are based on *Itogi vsesoiuznoi perepisi naseleniia 1970 goda,* IV (Moscow: n.p., 1973).
12. "Sociological Characteristics" p. 9. The attachment to Judaism of activists' parents does not include an identification with the Zionist movement that was expressed in the home. Grisha Feigin, for example, defines his home as "Zionist" (*Lamerhav,* May 25, 1971). His home, therefore, is not included in our category because no religious observance was practiced. In contrast, another former activist, Michael Zand, describes his house as "half Communist and half Jewish Orthodox" (*Ma'ariv,* July 3, 1971). Zand's home is considered to have been a "religious" one for the purposes of our definition.
13. "Sociological Characteristics," p. 9.

14. "Sociological Characteristics," p. 10.
15. According to the testimony of many activists, *Simhat Torah* was the chief festival on which the activists publicly demonstrated their national identification with Israel. "The mass neo-Zionist assemblies began on *Simhat Torah*," according to M. Perah (Lapid), "The Meetings at Rumboli," from his private archive.
    Yasha Kazakov has also affirmed this: "On the holidays, Jewish youth would come by the thousands to synagogues in Moscow, Leningrad, Riga and Kiev and stand there and sing and dance and identify publicly with Israel, before the very eyes of the secret police. That was a real demonstration." *Jerusalem Post*, February 18, 1970. Another related form of national endeavor was the *aliya* activists' meetings in homes of movement members on various festivals. See, for example, Hillel Shur's story, *Ma'ariv*, August 19, 1970.
16. "Sociological Characteristics," p. 10. A letter sent by engineer K. Rabinovich to *Pravda* reinforces these findings. He asserts that one of the reasons that impelled him to seek permission to settle in Israel was the impossibility of observing, in the USSR, the Jewish holidays which require public worship. He makes no mention of other activities, carried out in private. *Davar*, March 22, 1970.
17. "Sociological Characteristics," p. 10. Vladimir Borisov relates *(Ma'ariv,* November 28, 1960) that for many years during his childhood he did not know of Israel's existence. He did not know a word of Yiddish or Hebrew and had no idea that there had once been a Jewish state which had now been reborn. His experience more or less resembles that of many activists, such as Tina Brodetskaia *(Ma'ariv,* September 11, 1970) and Lazar Liubarskii. The latter joined the Jewish national movement when he began his studies for a degree in automotive engineering. At that time "he knew virtually nothing about Hebrew literature and culture or about Jewish history." See Moshe Decter, *The Lonely Course of Lazar Liubarsky* (Jerusalem: 1971, stencil).
18. The Holocaust left its imprint in one form or another on approximately 82 percent of the activists. It aroused about one-third of them to greater solidarity with the Jewish people. "Sociological Characteristics," p. 12.
19. For the impact of the Holocaust on the activists, see, for example, Izrail' Kleiner, *Anekdoticheskaia tragediia* (Tel Aviv: Krug, 1978), pp. 23–28.
20. According to the Soviet scientist Roy Medvedev in William Korey, *The Soviet Cage: Anti-Semitism in Russia* (New York: Viking Press, 1973). See also interview with Mikhail Polutsk, May 9, 1975, and others, CRD.
21. For the impact and implications of Golda Meyerson's arrival in Moscow, see Yaacov Ro'i, *Soviet Decision Making in Practice: The USSR and Israel 1947–1954* (New Brunswick, N.J.: Transaction Books, 1980), pp. 183–219.
22. As many as 23.5 percent said that the 1967 war had been a watershed event, leading them to become active in the national movement, ("Sociological Characteristics," p. 13) while half of them viewed the war as an extraordinary event which had generated in them a "powerful" (though not "overwhelming") emotional response. Some activists assert that, while they had been active in the

Jewish national movement even before the Six-Day War, that even wrought a "crucial change" in them. See among others the testimony of Raiza Palatnik (*Al hamishmar*, December 29, 1972). On the other hand, some began to be active under the influence of the "spirit" of the Six-Day War. According to Raia Kasieta: "It was in 1969. Although I had begun to aspire to *aliya* two years earlier, I made no special efforts because of my parents' vigorous objections. That year, a friend from Riga, Iosif Shnaider, brought me several records of songs from the Six-Day War. I taped them and listened to them for hours every day. I understood no Hebrew, but I did understand the enthusiasm and the heroism of the songs. Thus I decided that I would go to Israel no matter what!" *Yediot aharonot*, May 12, 1972.

23. Many activists recall particularly the arrival of the Israeli delegation to the International Youth Festival held in Moscow in 1957. "At the festival I met Israelis for the first time," Tina Brodetskaia relates. "Suddenly I saw many proud, free Jews who were completely different from the Jews of Russia. I grasped that the Jews of the Diaspora, including those in Russia, were 'creatures of the ghetto.' The meetings at the festival were crucial for me." *Lamerhav*, September 18, 1970.

24. "The Sinai Campaign of 1956 lit in him an 'internal fire.' Suddenly he notices that there were Jewish surnames and that his friends were Jewish." This motif in the story of an *aliya* activist (*Haaretz*, January 4, 1971) recurs from time to time in the stories of other activists.

25. Estrangement from the Soviet Union intensified in the wake of the Six-Day War. However, about one-third of the activists had felt a sense of alienation prior to the Six-Day War. "Sociological Characteristics," p. 30. It is noteworthy that this social alienation did not prevent the activists from promoting Jewish culture inside the USSR, not as a palliative, let alone a long-term solution, but as a means of reinforcing a sense of nationalism. Ibid., p. 33.

26. About 80 percent of the activists experienced anti-Semitism as children. "Sociological Characteristics," p. 14.

27. See for example, among numerous others, the testimony of Vitalii Rubin—"I was not accepted for post-graduate studies because of my nationality." CRD, February 1977.

28. Approximately 57 percent of the activists said they had had difficulty finding a place of employment because of their Jewishness: "Sociological Characteristics," p. 14. As Viktor Perlman relates: "I felt the full force of antisemitism when in 1951 all the institute's Jewish graduates, about 200 people, remained without appointments and were never given a job." Interview, Center for Research and Documentation on East European Jews, Hebrew University, May 1974.

29. 70 percent of the activists had adaptation problems of various sorts in their places of work, "Sociological Characteristics," p. 14.

30. "Sociological Characteristics," p. 15.

31. Various charges were leveled at the activists. Among the most frequent were accusations of "parasitism" (Leonid Zbalishanskii, Valerii Panov and Mark Azbel were among those accused of this), "vagrancy" (for example, Anatolii

Novikov), "hooliganism" (Aleksandr Feldman), "unlawful demonstrations," "alchoholism" (Ida Nudel was accused of having committed that offense), or writing anti-Soviet literature (for example, General Iosif Davidovich, Col. Lev Ostraikher, and Col. Naum Alshanskii were tried and jailed for this). *New York Times,* October 1, 1973.

32. The statement by Boris Kochubievskii, which was read out before his sentence was announced, reinforces the finding that trials conducted against activists sometimes actually fortified their spirit and their desire to work in the national movement for their emigration to Israel and that of their colleagues: "As long as I live, as long as I am capable of feeling, I shall do all I can to get to Israel. If you judges think that I merit imprisonment for this, then it does not matter to me: If I live until the day of my release, that day will once again find me ready to leave for the land of my fathers, even if I have to make the journey on foot." See "Protsess Borisa Kochubievskogo," in A. Rozhanskii, ed., *Antievreiskie protsessy v Sovetskom Soiuze (1969–1971)* (Jerusalem: CRD, 1979), pp. 20–23.

33. According to the findings, the chief reasons for emigration to Israel were: anti-Semitism (29 percent), fear and apprehension about their fate and their future (18 percent), absence of a distinctive Jewish way of life (15 percent), disappointment in the regime (9 percent), social difficulties (4 percent), and economic difficulties (4 percent). Only about 20 percent of the activists viewed Zionism as a central, paramount reason for their decision. "Sociological Characteristics," p. 36. These findings conflict with the conclusion of William Korey, who asserts in his book that love of Israel was the chief reason for the intensification of Jewish consciousness in the USSR, and only afterward "the new form of Russian antisemitism," which also led to enhanced awareness among the activists aspiring to settle in Israel. Other causes noted by Korey for the intensification of Jewish national consciousness were "the refusal of the Jews to assume that their culture and tradition will die in the Soviet Union" and "their deeply rooted and growing faith in Jewish unity." Korey, *The Soviet Cage,* pp. 98–101.

34. Since 1967, approximately 80 percent of the activists have listened to Israel Radio on a regular basis, as compared with 25 percent previously. "Sociological Characteristics," p. 17. Professor Tartakower, chairman of the World Hebrew Union, quoted findings that a daily average of about half a million persons listened to Israel Radio. *Davar,* February 10, 1970. This figure seems somewhat inordinate. However, one can accept Dr. Avic Eliav's point that listening to Israel Radio was a precept for every *aliya* activist and sympathizer of Israel. *Jerusalem Post,* January 18, 1971. For an interesting account of the techniques that were developed for listening to Israel Radio, see Izrail' Kleiner, *Anekdoticheskaia tragediia,* pp. 19–20.

35. Approximately 60 percent of the activists had read Leon Uris's novel *Exodus.* Half of them had read the writings of Zionist leader Ze'ev Jabotinsky and about one-quarter kept up with Israeli papers and journals, and the like. "Sociological Characteristics," p. 17. All the activists were familiar with *samizdat.* On the means of publication of *samizdat,* see below.

36. Approximately 85 percent of the activists were in correspondence with people in Israel. "Sociological Characteristics," p. 17.
37. Over half of the activists said they had met with Israeli representatives. Ibid., p. 17.
38. Many accounts exist of the various methods by which the activists met with correspondents. These meetings were generally secret, although some were held in public. The thousands of petitions published in the West were conveyed in this manner. See, for example, *Ha'aretz*, August 15, 1964, May 24, 1970, and January 5, 1971; *New York Times*, April 29, 1974.
39. Particularly noteworthy were the memorial ceremonies for Holocaust victims held at Babii Iar, Rumboli, and elsewhere. This activity, being public, may be included in the third category (see below). As of 1969 the memorial ceremony at Babii Iar was generally attended by over 2,000 Jews from throughout the Soviet Union, among them many *aliya* activists, and it became a demonstration of national identification. Many *aliya* activists tried to get to these ceremonies, despite the authorities' attempts to prevent their attendance. See, for example, *Davar*, October 1, 1974. On the meetings at Rumboli and on the national activity there since the beginning of the 1960s, see the testimony of M. Perah (Lapid), "The Meetings at Rumboli" (cf. note 15 above).
40. "Sociological Characteristics," p. 18. According to Prof. Tartakower, thousands of requests arrived in Israel from Jews in the Soviet Union for Hebrew schoolbooks and for dictionaries from Israel. He and his deputy, Haim Levanon, reported that the World Hebrew Union sent large numbers of Hebrew books to the Soviet Union. They added that the Union helped "bodies and organizations in Israel and worldwide to send gifts to Jews in the Soviet Union, such as records of Hebrew songs, postcards depicting Israeli scenes, Passover *haggadot* and even *noisemakers* for Purim. . . . The Union's offices receive letters written in good Hebrew, including one from a researcher who claims (and complains) that poor Hebrew is written in Israel." *Davar*, February 10, 1970.
41. Most of the farewells took place in private homes (approximately 70 percent), although some were public (on which, see below). "Sociological Characteristics," p. 21.
42. Ibid. This type of activity took many forms, of which the most typical was demonstrations in small groups. An example is the demonstration by three activists who distributed leaflets in front of the Communist party building in Moscow following the Yom Kippur War in which they maintained that they were "prisoners of war." Or the demonstrations in a Moscow synagogue in which Jewish activists carried torches made of paper and other flammable material, and cried out "Long live Jerusalem!" "Long live Dayan!" (*Ma'ariv*, January 23, 1970).
43. About six out of every ten activists took part in drawing up petitions, and seven out of every ten collected signatures. "Sociological Characteristics," p. 19. The first petition to be sent abroad (to the UN secretary-general) was apparently that of the group of eighteen from Georgia (August 1969), published in *Evreiskii samizdat*, II, pp. 1–3.

The first protest letter (known in the West) sent to a ranking Soviet official after the Six-Day War was the Letter of the 26 to the first secretary of the Lithuanian Communist party. See *Evrei i evreiskii narod*, I: *Petitskii, pis'ma i obrashcheniia evreev SSSR, 1968–1970* (Jerusalem: CRD, 1973), pp. 1–3.

44. See, for example, the public demand of thirteen Jews from Minsk that the authorities try for slander the author of an anti-Semitic poem. *Al hamishmar*, April 24, 1974.

45. There were two types of activity relating to samizdat. One, in which the activists received samizdat material for reading, was passive in nature and is included in the first category. Approximately 56 percent of all the activists took part in the actual preparation of samizdat materials. ("Sociological Characteristics," p. 19.) On this, see Dr. L. Dimerski-Tsigelman, "Attitudes Towards Jews in the U.S.S.R.," in *Antisemitism in the Soviet Union: Its Roots and Consequences* (Jerusalem: Hebrew University of Jerusalem, 1979), p. 123.

46. The first periodical journal was published in Riga in February 1970. See *Evreiskii samizdat* (CRD), 1–2.

47. The term "government representatives" includes militia forces, KGB personnel, or officials of various ministries. Approximately 54 percent of the activists were insulted in one way or another by representatives of the authorities. "Sociological Characteristics," p. 26.

48. Five percent of the activists alleged that they were beaten or physically assaulted. Ibid., p. 26.

49. Approximately 4 percent of the activists were dismissed from their jobs, while 10 percent were demoted. Ibid., p. 26. According to the estimate of the *Washington Post* (March 21, 1970), 40 percent of the approximately 300 Jewish activist intellectuals who had requested exit permits from the Soviet Union were dismissed from their jobs.

50. Over one-third of the spouses of persons fired from their jobs were also fired. "Sociological Characteristics," p. 26.

51. Ibid., p. 27.

52. A number of cases are known of activists who were expelled from the Party. See the testimonies of Iasha Cherniak and of Leizer Eisenshtat—the former was expelled in 1971, the latter in the spring of 1969. CRD.

53. "Sociological Characteristics," p. 29.

3
The Impact of Ideological Changes in the USSR on Different Generations of the Soviet Jewish Intelligentsia

Ludmilla Tsigelman

Over the first three postwar decades Soviet Jewry, suffering from government-inspired discriminatory policies, was more and more actively rejected by Soviet society. Nevertheless, the Jews remained de facto an integral part of this society and to a large degree their fate was determined by its development.

This essay will study the formation of Jewish national consciousness and the influence of changes in the ideological situation in the USSR on various generations of Soviet Jews. It seeks to examine the hypothesis that the distinctive features in the formation of Soviet Jewish national consciousness derive largely from the interaction between the Jews and their social environment in its various phases of evolution. In the development of a Jewish nationalist orientation each subsequent generation of Soviet Jews was influenced first by the general ideological situation which shaped the Soviet citizen's worldview, value system, and preferences and second by the official Soviet policy and attitude toward Jews and Judaism.

This chapter focuses on individuals whose conduct was guided by ideology and spiritual considerations. These were generally people with a higher education. Although relatively few in number, this elite formed the leadership of the Soviet Jewish *aliya* movement of the seventies. Hence the study of their nationalist motivation, their ideological and spiritual roots is essentially a study of the leadership group in the Soviet Jewish movement—its formation, composition in various generations, and future prospects.

The available material permits us, indeed, to distinguish between three basic periods or generations, although in fact the borders between each are vague and somewhat arbitrary. The first grouping, the "fathers," includes those who grew up in the prewar and war years (the thirties and early forties) and entered institutions of higher learning primarily in the first postwar decade; the second group—the "younger brothers" of the first, whose school years coincided with the fifties, started their higher education in the late fifties or early sixties. The generation of "sons" includes those who entered school in the late fifties and sixties.

In the lifetime of these three generations changes occurred not only in the ideological situation and in the Soviet Jews' status, but also in the reaction to these changes. Naturally, specific reactions depended on the individual's particular family background and personal characteristics. These determined the "coefficient of diffraction of environmental factors and the variety of ways through which members of various generations arrived at a nationalist position. Unfortunately, it is impossible to encompass the entire latitude with all its diversity; some of it is inevitably lost in distinguishing the general and typical features for each generation.

The Generation of "Fathers": Paths Toward National Identity

The generation of "fathers" grew up in the thirties and early forties, that is the period when the Soviet regime used both repression and ideological propaganda to establish and stabilize itself. The psyche and world outlook of gifted youth, including the Jewish segment, was strongly affected by the subordination of spiritual and intellectual processes to the ideological and by the growing information gap. They filled in the gap created by the deprivation of traditional, moral, and religious education with Marxist-Leninist ideology.

This generation, born under Soviet rule, received Marxist-Leninist ideology with its apologetics of social and national equality with genuine faith and enthusiasm. The youth of those years accepted the realization of the communist ideal as the primary task imparting meaning to all of human life. Often the influence of ideology went beyond the formation of a Marxist-Leninist worldview to the creation of a definite personality type whose intellectual and spiritual interests, emotions, and conscious strivings were subordinated to the realization of some social ideal, some suprapersonal task. This ideologically oriented personality type had long been common among the Russian intelligentsia, of which the Jews had constituted a significant segment, already prior to the 1917 Revolution. Now, in the Soviet period, the entire system of education and propaganda was directed at forming a personality type, who self-sacrificingly subordinated himself to the common cause.

One must keep in mind that the thirties, although a time of massive repressions, evoked massive enthusiasm. Among the most eager and sincere participants in this enthusiasm were Jewish youngsters, who were deeply impressed by the idea of serving an ideal and dedicating their life to its realization. Perhaps a typical Jewish inclination toward faith played some part in this, even though most of them grew up in assimilated, pro-Soviet families, the dominant norm among the Jewish population in the European parts of the Soviet Union. The national sensibilities of these Jewish youngsters were determined by their implacable opposition to anti-Semitism which, being in contradiction to the Marxist-Leninist apologetics of national equality, was perceived primarily as a malicious manifestation of anti-Sovietism.

When anti-Semitism was not an immediate concern, these youths were generally indifferent to their Jewishness. Often the same indifference prevailed among those who grew up in families which respected Jewish culture, spirituality, and traditions. They perceived their Jewishness as an antiquated attribute somehow related to their parents or grandparents but not relevant to themselves.

The late sinologist Vitalii Rubin grew up in a Jewish intelligentsia family in Moscow. His father, a philosopher noted for his work on Spinoza, knew and highly valued the Jewish spiritual tradition. Vitalii studied in a class of children selected for their ability and knowledge; more than half of the class was Jewish. "Understandably," writes Rubin, "the Jewish question in the generally accepted sense not only did not arise there, but also was absent in the negative antisemitic sense. All the Jews knew that they were Jewish but considered everything relating to Jewishness as a thing of the past. I remember relating to my father's stories about his childhood, *heder* (Jewish religious elementary school) and traditional Jewish upbringing as tales about something disappearing into the past, which did not concern me at all. There was no active intention of renouncing one's Jewishness. This question simply did not exist."[1]

Scientist Mark Perakh describes a similar situation in Odessa in the thirties. He recalls:

In my class, at least thirty out of thirty-five pupils were Jewish. Most knew some Yiddish. Although we spoke Russian among ourselves, our speech was sprinkled with many Yiddish words and expressions. I never experienced any antisemitism during all my school years. We did not feel separate from the rest of the "Soviet people." In school we did not study any Jewish history, but devoted a lot of time to Russian history and literature. We Jewish pupils perceived it as our history and literature, not realizing that we were strangers in the country. This was the paradox: we considered ourselves part of an indivisible Russian nation although we knew that we were Jews. Sayings in Yiddish and distinctive conduct coexisted in us with the feeling that we were living at home in our own country. I think that such a paradox had also been characteristic of prerevolutionary Odessa with its compact Jewish nucleus.

The writer Efraim Sevella recounts a similar experience in his childhood town of Bobruisk, where Jews predominated in the population and everyone in the town—Jews and non-Jews—spoke both Russian and Yiddish.

This Russian or Soviet patriotism was accompanied by an alienation from Jewishness which was the more natural and organic the more compact and meaningful was the surrounding and protecting Jewish majority. Paradoxically, the initial relative freedoms which enabled Jews to move to the bigger cities and enter all schools and institutes, including the most prestigious where they often constituted a majority in their various collectives, created the best conditions for the disintegration of the Jews as a nation, that is, they facilitated the decline of their national consciousness and hence their assimilation.

But assimilation is two-sided: ignoring one's Jewishness in a Jewish collective created only the illusion of absorption into another community. The milieu must also be willing to assimilate the Jew. True, the Jews were not universally repelled; indeed, nationality (as opposed to social origin) was not so significant in the prewar period. Contacts at work, the development of friendships, and mixed marriages gave the Jews the impression of belonging organically to a non-Jewish milieu.

Yet it is questionable how frequently the conditions facilitated real, as against illusory, assimilation. Moreover, we do not have sufficiently representative information on the frequency with which Jews ceased being Jews because they were protected by their own Jewish collectives. In the majority of cases in which people assert that they did not suffer from anti-Semitism in childhood, they are not describing the situation in mixed collectives; they belonged to Jewish collectives which involved them primarily in ideological and verbal relationships, but not in real ties, with the surrounding dominant nationality. The absence of negative emotions connected with Jewishness in this milieu became the source of indifference, which was conducive to a numbing of national sensibilities among many representatives of the generation growing up in the thirties.

National consciousness bore a different character when Jewish children encountered anti-Semitism;[2] here indifference was impossible and children had to choose between accepting or rejecting their Jewishness. They made this choice after the first encounter with anti-Semitism, which often resulted in a desire not to be a Jew. It is clear from the testimonies of those now in Israel that not only was this desire transient, but also that recognition of this striving as apostasy and self-shame often became the starting point for the formation of a nonconformist personality. Further encounters with anti-Semitism aroused such people to active opposition in which they asserted themselves as sovereign personalities and as Jews.[3]

Like any nonconformist behavior in a totalitarian society, active assertion of one's Jewishness in a hostile milieu could hardly become widespread among Soviet Jewish youth. The whole system of Soviet education was directed at creating a conformist personality, deprived not only of the ability to choose, but also of the ability to make independent judgments. Understandably, in such conditions, a conformist personality predominated, even in Jewish intelligentsia circles.

Jews adapted to the ideological situation and to the surrounding norms by distancing themselves from their Jewishness, sometimes even going to the extreme of Jewish self-hate and total rejection of their nationality. It is logical to assume that with the growth of official and popular anti-Semitism, this type of conformism would intensify and spread to ever wider circles.

Those who were able to withstand the hypnotic influence of mass indoctrination represent interesting exceptions, especially since their nonconformist views were formed in childhood, an age particularly susceptible to environmental influences.

The young nonconformists can be divided into three groups in accordance with their motivation and the nature of the families in which they grew up. The first and most numerous group consists of children from assimilated Soviet families living in the large cities of the country's central regions. The second group includes children from religious families where Jewish traditions were preserved. Since they were to some degree familiar with Jewish history and spirituality, they were able to retain a sentiment toward it. Under Soviet rule the number of such families constantly declined among the Ashkenazi Jews, although they continued to be found in larger numbers among Georgian, Bukharan, and Mountain Jews. The third group—as of 1940—consists of those from families living in, or coming from, the Western territories, that is, the areas annexed by the USSR during World War II. Such children (particularly from the Baltic states) were familiar not only with Jewish traditions but also with Zionist ideas and activity. These three groups formed the nucleus of the ideologically motivated *aliya*. Their interrelationships and their influence on the *aliya* process changed in the twenty-five or so years we are discussing, largely as a result of generational differences.

Children in the first group, raised in assimilated families where the parents were generally avid advocates of Soviet rule and frequently active in Soviet public life, based their opposition to anti-Semitism on faith in the justice and sincerity of the slogans of internationalism and national equality which were constantly and loudly proclaimed by Soviet propaganda. They perceived anti-Semitism as a species of national hatred and as an encroachment on the principle of national equality, and therefore as a form of anti-Sovietism. Volt Lomovskii, following his father's example, constructed the following syllogism: Internationalism, proclaimed by the Soviet government, is equivalent to social justice and anyone who defies it is an anti-Soviet enemy. Anti-Semites oppose internationalism and hence are acting against the government which enforces it. They are therefore anti-Soviet and must be opposed. The Jew who fought against anti-Semitism was thus defending not so much himself as the government from hostile encroachments. Although, of course, children did not construct such syllogisms, they reached this basic conclusion concerning the need to fight anti-Semitism.

Emil Liuboshits and Iuliia Gindelshtein-Sevella reacted similarly to anti-Semitism before and during the war, but they did not remain at the "patriotic-Soviet" stage. Iuliia, for example, tried to learn something about Jewish history through reading the Jewish Encyclopedia, the Bible, and books on Jewish history. In such cases the atmosphere in Jewish intelligentsia families, which retained a deep respect for all aspects of spiritual culture despite the materialistic spirit of the times, generally played an essential role. Knowledge of the heroic side of Jewish history made her ashamed of her earlier desire to renounce her Jewishness. Shame was replaced by pride in her national origins, in the hereditary connection with the Maccabean clan, who had led the armed resistance to the decrees of Antiochus Epiphanes against the Jewish religion in the second century B.C.E..

The turning to the Maccabees was deliberate. The most insulting aspect of Soviet anti-Semitism during the war years in particular was the accusation that the Jews displayed cowardice, namely that they "fought" in Tashkent and bought their military medals in the rear. These accusations were often addressed to people who were themselves at the front or lost their closest relatives in battle and to children whose relatives fought, were wounded, or perished at the front and in partisan units. These accusations troubled young people who had been brought up in the cult of self-sacrifice for their motherland. Sincerely respecting the mythologized Soviet heroes, they desperately needed to prove that Jews were neither cowards nor traitors. They could not ignore these insults and got into fights, sometimes utterly hopeless ones. Some lads, not waiting for the draft age, went voluntarily to the front. In several cases of outstanding heroism these young men died, disregarding elementary precautionary measures only so that they would not be suspected of being Jewish cowards.

In the school in Mogilev-Podolsk where Iona Degen studied in 1941, only four of his thirty Jewish classmates remained alive—all four invalids of World War II.[4] The majority of these thirty boys went to the front as volunteers aged sixteen and seventeen. The protest against the anti-Semitic slogan, "The Jews are hiding in Tashkent," which was heard almost as often as "Death to the German occupiers," he writes, was the hidden part of the iceberg, whose upper part was desperate bravery. Degen recalls Pavel Kogan, an original, talented poet whose verse has been published and is still being reissued.[5] Almost blind, despite the opposition of the conscription office, he nevertheless made it to the front. But the dangerous job of a military translator was insufficient; the division headquarters seemed to him like the deep rear. "I am almost certain," writes Degen, "that the motivation for his irrational act—Kogan went to the front line as the commander of a counterintelligence platoon and soon died near Novorossiisk—was the feeling which I knew so well—what if someone will think that a Jew is a coward, that a Jew is sitting in the rear."

The same striving to restore the worth of the Jews as a nation capable of resistance and heroism became the leitmotif among those Jewish youths whose Jewish consciousness developed under the influence of the Holocaust. Many were deeply disturbed that news about the horrors not only failed to arouse indignation against the criminals and sympathy for the Jews but instead became the source for new streams of hatred and scorn of the Jews. For these youths, anti-Semitism was not an abstraction, but a continuation of the same actions to which millions of their defenseless brethren had fallen victim. They experienced the death of millions not only as a tragedy but also as a national shame. Vitalii Svechinskii, who was fourteen years old at the end of the war, expressed feelings typical of his peers when they found out about the Holocaust: "No opposition, submission to fate. Yes, it is not a great honor to be a Jew!"

This honor could be restored only by active, armed struggle. The struggle for Jewish national dignity could truly be carried on only in Israel. They realized that the Soviet Union, although it welcomed in principle any struggle for independence and justice and recognized Israel's existence, would not grant Jews in the Soviet Union the possibility of defending their national dignity or of reestablishing justice. "We thought about Israel in the following terms," recalls Svechinskii, "There our lads are fighting for their own country, but we shall just sit here wearing out our trousers and continuing the Diaspora."

In 1949 Svechinskii and his schoolmates—boys from assimilated Moscow intelligentsia families—began to plan an illegal border crossing and flight to Israel. A year later all three were arrested and sentenced by a Moscow tribunal for "treason to the motherland and Jewish bourgeois nationalism."

David Khavkin developed an interest in Zionism on his own. In his midteens David realized that Jews must unite in order to withstand a hostile, destructive environment and assimilation. An active person by temperament, he sought out concrete ways of creating this unity. This led him to an active interest in Palestine and later in Israel. His conduct was also influenced by his father, a man who took pride in his Jewishness. David Khavkin (he was then not yet eighteen years old) took a photograph showing Golda Meir surrounded by Soviet Jews near the Moscow synagogue. Although not a member of any group at that time, Khavkin was familiar with a group of third-year students at the Moscow Medical Institute who were sentenced in 1950 to prison terms for pro-Jewish sentiments.

A group of boys aged sixteen and seventeen from the small Ukrainian town of Zhmerinka came to their own conclusions about the need for Jewish unity. A Zionist youth group was organized in the Zhmerinka ghetto during the war. After the arrival of Soviet troops during the war, the boys were sent to penal battalions and most perished. One of the survivors organized the youth again and the group renewed its existence in 1945 under the name Eynikeyt. Efraim Vol'f, who was only fourteen years old in 1947 when he joined the revived group, tells of their common striving to defend themselves and their nation from a repetition of the Holocaust and from local anti-Semitism. The Holocaust and local hostility toward Jews seemed to be sufficiently convincing arguments for national unity and for either the creation of an independent Jewish state or at least of a separate republic within the Soviet Union.

The similarity of childhood wartime experiences apparently explains the spontaneous formation of other youth groups with a similar program to that of Eynikeyt. In 1949, when the Zhmerinka group was arrested, a Lvov group "The Union of Jewish Youth" (SEM) was also suppressed. At the same time occurred the arrests of the Kiev schoolboy group, Dvasun. (The acronym is based on the Russian words for Saturday in November, the time when the group was started.) Vol'f met them in Kiev and in the Lukianovskaia prison.

Details on the extent and development of such groups are unlikely ever to be fully revealed. Their spontaneous formation in various locations suggests the potential basis, under legal open conditions, for a massive *aliya* to Israel even in the fifties. But the movement was crushed in its embryonic stages and the participants, despite their youth, were sentenced to long prison terms for "anti-Soviet behavior and Jewish bourgeois nationalism."

Even in their Zionism, these Jewish youths were distinctively not anti-Soviet; on the contrary, they counted on the Soviet Union as the basic force which could help them realize their plans. Vol'f mentions his group's drawing up an appeal to the Soviet government which spoke of Soviet help in the organization of a Jewish republic and in sending Jews to Palestine. In planning their flight to Israel, Svechinskii and his comrades did not change their attitude toward the Soviet Union. They considered that they were living "in a good country" and were generally satisfied, except, of course, with anti-Semitism, which at that time they thought had no connection with the government.

Their pro-Soviet attitude was completely sincere, and no matter how strange such an assertion appears now, the Jewish national striving of these completely assimilated Jewish youths was to a great extent the product of their Soviet upbringing, which cultivated the idea of service to country and people. "These Soviet attributes—concepts of honor, obligations to one's country, were not alien to us," recalls Svechinskii, "We grew up with this, it was our spiritual world."

This was the spiritual world of the ideologically oriented personality. We have already mentioned these youths' characteristic perception of their personal fate as a part of the national fate, the experiencing of social and national problems as deeply personal ones. Hence they reacted to the fascist genocide as a very personal national tragedy. Their conclusion was similarly organic: they themselves were obliged to do everything in their power to prevent the recurrence of their people's destruction.

Significantly, many youths could only come to this conclusion by overstepping the views and ideas which were tied directly or indirectly to Soviet propaganda. According to these views, communism and the Soviet motherland as its sole embodiment were the ideal which had to be served.

Many young Jewish men and women, without rejecting either communist ideals or Soviet-Russian patriotism, came to consider their primary life task the defence of *their* nation, the fight for its national self-preservation. This position derived logically from Marxist apologetics concerning national equality—if all nations are equal, then all patriotisms must also be equal. But at the time Soviet reality presented a different picture. "Proletarian internationalism" was interpreted in such a way as to justify ideologically the postwar strengthening of the Soviet Union as a world power. Official Soviet propaganda not only rejected any national patriotism other then Russian patriotism but also branded any other national ideology as a manifestation of "bourgeois nationalism." Jewish youths' interest in Jewish nationalism hence signified a departure from officially practiced ideology even though these young people remained loyal to the principles of Marxist internationalism.

This development shows that the ideologization of the "fathers' " generation was expressed not so much in dedication to a concrete ideology (in this case Marxism-Leninism) as in the formation of a personality type. The specific ideology changed, but not the striving to achieve fulfillment through subordinating oneself to the attainment of a suprapersonal idealistic goal. As Svechinskii tesifies: "For each of us the solution of our personal fate was part of the general plan. . . . For us justice consisted of our needing to be in Israel at that time, sharing the fate of our people."

Not all members of the "fathers' " generation followed such a direct path toward the awakening of their Jewish national consciousness. Several began their ideological and spiritual evolution with the discovery of the divergence between communist ideals and practice. The government-inspired anti-Semitic campaign was particularly painful for them. Those who had equated anti-Semitism with anti-Soviet behavior and seen Soviet rule as the natural antipode of any social injustice lost faith in their ideals and gave up their former political beliefs. In order to reach a Jewish nationalist viewpoint, many of the "fathers" reevaluated their ideological beliefs and passed through a dissident phase.

Jews came to dissidence from various circles, including nationally oriented ones. Those whose nationalist motivation predominated considered the link with the dissidents as secondary to the national idea. For many assimilated Jews, however, it often became a goal in itself and only a radical reevaluation of ideological and social positions (often connected with the failure of attempts to "humanize" the face of Soviet communism) made possible the transition to a nationalist position.

The autobiographical essay *The Tremor of Judaic Anxieties* by Aleksandr Voronel, one of the leaders of the *aliya* movement of the early 1970s and founder of the samizdat journal *Jews in the USSR*, reveals the typical stages in the spiritual development of these young Jews.[6] From their very childhood they felt such a degree of closeness to Russian culture and to Soviet social life that they did not question their right to participate in changing and improving it. Believing that communism offered an ideal model for such improvements, they strove to change society in conformity with this model. Following their disenchantment, they were forced to radically change their views and conduct.

In 1946, Voronel (then fourteen years old), motivated, like many of his peers by the desire to reestablish justice—not on the national but on the broad social plane—organized a group whose members distributed leaflets explaining to Soviet citizens the ways in which Soviet law and Marxist principles were being violated.

The attempts to bring Soviet practice into conformity with "scientific communism" generally led the youthful seekers of justice to the tribunal and further to forced labor camps. Jews constituted a significant segment of this group (for example, seven out of eight members of Voronel's group were Jews). Upon completion of their detention, the majority retained their former interest in social problems which sooner or later turned into a concern for national problems, for the fate of Soviet Jewry, and for the determination of their own personal fate within this framework—to a decision concerning repatriation to Israel.

Among those now living in Israel who followed such a path are Maia Ulanovskaia, sentenced at the age of eighteen to twenty-five years of imprisonment, and Dora Shturman, who in her youth served a five-year camp term for a work on Boris Pasternak and who dedicated the years after her imprisonment to studying the general systemic features of socialism and its specific Soviet characteristics.

Typically, many intellectuals from the "fathers' " generation arrived at a nationalist viewpoint via a transformation of their social and spiritual values. This process of change led them to a nationalist position in the sixties and seventies when they were already mature people. But even as their interests and views changed, they preserved the ideological orientation which had evolved during their youth.

An ideological orientation also predominated among the "hereditary Zionists," that is, those who grew up in homes with Jewish content and Zionist interests. Although similar in personality, they differed radically in their initial premises and spiritual evolution from their assimilated contemporaries. For example, Ester Lomovskaia and David Khavkin, who were brought up in Jewish-oriented families, initially and uncompromisingly rejected Soviet life. Like their parents, they categorically rejected a regime which destroyed all forms of Jewish national life. Unlike those youths whose national reorientation was an organic consequence of their Soviet upbringing, the Zionist views of Lomovskaia and others derived from their rejection of the entire Soviet system.

Despite their similar backgrounds, differences existed among the "hereditary Zionists" themselves in the formation of their national sensibility. These distinctions derived from differing environmental and social conditions in childhood.

Iosif Shnaider, for instance, grew up until the age of fourteen in pre-Soviet Latvia, where all forms of Jewish life continued to exist legally, where he was able to receive a Jewish education without hindrance, and where conflict with another hostile nationality was minimal. His contemporary, Ester Lomovskaia, grew up in Minsk, the capital of Soviet Belorussia, where even in the most favorable Soviet period—the early thirties—anti-Semitism continued to exist. Anti-Semitism was one of the strongest factors pushing Jews toward assimilation. Despite her family upbringing, when Ester Lomovskaia heard at age five that the Jews are bad people and "crucified Jesus," she came home in hysterics, denying both the crime and her Jewishness.

Shnaider had a higher threshold of sensitivity to anti-Semitism than did the youths who grew up in Soviet conditions. When at age fourteen he encountered a group of boys who screamed at him "Ab'gam" (an epithet aimed at deriding both his Jewish origin and Jewish mispronunciation of Russian), he genuinely thought they had erred and answered that he was not called Abram but Iosif. Only after catching the derisive nuances and intonation did he start a fight. But neither popular nor official anti-Semitism played a role in the formation of his Jewish national consciousness or in his decision to emigrate. His Zionism was a positive reaction built on Jewish values which had been instilled in his childhood. The Zionism of his Soviet peers developed more as a reaction to the Soviet system in general and to Soviet anti-Semitism in particular.

The generations which grew up under Soviet rule could formulate their Jewish national consciousness only by defining their attitude toward the Soviet system, even in Jewish-oriented families such as those of Lomovskaia and Khavkin. These families' acceptance of Jewish values was a corollary of their hostility toward the Soviet system as a system destroying these values. Nurturing no expectations of the regime, these children were free from the disillusionments which overtook those from pro-Soviet backgrounds. But such children were an exception; more commonly, as we have seen, ideologically oriented youths who grew up in the thirties and forties first accepted Soviet ideology, then turned toward dissident activity and ultimately toward Jewish values and Zionism.

National Consciousness of the Younger Generations of Soviet Jews

The following generations differed from the "fathers" in their approach toward Jewish nationalism. They were influenced by new factors, such as anti-Semitic campaigns which were obviously state-inspired, revelations about the Soviet regime, such as those disclosed at the Twentieth Party Congress, the rise and fall of the dissident movement, the devaluation of Marxist-Leninist ideology, indeed of any political ideology per se, paralleled by a greater interest in religious and metaphysical problems, and by the Jews' struggle for the right to emigrate.

Between the generations of fathers and sons lies an intermediary group —the "younger brothers" of the senior generation, whose school years coincided with the start of the state-conducted anti-Semitic campaigns.

Although ideologically oriented, this group was less dazzled than their "older brothers" by the Soviet system.

The proclaimed propaganda slogans of internationalism meant less to the "younger brothers" than the real, constantly intensifying state and popular anti-Semitism. The pogromist nature of the anticosmopolitan campaign and the "Doctors' Plot," the anti-Israeli direction of state anti-Semitism, and the increasingly clearer trend toward limiting Jews' access to higher education, the sciences, and other areas of qualified intellectual work naturally precluded any forms of pro-Soviet enthusiasm. In addition, they participated in the general critical atmosphere which developed from Khrushchev's and others' disclosures of state crimes and weaknesses.

An active response to state anti-Semitism on the one hand and a critical reevaluation of Marxist-Leninist ideology and the Soviet system as a whole on the other—these are the significant starting points in the spiritual and intellectual evolution of the "younger brothers." Like the "fathers' " generation, they also contain subgroups with differing ideological orientations. A first subgroup was more immersed in general democratic-social, political, and ideological problems. The second was chiefly concerned with the Soviet authorities' attitude toward the Jews and with the fate of Jewry itself. The first became involved in various forms of dissident activity. The second worked actively to combat state anti-Semitism. Its activities involved educational work, in particular the development and dissemination of Jewish samizdat.

In the late fifties and early sixties, before Jewish samizdat and the *aliya* struggle became widespread phenomena, a Jewish national orientation was characteristic of those from families which preserved elements of Jewish life, traditions, and national self-respect. Youth raised in assimilated families rarely came to nationalist positions independently. Their national reorientation was generally the result of their friends' and fellow students' educational activity.

One of these educators was Il'ia Voitovetskii, who grew up in a family that retained a positive attitude toward Judaism, Yiddish as a conversational tongue, and the memory of a Zionist uncle, Froim, who was shot in 1937. Suffering from earliest childhood from the anti-Semitism of peers and adults, including even his schoolteachers, Il'ia did not distinguish between popular and state-inspired anti-Semitism. While still a schoolboy he tried to protest against the Doctors' "Plot," and as a student in the late fifties he organized the Jewish youth in the Ural Polytechnical Institute. Trying to counter Soviet anti-Semitic policies and propaganda with positive Jewish knowledge, he attracted his fellow students to Jewish literature and music, to the study of Yiddish and Hebrew, and to listening to Israeli broadcasts. Many of these students came to the Urals from the Ukraine and other western regions where restrictions against Jews intensified in those years. Many were embarrassed by their Jewishness and tried to hide it. Voitovetskii's defense of Jewish national dignity influenced several to change their attitude: in his dormitory, which at first contained only one other "obvious" Jew, another four were gradually revealed. Two had preferred previously to be considered Russians, a third Moldavian, and a fourth Armenian.

Voitovetskii's active opposition to anti-Semitism and his organization of avowedly Jewish educational activity with a pro-Israel orientation attracted many young people in the second half of the fifties. In contrast, however, in this same Ural Polytechnical Institute another Jewish student, supported by his own group of like-minded students, presented to a Komsomol conference a program devoted chiefly to transforming the political order in the USSR. Although their national consciousness was aroused, some young Jewish intellectuals remained more interested in improving Soviet society. Assuming that national issues derived from social issues, they considered that the former would be resolved in a renewed, democratized Russia. This, in its general features was, for example, the credo of the Kievans Anatolii Partashnikov, Anatolii Feldman, and their two fellow activists who were sentenced in 1956 for anti-Soviet activity. They considered that freedom of emigration—including emigration to Israel—would be a consequence of general democratic reforms in the Soviet Union.

Thus the turn toward Israel, toward thoughts of *aliya*, often did not signify a withdrawal from social and political ideals. On the contrary, *aliya* often appeared to be a way to realize them. The less Jewish youth saw the possibility of realizing their ideals in the USSR, the more strongly they were attracted to Israel. The writer Iuliia Shmukler and the mathematician Pavel Vasilevskii describe Moscow youth groups in which such views evolved. The group which Iuliia joined upon entering an institute in 1956 included ten people—"Jews, half-Jews and 'transitional Jews' " (her name for those Jews who had a different nationality listed in their passport).

Organized in 1953, the group's actual leader, Lev Levitin, became a student in the physics department of Moscow University. Like Voronel, he began a fundamental study of Marxism and political economy while still a schoolboy and came to the conclusion that the Soviet system had nothing in common with socialism, but was a typical example of state capitalism. The entire group agreed with this conclusion. The constructive aspect—"what is to be done?" remained the most difficult question for them and for the circle of Pavel Vasilevskii, which the students from Levitin's group joined in 1960.

The group's interests were broad; the solutions to the problems concerning them focused on Israel.

When we discussed the fate of the world, Vasilevskii recalls, the expansion of the Soviet totalitarian system was a major concern. We perceived the West's extreme flaccidity, its Munich-like disposition. In our eyes Israel was the only country which, remaining democratic and socialist, demonstrated an ability to act, to show opposition. We remained convinced socialists and Israel's position as the first to realize a Fourier variant of socialism made it the place where one of the most acceptable contemporary alternatives had been tested. We were enthusiastic and proud that precisely Israel had proven that a free society, without waiving democracy, can exist and successfully fight violence and terror.

Strictly national motives were added to general social concerns. Vasilevskii believed that although the Soviet Jew was far removed from his national roots, he still regarded genocide as a real possibility. Vasilevskii and his companions became convinced that the Jewish question is insoluble in the Diaspora. He began studying Hebrew in the early sixties, feeling confident that the Soviet authorities, with their policy of repelling Jews, would sooner or later be forced to allow them to emigrate.

The ten members of the Vasilevskii group later followed various paths. Some, becoming involved in professional activity, turned away from social problems. One member of the group, Lev Regelson, converted to Russian Orthodoxy, joined the priesthood, and emigrated to the West. More typical, however, were those who turned to their own people and state in the first major wave of Soviet *aliya* to Israel. Among the first to emigrate to Israel— in 1971—were Feldman and Partashnikov. After completing their terms of detention for anti-Soviet activity in 1961, both adopted Jewish nationalist positions and regarded *aliya* as their primary objective.

In general, as the sixties proceeded, various forms of broad dissident activity lost their attraction and Jewish national issues became more vital. The ranks of the advocates of nationalism were increased by those from the "fathers' " generation who turned away from their pro-Soviet views and convictions and by those dissidents who, disillusioned with the possibilities for democratic changes in the USSR and doubting the right of the Jews actively to participate in this effort, turned to Jewish national problems. Their ranks were also filled by those youths who can legitimately be called the generation of "sons."

Unlike the "fathers" and their "younger brothers", the "sons" proceeded directly to a Jewish nationalist outlook, avoiding the stages of pro-Sovietism and dissidence. Although in the sixties young people criticized the Soviet system, this critique was not their most vital concern as it often was with the senior generations. The situation in the family of Maia Ulanovskaia and the late Anatolii Iakobson is representative. These two were exceptionally active political figures whose fate symbolized the fate of the ideologically oriented youth of their generation. Their son, familiar with his parents' way of life and circle of friends, which included many outstanding intellectuals and dissident leaders, nevertheless rejected his parents' values and preferences and turned to national concerns. These took the form of an interest in Israel and a striving to be there in his own country. This was his reply to the anti-Semitism which he encountered at the very beginning of his conscious life. As an eight-year-old during the Six-Day War, he already chose his path.[7] Another Moscow schoolboy, Zhenia Gendlin, reacted similarly.

The Six-Day War played an enormous role in strengthening the national self-esteem of Soviet Jewish youth. In the late sixties in Moscow and in other major cities, youth groups whose main interest was Israel sprang up spontaneously. Fira Kantor recalls that among Jewish students in Moscow the striving toward Israel in the late sixties resembled an epidemic. Her own decision to emigrate was provoked by a feeling of rootlessness, of "homelessness," which gradually intensified under the influence of local Judeophobia and state-inspired anti-Semitism (her documents were not accepted for university entrance because of an "unsuitable" family name).

The rejection of Soviet reality was limited to this decision to emigrate. Fira was not sufficiently interested in the nature of the Soviet order to consider how to change it. Fira and her rather wide circle of like-minded young Jews had practically no connection with the dissident movement or dissident ideology. "We were ordinary Jewish youth," she recalls, "who together studied Hebrew and prepared for our departure."[8]

In the late sixties and early seventies these youths frequently initiated the idea of repatriation within their families. In several instances an evaluation of the prospects for Jewish life in the Soviet Union, the decision to remain or depart, and in later years the choice between Israel and other Western countries became sources of disagreement between parents and their offspring. For example, Pinkhas Gil went alone to Jerusalem in 1971 at age nineteen. His parents and two sisters remained in Moscow. His motives for going to Israel were strictly national. He felt that a man cannot live alone; he must recognize to what group he belongs. The natural conclusion for those who wanted to remain Jews was to go to Israel. To be a Jew meant to follow the Jewish religion and tradition. He came to the recognition of his Jewishness as the primary element in his life on his own. Although Gil was interested in general social problems at some period, he quickly abandoned dissident activity because it was far removed from his personal goals.[9]

Jewish national consciousness determined the vital decision of many Jewish young people in that period, although they generally did not equate it with religious feelings. Of twenty-four youths who finished one of the Kiev mathematical schools in 1971, fifteen had already been living in Israel for several years by 1980. These youths decided on repatriation independently, as in the cases of Mark Lutsker and Iakov Vinaver, who left despite their parents' objections, after having served three-year prison terms for their refusal to serve in the Soviet army.

The generational conflict occurred most frequently in families where the parents had firmly adapted to Soviet conditions and were often more anti-Zionist and anti-Israel than even the Soviet media. In some cases, parents even turned in their sons who refused to serve in the Soviet army, declaring that they would rather see them in prison than in Israel.

The motivation of those who strove to reach Israel despite their parents' wishes was rather complex. They wished to avoid the dissatisfactions generated by both general Soviet conditions and anti-Semitism in particular: feelings of inadequacy in personal and civil matters, social problems, and difficulties in academic and professional placement and advancement. They were also attracted to Israel, which was romanticized after its victory in the Six-Day War, by the search for their own national, cultural, and spiritual roots.

A spiritual orientation influenced the national consciousness of two classmates from the above-mentioned Kiev mathematical school—Petr Kriksunov and Emanuil Gelman. Kriksunov, whose parents succeeded in creating a relatively isolated microworld, grew up in a milieu which emphasized intellectual and spiritual values. His linguistic talents were revealed rather early. For him word and text were authoritative representatives of national spirit and being. His acquaintance in his school years with Mandelshtam's works was decisive: the poet's symbolism, images, and ways of viewing the world seemed essentially Jewish. He found a remarkable correspondence between them and the figurative structure of the Bible.[10] Through this interest he came to identify personally with Jewishness. His feeling of metaphysical-spiritual kinship with the Jewish nation led him to a recognition of the need to unite his fate with his nation's and consequently to the idea of repatriation to Israel. The motivation of Gelman was similar.

A slightly different spiritual orientation—its national motivation was more historiosophical than literary in content—prevailed among a very small, closed circle of Moscow students who began to study Hebrew, the Bible, Jewish philosophy, and history immediately after entering Moscow University in 1964.

In this group social and political problems were secondary to philosophical and religious interests. Israel, reborn after a two thousand-year interruption in its historical life, was perceived as the embodiment and bearer of that spiritual principle which, it seemed, had been hopelessly lost both by the rational West and totalitarian Russia. They disapproved of the intelligentsia's (including Jews') involvement in Christianity and Orthodox ritual because they saw it as an avoidance of personal responsibility through immersion in a religion which stresses collective principles. In contrast the group was favorably inclined toward Judaism which, in their view, espoused an individualistic principle—man's personal and direct responsibility. By projecting their interpretation of Judaism onto the contemporary scene, they were able not only to establish their worldview, but also to define their attitude to the social entity—Soviet and Israeli—and to decide on their path in life. Their choices varied.

Some, having started from a metaphysical concept, made their way to a real Israel and remained there. These people were able to solve for themselves the problem of combining an idealized metahistorical Israel with its historic reality. Some fenced themselves off from any social units and tried, without leaving the USSR, to hide in their own socio-ecological niche, to withdraw into spiritual asceticism. Others, despite their initial critical attitude toward Russian Orthodoxy, later turned toward it.

Although the path of metaphysical, spiritual quests can hardly be called typical or widespread, it nevertheless deserves analysis since it reflects that reorientation of interests which became characteristic of elite intelligentsia circles in the late sixties and seventies and which in a certain way was reflected in the national motivation of various generations of the Jewish intelligentsia.

The De-ideologization of the Soviet Jewish Intelligentsia Under the Influence of Ideological Changes in the Sixties and Seventies

In the previous sections we examined each generation of the Soviet Jewish intellectual elite separately, focusing on the specific ideological factors influencing the Jewish national consciousness of each generation. In this section we shall deal with the ideological changes in the sixties and seventies which led to a de-ideologization among all generations. The de-ideologization took on two different forms—on the one hand, a heightened interest in religion and philosophy and on the other, a turn toward consumerism.

Beginning in the mid-sixties, the intelligentsia noticeably shifted its interests from ideological doctrines and social and political concepts to religious, philosophical, anthroposophical, historiosophical, and other metaphysical spheres. This process had its origin in an earlier amazing phenomenon which Ernst Neizvestnyi labeled catacomb culture.[11] In 1947, Neizvestnyi gathered together on his own initiative a group of people in Moscow interested in studying and solving all kinds of problems, but only in their metaphysical aspect. The content of this catacomb culture can be judged by the authors whom the group studied, such as Thomas Aquinas, Saint Augustine, Kierkegaard, and other existentialists; Aldous Huxley and George Orwell; representatives of the Russian spiritual-philosophical renaissance: Solov'ev, Berdiaev, Rozanov, and Bulgakov; and theosophists and anthroposophists such as A. Besant, E. Blavatskaia, and Rudolph Steiner. They were especially interested in the idea of unifying various religious systems, in partucular seeking an identity of meaning in the esoteric teachings of the East and of Chrisianity.

Such literature had been largely inaccessible in the Soviet Union and most intellectuals were unfamiliar with it. Once a circle such as this one started the process, the search for and distribution of such literature gathered its own momentum.[12] The process continually grew in scope and intensity in the sixties and seventies. This was prompted not only by the steady decline of interest in politico-ideological doctrines, but also by the sufficiently high level of the Soviet intellectual elite and by the increased exchange of information with the West. Worldwide ecological dangers and social crises also demanded a rethinking of general philosophical and humanistic problems.

Judaism and Jewish philosophy occupied an extremely minor position in this complex of religious and philosophical metaphysics, which were discussed in the sixties and seventies. The Jewish intelligentsia became acquainted with Jewish philosophy generally through the works of Russian religious philosophers such as Solov'ev, Bulgakov, and Rozanov. Prerevolutionary editions of Shestov's works also circulated secretly, but they were perceived primarily in the context of European existentialism, not in relation to the philosophical-ethical foundations of Judaism. Translated, samizdat editions of Buber's works were especially helpful for those particularly interested in Jewish problems, but they were but a drop in an alien ocean. Perhaps the Soviet Jewish intellectual's difficulty in obtaining Jewish philosophical literature explains why the move from ideology to metaphysics simultaneously signified an estrangement from Jewish national interests. At any rate, a significant part of the Jewish intellectual elite who were involved in the underground (catacomb) spiritual life in the USSR showed a marked indifference to Jewish problems.

Although common, this situation was neither all-encompassing nor entirely one-sided. Metaphysically inclined Soviet Jews might show an interest in ideology in general and in Jewish national problems in particular; ideologically or nationally oriented Jews might take an interest in other problems, including spiritual and cultural ones.

Like any other models, those of ideologically or spiritually oriented personalities are easily oversimplified. In reality, most people possess a complex of views and interests; one can speak of a personality type based on the dominance of certain elements. These dominants change under the influence of prevailing social preferences, spiritual processes, standards of conduct, and even fashions. The ideologically oriented personality, formed during the intensely ideological period of the Soviet government's formation and entrenchment in power, predominated among the first wave of Soviet *aliya* activists. The de-ideologization, which began with Khrushchev's disclosures and the accompanying increased interest in spiritual-metaphysical problems, created the conditions for a new personality type giving preference to philosophical and spiritual interests. These new abstract interests enabled intellectuals to retain a sense of honor while avoiding commitment to dangerous dissident and Jewish national concerns. At the same time, their aloofness from touchy political issues saved them from open involvement with the official ideology and its guardians.

For Jewish intellectuals such a switch in concerns signified a spiritual evolution which seldom involved an interest in Jewish national problems and even more rarely lead to making decisions about their life's course in accordance with the interests of the Jewish nation and its fate. Some became directly involved in Christianity.[13]

Presumably, the evolution of this type of personality is found significantly more often among the intellectual elite circles of "sons" than it was among such circles of "fathers." One can also assume, and observations seem to support this, that the "sons" more than the "fathers" manifest an interest not only in the philosophy of religion, but also in ritual and ceremonial observance. "More often," however, does not signify "many," and the conditions under which most Jewish sons are brought up suggest that the majority of them retain the characteristic Soviet spirit of religious ignorance and atheism.

Although the "fathers' " ideological orientation was determined by their childhood environment, this predisposition became significantly weaker in the late seventies and early eighties than it was in the years of active struggle for the very right to emigrate. In deciding to emigrate now, only a very small segment of the "fathers' " generation is guided by the same ideological and national motivation as their predecessors in the early seventies. Our survey reveals the same tendency among the "sons."

Although the "spiritualization" which replaced "ideologization" affected only the elite strata, it has a broader social significance because the elite's changed orientation diminishes the likelihood of their producing new leaders and ideologues with the Jewish national consciousness of those who initiated the first wave of *aliya*.

The future relationship between spiritualization and Jewish national consciousness remains unclear. Grigorii Pomerants offers a likely prediction concerning a revival of Jewish national consciousness among Jewish intellectuals who were attracted to Christianity. He considers that the continuation of the present policies toward the nationalities, and the polemic with the reviving Russian nationalism—both Soviet and non-Soviet, from Aleksandr Solzhenitsyn to Vladimir Osipov, will all the more frequently arouse the Jew in a Jew and create favorable conditions for the revival of Jewish religious separation.[14] It remains questionable whether in this instance a turn to Jewish identity and the Jewish religion will be combined with an intensification of Zionist strivings, or whether repatriation to Israel will remain outside or on the extreme periphery of such people's plans.

Not all intellectuals became involved in spiritual pursuits in the sixties and seventies. The loss of Jewish national motivation among many assimilated Soviet Jews was caused partly by the de-ideologization in Soviet society in the Brezhnev period, which was even more pronounced than in the Khrushchev era, plus the specifically Zionist de-ideologization of the latter half of the 1970s and the early 1980s. The factors leading to the general Soviet de-ideologization, which the average Jew was subject to from childhood in the same measure as any other Soviet citizen include: loss of faith in the communist ideal after Khrushchev's disclosures and the failure of the "Thaw" or liberalization associated with his name; the consequent devaluation of the social ideal as such; a growth in consumer demand stimulated both by the ideological vacuum and the constantly growing deficit of goods and services; and the replacement of the "hero" type as a model which the majority should try to emulate. The "fighter" who subordinates his life to the realization of some suprapersonal goal is replaced by the "acquirer," a man who possesses the hard-to-attain goods. With the growing demoralization in the Soviet Union, the amount of such possessions often testifies to one's place in the social hierarchy. Although an interest in consumerism may detract from an ideologically oriented interest in Jewish national consciousness it may lead to using one's Jewish identity as a means of leaving the Soviet Union. The pursuit of greater material satisfaction and security may partially explain the desire of many Soviet Jewish intellectuals to leave the Soviet Union for the more affluent West rather than for Israel.

The specific Zionist de-ideologization is usually explained by the negative information about Israel transmitted to the Soviet Union by Jews who have departed earlier. Although this information plays a role, information about absorption problems can neither create nor destroy ideological motivation. Could it decisively influence people who consider that they must share in their brethren's efforts and participate in the creation of a national state? It is more likely that in such a setting, negative information could become an additional argument for repatriation: who can help save the situation if not I, and when, if not now?

Such reasoning, however, would have the most impact on an ideological personality type who, under present Soviet conditions, appears only as an exception to the rule.

Conclusion

Those Soviet Jewish intellectuals who preserved an ideological type of personality provided the leadership for the large-scale *aliya* in the first half of the seventies.

The term "leadership" has a different meaning under Soviet conditions than it does in the West. The Jewish movement in the USSR could not acquire political leaders or an open organizational form since it did not meet with official approval. Hence leadership in the Jewish movement in the USSR had to be primarily ideological and this leadership became meaningful only when the leaders' ideals, ideas, and course of behavior were adopted by significantly broad circles. In other words, the leaders of the massive *aliya* movement of the early seventies turned out to be those whose ideological motivation was accepted by a sufficiently large number of Soviet Jews as a convincing argument in favor of *aliya*.

Ideological leadership was established through three basic types of dissident activity: (1) the struggle to emigrate, as a result of which not only was a breach opened in the Soviet emigration barrier, but also precedents were created which established standards of behavior, models to emulate for people who previously had not considered the possibility of such acts; (2) publishing—the creation and dissemination of uncensored samizdat literature; (3) scientific and educational activity—the organization of seminars, symposia, and circles for studying Hebrew, Jewish history, culture and religion.

The leadership group provided the impulse for two basic types of national ideological motivation: sociopolitical and cultural-religious. The sociopolitical motivation was expressed in the striving to live in Israel and strengthen it primarily as a refuge and guarantee against a possible repetition of the Holocaust. The creation of one's own state was evaluated as a unique chance for the historical rehabilitation of Jewry which had suffered not only tragedy but also the unexampled shame of mass annihilation. Adherents of a sociopolitical ideology also hoped that Israel could play a pioneering role in contemporary history by showing the way to the solution of social, economic, and ecological problems faced by Western powers. They believed that Israel demonstrated to the free world how to remain a democratic country, even while in the difficult situation of combating both terrorism within the country and the enmity of surrounding countries.

The hopes for Israel's special mission were based on a faith that it inherits and embodies spiritual and moral values scorned by both the utilitarian West and the totalitarian East. This faith brought the sociopolitical motivation closer to the cultural-religious, whose advocates sought to live in Israel in order to come closer to traditional Jewish forms of life, for the sake of a renaissance of Jewish cultural, spiritual, and religious values.

Although they have points of contact, the two motivations differ both in content and in their degree of influence on various generations of Soviet Jews. The leadership group of the first type is connected with the publication *Jews in the USSR* in the Soviet Union and with the journal *22* in Israel. That of the second type is associated with the journal *Tarbut* (Culture) in the USSR and with the journals *Sion, Menora,* and *Vozrozhdenie* (Renaissance) in Israel.

The sociopolitical ideology, which can be approximately equated with political Zionism, motivated the majority of leaders from the generation of "fathers," politicized by their Soviet upbringing and direct experience of the Holocaust. Politicization also affected many of the leaders from the generation of "younger brothers," whose mental development occurred during the period of disclosures about the Stalinist regime and the intensification of Soviet anti-Semitism. The generation of "sons" was significantly less attracted to political ideology.

The sociopolitical ideology had greater initial chances for success because of several factors. First, the sociopolitical approach was both familiar and legal in the USSR. The leaders could easily reorient this ideological approach toward a Jewish national ideology. Second, sociopolitical ideology can be translated into language accessible to the masses more easily than can other positions. Third, the ground for the reception of such an ideology in the USSR was well prepared—the lengthy period of Soviet history when political ideology subsumed all other forms of spiritual life for society and the individual.

The cultural-religious motivation, which held a subordinate position in the earlier years, acquired more proponents in the late 1970s when the devaluation of the social ideal in general and the Zionist-political one in particular became more perceptible. Despite a relative increase in its adherents, this ideology could not compare to sociopolitical ideology in absolute influence for several reasons. First, its leadership group was small and less prestigious. Second, the growth of this group was hindered by the attraction of Jewish intellectuals to Christianity or to other ecumenical or metaphysical doctrines unrelated to Jewish national interests. Presumably, people making their choice were influenced by the lack of interest in Jewish problems on the part of such influential figures of Jewish origin as Ernst Neizvestnyi, Grigorii Pomerants, Naum Korzhavin, and the late Aleksandr Galich. A third reason was the scorn for any religion which is rooted in the Soviet atheistic upbringing. The antipathy toward religion is often intensified in the educated Soviet Jew, who frequently equates Judaism with the life of the humiliating Sholem Aleichem *shtetl*.

Since the decreased prestige of sociopolitical ideology could not be compensated for on a large scale by cultural-religious motives, the sum of interest in Jewish national issues declined. The loss of that Jewish nationalist motivation which had originally led people to the idea of repatriation played a role in the transformation of large-scale *aliya* into large-scale emigration, although it is difficult to evaluate this influence since those Jews interested in emigration rather than *aliya* often differed from the other group in background and orientation.

Having explored the effects on Jewish national consciousness of ideological change in the USSR as a whole in the late sixties and early seventies, I should like to mention in conclusion the possible effect on this consciousness of a significant ideological development in the late seventies and the eighties—the intensification of Russian nationalist tendencies.

Unlike the situation in the forties and fifties, when the party apparatus initiated and supported the glorification of Russian nationalism and a concomitant anti-Semitism, in the late seventies and the eighties intellectuals produce—often at their own initiative—the basic conceptions of this ideology. Although they use philosophical, metaphysical, and metahistorical arguments, these authors' intellect and erudition lead them to a crude system in which the misfortunes and troubles of their own nation are explained by the vices and wiles of an antipode nation. The role of such an antipode is traditionally assigned to the Jews. According to one of the most widely spread current versions, the Jews, who have played a destructive role in world history in general and in Russian history in particular, are the basic and primary source of Russian misfortunes. Embodying universal evil, the Jews used the Revolution to settle accounts with the Russian people, destroying millions of human lives in the process. Lacking their own roots, they became the destroyers of the foundations of national being and culture.[15]

Soviet rule, driving the Jews from the ruling apparatus, defending the nation's spirit and culture from their encroachments, assumes the role of guardian of the foundations of national life.

This version of nationalism, first disseminated through samizdat, has gained more weight and influence among intellectuals through its reproduction in officially approved publications. It now determines the topic of table talk in ordinary intelligentsia company and the themes of gossip in innumerable smoking rooms, offices, and corridors of Soviet institutions. In other words, the Jews are now alienated from that professional and social milieu from which they had formerly selected friends and allies. Their rejection by their former circle of acquaintances is often motivated by ideological and existential claims against Judaism.

Some Soviet Jewish intellectuals see this development as an additional argument in favor of fleeing from one's Jewishness into assimilation, either in the USSR or, failing that, among intellectual circles in the West. Aleksandr Sukonik, for example, uses metaphysical and metahistorical arguments to castigate Judaism and Israel.[16] Acknowledgment of guilt before the Russian people and an appeal to expiate it became a motive for turning to Christianity, a cause for emigration, and an argument against repatriation to Israel.

The recent polemic on the sources and causes of the Revolution—its Russian national or Jewish imported nature—have produced a diametrically opposite position, expressed most clearly by Mikhail Kheifets, who immigrated to Israel at the beginning of 1980. Arguing with the Russian nationalist poet and publicist Stanislav Kuniaev,[17] Kheifets acknowledges both the guilt and degree of responsibility of those Jews who took part actively in the Revolution and consolidation of the regime. But we can expiate our fathers' and grandfathers' guilt in only one way—by forming and strengthening our own national state. Participation in the Revolution was an attempt to leave the Diaspora, but a false one, "in the final account a criminal one." This ought to be clear to the current generation. But do many recognize that the time has come to end the eternal Jewish playing at "others' weddings" and to create one's own history?

The newly revised questions about the essence of diaspora life, about the nature and fate of Judaism and Jewry intensify the Jewish national argumentation but simultaneously activate assimilationist tendencies. It is difficult to predict whether Jewish antinational or national motivation (in cultural-religious or political form) will acquire more influence. Clearly, however, these results depend not only on the ideological situation and spiritual atmosphere within the Soviet Union, but also on the conclusion and aims of those who have already left the USSR. The leadership groups outside the USSR to a large degree determine these views and aims. Their positions, which are expressed in the Israeli and émigré press, are themselves the subject of a separate study. One of the significant factors, however, in the formation of one or another ideological motivation, is the polemic surrounding the fate of Soviet Jewry, a polemic which encompasses not only topical political but also spiritual and metahistorical problems.

Notes

Questionnaires and interviews with Soviet Jewish immigrants to Israel served as research material for this study. The questionnaires and interviews were conducted under the auspices of the Center for Research and Documentation of East European Jewry of the Hebrew University (henceforth CRD) and are located in the Center archives. Unless otherwise indicated, the personal accounts cited in the text come from these interviews.

1. Vitalii Rubin was active in the struggle for the Jews' right of repatriation from the USSR. He organized the Moscow seminar on Jewish culture in 1974. After emigrating to Israel in 1976 he became a professor at the Hebrew University in Jerusalem until his death in a car accident in 1981. See Vitalii Rubin, *Dnevniki. pisma* (Diary. Letters). Jerusalem: Biblioteka-aliya, 1988.
2. Some notion of the frequency with which Jewish children experienced anti-Semitism in various periods of Soviet history can be found in the questionnaires, which contained the question: "Did you or any members of your family experience antisemitism in childhood caused by peers or adults?" Affirmative answers were given by 77.7 percent of activists and 74.2 percent of immigrants.

The data reveal not only the general total but also the changes in the quantity of anti-Semitic incidents in various periods. They show that anti-Semitism existed not only during the years of state-conducted anti-Semitic campaigns, but always persisted as a reserve which was brought to the forefront under "the most favorable circumstances."

The following table shows the incidence of anti-Semitism experienced by children who grew up in the various periods indicated in the left-hand column:

Table 3.1
Children and Anti-Semitism

1	2	3	4	5
Years	Percentage of activists who were aged 6–16 years	Percentage of activists experiencing anti-Semitism at that age	Percentage of immigrants who were aged 6–16 years	Percentage of immigrants experiencing anti-Semitism at that age
Until 1941	25.1	22.1	18.4	8.4
1941–1947	45.2	29.3	33.6	16.4
1948–1953	38.4	37.5	30.4	26.4
1954–1959	42.1	28.0	55.2	27.5
1960–1967	20.8	23.0	37.9	28.3
After 1967		20.3		41.0

Note: The second and fourth columns present the percentage of activists and the percentage of immigrants who were six to sixteen years old in the given periods. The third and fifth columns show the percentage of those who experienced anti-Semitism in those years.

Information in this table was obtained by the author from questionnaires and interviews with Soviet Jewish immigrants to Israel in connection with a research project entitled "The Rebirth of National Self-Consciousness of Soviet Jewry." These materials are now on file at the Center for Research and Documentation of East European Jewry of the Hebrew University of Jerusalem.

3. Descriptions of negative feelings toward Jewishness which then underwent a drastic reversal can be found in the interviews of Iulius Telesin, Volt Lomovskii, Ester Lomovskaia, and Iuliia Gindelshtein-Sevella, among others.
4. Degen's memoirs, the original of which are located at the CRD, have appeared in book form under the name *Iz doma rabstva* (From the House of Bondage). Tel Aviv: Moria, 1986. Degen, a professor of medicine, emigrated to Israel in 1977. In 1941, at the age of sixteen, he volunteered for the front and became an officer in the tank corps. He was wounded and decorated several times.
5. In the Gorbachev period of *glasnost'*, the Russian poet and publicist Stanislav Kuniaev published an article in which he writes about the phenomenon of rootlessness among certain poets, all the examples he brings being Jews, including Pavel Kogan—see *Nash sovremennik*, 8 (1987). In his protest against the award of the RSFSR State Prize to Kuniaev, the Soviet poet Evgenii Evtushenko talks, among others, of the "cold taunt" with which Kuniaev "jeers at young poets killed at the time at the front—P. Kogan, A. Kopshtein, N. Otrada and M. Kul'chitskii," *Literaturnaia gazeta*, January 13, 1988. The four poets Evtushenko saw fit to mention were all Jewish.
6. Aleksandr Voronel, *Trepet zabot iudeiskikh* (Jerusalem: Moscow-Jerusalem Publ. House, 1976). For *Jews in the USSR (Evrei v SSSR)*, see Stefani Hoffman,

"Jewish Samizdat and the Rise of Jewish National Consciousness" in this volume.
7. Maia Ulanovskaia, "Mosksovskii epilog," *Sion*, 27 (1979), pp. 28–29.
8. Interview with Fira Kantor, in *Aliia 70–kh*, ed. L. Dmerska-Tsigelman and L. Umanskaia (Jerusalem: n.p., 1978), pp. 178–82.
9. Interview with Pinkhas Gil, ibid., pp. 190–93.
10. In this connection see Maia Kaganskaia's article, "O Mandelshtame, poet iudeiskii," *Sion*, 20 (1977). For her work on Mandelshtam she had at her disposal unpublished verse by the poet which Kriksunov had obtained by traveling to Voronezh to see Nadezhda Mandelshtam.
11. "Vstrecha s Neizvestnym," *Kontinent*, 17 (1978).
12. During the ten years (1962–72) that I taught in various institutions of higher education in Kiev, I witnessed a gradual but clear reorientation among the most gifted students toward gnosio-logical, religious, and philosophical problems. This tendency was more noticeable among students in the natural sciences, who generally were on a higher level than those in the humanities. They read books on yoga and became interested in parapsychology. They obtained and reprinted prerevolutionary editions of Russian philosophers. Popular works included those of Sergei Averintsev and Grigorii Pomerants, and books and articles about the existentialism of Solov'ev, Iurii Davydov, Plama Gaidenko. Lively discussions—not by specialists—developed around the works of Iulii Shreider and Vasilii Nalimov on the borders of "competency" of the logical in the sphere of cognition of nature and phenomena of the human spirit,
13. According to Grigorii Pomerants, a writer familiar with the Moscow intellectual scene:

> Among my acquaintances are old *intelligenty* who have preserved loyalty to Russian Orthodoxy; not one who has remained faithful to Judaism. Educated Jews became complete atheists, and when they were caught by the opposite wave of a return to faith, they fell into the orbit of Christianity. In the absence of statistics, I can rely only on personal impressions: I am familiar with a Jewish priest, with several Jews turned Russian Orthodox, regular churchgoers, with one Adventist, and with one Catholic. Judaists began to appear among my contacts only after 1968, during the wave of Zionism. Generally they started with Christianity and turned to Judaism either in Israel or on the road to Israel, or were not religious people at all, but observed *national* religious customs. I think that an honest sociological questionnaire would show that among the intelligentsia segment of Moscow Jews there are more Russian Orthodox than Judaists even now. ("Son o spravedlivom vozmezdii," *Sintaksis*, 6 (1980), pp. 70–71)

14. Ibid.
15. A different, constructive tendency in Russian thought is connected with deepened national self-awareness and self-analysis, with the effort to explain the nation's vices and virtues through its own spiritual and material history. But this elite tendency, which is meagerly represented even in dissident literature (the works of A. Siniavskii and A. Zinov'ev) cannot in principle become officially acceptable and is unlikely to gain wide influence even among intellectuals.

Solzhenitsyn's works, which are interpreted in the spirit of egalitarian nationalism, enjoy almost absolute authority.

16. Aleksandr Sukonik, "Moi konsultant Bolotin," *Kontinent*, 3 (1975).
17. Cf. S. Kuniaev, "Legenda i vremia," report read on 21 December 1977, in the *Dom literatorov* in Moscow. Using the example of E. Bagritskii's "revolutionary euphoria," the report exposes Jewish hatred toward rooted Russian existence. Printed in the journal 22, 14 (Sept. 1980). In the same issue is M. Kheifets's reply, "Nashi obshchie uroki," pp. 156–66. For Kuniaev, see also note 5.

4

Jewish Samizdat at the End of the Forties: Fragments from Margarita Aliger's Poem *Your Victory*

Isai Averbukh

The phenomenon of uncensored literature and uncensored dissemination of information in the Soviet Union, popularly termed "samizdat," became widely known in the West in the second half of the sixties. Samizdat reflected the more open development of various opposition movements in the Soviet Union in this period. Similarly, Jewish samizdat became a significant manifestation of the Jewish national movement in the USSR. Having survived many years, silent and suppressed, the Jewish movement courageously announced its existence to the whole world in 1968 with a series of open letters by Soviet Jews. At this time works of Jewish samizdat and information about the existence of uncensored Jewish literature began to filter through to the West.

In a previous article I have examined the concepts "samizdat" and "Jewish samizdat."[1] Here I shall briefly define samizdat as any uncensored work produced under a totalitarian system, and Jewish samizdat as uncensored works on Jewish subjects created by Jews and disseminated by means of samizdat among Jews. Contemporary Jewish samizdat includes original and translated literature, material brought in from abroad, and recent copies of rare pre-Soviet works. (Since 1974 original Jewish samizdat in Russian has been reprinted in the series *Jewish Samizdat*, published by the Center for Research and Documentation of East European Jewry of the Hebrew University.)

Jewish samizdat, however, is not only a contemporary phenomenon. It existed long before the term designating it came into use. This article will describe an instance of Jewish samizdat in an earlier period which played an important role in arousing the national consciousness of Soviet Jewry. This is an uncensored fragment from the Jewish poetess, Margarita Aliger's long poem *Your Victory*. These verses were a protest against the revived anti-Semitism of the war years and the "anticosmopolitan" campaign of the late forties. During the war and, in particular, in the postwar period, a number of poems were published in the USSR which, to some degree or other, spoke of the Holocaust, yet none acquired such popularity as this fragment from Aliger's poem.

The poem *Your Victory* was first published in the journal *Znamia* in 1945 (No. 9). The *Short Jewish Encyclopedia* (in Russian) describes it in the following terms:

> The poem "Your Victory" occupies a special place in the work of Aliger. Trying to comprehend the tragic experience of the war, Aliger turns here for the first time to a Jewish theme. Aliger's poem reflected the deep ideological and emotional crisis of the Jewish communist intelligentsia caused by the catastrophic destruction of Jewry during the Second World War and the growth of open anti-Semitism in the USSR in the war years. Subjected to harsh criticism, it was later reprinted without the fragment dedicated to a Jewish theme.[2]

The fragment, which, with certain additions and variations was disseminated in samizdat, is given here in literal prose translation.[3]

> I traveled in the fall to Kama,
> To the distant little Tatar town.
> Mother had been evacuated there,
> And I hadn't seen her for a long time . . .
>
> Mama, mama, not a tear, not a word.
> Tears and words don't help.
> Left homeless in your old age,
> With what are you satisfied and alive? . . .
>
> Depriving the soul of rest and well-being,
> Across thousands of years
> A savage, charred resemblance has shown through
> With those who have no homeland,
>
> Whose innocence having perceived in the sentence
> Of an evil and unjust court,
> The Red Sea water shuddered,
> And the sea sighed and parted.

For whom God's sun generously
Baked the dry, unleavened bread . . .
How many miles, centuries and fates lay on the way
From Egypt to Russia?

Mama, mama, in foggy eternity
Along an unbeaten, fetid path,
How long did you wander under the sun and rain
Until the Promised Land?

You recognized this land in the night
And, falling down before the holy border,
Whispered, weeping, "I shall accept everything,
I shall not spare strength and love.

Give me only a wisp of settled life,
A hearth to warm the soul.
Mama, mama, you are in your homeland,
But the enemy has invaded its borders . . .

Lighting the stove and warming her hands,
Settling down to live anew,
My mother said, "We are Jews.
How did you dare forget that?"

Yet, I dared, you understand, I dared.
It was so cloudless all around.
I didn't have time to remember it,
Since childhood there was somehow never time.

You don't choose your motherland.
Beginning to see and breathe,
You receive your motherland on this earth
Irrevocably, like mother and father.

The days were blue-gray; with slanting rain . . .
Bad weather swept the streets . . .
I was born in the fall in Russia,
And Russia accepted me,

Suffused me with restless blood,
With the waters of a live spring,
Burned me with the unkind love
Of a wild Russian peasant.

It was difficult, it can be more difficult,
Let me only have enough strength for everything.
Can there really be a land more native
Than that land where one believed and loved?

Than that land which nurtured me,
Helped me to become big and proud.
It's true, mama, I forgot,
I could never imagine,

That we could look at the blue sky
Only little by little, surreptitiously,
Because it is you and I
Whom they are driving to Treblinka barefoot,

Suffocating with gas, exterminating in mobile gas-chambers,
Burning, shooting, hanging, and hacking to pieces,
Mixing with dirt and sand.

"We are a people prostrate in the dust,
We are a people cast down by the enemy . . ."
My people, I know about another . . .

At this point begins the samizdat version which differs sharply from the published one. Some of the stanzas are missing in the published version, and certain other lines contain major changes.[4]

Lorelei—the girl on the Rhine
The green chime of old strings . . .
What are we guilty of, Heinrich Heine?
In what way did we fail to please, Mendelssohn?

I shall ask Marx, Einstein,
Who were filled with wisdom,
Perhaps this secret of our guilt before eternity
Was revealed to them?

The charming canvases of Levitan,
The kind luminescence of birches . . .
Charlie Chaplin from the white screen,—
You answer my question:

Really everything that we were rich in,
Didn't we dispense without superfluous words?
What are we guilty of before the world,
Ehrenburg, Bagritskii, and Svetlov?*

They lived generously, not sparing their talents,
Not begrudging the best efforts of the soul.

---

* Famous Soviet writers of Jewish origin.

I shall ask the doctors and musicians,
Toilers great and small.

And the descendants of the proud Maccabees,
Faithful sons of their fathers,
Thousands of fighting Jews,
Brave officers and warriors.

Answer me in the name of the honor
Of a tribe persecuted over the centuries,
Lads, who disappeared without a trace,
Youths, who perished in battles.

The century-long horror of humiliation,
The lamentations of mothers and wives . . .
In the death camps of annihilation
Our people is tortured and burned.

Children crushed by tanks,
The label "Jude", the epithet "Zhid".
There are almost no more of us on earth,
Nothing will amaze us any longer.

We are Jews. How much grief and
Gloomy years in this word!
I don't know whether blood has a voice,
But I do know: blood has a color.

Foul riff-raff, branded for ever,
Reddened the earth with this color,
And human blood began to speak
At the hour of death in different languages.

Now I can hear the voice of blood,
The agonizing groan of my people.
Its fervent, subterranean call
Grows ever stronger, more savage, and stormier.

The manuscript in the possession of Tamar Dolzhanskaia contains several concluding stanzas to Aliger's poem which are missing in the manuscript in the possession of Alexander Donat and reproduced in his anthology from which the above is taken. They are:

The voice of blood. Our indelible blood
Is closely merged together,
And we have one road of revenge
And fury and love are indivisible.

> The knot of our age-old tie
> Is tightened more tightly by much blood—
> And our people, possessing arms,
> Thinking, passionate and alive.
>
> Life-loving, seething and hot,
> Will not be obliterated by any enemy.
> We live. It can't be otherwise!
> I speak to you in Russian:
> We live and breathe. Do you hear, mama?
> Do you hear, mother of children growing to adulthood?
> Your daughter stands easily and erect
> At the large crossroads . . .
> On land which contains many
> Of our tears, and blood and labor,
> On rich, strong, stern land,
> On land beloved forever.[5]

These verses were unacceptable to Soviet censorship. Although it was permissible in those years to damn fascism and sympathize with the innocent Jewish victims within the framework of the suffering and loss experienced by the entire Soviet nation, it was forbidden to express specific Jewish national pride.

The poem also hinted at another "seditious" subject—Soviet anti-Semitism against the local Jewish population during the war years.[6] Indeed, testimony from people who lived in the USSR in those years shows that many Jews perceived this theme of Soviet anti-Semitism in the poem.

People read and distributed the poem in handwritten and typed copies in Moscow, Leningrad, Kiev, Odessa, Riga, Kharkov, Novosibirsk, Alma-Ata, Tomsk, Kishinev, and other cities.[7] Presumably, these verses were known and disseminated in all areas of the Soviet Union where Jews lived who spoke and read Russian.

The popularity of these uncensored verses was enormous: I spoke with many people in gathering material for this chapter and not once did I meet a literate Jew who had reached adulthood in those years and did not know these verses. But most of the people who read and distributed them in samizdat thought they were an independent poem and did not suspect that they were the unpublished version of a fragment of a poem printed first in *Znamia* and later as a separate booklet.[8] In this instance, the samizdat edition apparently surpassed the official one both in its popularity and in the number of copies circulated. Some people thought that the entire fragment was an unpublished part of a poem by Aliger although they had neither read nor seen the poem itself. For example, Avram Shifrin, who in 1948 lived in Tula and worked in the prosecutor's office there, recalls that on one of his trips to Moscow a friend showed him Aliger's verses.

It was a few little pages, written by hand. He told me that Aliger had written a poem about those who had fought in the war—a heroic poem, etc. When she gave the poem to be published, in view of the fact that anti-Semitism had already begun, the part concerning the Jews was cut out. He had gotten hold of this part through friends and now he'd brought it to me. . . . I remember that afterwards I took it home and I typed those verses from the handwritten pages on the typewriter of the prosecutor of the Tula oblast'. . . . And then Senia—he worked in a factory which made copies of movies and which even in those times had a copying machine—used this machine to make numerous copies. And these made the rounds in Moscow.

But we simply did not realize that this was dangerous. Such a thought did not enter our heads—I remember that clearly. These verses just seemed powerful to us and we very much wanted to give Jews a feeling of pride. Later on I often found in Jewish homes the text which I myself had typed and Senia copied at his factory. Then I began to realize that this could be fraught with consequences. . . .

Shifrin's story reveals a characteristic detail: he and his friend were mistakenly convinced that Aliger's poem had first been published in 1948 but that the chapter about Jews was not passed for publication because of the "anticosmopolitan" campaign which had just begun.

Ester Lomovskaia, who lived with her family in Novosibirsk in the late forties, recalls that the manuscript copy of Aliger's verses was sent to them in a letter from Moscow relatives:

The content of these verses so moved us that father immediately copied them by hand and we soon all knew them by heart without having studied them specially. We were far from accepting everything in these verses, something provoked disagreement and even strong objections, but the very fact of the poem's appearance at that time was overwhelming. It was written with extraordinary sincerity, with deep bitterness and pain. Aliger wrote about the Jewish tragedy, about the Holocaust, and chiefly, about anti-Semitism, which was a completely forbidden theme, although at that time we all felt it keenly.

Moreover, this was being said not by someone from outside, standing on the side, but as if from within, by a person who had experienced it in her own life. At that time we neither saw nor knew of anything similar in contemporary Soviet literature.

Whenever Jewish acquaintances or friends came to our house, we always remembered to read them these verses and let them copy them. We were happy when we discovered that many were already familiar with the verses.

We didn't like the lines: "There are almost no more of us on earth, nothing will resurrect us any more" (that was the version we knew) because it seemed that she accepted painfully easily the situation that "There are almost no more of us on earth" and declared that "nothing will resurrect us any more." We didn't like the intonation of "What are we guilty of . . . in what way did we fail to please . . ." And finally, the following assertions provoked our protest: "It was so cloudless all around . . ." "Mama, mama, you are in your homeland . . ."; also the mention of Marx along with Einstein, "who were filled with wisdom" . . . etc.

But we saw that through these ideas, seasoned with the Soviet spirit, another thought was making its way (perhaps unconsciously contradicting them), one that was familiar to us, a feeling that was shared by us:

> Now I can hear the voice of blood,
> The agonizing groan of my people.
> Its fervent, subterranean call
> Grows ever stronger, more savage, and stormier.

In general, Aliger's verses produced a deep impression and became, as it were, a symbol of Jewish feelings. Later on, in our conversations with Jews, when we tried to develop their national consciousness, we also used Aliger's verse for this purpose. The text, which my father copied between 1946–48 (approximately), remained with us until our departure for Israel in 1971 when, along with other samizdat material, it was given to friends who remained.

Natal'ia Rubinshtein was still a child in the forties, but, although as yet unable to read Aliger's verses, she already knew them by heart as she heard them so often when her parents read them aloud at home. At the age of nine she often recited these verses at her parents' request for guests who visited their Leningrad home.

"I loved poetry from the time that I can remember myself," she recalls,

and I was moved that poetry—and beautiful poetry—could be written about Jews, a topic not quite forbidden or shameful but somehow strange and doubtful. At any rate, that's what I thought at that time. I shall give two examples to explain what could arouse such a feeling.

Once, in those years I accidentally discovered a poem entitled *The Jew,* in a book by Maiakovskii.[9] I read it with great interest, but later, when giving the book to a friend, I placed a bookmark on the relevant page and said: "Take a look at home." I didn't dare to open the book and simply show her the poem.

Another example was when my teacher, who gave me private lessons, once showed me some old Russian story about a pogrom, I flatly refused to read this story with her because it contained the word "Jew," which somehow was terribly difficult for me to pronounce out loud.

I cannot say that I was ashamed of my Jewishness. On the contrary. This fact aroused my intense curiosity, but in our life this subject was surrounded by some kind of mysterious and painful taboo. And in this respect Aliger's verse clarified much and articulated some very important things which had remained unexpressed. But, I repeat, I was not yet ten years old. Even so those verses stayed in my memory from then on.

While recording Natal'ia Rubinshtein's story, I asked her to recite the fragment from Aliger's poem just as she remembered it from her childhood in the late forties. The text which she recited corresponded exactly with the one published in Donat's anthology.

Boris Slovin, who lived in Riga in the late forties recalls:

In 1946 Margarita Aliger's poem *Your Victory* was published as a separate booklet. In 1947 I was using the Library of the Arts in Riga, when, quite by chance, I took Aliger's book. And lo and behold, I discovered a typewritten insert in the book containing the fragment which had not been included in the published text but which was well known to me from manuscript copies: I remembered it by heart. . . . Interestingly, the text typed on the insert was different from the one I remembered. It was not, as much as I understand of such matters, better quality poetry: it differed in its greater nationalism. This I remember well.

I, of course, immediately recopied this fragment. My copy then was passed on to others. Apparently, many versions of these verses existed: everyone added something of his own to them, and they turned into a kind of folk creation.

There were thousands of these manuscripts, as I shall now show. A few years after my discovery in the library, I was exiled to Siberia (in 1950) and in 1952 I was living in Tomsk. Tomsk is a student town and in those years many Jews who were not accepted into institutes of higher learning in the main cities went there to study. I tried to agitate for Zionism all the time but my arsenal of means was very poor and I would often produce Aliger's poem. And to my great surprise, it turned out that even Jews from distant, provincial towns knew these verses very well. The Jews who came to Tomsk from Kishinev also knew them.

Thus, for Soviet Jews in those years Aliger's verses became not only a support for their national pride, or a protest against anti-Semitism, but also in certain situations, as Ester Lomovskaia and Boris Slovin testify, an argument in support of Zionism. Naturally, such a phenomenon could not help but attract the attention of the punitive organs.

At the end of 1949 Moshe Giterman was expelled from the physics faculty of Kiev University after a Komsomol meeting at which his "nationalist activity" was condemned. One of the main charges was that Aliger's verses had been discovered in one of his student notebooks, copied out in Giterman's hand. They were discovered, apparently, by one of his classmates who reported the fact to the appropriate organs. The KGB worker who interrogated Giterman insisted that he name the person from whom he had received these verses. Giterman was saved from arrest, apparently, only by managing to go into hiding in a distant provincial town. Witnesses tell of several such instances when possession of Margarita Aliger's uncensored fragment caused trouble. In the forties and fifties the hand-written text often figured as evidence in the trials of "Jewish nationalists."[10]

In the late forties, during the "anticosmopolitan" campaign when the entire Soviet press seemed preoccupied only with furiously "exposing" hidden Jewish motifs in the works of Jewish writers, finding "nationalism" even where there was no trace of it, Aliger's poem could naturally not escape mention. Nikolai Gribachev's attack was particularly vicious:

Aside from a series of pseudo-philosophical works, M. Aliger has a decadent, subjectivist poem, "Your Victory." I remember how the officers of the border garrison, those from Stalingrad, were outraged when reading the seventeenth chapter in which the author describes her trip to visit her mother in Kama and at the same time discusses . . . Stalingrad.

> Mother had been evacuated then to Kama.
> And I hadn't seen her for a long time . . .

What grief! And at that time our marvelous youth were dying in the trenches near Stalingrad, their mothers received notices about the death of, perhaps, their only sons. . . . Well, all right, let her travel, let her enjoy nature if her conscience permits, but why all these empty words:

> We shall conquer!—was heard in the deathly groan,
> Under torture in the last terrible hour.
> And the officer didn't understand anything
> And, amazed, frightened us . . .

Who are those who are traveling to visit their mothers?[11]

Gribachev's attack seemed excessive even for those bad times; he barely conceals his logic of a common pogrom maker: "our marvelous youth were dying in the trenches," while *they* traveled to their mothers . . .

Gribachev continues:

... the decadent, hopelessly dismal poem "Your Victory" is reprinted in the Jubilee series[12] and again we read in it such "pearls":

> For whom God's sun generously
> Baked unleavened bread . . .

writes Aliger, introducing religious concepts and images into her poem. She intimately acknowledges:

> Suffused me with restless blood,
> With the waters of a live spring,
> Burned me with the unkind love
> Of a *wild* Russian peasant . . .

These are the alien, false words the poet picks to describe our people.[13]

Gribachev evidently did not come to such conclusions on his own initiative alone; possible danger to Aliger at the time was also obvious. The Jews who read and disseminated Aliger's verse in samizdat were often stimulated by such official criticism to spread this samizdat further. But how did Aliger herself react?

Valuable testimony was given me by the late writer David Dar who personally met the poetess in those years. Dar could not recall the exact date of his meeting with her, but only that it was "at the height of the 'anticosmopolitan' campaign," that is, in the late forties.

Margarita Iosifovna came to Leningrad and dropped in to visit me and Vera Fedorovna.[14] She told us about the anticosmopolitan campaign, and from her we first heard about the Moscow meetings of writers at which Iuzovskii, Gurevich, and others had been slated. I no longer remember all the details, but I remember that she spoke about it with great agitation and sorrow. One felt that it had deeply upset her personally. And it was then that she read us her verses on a Jewish theme, saying that they were an excerpt from a poem. At that time those lines sounded like a protest and seemed extremely bold and dangerous. I did not know then that they had already been published in a somewhat milder version several years ago. The verses which she read us that evening sounded completely fresh and up-to-date, and under no circumstances could have been published in the Soviet press. That I can say for sure, although I no longer remember them and never read them again.

I must say that to hear such verses from Aliger was a great surprise. Until then she had been a thoroughly loyal, orthodox poetess and belonged to that category of Jewish writers who actively disowned their Jewishness, in contrast to such people as Mikhail Svetlov or Iosif Utkin, who emphasized everywhere that they were Jews and even bragged about it. But Margarita Aliger, like many others, had always tried to appear Russian; her husband, Aleksandr Fadeev, was Russian and the lines "Burned me with the unkind love of a wild Russian peasant" are probably about him. The Jewish theme had not even made a brief appearance in all her previous poetry, and now there was this unexpected and strange outburst. Unexpected and strange, but perhaps the more instructive and valuable . . .

I must add that these verses were incredibly popular among the Leningrad intelligentsia; everyone knew them and everyone spoke about them, although I personally was convinced that they were never published.

I remember—after the meeting with Aliger—my talking about those verses with the Leningrad writer Boris Iosifovich Kastelianets, the music critic Moisei Iosifovich Iankovskii, and others. This was during the "anticosmopolitan" campaign, which agitated us all deeply and affected us personally.

Aliger never wrote anything similar to these verses again, at any rate nothing dedicated to a Jewish theme appeared by her either in samizdat or the official press. Moreover, she subsequently denied her authorship of the samizdat version of the fragment from the poem *Your Victory*.

In 1969 the American writer Alexander Donat visited Moscow in connection with his work on compiling an anthology *Jewish Subjects in Russian Poetry* and contacted Aliger by telephone. Telling her about his work, he informed her that he possessed an unpublished fragment from her poem "Your Victory," which he intended to include in his anthology and would like to meet with her to speak about it. Aliger replied that she did not know of any unpublished version of a fragment from her poem and she refused to meet him.[15]

Aliger's unwillingness to meet with strangers, especially on such a tricky subject, is understandable, but in connection with this incident, Aliger's own account in her reminiscences of Il'ia Ehrenburg (published in the USSR) is of particular interest:

We became acquainted on that evening in January or the beginning of February 1942 when he invited me to visit him in the military hotel "Moscow." . . . I read poems the whole evening. . . .

Once Ehrenburg phoned me—it was in the late fifties or early sixties, when he was writing about the war years in his book *People, Years, Life*. He called and asked me to recall the lines which he had liked on that distant evening. "I looked in your collections," said Il'ia Grigor'evich, "found the poem, but for some reason could not find those lines in it. But I remember them, remember them well, I remember the feeling from them. . . . Tell me, I'm not mistaken am I?" No, he was not mistaken. He never erred in matters of poetry, never forgot what he once liked. And he was very happy when I reminded him of those lines.[16]

What poem is she talking about here? Why did Aliger not mention its title? What were the lines, which Ehrenburg remembered so well from the meeting in 1942 which were omitted when the poem was published? According to the time when the verses were written this could very well be the poem "Your Victory"; and maybe Aliger did not mention the title because the lines which Ehrenburg "for some reason could not find" in the published text were only too well known to everybody?

In addition to the unpublished fragment from the poem *Your Victory*, an anonymous poem, *A Reply to Margarita Aliger*, was unofficially circulated fairly widely in the late forties. Some people who disseminated this poem in samizdat along with Aliger's verses thought that it was by Ehrenburg, but such a possibility can hardly be taken seriously. The poem is on a low artistic level, written unprofessionally, and does not have the slightest relation to Ehrenburg's style.

Such lines as "we are guilty of being intelligent," are in very bad taste, and the words that the misfortune of the Jewish people consists of "the fact that we are dispersed throughout the world and do not have one homeland," where the author hints at his Zionist views, could in no way have been uttered by Ehrenburg, who for many years had been stubbornly trying to defend the opposite view.

Nevertheless, despite its evident artistic weakness, this poem enjoyed wide popularity among Soviet Jews in the forties. People apparently found in these ingenuous lines what they had missed in Aliger's verses:

We shall live, and we shall yet be able,
Flashing our talents, to show
That our people is great, that we Jews
Have the right to live and flourish.
Our blood and tears gave this right,
The dead blessed us from the grave.
I believe: Our people's heart was resuscitated
For exploits and glory, for new life.
Our people is immortal. It shall bring forth
New Maccabees as an example for the future.
And I am proud, I am proud and do not regret,
That I am a Jew, comrade Aliger.[17]

This entire episode shows that even in the most difficult years of Stalinism Soviet Jews were never the "Jews of silence," as they were frequently called in the West. Condemned to forced assimilation and deprived of any possibility of openly creating and developing their own national culture, Soviet Jews did not cease to struggle: they strove to uphold and express their national essence in Jewish samizdat.

The remarkable upsurge of Soviet Jewish national consciousness in the early seventies was no accident; it was made possible by long years of persistent, painstaking, and dangerous work. The efforts to obtain and disseminate Aliger's samizdat verses were only one of the most outstanding examples of this activity.

Notes

1. "Jewish Samizdat and Methods of Preparing It," *Behinot* (Jerusalem), 8–9 (1979), pp. 52–67.
2. *Kratkaia evreiskaia entsiklopediia* (Jerusalem: Keter, 1976), vol. 1, p. 83.
3. The text of Aliger's verses is given according to the following edition: Aleksandr Donat, *Neopalimaia kupina, Evreiskie siuzhety v russkoi poezii. Antologiia* (New York: New York University Press, 1973), pp. 411–15.
4. For example, the following lines of the samizdat variant:

    We are Jews. How much grief and
    Gloomy years in this word!

    were replaced in the published version by:

    War broke out. We looked at the wide world
    More directly and sternly.

5. Tamar Dolzhanskaia, *Na odnoi volne, Evreiskie motivy v russkoi poezii* (Tel Aviv: Biblioteka Aliya, 1974), pp. 37–38.
6. Later, in less dangerous years after Stalin's death, Boris Slutskii wrote openly about this:

    The bullets passed by me,
    So that it could be said falsely:
    "The Jews didn't fight—
    They all returned alive."

7. See interviews with Boris Slovin, Avram Shifrin, Alexksandr Voronel, David Dar, Ester Lomovskaia, Vitalii Svechinskii, located in the Center for Research and Documentation of East European Jewry in the Hebrew University. All further references to these and other interviews come from this collection.
8. Margarita Aliger, *Tvoia pobeda, poema* (Moscow: Sovetskii pisatel', 1946).
9. Vladimir Maiakovskii, *Sobranie sochinenii* (Moscow: Gosizdat, 1958), vol. 7, pp. 244–47.

10. Interview with Moshe Giterman.
11. Nikolai Gribachev, "Za novyi pod"em sovetskoi poezii!" *Znamia*, 1 (1949), p. 172.
12. Special editions of poetry published in 1947.
13. Gribachev, "Za novyi pod"em."
14. David Dar was married to the famous Soviet writer Vera Panova.
15. The incident was described to me directly by A. Donat.
16. M. Aliger, "Nas sdruzhila poeziia," *Vospominaniia ob Erenburge* (Moscow: Sovietskii pisatel', 1975), p. 196.
17. Donat, *Neopalimaia kupina*, pp. 416–17.

5
Jewish Samizdat and the Rise of Jewish National Consciousness
Stefani Hoffman

The struggle of Soviet Jewry for the right to emigrate to Israel and for recognition of Jewish culture within the Soviet Union has generated a wealth of Jewish samizdat. When studying the Jewish samizdat from the late 1950s to the late 1970s (the period covered by this chapter) in relation to the rise of Jewish national consciousness in the Soviet Union, certain questions arise. What material was disseminated via samizdat and how was it selected and distributed? In what way did the samizdat itself encourage the development of Jewish consciousness? In what way does it reflect a maturing of this consciousness?

Samizdat literature by definition, encompasses works which are circulated within the Soviet Union without official permission.[1] Jewish samizdat, as distinguished from other forms of samizdat in the USSR, contains articles of specific Jewish interest and is designated for a primarily Jewish readership. The material itself is not written or prepared exclusively by Jews although Jewish authors predominate. Jewish activists acknowledge their indebtedness to the Russian democratic dissident movement for familiarizing them with methods of samizdat publication and dissemination. Several Jewish activists such as Mikhail Zand, Aleksandr Voronel, and Eduard Kuznetsov, originally participated in the democratic movement and gradually shifted their attention to the Jewish movement.

Information about the dissemination of samizdat material comes from transcripts of the various trials of Jewish activists, from personal testimony, and from a questionnaire distributed to 447 Jewish activists who emigrated to Israel.[2] Among these activists, who were interviewed in Israel in the early 1970s, just over 70 percent indicated that they had read some form of illegal publications on Jewish themes, and nearly 80 percent stated that they or some member of their family had helped disseminate samizdat literature.[3] One copy of a work would pass through many hands.[4] Moscow and Riga have been the main centers for the publication of Jewish samizdat; from there activists circulated the material throughout the USSR. For example, during their frequent trips to Moscow, Ester and Vol't Lomovskii obtained samizdat works, which they brought back to their home in Novosibirsk.[5] Trial testimony of witnesses from Leningrad, Vilnius, Odessa, Kishinev, Sverdlovsk, Samarkand, Sukhumi, Kharkov, and Minsk points to other cities reached by samizdat.[6] Jewish samizdat also existed in Soviet labor camps—in fact, one translation of Leon Uris's *Exodus* was made in a camp.[7]

The Jewish samizdat in these two decades can be divided into three periods according to the dominant type of material. In the first period, from the mid-fifties through the Six-Day War of 1967, samizdat consisted mainly of either translations of material brought in from the West or copies of Russian-language works of Jewish interest written before the Soviet period. In the second period, from the Six-Day War until the early seventies, Jewish samizdat concentrated on the struggle for *aliya*. Personal and group letters, legal documents, and transcripts of trials formed the core of this samizdat activity. In the third period, from the early seventies to the end of that decade, a new form of samizdat supplemented the earlier varieties, which also continued to circulate. The new samizdat offers original Russian-language works which go beyond the immediate problems of the *aliya* struggle to explore questions of Jewish identity, culture, religion, and history.

Samizdat up to and Including the Six-Day War

Samizdat becomes necessary only when official open publication of material is forbidden. Beginning in the mid-1920s the Soviet government increasingly restricted publication of material about Jewish themes and in Jewish languages, that is, in Yiddish and Hebrew.[8] Illegal preparation of Jewish material in Stalinist times was too dangerous to be widespread. Even the possession of such material often had grave consequences. In the World War II period, when Soviet censorship in general became looser, Jewish grief over the Holocaust found expression in samizdat works. The most notable was the poem by Margarita Aliger *Your Victory,* which made its way in manuscript form throughout the Soviet Union.[9]

Although the birth of the State of Israel deeply affected Soviet Jewry, it did not produce a wealth of illegal literature, only a few isolated pamphlets. Jewish samizdat first became a significant phenomenon after Stalin's death. The Khrushchevan "thaw" and de-Stalinization removed some of the dark fears of speaking out bred by the Stalinist "black years." The need to discuss Jewish topics became more acute in this period as Jewish intellectuals gradually realized that liberalization did not change Soviet anti-Semitic discrimination and suppression of Jewish culture.

The typical Soviet Jewish reader in the post-Stalinist period lacked the most elementary notions about Jewish culture, history, or religion.[10] Russian rather than Yiddish had become the native tongue. Starved for even the most elementary Jewish knowledge, the Soviet Jewish reader eagerly sought any material. People searched in bookstores and private collections for rare copies of prerevolutionary Jewish works in Russian, which were generally no longer available in public libraries. Following a tradition established by the Russian intelligentsia, they also turned to the West for material. Tourists were the main source of this Western literature,[11] although the copy of *Exodus* used in the labor camp translation was obtained from a Latvian or Lithuanian who had received it accidentally.[12]

The readers seized upon a range of eclectic material to satisfy their basic needs: political and educational writings by early leaders of political Zionism such as Theodor Herzl and Vladimir Jabotinsky, lyrical poetry by noted Russian-Jewish poets such as Haim Nahman Bialik and Shimon Frug (in Russian), and Israeli periodicals such as *Ariel* and *Shalom,* designed to bring information about Israeli culture, education, and social conditions to readers outside of Israel. Other samizdat literature included the Russian-Jewish historian Simon Dubnow's *History of the Jews,* and Western fiction (*Exodus,* Howard Fast's *My Glorious Brothers,* André Schwarz-Bart's *The Last of the Just*).[13] These works were not written with the contemporary Soviet reader in mind; yet certain factors explain their deep appeal. They warned of the dangers of assimilation, called for pride in Jewish nationhood based on the millennia-long Jewish history, and offered Soviet Jews models of action and belief.

The single samizdat book which had the profoundest effect on Soviet Jews was Leon Uris's *Exodus.* At least three translations circulated inside the USSR. Most Jewish activists interviewed in Israel testify to the overwhelming impression that it made on them. Some say that it literally caused their *aliya*. Others read it after their Zionist convictions had already crystallized. Many noted the inferior quality of the translation they read, the book's lack of literary merit, and its slow opening pages. Nevertheless, the story gradually absorbed them, and whatever the reader's stage of Zionist development, the book increased emotional involvement in Jewish life and intensified the desire to leave the USSR.

Exodus instilled in Soviet Jews pride in being Jewish; it presented heroic, idealistic Jewish figures—counterweights to the scheming, stooped villians presented by Soviet propaganda. Soviet Jews valued *Exodus* not only for the emotional uplift but also for the basic Jewish information supplied in a simplified, schematic manner. With the help of flashbacks, Uris offers a panorama of Jewish history—the first and second *aliya* from Russia, the Dreyfus affair, Herzl's Zionism, the first settlements in Palestine, Europe during the Holocaust, and, of course, the events surrounding the founding of the State of Israel. The book also mentions and explains the major Jewish festivals. The information and Zionist inspiration in the book were so important that one translation (made in Riga by Leah Slovin) purposely omitted the love story between the non-Jewish Kitty and Ari Ben Canaan as an unnecessary distraction.

Thematically, *Exodus* possessed double significance for Soviet Jews. The inspiring story of the establishment of Israel suggested parallels, modes of action for the contemporary Soviet Jew contemplating his own exodus. The biblical injunction "Let my people go," the epigraph of the first book in the novel, became the rallying cry of Soviet Jewry. They, like the Jews in Cyprus at the outset of the novel, had to fight against unreasonable outside forces preventing them from entering the Promised Land. The refugee children on the boat *Exodus* did not wait passively to reach Israel; they took their fate into their own hands and through their offensive brought world public attention to bear on their plight.

Exodus possessed another advantage—it emphasized a Jewishness founded more on proud nationalism than on religion. Its heroes are invariably nonreligious Jews, fiercely committed to their land. For Soviet Jewry, which had over the years grown distant from religion and had been constantly humiliated by Soviet attempts to deny the very existence of a Jewish nation or Jewish nationalism, *Exodus* provided a comprehensible way of identifying as a Jew. *Exodus* also contains a brief, but prophetic reference to Soviet Jewry near the end of the novel when Kitty predicts that the next large wave of *aliya* will come from the Soviet Union.

Howard Fast's novel about the Maccabean revolt, *My Glorious Brothers*, like *Exodus*, gave Soviet Jews a positive, heroic image of the Jew. The novel emphasizes the Jews' stubbornness, independence, and unique striving for freedom. The treatment of assimilation was also relevant to the contemporary Soviet scene. Fast portrays assimilation negatively—the urban Jew who tries to become Hellenized or assimilated is not merely repudiated but persecuted by the Hellenes. The assimilated Jew represents a retreat from genuine freedom back to slavery. The Soviet Jew could apply this message to his own situation where attempted assimilation was not only unsuccessful but resulted in the loss of independence and self-esteem.[14]

Howard Fast, like Uris, emphasizes nationalism over religion as the force uniting all Jews both within a given historic period and from one generation to another. The modern Soviet Jew, alienated from the more recent Jewish life of the *shtetl*, could look back to the Maccabees for a source of proud national identification, just as in *My Glorious Brothers*, Simon the Maccabee constantly refers back to the generation which went out of Egypt, leaving slavery behind. Indeed, later original Russian-language samizdat often refers proudly to the historic tie between modern Jews and the Maccabean fighters.

The reading of these fictional works often stimulated Soviet Jews to delve deeper into Jewish culture, to seek out poetry, history, political and educational writings. One of the most popular works was Jabotinsky's *Feuilletons*, a collection of speeches and essays on cultural and educational topics first published in 1911. Over 50 percent of the Jewish activists listed it among the illegal Jewish literature that they had read. Boris Slovin from Riga copied several articles from *Feuilletons* on a copying machine at his home in the early 1960s. He distributed them in Riga and also traveled with a full suitcase of Jabotinsky's articles and Bialik's poems to Moscow. Having obtained the name of a reliable Jewish activist—Arnold Neiborgen—he approached him after work and offered him the dangerous suitcase. Slovin asked him to distribute as many copies as he could and to burn any remaining ones. When they met a year later, Neiborgen explained that although he had not been able to distribute every copy, he did not have the heart to burn the remaining literature.[15]

The issues stirring Jabotinsky in the early 1900s were most timely to

Jewish intellectuals in the 1960s and 1970s: the lure of Russian culture, the problem of Jewish self-esteem, the lack of a proper Jewish education, and the question of assimilation. Jabotinsky urged his contemporaries to value their Jewishness, warning that the Jews' innate feeling and the Russians' natural inclinations would never allow the Jews to be "like them." "Our chief illness is self-hatred, our chief need—to develop self-respect: i.e., the basis of our national upbringing must henceforth be self-awareness."[16]

The typical Soviet Jew who rediscovered Jabotinsky regarded Russian as his mother tongue and had grown up with a strong attachment to Russian culture. Any knowledge of Hebrew was a recent acquisition. Jabotinsky dealt with this problem in an essay, "Jews and Russian literature." Although calling for a return to the Hebrew language, he also declared that the Jewishness of a work was determined not by the language in which it was written, but by the author's mood and by the audience for whom he was writing.[17]

Recognizing the attraction of Russian culture, Jabotinsky encouraged Russian Jews not to be overwhelmed by it, but to incorporate this culture into their Jewishness. Because the assimilated Jew of the time possessed insufficient knowledge of Jewish tradition to do this, Jabotinsky stressed the need for a solid Jewish education to overcome this ignorance.[18] His warning applied even more to the modern Soviet Jewish reader than to his original audience. His suggestions on what to study in Jewish tradition suited the Soviet Jew; he did not emphasize religion but pointed rather to the distant historic past, for example to the Maccabees, for Jewish identification.

In another article Jabotinsky expresses no surprise over Russian intelligentsia objections to the "flood" of Jews pouring into Russian literature. He interprets it as a sign of the intelligentsia's genuine feeling about Jews and an indication of future attempts to drive Jews out of Russian literature.[19] Soviet Jews, subject to discrimination in university admission and in professional advancement, saw Jabotinsky's predictions realized in their time.

In another article which became popular in samizdat, "I Don't Believe," Jabotinsky expressed doubts that future democratic societies would automatically eliminate the discrimination and oppression of minorities. Democracy, he points out, can protect large national groups against the threat of absolutism, but it will not automatically wipe out the inborn prejudices of these nationalities.[20] The Soviet Jew felt the problem even more acutely as the society in which he grew up did not even try to eradicate innate prejudices or to protect Jews against discrimination.

Taken as a whole, Jabotinsky's essays stimulated Soviet Jews to reevaluate their position in Soviet society: could they assimilate if they so desired, could they reasonably expect to attain self-esteem as Jews in this society, and could they make their Jewishness a source of pride?

Samizdat in the Fight for *Aliya*

The Six-Day War was a turning point in the development of Soviet Jewish national consciousness and of Jewish samizdat. Soviet Jewry did not need to reach back into the historic past for a source of Jewish national pride— Israel had demonstrated Jewish strength and daring in the face of impossible odds. Israel's bold victory stirred the national pride of many who had not previously identified as Jews. Soviet aid to the Arabs and a campaign of vilification against Israel intensified Jews' feeling of isolation within the USSR and increased the desire to leave the country.

The Six-Day War created a greater audience for samizdat, and Jewish activists tried to meet the increased demand by producing more copies of works such as *Exodus*. In the 1971 Kishinev trial, Anatolii Gol'dfeld was accused of holding one hundred copies of *Exodus* in his apartment for safekeeping and of distributing some of these copies to friends.[21]

Works describing the Six-Day War also appeared in samizdat. Translations of Western works, they were distributed mainly in excerpted form. In the seventies, excerpts also appeared in samizdat collections. One of the works, *The Aggressors* was written by L. Mnačko, a Czech émigré. Pro-Israeli, he described the war from a socialist, but anti-Soviet viewpoint. The two most popular works on the subject to appear in samizdat were *The Six Day War* by Randolph and Winston S. Churchill and *Swift Sword* by General S. L. Marshall. For the Soviet Jew, the opportunity to read about the details of the war was a way of reinforcing the pride which the Israeli victory instilled in him.

The rise in Jewish consciousness generated by the Six-Day War set the stage for the next period—from 1967 to 1972—a period of intense struggle for the right to emigrate to Israel. Samizdat from the earlier period now served as cultural preparation for *aliya* to Israel. The new samizdat in this period, according to Leah Slovin from Riga, was directed exclusively at "infecting" people with Zionism. "We were sure that the development of Jewish culture in Russia would harm our movement. We felt *aliya* was the only solution."[22] According to another activist, "The samizdat material helped Jews know Israel and Jewish life. We had to do this or there would have been no movement."[23]

Samizdat after the Six-Day War went beyond reproducing works obtained haphazardly and written either by Russian Jews already in the grave or by Westerners beyond the reach of Soviet power. The first new form of samizdat developed out of Soviet Jewry's letter-writing campaign. Although the Soviet authorities had permitted a modest amount of emigration ("reunification of families") before the Six-Day War, they ended this with the outbreak of the war. The frustrated would-be repatriates sent a flood of petitions to Soviet leaders, the UN, or leading Western and Israeli figures.[24] The petitions were directed not only to the addressee, who rarely responded, but also at Western public opinion. The letters were also aimed at Soviet Jewry itself—to inform and to encourage others to emigrate. Appeals were smuggled to the West, first by tourists and later by departing Soviet Jews, and read over broadcasts beamed to the USSR. Soviet Jews would copy down the broadcast text in order to reproduce it in samizdat, singly and in collections. Jewish activists traveling from one city to another also brought copies of petitions and appeals back and forth. Indeed, such material is included in lists of articles confiscated at the homes of various activists.

Names of the letter writers and signatories and their addresses were clearly displayed, not just for identification but to encourage others to overcome their own fear of stepping forth as Jews. At first there was some hesitation about having people from different cities sign the same letter, but this later became accepted when the intercity cooperation among Jewish activists became obvious.[25] The collective petitions demonstrated that Jews could work together to influence their own fate.

In the survey of activists cited above, over 76 percent stated that they had signed some form of petition or letter and almost 70 percent that they had solicited others' signatures for petitions.[26] Tina Brodetskaia, an initiator of a Moscow letter, notes that she went to Vilnius in January 1970 to see why no letters were coming from there. Two weeks later, she received a letter from seven Vilnius Jews and others soon followed.[27] The authors of these early letters understood the influence that their letter-writing activity could have on others. Tina Brodetskaia remarks that later on, others were less careful about the actual composition of the letters: "Only in our period did we put so much love and passion into each letter."[28]

The letters and petitions raised certain basic issues. The "Letter of the Moscow 39,"[29] written in response to the officially staged press conference of 4 March 1970, is typical of the genre. The press conference paraded a variety of famous cultural, military, and political figures of "Jewish nationality" who denounced Israel and contended that anti-Semitic discrimination did not exist in the USSR. The letter writers disagreed with the conference participants and pressed for the right to leave for Israel. They defended their right to decide their own fate and claimed that both Soviet and international law guaranteed them the right of repatriation to Israel. They moved the issue from the personal to the universal—anyone who wanted to leave had the right to do so. The emphasis on universal rights was aimed at both the Western audience and potential émigrés. The defense of Israel in the letter was designed more for the internal audience, continually barraged by Soviet anti-Israel propaganda.

Jewish national identity is another basic concern in the petitions. The "Letter of the 39" deals mildly with this issue, agreeing that every individual has the right to any degree of assimilation that he chooses. They themselves prefer a strong independent Jewish culture and express dismay over the degree of assimilation in the USSR. Other individual and group letters, using the Holocaust as an example, speak more sharply of the dangers of assimilation. Only a Jewish state, they declare, can truly protect Jewish life and culture.

In August 1969, David Khavkin from Moscow initiated an All-Union Coordinating Committee (*Vsesoiuznyi koordinatsionnyi komitet*) which worked together on all aspects of the Jewish movement. The coordinating committee took on the dissemination of samizdat as one of its tasks. Jewish activists from all over the USSR, who had met when serving camp sentences together, used their intercity connections to help circulate samizdat. For example, Anatolii Rubin, an ex-prisoner, obtained samizdat literature from friends in Riga, Moscow, and Leningrad, which he brought back to his native Minsk.[30]

At its November 1969 meeting in Riga, the committee decided to prepare its own samizdat journal—*Iton* (Hebrew for newspaper). *Iton alef* and *Iton bet* (i.e., *Iton a* and *b*) appeared in February and May of 1970. Prepared by individuals in various cities, the two issues were disseminated throughout the Soviet Union.

Significantly, the first article in *Iton alef* was original, not a translation. The author, however, remained anonymous, perhaps from fear of reprisals.[31] The topic of this brief article—assimilation—lies at the heart of the Soviet Jewish movement. The author notes that the inability to assimilate led Soviet Jews to rediscover their Jewish identity.

Iton attempts to stimulate *aliya*. Hence it has few articles about Jewish culture, religion, or history; instead it concentrates on material which encourages national identification with the State of Israel.

Translated articles (which predominate numerically over original ones) present a very positive picture of Israel. For example, the excerpt from Marshall's *Swift Sword* on Israel's citizen army shows the high degree of motivation and dedication of the "Israeli people's army." Amos Kenan's "Open Letter" (which also circulated separately), written by a self-acknowledged former leftist, challenged leftist attacks on Israel, including of course Soviet ones. Kenan concludes that no one will defend Jews except the Jews themselves.

Two unsigned articles at the end of *Iton alef* point out analogies between past and present. In one article, the author presents Purim and Pesah (the Passover) as national and folk more than as religious holidays. He elevates Pesah over Purim, because during Pesah the Jews initiated their own struggle for freedom instead of waiting for divine miracles. The author reminds the reader that the desire for freedom is insufficient—freedom must be won. The Jewish nation need not fear perishing in the desert because "there, beyond the desert, is your home."[32]

An article about the Warsaw ghetto military organization focuses more on the ideological issue of Jewish nationalism than on the individual, tragic losses of the ghetto uprising. The author portrays the ghetto fighters as conscious followers of the national idea of the Maccabees and Bar Kokhba who understood that "talk about solving the problems of minority nationalities in conditions of universal brotherhood was empty phraseology." They realized that the only solution to the Jewish predicament in Poland was for Jews to live in their own country. The author lets Soviet Jews reach their own conclusions about the situation of Jews in the USSR.

The second issue of *Iton* resembles the first, with even more emphasis on Israel. It includes several translations of Western articles on Israel. A short anonymous article points out the tragic destruction of Jewish life in the USSR. Describing an official ceremony on 29 September 1969 at Babii Iar to commemorate the Nazi massacre of Soviet citizens (including over 100,000 Jews), the author notes the Soviet authorities' deliberate refusal to recognize the Jewish aspect of this tragedy.

Iton bet initiates a more militant phase in the Jewish movement. Raising Soviet Jewish consciousness is not enough. The editors assert Soviet Jews' determination and right to seek repatriation to Israel and to overcome any official obstacles in their way. The translated article "Soviet Authorities Cannot Destroy the Jewish Spirit" quotes Golda Meir at a demonstration of solidarity with Soviet Jewry: "No matter what cruel means the Soviet Union will employ, it will not achieve its goal" (of breaking the Jewish spirit).[33]

An unsigned article "The Jews Cease to be Silent" introduces a section of individual letters and collective petitions. It declares that the time to weep over recent tragedies has passed. "The time has come to speak and demand. To demand what Moses in the name of God demanded of Pharaoh 'Let my people go.' "[34] After briefly describing the start of the letter-writing campaign, the article concludes, "Thus, ready for sacrifices, step by step, Soviet Jews have exposed the anti-Jewish, anti-humanist policy of the Soviet Union in striving for the right to live in the land of their ancestors, in the Homeland."[35] The letters militantly insist on the legal right to free emigration. Many letter writers challenge the statements made at the March 4 press conference about the freedom of Jewish cultural expression, but their criticism is a prelude to their request to leave, not a call for internal change.

At approximately the same time that Jews in Riga were preparing *Iton*, Moscow activists were bringing out *Iskhod* (Exodus), a compilation of documents. Four issues appeared in 1970–71. Similar collections followed it— three issues of *Vestnik iskhoda* (The Herald of Exodus) in 1971–72 and *Belaia kniga iskhoda* (The White Paper of the Exodus) in 1972.

These samizdat collections concentrate on the *aliya* struggle in all its intensity and relegate other aspects of Jewish consciousness and culture to the side. By publicizing all the difficulties on the road to repatriation, they strive to overcome them.

The two components influencing the editors—the liberal democratic movement and the Jewish movement—find expression in the dual epigraph on the title page: on one side a quote from the Book of Psalms, "If I forget thee, O Jerusalem, let my right hand lose its cunning" and on the other side—a quotation from the Universal Declaration of Human Rights on the right to free movement between countries.[36] The first quote suggests the deep emotional and historical roots of the Soviet Jewish national revival and the second reflects the democratic movement's emphasis on universalism and legality.

A series of quotes from Elie Wiesel's *The Jews of Silence* shows the development of the struggle. The first issue quotes Wiesel's statement that he set out for the Soviet Union "attracted by the Jews' silence and I carried back with me their cry." This issue contains the early petitions, appeals, and legal information on the documents needed for requests to travel to capitalist countries.

The second issue quotes Wiesel on the isolation of Soviet Jewry. "The very fact that we leave them alone in their fight with their backs to the wall, remains inexplicable to them." This issue aims not only at stiffening Soviet Jewish resistance but also at breaking down the wall of Western silence. The letters and petitions describe a process which has become wearisome. The petitioners have already turned to numerous individuals and institutions and are becoming tired of waiting. The writers do not request changes in the Soviet Union; they just want to be let out. Stress falls on the personal, human element—selected excerpts relate family tragedies in the USSR and the desire to rejoin close relatives in Israel.

In the third issue, hope breaks through the wall of isolation. The epigraph cites Wiesel's description of the joyous celebration of Simhat Torah in the Moscow synagogue, culminating in the cry of "anger and hope 'NEXT YEAR IN JERUSALEM!' " The determination to oppose increasing Soviet harassment receives full treatment. Letters include renunciation of Soviet citizenship and complaints of indifference to previous letters. Documents include protocols of searches and lists of confiscated material, including the letters of petition. A protocol of the search of Vladimir Slepak's apartment on 15 June 1970 (date of the Leningrad hijacking attempt) lists numerous petitions and letters among his possessions.

The fourth issue of *Iskhod* is devoted entirely to the Leningrad hijacking trial; two issues of *Vestnik iskhoda* deal primarily with related trials. The greater length of the second issue of *Vestnik iskhoda* testifies to the growing breadth and complexity of the movement. The editors carefully selected, arranged, and annotated documents with both the Western and Soviet reader in mind. Letters from arrested persons and their relatives appeal for immediate help. They also indicate how the West can influence Soviet Jewish consciousness by broadcasting Soviet Jews' appeals back to the Soviet

Union. Potential émigrés were encouraged by the efforts of their fellow Jews.[37]

A second section, "Jewish Groups Visit Soviet Institutions," points to the effectiveness of resolute action by Soviet Jews. It factually describes demonstrations and hunger strikes at public institutions in March 1971. A concluding note states that by the end of March 1971, most of the participants received permission to emigrate to Israel—that is, open protest produces results! A final section on official documents gives the Soviet reader practical information on departure procedures.

The third issue of *Vestnik iskhoda* (February 1972) reveals the intensification of the *aliya* struggle and the tragic fate of "refuseniks" (those refused exit visas). Appeals and letters from those sentenced in the various trials speak for themselves. The editors encouraged Soviet Jews to persevere with their appeals and demonstrations and urged Western readers to apply the pressure of world public opinion.

Two issues of *Belaia kniga iskhoda* in 1972 continue to focus exclusively on the *aliya* struggle. Based on genuine documents, the first volume illustrates "the incredible difficulties which Soviet Jews encounter on the road to repatriation: administrative obstacles, social ostracism, indifference, arbitrariness, and illegality."[38] The editors hoped to show the average Soviet Jew what to expect should he make the decision to emigrate. They also wanted to show Western society that, despite certain successes, Soviet Jews still faced enormous difficulties in realizing their desire for repatriation.[39]

This issue is no mere compilation. Documents are selected and arranged for effect; the editors accompany the documents with a running commentary addressed personally to "you," the reader. The tone is deliberately ironic, continually warning the reader not to exult at current victories in his struggle since he will invariably face new, unexpected obstacles. The work unfolds like a novelistic plot: it opens with the first stage—deciding to leave—passes through all ensuing difficulties, and ends with the final harassment at customs. An epilogue-like conclusion mentions those who end up in labor camps instead of the Promised Land.

The second *Belaia kniga iskhoda*, devoted to the events surrounding Nixon's visit to Moscow in 1972, aims more at the Western than at the Soviet Jewish audience. It appeals for Western understanding and help in overcoming obstacles. The style resembles compilations by the democratic movement—a straightforward record of events surrounding Nixon's visit which exposes the Soviet authorities' blatant violations of their own legal system.

Another form of samizdat in this period was designed exclusively for the Soviet Jewish reader. Letters from Israel sent by recent emigrants served as an antidote to official declarations about the unhappy lot of Soviet Jews in Israel. Ester Lomovskaia, whose son and father were able to emigrate to Israel before she did, recalls people staying at Mikhail Kalik's house until 4:00 A.M. while she read aloud her son's and father's letters from Israel. She made five typewritten copies of these letters and appended a commentary. "We traveled—they called us like first aid, if someone in the family did not want to go to Israel: 'Come with the letters.' . . . In Moscow we went to many people to read the letters—our group simply all loved to hear them."[40]

Samizdat in this period kept the West informed and provided distant cities in the USSR with basic information on Jewish topics and with helpful advice on emigration. Samizdat collections showed that no matter how great the obstacles, Soviet Jews were daring and succeeding in changing Soviet emigration policy.

Samizdat and the Question of Jewish Culture in the USSR

The years from 1970 to 1973 saw a dramatic increase in the number of Jews permitted to leave the USSR—from one thousand in 1970 to thirty-five thousand in 1973. After 1973, emigration began declining again and also changed in character—a large percentage of those who left were interested in emigrating to Western countries rather than to Israel. The Jewish activists still left in the USSR also became less homogeneous in outlook. Those who had emigrated to Israel in the early seventies regarded the problem of Jewish culture in the USSR as a closed book. In the survey of Jewish activists, over 85 percent responded negatively to the question: "Do you believe in the possibility of the existence of Jewish culture in the USSR?"[41] They regarded *aliya* as the only way to foster a healthy Jewish consciousness and to preserve Jewish culture. Nevertheless, in the mid-1970s emigration statistics showed that at current emigration rates most Soviet Jews would remain in the USSR in the foreseeable future. Therefore, while continuing strongly to support *aliya,* Jewish activists remaining in the USSR also seriously concerned themselves with the problem of developing Jewish culture in the USSR.

Jewish samizdat in this period reflected the new developments and also attempted to influence them. Two journals—*Evrei v SSSR* (Jews in the USSR)[42] and *Tarbut* (Culture—Hebrew) embody the new direction in samizdat.

Evrei v SSSR first appeared in October 1972 under the editorship of Aleksandr Voronel and Viktor Yakhot. Later, new editors replaced the original ones. These included Nina Voronel, Mikhail Agurskii, and Rafael Nudelman, all of whom emigrated to Israel. The last volume appeared in August 1979. According to Emil Liuboshits, the idea of starting the journal arose when Voronel was visiting him in Kharkov. Voronel initiated the project and began collecting material. Many participants in Voronel's scientific seminars helped in the preparation.[43]

Evrei v SSSR represented a departure from previous samizdat publications in various ways. First, the editors and contributors made no attempt to conceal their identity. Editors' names and addresses appear on the title page and an editors' note states that no anonymous works will be considered.

Second, unlike *Iskhod* or *Iton, Evrei v SSSR* contains primarily original works. Creativity flowers in many genres: essays, memoirs, sketches, poetry, short stories, and short plays.

Third, unlike earlier collections, the journal goes beyond the *aliya* struggle to broader problems of Jewish existence. The editors state their desire to study systematically the question of Jewish consciousness. Their proposed method reflects the scientific background of many of the editors: "it is necessary to gather sufficient representative material to separate the object from the subject of cognition and to distinguish between the multiplicity of observations and interpretations."[44] This proposal also reflects the relative naïveté of its editors about the depth, wealth, and subtlety of the Jewish tradition. Expansion of the format from issue to issue suggests growing awareness of the complexity of dealing with problems of Jewish consciousness. Four subdivisions suffice for the first issue: "From the Editors"; "Legal Questions"; "History"; and "Who Am I?" (personal statements about Jewish identity). The twelfth issue contains eleven subdivisions including new ones such as "Prose"; "Poetry"; "Overseas"; "Essays";

"Articles"; "Information"; "A Glance from the Side" (works by or interviews with non-Jews); "Bibliography"; and "Letters."

One of the journal's functions was to supplement the educative samizdat material already in circulation. A bibliography section lists Russian-language works on the history of the Jews; the history section offers information primarily on Russian-Jewish history—from early times (the seventh to eighth centuries CE) up to the present. Articles on general Jewish history (for example "Who are the Marranos?", in No. 5) often make explicit or implicit parallels with the modern Soviet situation.

Problems of *aliya*, although not central, also received serious attention. Legal advice and documents, petitions and appeals kept the reader informed on new stages in the *aliya* struggle.

The editors' eclectic approach gradually encompassed religion—the separate categories "Religion" and "Judaica" first appeared in the ninth issue. Some articles are purely factual—an explanation of the Jewish calendar or of the holiday of Purim; others offer Bible translations and commentary. These articles present religion as part of a reasoned intellectual exercise, rather than as an emotional experience.

Articles by and interviews with non-Jews, some of whom are openly anti-Semitic, contribute to the experimental method of presenting as many sides of the Jewish question as possible. Excerpts range from famous nineteenth-century writers such as Gogol and Dostoevsky to Soviet classics such as Aleksandr Fadeev and Sergei Vasil'ev. Interviews with contemporary Russian Orthodox spokesmen like Aleksandr Men' (a convert from Judaism to Christianity in his youth) and Gennadii Shimanov (active in the right-wing Russian religious movement), or a lecture by the anti-Semitic writer Valerii Emil'ianov can be more revealing than dozens of essays by Jews.

The journal focuses on the question of Jewish individual and national identity. The authors possess a Jewish consciousness which has been stimulated in part by earlier samizdat reading. The simple presentation of information is insufficient; articles analyze the Jewish experience, try to understand its meaning for the individual, and to generalize to the national level.

The section "Who am I?" offers individual perceptions. Ultimately, Jewish consciousness remains very subjective. The first issue presents, on the one hand, Larissa Bogoraz, who, despite the intellectual knowledge that she is a Jewess, cannot feel any emotional identification with her Jewishness, and, on the other hand, Mikhail Kliachkin who, having felt an irrational identification with the Jewish nation since childhood, finally decides to apply for an exit visa to Israel. Subsequent issues continue the dialogue in this and in other sections.

Some contributors regard their Jewishness as a form of alienation which they share with the intelligentsia of the country as a whole. Boris Khazanov, for example, does not want to separate his Jewish and his intelligentsia identity. He considers that those who become absorbed solely in Jewish questions severely limit their cultural horizons.[45]

Aleksandr Voronel, a physicist who subsequently emigrated to Israel, adopts an opposing viewpoint. In one of the most thoughtful and interesting essays in *Evrei v SSSR*, Voronel dissociates himself from the Russian intelligentsia and explains why the Jewish intellectual tradition is richer and more sophisticated than the Russian one. Voronel uses his personal experience as an analytic tool in constructing his generalizations.[46]

Several articles show that persistent anti-Semitism can stimulate Jewish consciousness. I. Domal'skii (pseudonym of the writer Mikhail Baital'skii) surveys the problem of anti-Semitism in the USSR and its ramifications for Jews who choose to remain in the Soviet Union. Using Soviet statistics, he points to an increase in anti-Semitic discrimination in academic professions and in access to institutions of higher learning. The individual who suffers from this policy must find a way of coming to terms with his Jewish identity.

Domal'skii's distress over anti-Semitism in the USSR is related to his concern with the moral decline of the country as a whole, and of the intelligentsia in particular. Although the intelligentsia should provide moral leadership, instead they officially or unofficially endorse anti-Semitism. He hopes that Jewish intellectuals can set an example which will help restore the intelligentsia's moral integrity.[47]

In urging Jewish intellectuals to become moral leaders, Domal'skii suggests that they examine the Jewish tradition for models of freedom, courage, integrity, and so forth. He and other contributors to *Evrei v SSSR* emphatically reject the Jewish *shtetl* experience as a source of Jewish identity.[48] This prejudice derives from an earlier generation of Jewish *intelligenty*: an excerpt from the poet Osip Mandelshtam, "Judaic Chaos" (No. 7), shows his discomfort with "unenlightened" Jewish relatives.

Unlike Mandelshtam who rejected his Jewish heritage in favor of the Russian, many of the writers in *Evrei v SSSR* assert their spiritual affinity with Jews of the Biblical and Mishnaic periods—the Israelites of the Exodus, the Maccabees, or the defenders of Masada.

The journal discusses another important subject—the role of a Jewish language in Jewish identity. The appearance of a serious Jewish journal in Russian reveals much: assimilation occurred most successfully in the language area. Yiddish, according to statistical evidence, has ceased to be Soviet Jews' native tongue.[49] Contemporary Jewish intellectuals display a strong attachment to the Russian language. Khazanov refers to it as his only homeland.[50] Bogoraz and others display similar sentiments. Their unwillingness to identify too strongly as Jews relates to their fear of losing contact with the Russian language and culture.

Those who have chosen a strong Jewish identity follow the pattern suggested in Jabotinsky's *Feuilletons*. They do not discourage or deny the Jewishness of works written in Russian, but they simultaneously urge the study of Hebrew. Iosif Begun points to the growing interest in Hebrew study as an important manifestation of "the renaissance of the national spirit among Soviet Jews. . . . And despite . . . all concealed and open opposition Jews are beginning to study Hebrew."[51]

The journal *Tarbut* first appeared in 1975 as a supplement to *Evrei v SSSR*. It continued to be published for several years, although the original editors—Feliks Dektor, Veniamin Fain, and Il'ia Rubin—emigrated to Israel.

The introduction to each issue of *Tarbut* urges readers, "Most important, don't be afraid." In emphasizing that Jewish culture in the USSR must be open and legal, the editors strive to make Soviet Jews feel an integral and normal part of world Jewry. Articles describe major Jewish communities and Jewish periodicals; a special section prints Jewish recipes and lists the dates of Jewish holidays.[52]

The editors show a deeper awareness of the role of religion in Jewish nationhood. Some issues are arranged thematically around holidays—the third issue around Hanukkah and the fifth around Pesah. The ninth issue contains several introductory articles on the Talmud.

Tarbut relies mainly on authoritative Western sources, but also reprints prerevolutionary Russian works (e.g., Joseph Klausner, "Literature in Hebrew in Russia, 1810–1910"; Vladimir Jabotinsky, "Four Sons"), some fiction and poetry, and informative articles by Soviet Jews.

The Symposium on Jewish Culture in the USSR which was supposed to take place in Moscow on 21–23 December 1976, best exemplifies the change in focus of the Jewish movement in the mid-seventies. After a month of preliminary harassment, the Soviet authorities cancelled the symposium, but the symposium's organizers published a samizdat white paper with the following sections: (1) A chronicle containing: (a) explanation of the reasons for convening the symposium, (b) description of organizational preparations, and (c) record of the KGB's fight against the symposium; (2) Documents of the symposium; (3) Declarations of the organizing committee on harassment of the symposium; (4) Excerpts from the Soviet press concerning the symposium; (5) Personal testimony of participants; (6) Reports prepared for the symposium. This format combines several genres previously used by Jewish samizdat; the compilation of public appeals and declarations; official documents related to harassment, searches, and arrests; and essays in the style of *Evrei v SSSR* presenting varying viewpoints on Jewish topics.

The organizers, like the Russian democratic dissidents, emphasize legalism. They detail all the illegal methods used against symposium participants and point to the blatant violation of the Helsinki Accords, which the Soviet Union had signed in 1975. They stress the legality of their own actions, which are based on "the strict observance of all Soviet laws and on fully publicizing all our actions. Also, we always base ourselves on the assumption that the authorities can have no grounds for opposing an undertaking which is cultural and national rather than political."[53]

The symposium, in effect, calls for a realistic reevaluation of the *aliya* movement. The organizers' appeal to Soviet Jews approvingly mentions those 100,000 Jews who have left the USSR to join in the mainstream of world Jewry, but notes that "the experience of recent years indicates that the majority of Soviet Jews presently remain and will continue to remain in the USSR for a long time." They remind Soviet Jews that the Soviet variety of assimilation is a form of degradation—that is, a loss of national self-respect without genuine acceptance into Soviet society. They suggest a return to Jewish self-respect, a revival of Jewish national consciousness, and the reestablishment of dying traditions through better Jewish education.[54] In the tradition of *Evrei v SSSR* symposium participants disapprovingly pass over the *shtetl* experience and the Yiddish language in the search for Jewish roots and speak of the "true Jewish culture and traditions which have an almost 4,000-year-long history."[55] They regard Yiddish, and official spokesmen for Yiddish such as A. Vergelis, editor of *Sovetish heymland*, as hindrances to the development of this true culture. Recognition of Yiddish as the official Jewish national language is used as an excuse to prevent the study of Hebrew.[56]

The symposium reports assiduously avoid political controversy. Topics include demographic surveys; aspects of Jewish musical, visual, and folk arts; Soviet treatment of Jewish topics in textbooks; religious, linguistic, and legal aspects of the national revival. Most reports stress the desperate situation of Jewish culture in the USSR caused by the abysmal lack of the most elementary knowledge. Participants such as Veniamin Fain, M. Zubin, and Aleksandr Lerner advocate a legal fight for a national cultural renaissance. They appeal to the West for help in providing nonpolitical cultural material. Their demands from the Soviet authorities include permission to teach Hebrew legally and to publish texts and periodicals on Jewish life; permission to hold seminars on Jewish culture and to maintain contact with the world Jewish community; and noninterference in broadcasts from Israel and other countries.[57] Although all these demands may, indeed, be technically legal, so far the Soviet authorities have not agreed to them.

Jewish samizdat in recent decades has helped encourage the revival of Jewish national consciousness in the USSR. At first, it satisfied a thirst for basic Jewish knowledge and stimulated interest in the Jewish heritage. Readers favored samizdat works which stressed Jewish heroism and nationalism—*Exodus, My Glorious Brothers,* and Jabotinsky's *Feuilletons.* Jews who had been brought up in an atmosphere of Great Russian nationalism which excluded them, eagerly substituted Jewish nationalism for the Russian variety.

The Six-Day War generated a burst of nationalism which increased the readership for Jewish samizdat. Samizdat in the late sixties and early seventies concentrated almost exclusively on the *aliya* struggle; activists produced documentary collections which simultaneously sought Western support and encouraged Soviet Jews to emigrate. These collections became more selective and sophisticated as the Jewish movement developed.

Like the Jewish movement as a whole, samizdat developed quickly. By the mid-seventies, Jewish samizdat had matured sufficiently to produce thought-provoking collections containing many original works. The writers in *Evrei v SSSR* are not satisfied simply with being proud of their Jewish nationality. They continually examine themselves and their position in Soviet society. They acknowledge the origins of their Jewish consciousness in Soviet anti-Semitic discriminatory practice, but discover that familiarity with Jewish history and historiography, arts, philosophy, and religion all contribute toward a firmer Jewish identity.

The articles in *Evrei v SSSR* show the distortions in contemporary Soviet Jewish consciousness: an inbred fear of appearing too Jewish; appalling ignorance of the Jewish heritage; and contempt for *shtetl* life and its achievements. *Tarbut* tries to overcome the imbalance by offering material leading to Jewish normalcy and to a feeling of unity with world Jewry.

Samizdat in the late 1970s faced new challenges: (1) More than 70 percent of Soviet Jews who were leaving the USSR were choosing other Western countries over Israel; how should samizdat deal with this problem of *neshira* ("dropping-out" in Hebrew)? (2) Despite the exodus of nearly 250,000 Jews in the seventies, the overwhelming majority of Soviet Jews remain in the USSR. Even if the peak emigration rate in 1979 of over 50,000 people were to be resumed and maintained, it would take many years before even half of Soviet Jewry would emigrate—if they were to choose to do so. Should samizdat writers ignore this often "silent majority"? If not, what stance should they take and how important is such cultural work in relation to the immediate problems of the *aliya* struggle?

These questions constituted an important element in the reports prepared for the Symposium on Jewish Culture and continued to preoccupy samizdat writers.[58] Many share the opinion of Aleksandr Lerner that this silent majority should not be ignored: "Although the renaissance of Jewish civilization in the USSR and a renewed adherence to it by the mass of Soviet Jewry seems improbable, we must try to save and preserve every Soviet Jew as a son of the Jewish nation and we don't have the right to bury hope for the success of this mission as long as even one Jew remains in the USSR."[59]

Samizdat thus has a threefold task: to encourage a minority to make *aliya* immediately; to arouse the Jewish consciousness of others sufficiently to help them make a more knowledgeable decision on whether to emigrate to Israel or to the West; to prevent the spark of Jewish feeling from dying out among those still far from attempting emigration, and to instill a more positive attitude toward Jewish identity among this group. Although most activists agree that the three goals are connected, they differ on which deserves the most attention at any given moment and on the means to achieve them.

Ultimately, the goal of Jewish samizdat is to eliminate its own raison d'être, that is, to attain a legal, open status for Jewish activity in the USSR with free access to international Jewish life. This goal still appears distant and Jewish samizdat continues to flourish.[60]

Notes

1. The publication and dissemination of samizdat works outside the Soviet Union constitute a topic in its own right that is beyond the scope of this chapter.
2. Questionnaire survey of 447 Jewish activists in Israel, Center for Research and Documentation of East European Jewry (CRD), Hebrew University, Jerusalem (henceforth referred to as "Questionnaire"). The questionnaire shows that the most popular methods of preparing samizdat material include preparation of additional typewritten copies, photo-reproduction or a combination of the two (Question no. 168).
3. Questionnaire, nos. 64 and 169.
4. For example, Ester Lomovskaia from Novosibirsk relates that she kept a samizdat library of fifty-five titles which she continually loaned out to people. Interview with Ester Lomovskaia, CRD, typescript, p. 24.
5. Vol't Lomovskii notes that the library which they assembled included basically the same works as were available in Moscow and Riga. Interview with Vol't Lomovskii, September 28, 1976, CRD, typescript, p. 65.
6. See A. Rozhanskii, ed., *Antievreiskie protesessy v Sovetskom Soiuze* (1969–1971), (Jerusalem: CRD, 1979), vols. 1, 2.
7. See interview with Avraham Shifrin, March 25, 1979, CRD.
8. For articles about literature in Hebrew and Yiddish in the Soviet period, see Y. A. Gilboa, "Hebrew Literature in the USSR," and C. Shmeruk, "Yiddish Literature in the USSR," in L. Kochan, ed., *The Jews in Soviet Russia Since 1917* (London: Oxford University Press, 1972), 2nd edition, pp. 216–31 and 232–68.
9. See Isai Averbukh, "Jewish Samizdat at the End of the Forties: Fragments from Margarita Aliger's Poem 'Your Victory'," in this volume.
10. This refers to the inhabitants of the European regions of the pre–World War II Soviet Union. In the areas such as the Baltic states and the Western Ukraine, which were annexed by the USSR in World War II, Jewish consciousness did survive. Those who had grown up there before the war had received a Jewish education in their youth. The non-Ashkenazi groups—that is, the Bukharan, Georgian, and Mountain Jews—also retained their Jewish consciousness.
11. Questionnaire, no. 65.
12. Shifrin interview, p. 29ff.
13. Questionnaire, no. 64.

14. Both *Exodus* and *My Glorious Brothers* were described as anti-Soviet in activists' trials. *Antievreiskie protesessy*, vol. 2, p. 864.
15. Author's interview with Boris Slovin, June 14, 1979.
16. V. Jabotinsky, "O natsional'nom vospitanii," *Fel'etony*, reprinted ed. (St. Petersburg: n.p., 1913), p. 14.
17. V. Jabotinsky, "O 'evreiakh i russkoi literature'," ibid., p. 66.
18. Jabotinsky, "O natsional'nom vospitanii," p. 19.
19. Jabotinsky, "Chetyre stat'i o Chirikovskom intsident'e," *Fel'etony*, pp. 71–100.
20. Jabotinsky, "Ne veriu," ibid., pp. 115–24.
21. *Antievreiskie protsessy*, vol. 2, p. 893.
22. Author's interview with Leah Slovin, June 14, 1979.
23. Polina Korenblit, quoted in Leonard Schroeter, *The Last Exodus* (New York: Universe Books, 1974), pp. 208–9.
24. See Shimon Redlich, "Haatzumot shel yehudei brit-ha-moetzot kebitui l'hitorerrut leumit (1968–1970)" (Petitions of Soviet Jews as an Expression of National Revival–1968–1970), *Behinot* (Jerusalem), 5 (1974), pp. 7–24.
25. Ester Lomovskaia interview, p. 41.
26. Questionnaire, nos. 170 and 171.
27. Interview with Tina Brodetskaia, June 27, 1976, CRD, typescript, p. 59.
28. Ibid., pp. 50, 57.
29. In the USSR it was known as the "Letter of the Moscow 40" since the signature of Iulius Telesin was added after it had been transmitted to the West. It is reproduced in *Iton bet* in *Evreiskii samizdat* (Jerusalem: CRD, 1974), vol. 1, p. 91ff.
30. Shroeter, *The Last Exodus*, p. 275.
31. In the first and second Leningrad trials of Jewish activists, Iosif Mendelevich was accused of writing this and subsequent anonymous articles.
32. "Purim i pesakh," *Iton alef*, reprinted in *Evreiskii samizdat*, vol. 1, p. 40.
33. Sara Khonig, "Sovetskie vlasti ne smogut sokrushit' evreiskii dukh," ibid., p. 83.
34. "Evrei perestaut molchat'!" ibid., p. 85.
35. Ibid., p. 89.
36. *Iskhod*, no. 1, reprinted in *Evreiskii samizdat*, vol. 2 (Jerusalem: CRD, 1974).
37. See for example, "Delo R. Palatnik (Odessa)," *Vestnik iskhoda*, reprinted in *Evreiskii samizdat*, vol. 3 (Jerusalem: CRD, 1974), p. 12.
38. "Ot sostavitelei," *Belaia kniga iskhoda*, reprinted in *Evreiskii samizdat*, vol. 5 (Jerusalem: CRD, 1974), p. 1.
39. Author's interview with Boris Orlov, May 1979.
40. Ester Lomovskaia interview, pp. 35–36.
41. Questionnaire, no. 195.
42. The issues of the journal were republished in Russian by the Center for Research and Documentation of East European Jewry, Hebrew University of Jerusalem, in the series *Evreiskii samizdat*.
43. Refuseniks who had lost their jobs initiated scientific seminars to discuss

material in their field. They also organized seminars on Jewish topics. Interview with E. Liuboshits, CRD, typescript, p. 10.
44. "Ot sostavitelei," *Evrei v SSSR*, no. 1, reprinted in *Evreiskii samizdat*, vol. 4 (Jerusalem: CRD, 1974), p. 1.
45. See B. Khazanov, "Novaia Rossiia," *Evrei v SSSR*, no. 7, reprinted in *Evreiskii samizdat*, vol. 10 (Jerusalem: CRD, 1976).
46. A. Voronel, "Trepet iudaiskikh zabot," *Evrei v SSSR*, nos. 10 and 11, reprinted in *Evreiskii samizdat*, vol. 12 (Jerusalem: CRD, 1977).
47. See I. Domal'skii, *Russkie evrei vchera i segodnia* (Jerusalem: Biblioteka Aliya, 1975).
48. Rejection of the *shtetl* is so pervasive that it can be found even where it makes very little sense, as in a manifesto by Jewish artists who exhibited in November–December 1975 in Leningrad and Moscow. In a short essay ("Stereotipy," no. 7, vol. 10) one contemporary writer points out the dangers of such stereotyped thinking.
49. See L. Hirszowicz, "Jewish Culture in the USSR Today" in this volume.
50. Khazanov, "Novaia Rossiia," p. 114.
51. I. Begun, "K istorii natsional'nogo iazyka sovetskikh evreev," *Evrei v SSSR*, no. 4, reprinted in *Evreiskii samizdat*, vol. 6 (Jerusalem: CRD, 1974), p. 105.
52. *Tarbut*, nos. 1–8, 1975–77, were reprinted in *Evreiskii samizdat*, vol. 18; *Tarbut*, nos. 9–12, 1977, in vol. 19; no. 13, 1979, in vol. 25.
53. "Dokumenty press-konferentsii 17 noiabria 1976g," *Belaia kniga o simpoziume: Evreiskaia kul'tura v SSSR. Sostoianie, Perspektivy*. Reprinted in *Evreiskii samizdat*, vol. 15, p. 39.
54. "Obrashcheniia k evreiam SSSR," in ibid., p. 35.
55. "Dokumenty," in ibid., p. 38.
56. P. Abramovich, "Nekotorye voprosy problemy izucheniia i prepodavaniia iazyka ivrit v SSSR," ibid., pp. 149–52.
57. M. Zubin, "Nekotorye perspektivy evreiskoi natsional'noi kul'tury v SSSR"; A. Lerner, "Emigratsiia ili tsivilizatsiia? Chto vazhnee?"; V. Fain, V. Prestin, P. Abramovich, Ts. Adoma, S. Admoni, "Blizhaishchii etap vozrozhdeniia evreiskoi kul'turnoi zhizni v SSSR," ibid.
58. A similar debate continues among Russian activist *olim* (immigrants to Israel) in the Israeli Russian-language press.
59. Lerner, "Emigratsiia," *Evreiskii samizdat*, vol. 15, p. 248.
60. This chapter deals with samizdat material only up until the end of the 1970s.

6

The Role of the Synagogue and Religion in the Jewish National Awakening

Yaacov Ro'i

The last Jewish cultural institutions in the Soviet Union were closed in 1948–49. From that time on the Jews have been deprived even of the minimal cultural autonomy enjoyed by other national minorities in the USSR. All that remained were the few synagogues which World War II and the Soviet regime had left unscathed. It was around these synagogues that the Jews concentrated a great deal of the activity that they felt able to indulge in during the 1950s and 1960s.[1]

This essay will endeavor to ascertain what role the synagogues in particular and Jewish religious ceremonies and festivals in general played in the history of the Jewish national awakening since the end of World War II. All sources agree that Soviet Jewry in this period was not essentially religious in either belief or practice: the Enlightenment and then the agnosticism that had gained so much ground in the czarist Russia of the late nineteenth and early twentieth century had been topped by several decades of communist rule and its atheist education. This does not mean that there were no Jews who sought to practice Judaism and preserve its precepts. Even in the most difficult periods there were, for example, Jews who observed the Sabbath and ate only *matzot* on the Passover (the special unleavened bread eaten on that festival).[2] Yet the vast majority of Jews had little or no religious orientation or inclination.

Nonetheless, many among them sought to identify as Jews and, having no other source of identification within the USSR, they did so by attending synagogue at least on the major festivals and by preserving some of the traditional Jewish rites. On the Sabbath the Jews who went to synagogue were mostly either religious Jews who went to pray or elderly Jews, pensioners, who wanted to be among, and meet with, fellow Jews. On the High Holy Days, and especially the Day of Atonement, other Jews came as well, Jews who had no association with anything Jewish and gave no expression to their Jewishness throughout the year, Jews who on this particular day felt a psychological need to associate themselves with their people and its tradition. Even in the camps Jewish prisoners who had no religious proclivities fasted on the Day of Atonement.[3] This was a gesture of national belonging rather than an act of religious faith. Yet, in this way religion, and the Jewish religion is in essence a national religion, helped the Jews find at least a partial solution to the anomalous situation in which they were placed under a regime that allowed them neither to be full-fledged Jews nor full-fledged Russians (let alone Ukrainians, Latvians, Georgians, and so forth).[4]

The Holocaust and the concomitant manifestations of anti-Semitism among the non-Jewish population, especially in the Ukraine, Belorussia, and the Baltic republics, followed by the official anti-Semitism of the late war and immediate postwar years, disenchanted many of those Jews who in the 1920s and 1930s had hoped that the Jewish problem was indeed solved in the Soviet Union and that they were becoming an integral part of a new supranational, communist society. Toward the end of World War II and in its immediate aftermath the synagogues would be filled on the major Jewish festivals[5] and on the occasion of special services held to commemorate the victims of the Holocaust.[6] Even in this period when it was still possible to go to the Jewish theater in Moscow or in Minsk and to attend Jewish concerts or literary evenings (in December 1947, for example, such evenings were held in a number of cities to commemorate the thirtieth anniversary of the death of the Hebrew writer Mendele Moikher Seforim),[7] the synagogue attracted thousands of Jews. They felt the need not only to meet and be among fellow Jews, but also to give vent to their pent-up feelings of sadness and anguish with the help of age-old rites that provided a last link with a past from which they felt artificially cut off. Young Jews who in the immediate postwar period met in small groups in various cities for some sort of Zionist activity turned to the synagogue as the sole place for disseminating their ideas.[8]

In this period the synagogue also meant a link, even though a somewhat flimsy one, with Jews outside the confines of the USSR and especially in Palestine. In Moscow's main Choral Synagogue a service held to commemorate the communities that had been annihilated in the Holocaust was a response to an appeal by the chief rabbi of Palestine, Rabbi Isaac Herzog, to Jewish communities the world over.[9] On the last Passover of the war, the president of the congregation, Samuil' Chobruitskii, read out a greetings cable from the Chief Rabbinate of Palestine together with a telegram from Stalin.[10] In 1946 the American Jewish publicist Ben-Zion Goldberg spoke inter alia about Palestine and the struggle of the *yishuv* (the Jewish community) there in a number of synagogues throughout the USSR, where he was visiting at the invitation of the Jewish Anti-Fascist Committee. Everywhere these references were greeted with stormy ovations.[11] On the Feast of Hanukkah in the winter of 1947–48, just a month after the United Nations General Assembly had decided on the establishment of a Jewish state in Palestine, Rabbi Shlomo Shlifer of the Moscow Choral Synagogue read out another message of greetings from Rabbi Herzog, noting that the redemption of the Jewish people had begun.[12] The peak of activity at the Moscow synagogue came after the birth of the Jewish state. On the first weekend following the event some two thousand Jews gathered spontaneously to congratulate each other and express their joy. Several weeks later an official service was held to mark the establishment of the State of Israel, at which the synagogue was packed. And finally, when Israel's first diplomatic envoy, Mrs. Golda Meyerson (later Meir) reached Moscow, she was welcomed with the well-known demonstrations of the High Holy Days (the New Year and Day of Atonement) of October 1948.[13] Both Golda Meir and the counselor of the Israeli legation, Mordecai Namir, have described the scenes of the High Holy Days in detail as well as the excitement and enthusiasm of the Israeli diplomats' first encounter with the leaders of the congregation of Moscow's main synagogue on a previous Sabbath (11 September 1948), when Mrs. Meyerson's meeting with Rabbi Shlifer was received with a tremendous ovation and cries of "The people of Israel lives," and when many of the worshipers actually accompanied the diplomats back to their hotel.[14]

The ecstasy of 1948 was stifled by the persecution and arrests of the following years, the "Black Years" of Stalin's last period. Undoubtedly the Jews had lost their sense of proportion on the above occasions and provocateurs who were present took advantage of this to present reports to the authorities that were used against many who participated in the 1948 demonstrations so that these people were arrested in the weeks and months that followed. Others came under surveillance following the demonstrations and were arrested later.[15] From this time on the synagogue authorities took every possible precaution to prevent a recurrence of any activity that could provide a pretext for the powers-that-be to act against the Jews as a whole and the synagogue in particular. Yet even in the 1949–53 period, with all the fear that prevailed, people came to the synagogues on festivals and holidays, especially the High Holy Days, when the congregation, which included young people, still spilled over from the packed buildings onto the street in front.[16] Something of the atmosphere of this period is perhaps best conveyed by recalling Rabbi Shlifer's request to his congregation to refrain from uttering the concluding prayer of the Day of Atonement: "Next year in Jerusalem!" The request made from the pulpit toward the end of the service in 1951 was of no avail and was not reiterated. In other towns, too, the rabbis received injunctions to a similar effect.[17] Indeed, this oath of fidelity to the Jewish messianic dream, uttered by the entire congregation in "a wild spontaneous cry, which seemed to rise from a single throat, a single heart," gave expression to the Jews' innermost feelings which were part of their spiritual life[18] and therefore allowed for no compromise.

As early as the winter of 1948–49 there were indications that the exuberant atmosphere that had marked the first encounters in the synagogue was changing. When members of the Israeli legation visited the Choral Synagogue on one evening of Hanukkah (1 January 1949), they felt that the congregation was keeping its distance and refraining from contact. The synagogue officials were prepared neither to receive a Jewish calendar nor to transmit a letter of thanks to the Great Synagogue in Tel Aviv for a Scroll of the Law it had sent to Moscow and which was transferred to the synagogue in a closed ceremony. At this time, significantly, rumors were being spread among the Jews in Moscow that the Israeli government was recalling Mrs. Meyerson because the excitement aroused among the local Jews by the visits to the synagogue of the envoy and the members of her staff was not to the liking of the Soviet authorities.[19] Such rumors presumably originated with the Ministry of Internal Security (MGB) and were intended to deter Jews from going to the synagogue.

On Passover 1949, which fell at the height of the anticosmopolitan campaign, the synagogue was in a state of gloom and depression. This mood improved slightly when the campaign let up somewhat by the Feast of Pentecost seven weeks later. Once again the congregants who filled the synagogue tried to approach the Israeli diplomats, although the wardens held them off, and once again a memorial prayer for those who had fallen in the struggle for Israel's independence was read out. Such a prayer had been read on the Day of Atonement of October 1948 and was read for the last time on the Day of Atonement of October 1949.

In 1949, and even more so in the following years, the worshipers in Moscow refrained from even the minimal personal contact which they had allowed themselves in the excitement of the first encounter. An occasional tightly screwed up piece of paper would, however, be unobtrusively transferred to the hand or pocket of one of the Israelis, telling of the plight of Soviet Jewry or asking for a message to be conveyed to a relative in Israel. A few words might even be hastily exchanged.[20] One Jew managed to tell one of the diplomats that the establishment of the State of Israel had evoked a profound Zionist awakening; another, that the existence of the state was of great significance to Soviet Jews. The very appearance of the Israeli legation staff, even without possibility of contact, was their greatest comfort and joy. Another Jew, from the town of Saratov, told the Israelis that he considered even in these harsh years that he could arouse interest in Israel simply by talking to local Jews in the synagogue. Indeed, the few synagogues that still existed and the institutions connected with them provided the opportunity for conversations concerning Israel.[21] In some places, especially in the Ukraine, in the smaller townships as well as in major cities, rabbis were interrogated and arrested on charges that in the synagogues the Jews, while pretending to be praying, in fact conducted political conversations and business transactions and, above all, showed undue interest in the Jewish community outside the USSR, notably in Israel. The rabbi of one small Ukrainian town, an invalid of World War II, was charged with maintaining ties with foreign agents, with receiving information from Israel, and with attempting to contact the Israel legation in Moscow.[22]

In Tbilisi, the capital of the Georgian SSR, members of the Israeli delegation who visited the town on Passover of 1951 found an atmosphere that was notably freer than elsewhere. Worshipers, especially in the synagogue where prayers were conducted according to the Georgian Jewish rite and custom (as distinct from the Ashkenazi) were not afraid to talk to the guests and both the leader of the congregation, the *hacham,* and its members showed great interest in Israel. From the conversations in the synagogue it was clear that many Jews listened to the "Voice of Israel" broadcasts; some even asked if and when they would be able to go to Israel. The Georgian Jews, perhaps because the population surrounding them had preserved more of its own traditions, had been better able to retain their religious practices and institutions than Jews in the other European parts of the USSR: many of them continued to be observing Jews, who even taught their children the rites and precepts of Judaism.[23]

The mid-1950s brought new hope to Soviet Jews. The common experience of Stalin's last Black Years, culminating in the "Doctors' Plot," had brought the Jews together and strengthened Jewish solidarity and awareness. Young Jews began appearing in the synagogues on the major festivals simply to display their identification with their Jewishness and to meet other Jews, there being virtually no other place or opportunity to do this. At the time of the Sinai War (October–November 1956), special *minyanim* (groups of at least ten men, the necessary quorum for Jewish communal service) convened to pray for Israel's welfare.[24]

Toward the end of the decade, as Jewish national consciousness grew and spread among the young, the identification with Jewish religious tradition acquired a new thrust. This growth of national consciousness was in part a result of the more relaxed atmosphere of the immediate post-Stalin years, in part a result of disappointment among Jews that the "Thaw" of de-Stalinization had brought no remedy to their own situation (discrimination, anti-Semitism), and in part a continuation of the above-mentioned dilemma which prevented the Jew from identifying with any official, authorized secular national culture. Although the antireligious campaign that gathered momentum in the latter part of the Khrushchev period (1958–64) brought at least a proportionate toll of victims among Jewish houses of worship and their custodians, it did not affect this trend.[25]

The fact that the disfavor with which the authorities regarded the Jewish religion in its various manifestations did not deter Jews was particularly evident with regard to the young generation that had reached political awareness and maturity after Stalin's death and had not experienced some of the more traumatic aspects of his rule. Although Jewish worshipers were charged not only with dishonesty and fraud and the use of synagogues for "nonreligious and illegal purposes," but also with allegiance to Israel, which meant disloyalty to the Soviet Union,[26] young Jews came in increasing numbers to the few synagogues that remained open to manifest their pride in being Jewish. In the synagogue alone Soviet Jews could demonstrate that the Jewish people lived on and refused to renounce its existence as a nation. For that they were ready to suffer interrogations, arrest, and even punitive measures in places of study or work. One visitor to the USSR wrote that Soviet policy compelled Jews who sought to retain allegiance to their people to demonstrate their Jewishness by participating in Jewish religious rites.[27]

In addition to the High Holy Days, the festivals that most attracted the youth were Passover, the festival of freedom and the Exodus from Egypt, being especially singled out by the Soviets as a holiday that gives rise to nationalist feelings,[28] and Simhat Torah (the rejoicing of the Law) when worshipers dance and sing with the Scrolls of the Law. Jews came to meet fellow Jews and talk with them, especially about Israel, to sing Jewish songs, and to dance. Elie Wiesel who visited the USSR in the fall of 1965 wrote that Simhat Torah was an event that Jews as a whole, and the youth in particular, looked forward to for a whole year. Even though the authorities tried to deter Jews from attending synagogue on this occasion, the Jews refused to stay away. In Moscow, for example, rumors were spread that those who had come to the synagogue on the High Holy Days a few weeks before had been photographed there; moreover, two large projectors had been installed to light up the street and the entry of the building. Nonetheless, parents came with small children and young people came in their thousands to identify, to give vent to long-repressed feelings. Fear was thrust aside. During the entire year Soviet Jews had neither occasion nor opportunity to sing. Once a year they sang with all their might, were genuinely happy, and could forget their surroundings and problems, kissing the Scrolls of the Law with enthusiasm and devotion. The singing and dancing that went on for hours, inside the synagogue and in the street outside, in a celebration that was protracted because no one wished it to end, enabled them to overcome their enemies and gave them the strength to endure.[29] This was, in the words of a Western correspondent, a true demonstration of Jewish solidarity.[30] In Riga a number of activists held open house on Jewish holidays, especially on the Passover, the first evening of which is a traditional family and social get-together to recount the biblical Exodus from Egypt. At first this was done quietly, but by the 1960s it would be announced openly in the synagogue who was holding open house and, as one such activist has recorded, "people came."[31]

Visitors who came to the USSR in the second half of the 1950s and the early and mid-1960s, and Soviet Jews who have since left the USSR have afforded us ample evidence of these "happenings." Some published their stories in book form (such as Aryeh L. Eliav, *Between Hammer and Sickle*, first published in Hebrew in 1958—Eliav had served in the Israeli Embassy in Moscow from 1958 to 1960, and Elie Wiesel, *The Jews of Silence*); others gave their stories to the media; and still others have told of their visits to the synagogue and the celebration of Jewish festivals in their reminiscences or in interviews by historians and other scholars. While it is not possible in the scope of a single chapter to give even a fair sample of all the evidence that has been amassed or do justice to what was in fact an extraordinary manifestation of the Jews' association with their roots, I shall attempt to describe its main aspects and discuss its historical significance.

The Israeli diplomats who served in Moscow in the years 1953–67 not only played an important part in bringing the story to the knowledge of the outside world. They also made their own contribution to its evolution. In Stalin's last years their movements and contacts throughout the USSR and in particular in the synagogues had been severely curtailed. With the return of the Israeli legation to the USSR in the latter half of 1953—relations had been severed in February of that year in the wake of the "Doctors' Plot" but were renewed in July (Stalin had died in March)—the Israelis were freer to move around than in the previous period. They visited the synagogues in Moscow and other cities which they toured, especially at times of the Jewish festivals, often bringing with them prayer books, shawls, and other items of worship that were unobtainable in the USSR, such as *etrogim* and *lulavim* (citrons and palm branches) for the Feast of Tabernacles, which they gave directly to the synagogue authorities, as well as small souvenirs of and brochures about Israel, and Hebrew newspapers. Despite the persistent obstructionism of the synagogue authorities who continued to seek the total isolation of the Israeli diplomats during and after the services, the little contact that was possible, and often even the mere presence of representatives of the State of Israel, gave Jews a moral boost and food for thought.[32] These encounters were often a turning point in their lives. The Israelis for their part realized at once that there was a somewhat freer atmosphere than under Stalin and that Jews were a little less afraid; some were even ready to give verbal expression to their aspirations to go to Israel and to look for the occasion to speak with the Israelis.

Gedalia Pecherskii, warden of the Leningrad synagogue as of January 1954 and later president of the congregation, records in his diary that in 1954 some 4,000 worshipers visited the synagogue on Simhat Torah, many of them young people, and a year later approximately 3,000. He put the number of Leningrad Jews who visited the synagogue on all the festivals in the fall of 1954 at about 10,000. Many of them came especially to see the

Israeli minister to Finland who spent the New Year in Leningrad. In May 1955 the Israeli ambassador in Moscow, Yosef Avidar, also visited the synagogue for the Pentecost (*Shavuot*): "a great and awesome day in my life," Pecherskii wrote.[33]

Often the attacks on synagogues printed in the Soviet press that served as pretexts for closing them down referred directly to the activities of the Israeli diplomats—a sure sign that the Soviet authorities were disturbed by their presence in the synagogues both in Moscow and elsewhere, and by the feelings these visits aroused among the worshipers. Some of the latter reportedly approached the local authorities asking that these visits of Israeli representatives be stopped, either out of a genuine fear that they might provide the authorities with an excuse for closing the local synagogue or—more probably—because specific pressure was applied on them to make such a request. The arrest of synagogue officials was often explained by their meetings with Israeli diplomats.[34] One Western correspondent reported that members of the Moscow synagogue were compelled "to sign 'spontaneous letters' to the Chief Rabbinate in Jerusalem, requesting that Israeli representatives should not appear in the synagogue since their behavior is 'unbecoming' and they 'violate the Sabbath.' "[35]

Nonetheless, the synagogue officials themselves did not invariably disavow their connection with Israel even in these troubled times. In April 1963 the Choral Synagogue held a memorial prayer in memory of Israeli president Yitzhak Ben Zvi, on the initiative of the Israeli embassy, at which foreign diplomats and even the Soviet Foreign Ministry were represented.[36] Perhaps this was part of the constant campaign of the Soviet authorities to compromise the synagogues and their officials, who surely could not have held such a service without permission from the Council for the Affairs of Religious Cults.

By the mid-1950s the "Thaw" of de-Stalinization had also led to the beginnings of foreign tourism to the USSR. At first these were chiefly delegations who came at the invitation of some public body or institution, but by the early 1960s individual tourists were also reaching the Soviet Union. Both groups included large numbers of Jews. Indeed, many of the Jewish members of foreign delegations sought specifically to investigate the situation of their coreligionists and even to extend a helping hand, while the individuals usually came to seek out relatives they had not seen for decades, or to look for childhood homes and parents' graves. Once more the synagogue was a natural meeting place. No visitor to the Soviet Union who visited a synagogue, especially on a festival, could come away indifferent. Each one, no matter when or where, felt the warmth and excitement of those who surrounded him, their longing and need for contact with fellow Jews from the world outside, and their cry to remember them and tell everything on returning to the West.[37] Jews in the Soviet Union for their part knew that in the synagogues they could meet Israelis and other foreign Jews and many of those who frequented the synagogues were attracted precisely by the opportunity for such encounters[38]—sometimes they knew in advance that a certain foreigner would be there and sometimes they came on the off chance, especially during the tourist season. The importance of these contacts with Jews from the outside world lay in the need to break through the isolation which the Soviet authorities endeavored to impose upon the Jewish population as part of the policy of assimilating the Jews. The Soviet Jew needed to feel both that the Jews in the West and in Israel were concerned about his lot and that a Jewish future was being built in these countries based on traditional Jewish customs and values.[39]

In 1956 two delegations of American rabbis came to the Soviet Union at the invitation of Rabbi Shlifer. On 23 June 1956 a delegation of the Rabbinical Council of America, headed by Rabbi David Hollander, visited the Moscow Choral Synagogue. After a sermon by Rabbi Shlifer in which he welcomed the delegation, Rabbi Hollander addressed the congregation in Yiddish. He stressed the bond between Orthodox Jewry in the United States and Soviet Jewry and promised not only that the former would never forget Soviet Jews but also that it would extend any assistance that might be called for. Jewish communities everywhere, he pointed out, were closely linked, the Torah providing the cement for these ties. Finally, he said that Jews had every reason to take pride in their Jewishness and must not belittle it under the pressure of environmental constraints. Rabbi Hollander's sermon caused considerable excitement in the synagogue. In Leningrad too, on the following Saturday, the appearance of the rabbis caused great excitement. When they left the synagogue, they found hundreds of Jews awaiting them in the street in a quiet demonstration that was full of unspoken entreaty. At the Jewish cemetery the Jews felt somewhat freer. The president of the Leningrad congregation, Gedalia Pecherskii, invited the rabbis to pray at the mass grave of ten thousand Jews who had died of starvation and cold during the siege of the city in World War II. Word got around of the visit and some eight hundred Jews came there. They beseeched the rabbis for help; some of them declared: "Get us out of here naked and empty-handed and we shall go up to Zion in joy." Rabbi Irving Kosloff, who was originally to be a member of one of the delegations but reached the Soviet Union at a later date, also spoke on a Sabbath morning at the Choral Synagogue and was likewise given an enthusiastic reception. Coming alone, he had more access to worshipers, who did not conceal their delight at the rabbi's visit. Many of them told of their hopes to leave the USSR, particularly to go to Israel.

A statement issued by the second delegation—of the New York Board of Rabbis—told the West for the first time of Soviet Jewry's total lack of the "physical means" for "transmitting a Jewish heritage" despite "the passionate desire by many parents to instill in the younger generation a love for God and loyalty to Jewish traditions." A number of the rabbis called specifically for "additional facilities for religious rituals and observances"; a broader application of "the policy adopted in principle to reunite Soviet residents with their immediate families abroad"; "formal religious education for the young"; and the opening of "avenues . . . to maintain religious and cultural contacts with world Jewry." Although the rabbis were able to establish very little contact with local Jews, except synagogue officials who were themselves usually under strict surveillance, their appearance in synagogues (in Moscow, Leningrad, Kiev, and Odessa) was a major breakthrough and they too received clandestine notes, describing the difficulties of the Soviet Jewish situation and the growing awareness among Soviet Jews, including the youth, that they had in fact no place and no future in the USSR.[40]

The effect of the appearance and address of these American rabbis was apparently so strong that it was not until 1965 that a further delegation, this time of the Rabbinical Council of America, headed by the president of the Council, Rabbi Israel Miller of New York, was allowed to address the Moscow congregation.[41]

Other official guests to the USSR included in November 1961, Senator Jacob Javits—then on his first visit to the USSR—who visited the main Moscow synagogue and was able to talk there with the worshipers (in Yiddish).[42]

A member of a group of Israeli tourists to the Soviet Union in 1962 reported on returning to Israel that his group had sat in the special, segregated box assigned for the Israeli ambassador and other diplomats, which had included on that Sabbath two American tourists with their three children who had come to visit relatives and an Israeli veterinary surgeon who was attending an international conference in Moscow. One worshiper (a man in his sixties) told him: "I am an Orthodox Jew and I pray to our Father in Heaven, but my glance is automatically attracted to the seating place of the people from Israel, from whom I draw strength, hope, and self-esteem. Perhaps were it not for them an old man like me would not come all the way from my distant apartment." Other worshipers asked to pass on regards to relatives in Israel; one young man complained that only the Jews could not meet to celebrate anniversaries of national writers or to enjoy their works, and another that stones were thrown at Jews in front of the synagogue and in other public places. One Jew who had come from another town to visit his son in Moscow asked for a Hebrew newspaper—he himself taught Hebrew in his hometown where he had also organized a group of Hebrew speakers.[43]

Throughout the 1960s and 1970s, however, many worshipers refrained from talking with foreigners on the synagogue premises in view of the constant surveillance of synagogue officials. One young man followed an American professor from the synagogue in Leningrad and told him that the remnants of Soviet Jewish life focused on the few remaining synagogues. Apart from the old who came to pray and study Torah and Talmud, young people also came either to say the memorial prayer in memory of deceased relatives or to find a Jewish atmosphere.[44] Indeed, synagogues continued to be filled, especially on festivals, throughout the 1960s and 1970s.

As Label Katz, president of B'nai B'rith told the B'nai B'rith annual conference on 13 November 1961, the synagogue had become the only regular meeting place for Jews. The synagogues, he said, attracted not only the orthodox but also young Soviet Jews who knew nothing whatever about Judaism, yet came to express their feelings in song and dance on the various Jewish festivals.[45] The Western press reported annually the great numbers of Jews who gathered in the synagogues and in the streets outside to demonstrate their Jewish identity, to celebrate Jewish festivals openly with their fellow Jews, and sometimes to meet Jews from abroad, from Israel, the United States, and elsewhere.[46] One correspondent wrote that every worshiper attested, whether deliberately or not, the ties between the individual Jew and the entire Soviet Jewish community.[47] The risks involved, particularly for the young—questioning, exclusion from the Komsomol, diminished chances of admission to university, disgrace in school or at work—clearly deterred large numbers who had not yet decided to identify openly as Jews. Yet there were hundreds, if not thousands, in every major city with a synagogue and a large Jewish population, who preferred the moral catharsis provided by the occasional visit to the synagogue to living in isolation from their Jewishness and in an environment in which being Jewish had solely negative meaning and connotations. One Jew who was not religious at all told his brother from Israel that he went to the synagogue every Sabbath and festival as a silent personal demonstration against the position of millions of Jewish citizens who were deprived of all educational and cultural institutions.[48]

Sometimes the meetings in the synagogue led to further activity. In the mid-1950s, after worshipers who were leaving the Riga synagogue were bombarded with a rotten watermelon by a "construction battalion" that was working in the vicinity, a so-called self-defense group was formed: on every festival or whenever one of the synagogue officials considered it necessary, ten to fifteen young men would patrol around the synagogue.[49] One young man who had attended the synagogue in Moscow on festivals since the age of thirteen began, as he reached adulthood, to feel surprised at how little the people who came to synagogue were prepared to do to realize their dream of emigration to Israel. In synagogue on the New Year of 1967 he and four other young men decided to take action in order to realize their *aliya*.[50]

A young Jewish person's first visit to the synagogue was not always an act of purposeful identification. Sometimes he or she came out of curiosity or at the suggestion of a friend or relative. In such instances the visit to synagogue often opened up new vistas, generated new questions: What am I doing here? Why are we all here? What does this place or occasion mean to me?

A few of the young Jews who began attending synagogue for nationalist reasons moved close to religion[51] or even became orthodox Jews. The specifically Jewish national values of Judaism attracted a number of young Jewish intellectuals.[52] A few even became Hasidim of Habad; until the 1970s there were communities of Hasidim—Habad and others—in Moscow, Leningrad, and Riga as well as Tashkent and Samarkand, who had traditionally emphasized the links between Judaism and *Eretz Yisrael* (the Land of Israel), and who taught the new recruits, as well as their own children, Hebrew, Yiddish, and Jewish law and precepts.[53] In the 1960s Jews from all over the country sent their sons to Samarkand and Tashkent where they could receive a Jewish education. The Habad *yeshiva* (rabbinical seminary) in Tashkent had between four and five hundred pupils. By the end of the decade considerable sums of money had been collected for Jewish education.[54] Sometimes young Jews first became religious and this led them to Zionist activity and Israel, since the Jewish religion, its prayers, and rites are intricately connected with the country.[55]

But these remained a small minority. For most of the youth, attending synagogue was an outlet for nationalist expression and identification. As one young Moscow activist, Yasha Kazakov, has recorded:

On almost every festival you can hear the Jewish father begging his son: "Please, do not go to the synagogue. What are you looking for there? You do not even know how to pray. Don't go. In any case you will not change the situation but you will cause trouble for yourself at work, at university! . . ." I know from my own experience and that of my friends that in these cases no one argues with his father, but simply goes to the synagogue. . . . It is impossible to argue with fear. My father is no longer able to go to synagogue, so I go for him too, for my father also has inside him, deep down, national feelings. . . .

When thousands of young Jewish people go to synagogue in Moscow, Leningrad, Riga, Kiev, and stand and sing and dance and identify openly with Israel in the face of the secret police—that is a real demonstration. And when I say "demonstration" I want you to understand that it's not the same as in the West. In democratic countries demonstrators—even the most aggressive ones—know that nothing really bad will happen to them, yet in the USSR even in the most tranquil of demonstrations, every demonstrator knows that the time may come when it will cause him real harm. . . . And nevertheless we demonstrated, and not always quietly. I remember that in one such demonstration in which I participated at the synagogue in Moscow, we collected paper and other inflammable material, made a torch, lit it, and bore it on high with all sorts of slogans such as, "Long live Jerusalem," "Long live Dayan," and so on. . . .

Once I decided to come to Israel, I decided that if I wanted to know the roots of our culture, I must look for them in its oldest sources, in the Bible and the Talmud. I understood, intuitively, that all the roots of our national feeling are to be found in the Jewish religion and I very much wanted to understand these roots and know their essence.

So Kazakov went to Rabbi Judah Leib Levin (who had succeeded Rabbi Shlifer on the latter's death in 1957) and asked to be enrolled in the *yeshiva*, the sole Jewish theological seminary in the USSR. (Not surprisingly he was not accepted.)[56]

An art student in Odessa conducted a propaganda campaign in his art school before Simhat Torah of the year 1971 and virtually all the Jewish students went to synagogue for the occasion. After prayers someone played the guitar and the young men and women began singing and dancing Jewish and Israeli songs. They then went out onto the street and someone shouted: "Who are we?" and everyone answered: "Israel." "Where are we going?" "To Israel!" This was a demonstration. (Not surprisingly the authorities summoned the students for questioning and intimidation.)[57]

In the camps too, those accused of Zionism (or, to be more precise, of nationalism and counterrevolutionary activity according to Article 58-10 of the RSFSR criminal code) made every effort to observe the Jewish holidays in one way or another. They received *matzot* for the Passover holiday. They conducted a Seder service on the first night of Passover, observed the Day of Atonement, and lit candles on Hanukkah. One prisoner of Zion who "sat" from 1955 to 1960 recalls that on the Eve of the Day of Atonement twelve Jewish prisoners persuaded the warden to lock them in a warehouse so that they could conduct the Kol Nidre service; the son of one of the prisoners had brought them a few prayer books for the festivals some days before.[58]

In the early 1970s, as the Jewish national movement took on new dimensions, the street in front of the synagogue often became more significant than the synagogue itself and the prayers held inside it, although Jews, like all Soviet citizens, are forbidden to meet in large groups or organize. As Jesse Zel Lurie, executive editor of *Hadassah Magazine*, wrote after a visit to the USSR, they obviate this prohibition by simply meeting on the street in front of the synagogue. The Sabbath morning services in Moscow, he reported, terminated at approximately one o'clock

and several hundred middle-aged and elderly men folded up their prayer shawls and, joined by a sprinkling of women, streamed into the streets. But they did not go home. This was Moscow Jewry's social hour. They talked and talked in Yiddish and Russian, joined by an equal number of young people who had not attended the services. The street was packed from sidewalk to sidewalk and the occasional car or truck had to crawl through the mass of humanity. This is the first small step toward the dangerous and irrevocable act of asking for an exit visa for Israel.[59]

The Jews whom a group of American Jewish youngsters met in 1970 outside the synagogues in Moscow, Leningrad, and Riga questioned them eagerly about Israel, stated their desire to go on *aliya*, and demanded that Jews in the West take up their cause. Rabbi Levin of the Moscow Choral Synagogue told the young tourists: "the young people identify with Judaism but are not religious and therefore do not enter the synagogue."[60]

One Moscow family who applied for exit visas in 1971 had had no Jewish background and had never celebrated any Jewish festival. With their decision to emigrate they decided also to change their life-style, to learn Hebrew, and visit the synagogue. Yet they did not go inside, preferring to gather with others on the empty lot opposite the synagogue which they called the "Jewish Community Center." There they sang songs, spoke about Israel, rejoiced with those who had been given permission to emigrate, and consoled those who had been refused.[61] This dichotomy between services inside the synagogue and the social gatherings outside of *aliya* activists and others who had committed themselves to a new future outside the Soviet Union reflected the tragedy of Soviet Jewish existence: the fear of those Jews who would remain in the USSR, but still wanted to take refuge in the synagogue and religion, that their very tenuous links with the few physical vestiges of Judaism might be jeopardized by the rash behavior of youngsters who had burned their bridges. The fact that Rabbi Levin himself made this distinction between those who worshiped inside the building and those who identified but had no religious roots and stayed outside is the most poignant manifestation of that fear. He may well have been told by the authorities to whom his post subordinated him that if the synagogue was to continue functioning the distinction must be made between worshipers who came to pray and Zionists who came to demonstrate their anti-Sovietism. The Soviet authorities themselves are faced with an obvious dilemma on this score: while aware of the central place filled by the synagogues in the Soviet Jewish national movement, they are unwilling to close the few remaining synagogues which also serve as evidence of their own tolerance to religion as a whole and Judaism in particular and of the fulfillment of their obligations toward freedom of conscience and worship, and so on. One Western tourist told of an Intourist guide who had taken two Americans to the Moscow synagogue on a Sabbath (the Intourist car was parked directly in front of the building).[62] I myself met a group of U.S. congressmen in the Leningrad synagogue on a weekday morning in August 1979.[63] Yet, at the same time, by the 1970s the authorities were visibly endeavoring to keep the celebration of Jewish festivals as inconspicuous as possible—in particular by trying to prevent Jews from congregating outside the synagogue during and after prayers.[64] One favorite means was causing various unpleasantnesses to young people who came to the synagogues, sometimes even evicting them from their place of study.[65]

The undisguisedly nationalist features of the Jewish religion, its orientation toward Zion and *Eretz Yisrael,* its stress on the mutual responsibility of Jews everywhere and on the singularity of the Chosen People, and the Jewish-historical aspect of its festivals made it a natural focus of and framework for the Jewish nationalist revival. This is particularly evident in the USSR where the Jews lack any other cultural or communal institution and are denied the right to organize. Moreover, the eschatological events of the twentieth century—the Bolsehvik Revolution, on the one hand, and the Holocaust and the establishment of the State of Israel, on the other—along with the exclusion and rejection of the Jews by the second generation of builders of the communist society accentuated the Russian-Jewish syndrome. As a result, many Jews returned in part to the traditions of their ancestors. Despite the basically nonreligious, nonbelieving nature of virtually the entire Jewish population, Jews want to understand who they are, why they are different from their non-Jewish neighbors, why the latter reject them, and what is the essence of Judaism and being Jewish. They therefore go to the synagogues, even—and on certain festivals especially—the young, second- and third-generation Soviet citizens, in flagrant contradiction to the ideology of the regime that at one and the same time rejects them and demands their total absorption. The Soviet theoreticians deny the relevance of religion to the circumstances of Soviet society; yet the Jews—as well as many other groups in the Soviet population which are beyond the scope of this chapter—have demonstrated a manifest interest in and attachment to their religious heritage.[66]

True, the number of orthodox, practicing Jews has necessarily been minimal in the USSR of post–World War II, although in the 1980s it has grown somewhat, perhaps as part of a broader turn to religion among various sectors of the Soviet population and particularly the intelligentsia. Very few Jews circumcise their sons, celebrate their Bar Mitzvah[67] (or even know what a Bar Mitzvah is), or hold a religious wedding, let alone observe the Sabbath. Yet large numbers celebrate the traditional Jewish festivals, fast on the Day of Atonement, and come together for the Seder on the first night of Passover to tell of the Biblical redemption from slavery and exile.[68] Many go to the synagogues if not to pray, then at least to identify as Jews and, what is even more surprising to the outside observer and presumably even more aggravating to the Soviet authorities, to rejoice in being Jewish. Others celebrate in less conventional ways, meeting in private homes or in places outside the major towns where they can hope to speak and sing more freely. In the first three decades after World War II the synagogues were a central meeting place for nationally minded Jews, and the ancient Jewish festivals the natural occasion for coming together. This will presumably continue to be so, but if the wrath of the Soviet authorities is vented on the synagogues, these Jews have developed their own special alternative and will continue to meet and celebrate Jewish festivals in their own way. The internal dynamics of the Soviet Jewish national movement have brought Jews back to their roots but in a way that is peculiar to the USSR, the result of their political and social ecology. It is the sense of an unbreakable bond, that even in conditions of total ignorance of Judaism and its precepts —no books, no schools, virtually no rabbis—has enabled Soviet Jews to preserve and even rekindle their attachment to their religion and at least some of its traditions as an integral part of their national awakening.

Notes

All interviews and other unpublished materials are (unless otherwise stated) in the archives of the Center for Research and Documentation of East European Jewry, the Hebrew University of Jerusalem.

1. Far be it from me to lessen in any way the other two main foci of such activity that developed mainly in the 1960s—the memorials to the victims of the Holocaust at Rumboli, Panerai, or Babii Iar, to which, unfortunately, this volume has been unable to dedicate separate treatment, and cultural performances, such as those of Nehama Lifshitz, and other activities, Hebrew speaking, or study circles, etc., which are dealt with in this volume.
2. One Jew who observed the Sabbath throughout, even choosing his professional career so as to enable him not to work on Saturdays, was Shneur Pinskii of Moscow, a Hasid of Habad—author's interview with Yisrael Pinskii, September 9, 1980, p. 8. In the camps, too, there were a few Jews who refused to work on the Sabbath—author's interview with Rabbi Mordekhai Hanzin, December 12, 1976 (Hanzin was arrested in 1935 and released in 1956). Another, much later, example was Yosef Mendelevich, sentenced for participating in the Leningrad hijacking attempt in 1970. A Jew who was pedantic about eating only *matzot* on Passover, Izrail' Kanson, was arrested in 1948 for approaching the Israeli legation for help to emigrate. Kanson likewise refused to let the camp barber shave his beard—testimony of Lipa Fischer, *Sappar b'mamlekhet gulag* (Barber in Gulag Camp, Heb.) (Tel Aviv: Alef, 1979), pp. 251–52.
3. Anatolii Rubin (of Minsk), "Moi put' v Izrail' " (My Road to Israel, published in Hebrew as *Magafayim humim, magafayim adumim* [Brown boots, red boots] [Tel Aviv: Dvir, 1977], p. 120). Rubin was one of many immigrants from the USSR who participated in a competition set by the Center for Research and

Documentation on East European Jewry, which invited these immigrants to contribute their reminiscences or testimonies to the Center archives.

4. For the inherent contradictions of the Soviet Jewish position, see Yaacov Ro'i, "The Soviet Jewish Anomaly," *Jerusalem Quarterly* 10 (Winter 1979), pp. 106–16.
5. For example, on the last Passover of the war—Jewish Telegraphic Agency, *Daily News Bulletin* (henceforth *JTA*), April 1, 1945. On a visit to Kharkov in October 1950, Israeli diplomats were told that the number of worshipers on Jewish festivals had been more than the synagogue could hold until its recent closing down by the authorities, after which Jews had to pray in small *minyanim* (a *minyan* is the quorum of ten men necessary for public prayer) held in private homes—Mordecai Namir, *Shelihut bemoskva* (Israeli Mission to Moscow, Tel Aviv: Am Oved, 1971), pp. 210–11.
6. At one such service held in March 1945 the packed synagogue included such Jewish notables as Foreign Minister Viacheslav Molotov's wife, Polina Zhemchuzhina, the wife of Marshal Aleksei Antonov, and General David Dragunskii —author's interview with Rabbi Elhanan Sorochkin, October 20, 1970.
7. *Kol ha'am*, January 30, 1948.
8. One such group that formed in the small Ukrainian town of Zhmerinka, for example, left pamphlets they had composed on Palestine in the synagogue where a few local Jews took them and read them. Most of the pamphlets were duly collected by the synagogue warden and handed to the NKVD, (People's Commissariat of Internal Affairs), as the members of the group discovered some years later when they were arrested and interrogated—author's interview with Meir Gelfond, February 27, 1973.
9. For the service, see also note 6 above.
10. *JTA*, April 1, 1945.
11. *Haliga lekishrei yedidut im SSSR* (The League for Friendly Relations with the USSR) 10 (November 1946).
12. *Folks-shtime* (Warsaw), January 10, 1948.
13. I have described these events in some detail in *Soviet Decision Making in Practice, The USSR and Israel 1947–1954* (New Brunswick, N.J.: Transaction Books, 1980), pp. 190–91, 193–95.
14. Golda Meir, *My Life* (Jerusalem and Tel Aviv: Steimatzky, 1975), pp. 206–8; Namir, *Shelihut bemoskva*, pp. 46–50.
15. Namir, *Shelihut bemoskva*, p. 331; author's interview with Yosef Neiman, June 19, 1968.
16. Namir, *Shelihut bemoskva*, p. 262–63, 314–15. On the Day of Atonement in 1952, the demand for the Kol Nidre service was so considerable that the Choral Synagogue filled up and a second service was held after the congregation that had attended the first service went home.
17. Author's interviews with former Israeli diplomats in Moscow.
18. Elie Wiesel, *The Jews of Silence* (New York: Holt, Rinehart & Winston, 1966), chapter 8.

THE ROLE OF THE SYNAGOGUE 131

19. Namir, *Shelihut bemoskva*, pp. 97–98 and 254.
20. Meir Kanevskii records having spoken with one of the members of the legation in the synagogue courtyard on the Day of Atonement of 1949—reminiscences of Meir Kanevskii, Yad Vashem Archives (Givatayim, Israel), February 1974, 3759.
21. Namir, *Shelihut bemoskva*, pp. 97–98, 254, 262–63 and passim; also author's interviews with former Israeli diplomats in Moscow.
22. *Lamerhav*, October 6, 1968 (from the reminiscences from a Soviet prison camp of Yosef Berger-Barzilai).
23. The rabbi of the Ashkenazi Jewish community in Georgia, who had come to Georgia in recent years, had been arrested in 1948 or 1949. At the end of 1952, the anti-Jewish campaign affected the Georgian Jews as well: synagogues were closed and the *hacham*, Emanuel Davidashvili, and some of the synagogue wardens were arrested—interview of Vera Yedidya with Fania Baazova, June 16, 1976.
24. Testimony of Rabbi Mordekhai Hanzin, *Hatzofe*, November 26, 1971.
25. By the end of this period there were thought to be only between fifty and sixty synagogues still in existence throughout the USSR, nearly one-half of them in Georgia, Dagestan, and Central Asia, although these areas had less than 10 percent of the country's Jewish population. In Georgia one case is known where the Jews physically prevented the razing of a synagogue by lying in the street that led to the synagogue when the bulldozers arrived—Wiesel, *The Jews of Silence*, chapter 9. For the position of the Jewish religion in the USSR, see Joshua Rothenberg, "Jewish Religion in the Soviet Union," in Lionel Kochan, ed., *The Jews in Soviet Russia Since 1917* (London: Oxford University Press, 1974), 2nd ed., pp. 159–87.

In the latter part of the Khrushchev period there were also attempts by the authorities to disrupt the baking of *matzot*, yet the hue and cry raised by Jews the world over and the vast, organized dispatch of *matzot* to the USSR from Israel and the United States merely served to highlight the ties that still linked the Jewish people throughout the world. See *Passover and Matzoth: A Case History of Soviet Policy*, Commission Study presented at the Ad Hoc Commission on the Rights of Soviet Jews, Carnegie International Center, New York, March 18, 1966.
26. "You are eating Russian bread but praying for Israel," a Kharkov policeman told one of the Jews when private *minyanim* were closed on the second day of the New Year (September 1958). A similar charge had been brought by the Lvov party organ which had claimed in December 1958 that when Jews eat their unleavened bread on Passover, they express the hope that they will eat it the following year in Jerusalem, on Israeli soil—*New York Times*, May 22, 1959.
27. *Davar*, January 27, 1964.
28. For example, *Sovetskaia Moldavia*, July 23, 1959, quoted by Neal Kovody in his Historical Afterword to Wiesel, *The Jews of Silence*, p. 153. For Passover in the USSR, see my article "Hag hapesah mul hamishtar hasovieti," (The Holiday of

Passover versus the Soviet Regime, Heb.), *Annual of Bar Ilan University: Studies in Judaica and Humanities*, vol. 24–25 (1988).
29. Wiesel, *The Jews of Silence*, chapters 3 and 4.
30. *New York Herald Tribune*, October 19, 1965.
31. Interview of Vera Yedidya with Gesia Kamaiskaia, p. 32; also interview of Yaacov Ro'i with David Garber who, with his wife Miriam, held such an open house.
32. The appearance of a member of the Israeli embassy in the Kiev synagogue and its electrifying effect on the Jews of the town have been described by Barukh Vaisman, *Yoman mahteret ivri*, (Hebrew Underground Diary, Heb.) (Ramat Gan: Masada, 1973), pp. 171–73. When another Israeli diplomat visited Kiev —Ambassador Avidar on the Day of Atonement, September 1955—Vaisman was able to transmit the first portions of his description of the Soviet Jewish situation in the 1950s that were first published in instalments in *Davar* under the title "El ahai bimedinat Yisrael" (To My Brothers in the State of Israel, Heb.) (ibid., pp. 256–57), and were later compiled in book form at first anonymously under the pseudonym Yehudi sovieti almoni (an unknown Soviet Jew) and later, after Vaisman's death, under his full name.

Many emigrants have testified to the importance of the presence of the Israeli diplomats in synagogues throughout the USSR. See, for example, author's interview with David Rom, May 10, 1976, p. 25; interview with Yosef Shnaider, p. 24; interview of Vera Yedidya with Gesia Kamaiskaia (p. 41); author's interview with Herman Branover, January 7, 1980, p. 8; reminiscences of Baruch Podolskii, Yad Vashem (Givatayim) 3792, p. 2.
33. From the unpublished diary of Gedalia Pecherskii.
34. *Yediot aharonot*, November 14, 1961, quoting *New York Herald Tribune*.
35. *Christian Science Monitor*, October 30, 1958. Similar complaints would be heard recurrently. In February 1962 a meeting of some two hundred congregants of the Moscow Choral Synagogue heard demands from Rabbi Levin and no less than twelve other speakers that the congregation refrain from contact with the Israeli diplomats. Rabbi Levin said the diplomats were welcome in the synagogue insofar as they came to pray—*Ma'ariv*, July 28, 1963. In 1963, worshipers in Moscow contested that the Israeli embassy staff traveled to the synagogue (travel on the Sabbath and festivals is forbidden by Jewish Law), caused a commotion by distributing written materials on the synagogue premises, and talked during service instead of praying—*Yediot aharonot*, July 26, 1963. For another such story, see *Ma'ariv*, Supplement, Passover 5730, April 20, 1970.
36. *Herut*, May 1, 1963.
37. Wiesel, *The Jews of Silence*, pp. 19–21.
38. E.g., author's interview with Eli Valk (Riga), January 6, 1976, pp. 9–10. Valk had received a traditional upbringing (cf. notes 51 and 67) and went to the synagogue on every festival. He recalls that from the very early 1960s, when still a boy of fifteen or sixteen, he would meet there with Jews from abroad including Israeli diplomats and tourists.

39. Wiesel, *The Jews of Silence*, chapter 7.
40. *New York Times*, June 25 and July 15, 1956: *New York Herald Tribune*, July 13, 1956; and private statement by Rabbis Hollander and Mowshowitz, July 29, 1956.
41. *New York Times*, July 26, 1965.
42. *New York Herald Tribune*, November 27, 1961.
43. *Davar*, November 2, 1962.
44. *Haaretz*, August 31, 1970.
45. *New York Herald Tribune*, November 14, 1961.
46. In the latter half of the 1960s Western journalists were invited to synagogue on these occasions to see that "Jewish expression is tolerated," unlike under Khrushchev, when "fire trucks and ambulances 'happened' to rush through when the dancing took place" in the street in front of the synagogue—*Washington Post*, March 26, 1967.
47. *Ma'ariv*, October 9, 1962.
48. *Davar*, November 2, 1962.
49. Interview with Yosef Shnaider, p. 9.
50. *Al hamishmar*, February 14, 1972.
51. One such young man recalls that in the mid-1960s he studied the Jewish prayer book and the main tenets of Jewish tradition, and began frequenting the synagogue every Sabbath—author's interview with Eli Valk, January 6, 1976, pp. 9–12. Another person whose nationalism brought him "toward God" was Miron Khazin of Odessa—interview of I. Averbuch with M. Khazin, September 1, 1977, p. 26.
52. *Ma'ariv*, March 19, 1971.
53. Cf., for example, author's interviews with Prof. Herman Branover, Natan Malkin, and Yisrael Pinskii. (Pinskii himself was born into a Habad family, see note 2 above.) These Hasidim prayed in separate, smaller halls in the synagogue premises or in *minyanim* in private homes. While the nuclei of the Habad groups in each town were mostly very small, they maintained contacts with their fellow Hasidim throughout the country. For the ability of the Hasidim to celebrate the Jewish festivals, even in the atmosphere of gloom and persecution that pervaded the Soviet Jewish community, and their obstinate perseverance in observing the precepts of the Jewish religion, see Wiesel, *The Jews of Silence*, chapter 3 and pp. 66–67.
54. Author's interview with Bezalel Shiff. Shiff himself worked full time in the *yeshiva*. In the mornings he taught one class of thirty boys, in the afternoon other boys who attended regular schools in the morning, and in the evening a group of young men.
55. Author's interview with Isai (Yeshayahu) Averbuch, December 9, 1975, p. 5.
56. *Ma'ariv*, January 23, 1970. No serious analytic study has yet been made of either of Moscow's late rabbis, Rabbi Shlifer and Rabbi Levin, both of whom were in their time very controversial figures, although we do have a very interesting book on the activities of the former written by his son-in-law,

Emanuel Mikhlin, *Hagahelet* (Jerusalem: Shamir, 1986). Certainly their position was not an enviable one, and surely their case is an outstanding example of the need to apply the old Jewish precept: Do not judge your friend until you are in his place. This is not the framework within which to analyze the motives and actions of these two men, but suffice it to bear in mind that the daughters of both have since come to Israel, that Rabbi Levin specifically instructed his wife and daughters to emigrate to Israel with their families, and according to the testimony of one of his daughters (*Ma'ariv*, January 26, 1973) helped a number of emigrants from his own private funds to make the necessary payments to enable them to leave the Soviet Union.

The Kol Yaacov Yeshiva opened by Rabbi Shlifer had a very checkered existence. At no time did it have more than twenty members and very often the authorities made things so difficult for its students that they numbered fewer than ten. Not surprisingly most of its alumni, at least those who studied there in their twenties, as against religious officials especially prepared for specific rabbinical or other religious posts by the authorities, have emigrated to Israel.

57. Interview of Yeshayahu Averbuch with Miron Khazin, September 1, 1977, pp. 35–36.
58. The reminiscences of Eliyahu Hoberman, section entitled "Di letzte tekufa" (The last period—Yid.), pp. 79–90 passim.
59. *New World Outlook* (January 1974).
60. *Ma'ariv*, August 7, 1970.
61. *Jerusalem Post*, February 8, 1974.
62. Sidney Du Groff, Moscow Report, *The American Zionist* (May 1974), pp. 12–14.
63. For my thoughts on Jewish religious life in the USSR after my visit there, see Yaacov Ro'i, "Jewish Religion in the USSR: Some Impressions," *Soviet Jewish Affairs* (May 1980), pp. 29–50. Even if these visits to the synagogues by foreign tourists and delegations take place as a result of pressure applied to the Soviets, the latter will hardly wish to place themselves in a position in which there will be no synagogues to show. The sight of a few elderly people praying timidly in a big and impressive building is from their point of view the best evidence that there is no real need for more synagogues and more and better religious services. The hue and cry that would follow the closing down of the remaining synagogues could be expected to be far more injurious to the USSR than their continued existence.
64. *Hatzofe*, March 28, 1975.
65. Author's interview with Natan Malkin, p. 8.
66. For the confluence of nationalism and religion in the Soviet Union, see my article, "Religion as an Obstacle to *Sblizhenie*: the Official View," *Soviet Union*, 14, no. 2, pp. 163–79.
67. In the Baltic republics, in particular, there seem to have been exceptions. One boy who celebrated his Bar Mitzvah in Riga was Eli Valk who read all the benedictions in the synagogue and afterward had a party at home—author's interview with Eli Valk, January 6, 1976, p. 12.

68. Although traditionally the Seder is celebrated by Jewish families in the home, in the special conditions of the USSR—lack of *haggadot,* the prayer book used to tell the story of the Exodus; ignorance of what to do on the occasion, because of the dearth of even a minimal religious education and the interruption of any religious tradition in so many families; the fear of certain members of many families to hold the ceremony at home; and the psychological need for Jews to come together—the Seder is often celebrated in the synagogue.

7

The Struggle for the Study of Hebrew
Vera Yedidya

One of the most striking features of the discrimination against the Jewish national minority in the Soviet Union is, and has long been, its cultural deprivation. None of the Jewish national languages[1] is taught in any school, nor is there any way for Jewish youth to learn those languages officially. Yet while Yiddish has known its ups and downs—at different periods there have been theaters, printed literature, and even, in the 1920s and early 1930s, schools—Hebrew has always been anathema to the Soviet authorities. This is probably because of Hebrew's special significance as the language of the Jewish religion, in which prayers are conducted, the Bible read in the synagogue, and the Code of Law studied by orthodox Jews the world over, and second as the language of the Jewish national movement, that sought at the beginning of the twentieth century to revive and rejuvenate the sole language that could form the basis for reuniting the entire Jewish people in its effort to attain national sovereignty after nearly 2,000 years.

The Soviet Constitution assures equal rights to "citizens of . . . different races and nationalities," including "the possibility to use their native language." It even insists that "any direct or indirect limitation" of these rights is "punishable by law."[2] Yet the Jews have been denied the right to use their national language.[3] Not only is Hebrew not taught in any school, there is also no Soviet Hebrew literature: no books, journals, or newspapers appear in Hebrew. While a few universities or institutes of higher learning teach Hebrew,[4] it is extremely difficult for Jews to be accepted to such studies even to those courses which are not intended solely for diplomats, security service employees, and military personnel.[5] The major ray of light in this entire gloomy picture was the appearance in 1963 of a Hebrew-

Russian dictionary, edited by Feliks Shapiro, which was followed in 1964 by a conference on Semitic languages held under the auspices of the Institute of Oriental Studies of the USSR Academy of Sciences, where stress was laid on "revival of the Hebrew language" as a unique event in the history of mankind" and "its extraordinary importance for Semitic and linguistic studies." At this conference the non-Jewish Hebraist scholar, Klavdiia Starkova of Leningrad, as well as the Jewish Isak Vinnikov demanded the building up of a substantial body of Hebrew scholars in order to enable the Soviet Union to catch up in the field of Hebrew studies, and called for the publication of a Hebrew textbook. At this conference both Mikhail Zand and Abram Rubinshtain delivered lectures on aspects of the Hebrew language and its study.[6] The subsequent conference on Semitic languages held in Tbilisi under the joint auspices of the Georgian SSR Academy of Sciences Institute of Oriental Studies and the University of Tbilisi in 1966 also included lectures by Zand and Rubinshtain; but although its proceedings were not published, it could not conceal the fact that none of the demands of its predecessor had been implemented.[7]

A significant portion of the Soviet Jewish population, however, had traditionally felt a particular attachment to Hebrew. In 1917 the Zionist movement was the strongest of all the political parties in the Jewish street.[8] The interest in Hebrew revived following the Soviet annexation during World War II of large areas where Hebrew education and culture had flourished until the eve of the war, and in the wake of the establishment of the State of Israel. The total repression of Yiddish culture in Stalin's last years meant that the movement of Jewish national awakening, deprived of the only language which the regime had permitted for the Ashkenazi Jewish population, turned once more to Hebrew as its sole, natural framework of activity.

The struggle to conduct lessons or courses in the Hebrew language has, then, become one of the central issues of the Jewish national movement in the USSR. The movement's activists have had to circumvent an unofficial but nevertheless prevalent prohibition on the use of Hebrew. Some chose to do so by way of a direct approach to the authorities, others preferred to conduct clandestine Hebrew lessons.

The requests made to the authorities to teach Hebrew privately—there being, as we have seen, no other way of teaching or studying the language —met with steady refusal (although the teaching of other languages was invariably endorsed). There was one major exception: in 1971 a number of

Moscow Hebrew teachers—including Viktor Pol'skii, Vladimir Prestin, Samuil Gurvits, and Pavel Abramovich—were given permission to give private Hebrew lessons. Yet late in 1972 their permits were rescinded, on the grounds that there was no curriculum for Hebrew language teaching in the USSR and that the initiation of such courses did not "correspond with the interests of the Soviet state."[9] In 1970 three teachers of Hebrew, also in Moscow—David Drabkin, Anatolii Dekatov, and Lev Shinkar'—succeeded in advertising their lessons on the municipal notice boards.[10] Their advertisements, however, were soon prohibited. In 1976 Pavel Abramovich paid the Moscow municipality advertisements department *(Mosgorspravka)* to post thirty notices about Hebrew classes. When the notices did not appear, Abramovich took his case to the municipal court, which rejected his request on the pretext that he was not a qualified Hebrew teacher. Abramovich presented to the court a certificate he had received from the *Brit Ivrit Olamit* (World Association for Hebrew Language and Culture)[11] and the notices duly appeared on the municipal notice board. By contrast Abramovich's attempts to advertise his lessons in the Moscow evening paper were to no avail.[12]

Despite all the obstacles in the path of studying Hebrew in the Soviet Union—the absence of any social framework for the study of Hebrew, the lack of permitted textbooks and other aids for studying the language, the jamming, among others, of Israeli broadcasts of Hebrew lessons, the fear of repression, and the actual administrative measures taken against those involved in teaching and studying the language—thousands of Soviet Jews have been able to study Hebrew. The purpose of this chapter is to survey the ways in which the Hebrew language fought for its survival and in recent years has actually undergone a renaissance among the Soviet Jewish population: numerous Hebrew study circles exist and Hebrew teachers operate in many Soviet cities, or at least they did until the early 1980s when repressive measures were again intensified. In this chapter I shall endeavor to describe this struggle not only in the 1970s, for which fairly abundant material exists,[13] but also in the entire period since the establishment of the State of Israel in 1948, and to evaluate its significance for the Jewish national awakening, using primarily interviews with Soviet emigrants who were active as teachers or students of Hebrew.

The thirty or so years which this chapter covers can be divided into different periods, each with its own special features that influenced, and were reflected in, the nature and quantity of Hebrew teaching. In the first period, from 1948 to the mid-fifties, most people studied Hebrew individually, in absolute secrecy, as dictated by the policy of terror, arrests, and persecution in Stalin's "Black Years," and the atmosphere of fear which it engendered. The only framework within which Hebrew was studied in groups was that of the prison camps. The second period, that begins with the "Thaw" of the immediate post-Stalin years, saw the formation of ties with the Israeli embassy (as the legation became in August 1954) and later with Israeli and other Jewish tourists from the West, who brought with them grammars, dictionaries, newspapers, and other materials for the study of Hebrew. It witnessed the beginnings of Hebrew broadcasts from Israel ("Kol Tsion Lagola")[14] which became increasingly popular, especially after the systematic jamming of Israeli Yiddish broadcasts. Moreover, with the liberation and rehabilitation of political prisoners, including many of the Jews who had been imprisoned under Stalin for Zionism, a few Jews began in the early 1960s to learn Hebrew in small groups, although most students of the language still studied by themselves. Only in the third period, beginning in 1967, did the study of Hebrew become a large-scale phenomenon, with organized circles or *ulpanim* operating in most of the large cities. In this period a new generation of Hebrew teachers came into being. Instead of, or in addition to, the older Zionists, who had learned the language in the pre-Soviet era, the new teachers were mostly young people, products of an anti-Zionist Soviet upbringing who had attained their Jewish consciousness in defiance of the regime and the values it sought to imbibe.

The immediate postwar period witnessed a revival of Jewish consciousness and a renewed interest in the Jewish national home in Palestine.[15] This interest—as well as the actual hope of emigration—was strengthened by the Soviet Union's support for the establishment of Israel, and Hebrew as the language of the new Jewish state, was a natural link with it. Moreover, the annexation during the war of the Western territories (the Baltic states, Western Belorussia, the Western Ukraine, the Transcarpathian region, Bessarabia, and Northern Bukovina) had added to the Soviet Union the Jewish communities of these areas, where the Zionist movements were very strong and where many Jews had been educated in Hebrew schools, spoke Hebrew, and were immersed in Hebrew culture. These people did not remain in their native areas in the war years for the exigencies first of the Soviet occupation and later of the Nazi threat dispersed them throughout the country. However, in some of these areas once the war was over and life had returned to normal, a few boys again began to learn Hebrew as they approached thirteen, the age of their Bar Mitzvah. Teachers went from house to house to instruct the boys in the Hebrew prayers and taught them the Hebrew alphabet.[16] In the Baltic republics as well, parents transmitted their knowledge of Hebrew to their children.[17] Among the Hasidim of "Habad," who were also scattered among a number of towns and constituted a very compact, militantly Jewish group (although numerically only a minute minority among the Jewish population), the study of Hebrew was a major factor in their study of Torah and their persistent struggle against assimilation. They were perhaps the only clearly defined group to persevere in the study and use of Hebrew as a living language, while maintaining the total secrecy that the times made compulsory.[18] Among the non-Ashkenazi Jews, the Georgians and the Bukharans in particular, Hebrew was also taught for religious purposes. However, even here conditions were such that Hebrew education was not systematic, merely enabling boys to perform their most elementary religious duties, usually without understanding the rites they had learned by heart.

In Moscow a small Hebrew circle was formed shortly after the war by Zvi Pregerzon, Zvi Plotkin, Isak Zaretskii, Meir Baazov, and Isak Kogan, all of whom spoke and wrote Hebrew fluently. They actually sent a letter to Moscow State University requesting it to open a department for the study of Hebraica. Yet one young man who joined the group, ostensibly to learn the language from Pregerzon, turned out to be a provacateur. He persuaded the group to send their writings to Israel and this advice, which originated with the security organs, led in late 1948–early 1949 to the arrest of the entire circle and their being sentenced to long terms of imprisonment.[19]

The son of one member of the circle, Vladimir Zaretskii, continued in his father's footsteps. In 1949, at the age of twenty-two, he gathered together a group of friends who believed, like him, that the Jews' place was in Israel and that it was therefore necessary to learn the language of that state. For a whole year Zaretskii taught his friends Hebrew, which he had learned as a boy, using a Hebrew-language grammar that had been published in Vilnius at the beginning of the century and from which his grandfather had studied. He also had in his possession a Russian-language Bible and children's stories which his father had written in Hebrew. He improved his own knowledge with the help of Israeli broadcasts using them, among others, to compile a Hebrew-Russian political dictionary. (Many years later, in 1965, Vladimir began teaching his own son who had now reached the age of eleven, the age at which he himself had begun learning Hebrew.)[20]

In Leningrad, at about the same time, Leonid Rutshtain tried, without success, to organize a Hebrew study circle among the students of the medical faculty: his fellow students were either not interested or afraid. Rutshtain, whose parents had been born in the Ukraine and who had received a Jewish education, knew a few words of Hebrew as well as some of Bialik's poems which his father had taught him. Undaunted by his failure, he started learning Hebrew from an acquaintance, from a prayer book and a Bible, but these studies were soon interrupted by his arrest (in 1950) for Zionism. (He had signed a request to the authorities to be allowed to volunteer to fight in the Israeli War of Independence and was sentenced to ten years.) After his release Rutshtain, who now lived in Moscow, returned to his study of Hebrew and became a Hebrew teacher in his own right.[21]

Even in the Soviet armed forces Jews formed circles to study Hebrew and Jewish history. The desire to become acquainted with Judaism and the Jewish people overcame the fear of the risk involved in such activity. Here again Jews from the annexed territories provided the main stimulus. It was thanks to a young officer who had been born and educated in Latvia, Grisha Feigin, that toward the end of 1948 a number of Jewish officers who were studying at the military academy in the town of Ul'ianovsk first became acquainted with the Hebrew alphabet. Feigin and his friends shared an attachment to Israel and would talk about Zionism. Feigin introduced his fellow officers to an inhabitant of Ul'ianovsk who knew both Jewish history and the Hebrew language, and in his house an underground group of army officers was organized called Bar Kokhba, whose purpose was to instill an attachment to Zion through the study of Zionist history and Hebrew. The nucleus of the group, among them Efim Shperber, Iosif Ginzburg, and Iasha Granovskii, formed clandestine Zionist circles of Jewish officers in a number of cities in the heartland of the RSFSR: Saratov, Kuibyshev, Stalingrad, Kazan', and Sverdlovsk, in addition to the one in Ul'ianovsk itself.[22] Each circle, consisting of between five and ten members, studied Hebrew from old books of prerevolutionary times. Pinhas Neiburger of Moscow, a professional photographer, made photocopies of these books at Feigin's request (Feigin had first met Neiburger in the military hospital where the two men were recuperating from wounds received toward the end of World War II).[23]

One of these circles studied Hebrew with a special thoroughness. Early in 1949 Efim Shul'ner, who before the war had been a pupil in a Hebrew gymnasium in Poland, was called up for reserve duty in the town where he lived, Sverdlovsk. In the military aviation club there he met Efim Shperber and, upon Feigin's urging, Shul'ner began to give Hebrew lessons to members of Shperber's group, made up of pilots, paratroopers, and reservists. Shul'ner taught his pupils individually and very occasionally they would meet in an apartment rented for the purpose. He operated in this way for approximately one year and had in all about thirty students.[24]

In 1949 Feigin was transferred, as part of his military service, to the Far East. Here too, in Vladivostok and Khabarovsk, he met with Jewish officers and soldiers and organized lessons in Hebrew and Jewish history. Although a number of members of these circles were arrested, none informed on Feigin and he was able to continue his activities until he left for Israel in 1970.[25]

However, in this period most people who desired to learn Hebrew were afraid to discuss their plan with their friends and relatives, let alone to operate within any sort of group, and therefore studied on their own. Moreover, those who knew Hebrew were rarely willing to teach others. Indicative of the atmosphere of the times is the story of Ihiel Abramzon who had been a Hebrew teacher in Riga before the war and moved to Moscow after it. In 1948 he was approached by someone in synagogue who asked him to teach him Hebrew. Abramzon refused out of sheer fear.[26] The more daring looked for Hebrew-language books in public libraries that still had old books from the czarist period, even though these books were often uninteresting and old-fashioned, and the request for such a book and its loan to a reader were noted by the librarians. It would take very little time for the security police to be on the track of readers of Hebrew books.[27] Even those who desired to read the only readily available Israeli newspaper, that of the Israeli Communist party *(Maki)*, had fears, despite its being a communist newspaper.[28]

A young student from Riga, German (Herman) Branover, who began his studies at the Leningrad Polytechnical Institute in 1949, discovered in the Saltykov-Shchedrin Library a number of Hebrew textbooks in Russian, that had been published in Vilnius before 1917. He spent long hours copying out exercises and compiling a Hebrew-Russian dictionary, and was subsequently joined by another student from the polytechnic. The two were eventually summoned to one of the offices of the library where they were asked why they were studying Hebrew. Branover said he simply felt an urge to learn the language. The two were rebuked and requested to cease their study of Hebrew.[29]

Many potential students of Hebrew were deterred by the risk involved and by the scarcity of material. Many Jews knew of people who had been arrested merely for requesting Hebrew material in a public library or for having a Hebrew book in their possession.[30] Nonetheless, the enterprising would still hunt for such books, in the flea markets, or secondhand bookstores. The owner of one such store in Kiev who bought private libraries would sell the Hebrew books he found in these collections to acquaintances he could trust. His store even became a meeting place for Jews seeking an opportunity to talk Hebrew.[31] Ben-Horin has recalled that in May 1948 he and a friend managed to obtain a Hebrew grammar published in Italy in the 1870s. However, their ignorance of Italian prevented them from using it.[32] One student at the Leningrad Polytechnical Institute (Samuil' Kochin) brought Hebrew books to Leningrad from Lithuania, where they had been hidden before the war. He too was arrested late in 1949 and sentenced to twenty-five years' imprisonment.[33] A Kiev neurologist, Izrail' Gutin, decided to compile a Hebrew-Russian medical dictionary. For this purpose he bought Hebrew books from non-Jews at the flea market or was given them by Jewish patients. Although he worked in complete secrecy, he abandoned his project in 1952 when an elderly Jew in the Podol neighborhood was arrested and sentenced to fifteen years in prison for having Bialik's poems. This was a clear warning to other owners of Hebrew books, many of whom simply burned them. Others hid them in various places. Gutin himself concealed his dictionary and books in a wooden shack.[34]

While the study of Hebrew became well-nigh impossible in Stalin's last years for those who remained "free," paradoxically, inside Soviet prisons, the language was studied with relative freedom. The Jews there formed a natural group of Hebrew speakers and students—and had less to lose than those outside prison. Many of them had been arrested for Zionism or "bourgeois nationalist tendencies and activities," and they sought each other out almost instinctively. In the camps, these Jews from different cities and different walks of life would spend their free time, allotted the prisoners at the end of the day's work, secretly teaching and studying Hebrew. In Vorkuta, for example, Zvi Pregerzon conducted a daily two-hour, oral Hebrew lesson. (There was, of course, no opportunity to write.) Meir Gel'fond, a young medical student from Vinnitsa (originally from

Zhmerinka), even succeeded in mastering the spoken language while in the camps. Besides Pregezson, Gel'fond recalls another Hebrew teacher, Jacques Feldman, a Romanian Communist who returned to his Jewish roots while in the Soviet prison camps and who taught his fellow Jews the Israeli national anthem *hatikva*.[35]

Such stories abound. Prisoner of Zion Vladimir Levitin met an elderly Orthodox Jew in a Siberian camp who would write out sentences of the Bible with a Russian translation under each Hebrew word. He also received daily lessons from another fellow prisoner, who had been assistant editor of the Yiddish newspaper of the Jewish Autonomous Region, *Birobidzhaner shtern*.[36] Moisei Krantz of Gomel, who knew some Hebrew from his childhood when he had studied in *heder* (a religious Jewish elementary school), met a fellow Jew in camp with whom he spoke and studied Hebrew secretly every morning before work.[37] An Orthodox Riga Jew, the painter Yitzhak Hayit, who had been arrested, among others, for conducting clandestine Hebrew lessons, continued to give lessons in the camps.[38]

What is clear from all these testimonies is that the study of Hebrew in the camps was of vital importance. It not only gave the Jewish prisoners a purpose, it endowed their camp experience with spiritual content and so helped them preserve those human qualities that Soviet camp inmates so readily lose. It also comprised a link among the Jewish prisoners and for many of them it was their first Jewish and Zionist education.

The second, post-Stalin, period is not a direct continuation of the Black Years. The intense activity and the hopes of emigration that characterized the 1948–1949 period were no more. The persecution of Stalin's last years had devastated the Zionist movement and Jewish culture. The few teachers of Hebrew were in the camps, the books—rare as they had been before— had been burned or hidden.

Yet, slowly a new edifice was created on the rubble of Jewish life. The resumption of diplomatic relations between Moscow and Jerusalem in an atmosphere of relatively relaxed tensions enabled Israeli diplomats to visit many towns throughout the country and create closer contact between Soviet Jews and the Israeli embassy staff. Moreover, Israeli sports, scientific, and cultural delegations began to visit the Soviet Union, also creating contacts with Soviet Jewry. (Previously such delegations had been rare and had been isolated from any contact with the population.) In particular, the Israelis now brought with them Hebrew grammars and textbooks, as well as newspapers and other aids for learning Hebrew. In addition, with the rehabilitation and amnesties of the mid-1950s, tens and perhaps hundreds of thousands of Jewish prisoners returned to the major Jewish centers as well as to the small towns. Many of them had become Zionists in the camps or, if they had been Zionists before, had had their Zionist convictions strengthened by their camp experience and had enhanced their knowledge of Jewish history and Hebrew. While some of these people decided that they had suffered enough privation and refrained from any activity that could possibly be interpreted as anti-Soviet, many considered it their obligation to transmit Jewish values and culture to the younger generation. One of these, Vol'f Rishal' of Moscow, who was released in 1956, searched for Hebrew books and newspapers in the Lenin Library, and made notes from them to distribute among his friends.[39] Moisei Krantz returned to Gomel in 1955 where he continued to teach the younger generation Hebrew, using prayer books as textbooks.[40] Another camp inmate of long standing, Izrail' Mintz, returned in 1963 to Moscow where he sought out other speakers of Hebrew, made clandestine translations from Hebrew to Russian, and began teaching the language to young people (on an individual basis). He made a point of equipping his pupils with the particular terms necessary for their professions. Many of these young people had become Hebrew teachers in their own right by the end of the decade.[41]

The Israeli embassy staff was a major source of material for studying Hebrew. Rishal' was among those who would meet members of the Israeli embassy in Moscow's main synagogue and receive from them Israeli newspapers and Hebrew textbooks. He also began teaching the language to acquaintances in Moscow.[42] In 1955, embassy members in the synagogue gave fifteen-year-old Boris Podol'skii a Hebrew-Russian, Russian-Hebrew dictionary and *Elef millim* (a popular Hebrew textbook, literally "A Thousand Words"). Podol'skii studied Hebrew for more than a year with Grigorii Zil'berman, a regular worshiper at the synagogue.[43]

Members of the Israeli delegation to the Sixth World Festival of Youth and Students held in Moscow in 1957 reported numerous instances of the Jews' interest in Hebrew. One Jew they met was learning Hebrew from the prerevolutionary journal *Hatekufa* in one of the reading rooms of the Lenin Library; an engineer begged them to give him a Hebrew dictionary "at any price"; and a mother visited the delegation with her two small children and tearfully asked for a Hebrew textbook. They came across students who wrote down the words of Israeli folk songs from records the Israelis were not allowed to distribute, as well as Jews who told the delegation that they listened to Israeli broadcasts in Hebrew or participated in underground Hebrew circles.[44]

The encounter with this large Israeli delegation aroused in many young Jews an intensified interest in their Jewishness, Israel, and the Hebrew language. Anatoli Rubin of Minsk journeyed specially to Moscow to meet the Israelis and received from them Hebrew pamphlets and dictionaries. (This encounter led to his imprisonment, see below.)[45] One young woman, Tina Brodetskaia of Moscow, excited by a performance of Israeli songs and dances by members of the delegation, went to the synagogue and asked Rabbi Levin to find her a Hebrew teacher. As a result, she too began to study the language with Grigorii Zil'berman.[46] Another young woman, Liliia Ontman, met the Israeli delegation as it passed through her hometown, Ungenyi (Moldavian SSR), on its way to Moscow and decided to study Hebrew. (She had some knowledge of the language from her grandmother.) She was, however, unable to proceed since she had no texts. In 1960, further motivated to study the language by the desire to listen to Israeli broadcasts in Hebrew (the Yiddish broadcasts were systematically jammed), she wrote to the Institute of Foreign Languages in Moscow requesting books for learning Hebrew or at least information about where she could learn it. In reply she was summoned to the KGB in Chernovtsy where she was studying and warned to desist. Later, in Kiev, where she was sent to do practical work, Liliia Ontman managed to obtain books (from one Aron Brand), but her family was afraid to keep the books at home and transferred them to an acquaintance, so once again her ambition to study Hebrew was frustrated.[47]

In 1959 a Hebrew circle was organized in Leningrad by Shoshana Zusman-Epshtain and Natan Tsirul'nikov, both of whom had made up their minds to emigrate to Israel, and until this became possible were resolved to study Hebrew and stimulate Jewish national consciousness among their friends. After a short-lived attempt to study by themselves from religious books (prayer books, the Bible, etc.) Tsirul'nikov asked a pensioner, one Prostakov (a former civil engineer, originally from Lithuania) who was a regular reader of Israeli newspapers at the Saltykov-Shchedrin Library if he would teach the group Hebrew. He agreed readily and taught them for over half a year, until the group's dispersal. The circle comprised some fifteen people who would meet for each lesson in the home of a different member so as not to arouse suspicion. Tsirul'nikov managed to "borrow" a pre-1917 textbook from the library and one of the group members, a radiologist, Aleksandr Tsadikov, made ten photocopies of it. On work trips to Moscow, Tsirul'nikov obtained other materials from the Israeli embassy. In March 1960, after one such meeting with an Israeli diplomat, he was arrested and sentenced to a year's imprisonment for distributing anti-Soviet materials. The group ceased to exist but its influence persisted and its members were among those who organized the *ulpanim* which came into being later in the 1960s (see below).[48] Liia Lur'e, who had been a leading light in the Hebrew circle and had listened to Israeli broadcasts since 1958, now began teaching Hebrew. Among her pupils were Gil'ia (Hillel) Butman and Solomon Drezner,[49] who later (in November 1966) organized a Zionist group in Leningrad. Butman continued to study Hebrew by himself from *Elef millim* after Liia Lur'e's death in 1960, and in 1967 became the teacher of one of Leningrad's first two *ulpanim* (see below). Still later, in a Leningrad prison cell (after the 1970 hijacking attempt), Butman was able to reconstruct 961 out of the 1,000 words listed in *Elef millim*.[50]

In the late 1950s Gennadii (Gedalia) Pecherskii, one of the wardens of the Leningrad synagogue, attempted to obtain official permission to study Hebrew. Believing that the Hebrew language was a vital part of Jewish education and could help to prevent the assimilation and acculturation of Soviet Jewish youth, he dreamt of founding a club in which young Jews could learn Hebrew, Yiddish, and Jewish history and literature. Along with a friend, one Fainitskii, he wrote to the Leningrad town soviet and the RSFSR Ministry of Education requesting permission to teach Hebrew. They received the reply that those bodies did not have the necessary authority, but Pecherskii was undaunted and encouraged a number of his friends, Evsei Dynkin, Ostrovskii, and Admoni, to write similar letters. He even found a Hebrew teacher, a member of Leningrad's old intelligentsia, the Russian orientalist Klavdiia Starkova (see above), who welcomed Pecherskii's plan and appended her signature to these letters. This activity eventually led to the arrest of Pecherskii and two of his friends in 1961, and Pecherskii's dream to legitimize the study of Hebrew remained unfulfilled.[51]

One of the very few Jews who actually taught Hebrew officially was Feliks Shapiro. Following the establishment of the State of Israel and of diplomatic ties between it and the USSR, Shapiro was asked in 1953, when he was already in his seventies, to teach Hebrew to foreign ministry personnel in a number of Moscow's institutes of higher learning. Confronted with the difficulty of teaching a language without teaching aids and dictionaries, Shapiro requested permission to compile a Hebrew-Russian dictionary. Although a Hebrew textbook was never published, the dictionary was eventually published in 1963, two years after Shapiro's death. This dictionary, which includes a grammatical survey by Professor B. M. Grande, is the only textbook for the study of Hebrew that has ever appeared in the USSR.[52] Jews rushed to buy the dictionary in the belief that it augured a new policy permitting the official study of Hebrew. Izrail' Mintz recalls: "I ran into people waiting in line to receive the dictionary. . . . None of them knew Hebrew. People were simply happy, as though a prayer book had appeared."[53]

In the 1960s it became possible for the first time to receive Hebrew textbooks and dictionaries through the post.[54] Tourists from Israel and the West also brought textbooks and records for the study of Hebrew.[55] Occasionally it was even possible to buy Hebrew textbooks published in Soviet bloc countries.[56] Many Jews were also helped by the Hebrew lessons broadcast by the "Voice of Israel."[57] Israeli textbooks also became available in some of the larger public libraries, not, of course, for taking home, but for reading on the spot. Thus, from 1966, Karl (Yehezkeel) Malkin and later also his brother Aleksandr read *Mori* (My Teacher) in Moscow's Lenin Library and the Library of Foreign Literature. However, when the demand for such books grew markedly, they disappeared from the catalog of books available to the public.[58]

Unlike in Moscow and Leningrad, there were many Jews in Latvia and Lithuania, particularly in the two capital cities, who knew Hebrew. People who were in their thirties in the mid-1950s had received a Hebrew education before the USSR annexed the Baltic republics in 1940. Even some of the younger generation had been taught the language by their parents after the annexation.[59] Eli Valk was taught to read and write Hebrew by his mother in preparation for his Bar Mitzvah in 1957. By 1965 Valk knew enough Hebrew to converse with foreign tourists. It was these people who after the Six-Day War translated Israeli newspaper articles and disseminated them among the local Jews.[60] Iakov Gurevich taught Hebrew in Riga to individual pupils from the early post-Stalin period until his departure for Israel in 1964.[61] David Garber, a leading Zionist activist in Riga, knew no Hebrew and, like Liliia Ontman, wanted to study the language in order to understand Hebrew broadcasts and to converse with Israeli tourists. In

1957 he was told that Moshe Shubin, a lawyer by profession who had been an active Zionist before the war, was about to open a circle for students of Hebrew. Garber joined his study group, along with three other people and they obtained books and dictionaries from the Israeli embassy. Boris Krechmar also taught Hebrew to a number of Riga Jews who departed for Israel in the second half of the 1950s. For lack of Hebrew textbooks Krechmar used a Russian-language primer, inscribing by hand the Hebrew translation of each word. By 1967 the study of Hebrew in Riga was well organized and the thirty or so families whose departure for Israel was delayed by the Six-Day War took advantage of this period of waiting to study Hebrew in small groups of two or three pupils.[62]

In other parts of the USSR, too, throughout this period, there were people who were taught Hebrew by their parents or grandparents, often without the help of any books at all. Thus, in Novosibirsk, Esfir Shmerler and her twelve-year-old son Iz'ia (Izrail') were taught Hebrew by Esfir's father in 1959 for over a year, which was as long as they could study the language without written materials.[63]

Riga activist Grisha Feigin (see above) decided to distribute copies of *Elef millim* to the Mountain Jews of Dagestan. In the winter of 1964 he went to Dagestan, along with Nisim Ilishaev, himself a Mountain Jew who lived in Moscow, and they distributed the books in the synagogues in Derbent, Kuba, and Makhachkala. At this time, small groups of Mountain Jews began meeting to study Hebrew and Jewish history. One such group of young people was taught Hebrew by the rabbi of Derbent, Abraham Agronov, in 1965. Unlike many of their Ashkenazi brethren the Mountain Jews grew up with at least a minimal knowledge of Hebrew, as they learned to read Hebrew in their childhood when they were taught to pray by their families.[64]

The Georgian Jews likewise attached considerable importance to teaching their children Hebrew. Most of the men at least were able to read Hebrew, by virtue of their religious education, although only a few understood more than a smattering of the language. In the early 1960s in Tbilisi a group was formed to produce a Hebrew-language textbook. Its members included Gershon and Mikhail Tsitsuashvili, and the writer Abram Mamistvalov. A Georgian Hebrew grammar was duly produced in 1964 or 1965, copied out in fifty or so copies, and distributed.[65] The Bukharan Jews also taught their children Hebrew as part of a religious education. Their children were taught either by grandparents, whose own Hebrew dated back to czarist times, or by Jews from Poland or the annexed territories who had found their way to Central Asia during World War II. Emma Graiver, formerly Khudaidutova, of Samarkand recalls that in her family all eleven siblings studied Hebrew as children, of course in total secrecy. She and her younger sister Riva were taught by a Polish Jew.[66]

In this period, too, Jewish prisoners studied in the camps. Barukh Vaisman of Kiev, a long-standing Zionist who was already in his seventies when he was arrested, was among those who taught Hebrew during his imprisonment. In camp, too, he composed a Hebrew-Hebrew pocket dictionary on very poor quality, crumpled paper, which was used by a large number of camp inmates who passed it among them from hand to hand.[67]

In Vorkuta the tradition of Pregerzon and others was continued by Mordekhai Shinkar', an Orthodox Jew from Lvov, and one Zeksler of Vilnius.[68] Boris Podol'skii's father, Semen, who was arrested in 1958, first began to learn Hebrew in prison camp. He met there an old Zionist from Kiev, Meir Draznin, who had a Hebrew-Hebrew dictionary. Boris recalls that his father copied entries from the dictionary into a notebook which he smuggled out from his camp to that of his son. Semen learned sufficient Hebrew from Draznin "for us to be able to converse in Hebrew when we did not want other prisoners to understand." In his camp, Boris met Abraham Shifrin, who in 1962 received by a very roundabout way a German Hebrew-language grammar.[69] Yet another Jewish prisoner who was taught Hebrew and Jewish history in the camp by veteran Zionists was Anatolii Rubin of Minsk (see above).[70]

Another political prisoner who had been sentenced in 1966 for Zionist activity, Solomon Dol'nik, relates how he convinced a fellow prisoner, an assimilated Jew who belonged to the Russian democratic movement, that, being a Jew, he should study Hebrew. Dol'nik began to teach him with the help of a dictionary he had obtained from a third camp inmate, an observant Jew from Leningrad by the name of Rafalovich, and, as a result of the study of Hebrew, his pupil began to move toward Jewish consciousness.[71]

In the period after the Six-Day War the Jewish national movement developed new momentum. The prominent trait of this period was the overcoming of the barrier of fear which had, among others, deterred so many Jews from studying Hebrew in the past. As a result of this new confidence, Jews began to organize in small study groups to learn Hebrew. Larger Hebrew circles which came to be known by the Hebrew term *ulpanim* also came into existence, many of their members being young men and women who had grown up in totally assimilated homes. Many of the teachers, too, were youngsters, a new generation who only recently had been pupils themselves, and who had managed to gain a relatively good knowledge of the language in their clandestine studies. Usually the pupils would pay a symbolic sum for tuition: this both helped pay expenses (mimeographing or xeroxing, the purchase of paper, etc.) and created a commitment among the pupils to persist in their studies.[72] In Moscow the Hebrew teachers would meet once every two weeks. Their meetings would be held in Hebrew and for each occasion a special topic of Jewish interest would be chosen for discussion.[73]

In this period the *ulpanim* spread throughout the country, even reaching towns that had not traditionally been centers of Jewish activity, such as Gorkii, Rostov, and Novosibirsk.[74] This network was made possible by the ties that were now formed among Jews from different towns, with the leadership remaining in the main centers: Moscow, Leningrad, Riga, and Vilnius.

Although the Israeli embassy no longer existed, following the severance of diplomatic relations by the USSR after the war, Israel continued to supply textbooks, dictionaries, and other study materials through the post and with the help of tourists.[75] Moreover, the "Voice of Israel" continued to broadcast Hebrew lessons which, despite jamming, most Hebrew students listened to regularly.[76]

Of particular importance was the fact that in this period the study of Hebrew was apparently condoned by the authorities, who virtually ignored the *ulpanim* and refrained from taking action against them. Some of the Hebrew teachers believed that this policy should be exploited quietly to broaden the network of Hebrew studies;[77] others thought that this was the time to request official permission to teach and study Hebrew.[78]

Thus, whatever the reasons for the authorities' relative lenience, by the end of the 1960s when emigration still seemed an unrealistic prospect, (except in the annexed territories from where there had been some emigration prior to the Six-Day War) the study of Hebrew became the most accepted framework for identification with Judaism and the State of Israel. The *ulpanim* became the framework not only for studying Hebrew, but also for learning about Jewish values and culture in general, as well as for discussing Israel's significance and problems. Originating in the desire to associate with Israel, the *ulpanim* in fact strengthened the identification with Israel of teachers and students alike. Moreover, these circles played a vital role by creating both an organizational basis for the Jewish national movement and a social framework that brought together people from different walks of life and different age groups, united by a single interest and purpose. By the time exit permits began to be received on a larger scale, new recruits came to the *ulpanim*, motivated now by practical considerations: preparing for life in Israel.

It is difficult to determine where exactly the first *ulpan* started in this period; but, it seems likely that the first circles appeared in Moscow and Leningrad. In these cities many of the *ulpanim* maintained a high level and continuity, even when teachers emigrated to Israel. The reason for this concentration of *ulpanim* in the USSR's two major cities, where the Jews were traditionally most acculturated in their surrounding non-Jewish society, was presumably that Moscow and Leningrad boasted a large Jewish intellectual elite that was well aware of the legal rights of the Soviet citizen and was less afraid of the reaction of the authorities to their activities than were their fellow Jews in most of the provincial towns. Moreover, the Jews of Moscow and Leningrad (particularly of Moscow) had connections with foreigners which strengthened their position, and also with non-Jewish dissident activists. Thus it came about that in Moscow in particular, and to a lesser extent also in Leningrad, there lived a number of Jews who became foci of Jewish activity, by virtue of both their knowledge of Israel and their instruction of young people in Hebrew and Jewish history.

In Leningrad the number of *ulpanim* multiplied quickly as of the fall of 1967. The first initiative was taken by David Chernoglaz, Vladimir Mogilever, and Aleksandr (Sasha) Blank. Blank had begun teaching himself Hebrew a year or two previously from *Elef millim* (to make sure that his accent was reasonably accurate he went several times to Moscow to talk to the former actress of the *Habima* (Hebrew theater), Hava Edel'man).[79] They ensured that their pupils took their studies seriously and maintained a high level by imposing a final examination at the end of each course. Six weeks later Gil'ia Butman and Solomon Drezner opened a second *ulpan*. They rented a room just outside Leningrad, hardly large enough for their fifteen or so pupils. *Elef millim*, in mimeograph, was again the textbook used; the pupils would come to class with just a few pages, because it was too unwieldy for the entire volume to be used in mimeographed form. Part of their studies would be to copy out pages from the textbook, thus providing further copies for new students.[80] Even in prison camp, Drezner (who was arrested in June 1970) managed to organize students to copy out Hebrew textbooks, and Hebrew was studied in a relatively systematic fashion, despite the obstacles imposed by the camp authorities.[81] Meanwhile, in Leningrad the first two *ulpanim* bred new ones. In 1969 alone, five new *ulpanim* developed out of Butman's *ulpan*;[82] indeed, it became regular practice for pupils who attained a certain level themselves to become teachers.

In Moscow the influence was felt of the older generation of teachers, a few veteran Zionists who had a good knowledge of Hebrew, such as Izrail' Mintz, Hava Edel'man, and Esfir Aizenshtat.[83] About this time, in the late 1960s, Hava Edel'man prepared a "commentary" to *Elef millim* to facilitate its use as the sole source for Hebrew lessons.[84] One of the first circles in the Soviet capital was started by David Khavkin. Early in 1967 Khavkin met Ihiel Abramzon (see above) in the synagogue and suggested to him that he teach Hebrew to a group of young people in Moscow. Abramzon taught in the *ulpan* until his *aliya* in 1971 and his first pupils included some of the leading figures of the growing *aliya* movement, such as Vladimir Prestin, Leonid Lipkovskii, and Iosif Begun. Once again, *Elef millim* was the main textbook and the pupils would mimeograph it themselves in secret. Abramzon also introduced his pupils to Hebrew literature, in particular Bialik's poems.[85]

Khavkin recruited other teachers as well. He and Yehezkeel Malkin, who had been studying Hebrew by himself for years (see above), decided to open further *ulpanim*, and in their quest for teachers Malkin turned to Mikhail (Misha) Trakhtenberg who had an excellent command of the language from his mother. In 1968 Trakhtenberg began teaching his first three pupils and soon became one of the most popular teachers in town. He devised his own method of teaching Hebrew, which became standard in the Soviet Union and was the method used to train future generations of Hebrew teachers. By the turn of the decade (1970) his first pupils had themselves become teachers and by the early 1970s had over a hundred pupils.[86] Vladimir Shakhnovskii was another teacher who elaborated a special method for teaching Hebrew, especially to enable beginners to advance by themselves; he was also very active in organizing new study circles in different parts of the USSR.[87]

For all these *ulpanim* the major difficulty remained the dearth of teaching materials. Pupils who emigrated to Israel left their books at the disposal of the *ulpanim*. The orientalist Mikhail Zand contributed some of his own books for use by the teachers. Used and new copies of the usual *Elef millim, Mori,* and *Hasafa haivrit* (The Hebrew language) were mimeographed and distributed.[88]

While most of the first teachers emigrated to Israel, some (Shakhnovskii, Prestin, Abramovich, and Begun) were refused exit permits for many years. Begun was sentenced in 1967 to three years' exile in Siberia for "parasitism" after he had several times requested the Moscow municipality finance department (Mosgorfin *upravelenie*) to register him as a private Hebrew teacher. In his letters to the municipality Begun supported his requests by referring to Lenin's position on the nationalities policy and in particular on the languages of the nationalities as well as to the CPSU Program which places no restriction on the use of the language of any Soviet national minority.[89]

Another teacher who fought an open struggle to legitimize the study of Hebrew was Vladimir Roginskii of Moscow. In 1972 he conducted a lengthy correspondence with the USSR Minister of Culture Ekatarina Furtseva, with various bodies connected with the export of books, and with the Soviet record company Gramplastinok asking a single question: Where in the USSR could a Hebrew book, record, newspaper, or magazine be purchased? The few replies he received were uniform: such materials could not be purchased in the Soviet Union since there was no demand. However, there were Yiddish books and records, and even a Yiddish journal.[90] Mikhail Nosovskii of Leningrad wrote in 1977 to the RSFSR minister of justice asking him how he could legally teach Hebrew with or without pay, to those who wanted to learn. He received a reply through the minister of education pointing out that Hebrew was not on the list of subjects taught in schools and therefore, according to law, could neither be taught nor studied.[91] In November 1972 a group of Moscow Jews wrote to the director general of UNESCO in France and the chairman of the USSR Commission for UNESCO Affairs, A. A. Smirnov, requesting help in gaining permission to learn to read and write in their national tongue, Hebrew. The only reply they received came in the form of exit permits for some of the letter's signatories.[92] Indeed, Lev (Levi) Ul'ianovskii has argued that in the 1970s a significant change for the better occurred in the status of the Hebrew language: when he was under investigation by the KGB and insisted on talking Hebrew, "the investigator did not reject outright my request to employ an interpreter," thus implying official recognition of the language.[93] Another victory was scored by Pavel Abramovich, a Hebrew teacher and refusenik of long standing, who in 1976, after having gone to court, was permitted to advertise on thirty Moscow notice boards: "I offer Hebrew lessons"[94] (see above).

In other towns, too, activists approached the local powers-that-be with similar requests. In the winter of 1970–71, a group of ten families in Sverdlovsk approached the local *oblast'* department of popular education for permission to conduct a course in Hebrew.[95] In Kaunas a group of young people actually received oral permission from the authorities to study Hebrew in the synagogue. Over forty people of various ages, some of whom already knew Hebrew, duly gathered there at the first meeting. So too did representatives of the government, who took considerable interest in the identity of the would-be students. They eventually told them that the authorities had no intention of preparing cadres for Israel and any further meeting for the purpose of studying Hebrew was prohibited. Five of the younger people decided nevertheless to learn Hebrew; one of them already had some knowledge of the language from *Mori* and *Elef millim* which had been provided by activists in Moscow.[96]

In Odessa young men and women turned to older people who knew Hebrew from pre-Soviet times. Thus, toward the end of the sixties Nahman Moredin received his first pupil, a young engineer called Petr Vaisblit, who brought him many other pupils. Other *ulpanim* started like a chain reaction: one pupil learned four hundred words and immediately opened his own *ulpan*.[97]

Ulpanim sprang up in like fashion in Riga, Vilnius, Kishinev, and Mukachevo (Muncacz) where, as we have seen, there were many Jews who had attended Hebrew gymnasiums before the annexation by the USSR and who had taught Hebrew to their children and their children's friends clandestinely for several years. Before June 1967 they had received textbooks and other study materials through the Israel embassy, and after the Six-Day War they continued to receive these materials through tourists. In some of these towns several *ulpanim* were functioning by the end of the 1960s.[98] In 1970 an attempt was made to teach Hebrew openly in Riga. A clubhouse was found to house an *ulpan* and two teachers were recruited, Rivka Aleksandrovich and Ben-Zion Shrofter. Once again the problem was solved—from the point of view of the authorities—by giving the teachers exit permits to Israel.[99]

In Kiev and Kishinev the first *ulpanim* were opened in 1969. In Kiev the first two teachers Evgeniia (Zhenia) Bukhina and Anatolii Gerenrot—were young people who had previously learned Hebrew from older Zionists in Kiev itself, such as Meir Draznin. The *ulpanim* in Kiev were initiated by Kiev's leading activists and their purpose, as explained by Zhenia, was to strengthen the ties among nationally oriented Jews. As the teachers' own knowledge of Hebrew was limited they would meet regularly to talk Hebrew. The moderator at these meetings was Hirsh Remenik, a veteran Zionist activist and father of one of the new young Hebrew teachers, Ita Remenik.[100] In Kishinev, on the other hand, the first *ulpanim* were set up by two local young people Arkadii Voloshin and Aleksandr Gal'perin, who during their studies in Leningrad had been pupils at *ulpanim* there. Upon their return to their hometown, they organized *ulpanim* where they taught Hebrew and Jewish history, celebrated Jewish festivals, and distributed materials on Israel. In 1970 the two men were arrested.[101]

In Minsk, as in Moscow, Kiev, and Odessa, there were a number of older Zionists who had learned Hebrew in their youth in a *heder* or *yeshiva*. One such person was Zefania Kipnis, who taught Hebrew individually to young people in their own homes. Among his pupils was Shmaryahu Gorelik who himself opened an *ulpan* which had twelve pupils. One day, when he was speaking Hebrew to a friend in the synagogue, he was overheard by Naum Al'shanskii, a retired army colonel *(polkovnik)* who, intending to emigrate to Israel, had started learning Hebrew from a copy of *Elef millim* which he had received from an American tourist. Al'shanskii asked Gorelik to teach him Hebrew, along with two other retired colonels, Lev Ovsishcher and Efim Davidovich. Both had renounced their rank in protest against the authorities' refusal to permit them to emigrate to Israel. Al'shanskii, meanwhile, whose name was known to American Jews as a would-be repatriate to Israel, received copies of *Mori* from Western tourists which he distributed among friends, not only in Minsk, but even in the Siberian town of Novisibirsk where he had acquaintances. Davidovich for his part made great progress in his study of Hebrew and began to teach other Jews whom he found through the synagogue. Deprived of his work and subjected to other ignominies because of his desire to leave for Israel, Davidovich had begun suffering from heart trouble. Yet he continued teaching Hebrew from his sickbed, explaining to his wife (who was also his doctor) that to teach Hebrew to young Jews was his new battlefront.[102]

By the late 1970s, former Hebrew teachers from the Soviet Union who had emigrated to Israel reported that in Moscow there were some thirty teachers of Hebrew with four to five hundred pupils, in Leningrad twelve teachers with a hundred pupils, and that Hebrew was also being taught in Kaunas, Kiev, Minsk, Tbilisi, Kharkov, Tashkent, and other cities.[103] Thus, the study and teaching of Hebrew developed rapidly after the Six-Day War, even though many difficulties faced those who sought to teach the language: study materials were still not easy to come by and many Jews continued to have qualms about participating in the unofficial *ulpanim* that began operating. But many of those who desired to do so were now able to learn Hebrew. Moreover, there was now a place, the synagogue or the synagogue courtyard, where it was possible to obtain information about the *ulpanim*, Hebrew teachers, and books. For a short period, in Moscow at least, a few Hebrew teachers were even officially recognized as such and a number of notices on the municipal advertisement boards announced the existence of Hebrew lessons. In this short period, the *ulpanim* mushroomed and boasted many hundreds of pupils. The authorities must have known of this activity, yet they refrained from intervening, as long as the Hebrew teachers showed restraint in their struggle for legitimacy.

The spread of the *ulpanim* to most of the cities with considerable Jewish populations, together with the rapid increase in the number of functioning *ulpanim*, created a new generation of Hebrew speakers, many of whom quickly became Hebrew teachers, ensuring the continuity of Hebrew teaching in the Soviet Union. In addition, the *ulpanim* provided a framework for discussions on Israel, *aliya,* and Jewish life in the Soviet Union. From the purely social point of view, they were also a meeting place for young Jews, who, through the *ulpanim,* gained a Jewish consciousness. Many even reached the decision to emigrate to Israel as a result of their study of the Hebrew language, which, in the conditions of the late 1960s and the 1970s in the Soviet Union, was often the sole chance for actively identifying as Jews.

The story of the struggle for the study of Hebrew in the Soviet Union is in many ways that of the Jewish national awakening in that country. The study of Hebrew was conceived by many Soviet Jews from the early period covered by this paper, and increasingly so from the late 1950s onward, as the major way of identifying with their national culture, which Soviet theory associated above all with language. This was especially true following the elimination of the vestiges of Yiddish culture in the USSR, which had in any case become less attractive to the younger generation of Soviet Jews as the language, on the one hand, of the *shtetl* and a way of life that had become anomalous and irrelevant and, on the other hand, of the *Evsektsiia*, of the Jewish section of the Russian Communist party (of Bolsheviks), that had served as the party's instrument for suppressing any autonomous Jewish existence. Hebrew symbolized the renaissance of the national culture as embodied in the new Jewish state, the language of Jewish independence. Knowledge of it enabled one to listen to Israeli broadcasts—Yiddish was mostly jammed and Russian programs only began to be broadcast in the 1960s—to learn Israeli songs and to read material that told of life in Israel and depicted its problems and achievements. Eventually, as the prospects of *aliya* improved, Jews began studying Hebrew in order to prepare for the new life in a free country of their own, where they would be neither strangers nor second-class citizens.

It is, therefore, not surprising that throughout the period in question Jews endeavored by a variety of means to surmount the obstacles the authorities placed in the path of those who sought to learn the language of their fathers. Sometimes the means had perforce to be devious, sometimes one paid a heavy price, but, on the whole, many among the young generation of Jewish intelligentsia saw in Hebrew and its study the most substantial vehicle available to them for asserting their national consciousness. Often they were helped in their endeavors, in the Western territories by parents, and in the areas that had been part of the Soviet Union prior to World War II, by grandparents or other pensioners, not a few of them erstwhile Prisoners of Zion, who had retained the knowledge of Hebrew they had acquired in their youth, so that in addition the study of Hebrew became a consolidating social factor that brought together Jews of different generations and walks of life. The considerable success of the movement for the study of Hebrew can only be explained by the combination of all three components. At first a trend that marked a considerable number of individuals throughout the length and breadth of the USSR, it became in the late 1960s and even more so in the 1970s the focus and yardstick of Jewish nationalist activity.

Notes

I wish to thank all those participants in the struggle for the survival of Hebrew in the Soviet Union who shared their experiences with me, and also Yaacov Ro'i for his assistance in preparing this chapter.

1. The Jewish languages spoken in the USSR are Yiddish; Judaeo-Georgian

which is an argot rather than a distinct language; Judaeo-Tadzhik, a dialect of Tadzhik; Judaeo-Tat; and Judaeo-Crimean Tatar or Krymchak.
2. The 1977 Constitution (Fundamental Law) of the USSR, Article 13, in David Lane, *Politics and Society in the USSR* (London: Martin Robertson, 1978), 2nd ed., Appendix C/2, pp. 560–61.
3. From time to time the Soviet Union has, however, claimed that it permits the study of Hebrew, e.g., *Izvestiia,* December 24, 1976, wrote: "In the USSR, as is well known, nobody is prohibited from studying any language—including *Ivrit* or Yiddish." The Russian language has traditionally used the term the Jewish language, *evreiskii iazyk,* to designate Yiddish, and the ancient Jewish language, *drevnyi evreiskii iazyk,* for Hebrew. Interestingly, *Izvestiia* used the Hebrew term *Ivrit.*

In the second half of the 1980s under Gorbachev the Soviet authorities have indicated a willingness to make some concessions regarding the study of Hebrew, notably under the auspices of the synagogues. This chapter was prepared prior to Gorbachev's rise to power and therefore these concessions have not been discussed here. Even at the time of going to press, moreover, it is still too early to assess their significance, impact, and implications.
4. In the early 1970s, for instance, Hebrew was being taught at Moscow State University: the Moscow Institute of International Relations; Leningrad State University; and Tbilisi State University—*Evreiskii samizdat* (Jerusalem: CRD), vol. 15 (1978), p. 41 and vol. 17 (1979), pp. 125–26. In addition, Hebrew was taught at the School of Foreign Languages, the KGB Institute of Foreign Languages, and the Higher Diplomatic Courses.
5. Two Jews who were accepted to the Department of Assyriology and Hebraica at Leningrad University in the late 1940s emigrated to Israel in the mid-1970s, Iakov Gruntfest and Anatolii Gezov-Ginzberg (now Amnon Ginezi). Gruntfest recalls that from 1949 Jews were no longer admitted to the department, which was closed down a year later on the pretext that the subject matter was not sufficiently relevant. For years it was impossible for him to find employment as an expert in Semitic languages, but in 1960 he was able to continue to study for his doctoral degree and in the ten years prior to his emigration he worked at the Leningrad Oriental Institute—Y. Gruntfest to the author, October 7, 1982. Gezov-Ginzburg for his part chose to study Hebrew on entering university in 1947 because he was already at that time planning *aliya* and could conceive of no other way of acquiring the language. Hebrew was taught with the help of European textbooks and his teacher was a Russian, Dr. Klavdiia Starkova (see below)—A. Ginezi to the author, October 5, 1982.
6. Zand had studied Oriental Studies at Moscow State University (1945–50). In 1946 he taught himself Hebrew with the help of a book he purchased in Chernovtsy that had been published in Cracow in German in 1889, *Hamedaber bil'shon amo.* (He Who Speaks the Language of His People)—author's conversation with M. Zand, July 3, 1982. Rubinshtain, who proofread the Shapiro Hebrew-Russian dictionary, conducted a course in Hebrew at Moscow University for Soviet foreign service and military personnel—author's interview

with Yisrael Mintz, January 5, 1982. For the paper of Vasilii Struve and Mikhail Korostovtsev, read at the conference by the latter and which talked of the revival of biblical Hebrew in Israel as a miracle, see *Semitskie iazyki, vypusk 2* (chapter 1). *Materialy pervoi konferentsii posemitskim iazykam,* 22–28, *oktiabria, 1964 g.* (Moscow: Nauka, 1965), pp. 36–37.

7. *Jewish Chronicle,* July 17, 1966, and conversation of Yaacov Ro'i with M. Zand, January 23, 1984.
8. It boasted a "membership" of 300,000 with some 12,000 local groups—J. B. Schechtman, "The U.S.S.R., Zionism, and Israel," in Lionel Kochan, ed., *The Jews in Soviet Russia Since 1917* (London: Oxford University Press, 1970), p. 101.
9. P. Abramovich, "Zaiavlenie dlia pechati ob izuchenii ivrita," *Evreiskii samizdat,* vol. 15, p. 41. Pol'skii has recorded that in the summer of 1971 he approached the *raionnyi otdel narodnogo obrazovaniia* (the district department of popular education) asking to be registered as a private teacher and to be allowed to pay the appropriate tax. The acceptance of this payment comprised official recognition of the legitimacy of teaching Hebrew. The refusal to accept further payments of tax, in 1972, indicated a reversion to the status quo ante in which the study of Hebrew was not recognized as legitimate. In Pol'skii's *ulpan* there were a number of groups of students, probably several score in all. Pol'skii had himself studied Hebrew on his own in 1965 from L. I. Rikliss's *Mori* (Tel Aviv: Hazvi, 1963). V. Pol'skii to the author, November 7, 1982.
10. P. Abramovich, "Nekotorye voprosy problemy izucheniia i prepodavaniia iazyka ivrit v USSR" (henceforth "Nekotorye voprosy"), *Evreiskii samizdat,* vol. 15, p. 151. Yehiel Abramson recalls that he heard in the Moscow synagogue that one of Dekatov's advertisements was on the boards in Pushkin Square— author's interview with Y. Abramson, November 25, 1982. Feliks Kantor, who was a student at Dekatov's official *ulpan* in the winter of 1970–71, remembers that there was a sign at the entrance to his apartment house with the word *ivrit* in cyrillic letters; the sign "annoyed" the neighbors who retaliated by insulting Dekatov's wife—author's interview with F. Kantor, November 24, 1982. For the activity of D. Drabkin, see "David Drabkin, Profile of an 'Activist,'" *Jews in Eastern Europe* (London), April 1972, vol. 5, no. 1, p. 21.
11. Iulii Margolin, "Vozvrozhdenie ivrita," *Evreiskii samizdat,* vol. 19 (1979), p. 264. *Brit Ivrit Olamit* is an international organization for the dissemination of Hebrew in the Diaspora. Its headquarters are in Jerusalem and it has branches in a large number of countries.
12. P. Abramovich, "Nekotorye voprosy," *Evreiskii samizdat,* vol. 15, pp. 151–52.
13. See, e.g., *Evreiskii Samizdat,* vols. 15, 17, 19.
14. "Kol Tsion Lagola" (The Voice of Zion to the Diaspora, Heb.) began broadcasting to the USSR in Yiddish and Hebrew in 1949. These broadcasts were not designed especially for the Soviet Union but were intended for Western and Eastern Europe in general. The broadcasts in Hebrew were transmitted on shortwave and lasted a quarter of an hour daily—Victor Graevsky (director

of "Israel Radio International Kol Israel External Services") to the author, October 17, 1982.
15. See, e.g., Yaacov Ro'i, *Soviet Decision Making in Practice: The USSR and Israel 1947–1954* (New Brunswick, N.J.: Transaction Books, 1980), pp. 183–217.
16. As recalled by the author's father, Shmuel Gotesman, who lived in Transcarpathia.
17. Boris Druk (now Dov Drori) recalls: "In Riga the youth began learning Hebrew in 1948. We of the older generation had been Zionists from childhood and we wanted our children to be Zionists as well. So we told them a great deal about Palestine and taught them our language—Hebrew." D. Drori to the author, October 28, 1982. Boris Iofis also acquired a knowledge of Hebrew from his father, David—author's conversation with B. Yafit, November 4, 1983.
18. Izrail' Pinskii grew up in a Moscow Habad family and as a child studied Hebrew and Torah with his father. Indeed, his father would teach children every day after work in an attempt to give them something of a Jewish education. Habad Hasidim were doing this in a number of Soviet cities (Moscow, Leningrad, Tashkent, Samarkand, and others)—interview of Y. Ro'i with Y. Pinskii, September 8, 1980. See also Y. Ro'i, "The Role of the Synagogue and Religion in the Jewish National Awakening" in this volume.
19. Jehuda Slutsky, "Zvi Preigerson," *Behinot*, no. 6, 1975, p. 91.
20. Z. Zaretsky to the author, October 4, 1982.
21. A. Rotem to the author, October 6, 1982. (After emigrating to Israel Leonid Rutshtain became Arye Rotem.)
22. Author's interview with G. Feigin, January 8, 1982. Feigin actually wrote a number of articles which he sent out to these circles entitled: "Turn Your Face to Zion," "Descendants of the Maccabees, Stand Erect," and "Zionism —the National Liberation Movement of the Jewish People."
23. Efim Shperber, a paratroop officer, and a pilot friend, Igor' Pischal'nik, made an attempt in February 1950 to cross into Turkey. Shperber eventually reached Israel, via Poland, in 1960 after serving eight years in a Soviet prison camp. Ginzburg died in 1958 in one of the camps while Granovskii disappeared during his term of imprisonment and his friends never found out his fate. Neiburger eventually died in Moscow several years after his release from prison camp in 1967—author's interviews with G. Feigin, January 8, 1982 and Haim (Efim) Shperber, January 24, 1982.
24. Author's joint interview with G. Feigin and H. Shperber, January 24, 1982.
25. Author's interview with G. Feigin, January 8, 1982. For Feigin's later activities in Riga, see p. 141.
26. Author's interview with Yehiel Abramson, November 25, 1982.
27. Ben-Horin, *Ma koreh sham* (What's Going On There, Heb.), Tel Aviv: Am Oved, 1970), p. 33, writes: "In at least three libraries in Leningrad there were good English books for the study of the Hebrew language. But when such a book was given to a reader, the librarians would note his name. I was apprehensive all the time that one bright day the authorities might manifest an

interest in the political profile of those who studied Hebrew. At no stage did I abandon my hope to leave for Israel and so I decided not to take the risk."
28. See, e.g., interview of Y. Alperovich with B. Podolsky, Yad Vashem, Givatayim, no. 3792, p. 14, in which Podolsky recalled: "In Moscow it was possible to get hold of the Israeli Communist party newspaper *Kol ha'am* only in the Lenin Library, but many were afraid to ask for an Israeli paper for fear that their names and other details would reach the KGB."
29. G. Branover, *Vozyvrashchenie* (The Return, Rus.) (New York: Free Press, 1977), pp. 183–84.
30. One of Ben-Horin's acquaintances who studied Hebrew in 1950 was arrested and convicted for having a Hebrew book in his home—*Ma koreh sham*, p. 32.
31. Yisrael Gutin, *Kur 'oni* (The Forge of Affliction, Heb.) (Tel Aviv: 'Eked, 1979), p. 29.
32. Ben-Horin, *Ma koreh sham*, p. 32.
33. Testimony of Shmuel Kochin in the archives of the Prisoners of Zion Association in Tel Aviv (henceforth PZA).
34. When, after Stalin's death, he opened the boxes in which he had concealed his books, Gutin found them rotten from damp, and he had to begin his work again from scratch.

    Gutin, b. 1903 in Belorussia, had studied in *yeshiva* as a boy and his excellent Hebrew dated from then. He taught his son Il'ia (Eliahu) Hebrew from the age of eleven. At the age of thirteen, at a family celebration of Israel's third Independence Day, Il'ia declared that before emigrating to Israel a Jew should know that the Jews had their own language and should learn that language—author's conversation with Yisrael Gutin, January 31, 1982, and Yisrael Gutin, *Kur 'oni*, p. 23.
35. Interview of Y. Ro'i with M. Gel'fond, January 21 and 26, 1982.
36. Levitin was born in Roslavl', near Moscow, but lived in Briansk until he enlisted in the Red Army. On his return to Briansk in 1944 he became a student and organized a small clandestine group of five members who wanted to reach Palestine. He was arrested in 1949—author's interview with V. Levitin, January 25, 1982.
37. Testimony of Moshe Krantz in PZA archives; and M. Krantz to the author, November 15, 1982. Isak Roitman and Yehezkel Polarevich also sought out Hebrew speakers during their camp experience—Y. Roitman to the author, October 22, 1982; and Y. Polarevich, *Hasippur hakatzar al hamavet haarokh* (A Short Story About a Long Death, Heb.) (Tel Aviv: Israel Ministry of Defence, 1978).
38. David Garber to the author, October 17, 1982.
39. Ze'ev Rishal to the author, February 1, 1982. Rishal, b. 1904 in Bessarabia, had studied Hebrew from the age of five.
40. M. Krantz to the author, November 15, 1982.
41. Author's interview with Y. Mintz, January 5, 1982.
42. Z. Rishal to the author, February 1, 1982.

43. Boris Podol'skii was born in Moscow in 1940 to a family deeply immersed in Yiddish culture. In 1958 he was arrested, along with his parents, Zil'berman (his Hebrew teacher) and another of the latter's pupils, Tina Brodetskaia (see below). This was Zil'berman's third arrest for Zionist activity in the course of a decade; born in the Ukraine, Zil'berman was an old-time Zionist—author's interview with B. Podolsky, January 3, 1982.
44. The source material relating to the 1957 Youth Festival has been provided by Yaacov Ro'i.
45. A. Rubin, "Moi put' v Izrail" (My Road to Israel, Rus.), CRD and A. Rubin, *Magafayim humim, magafayim adumim* (Brown Boots, Red Boots, Heb.) (Tel Aviv: Dvir, 1977), pp. 83–88.
46. Interview of Yitzhak Alperovich with Dora Poldolsky, May 1971, Yad Vashem, Givatayim, no. 3200/270, and author's conversation with T. Brodetskaia, November 1982.

    Several years later, in 1966, ex-prisoner Leonid Rutshtain (see above) also asked Rabbi Levin where to find a Hebrew teacher. Rabbi Levin pointed out an elderly Jew and Rutshtain studied Hebrew with him in a quiet corner of the synagogue—A. Rotem to the author, October 6, 1982.
47. L. Ontman to the author, November 12, 1982; testimony of L. Ontman in the PZA Archives; and author's conversation with A. Brand of Kiev, December 1, 1982. Liliia heard of Brand from friends in Kiev.
48. Tsirul'nikov, an electrical engineer, was born in 1910 in Belorussia. Although he had studied in *heder* as a boy he had forgotten the Hebrew he had learnt. From the mid-fifties he began visiting the Oriental Department of the Saltykov-Shchedrin Library which had a collection of Israeli books, including Hebrew textbooks.

    Aleksandr Tsadikov was born in 1938 in Leningrad. He taught himself Yiddish from books in the Saltykov-Shchedrin Library and in 1959, in his continued quest for his roots, he began to take an interest in Hebrew. He found in the library Pevsner's Russian-Hebrew dictionary and *Elef millim*. Every time he visited the library he copied out a lesson or two and eventually took out Israeli newspapers (*Kol ha'am* and *Lamathil*), as well as prerevolutionary books and newspapers. Although most of the readers in the Oriental Department were older people who tended to keep to themselves, the use of similar materials brought Tsadikov and Tsirul'nikov together and the former found his way to Tsirul'nikov's study circle—N. Tsirul'nikov to the author, December 5, 1982; Shoshana Zusman-Epshtain to the author, January 31, 1982; and A. Tsadikov to the author, November 19, 1982.
49. The two young men came to the Lur'es by chance in 1958. Butman had met Rosa (Shoshana) Zusman-Epshtain outside the synagogue on Simhat Torah and heard her talking about Israel, and she took him to Liia—Gilel' Butman, *Leningrad-Ierusalim s dolgoi peresadkoi* (Leningrad-Jerusalem With a Long Stopover, Rus), henceforth Butman, *Leningrad-Jerusalem* (Tel Aviv: Sifriyat Aliya, 1981), pp. 70–71 and 74.

50. Author's conversation with H. (formerly G.) Butman, April 6, 1982.
51. Author's interview with a Soviet immigrant who has asked to remain anonymous, February 10, 1982.
52. Z. Mohilever to the author, November 4, 1982, and Isai Sheinkar', "Iz noveishei istorii," (Recent History, Rus.), *Zemliaki*, Izdanie soiuza zemliachestv vykhodtsev iz SSSR, Tel Aviv, March 1981, p. 5. For Shapiro and his work, see *Evreiskii samizdat*, vols. 17 and 19. His dictionary *(Ivrit-russkii slovar')* was published in 1963 by Gosudarstvennoe izdatel'stvo inostrannykh i natsional'nykh slovarei. There were plans, following the publication of this dictionary, for a companion Russia-Hebrew dictionary to be edited by Rubinshtain, Zand, and Churlin of the Soviet Foreign Ministry Near Eastern Department who had served with the Soviet embassy in Tel Aviv and knew some Hebrew. The project was, however, never implemented—conversation of Yaacov Ro'i with M. Zand, January 23, 1984.
53. Author's interview with Y. Mintz, January 5, 1982.
54. Mintz received books from Israel as early as 1963.
55. M. Zand received Hebrew books from the Israel delegation to the World Youth Festival. E. Valk was given Hebrew study books and records by relatives from Israel who visited Riga in the 1960s—author's conversation with M. Zand, July 3, 1982, and interview of Y. Ro'i with E. Valk, January 6, 1976.
56. Boris Podol'skii and Iakov Gruntfest brought two or three Hebrew textbooks published in the GDR—author's interview with B. Podolsky and Y. Gruntfest to the author, October 7, 1982.
57. Among those who listened regularly to Hebrew broadcasts from Israel were Vladimir Zaretskii, Liia Levin, Gil'ia Butman, and Liliia Ontman. Mikhail Agurskii of Moscow, who began to study Hebrew in 1964 from Shlomo Kodesh's *Hasafa haivrit* (The Hebrew Language, Heb.) (see following note) which he received from an acquaintance, was also helped by the Israeli radio's Hebrew lessons—author's conversation with M. Agurskii, March 1982 and Agurskii to the author, December 13, 1982. Hebrew lessons began to be broadcast by the "Voice of Israel" in the early 1960s. In the course of time three courses were given, two prepared by Mordekhai Ben Sever for beginners and one by Shmuel Segal at a more advanced level. Each lesson lasted fifteen to twenty minutes and the whole course would last one year—Viktor Grajevski to the author, October 17, 1982.
58. Y. Malkin to the author, October 17, 1982. Malkin, like Tsadikov (see note 48), started by learning Yiddish (in 1955). In 1959, he received a Hebrew calendar from which he was able to learn Hebrew vocalization or pointing; the Hebrew letters represent consonants, the vowel sounds being rendered by signs accompanying each letter, usually beneath the letter. Malkin continued his study of Hebrew from Shlomo Kodesh's *Hasafa haivrit* which he obtained in 1966.

In 1961, Kodesh had been asked by Shaul Avigur to compile a Hebrew-language textbook for Jews in the USSR. The book was published in 1963 by

Kiryat Sefer (Jerusalem). Kodesh reports writing this book with a sense of a special mission—author's conversation with S. Kodesh, November 22, 1982.
59. David Garber to the author, November 21, 1982; see also note 17 above.
60. Interview of Y. Ro'i with E. Valk, January 6, 1976.
61. Author's conversation with Y. Guri (Ia. Gurevich), April 29, 1982.
62. David Garber to the author, November 21, 1982.
63. Ester Lomovskaia to the author, December 23, 1982. (Esfir Shmerler married Vol't Lomovskii after the death of her first husband.)
64. Author's interview with N. Ilishaev, February 4, 1982.
65. Author's interview with Gershon Ben-Oren (Tsitsuashvili), May 3, 1976. The interview appeared in *Hainteligentsia hayehudit bivrit hamoatzot* (Jewish Intelligentsia in the Soviet Union, Heb.), vol. 3, 1979, pp. 26–35.
66. Author's interview with Emma Graiver-Khudaidutova, February 1978.
67. Interview with Y. Shnaider, interviewer unknown, May 21, 1974.
   Vaisman was the author of a series of letters on the situation of Soviet Jewry that were smuggled out of the country in the mid-1950s; see Yaacov Ro'i, "The Role of the Synagogue and Religion in the Jewish National Awakening" in this volume, note 32.
68. Author's conversation with Mendel Kublanov, January 26, 1982.
69. Author's interview with B. Podolsky. Other pupils of Meir Draznin were Zhenia Bukhina and Anatolii Gerenrot, also of Kiev. Bukhina recalls that Draznin had a profound knowledge of Hebrew. After his release from camp he lived in permanent fear but nevertheless resumed teaching the language with the help of Kodesh's book which Zhenia received from the writer Zefania Kipnis—Zh. Bukhina to the author, November 17, 1982.
70. A. Rubin, "Moi put' v Izrail' " (see note 45).
71. Interview of Y. Alperovich with S. Dolnik, March 1974, Yad Vashem, Givatayim, no. 3789.
72. Author's interview with M. Goldblatt, March 11, 1982.
73. Ibid.
74. *Evreiskii samizdat*, vol. 15, p. 92; author's interview with Valerii Kukui, August 22, 1976; and E. Lomovskaia to the author, November 4, 1983. Lomovskaia has told how the first *ulpan* in Novosibirsk began, in 1969, on the initiative of the Lomovskii-Shmerler family, in whose home Israeli songs played on the tape recorder from morning to night. Its first teacher was Iz'ia (Izrail') Shmerler, a young man (son of Esfir Lomovskaia by her first marriage) who had learned Hebrew from his grandfather (see above). When he left for Israel his place was taken by Esfir's husband, Vol't Lomovskii, although he knew only a little more Hebrew than his pupils, until his own *aliya* in 1971. One person who studied Hebrew in Novosibirsk was Natan Pol'tinnikov, "Iyov minovosibirsk" (The Job from Novosibirsk, Heb.), *La'isha*, September 27, 1981.
75. Mikhail Goldblatt received Hebrew literature in the post in the early 1970s— author's interview with M. Goldblatt, March 11, 1982.

76. The jamming of Hebrew broadcasts began in 1969 when, following the letter of the eighteen Georgian Jewish families, the question of Soviet Jewry began to be discussed on the air. In previous years it had been Israeli policy not to touch on this issue directly. At first, jamming was selective both in time and place, and was especially strong in Moscow and Leningrad. In 1970 jamming became general and affected broadcasts in Russian, Yiddish, Georgian, Judaeo-Tadzhik, and Hebrew. The "Voice of Israel" made great efforts to overcome the jamming (by use of a powerful shortwave center and with numerous transmitters and frequencies) with varying degrees of success—V. Grajevski to the author. So important were these broadcasts to Soviet Jews that the painter Iosif Kuzskovskii painted a picture, entitled "33.3," portraying a Jew spellbound by the radio; 33.3 was the frequency used for the transmission of broadcasts from Israel to the Soviet Union—author's conversation with Eli Valk, June 7, 1982.
77. Author's interview with M. Goldblatt, March 11, 1982. This view was held, among others, by Vladimir (Dan) Roginskii, Evgenii Deborin, and Mikhail Gol'dblatt.
78. This view was held by Pavel Abramovich, Iosif Begun, Vladimir Prestin, and others (see above).
79. Interview of Yaacov Ro'i with S. Blank, August 8, 1982.
80. Butman, *Leningrad-Jerusalem*, pp. 115–16.
81. From lecture by Ze'ev Mohilever, "Hebrew Lessons in the Sixties" at a CRD symposium on "Jewish Samizdat in the Soviet Union," October 16, 1980.
82. Author's interview with Yisrael Mintz, January 5, 1982.
83. Mohilever, "Hebrew Lessons."
84. Butman, *Leningrad-Jerusalem*, p. 123.
85. Author's interview with Y. Abramson, November 25, 1982.
86. From lecture by Y. Palhan, "The Study of Hebrew in the Soviet Union" at a CRD symposium on "The Situation of Jewish Culture in the Soviet Union—Present and Future," January 11, 1979.
87. V. Shakhnovskii, "Advice on Methods of Studying Hebrew (For Beginners)," *Evreiskii samizdat*, vol. 17, pp. 81–84.
88. Author's interview with M. Goldblatt, March 11, 1982.
89. *Evreiskii samizdat*, vol. 17, pp. 128–29.
90. Ibid., p. 116. Besides the minister of culture and Gramplastinok, Roginskii wrote to the director of the Office for the Export and Import of Books, and to the director of the Central Soiuzpechat' Agency for Foreign Publications.
91. Ibid., pp. 122–23.
92. Ibid., pp. 112–41.
93. L. Ul'ianovskii, "Hebrew in the Soviet Union," in *The Jewish Intelligentsia in the USSR*, vol. 4 (Tel Aviv: Scientists Committee of the Israeli Public Council for Soviet Jewry, 1980), pp. 173–76.
94. *Evreiskii samizdat*, vol. 17, pp. 133–36.
95. Author's interview with V. Kukui, August 22, 1976.

96. Author's interview with M. Lifshits, November 4, 1983.
97. Author's interview with N. Moredin, February 17, 1977. In 1971 Khazin received a copy of *Mori* from a Swiss tourist, and from then on spent some five hours a day studying Hebrew. His friend Iz'ia Krasnov, teacher of an *ulpan*, examined him and found he had reached a level that enabled him to teach. When Krasnov left for Israel, Khazin replaced him—interview of Y. Averbukh with M. Khazin, September 1, 1977.
98. Author's conversation with Shaul Beilinson, April 21, 1982. In Mukachevo the first *ulpan* that was opened was short-lived. Mikhail Klainbart had received a number of copies of *Elef millim* from Moscow, and he and his brother began learning Hebrew from their father. Once Mikhail felt he was in a position to pass on his knowledge, he opened a Hebrew circle in 1972. It stopped functioning, however, when its three or four pupils left for Israel—author's conversation with Rivka Aleksandrovich, April 30, 1982.
99. Author's conversation with Rivka Aleksandrovich, April 30, 1982.
100. Zh. Bukhina to the author, November 17, 1982.
101. Testimony of Arkadii Voloshin in PZA Archives.
102. Author's interview with N. Al'shansky, April 19, 1982.
103. Palhan, "The Study of Hebrew," and author's interview with M. Goldblatt, March 11, 1982.

8
Nehama Lifshitz: Symbol of the Jewish National Awakening
Yaacov Ro'i

The last vestiges of Soviet Jewish culture which had survived the vicissitudes first of the 1930s and then of World War II were eliminated by the Soviet authorities in 1948–49. In a major campaign that was intended to deprive Soviet Jewry of even those tokens of national culture endorsed by the Soviet nationalities policy, and in effect to outlaw the Soviet Jewish national minority from the Soviet comity of nations, Yiddish publications (press and literature) were discontinued and theatrical and other public performances banned.[1]

It was only in the mid-fifties that a number of Yiddish actors and singers surfaced once more. At first they were allowed to appear in a very few public performances in a number of cities with large Jewish populations. Despite the poor quality of both the artists themselves and the programs they were permitted to present to their audiences, these performances invariably drew a full house. Tickets would be sold out as soon as the posters announcing the event were displayed and the audiences would include not only older-generation Jews who understood Yiddish but also youngsters curious for a glimpse of their national folklore.[2]

This chapter will focus on the struggle of the best-known of these artists to give her public as much of its national culture as Soviet conditions permitted and will attempt to evaluate her impact on the Jewish national awakening in the Soviet Union. Nehama Lifshitz, or Lifshitzaite as she was known, was born in Kaunas (Kovno) prior to the Soviet annexation of the Baltic states. During World War II she was evacuated to Uzbekistan where she became a member of the Komsomol and later of the Soviet Communist party. In 1946 she and her family returned to Kaunas, and in 1951 she completed her studies at the Vilnius Music Academy. (The Kaunas and Vilnius conservatories had been amalgamated in 1949.) While the majority of Yiddish artists had received their training mostly in Yiddish-language schools or institutes, and begun their careers before the war, Nehama was a product of the postwar period, of a time when there was no longer a possibility to train in Yiddish except at the Yiddish State Theater (Goset) in Moscow.[3] She began her career as a singer in a variety of Soviet languages —Lithuanian, Ukrainian, Uzbek, as well, of course, as Russian. From the beginning of her career in 1949 and until her emigration to Israel in 1969, her performances took place under the auspices of the Lithuanian SSR Philharmonic Society *(filarmoniaa)*; every singer in the USSR who did not teach in an educational institution had to be connected either with a theater or a philharmonic society. In 1955, in the period of the "thaw" that followed Stalin's death, Nehama Lifshitz began to prepare a program of Yiddish songs, an idea that was first put to her by a former Yiddish actor, Mark Braudo.[4] This was the beginning of a career that within a few years catapulted her into the center of the Jewish national movement and made her in many ways its focus, its symbol, and its heroine.

Nehama insists that her urge to sing in Yiddish seemed natural to her and to the members of her generation in the Baltic republics, who had been raised on Jewish culture and for whom Palestine and the places and people described in the Bible and throughout Jewish history were a part of themselves. They felt themselves to be a branch of the ancient tree of the Jewish people, unlike many of their contemporaries in those parts of the country which had belonged to the Soviet Union since the 1917 Revolution and who were only now rediscovering their "roots." Moreover, Nehama's desire to sing in Yiddish was regarded with understanding by the Lithuanians with whom she came into contact in the Philharmonic Society, in the Ministry of Culture, and even in the party establishment, including as prominent a figure as the Lithuanian party first secretary, Antanas Snieckus.[5]

At first, Nehama's intentions were primarily artistic. Although Yiddish culture was rich and variegated in both its literature and its songs, she felt that the Yiddish stage and the artists who began reappearing during the "thaw" did not always do it justice. She wanted to perform in Yiddish with the same professional virtuosity as she performed in other languages. She also decided to model her performances on the pattern she had learned during her studies: the first part of the program would be classical, the second made up of folk songs. At the outset, she sought to take into account three factors: the ignorance of Yiddish of at least some of her audience; the need to convey the Jewish content of her songs; and the restrictions placed by the regime on all Soviet performances.

Having virtually no knowledge of or access to Jewish songs—Nehama's own immediate contact with Jewish culture had come to an end with the Soviet "liberation" of Lithuania in 1940 and, needless to say, there was no possibility of acquiring Jewish music literature in the USSR in the mid-1950s—Braudo sent her to Moscow to the two Yiddish composers, Samuil' (Shaul) Senderei, who had just returned from a long period of imprisonment and exile, and Lev Pulver, who had been for many years the musical director at the Moscow Yiddish State Theater. The former agreed to harmonize eighteen songs for her for which the Jewish director of the Lithuanian Philharmonic Society, Balis Fedorovich, agreed that the Philharmonic Society should pay. From Pulver, Nehama ordered parts of "Shulamith," Shmuel Halkin's "Bar Kokhba," and Sholem Aleichem's "Shir hashirim" (The Song of Songs). She received the blessing of the Yiddish singer Moyshe (Mikhail) Apelbaum, then recuperating in a sanatorium at Druskenniki in Lithuania, and moral encouragement and sometimes actual help from the few Yiddish writers who were in Vilnius in the mid-1950s, in particular Hirsh Osherovich and Yosef Kotlyar.

Her first performance in Yiddish in Vilnius in March 1956 included a Yiddish translation of Rosina's aria in "The Barber of Seville," an Indian aria (of the Lakme tribe), and then "Bar Kokhba" and the "Song of Songs." In her early performances, Nehama also sang Verdi's "Violetta" in Yiddish, as well as some of Rimsky-Korsakov's romances, but later she was reluctant, as she put it, to waste valuable time on the Russian and other classics, and she sought to increase that part of the program devoted to Yiddish poets and writers. When she did occasionally sing a song in Lithuanian or Russian, it would have some additional implication for her audiences, for example, Dmitrii Pokras's "Warm Lands."[6]

In 1956 Nehama made her first appearance in the Latvian and Lithuanian Republics—in Riga, Daugavpils (Dvinsk), and Dzintari (a resort near Riga) in Latvia, and in Vilnius, Kaunas, and Klaipeda (Memel) in Lithuania—as well as in Leningrad, where she appeared in April with Veniamin Khaiatovskii in three successive concerts in one of Leningrad's most prestigious theaters. Toward the end of the year she also performed in Soviet Central Asia, in Uzbekistan—Tashkent, Samarkand, Namangan,

Andizhan, Kokand, Fergana, and Bukhara, cities in which Nehama found a "fine Jewish world"—and in Tadzhikistan (Dushanbe and Leninabad). Her tours were arranged (in return for the income of every third concert) by a Leningrad impresario, Lev Ravinov, who decided which cities she would appear in. In the following year, 1957, her tours extended to additional Union Republics: Estonia (Tallinn and Tartu), the RSFSR (Kaliningrad, Sovetsk, Chernikhovsk, and again, Leningrad), and Belorussia (the major Jewish centers except Minsk).

This was a significant achievement for both Nehama personally and for the cause of Yiddish "concerts," as such performances were called, and further successes soon followed. Early in 1958 Nehama won an all-Soviet prize for variety *(estradnyi)* artists in Moscow. The Lithuanian authorities tried to prevent her taking part in the competition by insisting, among other things, that she perform at least partly in Lithuanian. She was, however, encouraged to appear in Yiddish by Lithuanian People's Artist Aleksandra Staskaviciute and the Soviet Laureate singer Irma Iaunzem, who specialized in the folk songs of the smaller Soviet national minorities and had herself performed Yiddish songs. Nehama's actual appearance in the competition was made possible, in her own view, by the fact that no previous announcement was made of her intention to sing Yiddish songs.

Shortly after this success, on 12 and 13 May 1958, she appeared for the first time in the Soviet capital with a concert of her own. One of the performances during the competition had been open to the public, and word had gotten around among the surviving Yiddish cultural figures that there was a new star. All these figures, who had been left without professional work, and with no theater, journal, newspaper, or publishing house, came to Nehama's Moscow concerts, including Shmuel Halkin, the most important survivor of the cultural elite that had been arrested in 1948–49. They came backstage after the first performance where the daughter of Mikhoels, the founder of the Moscow Yiddish State Theater, told Nehama that she must continue the work of the generation of giants who had been cut down in their prime. The widows of Dovid Bergelson, Itzik Fefer, Der Nister, Perets Markish, Binyomin Zuskin, and Mikhoels brought her bouquets. In Nehama's own words, she became the tombstone of a nonexistent grave. Although in that year she appeared in fewer republics—Latvia, Lithuania, the RSFSR, and the Ukraine—she reached a number of towns in the two latter republics, in which over 75 percent of the Soviet Jewish population lived.

The great breakthrough came in 1959 when the hundredth anniversary celebration of the birth of the Yiddish writer Sholem Aleichem was celebrated. The Soviet authorities marked the centenary by permitting a relatively large number of Yiddish concerts, including performances by Emanuel Kaminka and Emil Gurvich. Nehama appeared in all the Union Republics except Georgia and Armenia (she was not to appear in Georgia until 1966). In Moscow she appeared in a concert to commemorate the centenary, along with leading Soviet artists and the American black singer Paul Robeson who sang, among other things, the anthem of the Jewish partisans. In the Ukraine she appeared in the major cities, including Chernovtsy (Czernowicz), Kharkov, and—in December—Kiev (see below). In Kharkov the demand was so great that the number of her performances was doubled (from four to eight) and the police called in to maintain order. There were still difficulties, however, although sometimes Nehama, as a Party member, was able to overcome them by turning directly, over the heads of the cultural establishment, to the local party officials: for example, when a scheduled performance in Smolensk was canceled on the grounds that it was too nationalistic, Nehama appealed to the Party authorities and was given permission to appear. On one occasion in Vilnius itself she was asked to announce that she could not appear due to illness, but she refused to comply and the concert took place. In Minsk, however, Belorussian Party Secretary for Propaganda Timofei Gorbunov categorically banned her from performing, despite the Sholom Aleichem celebrations. He was unmoved by the plea that it was necessary to disprove stories that Yiddish was prohibited in Minsk, the capital of Belorussia and the Belorussian town with the largest Jewish population. There was no place in Minsk, he said, for either gypsies or Jews. In Vinnitsa, too, part of her program was cut since her repertoire allegedly evoked undesirable nationalist, reactionary sentiment. While in Kiev she was summoned before a special Party committee to be told that the content of her concerts was unsuited to Soviet reality: not only were there no songs about Sputniks in her repertoire, but the nostalgia for the Jewish past was foreign to Jews who had grown up on Soviet culture. Indeed, following her first performance in Kiev, she was prevented from performing her usual programs for over half a year and obliged to appear with Soviet songs in Lithuanian, Russian, and Yiddish. Minister of Culture Nikolai Mikhailov informed all the Soviet republics that her performances were to be banned since her repertoire was "Zionist," "nationalist," and "decadent," and had a "negative effect on Soviet citizens." This was the general tenet of the argument the authorities used against her, namely that her songs and repertoire were chosen to suit her personal taste rather than the desires of her public. They preferred to ignore the fact that the size and enthusiasm of her audiences throughout the country belied this charge.

In 1959 and 1960 Nehama Lifshitz was sent abroad to demonstrate to the outside world that Yiddish culture was flourishing, or at least permitted, in the USSR: she appeared in Paris in March 1959, in Vienna in May 1959, and again in Paris, as well as in Brussels and Antwerp, in February 1960. In Paris in 1959 she was the only Soviet artist in her group who did not perform a single item in Russian. Her repertoire, moreover, was composed entirely of Jewish songs and not merely Yiddish versions of Russian songs. She clearly demonstrated her own nationalist sentiments and protested the official Soviet attitude to Yiddish culture.

In the following decade, until 1969, when she emigrated to Israel, there were years in which Nehama Lifshitz appeared more frequently and in more places, and years in which she was somewhat restricted. Generally, it was not easy for her to get permission to go to towns with a large Jewish population such as Kiev or Odessa. One friend who was closer to her from 1958 is convinced that the authorities wanted her to go to towns with few Jews to prove that there was no demand for Jewish culture.[7]

Nehama, for her part, sought to reach every place in the USSR where there might be Jews and bring them a taste of something Jewish. Indeed, there was hardly an important town in which she did not appear at one time or another during this period—from Kaliningrad to Birobidzhan and Khabarovsk, and from Murmansk to Dushanbe. In some cities, even outside Lithuania and Latvia, she would appear regularly every year, and sometimes even several times a year, notably in Moscow and Leningrad. And in response, the Jews would come to hear her, whatever the weather and whatever kind of hall or club she was performing in. Occasionally, in places where there was little or no Jewish consciousness, let alone activity, and where Nehama was not known, just a few score would come to hear her.[8] But usually, especially in the major centers and towns she had been to before, the halls were packed.

Her first performance in the Jewish centers of the Ukraine, both the big towns and the old, traditional smaller townships, in the fall and winter of 1959, and particularly in Kiev in December, made Nehama Lifshitz aware that her "concerts" were not only cultural events, but "happenings" of great nationalist significance, and a major instrument in arousing Jewish sentiment. In Odessa she had "southern, warm Yiddish-speaking audiences" and her concerts turned into demonstrations with speeches and greetings from the stage, and a festive atmosphere. In a letter to the orientalist geographer, Eliezer Gordonov, written in Nikolaev in September 1959, Nehama described how the large audiences she had had in Chernovtsy and Kishinev had made her feel as though she had been given wings. "It is impossible to describe the words. I only wish that one hundredth of all the good wishes that were showered on us is fulfilled. . . . I fear I am not worthy of this great success."[9] Her audiences demanded not only Yiddish but *Yiddishkeit* (Jewish content), and she was perceived not merely as a singer but as the bearer of a message. Made conscious of her responsibility as the personification of a great and awesome mission, Nehama lived for an entire decade haunted by visions and symbols—from biblical prophets to Soviet Jewish cultural martyrs—that became part of her.

Nehama would put together her program, in her words, "like a chemist, or perhaps an alchemist." Seeking to bring her Jewish, national message to her audiences without aggravating the censor,[10] she accompanied her songs with elaborate movements of her hands and body to help convey the meaning of her songs to those who knew no Yiddish. As one fan, himself a man with considerable artistic talent, has said, Nehama developed a special genre of her own. Being a natural actress, she transformed every song into a sketch, a miniature play that portrayed the Jewish culture she had absorbed in her childhood. Thus her performances became a dramatic presentation of the history of the Yiddish, and to an extent even of the Hebrew, culture of Eastern Europe. Hava Edelman of Moscow, who had been an actress in the Hebrew theater Habima in the 1920s and normally avoided Yiddish concerts because she thought them amateurish, would never miss Nehama's performances and saw her as a real star.[11] Nehama's programs included old Yiddish melodies, often with new adaptations by Soviet Jewish composers and writers—Perets Markish, Leyb Kvitko, Dovid Hofshteyn, Shmuel Halkin. But everything she used, whether classic or folklore, was presented in such a way as to stir up the long-suppressed Jewish sentiments that the older generation still harbored, and remind them of the destroyed *shtetls,* of their childhood homes, and the traditions and stories on which they had grown up; and to remind the younger generation of the horrors of the Holocaust and its implications for the Jewish people, and to arouse their curiosity about the Jewish past.

Early in 1959 Nehama Lifshitz took a very bold step—to sing in

Hebrew, a language that was in effect totally prohibited. Foiling the censor by asking no questions, she simply included Hebrew songs in her program. On March 4, in a concert held in the large Leninskii Komsomol Theater in Moscow (approximately 1,200 seats), within the framework of the Sholem Aleichem celebrations, Nehama, in the role of the singer Reizele in Sholem Aleichem's "Wandering Stars," sang a number of songs in Israeli Hebrew,[12] "Ani havatselet hasharon," "Hinakh yafa re'ayati," and "Hamavdil." The house was packed, people sitting on the steps in the aisles and in the orchestra stand. Nehama was called upon to sing many of her songs a second time and to prolong the program. Thus, for the first time since the Habima Theater Company had left the USSR in 1927, the Hebrew language was heard on the Soviet stage.[13] Following the excitement aroused by this first concert, which was enhanced by encounters of Moscow Jews with Israeli diplomats who attended the event and as many of Nehama's subsequent performances as they could (see below), the second concert, scheduled for March 8, was canceled. Two further concerts were held in smaller halls (that held 500 and 700, respectively) on March 10 and 11.

Hebrew now became an important element in Nehama's performances, especially from 1964 onward. In February 1964, she appeared in Moscow with a new repertoire, including in the program, "an Oriental Arab tune, words by Zalman Shneur in the Hebrew original, 'Yad anuga hayeta li,' " as the song was described in a book of songs and adaptations by Mikhail Gnesin published in the USSR in 1924, that Nehama had found among her music books. She continued with four songs by the poet Haim Nahman Bialik in Yiddish and concluded with the Hebrew folk song "Eli, eli, lama azavtani" (My God, My God, Why Have You Abandoned Me?), which brought the audience to a pitch of excitement with the final verse: Judaism's central declaration of faith—the "Shema yisrael"—"Hear O Israel, God is our Lord, God Is One." Nehama has called her new program "a careful beginning for breaking down the walls." She also made considerable use of the anthology of "progressive" Israeli verse published in the USSR in Russian by the Israeli communist writer Alexander Pen, which included his own "Adama admati," the poetess Rahel's "Veulai," and Avraham Shlonsky's "Harei Gilboa."[14] The Hebrew songs she sang often became material for the teaching of the Hebrew language with the opening of *ulpanim* in the latter half of the 1960s.[15]

Nehama usually prepared her programs herself. Occasionally she consulted with her friend Gordonov, with whom she had become acquainted at her first Moscow performance in May 1959, until his emigration to Israel in 1964, or with her father, Yehuda Hirsh Lifshitz. From another friend, Eliezer Podriadchik, she learnt much about Yiddish culture and folklore. She received ideas, inspiration, and encouragement from the surviving Yiddish writers and composers with whom she was in contact. In addition to Osherovich and Kotlyar in Vilnius, these included particularly Halkin, Pulver,[16] and Lev Kagan, who helped her adapt old Jewish songs from records and recordings, the Yiddish poet and writer Yosef Kerler, who had in his possession texts of songs which he let Nehama use, and Motl Saktsier.[17] In fact, through her performances she came into direct contact with most of the surviving Yiddish cultural world, not only in Moscow, Riga, and Vilnius but also in other towns. To her first performance in Kiev came the Yiddish writer Itzik Kipnis, the poetess Riva (Rivka) Balasnaia, and the widow of Dovid Hofshteyn, Feige. In Moscow the daughter of Solomon Mikhoels invited her to appear at an evening held at the Actors' House late in 1960 to commemorate the seventieth anniversary of Mikhoels's birth, together with the cellist Mstislav Rostropovich, the singer Sergei Kozlovskii, and the pianist Iakov Flier.

At the beginning Nehama would appear with another singer, at first Ino Topper (who had studied with her) until he left the Soviet Union early in 1957 with the Polish repatriation of 1956–59, and then Veniamin Khaiatovskii; later, when she was persuaded by the singer Mikhail Aleksandrovich that she could carry the evening alone, she would appear simply with a pianist and an announcer who read out a Russian summary of the songs. Sometimes the Russian summary was met with cries of "Yiddish, Yiddish! Why Russian? We understand Yiddish." For every song, in Yiddish and Hebrew, she would write out her own version, in order to adapt the song to the circumstances in which she was performing and the message she was seeking to transmit.

On various occasions when she was being interrogated by the KGB, she was asked why the words were written in her handwriting between the lines of the notes. Indeed, she had constant trouble with the authorities:[18] there would always be someone at her concerts ready to explain to the authorities what in fact Nehama was doing and what the words meant. (The informers were not always precise: for example, the "Hear O Israel, God is our Lord, God is One" was translated by them as "Hear, O State of Israel . . .") She would do her best to correct misunderstandings, although she herself knew little Hebrew and had had to learn painstakingly the meaning of what she was singing. However, for the most part, it was not the Hebrew language itself that disturbed the censor. (Nehama actually performed in Hebrew at an evening at the Writers' House in Moscow in January 1966, organized by the Writers' Union to commemorate the seventy-fifth anniversary of the birth of the Yiddish writer of children's stories, Leyb Kvitko.) It was the content of her songs that troubled the authorities. Thus, Alexander Pen's anthology which included the poets Rahel, Yaacov Fichman, and Avraham Shlonsky caused no difficulties. On the other hand, "when I wanted to sing Ravel's *Kaddish,* I was prevented from appearing." Popular Yiddish songs, too, were often taken out of her repertoire, to be replaced by songs in Russian or Lithuanian. Objection was taken to Itzik Manger, Bialik, and others whom Nehama insisted upon singing as the Jewish classics, comparable to Tolstoy, Pushkin, or Gorky who, as she constantly maintained, were performed freely, even though they also were not representatives of the Russian proletariat. Throughout the 1960s, as in earlier years, she would be told that her songs alienated the Jews from contemporary reality: instead of trying to wring tears from them, she should sing about peace and the free Jewish life in the Soviet Union. Nonetheless, the official position was not consistent even on this point. Israeli diplomats who in 1965 visited Frunze, the capital city of the Kirgiz SSR, were greeted with a forty-five-minute radio broadcast of one of Nehama's concerts, including "My God, My God."[19]

Although she appeared alone, Nehama had contacts with other Yiddish performing artists in Moscow and Riga and, in particular, with the singer Siddi Tal in Chernovtsy and her husband, Pinhas Falik, who was director of the Philharmonic Orchestra there. Whenever Nehama's performances were stopped by the authorities Falik would help her start again in Chernovtsy. In addition, Nehama was in contact with the Yiddish amateur drama groups that came into being, some for only very short periods, in different centers: the Vilnius and Kaunus collectives, the Riga drama group and choir conducted by Izrail' Abramis (a violin teacher), the Leningrad amateur group, and later the Kishinev and Tallinn collectives. She would send them the music for their repertoires which was normally unobtainable in the USSR and, as we have seen, had usually been especially adapted for her concerts. Toward the end of 1960 Nehama even appeared with the Riga choir at two concerts (in the university auditorium and at a radio plant) with the permission of the Vilnius Philharmonic authorities: the choir had achieved, in her view, a professional level.

Nehama thought that there was perhaps no special need for her performances in Vilnius where Jews spoke Yiddish openly and sang Hebrew songs at home. This was not, however, the opinion of her audiences. Her tours of Lithuanian and Latvian towns moreover, usually included "happenings" in private homes at which dozens of Jews would take the opportunity to sing together. At her first concerts in Riga she met local Yiddish cultural activists—the actors Eines Feivel Aronas and Dina Roitkop, and Dina's husband, Eliezer Podriadchik (see above). Later on, in the 1960s Nehama also established contact with a group of Rigan Jews who on their own initiative were photographing writings of Zionist leaders and other materials they had received from Israel and disseminating them throughout the USSR. Thus she met with Lidiia (Leah) Slovina who was responsible for dissemination, Iosif Shnaider, the photographer, as well as Miriam and David Garber, Mark Blum, and David Zil'berman.[20] Shnaider asked Nehama to transmit to the Israeli embassy the addresses of the new camps for political prisoners in Mordovia and Karaganda, where there were Zionists from both the Stalin and the Khrushchev periods. Shnaider wanted these addresses to be passed on to the International Red Cross so that these prisoners could be sent parcels, including *matzot* for Passover and feel they were not forgotten.

Nehama found a very different situation in other parts of the country. In most places there was no evidence of even a remnant of Jewish culture. At first her audiences usually comprised mostly older people, but, as time passed, more and more young people would attend—although at her first performance in Moscow the audience already included a notable number of young people. Those who understood no Yiddish were helped by their friends or relatives, who translated the songs into Russian, as well as by Nehama's own movements as she acted out her songs. Yet, the actual content of the song was mostly secondary to the experience of a direct—and often initial—encounter with living Jewish culture enhanced by Nehama's moving and sensitive performance.

Often after the concerts Nehama would meet the people who came to hear her perform, talk with them, or exchange greetings in Hebrew with the children. With some of them she developed a genuine friendship.[21] The Jews in the various towns she toured would come to her to learn new songs and in the towns she visited regularly her hotel room became a virtual Jewish club, a hub of activity.

In some of these towns she also went to private homes to meet and talk in a more intimate atmosphere. These were homes where very often small momentos of Israel had been carefully preserved, a piece of Bezalel work, a candelabrum, or simply a small piece of wrapping paper from an Elite chocolate bar or a package of Dubek cigarettes. All these "treasures" embodied the deep yearning for Jewish culture and contact with the Jewish world outside—and the Jewish state in particular—that Nehama found everywhere.

The most poignant encounter was her first performance in Kiev (December 1959). Jewish cultural events were very rare in the Ukrainian capital. The large hall was so packed that there was no standing room at all. Nehama concluded her concert with the "Lullaby to Babii Iar" by a Jewish poet from Kiev, Shayke Driz, set to music by Riva Boiarskaia (also of Kiev). Nehama usually sang this particular song last, as she found it difficult to continue singing after it. But to sing about Babii Iar in Kiev was not like singing about it elsewhere. Here no one applauded. The hall seemed to be electrified. The entire audience rose to its feet like one man and stood in absolute silence, in the atmosphere of fear that characterized the Jews of Kiev. In Nehama's words, this was a "curtain of tears." As she left the hall people stood outside, still silently weeping, in order to touch her hand or sleeve as though she were some holy person.[22] After this experience, Nehama could not sleep for nights. She became physically sick, and as she lay in bed and relived that evening over and over, she came to the conclusion that she must give as much as possible to her audiences who were hungry for every word, every inference about the silent Soviet Jewish tragedy. The revolutionary poet Vladimir Maiakovskii had written that "song and verse are bomb and banner." She had learnt that every legal factor that could serve the cause must be exploited. Nehama was applying these teachings with her performances. As she told an audience in Vilnius in January 1961: "I believe and hope that with my songs I am fulfilling a certain mission."[23] For this she won the respect, the love, and the confidence of Jews throughout the USSR, especially the youth. They were not deterred by the fact that after her concerts there would be interrogations and arrests, and that Nehama herself was under open surveillance.[24]

As Nehama became a symbol of their Jewish identity and feelings, many Jews came to her for a kind word or a feeling of hope and encouragement. Even after she made *aliya* to Israel, she would be approached by emigrants from the Soviet Union for whom she continued to represent a source of strength, solace, and warmth in the difficulties of adjusting to a new life.

Many Soviet Jews have borne witness to the considerable influence

Nehama exerted. Her performances were a source of encouragement to Jews already "contaminated" with Zionist inclinations who dreamt of *aliya*. They also lit a spark among those who, while thirsty for Jewish culture and content, had not yet dared to draw any practical conclusions from either their aspirations or their systematic frustration by the Soviet establishment.[25]

Yosef Kerler has described Nehama in these words: other singers evoked a tearful nostalgia for the past, but "Nehama aroused something new. Soviet Jews, especially youngsters, who know nothing about Judaism, let alone Zionism, began to think and to seek. . . . She would sing and suddenly you began to ponder upon your situation, the situation of the Jews in the Soviet Union." In Nehama's songs, "there was a call. This is what made her different from all the others."[26]

Another close friend and admirer, Asher (formerly Aleksandr or Sasha) Blank of Leningrad, calls Nehama a phenomenon which occurs once in a century. It was as though Soviet Jewry was waiting for something without knowing precisely for what. He argues that unless this is understood it is difficult to explain why hundreds of young people thronged to her concerts to hear her singing in a language they did not know. In Blank's view, Nehama was the match that ignited the explosion.[27]

It was, then, not surprising that Nehama was regarded by Jews as their "national singer,"[28] who articulated their national message. As one *aliya* activist has pointed out—each of her concerts was "a demonstration,"[29] an opportunity for celebrating the Jewish national tradition in a milieu where anything connected with Jewish culture and identity was virtually taboo.[30] As the sixties wore on, in the intermission the audiences would dance the *hora* (an Israeli circle dance) in the theater foyer.[31] Nehama's impact was perhaps the greater because she was younger than the other Yiddish performers and talented enough to have gone on the Russian or Lithuanian stage, where she would have been able to achieve much more on the purely professional level. She was probably the only person of her generation in the USSR to take up Jewish music as a profession.

An Israeli delegation to the USSR in 1965 attended one of two concerts she gave in the 1,500—seat Tchaikovsky Hall in Moscow. On the way to the concert, the Israelis noticed how many people were flocking there, and on entering they found the foyer packed with the kind of audience that could be found in Jewish theaters anywhere, except that it included a large number of young people. Inside the hall the atmosphere was tense. Nehama began in Yiddish: a Jewish lullaby, a song about Jewish life, then "Undzer shtetl brent" (Our Small Town is Burning, Yid.) about the Jewish townships that were no more, then Glick's song of the Jewish partisans. A tremor passed through the audience, but they remained quiet, until, all of a sudden she switched to Hebrew, and both she and her audience became transformed. Nehama seemed to have come more intensely alive while at the end of each song the audience applauded wildly for several minutes. Every few minutes someone would make his way to the stage and present Nehama with a bouquet, and the flowers piled up on the piano. Then written requests began arriving on the stage. She would read them out and start a new song. The official program had long been finished, but Nehama continued just as long as she was physically capable of singing. Afterward the Israelis visited her backstage where she was handing out autographs and receiving hugs and kisses. The Israeli ambassador and his wife gave her records with more songs. Nehama had given the Jews of Moscow a rare opportunity to express their feeling of Jewish identity and their longing for Israel and the Hebrew language.[32]

One of the diplomats who served with the Israeli embassy from late 1964 until the severance of relations at the end of the Six-Day War has called Nehama "an institution." By far the most important of the Yiddish artists, she was not only the first to include Hebrew in her programs but she alone persistently refused to pay lip service to the regime by singing songs that smacked of "socialist realism" even if she could not totally avoid singing some Soviet pieces. Although she did not appear in Russian and although most of the younger generation knew neither Yiddish nor Hebrew, she became their idol. In Riga young Jews donated blood in order to buy gold (on the black market) from which they made her a Star of David that they presented to her on a handmade necklace. In the words of Elie Wiesel who attended one of her concerts on his first, 1965, visit to the USSR, she was "the queen of Soviet Jewry." Even the Georgian and Bukharan Jews came to hear her sing and felt that her songs were their songs. When she appeared in Moscow's Tchaikovsky Hall on 30 May 1967, in the days of tension prior to the Six-Day War, with the entire Kaddish by Ravel (not only the tune, but also the words), the audience's ecstasy knew no bounds.[33]

In the early stages of her career, Nehama Lifshitz was criticized by some of the best-known Zionist activists. They claimed that she was in effect serving the interests of the Soviets by demonstrating that it was possible to create a Jewish culture in the USSR, and therefore there was no need for the Jews to go to Israel. One such person was a former Prisoner of Zion, Yehezkel Polarevich. Yet when he actually came to Nehama's performances and heard her explain that the inclusion of a few carefully selected Soviet songs in her program was simply lip service (*gospostavka*), a prerequisite for appearing at all on the Soviet stage—and even these, she hoped, would pass on the message she was seeking to transmit—he became convinced both of Nehama's devotion to her people and of the value of her concerts for the Jewish national awakening, of which the ultimate goal was *aliya* to Israel, and he even gave her new songs. She became for him a "Joan of Arc."[34]

Nehama's concerts were not only the occasion for Soviet Jews to hear Hebrew and Yiddish, get a taste of the Jewish culture for which they yearned, identify with their Jewishness, and give vent to their repressed, national feelings. They also enabled Jews to meet each other and to meet Israeli diplomats and tourists for which there was ordinarily very little opportunity.[35]

These encounters became increasingly common as the 1960s wore on, and helped to break down the barriers of fear and reservation among Jews, especially in Moscow, Riga, and Vilnius. They also enabled Jews to inform each other about other activities. At one of her concerts in Moscow, for instance, a note was passed from hand to hand announcing lessons in Yiddish for adults and children.[36]

An important factor in Nehama's career was her connection with the Israeli embassy. She first met with members of the embassy staff during her first visit to Moscow in 1958, and over the years these contacts deepened until the severance of diplomatic relations between Israel and the Soviet Union in June 1967. The Israeli diplomats gave Nehama records, sheet music, and books—everything she needed for her performances. Her first record of Hebrew songs was given her in Odessa by the Israeli diplomat, Eliyahu Hazan. Nehama, for her part, informed the embassy of her touring plans and the Israeli diplomats who regularly attended her concerts in Moscow tried to attend in other cities as well, as Nehama's performances provided the opportunity they were constantly seeking to meet large numbers of Jews. One of her concerts in Kishinev was canceled even though between six and seven thousand tickets had been sold, because a member of the Israeli embassy and his wife had come for the occasion. Nehama was told specifically that the authorities did not want the Israelis to make contacts with the local Jewish population. Although it was a fine day, the concert was canceled because of "rain." On another occasion in 1960 Nehama's tour to Lvov was postponed so that it would not coincide with the visit to that city of Israeli diplomats. Nehama was able to maintain her contacts with the embassy quite openly because she had been instructed by the Soviet authorities to come close to the Israeli diplomats in order to find out about their contacts with "underground Zionist groupings." Nehama was a party member and regarded herself as a loyal Soviet citizen, but she had always sought to make it clear to the many representatives of Soviet officialdom with whom she came into contact, that she could never betray her own people. The position into which she was gradually placed by the KGB became untenable for her and she made her choice. As she told a KGB official: "I naturally prefer my own mother to yours, just as you prefer yours to mine." Very quickly she came to regard the embassy as the real source of authority for her. She would have defected in Paris in 1959 had she not been told by Israeli diplomats that she should continue with her mission in the USSR. She took this, she recalls, like an order from a superior. Later she was asked by the KGB to refrain from meeting the Israelis.[37] She agreed not to initiate encounters but insisted that she could not prevent them from attending performances or even from coming backstage; nor could she avoid chance meetings.

It was only in the fall of 1966 that Nehama Lifshitz filed her first application to emigrate to Israel. (In this period there was a certain alleviation in what had hitherto been a virtual ban on emigration: in the years 1964–June 1967, some 3,000 Jews left the USSR, most of them from the Baltic republics.) Not surprisingly, as a result of her application, her performances were canceled for several months. In the period immediately after the Six-Day War when she was again prevented from appearing before Jewish audiences—but still obliged to perform—she fulfilled her quota of performances by singing in Yiddish to Lithuanian audiences who would bring her flowers in honor of Israel's victory.

By the fall of 1967, Nehama was appearing as usual. In letters to friends from this period, she told of seven performances in five different Siberian cities within nine days, as well as of tours in Lithuania and the south.[38] In late January 1969 she made her last tour—in Central Asia—although she gave one more, final performance in Moscow, at the Physics Institute, in February. By this time she already had her exit permit and in March she left the USSR.[39]

The Soviet authorities, Nehama thinks in retrospect, made a grave error in allowing her performances. They had planned a purely propaganda role for her, of demonstrating that Jewish culture was flourishing in the Soviet Union, both to make the Soviet Jews content with their lot and to show the world outside that there was no anti-Jewish discrimination in the USSR. (Soviet English-language publications produced and distributed by Soviet embassies in Western capitals carried articles on Nehama from time to time.)[40] Yet, as she puts it, the Soviets failed to take into account that "spark of something Jewish" which the regime strove to suppress but which, in many cases, led Soviet Jews to turn their backs on the USSR and to embark on the difficult struggle for *aliya*. As she looks back on her career and forward to the future of Soviet Jewry, Nehama is convinced of the great need that Soviet Jews will continue to have for Jewish songs. She points out the poignant relevance to the Soviet environment of the biblical commandment: "Take care lest you abandon the Levites." (The Levites were the singers and the musicians in the ancient Temple.) Powerful forces attract the Jews of the USSR to their people and the fact that Jewish culture barely exists does not lessen the strength of that attraction. On the contrary, the lure of forbidden fruit is all the stronger for the youth.

Nehama's career, then, did not only embody a persistent personal struggle and the individual dilemma of presenting Jewish culture in the Soviet Union. It also exemplified the dilemma of the Soviet establishment: the difficulty of allowing the Jews a small, controlled, portion of their culture in order to satisfy foreign visitors, yet without thereby providing Soviet Jews with a focus for all their latent national feelings—the moral support, the anchorage, which they sought and needed, and the ability to identify with a culture they could call their own. Thus, the more talented and sensitive the artists whom the Soviets cultivated to fulfill their purpose and the higher their artistic and human level, the more difficult it was to control them, to limit their appeal to their audience, and to restrain their own yearning for freer expression of their national cultural heritage. Most important, Nehama's career also embodied the national dilemma of Soviet Jews, especially of the young, and the anomaly of their position in the Soviet Union. They were not satisfied by the glimpse of their national culture which Nehama's performances provided. This glimpse merely made them all the more insistent and vociferous in their struggle to find their roots, to implement the right guaranteed by the Soviet Constitution for all ethnic groupings of developing their national culture and studying their national tongue, and also to learn about the Jewish state, where these were the official culture and language, and about the Jewish world outside, where every Jew was free to decide whether to adopt, or reject, his national tradition. Nehama's career had propelled her and many among her audiences to an increasingly nationalist orientation and to the conclusion that only by emigrating could they find the national and cultural fulfillment they sought.

Notes

1. For these trends and events, see Yaacov Ro'i, *Soviet Decision Making in Practice, Soviet-Israeli Relations 1947–54* (New Brunswick, N.J.: Transaction Books, 1980), chapter 7 and 8. For the last Yiddish performances to take place in the Stalin period, see also Benjamin Pinkus, *The Soviet Government and the Jews 1948–1967* (Cambridge: Cambridge University Press, 1984), chapter 7.
2. Roi, *Soviet Decision Making*, p. 492, note 9. For a detailed survey of Jewish cultural activity in the USSR, see Benjamin Pinkus, "Jewish Culture in the USSR, 1939–1967," *Shvut* (Heb.), vol. 3, 1975, pp. 17–34.
3. Nehama told the author that early on in her training she contemplated studying at the Yiddish State Theater in Moscow, but was dissuaded from doing so for reasons of personal security, advice that turned out to be most pertinent.
4. Unless otherwise stated, the source material for this paper has been taken from two interviews of the author with Ms. Lifshitz (in 1976 and 1980); from her reminiscences in Bet Hatefutsot, Tel Aviv University (in/170,7)—reminiscences which unfortunately do not go beyond 1963; and from a talk which Ms. Lifshits gave at a symposium held in Beersheba under the auspices of the Hebrew University's Center for Research and Documentation of East European Jewry (henceforth CRD) on January 11, 1979, to mark the first anniversary of the death of Shaul Avigur.
5. First secretary of the Lithuanian SSR Communist party from 1940 until his death in 1974.
6. Nehama once told Pokras that the anthem of the Jewish partisans was based on his music. Pokras was very moved, telling Nehama that the melody concerned had originally been an adaptation of a Jewish tune.
7. Author's interview with Asher Blank, August 8, 1982.
8. At a performance in Ufa, for example, in the early 1960s, there was just a handful of people—interview of Yisrael Mintz with Yisrael Liast, July 21, 1978 Oral History Division, ([henceforth OHD] 27.129). Nehama herself never knew whether her occasional failure to attract a crowd was the result of a total dearth of Jews in that particular place, or of a Jewish population which had no desire to underline its Jewishness by attending a Jewish concert, or simply of

faulty advertising—the posters announcing her concert night, for instance, omitted to state that she was singing in Yiddish.
9. N. Lifshitz to E. Gordonov, September 21, 1959. (Nehama kindly allowed me to read her letters to Gordonov for the purpose of this chapter.)
10. At the beginning of each year, every Soviet artist draws up his or her programs for the entire year, although the programs, or at least some items, would usually be checked again during the course of the year. While the artist can always shorten his program, it is very difficult to add to it.
11. Author's interview with A. Blank, August 8, 1982.
12. The Hebrew that is used in Europe and America was traditionally spoken with an Ashkenazi accent, while in Israel the Sephardi accent is used, although there are variations within each accent.
13. Nehama's evaluation of the event is undoubtedly correct, although her facts are not totally right: at least one foreign artist, the American Jewish tenor Jan Peerce, had sung in Hebrew in the USSR in 1956.
14. In the years 1964–65 a few books of Israeli prose and verse appeared in the Soviet Union in Russian translation for the first (and until the time of writing —1989—last) time. These books included *Rasskazy izrail'skikh pisatelei* (Stories of Israeli Writers) (Moscow; Progress Publishers, 1965); Aleksandr Pen, *Serdtse v puti* (Journeying Heart) (Moscow; Khudozhestvennaia literatura, 1965); and *Iskatel' zhemchuga* (The Pearl-Diver) (Moscow: Nauka, 1966).
15. Author's interview with A. Blank, August 8, 1982.
16. In a letter to a Leningrad friend she wrote in 1958 that Pulver, who was in Vilnius at the time, was helping her prepare the music for "Wandering Stars" —N. Lifshitz to A. Blank, July 19, 1958. (The letter is in the possession of Dr. Blank.)
17. Author's interview with Yosef and Anna Kerler, April 11, 1983.
18. When Nehama was first summoned to the KGB in 1957 she was told that the KGB's Lithuanian Department reserved for itself the right to interrogate her concerning her meetings and contacts. As early as this she was asked if she wished to appear abroad, and when her tours were being planned and later on her return, there were endless talks and questionings. For KGB pressure on Nehama in connection with the Israeli embassy in Moscow, see below.
19. Author's interview with a former member of the Israeli embassy.
20. Interview with David Zilberman (undated), CRD. (Apparently as a result of a typist's error the name of the interviewer was not recorded.)
21. Author's interview with Boris Gimelfarb.
22. This description of Nehama's first appearance in Kiev is based partly on her own reminiscences and partly on the testimony of Feige Hofstein—author's interview with her, October 10, 1982. In Mrs. Hofstein's words: "The audience was taken by storm by Nehama's appearance. Kiev had awaited her for a long time. And here she was at last, small, young, delicate, with enchanting eyes, a special charm, and singing that was full of expression."
23. Author's interview with Yaakov Sharett, September 8, 1981.

24. One girl, who became friendly with Nehama on KGB orders to report on her activities, told her an interesting story: she had been recruited by the KGB together with a number of other Jewish boys and girls who, during the traditional celebrations held by Moscow's young people on the completion of their ten years' schooling (dancing in Red Square), had danced the *hora* (an Israeli circle dance) and sung Jewish songs. (This was after the 1957 Youth Festival in which an Israeli delegation had participated.) They were released from detention after agreeing to "help the Soviet organs against enemies and nationalists."
25. Author's interview with Eliahu Hoberman, May 14, 1968.
26. Author's interview with Yosef and Anna Kerler, April 11, 1983.
27. Author's interview with A. Blank, August 8, 1982.
28. Interview of Yisrael Mintz with Michael Margulis, March 17, 1968 (OHD, 20.129), p. 13.
29. Author's interview with Meir Gelfond, January 21, 1982. Gelfond, who lived in Moscow from 1958 until he emigrated in 1971, attended all of Nehama's concerts in the Soviet capital.
30. Author's interview with Yosef and Anna Kerler, April 11, 1983.
31. Author's interview with Yosef Khorol, May 13, 1976.
32. *Yediot aharonot,* July 13, 1965.
33. Author's interview with a former member of the Israeli embassy and with Elie Wiesel, May 25, 1983.
34. Author's interview with Y. Polarevich, May 12, 1985.
35. See my chapter "The Role of the Synagogue and Religion in the Jewish National Awakening" in this volume.
36. The Israeli delegation which attended her concert in 1965 found a typewritten copy of the note on their seats at the end of the intermission. It read: "Comrades wishing to learn, or to teach their children, to read and write in spoken Yiddish [sic] are requested to send by mail their home address or telephone number and the age of whomever wishes to learn, to the following address: . . . signed G. M. Gnesin.' The heading of the note read: 'Please sign and pass on to others.' "—*Yediot aharonot,* July 13, 1965.
37. She was made aware of how efficient was the KGB's surveillance of both herself and the members of the Israeli embassy when she was shown photocopies of letters she had given Israeli diplomats on various occasions at the request of Jewish activists and others.
38. N. Lifshitz to A. Blank from Kuibyshev, undated; and to E. Gordonov, September 19 and 26, 1967. In the latter letter to Gordonov, she told of performances in the Lithuanian SSR (Vilnius, Kaunas, Druskenniki, Shavli, Klaipeda) and of an approaching tour—in October—that would include Odessa, Kherson, and the Crimea.
39. In Israel Nehama appeared only rarely. She had sung in the Soviet Union almost as a mission. Once she had arrived in Israel the mission no longer existed. In her own words, she felt like a partizan when the war was over.

Having nothing to sing for, something snapped inside her. Certainly, too, she was physically exhausted after more than a decade of incessant activity. So, she changed her profession and became a librarian in the Tel Aviv municipal music library.

40. E.g., *U.S.S.R.*, August 1960.

III
JEWISH THEMES AND MOTIVES IN OFFICIALLY PUBLISHED LITERATURE

9
Twenty-five Years of *Sovetish heymland:* Impressions and Criticism
Chone Shmeruk

The August 1986 issue of *Sovetish heymland* marked the celebration of the twenty-fifth anniversary of the "literary-artistic" Yiddish monthly published in Moscow under the official auspices of the Soviet Writers' Union. *Sovetish heymland* first appeared in July–August 1961 as a semimonthly journal.

At the end of 1948 the remnants of Jewish culture which had managed to survive World War II and the destruction of the Jews in the Soviet Union were ruthlessly and almost completely liquidated. Many of the Soviet Yiddish writers were arrested. On 12 August 1952, a group which included the leading Yiddish writers in the Soviet Union (among them Dovid Bergelson, Dovid Hofshteyn, Perets Markish, Shmuel Persov, Itzik Fefer, and Leyb Kvitko) were executed under false accusations, while many of their friends were taken to waste away in Soviet prison camps. After the death of Stalin, in the days of the "thaw," those writers who had survived were freed and official statements began to appear in Soviet newspapers announcing the "rehabilitation" of writers who were no longer living and the publication of their literary legacy. A fierce struggle was begun by the survivors of the Yiddish cultural activists in the Soviet Union for the renewal of their culture. Foremost among their demands was the resumption of publication of the works of Yiddish authors and permission to reinstate some sort of periodic platform in Yiddish.

This struggle was supported by the efforts of various circles and individuals in the West, among them communist activists and sympathizers of the Soviet Union. Nevertheless, only in 1961, after years of protest and evasions by the Soviet regime, was the publication of *Sovetish heymland* permitted, over five years after the famous Secret Speech of Nikita Khrushchev at the Party's Twentieth Congress, in which he did not even find it proper to mention the wrong which Stalin had done to Yiddish culture.

The publication of the magazine in Yiddish represented a new recognition by the Soviet regime of the essential legitimacy of Yiddish culture, despite the fact that from the beginning it was clear that this restored recognition would be a limited one compared to the situation in the Soviet Union before World War II and even in the immediate postwar period.

Sovetish heymland has appeared regularly since 1961 and expanded in several aspects. In January 1965 the semimonthly journal became a monthly and its volume has increased from 128 pages at the beginning to 170 pages or more. Since January 1980 a separate 64-page booklet named the "Bibliotek," or the library, of *Sovetish heymland* has been added to every monthly issue. Each booklet is devoted to a particular topic or author; over the years the Biblyotek has covered the entire range of issues that *Sovetish heymland* has embraced. Both the journal itself and the additional booklet appear in an attractive eye-catching form. They are known, moreover, for their adherence to a proper Yiddish, germane to all.[1]

Since its foundation, the editor of the journal, and its "library," has been the poet Aharon Vergelis, a man of great energy and ability, and a faithful representative of the Soviet regime regarding all that concerns the situation and problems of Soviet Jewry. In his opening words of the festive anniversary issue, the editor boastfully presented the following data concerning the contents of over 280 issues of the journal which had appeared since its establishment. They had included:

76 novels
109 full-length stories
1,478 short stories and novellas
65 long poems
6,680 poems
28 plays
1,628 review articles on art and literature.

In addition to these, 127 books had appeared in Yiddish in the USSR during these years, most of them works of Yiddish authors which had previously appeared in the pages of *Sovetish heymland*.[2] The numbers are highly impressive. The material itself which stands behind them is evaluated in the West from time to time in sporadic reviews and summaries that address themselves to just a few issues or are devoted to a specific topic or composition.[3] Until now no thorough study has been conducted to determine the nature of this large literary harvest and to seriously estimate the full scope of its literary-artistic value, its ideological and political direction, and, perhaps most interesting, its importance and significance in the realm of Jewish national culture.

As a regular reader of *Sovetish heymland* I will allow myself to take the risk of making a few generalizations, based on my impressions over a period of many years. There is no doubt that *Sovetish heymland*, along with the publications associated with it, serves as an instrument of Soviet propaganda. Its anti-Zionist attitude is revealed in the most uncurbed and at times even venomous attacks against the State of Israel which make their way even into the fiction and poetry published in the journal.[4] Indeed, in everything published in *Sovetish heymland*, the Soviet patriotic position is in the forefront. The recurrent eulogies of the Jews' prominent role in the October Revolution and the building of the Soviet state and, in particular, of the heroism and sacrifice of the Jewish soldiers and officers who served in World War II are an obvious expression of this apologetic position.[5] What is surprising is the small number of published items concerning the years 1948–53, a black, fateful period for the Jews of the Soviet Union and these few items reveal very little concerning, indeed hardly acknowledge the fate of, the Yiddish authors in that period. Along with the daily paper *Birobidzhaner shtern*, *Sovetish heymland* also serves as an organ of what is still maintained as the "Autonomous Jewish Region" in the Soviet Far East, for the 10,166 Jewish residents who remained there as of 1979. Grotesque though it may seem, the Moscow Yiddish monthly still refers to Birobidzhan as a Jewish center and publishes much material on it, including works of authors who have remained in the region.[6]

Nevertheless, one may find in almost every issue works whose artistic value and conceptual worth are unquestionable. In *Sovetish heymland* the first volume of the well-known novel by Eli Shekhtman, *The Eve*, was serialized for the first time[7] as was Natan Zabara's novel, *The Day Is Still Long*.[8] Further, texts of Sholem Aleichem which do not appear in any of his published books have been printed in *Sovetish heymland*,[9] along with other works from the legacies of Soviet Yiddish writers, the victims of the "Black Years."[10] And though these publications may be suspected of falsification as a result of cutting by the Soviet censorship,[11] they nevertheless retain their value as an expression of the effort to publish important works which would otherwise be forgotten. In *Sovetish heymland* documentary material is regularly published along with valuable studies on Yiddish [12] and Hebrew literature, particularly poetic texts of the Middle Ages from the manuscript holdings of Soviet libraries. [13] The magazine provides information on current Jewish studies initiated in the Soviet Union. Several times, too, a series of lessons are published in the journal for those interested in learning Yiddish. [14]

Thus, despite the well-known tendentiousness of a considerable portion of the works published in the magazine, *Sovetish heymland* is nonetheless worthy of serious consideration. And I believe, as I have noted on a number of previous occasions, that a thorough study of the journal will probably confirm my basic positive evaluation of *Sovetish heymland* as a valuable expression of Jewish creativity.

On this occasion I would like to emphasize my observations concerning the next generation who will, in time, become the contributors to *Sovetish heymland*. These comments cannot be separated from more general evaluations of the trends and directions which characterize the legitimate and official expression of Jewish culture in the Soviet Union today. I stress the terms "legitimate and official" since I am not dealing here with the problems of the Jewish samizdat or other expressions of Jewish culture which are not recognized by the Soviet regime.

In the first issue of *Sovetish heymland*, published in 1961, there appeared on the inside cover a list of Soviet Yiddish writers whose contributions would be appearing in the coming issues of the new journal. Although the absence from the list of those authors who had perished in the years 1948–52 was very blatant, the 111 names which did appear were to ensure the continued publication of the journal up to our very day, despite the high average age of the writers. Yet if we check that list today, it becomes apparent that one-third of the writers are no longer living. Further, fifteen of the writers left the Soviet Union for Israel during the great wave of *aliya* of the 1970s. [15] The decline in the number of "old-timers" [16] over twenty-five years is, of course, a natural phenomenon, which certainly does not only apply to Yiddish writers in the Soviet Union. In Israel, the United States, and other centers of Yiddish literature, the situation is similar. What differentiates *Sovetish heymland*, and the circle connected to the journal, is the effort to create in present-day Soviet conditions a young literary generation which will be able in the future to carry on the publication of the journal, when those who fulfill that task today will no longer be with us.

Throughout its existence it has been well known that the editor of *Sovetish heymland* has tried to find and train young people to fulfill this task in conjunction with the aging writers.[17] From time to time new names appear in the journal. And, as happens in other places in the world, Vergelis was recently able to boast of a non-Jewish poet who composes poems in a flawless Yiddish.[18] Nevertheless, all this was not sufficient to guarantee the future, and in 1981 a Jewish Department of Higher Literary Studies was set up at the Maksim Gorky Literary Institute in Moscow. The pro-rector of the Institute defined the program as "a school for Jewish or Yiddish editors."[19] Those accepted for the program held degrees in various fields. Since 1981, the fruits of their efforts have been published in *Sovetish heymland*. An entire issue (July 1986) was comprised entirely of the writings of the students of the department and other young writers.[20]

The editor of *Sovetish heymland* has deemed it fit on several occasions to draw attention explicitly and by allusion to this new cadre, comparing it boastfully with the miserable condition of Yiddish outside the Soviet Union. Pointing to the impotence of Yiddish literature beyond the confines of the USSR, Vergelis wrote in his introduction to the issue of the young writers:

> We are now, after twenty-five years, harvesting the first fruits of our labor and the regeneration of Soviet Yiddish literature. In order that everyone should be able to fully appreciate this development, we have decided to take an exceptional step in the history of Yiddish literature—we have devoted a special issue of *Sovetish heymland* to the young "brigade." When the reader, both here and abroad, looks through the pages of this issue, a remarkable phenomenon will be revealed to him: all thirty-one of the young contributors were born after the war when Yiddish schools no longer existed. Yet all of them write in a reasonable Yiddish, some in a freer style and others still making stylistic-lexical efforts, but the writing and the creation are apace.[21]

Emphasis was also placed on this achievement in the half-jubilee celebrations in Moscow to which guests from abroad were invited. We know this from the reportage of Yosef Lipsky in the Israeli Hebrew daily *Al hamishmar*, who pointed out in the subtitle to his article: "all of a sudden it appears that there are Yiddish writers in the Soviet Union, even young ones."[22]

In our attempt to evaluate the works which appeared in the "young writers' " issue, it seems fitting to point out that these works did not differ in form or content from the material regularly published in *Sovetish heymland*. And bearing in mind that these young writers are just beginning their literary endeavors, this phenomenon is certainly a cause for surprise.

The journal opens with a piece of prose written by Boris Sandler, "In the Brief Moment Between Today and Tomorrow" (pp. 7–31). The author was born in Moldavia in 1950. Despite his efforts to diverge in a few passages from the common, accepted "realistic" standards, there is no real innovation in his writing. The story is about the failed venture of a young man who left the USSR for Netanya in Israel. His plight is described through excerpts from his letters to which are added the reflections of the narrator, the recipient of these letters, on the happy past which they shared in the Soviet Union. In the background of this story there are reminiscent echoes of the Holocaust and the problem of the continuity of Jewish popular tradition in the Soviet Union. This is clearly a propagandist effort in the form of a story which succeeds neither in convincing the reader nor in stirring up his confidence in the author. A story such as this does not show great promise as the opening of the special issue of *Sovetish heymland*. Indeed, the works of other contributors are of the same genre: there is a story about a refusenik "who worked at a mail box" and by the end of the story understands that he was wrong in wanting to emigrate, changes his plans, and stays in the USSR as a faithful citizen;[23] another story tells of a young man, a member of the Komsomol, who is sent by them from Moscow to Riga and there meets his true love;[24] another shallow story includes an attack on the United States, with the declaration that "the Jewish question" is a problem of American Jewry and not of Soviet Jewry;[25] and there is an interview with a "positive" Jew who helps build up the Autonomous Jewish Region in Birobidzhan. He is the son and grandson of old-timers who settled there in 1928.[26]

Among the poems, too, it is difficult to find true innovation either in form or content. Poems are still written about Birobidzhan and revolutionary Cuba.[27] Nevertheless, here and there one may find a few refreshing lines of some young talented poet.

On the whole, it is certainly possible to agree with Vergelis in the opening article of the young writers' issue:

"Their program is the literary-artistic and conceptual program of our forum, the journal *Sovetish heymland*. The importance of this lies in the fact that the young Yiddish writers in the Soviet Union are not the representatives of some "lost generation." They have not emerged from any disappointment but straight from real life, they are their grandparents' grandchildren, the sons of their fathers, and they are prepared right now to take some of the responsibility upon themselves and do it with understanding."

Certainly, most of their works confirm Vergelis's somewhat questionable praise in his presentation of the group of young people who toe the traditional line of *Sovetish heymland,* without any doubts or thoughts as to the possibility of innovation or change. Nevertheless, within this special issue some changes are discernible in the official cultural-literary system whose importance should not be ignored. These are manifest principally in the realms of Judaica and literary criticism.

Within the group of young writers, those who are especially able have turned not to fiction and poetry but rather to popular forms of scientific information and to criticism. In this particular issue several very interesting articles of this sort appear, such as a survey and review of a most important bibliographic work on the history of the Hebrew book, published in Moscow in 1985, which gives a detailed description of the Hebrew incunables preserved in Soviet libraries.[28] We find here, also, a short survey of the Jewish treasures, in Hebrew and Yiddish, of the public library in Leningrad.[29] Another very interesting article is the work of a young scholar on the emergence of modern Hebrew;[30] of great value is the information included in an article which reviews the contents of a bio-bibliographic dictionary of historians of the freedom movements in czarist Russia, in which an honorable place is devoted to Jewish historians like Gessen, Tsinberg, Doytch, Bukhbinder, Kirzhnits, Rafes, and Zaslavsky who were forgotten because they were ejected from Soviet historiography after the 1920s.[31] Nor should one disparage the information in the article on Jewish demography in Latvia and Estonia which appeared in a volume in Russian in 1985.[32] All of these were published in the "young writers' " issue of *Sovetish heymland.*

And if we add to this the extremely interesting survey of yet another young man, Igor Krupnik, on the contribution of Soviet scholars of the young generation to the development of Jewish studies in the Soviet Union, together with the observations of Leyb Vilsker, which appeared in the November 1986 issue of *Sovetish heymland,* we obtain a picture of an obvious expansion in the field of Jewish studies.[33] All this is presented in the journal with an awareness that in certain areas this is not a generation continuing in the footsteps of its predecessors but rather a new creation in a field whose very existence had been intentionally curtailed in the Soviet Union. It should also be stressed that the previous language barriers have been removed in this field—studies on the Hebrew language, on Jewish demography, and on Jewish historians are conducted and published in Russian, and then discussed and reviewed in the journal in Yiddish.

One review which stands out for its unconventional opinions concerns a collection of stories in Yiddish by Boris Sandler, published in book form in 1986, *Treplekh aroyf tsu a nes* (Stairs to a Miracle);[34] the book contains Sandler's aforementioned story. Fayina Grimberg, the author of the review, was born in 1951 in Tashkent where she was still living. Her article contains a most meaningful, and one can even say provocative, title in the context of this issue: "Is this a literature of a linguistic experiment?"[35] What does Fayina Grimberg mean? Unlike the writers of the previous generation for whom Yiddish was a daily communicative medium, Grimberg, speaking of Boris Sandler, claims:

"A young writer has also appeared to whom Russian has in fact been his first language since childhood, a writer who received his education in this language from primary school and through university. Thus the legitimate question is raised: what caused this young man to write in Yiddish?" (p. 88). Fayina Grimberg's answer is not straightforward. She presents a number of possibilities among which she mentions the desire to return to the heritage of his fathers in order to cultivate it. She goes on to explain this in relation to the narrator in Sandler's stories who is identified here with the story's author:

He lives in a period in which the Russian language has gained an increasingly wide natural status as the medium of communication between nations. It is natural for young people to be the primary carriers of this language. Yet, at the same time, this is also a period in which developed socialism provides extensive possibilities for the development and flourishing of the literature of the various nationalities in the Soviet Union. (Ibid.)

Grimberg's comments are presented here in the broader context of the nationality problem in the Soviet Union and not as a specifically Jewish problem. Indeed, it would be worthwhile to check to what extent the courses for young Yiddish writers and editors are exceptional in a society in which not only the Jews are in danger of losing their national-lingual identity. And if, in fact, such is the case, a major opening has been made in the efforts to make the preservation of the Jewish heritage a legitimate aspiration from the point of view of the Soviet regime. It is worthwhile noting, furthermore, that the reviewer is not aware of the fact that this is not, in its general sense, a particularly Soviet phenomenon, that "developed socialism" has no influence on the parallel trend among Jewish youth in the West, where Yiddish is also not their first language, yet whose interest in Yiddish and its heritage is increasing.

Nevertheless, the train of thought of the writer is not simplistic at all. She sees in the return to Yiddish among these "native" Russian speakers an experiment whose significance has not yet been proved. This can be deduced from her demand that the works written and published in Yiddish by these young writers be judged according to the accepted level of Russian-language literary journals and not valued with apologetic criteria solely because they are written in Yiddish (p. 92).

From our point of view the most interesting point is Fayina Grimberg's bold suggestion concerning the possibility of creating bilingually in Yiddish and Russian. She supports her suggestion by pointing to Tolstoy's "bilingual" *War and Peace* and to a multilingual work by an Austrian author in which English, French, Italian, and German appear together. She concludes her suggestion with a question: "Why can't the young Yiddish writers use this solution?" Fayina Grimberg does not explain her intentions, but she clearly believes that the linguistic potential of these writers should be fully utilized. To this end they should be given the chance to express themselves in both Russian and Yiddish, according to the lingual situation pervading in Soviet Jewish society, paralleling the situation of other minorities in this multinational state. At first glance, Fayina Grimberg's suggestion may seem a curious experiment which has no real chance of acceptance or success. Yet it appears that the combining of Yiddish and Russian and its subsequent possibilities are gaining the attention not only of this critic of Sandler's book.[36]

Another young contributor is Vladimir Tshernin, who decided to return to his Jewish name and now signs his works as Velvl Tshernin.[37] He belongs to the group who participated in the courses of the Gorky Institute in Moscow. He was born in 1958, is a professional ethnographer, and a graduate of Moscow University's history department. Tshernin works on the editorial staff of *Sovetish heymland*. He has already gained prominence among the pages of the journal in a number of works—poetry, criticism,

articles on the ethnography of non-Ashkenazi Jews in the Soviet Union—
and in a series of interviews with people connected with Jewish culture and
art in the Soviet Union. To the November 1986 issue of *Sovetish heymland,*
a booklet was attached entitled: "Dialogues on Jewish Culture in the Soviet
Union."[38] This is actually a collection of interviews which Tshernin conducted and which were previously published in *Sovetish heymland.* Yet their
concentration in a single booklet stressed even further the clear direction of
the interviewer in his stubborn questioning of actors and other representatives of the Jewish theater. It appears that the possibility of holding performances in a combination of Yiddish and Russian is discussed in this series
of interviews, not solely as a possibility for the future. In the Moscow
Jewish Drama Group this is already being done in practice. This group is
comprised of young actors, most of them graduates of drama schools in
Moscow. They perform plays on Jewish subjects in whose presentation in
Yiddish "the Russian language is inserted." The director of the theater
presented this lingual combination as one of the directions for the group's
experimental quests and explained:

> The words of the character in Yiddish and the supporting explanation in Russian
> must be spread out to fit the context of the given drama so that they come across in
> a natural manner. (P. 4)

It is impossible to expound on this innovation without being able to test
its practical application in the theater.[39] Nevertheless, it is clear that it
parallels the suggestion of Fayina Grimberg.

It is also obvious that there is opposition to the use of Russian in Yiddish
performances. The director of the theater in Birobidzhan and the representatives of the Vilnius group expressed their negative attitude. The latter
explain their opposition to the use of Russian and their theater's faithful
adherence to Yiddish by the fact that the Lithuanian Jews, for whom they
perform, are less assimilated than the Jewish audiences in Moscow. Nevertheless, the people of Vilnius are aware that the Jewish youth is more likely
to attend a concert or dance performance than a play in which comprehen-
sion of Yiddish is vital to understanding the text. This issue crops up in all
the interviews and in the discussions with actors who perform only in
Russian with material which has been translated from Yiddish, particularly
works of Sholem Aleichem; it is apparent that these performances enjoy
great success in Moscow.

This situation becomes self-evident if we bear in mind that the number of Yiddish speakers among the Jews of the Soviet Union is diminishing drastically. The postwar census figures are well known. The number of readers and purchasers of *Sovetish heymland* has diminished correspondingly with the passing of the years. When the journal first appeared in 1961, 25,000 copies were printed; in 1966 the number fell to 16,000; in 1971 to 10,000; in 1977 to 9,000; in 1978 to 7,000; and since 1985 only 5,000 copies of each issue are printed.[40] These figures include a sizable number of copies which are sent abroad. Further, one may assume that a significant number of subscribers began to buy the journal as of 1977 when summaries in Russian were included.

Against the background of the decline of the Yiddish-reading public, special significance must be attached to the appearance of the annual volume *God za godom* (Year After Year) comprising almost entirely Russian translations of items which appeared during the course of the year in *Sovetish heymland*. The selection of what is to be translated is done by the editorial board of *Sovetish heymland*. So far two volumes have appeared, for 1985 and 1986, each in an edition of 30,000 copies.[41] Whatever may be the attitude of *Sovetish heymland* to Jewish literature and culture in Russian (see below), it is clear that the Russian language is now recognized as a real and legitimate medium in the official polysystem of Jewish culture in the Soviet Union.

Nevertheless, one must not see translations from Yiddish or the various combinations presented here of Yiddish and Russian as the essential issue. Over the past few years we have witnessed the fact that a literature in Russian, with an openly Jewish orientation and addressing itself manifestly to specifically Jewish issues, has enjoyed widespread and deep appreciation among the Jews of the Soviet Union and abroad. A few years ago Anatolii Rybakov's novel on the Holocaust, *Heavy Sands*, won great attention.[42] Another example is Grigorii Kanovich who made a name for himself with his Jewish novels, which are snatched up by his readers in the Soviet Union as soon as they appear.[43] The novel by Dina Kalinovskaia should also be mentioned here.[44]

Critics in the Soviet Union point out that these novels which focus on Jewish themes consitute what one may call a resurrection of the Jewish-Russian literature which flourished in the period before the Revolution. And although Rybakov and Kanovich are, without a doubt, also addressing the non-Jewish reader, it is unquestionable that their primary interest is the Jewish reader who is searching for his Jewish roots in the not-too-distant past. These authors have succeeded in presenting their readers with outstanding pieces of literature which stir both the heart and the imagination. These works represent the most meaningful innovation in the polysystem of Jewish culture in the Soviet Union in the past few years.

The reactions of the sector of the Jewish establishment which centers on *Sovetish heymland* are not quite clear. Anatolii Rybakov's book was translated into Yiddish and published in *Sovetish heymland*,[45] while Dina Kalinovskaia's novel appeared in shortened form in Yiddish in *Sovetish heymland*, prior to its publication in the original Russian.[46]

Yet Vergelis himself has gone on record as saying that "a culture can develop only in its own national language. Marshak, Bagritskii, Babel, in his view, are representatives of Russian culture, while a recording of Jewish songs performed by a Russian singer in the Russian language is a product of Russian culture. Vergelis is reported to have insisted that it is impossible to conceive of Jewish theater in Russian since the translation destroys the content of the composition.[47] Moreover, no translations of Kanovich's books, which have been very popular among Jews, have been published in the journal,[48] and reviews of his books, written by regular contributors to *Sovetish heymland*, are published in other Yiddish forums. Moyshe Byelenki[49] and Berl Royzn[50] published their very favorable reviews in the Warsaw *Folks-shtime*, while Velvl Tshernin, who works on the journal's staff, had his enthusiastic review on one of Kanovich's books published in the *Birobidzhaner shtern*.[51]

Translations of parts of Kanovich's book also appeared in *Birobidzhaner shtern*, as well as a lengthy, special interview with the author.[52] In this interview Kanovich states:

> My fate, be it what it may, does not stand alone, apart from the fate of the Jewish people. . . . My fate is strongly connected, perhaps one can say inseparably, with the living, and, it could be, even with the dead, in Babii Iar and Ponerai, with my fathers and my fathers' fathers.

In the course of this interview Kanovich took the opportunity to announce the new novel on which he is presently working entitled, *A Kid for Two Zuzim* (the refrain from *Had gadya* sung at the Passover Seder service).[53]

And so, Tshernin had to go as far as Birobidzhan in order to publish a favorable review of Kanovich's book, and on the occasion strayed into a discussion of a fundamental problem which digressed far afield from the specific subject of his article. These are the words of this young Soviet Jewish writer:

I am reminded that the three classics began their careers in Yiddish, not because they didn't know Hebrew or Russian, but rather because they wanted to speak with their people in its own language, in a language which it understood. Who would dare to say that for this reason the Hebrew poetry of Bialik has no value? No one. But the position of Sholem Aleichem, Mendele Moykher Seforim and Y. L. Perets, was clear and well founded. In our days one can't ignore the fact that the Jewish people in the Soviet Union speaks and reads mostly in Russian. Does this testify that Yiddish literature is no longer of any value today? Not at all. Yet, nevertheless, one must recognize the fact that in our day Jewish literature in the Russian language is as natural as was Jewish literature in Yiddish at the end of the 19th century. There is no contradiction in this. Why shouldn't a people be able to create its literature in several languages?

Was Tshernin forced to publish his remarks in *Birobidzhaner shtern* because the editor of *Sovetish heymland* did not agree with his opinion? Or because he had some objection to Kanovich? Does the opposition of *Sovetish heymland* to Jewish culture in Russian or certain of its manifestations carry any weight? Will the editors of *Sovetish heymland* be given the right to preserve the birthright or hegemony of Yiddish within the Jewish cultural polysystem in the USSR? We do not have any clear-cut answers to these questions. Nor do possible answers have any fundamental importance in light of the very clear indications presented by the linguistic-cultural reality of the Soviet Jews.

Many signs point to the fact that in the Soviet Union possibilities have been opening up of late for the creation of a trilingual Jewish culture: Yiddish, Russian, and Hebrew, as existed quite naturally in czarist Russia and even after the Revolution in the 1920s, although with different emphases. It could be that in *Sovetish heymland* not everyone is satisfied with the present state of affairs, yet clearly those who are dissatisfied cannot ignore developing trends. Let us hope that at least those of us who are outside the Soviet Union will be able to comprehend them in order to aid in the cultivation of all the expressions of this culture.

Notes

1. Compare, Mordechai Shekhter, "Dos loshn fun *Sovetish heymland,*" "Yidishe shprakh," 29 (1969–1970), pp. 10–42; 30(1971), pp. 32–65.
2. *Sovetish heymland,* 8(1986), p. 4.
3. See, for example: Josef and Abraham Brumberg, *Sovetish heymland—An Analysis* (New York, 1966); H. Sloves, "Oysruf-tseykhns, freg-tseykhns un klamern (finf yor 'Sovetish heymland')" *Yidishe kultur,* 8 (1966), pp. 4–17. See also note 1. Moyshe Abramovitsh (= Ch. Shmeruk), "Ktav ha'et hasovieti hehadash be'idish: nituah shlosh hahovrot harishonot shel *Sovetish heymland,*" *Molad,* 163 (January–February 1962), pp. 11–17. (The article appeared also in French in *Les Juifs en Europe de l'est,* 9–10 (April–May 1962), pp. 27–46.) See also Ch. Shmeruk and Michael Zand, *Tarbut yehudit bivrit hamoatzot* (The Institute of Contemporary Judaism, Hebrew University of Jerusalem, 1973); also, B. Gidvitz, "Less than Meets the Eye: On the State of Yiddish Culture in the Soviet Union," in *Moment,* vol. 9, no. 10 (1984).
4. For the extent of this trend, see the section, "Kean antisovetizm un tsiyenizm," in *20 yor "Sovetish heymland," biblyografisher ontsayger,* vol. 2 (Moscow, 1986) (Bibliotek fun *Sovetish heymland*), 8(68), pp. 9–19. Nor does this cover the belletristics on this subject; see, for example, pp. 196.
5. For the dimensions of this last subject, compare "Vegn heldnfun Sovetnfarband" and "Oyf milkhome-temes" in *20 yor "Sovetish heymland," biblyografisher ontsayqer,* vol. 3 (Moscow, 1986) (Bibliotek fun *Sovetish heymland,* 9[69]), pp. 43–51 (Moscow, 1986). Here, too, the belletristics are omitted.
6. See the "Yidishe oytonome gegnt" in the above-mentioned pamphlet, pp. 38–39. Concerning the problem, which exists up to this day, of the treatment of the destruction of Yiddish culture at the end of the 1940s and the executions which took place, see the interview with A. Vergelis,"Yiddish Given More Support by Gorbachev," *New York Times,* May 5, 1987, p. A15. The number of Birobidzhan's Jewish residents is as in the 1979 census, because at the time of going to press, the 1989 census data have not yet been published.
7. The first volume was printed in issues 1–5 (1962). The book was published in its entirety in Tel Aviv in 1983. Shekhtman's name was banned in the USSR and did not appear in *20 yor "Sovetish heymland," biblyografisher ontsayger* (Moscow, 1981) (= Bibliotek fun *Sovetish heymland,* 8, 1981). This applied also to *all* authors who emigrated from the USSR to Israel (see note 15); the "purged" authors were also treated this way in the 1930s. Then even the pages of periodicals in which their articles appeared were removed and their names erased from the journals' tables of contents.
8. The book was printed in issues 9, 10 (1972); 9, 10 (1973); and 1, 2, 3 (1975). The rest appeared in book form. For some reason Zabara's name, too, disappeared from the booklet mentioned in the previous note.
9. See p. 26 of the aforementioned bibliographical booklet.
10. Compare the list of authors in the aforementioned booklet.
11. See, for example, Dalya Kaufman,"Sholem Aleichem in Ratnfarband" *Yerusha-*

layimer almanakh, 1 (1973), pp. 171–72; Ch. Shmeruk, "Shnei nusakhim meharoman shel Peretz Markish, *Trot fun 'doyres'*," *Behinot*, 1 (1979), pp. 180–89.
12. See the second bibliographical booklet—8 (1968), pp. 19–61.
13. Leyb Vilsker's research in this field, published in the pages of *Sovetish heymland*, earned him a name among researchers of Judaica. His work was gathered in two booklets put out by the journal *Antdekte oytsres* (Moscow, 1981) (Bibliotek 9, 1981) and *Antdekte oytsres* (Moscow, 1985) (Bibliotek 3[51], 1985).
14. By E. Falkovitsh as of issue 1 (1974) and issue 7 (1977), and by Shimon Sandler as of issue 3 (1979). Sandler's series was gathered in the four booklets of *Limudim fun yidish* (Moscow, 1980–85) (Bibliotek 8, 1980; 8, 1983; 7, 1983; 9, 1985).
15. The fifteen are: Hirsh Osherovitsh, Rokhl Boymvol, Leyzer Vilenkin, Meyir Kharats, Zyame Telesin, Yosef Tsherniak, Yankl Yakir, Meyir Yelin, Khayim Maltinski, Motl Saktsier, Eliezer Podryadtshik, Yosef Kerler, Efroyim Roytman, Shloyme Roytman, and Eli Shekhtman. These are all names which were omitted in the bibliographical booklets mentioned above; see also note 7.
16. The data available from the anthology of poetry translated from Yiddish, published in 1985 in Moscow (*Sovetskaia evreiskaia poeziia*), highlight this phenomenon. There appear in this volume thirteen living Soviet Yiddish poets, among whom the youngest is Max Ryant, who is presently sixty-five years old (born 1923).
17. See, for example, in issue 10 (1965), pp. 102–16.
18. A. Belousov; his works were listed in the bibliographical booklet of 1981, p. 36.
19. See the introduction of the pro-rector of the Institute, Nikolai Gorbachev, "A shul fun yidishe redaktorn," *Sovetish heymland*, 10(1982), pp. 97–98. As a follow-up to the article, works of some of the participants in these courses appeared in the same issue, marking the start of the department's second school year.
20. Vergelis, in his *New York Times* interview, mentioned above in note 6, promised that the July issue of every year would be dedicated to the works of young writers.
21. A Vergelis, "Nemt zikh on mit koykhes, yunge shprotzlingen," *Sovetish heymland*, 7 (1986), p. 5. See also Vergelis's work, "A fertl yorhundert," *Sovetish heymland*, 8 (1980), pp. 4–5 and the *New York Times* interview in which he reiterated many of these statements.
22. Yosef Lipsky,"Yiddish is alive and well in Moscow," *Al hamishmar*, November 6, 1986. For the guests and the texts of their speeches, see *Sovetish heymland*, 1(1987), pp. 8–30, and similarly 2 (1987), pp. 112–24.
23. G. Estraykh, "Alte opgeribene trep," *Sovetish heymland*, 7(1986), pp. 55–58.
24. D. Yushkovski, "A studentisher shir-hashirim," ibid., pp. 67–70.
25. Y. Dekhtyar, "Morgn shteyt undz for a nayer tog," ibid., pp. 71–73.
26. B. Kushnir, "Der mentsh iz barimt mit zayn mi," ibid., pp. 82–84. The story of Dekhtyar also focuses on Birobidzhan.

27. V. Tshernin, "Kuba," "Der tsug," ibid., p. 49.
28. S. Kolyakov, "A nay bukh vegn hebreishe inkunabeln," ibid., pp. 97–98. For the great value of the book, see Chimen Abramsky's review in *Soviet Jewish Affairs*, vol. 17, no. 1 (Spring 1987), pp. 53–60.
29. A. Markova, "In der leningrader efntlekher bibliyotek," *Sovetish heymland*, 7(1986), p. 126.
30. M. Aykhenvald, "Di oisfuremung fun haynttsaytikn ivris als shprakheksperiment," ibid., pp. 122–25.
31. A. Lokshin, "Di historiker fun der bafrayungs-bavegung in Russland," ibid., pp. 99–100.
32. M. Kupovetski, "Eynike ongabn vegn yidn in Letland un Estland," ibid., pp. 127–30.
33. Igor Krupnik, "Der tsushtayer funem yungn dor sovetishe gelernte in der antviklung fun der yudaik in FSSR (iberzikht)," *Sovetish heymland*, 11(1986), pp. 71–81; L. Vilsker, "Bamerkungen tsu di arbetn fun tsvey yunge gelernte in dem yugentlekhn numer fun *Sovetish heymland*—yuli, 1986," *Sovetish heymland*, 7 (1986), pp. 77–80. Chimen Abramsky also observed this new development in Jewish studies in the USSR; see his review mentioned in note 28, p. 58. Krupnik's article appeared in English translation in *Soviet Jewish Affairs*, vol. 17, no. 1 (Spring 1987), pp. 122–25 with L. Hirszowicz's introduction and notes.
34. Moscow: Farlag Sovetski pisatel, 1986. The number of copies published was 1,100.
35. *Sovetish heymland*, 9(1986), pp. 87–92.
36. As if in order to put this proposal into effect, *Sovetish heymland*, 3(1987), published a story of G. Estraykh, in which, in a Yiddish context, words in direct speech are rendered in Russian, in accordance with the language of the speaker. See "Di bobe Basheve," p. 107, in *Sovetish heymland*, 3(1987), p. 107. A translation into Yiddish appears at the bottom of the page.
37. As of the article in *Sovetish heymland*, 11(1983), p. 149.
38. Bibliotek 11, 1980.
39. In his *New York Times* interview Vergelis mentions the two Moscow theaters which combine Yiddish and Russian in their performances. But it seems that Vergelis himself has reservations on this matter. Compare the discussion in *Sovetish heymland*, 4(1987), pp. 125–30, and Vergelis's statements on p. 129. This innovation in the dramatic theater of Moscow was also discussed in Warsaw's *Folks-shtime* on March 14 and April 11, 1987. The first item tells us that "all of the performances, except Tevia the Milkman which is performed only in Yiddish, are in Yiddish and Russian." The bilingual idea which was introduced by Yakov Gubyenko has no parallel in the tradition of the Jewish theater in Russia. The first time that it was implemented was in the play *The Women's Tailor* (see note 44). The director claims that the plays performed in Yiddish alone are not understood by the spectators. ". . . it was therefore decided to perform in two languages."
40. The data are all derived from the annual *Pechat' SSSR, statisticheskie materialy*

(Moscow: Kniga; later Statistika). The last issue that I have seen relates to the year 1985.
41. *God za godom. Literatunyi ezhegodnik. Po materialam zhurnala "Sovetish heymland."* Pod obshchei redaktsiei Arona Vergelisa. 1/85, 2/86. (Moscow: Sovetskii pisatel'.) This annual volume also appears in English and French translations.
42. The novel has been translated into Hebrew by Am Oved's library for subscribers, Sifria La'am, Tel Aviv, 1983.
43. One of his novels, too, has appeared in Hebrew entitled *Nerot baruah* (Candles in the Wind) (Tel Aviv; n.p., 1985).
44. Her novel appeared for the first time in a shortened translation from Russian to Yiddish under the title "Alte layt," *Sovetish heymland*, 2(1975), pp. 55–99; 3(1975), pp. 42–77. The Russian original appeared only in 1980 in the journal *Druzhba narodov*, 8(1980), pp. 22–106, entitled "O subbota!" In the first Russian-language annual volume of *Sovetish heymland* (see note 41), her most interesting "Jewish" story appeared, entitled "Risunok na dne," which deals with the preservation of traditions and family relics by Soviet Jews against the background of the Holocaust (*God za godom*, 1/85, pp. 49–75). Russian literature on Jewish themes written by Jews is not limited to the stories mentioned here, and is worthy of special attention and of in-depth research. Here we will mention also the play on the period of the Holocaust by Aleksandr Borshchagovskii, *Damskii portnoi* (The Women's Tailor) *Teatr*, 10 (1980), pp. 142–67, also known by the name of "Night in Babii Iar." This is the play which was performed in Yiddish and Russian in the Moscow Theater (see note 39).
45. "A shverer zamd," *Sovetish heymland*, 4, 5, and 6 (1979).
46. See note 44.
47. "You Are Disturbing Us in Your Activities." *Yehudei brit hamoatzot*, vol. 10 (1987), p. 217.
48. The absence of translations into Yiddish of Kanovich's books is noted with resentment in an article by L. Shkolnik in *Birobidzhaner shtern*, August 17, 1986.
49. Moyshe Byelenki, "Dervakhung (anshtot a retsenzye)," *Folks-shtime*, November 30, 1985.
50. Berl Royzn, "Naye kinstlerishe dergreykhungen fun der rusish-yidisher literatur," *Folks-shtime*, November 12, 1983; and "A bukh vos regt dem gedank," *Folks-shtime*, March 9, 1986.
51. Velv'l Tshernin, "Ven der bukh iz durkhgeleyent," *Birobidzhaner shtern*, September 29, 1985. E. Shulman has already drawn attention to Tshernin and this article in particular. In "Velv'l Tshernin—a yunger yidisher shrayber in Rusland," *Der veker*, July–August–September 1985, pp. 11–12.
52. L. Koval, "Tsvey trefungen mit Grigori Kanovitshn," in *Birobidzshaner shtern*, April 27, 1986. See also the report of the author's meeting with his readers in Vilnius, *Folks-shtime*, November 23, 1985.
53. See Hirsh Smalyakov, "G. Kanovitsh un zayn nayester roman, A tsigele for tsvey gildn," *Folks-shtime*, October 17, 1987. The first part of this novel appeared in Russian in the monthly *Sovetskaia Litva*, nos. 6–8, 1987.

10

The Role of Officially Published Russian Literature in the Reawakening of Jewish National Consciousness (1953–1970)

Shimon Markish

In 1968 the newspaper *Leninskoe znamia*, the organ of the Moscow *obkom* (*oblast* [regional] party committee) and of the Moscow *oblast' ispolkom* (executive committee) published the following poem entitled *Soiuz* (meaning both "union" and "conjunction"):[1]

> Like a breath of warmth in January
> Or the desperate will of beasts of burden,
> There is nothing more enigmatic in the dictionary
> Than words of one letter or one sound.
>
> There is one—and only it is endowed
> With the sovereign power to overcome differences
> It combines night with day,
> Peace with war and downfall with greatness.
>
> It contains your anxieties and mine,
> In this "I" lies our union and support . . .
> I found out: far away in Asia
> There is a people called "I."
>
> Just think: both death and conception,
> The everyday routine of childhood, the allotment, the courtyard
> The rejection of lies and the understanding
> Of compassion, fearlessness, and good,
>
> And the freedom, the ecstasy and the desperation
> Of our human family,—

All has its place and is mightily fused
In this small tribe "I."

And when in an alien heathen temple
A mother approaches the altar,
It is I,—all the stronger and more universal,—
That speaks about myself with her.

Without conjunctions the dictionary would fall mute,
And I know: everything would be out of joint,
Mankind would not be able to exist
Without the people called "I."

1967

Soon afterward the poem was reprinted by the respected literary journal *Moskva*. The poem was written by Semen Lipkin, a very well-known and successful translator of poetry, who translated almost exclusively from the languages of Soviet Central Asia and the Caucasus, from Kalmyk and Tatar. He translated both classical and folk works (national epics), as well as contemporary poets and the verse epistles to Comrade Stalin—the anonymous, but extensive expression of gratitude and enthusiasm which the Uzbeks, Tadzhiks, and other peoples had sent to the Kremlin on the occasion of the so-called "Decades of National Art"[2] in Moscow. In his youth—Lipkin was born in Odessa in 1911—he had also written and published a few of his own works, under the patronage of his illustrious fellow Odessan, the poet Eduard Bagritskii. During the Second World War too, he published a book of feature stories about the war, and after the war several prose versions for children of folk poetry of the East and one collection of original poems, in 1967. Yet, while he was known in his own professional circle as a dedicated and prolific, even though somewhat boring writer,[3] the reader, the multimillion consumers of newspapers, magazines, and books, barely knew Semen Lipkin's name, along with the names of other translators.

The poetess Anna Akhmatova, who died two years before the publication of *Soiuz*, often said (including in the presence of this writer) that Semen Lipkin was one of the five top contemporary poets in Russian. What she had in mind, however, was not his published work, but the poems which he had written for close friends or for his desk drawer and which had never been published. Later, indeed, Lipkin rebelled, was banned and expunged from the writers' "book of the living," so that he became a non-person, and his hitherto private poetic works, both short and long, were published in Russian in Europe and in the United States. Thus Akhmatova's evaluation may now be tested and confirmed. Yet all this occurred a good ten years later; in 1968 Lipkin was generally considered a dependable member of the literary "establishment" who knew his place and valued it.

The scandal which developed following the publication of "Soiuz" was therefore quite unexpected.

The newspaper *Sovetskaia Rossiia*, which, as the party organ of the RSFSR, was one of the country's central newspapers and a notch above *Leninskoe znamia*, published a long article by the Belorussian writer Ivan Shamiakin exposing Lipkin as a bourgeois nationalist.[4] Although the article did not specify just what kind of a nationalist he was, Shamiakin gave even the unsophisticated reader a broad enough hint when he referred to Lipkin by his first name and patronymic—Semen Izrailevich. (By the rules of the game operative in the Soviet press, usually only the top bosses are referred to in that way, for example: Iosif Vissarionovich [Stalin], Lavrentil Pavlovich [Beriia], Nikita Sergeevich [Khrushchev], Leonid Il'ich [Brezhnev], Iurii Vladimirovich [Andropov], Konstantin Ustinovich [Chernenko].) Accordingly, in the poem *Soiuz*, "I" was a camouflaged way of referring to Israel, and Lipkin, far from being a dependable translator, was a crafty Zionist. Furthermore, the date underneath the poem was in itself eloquent. 1967 was the year of the Six-Day War. Shamiakin did not state all this in so many words, but his message could be read between the lines without much difficulty.

What punitive measures were taken with regard to the paper *Leninskoe znamia* are unknown to me, but I do not know that the head of the poetry division of the magazine *Moskva* was fired.

At that time one of the staff of the journal *Aziia i Afrika segodnia* was a young man by the name of Aleksandr Polishchuk, who was then interested in Jewish problems (he now lives somewhere in the United States and, if my information is correct, is currently interested in Pentecostalists and other Christian sects persecuted in the USSR). Together with the orientalist and translator Mikhail Kurgantsev (who is also of Jewish origin), Polishchuk wrote for his magazine a brief article called "What is the People I," which, without a single reference to Lipkin's poem, revealed that in the jungles of southwest China there lived a tribe called I and described the mores and customs of this tribe. Word of this article reached the science department (or perhaps the press department) of the Party Central Committee, and the assistant editor of the journal was given a thorough dressing-down: he was hauled over the coals and told that it was no use pretending to be a simpleton and that it was clear to anyone which I Lipkin had in mind and what was the real purpose of the article by Kurgantsev and Polishchuk. Needless to say, their article did not see the light of day.

I read Shamiakin's article and the poem which provoked it many years ago (in 1968) when the events were fresh, and learned then, too, of the failed exploit of Polishchuk and Kurgantsev from my friend Mikhail Zand, currently a professor at the Hebrew University and then a junior research worker at the Institute of the Peoples of Asia and Africa of the USSR Academy of Sciences.[5] I was a "conscious" Jew, and had no need to be "reborn" or "awakened," but even so the stir caused by the poem *Soiuz* seemed to be artificial. Even after Zand, who knew Lipkin far better than I, told me in confidence that the poem had indeed been written on the occasion of the Six-Day War, when everyone who felt Jewish could think of nothing but the danger threatening the Jewish people, I continued to doubt whether the poet's intention was really clear to everyone. Would it not be more correct to say that whereas he failed to obviate the vigilance of the anti-Semites, the sensitivity of the Jewish reader to his allusions remains in the realm of indemonstrable hypotheses?

I continue to have doubts on this score even today.

Herein lies one of the main and insoluble difficulties of the topic of my chapter. We do not have criteria for making even a vaguely objective (let alone a strictly scientific) assessment of what influence this literature, which passed the censor and was published, had on those who several years later rushed in large numbers to OVIR (the Soviet exit visa office) or on those who, although not aiming to leave the Soviet Union, remembered their origin, were horrified at how assimilated they had become, and turned to Jewish civilization in some form or other—whether exclusively religious, purely secular, or a mixture of the two. All one can do is to rely on one's own intuition and judgment. Thus Professor Zand considers that just about the first Zionist work to break past the censor was the poem by my brother David Markish published in the magazine *Iunost'* in 1964. The poem was entitled "Easy is the first step into the desert . . ." ("Legok pervyi shag v pustyniu . . .") and related the ecstasy of freedom amidst the desert sands. Naturally David Markish was referring to the Exodus, to the sandy wastes of the Sinai and not the Kara-Kum or Kizil-Kum deserts of Soviet Central Asia; his entire personal and artistic life has made this evident. But I do not think that he was very successful in conveying his thoughts to the reader or infecting him with his own enthusiasm. Such allusions and associations have of necessity to be very vague and heavily veiled, otherwise they have no chance of sneaking through the heavy barbed wire of the censorship. And this was the case with all the positive components out of which the sense of Jewish national affiliation took shape.

In contrast, literary works about the Holocaust, even though permitted in only the most minute "doses" and screened with utmost caution, did not require such camouflage and thus their effectiveness, in my opinion, was much greater. For example, Semen Lipkin himself in the late sixties published the following three stanzas in one of the volumes of the annual *Den' poezii*:

Ashes

I was an extinguished ash
Without thought, face or speech,
But I started out on my earthly path
From the womb of my mother—the oven.

I had not yet understood life,
Nor mourned my previous life,
I walked amidst the Bavarian grass
And the de-populated barracks.

In the twilight slowly passed by
The Volkswagens and Mercedes.
And I whispered: "They burned me.
How can I get to Odessa?"

The date was again 1967. Although there is no Zionism here, this poem is immeasurably more Jewish than the coded *Soiuz*. Just because of its complete openness, its unadorned simplicity, the poem has a poignant effect of such force that it is quite impossible to remain indifferent to it. It seems that the most dulled soul encased in an apparently impermeable crust of assimilation would have to respond: "yes, indeed, that's how I feel . . . I too am with you." No matter how weak the response, it might well become the first step on the path toward what is often called (too bombastically and solemnly for my taste) the national rebirth.

The reader may object that my topic as stated in my title refers not to the propaganda effect of writing, but to self-expression, not to the reader, but to the writer. My answer is that the possibilities of self-expression for a

Jewish writer writing in Russian are minimal, if not totally nonexistent, and Russian-Jewish literature has not existed since the 1930s (I mean officially published literature, since secret or samizdat works are beyond the scope of this chapter). Who among the huge cohort of writers, who consider themselves Russian-Jewish writers and who now live in Jerusalem and West Berlin, in Tiberias and Paris, in Tel Aviv and Los Angeles, were clever enough to sneak even one Jewish line into a Soviet magazine or publication? This is in no way meant to disparage them but simply is a reminder of the way things are.

Therefore, I am obliged to exclude good intentions from my consideration.

I shall attempt to describe and systematize (without forgetting how subjective this must be) those phenomena and tendencies in belles lettres and literary criticism which might have had some influence on the formation of a new national consciousness among Russian-speaking Jews who during the period between the death of Stalin and the beginning of the large-scale emigration (1953–70) lived within the orbit of Russian culture. (This definition or category is intended to exclude the survivors in the former western provinces of the Russian Empire and in Moldavia: the degree to which the Jews of Tallinn (Estonia) or Kishinev (Moldavia) were Russian-speaking and related to Russian culture in the postwar period is somewhat problematic.)

The terror of the postwar years (1946–53) was of a scale that was unmatched in the history of Soviet rule. It was also the most effective, since the demoralization of the individual (the totality of fear and self-surrender), the destruction of every social structure, and the transformation of society into an amorphous mass reached their apogee. The state-encouraged anti-Semitism, and state-approved or incited pogroms of that time should be examined precisely in that broader context. Every Soviet "citizen" (the very term lost all meaning, for the citizen had become the slave of the state) was obliged—under threat of political extinction—to forget himself, his individuality, and his past, and to turn into a will-less, voiceless, and memoryless particle. The particularly cruel persecution of the Jew, the special derision aimed at him, were not only a function of traditional Russian or Stalin's personal anti-Semitism, nor merely an instructive example or a safety valve. They amounted to a recognition that the Jew possesses a particular ability to resist total leveling, a particularly stubborn individualism (both on the personal and on the national level).

The ability is real, not imagined, but nevertheless limited by the temptation to conform and assimilate, which has been present throughout Jewish history, along with the tendency to nonconformism. As a result, by the end of the Stalin era all manifestations of Jewishness had disappeared or, at best, were well hidden, and even the word "Jew" was uttered in a whisper like something unseemly or shameful.

Solzhenitsyn has written an article called: "The Return of Breathing and Consciousness."[6] This title formulates with wonderful precision the spiritual process in the USSR after the death of Stalin, and in particular what occurred among Soviet Jews who began to regain consciousness, to remember who they were, to seek out their lost identity—and Russian literature was noticeably helpful in this difficult task.

It would not be correct to say that Jewish characters or situations completely disappeared from Russian literature during the last part of Stalin's rule. The reason for this is evident: The more intolerable reality became, the more strictly was decorum observed and the deception maintained in what I call the "second reality," that is, in ceremonies, spectacles, and art. For example, on 20 December 1952, in the interval between the execution of the "Zionists" who were convicted in the Slansky-Gemeinder trial in Prague and the announcement of the unmasking of the Jewish "Doctors' Plot" in Moscow, the Stalin Prize for "encouraging peace between nations" was awarded to Il'ia Ehrenburg. The actual presentation of the prize (with an appropriate speech by the laureate) took place immediately after the announcement about the doctor-murderers. Here, both on the level of ceremony and on the level of literature was the required "positive" Jew whom Ehrenburg had depicted in the character of Osip Al'per, in *Buria* (The Storm, 1947) who reappeared in *Deviatyi val* (The Ninth Wave, 1951); the former had received the Stalin Prize, first class for literature in 1948. Moreover, completely respectable Russian writers, not only the (still!) suspect Ehrenburg, depicted impeccable Jews. The classic of socialist realism and one of the most outstanding examples of Stalinist literature is Vasilii Azhaev's novel *Daleko ot Moskvy* (Far from Moscow), which was awarded the Stalin prize first class for 1949, and depicted the splendid Party organizer and construction worker, Zalkind. I do not know whether these images of "valuable Jews" inspired with optimism and Soviet patriotism those who had just lived through one pogrom and were now awaiting another, but I think not. I also believe that in this case the Jewish reader reacted to Azhaev just as he reacted to Ehrenburg.

However, even at that time, there appeared books which, I am convinced, helped to form the Jewish national consciousness. I shall mention two examples.

In 1945 *Novyi mir* printed the beginning of Konstantin Paustovskii's autobiographical epic which eventually received the title *Povest' o zhizni* (The Story of My Life); the first part was called "Dalekie gody" (Distant Years). Paustovskii grew up in the Ukraine and in his memoirs about his childhood appear numerous Jewish figures and episodes depicted with considerable warmth. However, it is not these episodes which I have in mind (such scenes do more to irritate the anti-Semites than to gladden the hearts of Jews), but the place where Paustovskii describes graduating from the gymnasium in Kiev:

> Before the exams we arranged a meeting in the park. We invited to it all the gymnasium students in our class except the Jews, who were supposed to know nothing about it.
> At the meeting it was decided that the best Russian and Polish students would make an effort to receive the equivalent of a "4" rather than the top "5" in at least one subject in order *not* to win a gold medal. We decided to let the Jewish students win all the gold medals, since without these medals they were not admitted to university.

When Soviet Jews read these paragraphs in 1949 or 1952, I doubt whether they paused to think that our current situation resembled the prerevolutionary one; they did not have to be reminded of that. But rather they thought that in the contemporary Soviet Union you could not find Russian students who would agree to give up their medals for a Jew. Their awareness of their greatly increasing isolation, abandonment, and helplessness pushed Soviet Jews inevitably toward a search for something of their own which could not be taken away from them at the whim of their enemies or former friends.

But where could they find something of their own? Where could they look for it? Where could they read in Russian about Jews other than Zalkind or Al'per who were alienated from their people, Jews in name only? Against the background of silence about Jewish civilization decreed by the censor, the appearance in 1947 of the thick volume *Istoriia moei zhizni* (History of My Life) by Aleksei Svirskii was a miracle. Aleksei Ivanovich Svirskii, who died during the Second World War at just under eighty, was a well-known Russian-Jewish writer. Although he converted to Christianity in his youth, he never abandoned Jewish subject matter and always preserved his Jewish outlook (despite his Marxist views and party membership). He began writing *Istoriia moei zhizni* in 1928 and he continued working on it until his death. I do not know how much of his manuscript was included in the volume published in 1947. However, the volume covers the childhood and youth of the author-narrator and concludes with his conversion, that is, its subject matter comprises the most Jewish part of the narration. This book, issued apparently as a sign of respect to the memory of a writer who was considered a revolutionary and a realist of the Gorky school (after the beginning of the anticosmopolitan campaign in 1949 such merits were disregarded and the book would not have appeared!), was an unexpected joy, a priceless gift for the younger generation of Jews. Despite the restricted point of view, unavoidable in any autobiography, and despite the inevitable one-sidedness of perception and partiality of judgment expressed in the outright rejection of traditional forms of Jewish existence (not to mention Jewish ways of living), Svirskii gave Jews a glimpse of their past, from which they had been completely cut off. I cannot check whether *Istoriia moei zhizni* has ever been reprinted (I seriously doubt it), but in any case it remains the most Jewish work published after the war. This is borne out by comparing it to another "Jewish autobiography," Aleksandra Iakovlevna Brushtein's *Doroga vkhodit v dal'* (The Road Slips Away into the Distance) which was published after Stalin's death in 1957. After a long and successful career as a playwright for children and young people, Aleksandra Brushtein recorded her childhood in the Pale of Settlement, regarding it in a detached way (although not without a touch of nostalgia, which is only to be expected from someone advanced in years). This Soviet Russian writer tells about the girl from an assimilated Jewish intelligentsia family she had been so very long ago, and looks back on the path she has traversed. Although Brushtein never belonged to Russian-Jewish culture, as distinct from Svirskii who was a part of it (no matter how modest), those crumbs of Jewishness which one could glean from her work had their significance for starving Jewish minds and hearts.

As for anti-Semitism, which was the most powerful factor in Soviet circumstances for arousing Jewish consciousness, while it raged in the "first reality," it had no access to the "second reality," at least in an undisguised vein. To be more precise, it had no place either in official ritual or in socialist-realist belles lettres of any kind, so that the most inveterate and outspoken anti-Semites such as Aleksei Surov, Mikhail Bubennov, and

Anatolii Sofronov,[7] could not express their innermost feelings in their novels or plays. Even the literary critics who exhibited incredible baseness in "exterminating" the homeless cosmopolitans, had to limit themselves to insinuations. The most transparent of these was the so-called "unmasking by parenthesis" in which to a quite proper-sounding literary pseudonym was added—in parenthesis—the author's original, Jewish name, for example B. Iakovlev (Gol'zman). (Occasionally this led to amusing incidents and, in passing, I would like to mention one which I believe is not particularly well known: Nikolai Davydovich Otten, a Russian critic, prose, and scenario writer, happened to be included among the cosmopolitans. His real name was Potashinskii and his father had been a senator in the czarist period. Nikolai Davydovich made the rounds of all the editorial boards demanding that he be "unmasked by parenthesis" but to no avail.) However, even this device was soon banned, on the personal order of Stalin, so it was rumored, which is quite credible: the creator of the inviolable friendship of the Soviet peoples was not only a hypocrite, but also the most vigilant guardian of order and decency. Open, black on white, anti-Semitism would be an outright violation of order in the kingdom of triumphant socialism.

The last exploit of the Stalinist hawks of literary criticism during the life-time of the leader was the destruction of Vasilii Grossman for his novel *Za pravoe delo* (For the Right Cause). It was a clear-cut case: the author was a Jew and so was the main hero of the novel. Furthermore, Jew baiting had begun in February 1953 after the arrest of the doctor-murderers had been announced and after the sacramental words "Jewish bourgeois nationalism" had been publicly pronounced in all the newspapers and journals. Nonetheless, no one yet dared to call things by their true names, neither the completely ignorant Bubennov in *Pravda,* nor the refined Marietta Shaginian in *Izvestiia,* nor the party hack Lektorskii in the "theoretical organ," *Kommunist.*[8] (People may remind me of the monstrous Goebbels-like caricature and the feuilleton of Vasilii Ardamatskii "Pinia from Zhmerinka" which appeared in *Krokodil* in January–February 1953. However, I consider these to be the exception that proves the rule, an initiative from below, a trial balloon by the most zealous and impatient pogromists.)

Of course, there is no doubt that it was literary criticism which was the most anti-Semitic genre of the later Stalin period and, consequently, should have been—in theory—the most effective means of Jewish national education. But we should not forget two circumstances: that criticism is the fare of the few, as works of criticism do not interest the ordinary reader, and that the total horror of reality, the knife at the Jews' throats, was incomparably more meaningful and real than veiled anti-Semitic literary excercises.

It is with this emotional baggage that the Jews entered the post-Stalin era, the era of the "Thaw," as it is usually called after the phrase coined by Il'ia Ehrenburg. Indeed, I shall begin with him—with his Jewish name and his role as a Jew.

First, some words about Ehrenburg's role under Stalin. Clearly then, he played the role of *"shirmach"* (from the word *shirma,* meaning screen), which in thieves' slang refers to the member of the gang whose job it is to distract people's attention when the robbery is taking place and serves as a screen for his accomplices. Ehrenburg admitted as much in his memoirs, *Liudi, gody, zhizn'* (People, Years, Life), when he wrote that his silence in Paris after the arrest of the Jewish writers, after the beginning of the anticosmopolitan campaign, had been a lie (book five, chapter 17).[9] It is true that an article carrying his name appeared in *Pravda* ("About One Letter," 21 September 1948), in which he dissociated himself from the newly established State of Israel and warned Soviet Jews not to delude themselves with fantasies and not to place any hopes on their ancient homeland. But to accuse Ehrenburg of complicity in the murder of the Jewish intelligentsia (1949–52) is slander for which there is no evidence at all. What is of even greater significance is that he was the only major writer —and one who was particularly popular—who repeatedly reminded his reader: "I am a Jew." No one can testify that this was done on orders from the ideological authorities, but even if this were so (which I doubt), Ehrenburg's insistent reminders helped keep alive among the masses of simple, ordinary Jews, among the *people,* the barely flickering flame of their national consciousness which was being extinguished from all sides. In that lies Ehrenburg's great contribution which it would be foolish to deny.

I shall now consider the role of his Jewish name. Like their brethren throughout the world, Soviet Jews continually searched for famous fellow Jews and prided themselves on them. They would most assiduously scan the lists of Stalin prizewinners, candidate members of the USSR Academy of Science, and lists of Heroes of the Soviet Union or of Socialist Labor. Even if this "fellow tribesman" were the executioner Kaganovich or Mekhlis,[10] he was still one of theirs. It may be foolish, senseless, even unworthy, but this is a fact of national psychology (not only of Jews), a factor of national solidarity. In a period of totalitarian amorphousness, such quests also tend to be amorphous, random; they become more selective as soon as totalitarianism relaxes even in the slightest degree and the process of social crystallization begins. It can be assumed with a fairly high degree of certainty that hatred of the postwar Stalinist regime was the predominant emotion and frame of mind of Soviet Jewry after living through the "anticosmopolitan" terror. (It would be proper to speak of widespread hatred of Stalin personally, one that was not merely confined to the intelligentsia, only after Khrushchev's revelations.) It can also be assumed that this feeling was far more intense among Jews than among other peoples of the Soviet Union (except, of course, those who had been totally "repressed" as "accomplices of the Nazi occupiers,"—the Chechens, Crimean Tatars, and about ten others).[11] For this reason the first denunciations of the regime were viewed by Jews not only in a social, but also in a national context (as was the case later with attempts to rehabilitate Stalinism), in particular if such denunciations were made by someone with a Jewish name.

The first step toward de-Stalinization in Soviet literature was the article by Vladimir Pomerantsev "Ob iskrennosti v literature" (About Sincerity in Literature) published by *Novyi mir* in December 1953, and the second was the review by Mikhail Lifshits "Dnevnik Marietty Shaginian" (The Diary of Marietta Shaginian) which appeared three months later in the same journal. Mikhail Lifshits, one of the most faithful and orthodox of Soviet Marxists, a disciple of Georg Lukacs and supreme authority on questions of Marxist esthetics, had completely "clammed up" after the war. He had published the first volume of his anthology *Marks i Engel's ob iskusstve* (Marx and Engels on Art) in 1938, but the second volume appeared only twenty years later, in 1957. His short review of Marietta Shaginian's book of travel sketches *Puteshestvie po Sovetskoi Armenii* (Journey Through Soviet Armenia), which was awarded a Stalin Prize (third class) for 1951, marked the end to his long silence. There was no doubt whatsoever that this subject was a mere pretext for Lifshits, but it was a suitable one. Marietta Shaginian in the course of her impressively long life had changed her convictions and views with singular facility and dexterity; she had the fortunate knack of being able to wax enthusiastic about each new change in the general ideological line which inevitably also became a change in her own intellectual and professional, writer's career. In the new edition of her sketches which appeared in 1952, she had managed to include more than a few ecstatic pages about the latest brilliant revelation of Stalin to the Soviet people and the whole world in the same year in his article *Ekonomicheskie problemy sotsializma v SSSR* (The Economic Problems of Socialism in the USSR).

Lifshits's brutal sarcasm about Shaginian's ecstasies was not, on the surface, directed at Stalin, but he expressed here all the hatred—stored up during the many years of enforced silence—of an orthodox stalwart for the usurper and distorter of the "Single True Teaching" (as Solzhenitsyn would have put it), and it is impossible not to sense this when reading his review. It was not without reason that this modest review was immediately noticed and brutally torn apart in the organ of the Union of Writers, *Literaturnaia gazeta*, and when Aleksandr Tvardovskii, then editor of *Novyi mir*, was dismissed from his post (in August 1954), Lifshits's review was one of the main crimes he was accused of.

I am well aware that Mikhail Lifshits's article did not reach a broad readership and that the scandal it aroused remained in the sphere of literature. Nevertheless, this incident seems to be a good example of Jewish sensitivity to Jewish names. What had happened was that an adamant Marxist who had spent many years in disgrace had attacked a despicable Stalinist toady, and, indirectly, Stalin himself. However, Jewish intellectuals who in one way or another belonged to the literary world read into his text an additional, specific, and, in reality nonexistent, message: the beginning of Jewish resistance. After having been beaten almost to death for so many years and had not even been allowed to scream from pain and now, just look, Jewish intellectuals were beginning to snap back! And this message which had been invented and imagined by them was no less important for them than the genuine, real one. In this way de-Stalinization in Soviet Russian literature gave a real boost to the Jewish national awakening and the participation in this process of Jews—and first of all Ehrenburg—was of primary importance.

It would be difficult for someone reading Ehrenburg's *Ottepel'* (The Thaw) for the first time today, just as it is for someone rereading it after thirty years (the first part was published in May 1954) to imagine what a bombshell it was on publication. I shall not discuss its artistic "merits," but only its content, the new spirit it heralded. Today its message seems ludicrously timid, but at that time it appeared subversive, even revolutionary. It was not without reason that the conservatives attacked Ehrenburg, all of them, starting with the sly opportunist Konstantin Simonov; and it was not without reason that the second part of *Ottepel'* was published only two years later, after Khrushchev's speech at the Twentieth Party Congress. In contrast to Lifshits's article which was buried away in the pages of *Novyi mir*, *Ottepel'* was read by millions of people (even though it was published in a separate edition only in 1956). It was talked about everywhere, and was accessible and comprehensible to everybody (partly just because of its artistic impotence, its primitiveness). It heralded not only the end of the hellish Stalinist freeze, but also hopes that everything would be set right, that everything would be fine. False, deceptive hopes? Of course! But they were absolutely necessary at such a critical time. As the Prophet Isaiah said: "Comfort ye, comfort ye my people!" (Isa. 40:1). The character in *Ottepel'* of Vera Grigor'evna Sherer, a former army doctor and daughter of a *shtetl* shoemaker, who had lost all her relatives when Orsha was occupied by the Germans, and who was now tending the sick in a provincial city, seemed to us somehow quite different from the bland, boringly upright earlier Ehrenburg hero, Al'per in *Buria* and *Dveiatyi val* (although today anyone can see that Sherer is just as unimpressive). She must have seemed different then because in one of the first pages, along with references to the arrests of 1936, one read the following dialogue between Dr. Sherer and Lena, the mother of a sick girl:

"It's just flu, her lungs are clear." Lena rejoiced at this news, but since she was in such a state she spoke her thoughts aloud: "But you aren't making a mistake, are you? She's breathing rather strangely." Vera Grigor'evna suddenly flew into a rage: "If you don't trust me, why did you call me?" Lena blushed: "Forgive me, I don't know what I'm saying. Really, I didn't mean to insult you. This is awful! . . ." Tears appeared in Vera Grigor'evna's eyes and she said quietly: "Forgive me, it's my fault. My nerves got the better of me. These days sometimes you have to hear such . . . you know, after the announcements . . . It's not right when a doctor acts the way I am acting."

And a little further we read this exchange between Lena and her husband:

Lena began to tell about Vera Grigor'evna. He said nothing. Lena persisted: "Well, what do you think? Isn't it disgraceful? What does she have to do with the case?" Ivan Vasil'evich said soothingly: "What are you getting worked up about? After all, I told you myself to call Sherer. I have nothing against her, people say she's a good doctor. But you mustn't trust them too much, that's for certain."

As toothless and colorless as all this seems today, at that time it gladdened our hearts and straightened our usually stooped backs. Yes, Jews responded, we're Jews, like Sherer, like Il'ia Ehrenburg, and there is no need to hide it or keep quiet about it. We shall remain ourselves, Jews, we will resist, we will hold out! It seems to me that this *resolution to hold out* was the most important thing in these first post-Stalin years.

Similarly, it seems to me that Ehrenburg's six-volume memoirs (*Liudi, gody, zhizn'* [People, Years, Life], 1960–65) also had a major role in maintaining and increasing Jewish consciousness, despite all the concessions to the censor, all the subterfuges, ruses, omissions, fictions, and attempts at self-justification of which Ehrenburg has been accused and to which he himself has admitted, at least to some degree. When the author says on the last page of the last part of the work to be published: "I wanted to tell about the life I have lived, about the people I have met, this might give some readers something to think about and help them understand something," I utterly believe him and I know to what extent the indefinite "some" and "something" apply to the young generation of Soviet Jews.

It is not just that in this work anti-Stalinism assumed the concrete features of an exposure of postwar anti-Semitism (and even of anti-Semitism during the war), nor that Ehrenburg in many places gave detailed accounts of the "Black Years" of Soviet Jewry (the murder of Mikhoels, the destruction of the Jewish intelligentsia, the "Doctors' Plot," the mass persecutions of 1949–53). Nor is it just that Ehrenburg called the end of 1948 and the beginning of 1949, when the Jewish Anti-Fascist Committee was dissolved, when "Perets Markish, Kvitko, Bergelson, Fefer, et al." were arrested, when the "anticosmopolitan campaign" began and when he himself shamefully said nothing about all this in Paris, submissively playing his role of *shirmach*, "the most painful months in my whole life" and confesses: "I interrupted my work on the book for a long time trying to summon up the courage to embark on this chapter. I should have been glad enough to omit it altogether. But life is not like a set of galley proofs; what you live through cannot be deleted." What is far more significant is that in this work he clearly formulated his Jewish credo, his position as a Jew, even if assimilated, alienated, hostile to Zionism, and indifferent to Israel, yet still a Jew: "I have never concealed my origin. There were times when I did not give it a thought, and others when I said whenever I could: 'I am a Jew'; for to my mind solidarity with the persecuted is the first principle of humanitarianism." And a little further: "so long as there is a single anti-Semite in the world I shall declare that I am a Jew."[12] Undoubtedly this credo is as elementary as the A-B-C, yet no one but Ehrenburg could openly, publicly, via millions of copies of his work, give Soviet Jewish youth this elementary lesson in national education.

But even this was not his most important service.

Ehrenburg "drew" a large number of portraits, of varying length and value, but united by a common feature, the Jewishness of each of the subjects: the tea merchant, patron of the arts, and poet "Amari"-Mikhail Tsetlin, the painter Amedeo Modigliani, the writer Mikhail Gershenzon, the artist and stage designer Aleksandr Tyshler, Perets Markish, Mikhoels, the writer Isak Babel, the poet Julian Tuwim, the writer Joseph Roth, the artist Pascin (Julius Pinkas), and many others. The degree of closeness of these creative figures to their people of origin varied, but for each of them their Judaism was something important, indeed essential. And although, in his discussion of "what is often called the 'Jewish Question'," (book 6, chapter 15), Ehrenburg asserts, "I was very devoted to the Italian Modigliani. He once told me that he was a Jew but for me he was forever associated with the anxiety of the pre-war years and with the art of the Italian Renaissance; certainly not with Yahveh" (the ancient God of the Hebrews);[13] yet in the separate chapter about Modigliani (book 1, chapter 20) the artist tells the author about his forebears, reads him sonnets by the Jewish poet Emmanuele Romano, and describes the humiliation of Jews during the medieval carnivals. Moreover, in the chapter on Julian Tuwim (book 3, chapter 3) Ehrenburg quotes in considerable detail and not for the first time Tuwim's famous article: "We the Polish Jews." It is thanks to Ehrenburg that this article reached Soviet Jews and became their manifesto as well. Ehrenburg paraphrases Tuwim as follows: "The blood of the Jews flows in deep, broad streams, the dark streams flow together in a turbulent, foaming river, and in this new Jordan I accept holy baptism—the bloody, burning brotherhood in martyrdom of the Jews . . ." Ehrenburg adds: "These words . . . were copied by thousands of people. I read them in 1944 and for a long time could not speak to anyone: Tuwim's words were the vow and the curse that lived in the hearts of many."[14]

He was right: these words transmitted by Ehrenburg awoke the hearts of many thousands of assimilated Jews who had forgotten their origin, just as his gallery of portraits showed (despite their author's ideological setting) that Jews are one people, single and indivisible, and that Modigliani is a brother of Babel, Tuwim, and Markish, and even of Mikhail Kol'tsov.[15]

I certainly have no intention of writing a panegyric to Ehrenburg; from a Jewish perspective his path is quite contradictory and insufficiently clear.

However, I am convinced that no other book in Soviet Russian literature in the fifteen years after the death of Stalin did as much for the Jewish awakening as *Liudi, gody, zhizn'*. This is all the more significant since Ehrenburg did not describe a particularly Jewish past, neither the traditional *shtetl* nor a city of assimilated Jews like Odessa. Indeed, there was no one left to write about the traditional past. The last generation of Russian-Jewish writers had passed from the scene, perished, been executed or, at best, fallen silent like dead men. Writers who were Jewish by birth became Russian writers without a trace of Jewishness left; either they quite forgot Jewish life or recorded it very faintly, as in the memoirs of Samuil Marshak, V *nachale zhizni* (At the Beginning of Life), which appeared in 1960, who in his youth, before the Revolution, had been an ardent Zionist. It was, as it were, to make up for the lack of anyone Jewish who could write of the traditional Jewish past that the real epic of Russified Jewish life in Southern Russia, in the southern part of the Pale of Settlement, was composed by Konstantin Georgievich Paustovskii in his *Povest' o zhizni* (see above). I believe, in fact, that we are indebted to the Russian Paustovskii almost as much as to the Jew Ehrenburg, among others, for his "resurrection" of Babel', one of the main heroes of the second half of *Povest'*.

Babel's regaining his rightful place in literature was an event of supreme importance. The first edition of his work after his posthumous rehabilitation appeared in 1957 with a preface by Ehrenburg. The apogee of Russian-Jewish literature and its conclusion, Isak Babel' had a decisive influence on an entire new generation of Jewish writers who began working underground in the late fifties and sixties, and emerged in public in Israel and in the West in the seventies. However, both these underground writers and Babel', the resurrected classic, are outside the bounds of the present chapter.

Our discussion of Ehrenburg's memoirs cannot be complete without our noting that the destruction of European Jewry does not exist in them *as a separate topic*. It is mentioned only in connection with *The Black Book*, prepared for publication by Ehrenburg and Vasilii Grossman but not permitted to be published.[16] This is not surprising—the topic of the Holocaust had been strictly banned by the censor: the murder of six million Jews by Hitler and his minions had remained taboo for over a decade and a half. It was now even permitted to write about the Soviet prison camps (Solzhenitsyn's *Ivan Denisovich* appeared in 1962), but the murder of six million Jews by Hitler and his minions was still taboo. Evgenii Evtushenko's poem *Babii Iar* (September 1961) was therefore a political bombshell which provoked an unprecedented roar of anger from the ideological authorities and anti-Semitic writers and critics, and cost the editor in chief of *Literaturnaia gazeta* his job. Anatolii Kuznetsov's novel of the same name (*Babii Iar;* 1966) was the sole work of Russian prose in the period under discussion devoted to the Holocaust. The anti-Semitic ban on the topic of Jewish martyrdom together with Soviet Jews' razor-sharp sensitivity to the slightest word of truth about it transformed both Kuznetsov and, especially, Evtushenko virtually into their national heroes. (The same applies to Viktor Nekrasov although only one of his speeches, also about Babii Iar, made it into print.)

We have now reached the question of anti-Semitism in post-Stalin literature. As I have written above, in the preceding period, direct anti-Semitic remarks were not permitted to be published, but now for various reasons (not the least of which was the general relaxation of the totalitarian grip) they began to appear. The change could be seen above all in scientific and semiscientific publications (mostly, but not exclusively, after the Six-Day War) which are not my concern here. However, belles lettres and literary criticism also contributed their mite. Perhaps the best-known examples were Ivan Shevtsov's novels *Tlia* (The Louse) and *Vo imia ottsa i syna* (In the Name of the Father and the Son). The unabashedly Black Hundred—like[17] views of Shevtsov, who was a protégé of Politburo member Dmitrii Polianskii—went so far that *Pravda* became involved in the matter and chastised the writer for violating the party's policy of friendship among Soviet peoples and even placed him on the same level as the "anti-Soviet" Solzhenitsyn. However, Shevtsov was merely religiously following the formula worked out during the last days of Stalin's life in preparation for the nationwide pogrom that was to follow the announcement of the "Doctors' Plot." The formula was simple: all Jews are Zionists, clandestine or overt, hirelings of capital, members of an international conspiracy (a variation of the theme of the "Protocols of the Elders of Zion"). As such they had been members of the opposition groups within the party which had fought against the Lenin-Stalin line and had always been the nucleus of all opposition blocs and platforms; while today they were trying to poison Soviet youth, and indeed all of Soviet society with the corrupt spirit of the West; and with their weapon of ideological sabotage they were paving the way for the defeat of the homeland of socialism in the coming final confrontation with imperialism. Indeed, Ivan Shevtsov was always a loyal Stalinist, and his anti-Semitism was only one part of his efforts to restore "Stalinist norms."

It is very curious that the reputation of rabid anti-Semite was attached to Vsevolod Kochetov, the literary model for the quite ungifted and extremely primitive Shevtsov; *Oktiabr'*, the journal of which Kochetov was editor in chief, had a similar reputation. This reputation was unquestioned by any of the liberal intelligentsia who, as a rule, had not read Kochetov. If you read him or reread him with the least objectivity, you realize that in his notorious novels (even in the most notorious of them *Chego zhe ty khochesh'?* [What Do You Want?]) there is not a trace of anti-Semitism. Granted, his prose style is very bad, although this is not the utter literary pulp of Shevtsov. His writing is strictly conservative, even reactionary (by the standards of the Khrushchev period), but in its own way it is daring since Kochetov is not afraid to defend Stalin even at the height of the exposure of Stalin's "errors." Kochetov, essentially, is a resolutely anti-intelligentsia writer. But Stalinism, or its literary counterpart socialist realism (and Kochetov should be recognized, without any irony, as one of the real classics of socialist realism), has been so closely linked with anti-Semitism that any attempt to revert to Stalinism has been considered anti-Semitic regardless of both the specific content of such an attempt and the personal qualities of whoever makes the attempt. Indeed, Kochetov himself was never anti-Semitic in his personal relations, as many people, including the émigré writer Vladimir Maksimov, have testified.

In contrast to *Oktiabr'*, certain literary journals were real hotbeds of Jew baiting. Such was *Ogonek*, with its circulation of millions, whose main editor, Anatolii Sofronov, was an inveterate anti-Semite. Sofronov was a man without any convictions or principles and his anti-Semitism was more of the everyday market or streetcar variety than one based on any set of ideas. There is nothing particularly reprehensible in his own poems or plays, but *Ogonek* published, for example, articles blaming the suicide of Maiakovskii on a Jewish conspiracy of critics and the Jewish cupidity of Lili Brik. Another example was the journal *Druzhba narodov* of which in 1960 Vasilii Smirnov was appointed chief editor, a man who not only did not conceal, but even advertised his hatred for Jews and for all non-Russians, that is, precisely for all those peoples whose friendship—and friendship toward whom—his journal was supposed to embody and extol. (This case is recounted in detail by Svirskii in *Zalozhniki* [*Hostages*, Rus.; Paris: Les Editeurs, 1974].) During the 1960s yet another journal, *Molodaia gvardiia*, became a bastion of Russian chauvinists.

I have mentioned these events on the literary periphery because they became widely known, if only among the limited circle of the intelligentsia.

These rabidly anti-Semitic writers, along with pogrom-inciting writings, undoubtedly contributed greatly to what became the massive flow of Jewish emigration of the 1970s.

The Ukrainian writer Anatolii Dimarov is a clear case of virulent anti-Semitism in literature which passed the Soviet censor. Indeed, both Grigorii Svirskii in his documentary novel *Zalozhniki* and the American professor Maurice Friedberg, in his work *The Jew in Post-Stalin Soviet Literature* (Washington, 1970), a must for anyone seriously interested in our subject, discuss Dimarov's novel *Shchliakhami zhittia* (In the Paths of Life, Ukr., 1963). Here we find a pure, so to speak, in vitro, instance of Black Hundred attitudes, combining the traditions of Kostomarov, Krushevan, and Stalin's favorite, Chesnokov.[18] But I am concerned here with *Russian* literature and, as far as I know, Dimarov's work has not been translated into Russian. Yet, Dimarov is a respected member of the multinational Soviet literary fraternity and in 1982, on the occasion of his sixtieth birthday, laudatory articles about him appeared in newspapers and journals, so it is possible that his novel *Shchliakhami zhittia* has in fact reached Russian readers.

A discussion of officially published Russian literature in the context of the reawakening of Jewish consciousness would not be complete without mentioning works translated from the languages of the Soviet nationalities which are authentically Jewish in spirit and idea. I do not mean the renewed publication of translations from Yiddish (as of 1959)—this is a topic in itself, but, for example, the translation of such works as the tales of Itshak Meras or the documentary prose of Mariia Rol'nikaite, both originally written in Lithuanian.

However, among translations into Russian perhaps the most influential aids to Soviet Jews' national education in the post-Stalin era were works translated from West European languages. While it was quite forbidden for authors writing in Russian to touch on Jewish history or Jewish civilization, Lion Feuchtwanger, for example, was entirely a product of that civilization, and in the second half of the 1950s and in the 1960s his works were published in the USSR many times. All of his novels with the exception of *Jephthas Tochter* (Jephtha's Daughter) were published or republished within this fifteen-year period, and his collected works in twelve volumes were published in an edition of 300,000 copies. In all, this comprised a kind of compendium of Jewish history from the beginning of the Christian era to the Nazi persecutions. Most Jews of my generation and of the generation after mine experienced the fascination of Feuchtwanger, if not always as a writer at least as a Jew. As for myself, to this day I take pride in the fact that I translated his last novel about Josephus and compiled the notes to the whole trilogy about him. While doing this work, for the first time in my life I felt the true meaning of the lofty words which have been so perverted by ideology and propaganda: to labor for one's people. Indeed, Feuchtwanger's significance for the Jewish movement of the 1970s has been treated by Western scholars (including Maurice Friedberg, in A *Decade of Euphoria: Western Literature in Post-Stalin Russia* [1977]) and by Soviet Jewish émigrés.

I shall limit myself to Feuchtwanger, as translations of Western works divert us from the question we are examining. In trying to answer that question, I can state that the limited relaxation of totalitarianism after Stalin, which led to the "Thaw" in literature and enabled the publication of a few works which dealt with hitherto taboo subjects, including the Holocaust and anti-Semitism, helped liberate Soviet citizens from the stupefying effect of total fear and, in this sense, undoubtedly also aided the Jewish awakening.

I began with an example of this last point and I should like to conclude with similar illustrations. An outstanding example was Boris Slutskii who had become very well known, even famous at that time, and was considered a democratic, plebian poet, almost a populist, *mutatis mutandis*. Whole cycles of his anti-Stalinist and Jewish poems were circulating very widely in samizdat. These poems were "Jewish" in a particular sense: they were composed by a completely Russified poet who but vaguely remembered the Jewish atmosphere of the 1920s and 1930s and was protesting against state anti-Semitism. In some poems themes appeared or were even intertwined. In the year after the Twenty-second Party Congress at which the criticism of Stalin reached its apogee, *Literaturnaia gazeta* published Slutskii's poem "Khoziain" (The Boss). Here are some excerpts:

> But my boss did not like me,
> Did not know or hear or see me,
> But still he feared me, like fire,
> And murkily, morosely hated me.
>
> I carried his portrait everywhere,
> I hung it in my dug-out and in my tent,
> I gazed and gazed and never tired of gazing at it . . .
> And with every year more and more rarely
> Did his dislike hurt me . . .
>
> Such as I bosses do not like.

In November 1962 this poem was taken as just another gob of spit on the tyrant's grave, although within the context of the cycle of his Jewish poems it had quite another resonance. But that cycle remained—and remains even today—little known. Samizdat, even the most widely distributed, remains accessible only to the select few so that Slutskii's "I" and "such as I" were understood only by very few readers.

In the summer of 1965 the provincial journal *Literaturnaia Armeniia* published Vasilii Grossman's travel notes on Armenia. In a slightly abridged form they were republished in Moscow two years later, in a collection of stories. The work contains "Jewish pages" which are penetrating and profound. You react to them immediately and instinctively. But their true meaning, their true depth and significance are hidden even from the most sensitive Jewish reader if he is not familiar with Grossman's masterpiece, his novel *Zhizn' i sud'ba* (Life and Fate) which was confiscated by the KGB in 1961 and published only in 1980 in Switzerland. This novel introduces us to the best, the purest, and the most powerful Russian writer of Jewish fate, for whom the work on Armenia was not a casual sketch, but his literary and political testament.

Grossman was the most outstanding example of the Soviet Jewish national awakening, and perhaps this was because he belonged to the older generation, created, assimilated, and also perverted and morally destroyed by the Revolution and Soviet rule. In this case one may really speak of a rebirth, only not a national one, but a human one, in the universal sense. Yet the human rebirth was the result of a national awakening—caused first by Hitler's genocide, the Holocaust, and then by Stalin's "Black Years."

If Grossman's work had been officially published in the Soviet Union, its significance would have been incalculable. Indeed, it is hard to imagine what its consequences would have been, what impact it would have had.

But it was not published there.

To sum up, it is fairly clear that instances of officially condoned anti-Semitism in the post-Stalin era along with the unwritten ban on Jewish themes increased the Jews' sense of alienation from Soviet society and thus played an important role in stimulating the Soviet Jewish national awakening.

It is more difficult to determine the influence of *positive* references to things Jewish which managed to pass the censor. Attempts by Russian-Jewish writers to touch on Jewish themes were certainly very welcome to

Soviet Jews and, in the context of the official silence on these subjects, every such instance had a special resonance. However, these attempts were rare and often so carefully camouflaged that they not only slipped past the censor, but escaped the reader's notice as well.

All in all, however, the limited relaxation of totalitarianism after Stalin, which led to the "Thaw" in literature and enabled the publication of a few works which dealt with hitherto taboo subjects, including the Holocaust and anti-Semitism, helped liberate Soviet citizens from the stupefying effects of total fear and in this sense they, too, undoubtedly aided the Jewish awakening.

Notes

1. The Russian "i" means "and," i.e., a conjunction.
2. In each of the postwar years a Decade of National Art would be dedicated to one of the titular nationalities of a union or autonomous republic.
3. His translations of works of the East are certainly not the most amusing material. Not for nothing did a colleague of Lipkin's, Arsenii Tarkovskii, one of the most venerable Russian poets, once exclaim in desperation: "O translations of the East, how my head aches from you!"
4. The publication of these works was mainly due to the efforts of Professor Efim Etkind, now living in Paris.
5. Professor Zand has recently refreshed my memory about this matter, for which I am sincerely grateful.
6. The article appeared in the anthology *Iz-pod glyb* ("From under the Rubble," Rus.) (Paris: YMCA Press, 1974).
7. Surov and Bubennov were both literary figures (Surov was a playwright, Bubennov a writer) who filled central roles in the anticosmopolitan campaign. Bubennov was the author of the *Pravda* article (February 13, 1953) which ruined Vasilii Grossman (see below). For Sofronov, see also pp. 220.
8. A. Lektorskii's article appeared in *Kommunist*, 3 (1953), pp. 106–15.
9. Anatolii Goldberg, in his recently published biography of Ehrenburg, has written in detail of Ehrenburg's lies in the West (in Britain and France) in these years.
10. Lazar Kaganovich was the most prominent Jewish member of the Soviet hierarchy in the postwar period. He was a full member of the Politburo and filled a number of important posts until ousted by Khrushchev in 1957 for belonging to the "antiparty group" led by Malenkov and Molotov which sought to overthrow the first secretary.

    Lev Mekhlis had worked on the staff of the Central Committee in the 1920s, been head of the Chief Political Administration of the Armed Forces (1937–40), and served first as commissar and later as minister of state control.

11. The deportation of a number of nationalities by Stalin in the war years from their national territories to Siberia or Central Asia has been the topic of a number of books.
12. The quotations are from Ilya Ehrenburg, *Men, Years—Life*, vol. 6, *Post-war Years 1945–1954* (London: MacGibbon & Kee, 1966), pp. 124, 127, and 131.
13. Ibid., p. 127.
14. Ibid., vol. 3, *Truce: 1921–33* (London: MacGibbon & Kee, 1963), p. 34.
15. Mikhail Kol'tsov (1898–1942), writer and journalist, became a regular correspondent and columnist for *Pravda* in 1922. He founded and edited the popular magazine *Ogonek* and edited the satirical magazine *Krokodil* (1934–38). He also wrote a book on the Spanish Civil War, *Spanish Diary* (1938). He disappeared during the purges of 1938 and was posthumously rehabilitated in 1956–57. Ehrenburg described him in his memoirs.
16. The *Black Book* was published in full in Israel by Yad Vashem and the Israel Research Institute of Contemporary Soviety Jerusalem, in 1981.
17. The Black Hundreds (an arm of the right-wing Union of the Russian People, founded in 1905) were armed gangs who initiated pogroms against Jews and members of the radical intelligentsia during and after the 1905 revolution in Russia.
18. Nikolai Kostomarov, nineteenth-century Russian historian, described the Jews of the Ukraine as oppressors of the Russian population, attributed considerable significance to the negative role of the Jews in the evolution of the Cossack movement, and gave credence to historic and contemporary blood libels, i.e., charges that Jews killed non-Jewish children in order to use their blood for ritual purposes.

Pavolakii Krushevan was a journalist and publicist whose organ, published in the Moldavian town of Kishinev, was a forum for Jew baiting, including calls to anti-Jewish violence. The 1903 pogrom in Kishinev was widely thought to have resulted from Krushevan's agitational activity.

D. I. Chesnokov, the ideologist of Stalin's last purge, became a member of the Party Presidium (as the Politburo was renamed) at the Nineteenth Party Congress in 1952 and fell into obscurity immediately after Stalin's death.

IV
PERSONAL TESTIMONIES

11

Background to the Present Jewish Cultural Movement in the Soviet Union

Benjamin Fain

The new Jewish cultural movement which started in the USSR in the mid-seventies has its origins on the one hand in such great historical events and trends as the creation of a Jewish state and *aliya,* and on the other hand in such negative phenomena as the postwar renewal of anti-Semitism in the Soviet Union and that country's policy of the cultural genocide of the Jewish people. However, the so-called "drop-out" phenomenon or *neshira* provided the immediate stimulus for the birth of the present cultural movement. (*Neshira* or "drop-out" rate refers to the number of Jews who leave the Soviet Union on a visa for Israel but settle elsewhere.) It is therefore important for our topic to understand the rise and decline of *aliya* from the Soviet Union.

It is generally accepted that after the Six-Day War the Jewish spark in the hearts of Soviet Jews flared up and produced a miracle: Jews who were totally assimilated after more than fifty years under the Soviet regime and who were cut off from world Jewry were suddenly imbued with the Zionist idea and succeeded in pulling down the iron curtain. *Aliya*—repatriation to Israel—began. However, after 1974 the stream of migration suddenly changed its course. More and more Jews emigrated to the United States and other countries. Very soon the percentage of "dropouts" reached a catastrophic 70 to 80 percent.

Though this picture contains some elements of truth, as a whole it seems to me to be incorrect.

Soviet Jewry is not a homogeneous entity. Roughly speaking, it may be divided into three groups. The first group consists of Jews who were living in the "Western regions" which were annexed to the Soviet Union in the course of World War II (the Baltic republics, Western Ukraine, Bessarabia, and Northern Bukovina). These Jews have lived for only a relatively short period under the Soviet regime and the Soviets have not succeeded in destroying their cultural heritage. This region, which includes Vilna and Kovno, was a great traditional center of Jewish learning.

The second group is that of the less acculturated Jews who live in the Caucasus and in Central Asia where Russification was generally imposed more gradually by the authorities. These Jews managed to preserve their way of life and many of them retained ties to Jewish tradition.

The third group represents the bulk of Soviet Jewry. These are the Jews who live in the European part of the RSFSR, in Belorussia, and in the Eastern Ukraine, in such cities as Moscow, Leningrad, Minsk, Odessa, Kiev, and Kharkov. These are fully assimilated Jews. The only reminders of their Jewishness are the entries in their internal passports, anti-Jewish discrimination, and anti-Semitic campaigns in the press.

The Jews of the first two groups (with a high Jewish identity) created internal pressure on the authorities during the period of détente. With the support of public opinion in the West this resulted in mass emigration to Israel. In some regions more than 50 percent of the Jewish population repatriated to Israel. At a certain stage a new stream of emigration started —from the Russian heartland, Belorussia, and the Eastern Ukraine. It started on a massive scale in 1974. From the beginning, this stream was largely oriented toward the United States and other countries, and not to Israel. In other words, this stream began with a high percentage of "dropouts" and with a tendency for this percentage to increase.

What happened meanwhile to the stream from regions with a high Jewish motivation? It began to dry up due to natural causes. It came under the influence of the "drop-out" tendencies of the third group, yet *neshira* in this stream remained at a much lower level. For example, in 1979 *neshira* among emigrants from Tbilisi reached 32 percent, from Chernovtsy 24 percent, and from Kovno 11.5 percent, whereas in the same year "dropouts" from Kharkov accounted for 90.6 percent of all emigrants; from Odessa for 97 percent, and from Leningrad for 86.2 percent.

The table of percentages of "dropouts" from the twenty cities which provided 75 percent of Jewish emigration from the USSR from 1968 to 1980 is highly illustrative (see table 11.1). The number in parentheses indicates to which of the three groups the cities belong.

Table 11.1
Percentage of "Dropouts" During the Period 1968–1980[1]

Odessa (3)	82.7	Vilna (1)	8.0
Kiev (3)	79.4	Dushanbe (2)	8.0
Leningrad (3)	74.1	Chernovtsy (1)	7.6
Minsk (3)	65.5	Mukachevo (1)	5.3
Moscow (3)	62.9	Kovno (1)	5.2
Lvov (1)	56.5	Samarkand (2)	4.5
Tashkent (2)	34.4	Sukhumi (2)	1.7
Riga (1)	32.7	Kutaisi (2)	0.7
Kishinev (1)	19.3	Derbent (2)	0.7

This presents a picture which is quite different from the widespread myth. Thus, Jews with a comparatively high Jewish identity repatriated to Israel, while the majority of assimilated Jews emigrated to other countries. Therefore the miracle was not the sudden national reawakening of the assimilated Jew (though this, too, did happen here and there). The miracle (if one occurred at all) was the breaking through the iron curtain by Jews with a high Jewish identity. All in all, in the period 1968–80 more than 160,000 Jews repatriated to Israel, and over 100,000 assimilated Jews migrated to other countries. It should be pointed out that we are dealing with a statistical tendency: therefore the personal story of this or that person whose destiny contradicts this tendency is irrelevant. For fairness's sake it must be mentioned that activists and heroes of the movement belonging to the third group are not less numerous, in percentage terms, that those in the first two groups.

The above picture, or more exactly the emerging tendency, became clear to us—a group of activists in Moscow, including Vladimir Prestin, Yosef Begun, Leonid Volvovskii, Pavel Abramovich, and myself—as early as the end of 1974, when *neshira* had only just started. We realized that it was an illusion to think it was enough for the gates to be opened and that two million Jews would then go to Israel. We also understood that there was no immediate solution to the "drop-out" problem. We concluded that in order to raise Jewish identity among the assimilated Jews, we had to conduct educational work among them. We began spreading Jewishness by circulating samizdat, books, cassettes, and so on. However, we soon realised that despite the importance and usefulness of this activity, it could not measure up to the scale of the problem. Therefore, in the spring of 1976, we started an ambitious venture: the "Symposium of Jewish Culture in the USSR: Its Present State and Future Prospects." During the six months of preparation (before the authorities began with massive repressions) we succeeded in informing a great number of scholars and organizations abroad. At the same time we also invited relevant Soviet organizations (the Ministry of Culture, the Moscow Synagogue) since everything we did was in strict accordance with Soviet law.

In the framework of preparations for the symposium we conducted a sociological survey among more than 1,500 Jews in the various regions of the USSR. The survey was concerned with various aspects of Jewish life in the Soviet Union and Jews' attitudes toward them. Detailed results of this survey were published in 1984 under the title "Jewishness in the Soviet Union. Report of an Empirical Study." From the survey it emerged that despite a very low level of Jewish knowledge of any sort, there was great interest in Jewish subjects. To the question whether the respondent would like to buy a book on Jewish history (if one were available) 95 percent answered positively. Over 50 percent claimed that they would like to study Hebrew (or have their children study the language). The survey showed a relatively high level of Jewish identity among the first two groups discussed above.

During the period of preparation, the intention to hold the symposium became well known both in the West and among Soviet Jews. Western radio stations in Russian gave it a great deal of attention. Not unexpectedly, the symposium was suppressed by the authorities and house arrest was imposed on its organizers and speakers.

By that time, the movement of *tarbutniks* (activists in the struggle for Jewish culture in the USSR) had crystallized. At this point I would like to describe the general ideology of the movement.

1. Its aim was, and remains, to revive a tradition that unites the Jews as a people. Jewish "knowledge" for dissemination among Jews should include Jewish history, Judaism, and Hebrew.
2. Cultural aid by Israel and Jewish communities in the West is a necessary condition for success in spreading Jewish knowledge among Soviet Jews. Such aid, without political undertones, entirely conforms with Soviet law and international agreements signed by the Soviet Union.

3. The struggle for the legalization of Jewish culture in the Soviet Union is central to the success of this venture.

It must be stressed that by suppressing any glimmering of Jewish culture, the Soviet authorities violate their own laws. Therefore, the announcement of these violations, their discussion at international meetings in which the USSR participates, is of paramount importance. The attention of international organizations must be attracted to the suppression of the national cultural rights of Soviet Jews. All this can and must become the subject of a wide public campaign for the legalization of Jewish culture in the USSR. In this respect, Israel and the Jewish communities of the West must play a major role.

The symposium was a challenge. How did the Soviet authorities, Israel, and the Jewish communities outside the Soviet Union and Soviet Jews themselves respond to this challenge? It is common knowledge that the Soviet authorities conduct persistent and intensive anti-Semitic campaigns and that there is discrimination against Jews in all walks of Soviet life. World public opinion has paid less attention to another side of the authorities' war against Soviet Jews. Yosef Begun was among the first who tried to attract the attention of public opinion to the "cultural genocide" being carried out against the Jewish people. The notion of cultural genocide was used by the Soviets (Yosef Begun "discovered" this in one of his articles) and defined as follows: "National cultural genocide is the destruction of all that binds a certain group of people into a unified nation or into a people, the destruction of its language, literature, and art, the destruction of historic monuments, etc."[2] Ironically this exactly describes the attitude of the Soviet authorities toward Jewish culture. In February 1981, over 125 Soviet Jewish activists sent a letter to the Twenty-Sixth Congress of the Soviet Communist Party detailing the Kremlin's systematic attempt to exterminate Soviet Jewish life. They wrote:

> The Jews are almost completely deprived of the possibility of studying and using their national language. . . . The authorities refuse to legalize the private teaching of Hebrew and often interfere with it, subjecting both teachers and students to repression. . . . Jews residing in the USSR are, as a result, threatened by complete linguistic assimilation. . . . Soviet Jews are practically cut off from their national history. Not one book on Jewish history, except for a series of studies dealing with the ancient period, has been published in the USSR, and they are often confiscated from foreign tourists wishing to bring them into the USSR. . . . There is not one

museum dealing with Jewish history, culture or ethnography, and no existing Soviet museum has a special section dealing with these subjects. Not even one paragraph devoted to Jews has been included in school text books, even those on ancient history. . . . Jewish folklore, both literary and musical, is hardly collected. . . . National Jewish culture has not been included as an organic part of the official cultural framework of the USSR. The most important channel of popularizing cultural values, television, has never been made available for presenting the culture of the Jewish people to the general public. . . . Cultural exchanges with other countries do not exist. Soviet media, with the exception of *Sovetish heymland*, which is inaccessible both to non-Jews and to the majority of the Jews because of the language barrier, takes no notice of anything concerning the cultural life of Jews living abroad. . . . Attempts by Soviet Jews to restore certain elements of Jewish culture . . . meet with repression by the KGB. . . . The fact that the KGB is almost the sole state organization that has a special section dealing with the whole range of the national problems of Soviet Jews is a sinister and paradoxical symbol of the national status of Soviet Jewry.[3]

This letter was written in 1981, only four years after the symposium was due to be held. Yosef Begun was one of those who signed this letter. He has been tried three times, most recently in 1982, when he was sentenced to twelve years' deprivation of freedom (seven years in prison and five in exile under a special regime). In total he has been sentenced to seventeen years' deprivation of freedom for his commitment to the traditions of his people. [since this paper was delivered Begun has been released (in early 1987) and emigrated to Israel (early 1988)]. His story is a terrible illustration of national cultural genocide in the USSR. There are many other examples of the brutal war against any attempts at a Jewish cultural revival.

I have my own personal examples of manifestations of this cultural genocide. One of them is connected with the symposium. During a search in my flat in Moscow, the KGB officer classified the material to be confiscated according to the following classifications: "This is the symposium, this is Jewish culture, this is the symposium, this is Jewish culture . . ." He did not even try to conceal the authorities' intention that everything connected with Jewish culture should be confiscated.

It would not be true to say that what I have described so far depicts the *only* response of the Soviet authorities to the challenge presented by the symposium. It must be realized that the symposium touched upon a very sensitive issue of Soviet domestic policy—the attitude toward national minorities. It is for this reason that the authorities were now forced to take a number of positive measures in connection with Jewish culture. I quote again from the above-mentioned letter sent to the Kremlin by Jewish activists:

> State-supported Yiddish drama groups have been formed. The sole Yiddish publication, *Sovetish heymland,* has started publishing summaries and occasionally even translations of some of their articles in Russian. Works of fiction on Jewish subjects have again been published in central literary magazines after a ten years' absence, and the number of Yiddish gramophone records in the USSR has increased to a certain extent. In spite of these positive developments, no sufficient conditions for the preservation, study, propagation, and development of Jewish culture have been created in the USSR."

The Soviet response can be summarized as follows: The authorities continued their cultural genocide policy where such crucial elements of Jewish culture as history, religion, and Hebrew are concerned. On the other hand, they agreed to certain improvements in the more marginal elements of the Jewish cultural issue.

The response of Soviet Jews to the problem of Jewish culture and cultural genocide conducted against it has been quite unequivocal. Great interest in everything connected with Jewish culture was already revealed in the sociological study conducted before the symposium. But at that time there was much discussion among Jewish activists about the necessity of struggling for Jewish cultural rights. Now, ten years after the symposium, although the discussion continues, Jewish culture has become one of the main issues of Jewish activism.

What was the response of the State of Israel and the Jewish communities of the West to this movement which arose without their blessing and inspiration (contrary to Soviet propaganda claims)? And what was their response to the cultural genocide against Jewish culture in the Soviet Union? The contribution made by Israel and the Jewish communities of the West to the struggle for Jewish culture in the USSR and to supplying Soviet Jewry with Jewish cultural material by no means measured up to the scale of the problem.

What we felt was expressed in addresses prepared for the Moscow symposium in 1976:

> Only a lack of understanding of our problems can explain the minimal assistance which we have received from the Jewish communities in the West for the cultural needs of the Jews in the USSR. One of the reasons may be the little understanding

Western Jews have of the plight in which Soviet Jews find themselves. . . . Only with difficulty will one find among the more than two millian (Soviet) Jews a few hundred families who possess any material on Jewish history, and in most cases this is prerevolution. The Bible is a rare book in Jewish homes. Already several generations of Jews are without any inkling about their past.[4]

I must state, to my regret, that things have changed little. The assessment of my friends in Moscow of the role of Western Jewish communities today is almost the same as it was in 1976.

To summarize: the Jewish cultural movement in the USSR arose as a response to the incipient growth of the "drop-out" phenomenon. But, as a matter of fact, its creation was essential to fill a void in the Jewish national movement. Jewish education is the only way to assure the continuation of Jews as Jews in the Soviet Union. It is important for the increase in *aliya* and, in the long run, for the curbing of *neshira*. Today, as the gates of the Soviet Union are in fact closed—and this against a backdrop of 70 to 80 percent *neshira* of those who do get out—Jewish self-education and the struggle for its legalization are the most important elements in our fight to save Soviet Jewry from cultural genocide and for *aliya*.

Notes

1. See Z. Alexander, "Jewish Emigration from the USSR in 1980," Soviet Jewish Affairs, vol. 11(3), 1981, p. 17.
2. M. N. Andriukhin, "Genocide in the Policy of Imperialist States" (Moscow: Znanie, 1967).
3. *Jerusalem Post*, May 2, 1981.
4. Fain, Prestin, Abramovich et al., *Evreiskii samizdat*, vol. 15, (Jerusalem: CRD, 1978), p. 306.

A Call From Benjamin Fain: Moscow, 15 December 1976

The Moscow Cultural Symposium, organized by Benjamin Fain and Vladimir Prestin in December 1976, was the first major effort at establishing cultural and religious rights for Soviet Jews. Despite the fact that hundreds of the expected participants were placed under house arrest, the Seminar was attended by fifty people.

Opening Statement, Benjamin Fain, Chairman Moscow Conference:

Jews around the world are experiencing a period of flowering of Jewish culture and a series of miracles are occurring: the rebirth of a Jewish State; and Hebrew has become

BACKGROUND TO THE JEWISH CULTURAL MOVEMENT 243

the spoken language of the citizens of Israel, and the language of many Diaspora Jews. In contrast to this Renaissance of world Jewry is the condition of Jewish culture in the Soviet Union. Its problems have been discussed at numerous conferences. Our Symposium, however, differs from others. It is the first one in many years to be held in Moscow, and its aim is not only to present the state of Jewish culture but to discuss how it can be reborn and developed.

How do we see the present state of Jewish culture in the USSR? At present, there are in Russia a number of synagogues; a small number of books published in the Yiddish language; a newspaper called *Sovetish heymland;* one regional newspaper; and one or two semiprofessional artistic ensembles. That is all. These are "leftovers" from a sometime flourishing Yiddish culture, especially in the first years after the Revolution. The proponents of that culture used to fight against a culture in Hebrew. This Yiddish culture suffered a decline after World War II from which it has never recovered. In effect, the culture is dying. Most of its supporters are elderly. There are no schools to study the Yiddish language or people who are interested in doing so. Any attempt in the Soviet Union to become acquainted with Jewish culture is made within an atmosphere of fear and danger to Jews. This fear is intensified by anti-Zionist propaganda on the one hand, and lack of Jewish publications of a positive Jewish nature on the other. The atmosphere of fear, lack of Jewish expression, lack of Jewish culture, and a low birth rate are all symptoms affecting Soviet Jewry today. One of the papers of the Symposium is devoted to statistical prognosis. It shows that there is a constant reduction in Judaism. At the same time another tendency can be observed. More and more Jews have a yearning for their true culture. One of the most significant manifestations of this phenomenon is the celebration of Simhat Torah in Moscow. The incredible happens. Over 10,000 Jews demonstrate their devotion and interest in the tradition of their people.

There are other manifestations of their interest, but not such obvious ones. For example, many Jews collect Jewish history books, either rare prerevolutionary copies or books from abroad. They reprint them as well as other materials on Jewish subjects. All this is copied and disseminated. The typed magazine *Tarbut,* whose purpose is Jewish enlightenment in history, religion, art, and language, is in great demand. The Jewish Art Show in Leningrad attracted thousands of Jewish visitors. Spontaneous artistic ensembles are created with Jewish music and songs. Many unofficial seminars of Jewish history and culture exist. In Moscow and in many other cities there are Hebrew language study groups, etc. This is proof of our interest in the culture and tradition of the Jewish people. In March 1976, a group of enthusiasts carrying on the wave of this interest decided to arrange a Symposium devoted to the present state of Jewish culture and its future prospects in the USSR. This group eventually organized a committee for the Symposium. The preparation for the Symposium was open and legal. Invitations were sent to many scholars and rabbis abroad, as well as to many leading figures in Soviet culture and official Soviet organizations. Jewish scholars in the USSR were also invited. On 17 November 1976, a press conference for the Symposium was arranged by its organizers. Soviet journalists, correspondents of the Western Communist press, and other Western correspondents were invited to attend the news conference. Only the Western correspondents showed up. One of the questions they raised was the attitude of the Soviet government to the Symposium. At that time we had no answer to that question because our letters and invitations to the Soviet authorities which had been sent four to five months earlier had never been answered. The answer came a bit later. From 23 to 25 November 1976, the apartments of the organizers were searched. All materials concerning the Symposium and Jewish culture were confiscated. This was followed by an announcement of TASS which explained that the searches were legal and that the confiscated material testified to the fact that it was inspired by Zionist centers and aimed at inflaming national disunity. The next step by the authorities was an invitation by the deputy minister of culture to meet with the editor of *Sovetish heymland*. This was the first official reaction by the Soviet authorities. They stated that they would not participate in the Symposium. TASS called it "Symposium—a Provocation." From that time on the preparation for the Symposium became a struggle of a small group of individuals against a well-trained army in psychological and other forms of warfare. At the same time the Soviet press came out with a series of articles on the present state of Jewish culture in the USSR.

Because of this widespread campaign, we feel that the Symposium has actually begun. The Soviet press described the state of Jewish culture as flourishing. Or at least as very satisfactory. I do not intend to give a complete answer to all these allegations here. However, we would like to state the following:

1. The Soviet Jews have almost no access to the "Book of Books"—the Bible which they created.
2. Russian Jews have no access to their history.
3. Russian Jews have no legal right to study Hebrew, the language of their forefathers.
4. Russian Jews have practically no access to their art, literature, theater, and music.

At present, according to the program of the Symposium, there are about eighty papers to be delivered. More than forty are by Soviet authors. These papers present a variety of ideas on the possibility of developing Jewish culture in the Soviet Union. Some of the points emphasized in almost every paper are:

1. Religion is an important element of Jewish culture and must have an important role in the future rebirth of Jewish culture. For some Soviet Jews it may mean familiarization with religion, Judaism, and its philosophy. For others it may become a part of their cultural baggage, whereas, for many, it means a first step in their contact with the Jewish religion.
2. Jewish culture in the USSR is practically nonexistent. At the same time Jewish culture in Israel and in Western countries is flourishing. Therefore, any development of Jewish culture here must be based on the help of our brethren abroad. This help is within the Jewish tradition, the legal provisions of our Constitution, and the Helsinki Agreement.
3. Jewish cultural rebirth has a legal basis. It is defined by international agreements signed by the Soviet Union, the Helsinki Agreement of civil and political rights which state that national minorities have a right to develop their culture.

I wish to emphasize that our problem is that of national minorities. It is essential to fight for these rights. The struggle must be conducted primarily by Soviet Jews, but the support of Jews and non-Jews is essential. Our work of preparation for the Symposium once again proves that international agreements and practice are two different things.

In one of the papers a plan is laid for self-education in the fields of religion, history, art, language, and music through books on these subjects which are nonexistent in the Soviet Union and must be translated from Hebrew and English. We envision a long period of struggle in front of us for the legitimate distribution of these cultural treasures. This action is in accordance with the spirit and letter of the Helsinki Agreement.

In other papers it is suggested that religious centers of a new type should be created. They differ from the official synagogues that are under the control of the Soviet government. It was also suggested that many cultural institutions and learned societies be created and that it is our task to press for the creation of such institutions which were promised in the international agreements.

In conclusion, I wish to emphasize again that we are gathered here to discuss problems of Jewish cultural rebirth. However, the Symposium for us is not just a call for the discussion of this question, but an important *precedent* for the development of Jewish culture. Another step, perhaps a big one, along the road of Jewish rebirth.

Translated from Russian

While Benjamin Fain was being questioned in the Moscow procurator's office on 15 December 1976, his home was searched and Fain's opening statement confiscated. He later reconstructed the essential points of his opening remarks from memory.

12

A Brief Survey of the History of Hebrew Teaching in the USSR

Mark Drachinsky

The following is a discussion, conducted in Hebrew, between a Moscow Jew and a tourist in the back of the synagogue on Arkhipova Street in Moscow. The tourist, an American Jew who lived in Israel, spoke fluently and with a rich vocabulary. The Muscovite's Hebrew was no less fluent, and at one point the guest asked, "How long did you study in order to speak such fine Hebrew?" The Muscovite replied, "A pretty long time—it took me a full year of studying Hebrew until I was able to teach it." The stunned guest admitted that it took him many years after he had moved to Israel before he was able to converse in Hebrew.

The Muscovite in this story was a Hebrew teacher, presently a Prisoner a Zion, Aleksei Magarik.[1] His is not an exceptional case. The high level of instruction, the deep interest, and the strong incentive for learning Hebrew have resulted in many people in the Soviet Union, young and old, mastering this simultaneously ancient and modern language, although it is suffering from a severe and frighteningly rapid campaign for its obliteration on the part of the Soviet authorities.

This repression of a language has been going on in the midst of the spiritual barrenness prevalent in the Soviet Union. The conditions for Jewish study are sorely deficient. As is well known, there are no official Jewish schools in the Soviet Union. There is no framework for Jewish community life. The study of Hebrew is forbidden and even Yiddish cannot be studied. The history books available in the schools and universities make no mention of the Jewish people or the State of Israel, yet slander of the State of Israel is widespread. It is in this desolate atmosphere that the third generation of Soviet Jews has been raised. These Jews, like their parents and grandparents before them, receive no Jewish education, although they live in a country which eighty years ago was one of the centers of Hebrew culture, a country from which emerged the Hebrew language's great poets and authors, Bialik, Chernikhovsky, Mendele Moikher Seforim, and others.

With the victory of the anticzarist revolution in February 1917, the Jews of Russia were granted equal rights as Russian citizens, and the degrading laws of the Pale of Settlement were abandoned. Yet, after only a few months, in October of the same year, the Bolshevik Revolution brought to power a party which viewed every independent culture, as well as every expression of independent thought, as a dangerous threat to its rule. According to Soviet law, a Jew may be granted the complete rights of a Soviet citizen provided that he ceases to be a Jew: that he alienates himself from the traditions of his fathers and publically renounces his age-old heritage.

In the Soviet Union Hebrew was condemned as a language of the bourgeoisie and Zionism as an emissary of world imperialism. The Zionist movement was and remains in dire straits. Teachers of Jewish law and the Hebrew language were thrown into labor camps. In the front line of the oppressors stood the *Evsektsiia*, the Jewish division or section of the Communist party. Throughout the country synagogues and houses of Jewish study were shut down or desecrated. Despite the horrible conditions, however, a number of *heders* were run in secret in which *melamdim* (the term used for teachers in *heders*) taught children the holy language and the traditions of their fathers.

With the changes that came with the Revolution and the civil war, the Baltic states—Lithuania, Latvia and Estonia (which were previously included in the czarist Empire)—gained independence. The Jewish culture within these states continued to flourish until they became a part of the USSR in 1940. Elementary and high schools in which the Hebrew language and literature were taught existed in these states in the 1920s and 1930s. A relative of mine from Riga, who speaks a fluent Sephardi Hebrew, told me that in her hometown there used to be schools that taught Ashkenazi Hebrew and those that taught Sephardi, or Israeli, Hebrew.

Within the course of a single year, however, between the Soviet occupation of the Baltic states in 1940 and the Nazi occupation in 1941, the Soviets did their utmost to "equate" the Baltic population with the rest of the country through the denial of equal rights and the suppression of national cultures. Whatever traces of Jewish culture the Soviets did not manage to erase, the Nazi Germans finished off through the physical destruction of the Jews there.[2]

And yet, although the horrors suffered by the Baltic Jews over the past few decades were even worse than those suffered by the Jews of Russia, there were a few knowledgeable people, versed in Hebrew culture, who managed to survive both the Stalin and the Nazi destructions. There are testimonies from the fifties and sixties of elderly people, mostly from Lithuania, who had studied Hebrew in their hometowns. Most of them were by profession shoemakers, builders, pharmacists, and the like, who later managed to teach Hebrew, based only on what they had learned in their youth during their home countries' period of independence. Most of these teachers remained unknown for a number of reasons: because their efforts took place before the great surge of Hebrew study began, because almost all of them managed to go to Israel with relatively little difficulty in the early seventies, or because they taught on an individual basis at the invitation of the student, and only rarely on a group level.

The establishment of the State of Israel in 1948 helped to stir up nationalistic feelings among Soviet Jews. Suddenly a great number of young people emerged requesting visas to emigrate to Israel. The Jews were perplexed: Stalin was still alive and anti-Jewish terror was at its height, yet, on the other hand, at the United Nations the USSR had voted in favor of establishing a Jewish state. Thus no one could guess how the Soviet regime would react to this sudden surge of requests for emigration visas.

In 1948 a group of students from an institution in Leningrad wrote a letter to a top Soviet official requesting permission to go to Israel. As a result of that letter the group was placed under surveillance and in 1950 its members were arrested for treason. One of the group whom I know, Leonid Rutshtein, was sentenced to ten years in a prison camp. Two years after the death of Stalin, the Soviet authorities found that Rutshtein had indeed committed no act of treason and he was freed. He served a total of five years.

In the mid-sixties when Leonid Rutshtein was living in Moscow and working as a certified physician, he met an elderly man who had come from Latvia before its absorption into the Soviet Union, a graduate of one of the Hebrew gymnasiums of Riga who spoke fluent Hebrew. With him Rutshtein studied in secret the language of his fathers. Later he began studying on his own with a group of friends. During this period there was another group of Hebrew students of whom Moshe Palhan (Trakhtman) was the instructor. It may be fairly asserted that these groups, and most likely others like them, were the pioneers of a new major trend of Hebrew study in the USSR. I would like to point out, by the way, that Leonid Rutshtein moved to Israel with his family in 1970. Upon his arrival he changed his name to Aryeh Rotem and he now lives in Petah Tikvah and works in Beilinson Hospital.

This is not the time or place to trace the effects of the Six-Day War on Jewish identity in the Soviet Union. The establishment of the *aliya* movement, the attempted hijacking of a plane by *aliya* activists, and the Leningrad trials were all historical events that in some way helped bring about the opening of the gates and the beginning of the mass emigration of Jews from the Soviet Union. For our discussion it is important to note that from the end of the 1960s and throughout the 1970s Hebrew study groups continued to flourish although exit visas were comparatively easy to obtain, since even during this period in which thousands were leaving there were still hundreds whose requests for visas were rejected. The number of refuseniks has apparently grown from hundreds to thousands over the past decade.

To return to the 1960s and 1970s: most of the teachers of that period were swept up in the giant wave of *aliya* and left the Soviet Union. Their pupils quickly turned into teachers and almost as quickly into emigrants on their way to Israel. Thus the "generations" of this network changed rapidly. The teachers themselves had little time in which to master the language and even less time to gain any teaching experience. I remember cases in which someone who had completed the first five lessons of the Hebrew book, *Elef millim* (1,000 Words), would be teaching his friend who had completed only two lessons. The incentive of the students was clearly defined in most cases. They were preparing themselves for *aliya* and for their subsequent absorption into Israeli society. They hurried to learn what they could of the language which would soon be their means of communication in their new homeland.

It is understandable that under these conditions only those teachers who were refused exit visas were able to teach in a more permanent manner. Thus it is no surprise that these refuseniks stood at the head of what we may call the "Hebrew community" in the USSR. They taught many students, established "clubs" and seminars devoted to Hebrew study, and, of course, gained a great deal of teaching experience. However, I must point out that there were a few teachers who were not refuseniks. One good example is that of an acquaintance of mine, one of the leading teachers in Moscow, who has been teaching Hebrew for over ten years and who, to this day, has never made the decision to move to Israel or applied for an exit visa.

During the 1970s the nature of Hebrew study in the Soviet Union was fairly well consolidated and remains so up to today.:

- The study group gathers for a lesson in the apartment of one of the students, or that of the teacher. From time to time they try to change the location of the lesson, yet this is not always possible.
- The average group convenes once a week. A few groups try to meet more often, but never more than twice a week. For my beginners' groups I usually gave six lessons per month: every week a basic lesson in spoken Hebrew and every two weeks a lesson in grammar. In the summer *ulpanim*, however, studies are more intensive. In these *ulpanim* Jews from different areas meet at a vacation resort and lessons are given almost every day for a month or two.

Most of the teachers do not try to hide the fact that they teach Hebrew since the study of a foreign language is not officially forbidden by law. Nevertheless, they do try to keep secret the place, date, and time of the meetings, in addition to the names of the students, in order to prevent harassment in the form of an unpleasant visit from the KGB. For this reason it is difficult to organize Hebrew lessons by phone, since the phones of known *aliya* activists are usually tapped. Nevertheless, not all teachers agree with these precautions and there are those who insist on speaking freely on the phone despite the known risks. It is difficult to decide which method is better. In any case the situation is a delicate one and every teacher must consider not only his own opinion but also the position and demands of his students, not all of whom are refuseniks who are willing to burn all their bridges behind them in the Soviet Union. In fact, in the 1980s many people joined the Hebrew community who had no plans of moving to Israel.

In the classes a strong emphasis is placed on the ability to converse in Hebrew and to express oneself on various subjects in that language. It is common for students to begin speaking during the first few lessons, even with only ten words or so at their disposal. The teachers usually try to avoid translating full sentences from Russian into Hebrew so that students will free themselves from their attachment to the structure and idioms of the

Russian language and will begin as early as possible to "think in Hebrew." In the first stages, for example, the teachers translate Hebrew words into Russian. Later, however, new Hebrew words are explained in Hebrew and the students are then asked to provide the Russian translation. The study of grammar is very limited, and only its practical application is emphasized. I, for example, taught more grammar than most of my colleagues.

In many groups the students are asked to prepare a story with a given vocabulary which they must read aloud during the next lesson. As opposed to the average twenty students who make up most *ulpan* classes in Israel, the average class in the Soviet Union is made up of only four or five students. In these small classes the story is a very successful method of learning. Nevertheless, I do not think that this method is suitable for larger groups, since it would take up a large amount of time and students would lose interest while so many others are presenting their papers.

Hebrew books are always scarce. The most popular method of copying is by photography since duplication by Xerox machines is forbidden in the Soviet Union. The easiest method, and one which has proved quite useful, is to record the lessons. Teachers often record Israeli broadcasts, read aloud selections from Israeli stories, and so forth. During the 1980s the amount of Hebrew literature available to the Hebrew Community of the Soviet Union has grown, yet there is still a great scarcity of this material, especially outside Moscow and Leningrad.

I would like to take advantage of this opportunity to point out that here in Israel I have not managed to find the same lessons which have proved so successful in the Soviet Union. I have asked many of the professional teachers here. A few teachers know of one lesson by the name of "Look and Listen" which includes books, records, and pictures, but most have only heard of it and know nothing of its content and its quality. There are other lessons as well of which no one in Israel has heard, and I finally came to the conclusion that they simply have not been published here. For example, there was one recorded lesson composed in the style of a conversation which we called "The Dialogues" or "Love in Basic Hebrew"—we did not know its real name since it arrived in the USSR on unmarked cassettes. There is another recording whose name is unknown in the Soviet Union of which only the second half exists, and the quality of the recording itself is quite poor. I was asked by some friends in the Soviet Union to find it here and send it to them in its entirety, including tapes and texts. The hero of these stories is an American boy who corresponds with an Israeli girl named

Yardena. He later comes to Israel and they carry on their conversations in basic Hebrew. In the 1970s many teachers used the old *Elef millim.* Today it is hardly used. Instead there are other books: "I Am in Israel," "The Student's Conversation Guide," "Conversations," and this book which I mentioned whose title is unknown. The most popular course, at least in Moscow, is "Look and Listen." The more advanced levels use texts such as "Shalom from Jerusalem," issues of *Gesher* and *Hulia,* and regular books in Hebrew which are extremely difficult to obtain.

By the 1970s students and teachers alike began to feel the need to develop a better network of communication in order to expose students to a greater variety of teaching methods. WIth the goal of improving the students' Hebrew and the quality of instruction, two types of "clubs" were established—one of teachers and one of students (with the guidance of one or two teachers). These clubs were called "Teachers' Talk" or "Student Talk." They met on weekends at private apartments. One of the participants would usually give a lecture in Hebrew followed by group discussion. Aleksei Magarik, for example, a Prisioner of Zion whom I mentioned earlier, once gave a lecture of this sort on the "Muscovite Hebrew Dialect."

During this period kindergartens for Jewish children also began to appear, along with Sunday schools in which Hebrew was studied together with the usual religious subjects.

By the end of the 1970s the massive emigration of Jews from the Soviet Union had come to a halt. Since then all that has remained of Jewish emigration is a small stream of the few lucky individuals who manage to leave. A tremendous number of Jews have found themselves in the "refusenik" category.

Out of these conditions a new goal has emerged among the members of the Hebrew Community: not only to study Hebrew in order to prepare for life in Israel, but also in order to protect the language itself from disappearing altogether among the Jews of the Soviet Union. Today many Jews have joined the Hebrew Community who are hesitant about requesting exit visas due to the slim chance of receiving a positive answer and the likelihood, on the other hand, of losing one's job. Some Jews come to study who have no thoughts at all of moving to Israel or are even determined to stay in the Soviet Union, yet they wish to protect or express their Jewishness through studying Hebrew. In addition, over the past few years the phenomenon of a religious revival (*Ba'ale tshuva*) has gained great momentum and has increased the number of people who study Hebrew but have no intention of emigrating (although for most of them the desire to fulfill the precepts of the Torah includes the desire to live in the Promised Land). In the early and mid-1980s the average level of Hebrew among Soviet Jews was much higher than it was in the 1970s, since now there were teachers, longtime refuseniks, who entered the decade of the eighties with an almost full command of the Hebrew language. Another unique factor of Hebrew study in the Soviet Union today is the concern among students to acquire an Israeli accent and idiom. More and more Soviet Jews today try to abandon the tendency to pronounce words incorrectly with their natural Russian accent.

The Hebrew study seminars have increased in both number and quality despite the obstacles imposed by the Soviet authorities. There are also seminars whose participants wish not so much to improve their spoken Hebrew but rather to examine the cultural history of Hebrew and other Semitic languages (although the lectures and discussions are conducted in Hebrew).

I will not go into the matter of Soviet oppression which is a subject unto itself. I will only mention that lately the Soviet authorities are no longer satisfied with breaking in on lessons and club meetings, or with threats and damaging calls to places of employment. Today, the authorities have no qualms about fabricating cases by planting drugs or making accusations of anti-Soviet propagandizing based on the fact that a Hebrew book was found in the apartment of the accused. Prisoners of Zion of today whose conditions range from poor to dangerous—Yosef Begun, Iulii Edelshtein, Ari Volvovskii, Aleksei Magarik, Ruald Zelichonok—were all teachers of Hebrew. (Between the date of the lecture on which this chapter was based and its editing for publication all have been released.)

The Hebrew of the Soviet Hebrew Community is different from that of the Israeli Hebrew, since the two groups learn from completely different sources. Nevertheless, the Soviet student is influenced by modern Israeli Hebrew, through listening to recordings from Kol Yisrael's Second Program ("Reshet Bet") and through conversations with Hebrew-speaking tourists who learned to speak Hebrew in Israel. This sometimes creates interesting paradoxes. I have met students who have devoted their efforts to mastering Israeli slang, and in the outskirts of Moscow one can hear extraordinary examples of the latest Israeli idioms. Or I have met people who have mastered a Hebrew so rich that it is rarely heard in Israel. On the other hand, most Soviet Hebrew speakers fall into entirely different errors from those of the Israeli, and there are well-known Hebrew phrases which the Soviet student may never encounter. Similarly, I myself have often been guilty of making incorrect use of the definitive "hey"—the definite article —which is one of the most difficult errors to overcome among Soviet Hebrew students since it is a linguistic phenomenon not found in any of the Soviet languages spoken by Jews—Russian, Georgian, Latvian, and so forth.

As an example of "Muscovite" Hebrew I would like to read a poem which was written in Hebrew by a former student of mine and sent to me here in Israel.[3] Notice the use, or, more precisely, the absence of the definitive "hey." Yet try to appreciate, at the same time, her ability to express herself in a language which is not her mother tongue. Before reading the poem I would like to express my wish for further successes of the Hebrew language in the Soviet Union, as well as for the immediate release of the Prisoners of Zion and the quick successful *aliya* of the Hebrew-speaking Community.

Notes

The original lecture on which this chapter is based was given in Hebrew eighteen months after Drachinsky's *aliya*.

1. Magarik was released in September 1987 and has since emigrated to Israel.
2. The story of the Jews in the other "Western territories" (Western Ukraine and Belorussia, Northern Bukovina and Bessarabia which belonged to Poland and Romania until annexed by the USSR) is similar to that of the Baltic Jews.
3. The editors have omitted the poem since an English rendering could not convey the points Drachinksy was trying to make.

13

Jewish Samizdat
Alexander Voronel

The first time my wife and I saw specifically Jewish samizdat material was in 1969 in the apartment of the late Meir Gelfond, where it was kept in a disorderly medley together with Sakharov's letters and Solzhenitsyn's short stories. At that time in our social circles Jewish interests were not yet distinct from the general push for civil rights.

However, *Exodus*, André Schwarz-Bart's novel *The Last of the Just*, and the fearless letters by Jewish activists constituted an uncommon stand which contrasted clearly with the general background and which aroused a yearning for faraway places. The Jewish samizdat, even in its embryo stages, violated the Russian stereotype and appealed to one's sense of novelty. The novelty consisted in regarding oneself outside the framework of those relationships between the people and the authorities, which had been imposed on society by the entire history of the regime. It implied rather the beginning of one's own history together with one's own people. It meant, in other words, withdrawing from the USSR without waiting for *their* permission. This is essentially the ideology of the Exodus, and while it was well matured in Meir's circle of friends, for me, as well as for the overwhelming majority of Soviet Jews, the idea was perfectly new.

At the very beginning of 1971 Meir, who must have decided that Nina and I were sufficiently seasoned, asked us if the protocols of the first Leningrad trial could be retyped in our apartment. Iuliia Viner did the typing, and I, as the owner of the apartment, had the opportunity to be among the first readers.

On this occasion, it should be remarked, the Jewish people had luck. The heroes of the first trial were true heroes, and one could not help feeling compassionate excitement while reading the protocols. Even then, against this stirring background, I felt my heart clearly missing a beat when I started reading the interrogation of Iosif Mendelevich. Mendelevich, it turned out, was the first to have undertaken issuing the Russian-language Jewish magazine *Iton*. For me, then, this was the call of destiny, the word from heaven.

To characterize that time properly, it seems to me of great importance, however strange it may appear now, that the trial did not give rise to despondency or fear, which might have been quite in place in view of the draconian sentences passed against the accused. On the contrary, it *confirmed them in the confidence that their cause had to be pursued* no matter what. I shall not endeavor here to analyze the causes of this phenomenon, yet I do believe that the trial made just this impression on a great many Jews in the USSR and thus predetermined the initial achievements of the major movement.

The movement's successes in the following year or two had consequences that nobody could have foreseen:

1. The majority of the leaders as well as those who in the earlier years had had reason to call themselves Zionists left the USSR.
2. Little by little the interests of the Jews were reduced to the practical problems of emigration and the technical, rational preparation for the event: how to get the formal invitation, how to smuggle out one's documents, and how to get the necessary sum of money from the Dutch embassy. Later this also included how to tip the customs official, the problem of what one had to buy before departure, what was to be taken along, and what left behind.

German Andreev (alias German Fain), who presently publishes literary reviews in the Paris newspaper *Russkaia mysl'*, reproached me bitterly in 1972 for the lack of a sense of responsibility for the well-being of every Jew, which sense of responsibility should, he believed, be characteristic of true Zionists. Well, the lack of this sense must have been the reason why I refused to discuss with him how to take his favorite antique wardrobe out of the country. I do not know to this day whether he finally sacrificed the wardrobe or whether he remains its proud owner.

Because of this tendency—the concentration on the technicalities of emigration—Jewish samizdat almost disappeared in 1972. It seemed in the fever of those busy months that there was nothing to discuss. "Leaving" was the only aspiration. Where to? Each one of us knew. [At this point all emigration was to Israel. — Ed.]

By that time there had accumulated in Moscow a large group of refuseniks, most of them former thriving specialists in the physical sciences, who were denied by the authorities the right to be Jewish and to join the general stream. It was as though nature to some extent took revenge on those people who had until then been able to elude manifestations of anti-Semitism. This group, delivered from everyday intellectual effort and fear of losing their jobs (for almost all of them had by that time been dismissed from their positions), and unable to make plans for the future, became a fertile medium which produced a new generation of Zionists.

The idea of publishing the collections of articles known as *Evrei v SSSR* (Jews in the USSR) matured in the course of my talks with Viktor Yakhot in the summer of 1972.

Loyal to the spirit of our profession as scientists, we understood the role of samizdat as a form of getting to know ourselves, as self-instruction and self-education for a new role. Fully realizing that what was taking place was in fact an Exodus, we asked ourselves *who* was departing, *whence*, and *where*. The political routine of our daily existence prompted ready answers to all these questions that were too easy for our scientific honesty to accept. We made up our minds to study the available empirical materials (i.e., the self-consciousness of Soviet Jews) and analyze them against the background of the historical scheme (i.e., Jewish history, in general, and the history of Russian Jews, in particular). It was our intention to provide Soviet Jews with cultural material to compensate for their dearth of national self-consciousness that was the result of the total silence of Soviet publications on Jewish history and culture, and that might stimulate them to rethinking the humanitarian meaning of the tremendous change in their fate that was taking place in the 1970s.

Our experience of over a year suggested that the collection of articles should be designed basically for those who were not yet ready for emigration, rather than for those who were already packing their suitcases. Our idea did not inspire any particular enthusiasm among the leaders of the older generation. The causes for their veiled opposition are extremely interesting, since later they played an equally important role in resisting the activity of the next intellectual group headed by Benjamin Fain.

The principal argument against the magazine, samizdat, or any other cultural initiative, with the exception of the study of Hebrew, was that it was in fact tantamount to a form of dissident activity ("democratic" was the definition at the time) which would lead not to an exodus, but rather to an adaptation to Soviet conditions and life (or, for radicals, to the adaptation of the Soviet way of life to one's cultural requirements). Any attempt to study contemporary life was not welcome. For the true task, the traditionalist older generation maintained, consisted in total rejection of Soviet life. Strange as it may seem, the people who advocated total rejection overlooked the fact that this meant they were ready to reject the greater part of Soviet Jewry who still professed conventional Soviet ideas. I, on the other hand, believe there are enough Jews in the USSR for whom Jewish cultural-educational activity makes sense, indeed is absolutely necessary.

Quite a few well-known people contributed to the first issues of the magazine: Nina Voronel' and Aleksandr Temkin, Vitalii Mil'man and Dmitrii Segal, Aleksandr Radovskii and Liia Vladimirova, Iosif Begun, Mark Azbel', Viktor Brailovskii, Melik Agurskii, Feliks Kandel', Bella Ram, and Iuliia Shmukler. Almost from the very start, the refusenik group looked on the magazine as their creation. Moishe Giterman, Aleksandr Lunts, Azbel', Boris Orlov, and Brailovskii had their names listed on the cover, which signified both solidarity and responsibility, the confines of which could extend as far as Siberia. Years later (in 1980) Brailovskii was sentenced to five years' exile for his participation in, and especially for his fearless approval of, the publication of the magazine. By that time, thanks to Brailovskii, Emma Sotnikova, and Vladimir Lazaris, twenty numbers of *Evrei v SSSR* had appeared.

Nearly from the very beginning the small group responsible for the journal was joined by Rafail Nudel'man and later also by the late Il'ia Rubin who transformed our collection of articles from a purely intellectual undertaking into a professional periodical which attracted the interest of a wide circle of readers. Invaluable assistance was also rendered by three older persons, now, unfortunately, no longer with us, who put into the project all their unspent energy and talent, which otherwise could not have found appropriate expression in Soviet conditions: first of all, Mikhail Baital'skii (Domal'skii in our publications), then A. Volin (this pen name we cannot yet disclose), and finally Sara Shapiro who typed up all the first nine issues in a tremendous effort. Each number that she produced in seven copies on her ancient Underwood she had to retype at least three or four times. She made almost no typing errors; all those that appeared in the Jerusalem edition of the *Evreiskii samizdat* (Jewish Samizdat) are entirely our fault or that of the Hebrew University of Jerusalem. Each number that I have been able to trace was printed in twenty copies and found its way to Moscow, Leningrad, Kiev, Minsk, Kharkov, Riga, and Baku. Individual numbers turned up in other cities as well. The address of the editorial board was on the cover, so that we got feedback. We have collected quite a library of reminiscences as well as various letters. Altogether more than five thousand pages were published in *Evrei v SSSR* by more than one hundred authors. The "Jews of silence" showed that they were not altogether silent. An analysis of the material would demonstrate the spectrum of views, the nature of the problems, and the level of consciousness of Soviet Jews.

It should, however, be stressed that this material characterizes a specific group of "Soviet" Jews as opposed to "Western," Baltic, or Bessarabian Jews, on the one hand, and "Oriental," Georgian, Mountain, and Bukharan Jews on the other, Jews who had become deeply rooted in Soviet cultural and social life of which they had been an integral part for several generations. It is mainly for them that the question "Who am I?" which permeated all the early issues of the journal turned out to be so complex. Numerous immature answers to this question stimulated the readers to get a deeper insight into their own self and make the choice between Russian and Jewish identity which could be expressed verbally only inadequately. Altogether the journal legalized for the "Soviet" Jew the very concept of Jewishness, the long years of his education having deprived him of any sense of Jewish belongingness or of the feeling that such a belongingness is perfectly reputable. I remember a prominent writer who, having read several numbers of the magazine, admitted that for the first time in his life he felt he could think of his origin as something positive.

It should be mentioned that this new self-image of the Soviet Jews is commonly attributed to the influence of the Six-Day War, and I agree that this is correct in principle. Yet, it seems to me that the student of historical phenomena should be interested not so much in the general causes which are always more or less clear (the State of Israel came into being as a consequence of the Holocaust, but it was not created by the victims of the Holocaust, and unless one analyzes the history of the *yishuv*, the creation of the state will remain an enigma), but rather in the specific manifestation of these causes, which are far from providing simple explanations. By way of example, the assumption that a ship ran aground as a consequence of the influence of the moon, though being correct (as low tide is brought about by the gravitational attraction of the moon), does not contribute to understanding the topic under discussion, unless one takes into consideration the tide cycle and the local relief of the sea bottom, to say nothing of the possibility that the captain might have been drunk. In the case of Soviet Jews, their own history must be analyzed if one is to understand how the Six-Day War affected them. The fact that by the late 1960s an anti-Semitic policy had been openly practiced in the USSR for twenty years, that the period was that of the Brezhnev administration, and that drastic changes in the sphere of higher education were taking place in Soviet society just then could have as much influence on the situation and psychology of Soviet Jews as did the Six-Day War. And if one takes into account the 1968 events in Poland and Czechoslovakia, it may be suggested that the Six-Day War and its role took real shape in the minds of Soviet Jews concurrently with the prospect of becoming scapegoats.

In any case, this new awareness of Soviet Jews had to be expressed in literary form in order to be really comprehended. *Evrei v SSSR* did what it could to fulfill this cultural assignment.

The second cultural task of samizdat, which still remains far from being either solved or fully comprehended, was that of integrating our Jewish heritage with our European-oriented, aesthetically Russian, but ethically undetermined, Soviet culture. Almost all our original authors tackled this problem in some way, although the share of the Jewish and of the Russian differed with each individual author. Rafail Nudel'man tried to formulate this issue theoretically (under the pen name E. Liubov, "Who am I?", no. 6, 1973): "The integral identity of a Soviet Jew is one of total contradiction. An unequivocal self-determination means for him the forced amputation of one of the inalienable aspects of his identity and, as a result, violation of the integrity which is unendurable for the Jewish national character." In my opinion, a long time will pass till this truth becomes generally accepted in Soviet Jewish circles, but certain progress in this direction has been made.

The enormous cultural problems we were facing could not be solved by literary means alone. I want to mention the seminars in the humanities which were initiated by Vitalii Rubin and where a great many of the ideas, which were later expressed in our journal, took shape. Il'ia (Eliahu) Essas's religious seminar subsequently branched off from these seminars. When we started discussing our Jewish heritage, the monstrous cultural ignorance of the majority of Soviet Jews became apparent and hence the necessity to popularize elementary Jewish knowledge and Judaism. This led Feliks

Dektor to his decision to create a separate samizdat publication—the journal *Tarbut,* and Benjamin Fain to the idea of consolidating all the available cultural forces in order to disseminate the Jewish heritage among Soviet Jews, irrespective of their plans concerning emigration. This, however, is another chapter, which is outside the scope of my personal experience.

To conclude, I should like to emphasize that the nature of the cultural problems that Soviet Jews are facing now remains the same as it was at the outset: to find their *own path* to bring them closer to Judaism and Israel, without suffering irreversible cultural losses. In other words, Soviet Jews must continue exploring the possibility of contributing to culture by all available means and not only of "taking" from it.

The past years have seen changes in the people involved, in the situation within the USSR, and, of course, in the relationship between Soviet Jews and Israel. Of all the free Russian-language publications in Israel and the multitude of underground literature circulating among the Jews in the USSR, the sole historical heir to *Evrei v SSSR* and the entire Jewish samizdat of the 1970s, is the journal 22. This journal is a living testimony to the fact that the Soviet Jews have maintained their penchant for the ideological formulation of their problems and that the distinctiveness of our group—the Russian Jews—is still recognizable and, I believe, still has a rich future. Therefore, everything published in the Russian language in Israel, whatever we may think of it at present, can play a major, hardly predictable role in the life of Russian Jewry.

14

The Moscow Symposium: Ten Years Later
Eliahu Essas

Ten years ago a group of Jewish activists in Moscow called for a symposium on Jewish culture in Moscow. Although the invited foreign scholars were not allowed to enter the USSR and all the organizers were put under house arrest, the prepared materials were delivered in unofficial seminars on Jewish culture in Moscow. Moreover, the symposium aroused wide public interest in the Soviet Jewish cultural situation.

The event itself and subsequent developments must be discussed within the framework of an analysis of Soviet Jewish history. The real significance of the symposium can be understood only in the context of what has happened to Soviet Jews during the whole Soviet period.

Jewish education ceased to exist officially in the USSR in the early twenties. All religious schools were shut down, and the unofficial remnants were quickly destroyed. Jewish cultural life was crushed. In the thirties even the official communist schools in Yiddish were closed. Tens of thousands of rabbis, educators, and students were arrested and jailed.

Soviet Jews suffered a great deal during the Stalin purges, when hundreds of thousands of Jews were sent to camps and the Jewish spirit was largely destroyed. After Stalin's death Jewish life was not renewed and until the seventies it was almost totally paralyzed. There were, however, courageous individuals who tried to teach their children, but all this was conducted in secrecy and did not influence the vast majority of Soviet Jews.

The national revival which was greatly influenced by the Six-Day War embraced large segments of Soviet Jewry. This did not bring any immediate change in the cultural and religious spheres. The awakened desire to repatriate to Israel became a goal in itself. Most of the Jews who applied to leave in the early seventies were allowed to do so. Most of those who started looking for their national identity found its expression in their desire to repatriate.

The Jewish activists, almost exclusively refuseniks, were united in their struggle to leave. It was natural that the initiative to look for other expressions of national identity came from them. Being years in refusal and outcasts of Soviet society, they became semifree and turned their attention to searching for their roots. Aside from the Hebrew lessons, soon there were seminars on Jewish history and eventually some of the activists reached the conclusion that the time had come to demand a revival of Jewish cultural life in the USSR. A minority opposed the idea out of fear that it might detract from the struggle for repatriation. It is important to emphasize that the latter group has by now almost entirely disappeared from the scene of Soviet Jewish activism.

I prepared a detailed program for the gradual revival of Jewish life in the USSR. The short version of my program appeared in the symposium materials. The full version was confiscated by the KGB. My emphasis was on creating Hebrew and Judaic study groups within the framework of activity permitted by Soviet law. I was convinced that there was enormous interest among Soviet Jews to embrace their heritage, and intended to use the symposium as a springboard.

Many of those in the West who were concerned about the emigration problem alone began to consider the basic needs of Soviet Jews to develop their national identity. The symposium helped Jewish leaders abroad to study carefully the problems we were trying to raise.

Jewish activism in the USSR gradually started to become transformed into a search for spiritual depth. It became natural for many Hebrew pupils to use their knowledge of the language in order to approach Jewish traditional literature.

I started teaching Torah in unofficial classes in 1977, a few months after the symposium was suppressed. Dozens of young Jewish intellectuals and students expressed their desire to attend these studies. Within less than a year some of them were able to teach others. Meanwhile, we started learning Talmud with the most advanced pupils. The chain reaction became obvious a few years later when I met Jews whom I had never seen before learning Mishnah in the Moscow subway. These were students of my students.

There are more than five hundred young observant families today in the

USSR. Although the main religious activism is centered in Moscow, there are dozens of young religious families in Leningrad, Riga, Odessa, and Vilinus, and one can find religious Jews today even in Erevan and Novosibirsk.

There are tens of thousands who are under the influence of this hard core: that is, their relatives and friends, many of whom are themselves beginning to read books. This finds expression in the high attendance at Simhat Torah celebrations. Over twenty thousand come to Moscow's Choral Synagogue every year. Between seven and eight thousand come in Leningrad. In 1985 there were almost three thousand Jews at the Vilnius synagogue on Simhat Torah, almost half of them young people aged fifteen to twenty-five. This is especially significant if one bears in mind that there are only ten thousand Jews in Vilnius today. It shows how great the reservoir of Jewish spiritual potential is in the USSR.

This influences the whole Jewish population of the USSR. Although the assimilation rate is nearly 30 percent, the Jewish awareness of the young generation seems to be higher than that of their parents. All the religious activists today come from families with no Jewish educational background.

The outstanding Moscow Torah teacher, Chaim Briskman, came to my class in 1980. Today (i.e., December 1986) he leads a high-level *yeshiva* group which combines Talmud studies with the latest rabbinical literature. He was arrested at the end of 1980 during a KGB raid on one of our lessons and was expelled from his university. A dedicated and faithful Jew, he has advanced rapidly and today, at twenty-seven, is widely admired for his knowledge and leadership.

Mikhail Khanin, who has a Ph.D. in philosophy and recently arrived in Israel (1986), had studied to be a Scribe (*Sofer stam*) and together with an older man served the whole community of Moscow. Shimon Iantovskii belongs to the older generation. He is a World War II veteran who decided to leave for Israel in the mid-seventies. After starting Hebrew studies, he discovered the old-new world of Judaism. Today he is one of the most active religious Jews in Moscow. [Iantovskii emigrated to Israel in 1987.]

There are dozens of Torah study groups in Moscow at different levels, including special women's groups, which attract considerable interest. Books and articles are being translated and printed unofficially.

The authorities tried to prevent the proliferation of Judaic study groups. Many attempts were made to break them up, but the results can be judged by the facts and numbers which I have presented here.

Ten years after the symposium on Jewish culture a great deal of Jewish activism in the USSR has a religious character. The Soviet Jewish community is probably the only one in which most of the leading Jewish activists are observant. This does not hold true for any other community in the world. It is also certainly significant that of the religious Jews, there are almost no dropouts among those who have left the USSR.

A gradual step-by-step approach must be used in the further advancement of Jewish life in the USSR, including the necessity to demand legalization of some Jewish cultural and religious activities.

15

Soviet Jewish Culture Today: A Personal Israeli Account

Erez Biton

With an almost empty suitcase and a heart filled with apprehension I set off for Moscow by way of Romania. My close friends cautioned me: "Don't take any books, lists, or newspapers, especially anything in Hebrew; don't make calls directly from the hotel and when you meet with Jews there be extra careful. Remember that over there, in Russia, you can expect to be constantly trailed by the KGB and they have devices that can let them know your whereabouts and activities at any time."

Looking back, I am sorry now that I did not take any Hebrew reading material with me to Moscow, something which the Jews there are so in need of. In my meetings with the Jews of Moscow they told me that those fears are excessive: "After all, they won't put you in jail. The worst thing that they'd do would be to simply take the books away."

Throughout my visit I was driven by a great curiosity, both personal and professional as a journalist, to become acquainted with Soviet society. I was similarly driven by my identification with the fate of the Jews there and my desire to know them and their struggle.

October 15, 1986:

I changed a ruble into two-kopek coins in order to make contacts from a public phone. In Israel they had warned me not to make calls of that sort from the hotel since the phones are tapped. I called every number I had memorized, but there was no answer at any of them. Later on, when my Israeli friends heard that I was going to call the Begun family they were shocked and begged me to refrain from calling, since by doing so I could endanger the entire delegation. From that point on I decided to make these contacts with Jews on my own by taking the risk of calling from the hotel, simply because I had no chance of getting to a public phone alone. I tried the Beguns' number again. On the other end of the line Barukh Begun answered. I explained to him that I was a poet and a journalist from Israel and that I would like to meet with him.

I told him that, being blind, I would appreciate his coming to meet me at the hotel. "No problem," he answered in a beginner's Hebrew. "Just tell me how I can recognize you." I said that I have a beard and a handbag over my left shoulder. "We'll have to go from there to your house since it's forbidden to bring strangers into the hotel rooms," I added.

Barukh Begun took me in a cab to the house of Ina Begun, the wife of his father, Yosef. On the way we passed the building of the KGB. "We know the KGB people. For the most part they don't conceal themselves, they follow us openly. They maintain a special division for Jewish matters. We've learned to live with the trails." I ask him whether they might be following us now. "They certainly could be," he answered, "they do it whenever they like."

As each day passed in Moscow, my fear diminished. I ventured out more and more to as many meetings with Jews as I could manage, in their homes, in the street, in the synagogue, and by phone calls, I called them from the hotel and often they called me.

Why the Soviet authorities allowed me to meet with the Jews so freely, I still do not know. I am almost certain that my stand on Soviet Jewry, namely that every Jew who wishes to leave the Soviet Union should have the right to do so, is well known to them since it has been published more than once in the Israeli papers. It is also nearly certain that the Soviets were not unaware of the meetings I held with Jews during my visit to Moscow. In fact, all of the Jews with whom I met assumed that our activities were under surveillance. Some of them, mostly refuseniks and relatives of Prisoners of Zion, told me openly that their phones were constantly tapped and that the authorities without a doubt listened in on our conversations when they called me at the hotel.

On the night after Yom Kippur I made the acquaintance of Mikhail Chlenov, a Hebrew teacher. I sensed something unusual about him during our brief meeting at the home of the Arkadii family. He invited me to his home, yet he did not offer to come and pick me up from the hotel, as all the other Jews with whom I met had done. Rather, he recorded his address on a tape recorder and suggested that I play the address for the cab driver to hear. I agreed, knowing, however, that on such a journey, alone, I was likely to be afraid. Nevertheless, my curiosity was stronger than my fear . . .

. . . I sit next to the driver and each time we stop at a traffic light I hold the tape recorder toward him and play Chlenov's instructions. The driver murmurs something and continues, half an hour, forty minutes; in my mind I am already imagining the unpleasant possibilities. After nearly an hour the driver stops the cab, but Chlenov is not there waiting for me. I decide not to pay the driver until I find Chlenov. To my surprise a woman suddenly comes running out. I play for her the recording of the address. She slips into a house nearby and returns to me with Mikhail Chlenov. I breathe a deep sigh of relief.

Once we are inside, I notice something else which is unusual in Chlenov's behavior; he brings me into his home, yet refrains from introducing me to his wife and children. Rather, he takes me into his private study; I can hear his wife and children closed up in the other rooms of the apartment. A strange reception compared to the other Jews who were happy to present their children upon my arrival at their homes. Yet here—the opposite.

After a few days the mystery is solved. I am told that Chlenov's wife is not Jewish and is actually against his Hebrew and Jewish-oriented activities. Chlenov has not submitted a request to emigrate to Israel. Nevertheless, he is thought of as one of the central pillars of Hebrew study today. Chlenov himself proudly notes that he was Shcharansky's first Hebrew teacher.

By profession, Chlenov is an anthropologist. He spent two years doing research in Indonesia and travels for short periods to the northern regions of the Soviet Union which are inhabited by Eskimos.

Chlenov is constantly walking that thin line between his identification with Jewish culture and his will to realize his professional goals as an anthropologist. He has been offered a position in the Soviet diplomatic corps but has declined.

The Hebrew language is taught in three universities in the Soviet Union: in Moscow, Leningrad, and Tbilisi, capital of the Georgian SSR. Less than one hundred students study Hebrew within this framework. This information was presented to me by Dr. Dmitrii Prokof'ev, an expert in Hebrew with whom it was suggested that I meet. Over the past few years he has emerged as a top Hebrew-Russian translator and serves as the head announcer on the Hebrew Hour of Moscow Radio.

In my meeting with Prokof'ev, and with his co-announcer on Moscow Radio, Valerii Silver, Prokof'ev astonished me with his expertise on the subject of Israeli culture and particularly on Israeli theater. He wrote his doctoral thesis on post-1967 Israeli drama. Our conversation, all in faultless Hebrew, opened with a discussion of the plays of Hanokh Levin.

"I think," Prokof'ev told me, "that in the plays of Hanokh Levin there is something unquestionably Brechtian."

He will not accept my opinion that the writings of Hanokh Levin are essentially Jewish and that their source lies in Yiddish theater. "Is the culture which is produced in Israel today actually taken from Jewish sources?" he asked provocatively. "Take, for example, Amos Kenan, who once wrote that he feels like an American who writes in Hebrew. We in Russia are in favor of preserving the heritage of a culture."

Prokof'ev's friend Valerii, a young Jew, is the son of Ditza Silver, who was also an announcer on the Hebrew Hour and died a few years ago. He also speaks modern Hebrew and tells me about his mother who was a third generation *sabra* (native-born Israeli) . . .

All in all, I met with close to eighty refuseniks. I also delivered two lectures on Hebrew literature and social problems in Israel and was impressed by my audience's great familiarity with Israeli current events. They rarely miss listening to the "Voice of Israel" and most of them speak Hebrew beautifully. There, in Moscow, I fell in love anew with the Hebrew language and with the land of Israel. From there Israel looked absolutely faultless.

We spoke of the drop-out phenomenon and Jewish identity in the Soviet Union, of intermarriage, of the horrible anti-Semitism in the Ukraine, and of their feeling that the pressure exerted by the Soviet regime toward Hebrew teachers has relaxed somewhat.

Although I did not get the chance to meet with the poet Evgenii Evtushenko who was on tour in Burma, I nevertheless was granted admission to the Soviet Writers' Union. In addition to the central office of Soviet writers' affairs, the Union is divided into national divisions, each of which is responsible for the writers of a given republic. I was hosted by the Uzbek division, headed by Kamran Khakimov. Since Israel is considered an Oriental state, I was greeted by the Union's experts in Eastern culture.

My hosts open the discussion with the subject of Sholem Aleichem whose play *Tevia the Milkman* was shown twice last year on Soviet television.

I ask them about the nature of the relations between Russian literature and Uzbek literature, and whether there is not a dominance of Russian culture over that of the smaller republics. Khakimov answered that just the opposite is true: that there is a mutual influence between the literature of the different cultures. There are Uzbek writers who are known throughout the Soviet Union, and who thus have an influence on Russian literature. There are even Jews who write in Uzbek. The most famous of these is Iakov Khaimov.

At the end of my visit there I was asked to convey greetings to the Writers Union of Israel along with a proposal for joint activities, such as translating Hebrew poetry and prose into Russian.

On my last day in Moscow I held a sort of marathon of meetings with Jews at the hotel. Every half hour another would arrive with his request or inquiry. Elazar Iosipovich, a very close friend, came and we parted with kisses and a promise that my four-year-old son Asaf would write with pictures to Ariel, his four-year-old son. He asked me when I get back to Israel to emphasize the idea of granting Israeli citizenship to Soviet Jews. And Lula came, asking questions in Hebrew: "What's the difference in Hebrew between 'landing' a plane and 'bringing down' a plane?" And young Sasha Yitzhak ben Avraham Karlin, to whom I gave my prayer shawl in the synagogue on Succot, felt a deep need to come and thank me, indeed even to hug me, out of love and gratitude.

I will always remember that last night when I met with a young Jew on a bench on a rainy Moscow street, a tape recorder in my hand, and he, B. B., cried out his curses against anti-Semitism.

All of these images dwell within me and demand that I speak of them again and again.

V
REGIME POLICY

16

Jewish Culture in the USSR Today

Lukasz Hirszowicz

The whole of Soviet policy toward Jewish culture, as shaped after Stalin's death, has been more an answer to internal and external pressures than to the need for national cultural expression of the Soviet Jewish community. The main pillars of that policy are the Yiddish language and the Jewish Autonomous Region of Birobidzhan. However, as a result of processes of acculturation and deliberate Soviet policies since the 1930s, Yiddish is known only by a minority of Soviet Jews, and the moderate support extended to some cultural activities in Yiddish is interlinked with the virtual denial of similar activities in Russian and Hebrew. And although Birobidzhan has completely failed as a Jewish endeavor, for which again deliberate Soviet policies are at least partly responsible, it is still presented as an appropriate base of Jewish culture, as a pretext for limiting or preventing Jewish cultural activities in the large Jewish concentrations in the great cities of the USSR. The contemporary Soviet scene with respect to Jewish national culture should be viewed in this light.

The last few years have witnessed a wave of national demands in the USSR. These have not only manifested themselves in demonstrations and, in some cases, rioting—by Kazakhs, Georgians, Armenians, Azerbaidzhanis, Balts, Crimean Tatars, and Yakuts—but also in the press. The demands would seem to foreshadow positive policy changes toward nationality cultures. Such changes should also favor an improvement in the field of Jewish culture, but Jewish culture occupies a special position.

This is an abbreviated version of Lukasz Hirszowicz's essay, without notes.

Cultural Characteristics of Soviet Jewry

The Jews are recognized as a Soviet nationality. They rank sixteenth in size among the over one hundred nationalities of the Soviet Union. According to the 1979 census they numbered 1,810,876 but many observers believe the actual figure is higher; some estimate it at 2,500,000. The Jews' status as a Soviet nationality is confirmed by the existence of the Jewish Autonomous Region of Birobidzhan which is situated in the Russian Republic (the RSFSR). The existence of this entity is, however, only of symbolic importance: according to the 1979 census, it was inhabited by 10,166 Jews, 0.56 percent of the Soviet Jewish population. This Jewish symbol was recently strengthened by the reintroduction of bilingual—Russian and Yiddish— plaques on official buildings in Birobidzhan, some teaching of Yiddish, and a change in the policies of the newspaper *Birobidzhaner shtern* (see below).

A considerable proportion of Soviet Jewry resides in large urban centers. According to published data of the 1970 census (equivalent data of the 1979 census are available only for a few cities), 26 percent of the Jews inhabited the three capital cities—Moscow (251,500), Leningrad (162,600), and Kiev (152,000). A further 13 percent of Jews lived in the remaining thirteen Soviet republican capitals. Republican capitals with large Jewish populations are: Tashkent (55,800), Kishinev (49,900), Minsk (47,100), and Riga (20,600). (The available 1979 census figures put the number of Jewish inhabitants of Leningrad at 143,000, Kishinev at 42,800, and Vilnius at 10,700.)

Sizable Jewish populations, probably larger than in most republican capitals, exist in Odessa, Kharkov, and Dnepropetrovsk in the Ukraine, and Gomel in Belorussia. There are no available data on the number of Jews in these cities. According to the 1979 census, the Jewish population of the *oblast* (region) of Odessa was 92,200, that of Kharkov, 64,100, Dnepropetrovsk, 61,000, and Gomel 18,400.

Soviet Jewry is a relatively well-educated group. According to the 1970 census, 239 per 1,000 urban Jews over the age of ten had completed higher education and 521 had more than secondary education. The 1979 census figures on the level of education of Jewish women of ten years or over indicate that 871 in every thousand have higher and secondary specialist education. While a higher level of education draws people closer to the country's dominant, that is, Russian, culture, it also creates in them a deeper awareness of their own values and culture.

Further cultural determinants of the Jewish community are religion and language.

Judaism is a recognized religion in the USSR. Since in Soviet law—but not in practice—religion is regarded as an individual's private affair, no figures are available for membership of religious communities, synagogue attendance, religious marriages, burials, and the like. According to a semi-official assessment which can be found in Soviet publications, there are approximately 60,000 Jews actively practicing Judaism in the USSR. But this figure cannot cover more than a fraction of those for whom observance of religious customs and precepts is a part of their culture as individuals or as members of a family.

Several languages are recognized as Jewish languages in the USSR; for some time after the Revolution an educational network, press, and publications existed in these languages. The principal Jewish language is Yiddish, the language of the Ashkenazi Jews, who constitute over 90 percent of Soviet Jewry. The Oriental Jewish communities—the Georgian, Bukharan and Mountain Jews, and the Krymchaks—speak their own languages. Hebrew, which is common to all Jewish communities and which has enjoyed a remarkable revival since the nineteenth century, is not recognized as a Soviet minority language.

According to the 1979 census, 14.24 percent of Soviet Jews claimed a Jewish language as their mother tongue; an additional 5.35 percent claimed one as their second language. The census figures also reveal that 97.03 percent of Soviet Jews know Russian, making them linguistically the most Russified minority in the USSR. The figures demonstrate that at least one-fifth of Soviet Jewry is interested in their national language and culture. Reports by many observers of the Soviet scene, including foreign correspondents, indicate that a much larger number would like to enjoy their culture in Russian.

Linguistic assimilation (in the great majority of cases, to the Russian language) and bilingualism are stated objectives of Soviet policy. Many works of importance for the respective national cultures now appear in the Russian language. In the Jewish case, the elimination of national education and culture, and the exile and physical liquidation of many leading cultural activists were ordered under Stalin by administrative fiat. Nonetheless, internal pressures since Stalin's death, pressures which brought about the restoration of some semblance of Jewish cultural life despite the avowed intentions of the Soviet authorities, bear testimony to the strong attachment of many Soviet Jews to their national culture, though strong assimilationist attitudes can also be found among the Jewish community.

Parallel to the emigration movement, a cultural and cultural-religious movement emerged among Soviet Jewry expressed in Jewish samizdat, the study of Hebrew, the study of Jewish religious texts, seminars on Jewish history and culture, and the organization of a variety of cultural events, for example, celebration of Jewish festivals, concerts, and the staging of plays. This movement, as far as can be ascertained, reaches well beyond the circles of Yiddish-oriented Jews, and beyond Zionist activists and emigration-oriented Jews. Under Gorbachev's *glasnost'*, this kind of grass-roots initiative may finally prove successful.

Jewish Creativity

Jewish creativity in the USSR is dealt with in this chapter under the following headings: plastic and applied arts; performing arts; literature; Jewish scholarship; and cultural heritage.

Plastic and Applied Arts Jewish fine art—whether creativity by Jewish artists or creativity on Jewish themes—has a remarkable tradition in Russia and is highlighted by talents of world renown, such as Chagall, Lissitzky, Levitan, and Antokolsky. Until recent years, many well-known artists were active in the USSR, for example Anatolii (Tanhum) Kaplan—painter, ceramic and graphic artist; Aleksandr Tyshler—painter and scenographer; Zinovii Tolkachev—painter, whose works include Holocaust themes; Peisakh Krivorutskii and Iosif Chaikov—sculptors; and Gershon Kravtsov—graphic artist. Artists of the younger generation display an interest in Jewish themes too. Some of these are recognized Soviet artists, for example Luiza Sherenshtein and Semen Gruzberg from Lvov, Elia Remeniuk from Tbilisi, Samuelis Rosinas from Vilnius, and Milia Galkin and Gersh Inger from Moscow. Others, who are connected with "unofficial" Soviet art, became known to the wider public at the time of the much-publicized open-air Moscow exhibition of 1975, and the exhibition in a Leningrad private apartment in 1976. The Leningrad exhibition involved Jewish subjects only. It should be noted that the authorities removed several paintings of Jewish content from the Moscow exhibition on the basis that they were of Zionist inspiration.

There is no Jewish art gallery or exhibition hall anywhere in the USSR;

no authorized Jewish art exhibitions have taken place. The only way Jewish artists can exhibit works on Jewish subjects is by including them among their other works. Occasionally, works by Jewish artists are exhibited in a small way at the editorial offices of *Sovetish heymland,* and the Yiddish monthly publishes from time to time poor-quality reproductions. As far as is known, there are no other specific places where exhibitions of works on Jewish subjects can be held, and no arrangements exist for collective exhibitions or other creative meetings for these artists.

The USSR embraces territories with a long and rich Jewish history, including cities of major Jewish significance such as Vilnius, Odessa, Lvov, and Bukhara. The western parts of the USSR, where a large Jewish population was concentrated, were subjected to Nazi occupation in 1941–44 and various buildings and sites of Jewish historical significance have remained, as well as sites of mass executions such as those in Kiev, Minsk, Vilnius, Riga, Lvov, and Odessa.

Jewish historical sites in the USSR are generally in a state of neglect. Most Holocaust sites are not marked appropriately. The few monuments that have been erected on such sites, with the exception of those of the immediate postwar years and commemoration stones in some Jewish cemeteries, contain no reference to the Jewishness of the victims, even where the victims were exclusively Jewish. With one notable exception—that of Rumboli near Riga—the Soviet authorities have not subsequently permitted the Jews to erect monuments of their own.

The Performing Arts Performing arts, both in religious and secular form, were an integral part of Jewish cultural life under the czars and in the early years of the Soviet regime. Film, a new branch of the performing arts, made its appearance after the Revolution.

The Nazi occupation was a severe blow also to the Jewish performing arts. After the war, a brief period of revival was cut short by the Soviet authorities. All Jewish theaters were shut down. Many actors were liquidated or exiled. In the late 1940s and the 1950s all that remained of Jewish performing arts was a small number of "concerts" by singers. Following efforts by surviving Jewish actors, supported by cultural and political figures in the USSR and the West, a limited restoration of the Jewish performing arts was permitted, partly on a professional basis and partly on a semiprofessional or amateur basis.

At present, Soviet Jewry is served by only two professional theatrical bodies—the Moscow Jewish Dramatic Ensemble, formed in 1961 and recently renamed the Jewish Drama Studio Theater, and the Jewish Chamber Music Theater, which came into existence in 1978 and is officially based in Birobidzhan; the "show group" *Freylakhs*, which was formed in the early 1980s, is also officially based in Birobidzhan. But this is no more than an administrative device: the two establishments perform only occasionally in Birobidzhan. These performing groups are traveling companies that give a few score performances each year throughout the USSR. Only the Drama Studio which stages Yiddish and bilingual performances has recently acquired a hall of its own in Moscow's Varshavskoe shosse. As long as there are no other professional theaters or variety ensembles in the USSR, the natural place for them would be Moscow, where they rehearse and where they have the largest potential audience.

There are also a number of amateur performing arts establishments. Two of these—the theater of Vilnius (since 1957) and that of Birobidzhan (since 1965)—boast a great variety of activities. Amateur companies, including choir, drama, dance, and music, have existed at various times in other Soviet Jewish centers, for example Riga in 1957–63, Kaunas until 1971 and since 1976, Leningrad until 1971, and Kishinev until 1972. Theatrical activity is also reported to have taken place in Chernovtsy and Tallinn. At present, it would appear, regular amateur companies exist only in Vilnius, Kaunas, and Birobidzhan and they too give only a few performances per year.

There have been fruitless attempts to establish Jewish theatrical establishments in other centers too. In particular, there are no such establishments in Kiev and Minsk, which had Jewish theaters until the late 1940s, and where there are large Jewish populations. In March 1967 a group of Jewish actors is reported to have sought to establish a theater in Kiev to serve the whole of the Ukraine. Their attempts were renewed after 1973; and in 1982 they unofficially submitted a complaint to the UN requesting support for the project.

There are in the USSR a number of singers, musicians, and composers whose repertoires include Jewish songs and music; some even concentrate on Jewish items. In particular, Jewish folk music is of interest to composers and musicologists. The young Georgian composer Iosif Bardonoshvili has set to music medieval Hebrew poems which appeared in Georgian translation and some composers have set to music lyrics by Yiddish writers.

However, these artists give only occasional concerts and only rarely are some of their works published or issued on records.

Jewish plays, concerts, and records are enormously popular in the USSR. Reports on the situation in Moscow (and formerly Leningrad) occasionally appear in the Western press. *Sovetish heymland* and the Warsaw Jewish paper *Folks-shtime* give details of the enthusiastic reception accorded the Jewish performing arts in other centers. As so few companies and artists serve such a large community in such a vast territory, even towns with large Jewish populations have only two or three functions a year and some none at all for many years. For instance, there have been no official Jewish performances in Leningrad, Kiev, and Minsk for a long time.

A new element was added with the emergence of "unofficial" Jewish cultural activism. Amateur theater groups have emerged in many cities, several of them acquiring a more solid character at one time or another. Unsuccessful attempts were made to incorporate the work of some of these groups into the usual Soviet local framework of amateur performers. Also, ad hoc events take place on various Jewish festivals and anniversaries, in particular, so-called *Purim-shpils* on the occasion of the festival of Purim. These performances, which take place in private homes or on private outings, are given before very small audiences, mostly in Russian or Hebrew, and their number, too, is very small.

Like other Jewish "unofficial" cultural activities, the "unofficial" Jewish performing arts have been subjected to repression. In 1984, for example, several Jewish activists connected with *Purim-shpils* were arrested. The Georgian-Jewish musicians' group, "The Phantom," faced an intensified KGB campaign against them in 1985. But with the policy of *glasnost'*, repression has declined. In 1987 concerts of Jewish music were held in private homes in Leningrad and the organizers were reportedly offered the use of premises controlled by a local district authority.

With regard to the existing theatrical establishments, the principal complaint is still the relatively small number of performances, although the situation concerning Jewish theatrical performances in Moscow has improved in recent years. Also some, though by no means all, of the (unofficial) Jewish centers which were virtually out of bounds have been visited by one or another of the Jewish companies in the last few years.

Soviet Jewish theater companies have not been able to perform outside the USSR, with the exception of recent tours of the GDR, Czechoslovakia, and North America. Records of plays, including musicals, are rarely issued and are seldom available abroad. Nor have foreign Jewish theaters or non-Soviet performers with a Jewish repertoire ever been allowed to perform in the USSR, even those from the Soviet bloc countries. Soviet singers and musicians who have a Jewish repertoire are also not known outside the USSR and their records are virtually unobtainable abroad. In this field, the situation was marginally better before the USSR severed relations with Israel in 1967. Now that some Soviet companies have performed in Israel, there is perhaps hope for reciprocity on the part of the USSR.

Literature In the mid-1970s there were about seventy Yiddish writers in the USSR. (In the 1920s and 1930s there were over three hundred.) Very few of these writers wrote nonfiction, and virtually none of them had any nonfiction published, with the exception of a few items of literary criticism. The number of writers in Russian and other non-Jewish languages who deal with Jewish themes is also very limited, if one excludes anti-Zionist works.

There are only two Yiddish periodicals in the USSR; the monthly *Sovetish heymland* with a print run of four thousand, and the four-page regional newspaper *Birobidzhaner shtern*, which appears five times a week in Birobidzhan in twelve thousand copies (and is the only Soviet regional newspaper for which foreign subscriptions are accepted).

Sovetish heymland has been legitimately criticized for anti-Zionist items it has published, including *Di tsayt* (Time), a novel by its editor, Aron Vergelis. But *Sovetish heymland* has also always had a strong Jewish content, and this was enriched in the last year with the publication of articles popularizing Jewish scholarship. The March 1988 issue announced the serialization as from July of Sholem Aleichem's novel *Der blutiker shpas* (The Bloody Joke) which has never previously appeared in book form in the USSR. *Sovetish heymland* also intends to publish a new section on "the history of the Jewish people," a subject virtually nonexistent in the USSR for many decades.

Sovetish heymland is continuing its efforts to secure the continuity of Yiddish publications in the USSR. In this context, a meeting of young Yiddish writers should be mentioned; it follows from the report published in *Sovetish heymland* (in its November 1987 issue) that further conferences of a similar nature are contemplated.

There has also been a marginal change in *Birobidzhaner shtern*. For

Table 16.1
Books Published in Languages of Selected Nationalities and Print Runs, 1981–1986

Nationality & population	Number of books published in 1981–86	Combined print run
Bashkirs (1,751,000)	798	6,991,400
Chuvashes (1,371,000)	470	3,344,800
Poles (1,151,000)	585	24,742,700
Estonians (1,020,000)	8,091	75,026,800
Jews (1,811,000)	41	61,000

decades, this paper contained very little Jewish content apart from the odd item contributed by a Yiddish writer. The reader was reminded that this was a paper of the Jewish Autonomous Region by the Jewish names of outstanding workers and some local party and government officials. Today virtually every issue contains news about Jewish life elsewhere in the USSR, which is not easily available from any other source.

There also appears in the USSR an annual publication in Tat, the language of the Mountain Jews of the Caucasus. This publication, *Vatan sovetimu*, has a print run of up to one thousand. But its publication is irregular and the Mountain Jews are presented as a non-Jewish ethnic group of Tats who professed Judaism in former times.

Whatever opinion Soviet Yiddish establishment leaders may have, the Soviet authorities regard Yiddish literature as a vestigial phenomenon. This is clear from the number of books published in Yiddish in the USSR and their combined print run. Table 16.1 juxtaposes the number and print run of books in Yiddish with the number and print run of books published in the languages of other Soviet nationalities, which, according to the 1979 census, are similar in size to the Jewish minority. The table covers the years 1981–86. In the years 1947 and 1948, 112 and 117 Yiddish books, respectively, were published in the USSR.

Each of these nationalities has a different status. The Estonians have a union republic, the Bashkirs and Chuvashes have their own autonomous republics within the RSFSR, while the Poles are a dispersed nationality as are the Jews, without, however, an autonomous region in their name. Even the Koreans, a dispersed nationality with only 389,000 souls—less than a quarter of the Jewish population according to the 1979 census—had 58 books published in 1981–86 with a combined print run of 309,300.

If one takes into account the linguistic composition of Soviet Jewry, then translations of Yiddish writers in Russian (and other Soviet languages), as well as books on Jewish themes written in Russian (and other Soviet languages), such as A. Rybakov's *Tiazhelyi pesok* (Heavy Sands, 1978), are of greater interest to the reading public. (This is not to say that these publications are produced for or read by an exclusively Jewish public.) In 1958–79, 444 such translations were published of which 313 were into Russian. This is a total of 20 books per year. Among them were no studies of history or the history of literature, except for 9 volumes of literary criticism (104,800 copies). The situation deteriorated subsequently.

There were 100 such translations in 1980–86, that is, an average of less than 15 per annum. These 100 translations from Jewish literature in 1980–86 should be compared with the number of books translated from new and/or small literatures such as those of the Ossetians (117 books), Chuvashes (114 books), Kabardinians (74 books), and Avars (104 books). If one considers the rich reservoir of Jewish literature, this clearly indicates discriminatory treatment.

An important development has taken place in recent years in the field of Jewish publication in the Russian language. In 1985 a literary annual entitled *God za godom* (Year After Year) was printed in Russian in 30,000 copies; it also has French and English editions. The annual reprints material which has appeared in *Sovetish heymland* plus a small number of new items. It includes photographs of contributors, illustrations, reproductions of work by Jewish graphic artists, and interesting old photographic material. So far three issues of the annual have appeared and the editors have expressed the hope that in the future it will appear twice a year or even as a quarterly.

For the further fate of Yiddish literature in the USSR the educational network is of fundamental importance. From 1948 until recently no Yiddish was taught in any educational establishment in the USSR; in fact, Yiddish schools were being closed down as early as the 1930s. In this respect, there have been some—though very minor—positive developments in recent years. A center for Yiddish literature began to operate at Moscow's Gorky

Institute of World Literature in 1979 with an intake of five students; Yiddish became an optional subject in a few Birobidzhan schools in 1980; a Yiddish primer was published in 1982; the preparation of further textbooks was announced, as was a decision to open a teacher-training college for Yiddish lecturers in Birobidzhan; there was a report about a course for Yiddish editors in Khabarovsk, capital of the province in which the Jewish Autonomous Region is situated; and a Russian-Yiddish dictionary appeared in 1984 after a long delay.

No comprehensive data on the sale of *Sovetish heymland* and Yiddish books are available. (For the print-run of *Sovetish heymland* see p. 201.) The Yiddish primer, which was printed in Moscow in an edition of 5,000 copies for the Khabarovsk Book Publishers, appears to be available in large centers in the USSR.

To what extent works by Yiddish writers are available in general Soviet libraries is also unknown. One would assume that the newly published translations which have relatively large print runs—from hundreds of thousands to a million or more for children's books (for instance, by Leyb Kvitko or Shayke Driz) to a few thousand for a volume of poetry—are available at least in the larger and medium-sized Soviet towns. However, a serious interest in Jewish literature and history is much more difficult to satisfy. With the exception of the Sholem Aleichem Library in Birobidzhan and the Nekrasov Library in Moscow, we are not aware of any Jewish libraries or Soviet libraries with a special Yiddish or Jewish department for the use of the general public. A recent development should be noted in this field. In 1987 a Jewish library containing several hundred books in Russian, Yiddish, Hebrew, and other languages was opened in a private apartment in Moscow. The authorities neither encouraged nor suppressed this activity.

Literary creativity in Hebrew was virtually eliminated in the USSR in the 1920s, though a few writers, such as Elisha Rudin and Zvi Pregerzon, continued to lead a semiclandestine existence. Interest in Hebrew literature has, however, continued throughout the Soviet period, and a few scholarly works appeared on ancient and medieval (e.g., the Dead Sea Scrolls and the poetry of Yehuda Halevy) Hebrew literature. Some translations, including Yiddish ones, of modern Hebrew Israeli literature also appeared.

The emergence of "unofficial" Jewish activism since 1967 has increased the interest of Soviet Jews in Hebrew literature, ancient and modern alike. Existing facilities for the study of Hebrew are restricted to three institutes of higher education (in Moscow, in Leningrad, and in Tbilisi), to which, moreover, admission of Jews is extremely limited. No facilities for Hebrew teaching on a lower level exist anywhere. As a result, there emerged a network of private Hebrew study groups and classes. These grass-roots initiatives have become an object of persistent repression. Another element in Soviet repressive measures against "unofficial" Jewish culture is the confiscation of cultural material in private homes and efforts to prevent the influx of such material from abroad. In the 1970s and 1980s the Soviet authorities interfered with the sending or bringing in of books of Jewish interest, teaching manuals, prayer books, other religious books, music cassettes, or even postcards, which by no stretch of the imagination can be classified as pornography or anti-Soviet propaganda.

The drive against Hebrew material sent to Soviet Jews bordered on the absurd: the authorities confiscated classic children's books in Hebrew translation, for example Hebrew editions of books by Jack London, Robert Louis Stevenson, and Alphonse Daudet, and Hebrew translations of works by Yiddish writers which were available in the USSR in the original and in Russian translation. Curiously, even the Hebrew-Russian dictionary by Feliks Shapiro, which was published by the Soviets themselves in 1963, has been confiscated. Visitors and tourists who brought with them Jewish books, postcards, or religious articles suffered harassment and the offending items were confiscated. These practices have virtually ceased in the last two years (1986–87). In general, under the policy of *glasnost'* Jewish unofficial cultural activities have been subject to less harassment, though they have not been legalized.

Jewish Scholarship A comparatively recent development is the emergence of a younger generation of Soviet scholars working in the field of Judaica. Although a few Jewish scholars survived the "Black Years" of Soviet Jewry and have been active in the post-Stalin period—for example, the recently deceased Iosif Amusin, a Dead Sea Scrolls specialist, and Leyb Vilsker and his wife Gita Gluskina, specialists in Hebrew and medieval literature—in many fields continuity with the previous generation was completely interrupted and in others considerably weakened. Nevertheless, in the 1980s a new generation of scholars, born mostly in the 1950s, have turned to Jewish studies, acquiring the necessary preparation through their own efforts. A relatively strong group in which scholars from Tbilisi as well as Moscow and Leningrad are well represented works in the field of Hebrew studies and general Semitology. One of the young Hebrew scholars is Aleksandra Aikhenvald, of the Oriental Institute of the Soviet Academy of Sciences in Moscow and the great-granddaughter of Iulii Isaevich Aikhenvald, a celebrated Russian literary critic and essayist (who was expelled in 1922). Her monograph *Sovremennyi iazyk ivrit* (The Modern Language of Ivrit) is scheduled to be published at the beginning of 1989. The young Leningrad Hebraist Shimon Iakerson published a catalog of Hebrew incunabula holdings in the library of the Leningrad branch of the Oriental Institute (of the Soviet Academy of Sciences) and is engaged in producing similar catalogs for other Soviet collections.

Another field of research is Jewish ethnography and demography, which virtually ceased to exist after the publication of Lev Zinger's *Dos oyigerikhte folk* (The Restored People), which appeared shortly before the closure of the Emes publishing house in 1948. The young ethnographers include Velvl Chernin, an editorial staff member of *Sovetish heymland*, and Igor Krupnik, a research fellow of the Institute of Ethnography of the Soviet Academy of Sciences. There has also been important work undertaken in the field of Jewish folk music, particularly by Professor Max Goldin of Riga. However, many important fields of Jewish studies, including Jewish history and the Yiddish language, barely exist. Publications by the young scholars are mostly brief communiqués, notes, summaries of theses, and the like, and they appear in collections of very limited editions. The important Iakerson catalog of Hebrew incunabula, which is of great scholarly value, is a cheaply produced volume using poor-quality paper and printing and very inferior to other catalogs produced in the USSR. With one exception there is at the present time no academic research institute in the USSR devoted primarily to Jewish studies and there are not even Judaica departments at any scholarly institution. The sole exception is the Israel Section of the Institute of Oriental Studies of the USSR Academy of Sciences, which continues to serve mainly political and propaganda purposes.

The existence of a group of young scholars, perhaps numbering a few dozen, could be of considerable value for the cultural life of the general Jewish community. But there exists no framework for it, and, with the exception of a few articles in *Sovetish heymland* and the occasional book publication, there is no link between the work of these scholars and the Soviet Jewish population.

Cultural Heritage In Soviet education and public life the cultural heritage of the Jewish minority is generally passed over in silence; at present there are no Jewish museums, with the exception of the Sholem Aleichem Museum in the writer's birthplace, the Ukrainian town of Pereiaslav Khmel'nitskii; the forthcoming establishment of the Marc Chagall Museum in Vitebsk was announced on the centenary of his birth in 1987.

We have information on a considerable collection of Judaica in the vaults of existing museums; for example there is an important collection in the Leningrad State Museum of the History of Religion and Atheism which was recently described by Tatiana Gelfman. In this field an unofficial activity should be noted: an exhibition of photographs of cemeteries, nonfunctioning synagogues, and religious artefacts was held in the home of Semen Iantovskii, an elderly refusenik, the result of many years of research by him and younger colleagues. Many of Iantovskii's exhibits have become part of a Jewish museum in another private apartment in Moscow. In this unofficial initiative, as with the Jewish library, individuals outside the circle of *aliya* activists are involved.

The Jewish Autonomous Region of Birobidzhan cannot serve as a cultural center for Soviet Jewry and does not attempt to fulfill this function. It can be said rather to have a negative effect on Jewish cultural life in the major Jewish centers, insofar as the local authorities use its existence as a pretext for their own lack of activity and for preventing the activities of individuals who are concerned with Jewish culture.

Sovetish heymland editor Aron Vergelis has declared a desire to be active in the wider field of Jewish culture:

> *Sovetish heymland* differs noticeably in character from other Soviet periodicals. This is natural for we are the only journal appearing in a Jewish language in our country, which is obliged to deal with a variety of literary, socio-political, cultural instructive, and even educational problems, some of which are normally dealt with by several weeklies.

Sovetish heymland and Vergelis have indeed organized small artistic soirées and exhibitions on the journal's premises. They were also involved with many of the official Jewish cultural activities, especially those in Moscow. But all these activities fall short of the considerable needs of the Jewish minority in this area.

Some of the cultural requirements of an important segment of the Soviet

Jewish population can be satisfied in a religious framework. The publication in 1978 of a 200-page Jewish Religious Calendar by the Moscow Religious Society, which included much information on Jewish themes, was in answer to these needs. But such events are rare.

The teaching of Jewish subjects in general may benefit from the more liberal approach to religion which was publicly expressed by the head of the Council for Religious Affairs of the USSR Council of Ministers, Konstantin Kharchev, in January 1988, but shortly afterward the ban on teaching religion to children and teenagers was reiterated.

There have been some opportunities for informal Jewish religious study at the Moscow synagogue, in addition to what is sometimes described as the *yeshiva*, but two scholars who offered lessons—Izrail Shvartsblat and Abraham Miller—have recently died. In 1987 the Leningrad synagogue acquired permission to give lessons on Judaism on its premises. In 1988 Moscow's Rabbi Adolf Shaevich and Cantor Vladimir (Ze'ev) Plis were sent to the United States on a three-month stipend to study at New York's Yeshiva University. Hopefully, this will have a positive impact on religious culture in Moscow.

Some party and municipal authorities have shown a more positive attitude toward Jewish cultural activities, as witnessed by the activities of the Jewish amateur groups of Vilnius and Kaunas. Jewish cultural needs in most areas in the USSR have, however, not only been neglected but actively suppressed. For example, in recent years, a number of books and albums have been published on Soviet cities which were once important Jewish centers. A photo album on Vilnius, the "Jerusalem of Lithuania" in Jewish parlance, encyclopedias of Minsk and Kishinev, and a Grodno guidebook contain no testimony to the fact that Jewish populations had ever existed there. The same applies to publications concerning the Second World War.

An Interesting Initiative Against this background, it is of interest that a different approach to the Jewish past has emerged in Vilnius. Previous Soviet policy was to erase traces of Jewish life in this city: the so-called Goan's Synagogue built in the early seventeenth century was destroyed in 1946, the Jewish Museum was closed down in 1949, and at that time the Jewish inscription at Panerai (the site of the massacre of the Jews by the Nazis) was removed. The names of streets with a historical Jewish connection were changed with, it seems, a sole exception—Finn Street, named after Shmuel Yosef Finn (1818–1890). (It was generally—and wrongly—

assumed that the street was named after Finland.) Nevertheless, Vilnius, as well as Kaunas, was among the very few centers in the USSR where some semblance of organized Jewish life was permitted. In the 1970s it became an important center of the Jewish national renaissance and emigration.

On 5 January 1988, a meeting of Jewish and Lithuanian academics, writers, and cultural figures took place in Vilnius in the hall of the Zinija, the Lithuanian branch of the All Union Znanie (Knowledge) Society. The meeting was initiated by a group of Jews led by the young scholar Emanuelis Zingeris, who is known for his work on Jewish-Lithuanian literary links. This general meeting of supporters of Jewish culture in Lithuania attached to the Lithuanian Cultural Fund was opened by the chairman of the Fund, Professor Ceslavas Kudaba, and chaired by the vice-chairman, Gerintas Tarvidas. The meeting suggested reopening the Jewish Museum, creating a library and a hall for Jewish cultural events, commemorating ghettos and Holocuast sites, restoring Jewish names to certain streets in Vilnius and Kaunas, funding two or three posts at the Lithuanian Academy of Sciences for scholars of Judaica, and establishing contacts with Jewish centers in other countries, especially Poland.

Outlook for the Future

One should not be deluded into thinking that the activities described above reach anything more than a relatively small minority of Soviet Jews or, for that matter, potentially interested non-Jews.

The future of Jewish culture in the USSR depends to a large degree on the fate of the policies of *glasnost'* and democratization. Before these policies took effect, Jewish culture was in the hands of the Soviet Yiddish establishment or was pursued by Jewish activists. While recognizing the role of the Yiddish establishment in keeping alive some rudiments of Jewish culture, it appears unable for one reason or another to take advantage of the new possibilities and opportunities.

The services of Jewish activists to Jewish culture in the USSR have been considerable. However, Jewish activists first mentally and then physically cut themselves off from the USSR.

In the last two to three years the possibility has emerged for Jews who neither subscribe to the approach of the Yiddish establishment nor are necessarily emigration-oriented, to engage actively in the pursuit of Jewish culture. They may join the movement of the so-called informal associations now proliferating in the USSR and in fact some such groups meet in private to discuss Jewish cultural matters.

However, in the final analysis, it is the policies of the authorities which may give Jewish culture a decisive boost.

17

Soviet Government Policy Toward the Exterritorial National Minorities: Comparison Between the Jews and the Germans

Benjamin Pinkus

Comparative research on the national problem in the Soviet Union is still in its beginning stages. Lacunae in the research of exterritorial national minorities are all the more apparent due to the special difficulties arising from the poor statistical data published in the Soviet Union concerning this particular type of minority. From time to time some articles are published by Western scholars, comparing two or more nations from the political-legal perspective, or in light of the official policy adopted toward them, but in most cases the articles are purely tendentious, aimed at proving how one national minority is discriminated against in comparison with another of the same type.[1]

The use of the term "exterritorial national minority" in describing the situation of the Jews and the Germans is not incidental. It seems especially suitable, as it reflects the dispersion of these two national minorities and the nonexistence, or merely partial existence, of a national federative unit of their own, and it highlights the likelihood that these nations will be the first targets of the assimilation process, be it voluntary or compulsory, since national rights in the USSR have traditionally been associated with the territory in which the grouping in question is concentrated.

The other common terms used in research on the national problem in the Soviet Union, such as "ethnic minority," "national minority," "foreign national minority," "ethnicos," or "mobilized Diaspora" are less suitable and sometimes cause ambiguity in a complex and problematic issue such as the national one.[2] Terms such as "ethnic minority," or "ethnicos," generally refer to national communities with a low national public and self-image, or to groups on the verge of a separate national formation, while "national minority" is too general and can refer to any nation in the Soviet Union except for the majority one—that is, the Great Russians. As to the terms "foreign national minority" and "mobilized Diaspora," they are not only ambiguous, but also have a suspicious connotation especially in authoritative regimes, which are suspect of all forms of "dual loyalty" such as contacts with the mother country or with other dispersions outside the country in question. Finally, it is important to emphasize that from the point of view of the classification of the various nations in the Soviet Union, great importance is attached to the existence (or nonexistence) of a territory containing a strong federative unit (union or autonomous republic) as well as the main concentration of the national minority. It is therefore perhaps most relevant to divide the nations in the Soviet Union into three categories: territorial nations, semiterritorial nations, and exterritorial nations.

The comparison between the Jews and the Germans in the Soviet Union is almost self-evident, due to the great similarities between these two national minorities. Today they constitute the two main "emigrating nations," anticipating the right of mass emigration from the Soviet Union. Second, they have many common national characteristics. For example, they both came to Russia in considerable numbers in the same historical period (the Germans beginning from 1763 and the Jews from 1772). They have a similar legal and political status as exterritorial national minorities with a partially federative past or present (the Autonomous German Republic of the Volga until 1941 and Birobidzhan since 1928), and continual relations with the mother nation (East and West Germany for the Germans, and Israel for the Jews). Third, they are almost equal in number—each approximately two million. Finally, the Jews and the Germans, due to historical circumstances and their unique situation in the Soviet Union, are among the most deprived nations and suffer from a past trauma caused by the action of the government and/or the attitude of certain segments of the surrounding environment.

Nevertheless, there are considerable differences in the demographic, socioeconomic, and cultural-religious spheres, as well as in their different geographic concentrations: the Jews in the large cities of the European republics, and the Germans, nearly 50 percent of whom are rural in Siberia and the Asian republics.

Official Soviet policy toward national minorities is expressed in both the long and the short run by three main factors: legal-political status; society and economy; and religion, education, and culture.

We shall focus our discussion on these three factors since they highlight the common lot and the basic differences between Jews and Germans as objects of the USSR's nationalities policy, rather than on the complex of problems arising from the impact of foreign factors on national Soviet policy, and shall conclude with possible solutions to the Jewish and German problem in the Soviet Union.

Legal-Political Status

The legal-political status of the exterritorial national minorities, like that of other national minorities, was determined as a temporary compromise between Marxist-Leninist national theory and the pragmatic attitude of the Bolshevik regime which resulted from the historical political reality of the 1920s. The main attempt to bring about a synthesis of contradicting doctrines, the doctrine of national-cultural autonomy based on the exterritorial principle, and the Leninist-Stalinist theory of regional autonomy based on the territorial principle, did not succeed and caused inconsistency, indecision, and many complications which are still evident today.[3] The Jews and the Germans were indeed recognized in certain periods as possessing national-territorial units which implied an appropriate legal-political status and helped them to attain certain rights, but in 1941 the Germans lost their autonomous republic in which, in any case, only about 30 percent of all Soviet Germans resided, while the percentage of the Jews residing in Birobidzhan, the autonomous Jewish district, has always been very low. It is, therefore, not surprising that the Soviet authorities began to classify these two groupings as exterritorial national minorities, that is, minorities which have lost their national attributes. This trend was intensified from the end of the thirties with the change in Stalin's nationalities policy which abolished the autonomous administrative institutions and drastically diminished both the educational system and the national cultural framework.

Other factors, such as the USSR's antireligious policy adversely affected the national existence of the exterritorial minorities, since, having no territorial unit, they were the most seriously influenced by the institutional implications of this policy. This was less poignant for the Germans than for the Jews, whose link between religion and nation was especially close and manifest.[4] At the same time, another factor had an opposite influence on the legal-political status of the exterritorial minorities although this was not the initial intention of the authorities. This factor was the "passportization" enforced in December 1932, which obligated every urban dweller to hold an internal passport in which he declared his nationality (Article 5). A further most important factor that had a similar effect was the determination of nationality according to population census. In the census returns Soviet citizens identify themselves as belonging to a certain nationality and the measure of their link to the national tongue; census data provide some of the most significant information available concerning the number of people who regard themselves as belonging to each national grouping.

The formal legal-political status of the Jews did not change during World War II or in its aftermath. In contrast, a substantial transformation in the status of the Germans took place during the years 1941–1955. This change was due to the deportation of approximately 800,000 to 900,000 Germans from the Volga region, the Ukraine, the Crimea, and the Caucasus. (Minorities so deported and subjected to a "deportation regime" between 1937 and 1949, included the Koreans, the Crimean Tatars, the Germans, the Chechens, the Balkars, the Kalmyks, the Ingush, the Meskhetians, and the Greeks.) Their exile was to be permanent and the deportees were under the constant supervision of the NKVD. Those who violated the deportation regime rules were severely punished.[5] The practical result of the deportation regime was the automatic abolition of all civil rights, loss of representation in local and central administrative institutions, loss of positions in the civil service, the often intentional splitting-up of families, denial of freedom of movement and correspondence and, of course, abolition of all educational and cultural institutions in the German language. In addition, Germans were no longer able in fact to send their children to educational institutions, either at the high school or university level. It is noteworthy, for the sake of comparison, that in the postwar years (the late 1940s and early 1950s) the Jews, too, although they maintained their nominal legal-political status, lost all their cultural institutions, were imprisoned in large numbers and suffered a severe decline in their representation and advancement both in institutions of higher learning and in the government.

During the Khrushchev period, in the context of the relative liberalization of government and of changes in foreign policy, a rehabilitation of the Germans was begun. The main process lasted approximately ten years, from 1955 until 1964, although it was supplemented by further legislation in November 1972.⁶ The mere fact that the rehabilitation process was protracted over such a long period calls for explanation, but the more important question is whether or not the Germans indeed attained a full rehabilitation. The ordinances themselves (of 13 December 1955, 29 August 1964, and 3 November 1972) could not bring about a full rehabilitation of the Germans as they did not include an injunction to rehabilitate the German Republic of the Volga, did not enable the Germans to return to the places of residence from which they had been exiled, and did not include any restitution or payment for damages and property lost or expropriated during the deportation. Nevertheless, the ordinances provided a moral-political rehabilitation by officially abolishing the collective accusation of treason and cooperation with an enemy government and by promising assistance in developing the national culture.

What are the reasons why some exiled nations enjoyed a full rehabilitation whereas with others (the Germans, the Crimean Tatars, and the Meskhetians) rehabilitation was only partial? First, while external factors (such as West German pressure) did play a role in the rehabilitation of the Germans, it was not the primary one, the weight of domestic considerations being much greater. Second, a general mistrust if not actually an active hatred of the Germans (and the Crimean Tatars) on the part of the population at large, played a very important role. Third, the return of the Germans (and the Crimean Tatars) to their former places of residence would have been detrimental to the Slavic population which inhabited these areas, whereas the return of the other nations (except the Meskhetians) seemed actually desirable, as it weakened the Caucasian republics. Fourth, the large number of the Germans and their economic importance in their new places of residence had a certain influence when it came to adopting the decision that they remain in these areas, as chairman of the USSR Supreme Soviet Anastas Mikoian admitted in a conversation with a Soviet German delegation in June 1965. He also claimed that it would be impossible to make amends for a historical injustice. That which had been done could not be undone.⁷ Finally, it seems that the persistent struggle of the Chechens, for example in the years 1955–56, to return to their homeland, a struggle which culminated in a mass escape from the area to which they had been deported in Kazakhstan and Kirgiziia back to their homeland, as opposed to the lack of struggle on the part of the Germans in that period, was probably the crucial factor.

The new policy concerning the nationalities problem, a policy which was carried out under the slogan "Back to Lenin," was supposed also to symbolize the beginning of a revision of Soviet historiography. In the scientific-theoretical field, two conflicting approaches to the special problem of the exterritorial national minorities were employed in the post-Stalin period.

The ethnographer S. Tokarev totally revised Stalin's definition of a nation. Tokarev rejected the use of the "attributes" which Stalin had introduced to determine the existence of a nation, and preferred the larger and more flexible category "social relations." Further, the attributes he used, such as common origin and religion, were rejected by Lenin and Stalin. Consequently, the exterritorial nations, which do not possess a common territory or economy, may nevertheless be included in the category of "nation."[8]

Contrary to Tokarev, the philosopher I. Tsamerian and the ethnographer V. Kozlov[9] claimed that this attitude lacked any basis because a common origin or destiny is no more than a combination of feeble images. A decline in the importance of the exterritorial national minorities was highlighted by the various classifications of ethnic community which were published in the sixties and seventies. According to Tsamerian's classification, in addition to normal nations and smaller peoples, there exist national and ethnic groups which are detached from the mass of their nation and live in an international environment. In Tsamerian's view, if such a group is relatively large and lives in a more or less concentrated form, it is not essentially different from a socialist nation, whereas groups that are scattered in various national regions assimilate into the nationalities among whom they live.[10]

One of the principal ethnographers in the Soviet Union, Iu. Bromlei, devoted special attention to the issue of dispersed nations, that is, the cohesive Diasporas living outside the territorial framework of the ethnicos. Even if there is a possibility that parts of an ethnicos become engulfed in the nations among whom they live, especially by a high rate of intermarriage, Bromlei does not regard this as a necessary process, and its outcome will depend on a large number of complex factors.[11]

A significant indicator of the administration's attitude to certain national minorities is the reflection of their image in the mass media, which, in every period, conduct themselves in accordance with the accepted political line. There is great resemblance between the description of the Jews in the media and that of the Germans, although in terms of quantity and the devastating nature of the attacks upon them, the position of the Jews is much more difficult.[12]

The last sphere in which the legal-political status of the various nationalities and the attitude of the state toward them can be examined is their representation in the party and in state institutions, Until 1955, the Germans had no representation in any party or government institution. Although, moreover, old pre-1941 party members were not expelled, new members were not admitted. As late as 1984, the party had only 73,500 German members,[13] whereas in 1976, it had 294,774 Jewish members, comprising 1.9 percent of the total members and candidates.[14] According to the 1979 census the Jews comprised 0.7 percent of the total population.

A few conclusions may be drawn from these data. Many complex and sometimes even contradictory factors influence the proportional representation of ethnic groupings in the CPSU, in our case the overrepresentation of the Jews and the underrepresentation of the Germans (and Poles) and, likewise, as we shall see, in government institutions. The "historical" factor (i.e., the large number of Jewish party members in the past) continued to have an impact in the post-Stalin period. Moreover, Jews today are a manifestly urban population (97 percent), whereas most of the Germans are villagers (60 percent in 1959 and approximately 50 percent in 1979) and the proportion of party members in the cities is far greater than in the countryside. The Jewish population has a large bureaucratic and technocratic intelligentsia, whereas amongst the Germans this class is very small (even as late as the 1970s), and it is from this particular class that most of the party members are mobilized. Yet the principal influence on the situation of the Germans was their exile and the mistrust harbored toward them which persisted even after rehabilitation. Undoubtedly, the number of Jewish party members which seems to have decreased both proportionally and absolutely over recent years, will continue to decrease due both to Jewish emigration and a growing mistrust of the Jews in general. On the other hand, the number of German party members will probably increase, even though they too belong to an emigrating nation. With the continuation of these trends, the gap between the number of Jewish and German party members will gradually close.

Until the beginning of the 1970s the Germans had no representation in any of the local (republican) or central party institutions. During recent years more and more German names have appeared in the role of regional secretaries in Kazakhstan and Siberia which have large German populations. Nevertheless, at the higher levels there are still no Germans in the central party bureaucracy, although at the republican level there has been some change.

As for the Jews, although they did hold important positions in the party as late as the second half of the 1930s, a drastic diminishing of their representation began after 1939 and continued even more sharply through the 1950s. It is important to note that during the Brezhnev epoch a significant improvement in the Jewish representation on the Central Committee took place and in 1976 their situation returned to what it had been in 1956 (four members on the Central Committee).

With the change in the Khrushchev policy of introducing national quotas in state institutions, the number of Jews in the USSR Supreme Soviet was reduced in 1958 to five (in 1950 there had been eight delegates and in 1954, seven), thus comprising only 0.36 percent of the Supreme Soviet, while, according to the 1959 census, they comprised 0.9 percent of the entire population. In 1978 their representation was further reduced to only four delegates, in spite of the fact that Jews have a national autonomous region which sends five delegates to the Supreme Soviet. The Germans had no representation in the Supreme Soviet until the second half of the 1960s. In 1970, the Germans had two delegates and at the beginning of the 1980s a third was added.[15]

The gap between the Jews and the Germans in the Supreme Soviet—although a diminishing one—derives from two principal causes, namely, the existence, on the one hand, of the Jewish autonomous region and, on the other, of the exile policy toward the Germans, the impact of which has continued even after the abolition of all restrictions against the Germans. In terms of their social composition, too, there is a difference between the Jewish delegates and the Germans. The Jews are almost all employed in technology, science, literature or the arts, whereas the Germans are mainly heads of *kolkhozy* (collective farms), and outstanding dairy workers.

At the lower level, that of the local soviets, the situation has changed. Among the Jews, the slow but steady decrease in their representation continues, from 7,624 delegates in 1959, to 4,591 in 1975, and 3,685 in 1983. The figures relating to the Germans show an opposite process: in 1967 there were 12,536 German delegates and in 1983, 17,600.[16] These figures may be explained by the difference in the socioeconomic structure of both nations.

There are major differences between the Jews and the Germans in the central and republic administrations. In the twenties and thirties the Jews held key positions in all branches of the civil, military, and police administrations (and thus, in fact, replaced the Germans who had held similar positions in the czar's regime). Apart from the Autonomous German Republic of the Volga, the Germans had only a few representatives at the republican level in the Ukraine and no representation at all at the central all-Soviet level. The gradual decrease of Jewish representation in the central administration began in the 1950s, and today virtually no Jews remain in the more sensitive ministries. The Germans have no representation in the central institutions of the Soviet Union and until the 1980s there were no known ministers of German origin serving in the Kazakh SSR in which more than a million Germans reside. From this we may conclude that, besides the feelings of suspicion toward the Germans and besides their social structure, there seems to have been a specific decision not to admit them into the "national quotas" in this field.

Socioeconomic Policy

The first prominent issue in this realm is the Soviet policy concerning the publication of statistics. Beginning in the 1950s, the publicizing of partial data on the educational and occupational situation of the national minorities was resumed. There are more data concerning the Jews than the Germans, probably due to the legal status of the Jews as a national minority with a federative unit, and for propaganda purposes outside the Soviet Union, whereas the mere presence of the Germans in the Soviet Union had not been publicized until the second half of the 1960s.

Today, the central question in examining the national problem in the Soviet Union is whether a planned and formulated high-level policy in the socioeconomic sphere exists which takes into account the national element in the context of the distribution of resources, and in the granting of privileges to certain nationalities (such as the Russians and other Slavic nations in the non-Slavic republics), and the discrimination of others. This is undoubtedly one of the most difficult and complex issues for research due to the attempts of the Soviet regime to prove that its policy is one of complete equality for all nationalities, which means that information in this realm is obfuscated by the authorities.[17]

Yet we are interested in a more specific question: does the Soviet administration apply a special policy toward the exterritorial national minorities scattered throughout the various republics? This question can be examined through published data in spheres such as education, professional composition, and economic structure. The war and the deportation caused immeasurable damage to an entire generation of Germans, those who were born in the years 1930–45. A study carried out in the Novosibirsk *oblast* (region) in 1967 revealed that 11.6 percent of its German inhabitants had received no education, 21.5 percent attended grades 1 to 3, and 42.6 percent attended grades 1 to 6, although in the 1920s the Germans had been considered one of the nations with a particularly low percentage of illiterates.[18] As to higher learning among the Germans, the only available data are from the Kirgiz SSR, where in 1970 approximately 70,000 Germans lived. From this data one may conclude that the Soviet regime had decided to repair the damage caused to the Germans by encouraging higher education among them, mainly through the granting of high entry quotas in institutes of higher education.

According to the data concerning approximately 95 percent of Soviet Jews, in 1939 330 Jews aged ten and above, out of 1,000, had studied beyond grade 7, whereas in the population as a whole 83 attained this standard and, in the general urban population, 181.[19] In 1935, 13.3 percent of all the students in the country were Jewish (79,900 out of 563,000), while in 1960, the 77,177 Jewish students who attended university comprised only 3.2 percent of the total number of students. From 1951 a constant decline is evident both in the number of Jewish students and in their percentage among the other students. In 1976 there were only 66,900 Jewish students who constituted only 1.4 percent of all students, that is, less than their percentage in the urban population in 1970, which was 1.5 percent. The drastic decline in the number of Jewish students derived undoubtedly from the discriminatory policy against them in institutions of higher learning, a policy which meant that in addition to the general quotas, Jews were not accepted to the more important institutions and the more prestigious faculties.

From this brief discussion it is evident that there is discrimination in favor of the Germans in the realm of higher education due to the Soviets' effort to make amends and to improve their very slight participation in this sphere; while simultaneously there is discrimination against Jews who come up against all kinds of devious obstacles when seeking acceptance to institutions of higher learning. (According to reports of Jewish emigrants, this situation seems to have been somewhat mitigated in the mid-1980s.)

A similar situation exists among "scientific workers." Whereas the number of Jewish scientific workers diminished from 15.5 percent in 1950 to 5.7 percent in 1975, among the Germans there has been a slow increase since the early 1970s. Even so, many years will pass until the latter reach the average rate of the other nationalities of European origin in the Soviet Union.

Finally, the Soviet Germans' standard of living today is considerably higher than it was in the 1950s, owing to hard work and their improved qualifications. But in comparison with the European population of the Soviet Union, and certainly with the Jews, the standard of living is still low, as can be seen by the level of average family income and the possession of durable goods.

Education and Culture

This sphere is the most important, and perhaps the most convenient for examining the national policy of the Soviet administration. Both Jewish and German education were totally eliminated in the 1940s (that of the Germans in 1941 and of the Jews in 1948–49). Some slight efforts to renew the education and culture of Jews and Germans began in 1955–56, notably through the endeavors of foreign powers and Western public opinion, that sought to take advantage of the congenial internal constellation of this period. Official Soviet spokesmen usually denied that any national problem still existed in the Soviet Union.[20] Khrushchev insisted that the Jews were scattered all over the Soviet Union and therefore establishing Yiddish schools would involve a large expenditure. Moreover, in his opinion, the Jews were not at all interested in sending their children to Yiddish schools. All the efforts of Yiddish writers and artists in the Soviet Union and Jewish and non-Jewish circles in the West were in vain; only in the 1980s have we witnessed the opening of three Yiddish classes in high schools in Birobidzhan and the publication of a Russian-Yiddish dictionary. The opening up of a Yiddish education network in other regions is still a long way off and it is doubtful whether enough parents could be found who would wish to send their children to study this language. The condition of the Hebrew language in the Soviet Union is paradoxical: on the one hand the language is studied in some universities (Moscow, Leningrad, and Tbilisi), in theological seminaries, and in the Kol Yaacov Yeshiva; on the other hand, in practice Jews are not officially permitted, either within the education system or privately, to study Hebrew.[21] Despite the constant struggle against Hebrew teachers, thousands of Jews in the Soviet Union have learned Hebrew over the past twenty years, and in spite of all the difficulties, they have accomplished impressive achievements.[22]

As for the Germans, the first step toward their cultural "rehabilitation" in the Soviet Union was accomplished in 1956 when the German language was introduced as a foreign language into the school curricula in Kazakhstan and Siberia. On 9 April 1957, the Ministry of Education of the RFSFR published an ordinance introducing the German language "as a mother tongue for children and adults of the German nationality."[23] On the surface, the ordinance enabled parents located in an area with a German concentration to choose between establishing schools in which all studies would be conducted in the mother tongue and establishing special classes for instruction of the mother tongue in the regular schools. In fact, due to the fear which persisted as a legacy of the Stalin period and the lack of any central German body, such as the German Section in the Communist party (RCP[b]) in the twenties, no German schools have been established. The increase in the number of students of German origin who studied their mother tongue in the general schools was slow during the second half of the 1950s but more rapid during the 1960s. As of 1974 statistics relating to the number of students who study German as their mother tongue ceased to be published. During the peak years of 1968–72, approximately 35 percent of the total number of German pupils in Kirgiziia learned German as their mother tongue, approximately 25 percent in Kazakhstan, and only 10 percent in the RSFSR.

Why did the Soviet authorities enable the Germans and, in certain areas, the Poles and the Hungarians, to establish schools or classes in their mother tongue, while the Jews and other exterritorial national minorities were denied this opportunity (outside Birobidzhan)? There is no official explanation to serve as an answer, direct or indirect, and we must therefore draw conclusions from the historical background and from the national policy of the post-Stalin era. First, it is important to note that during the 1920s and 1930s, decades that comprised a relatively constructive period from the point of view of endeavors to solve the national problem, certain national minorities, due to external and internal influences, enjoyed more benefits than others. There were also republics (such as the Ukraine and Belorussia) which provided more convenient conditions for facilitating a minority's national existence than others (such as the RSFSR). Second, Khrushchev's basically negative attitude concerning a possible resuscitation of Jewish education in the Soviet Union, which was adopted also by his immediate successors, was an important factor. Third, there was a feeling among the Soviet leadership that a historical injustice had been done to the Germans, more than to the Jews. Fourth, Adenauer's visit to the Soviet Union in September 1955, probably contributed to the relatively favorable position regarding the Germans, especially in the sphere of education and culture. Finally, it seems that both the domestic and foreign Jewish pressure to renew the Yiddish school network was not powerful enough, the latter perhaps as a result of the public and covert opposition of Zionist circles and the State of Israel to renewing Yiddish culture rather than Hebrew.

There is a parallel process both in time and in form in the renewal of Yiddish and German literature; nevertheless, some differences do exist. The renewal of Yiddish literature and journalism was slow and encountered many obstacles. The first turning point was the rehabilitation, during the years 1955–56, of Jewish writers, not a few of whom had been executed in the Stalin period. The authors who survived, many of whom were now released from labor camps, were encouraged by the Twentieth Party Congress and the support of liberal circles in the Soviet Union to apply to the Soviet Writers' Union, requesting it to take action directed toward renewing publications in Yiddish.[24] The first book in Yiddish, however, was published only in 1959. The long-anticipated daily newspaper, so long-anticipated, never appeared at all, and the literary magazine, *Sovetish heymland*, was first published only in 1961. In the years 1959–64 only seven books were published in Yiddish, while during the short transition period of 1965–67, in which no new policy was elaborated, sixteen books were published in Yiddish. In the twenty years from 1959 to 1978, one Soviet source writes that 85 Yiddish books were published, and another 124, in addition to the periodical *Sovetish heymland*, of which 25,000 copies were printed in 1961 and progressively fewer since then. The newspaper, *Birobidzhaner shtern*, of Birobidzhan has had a regular distribution of 12,000 copies. An estimated 100 Jewish writers publish in Yiddish books and periodicals in the latter half of the 1980s.[25]

The main German writers of the twenties and thirties also disappeared during the maelstrom of the purges and deportation. Those who survived were forced to cease their German literary activity completely until 1955. In December 1955, the first German Soviet newspaper, *Arbeit*, was established in Barnaul in Siberia. In 1957 a central German newspaper *Neues Leben*, was first issued in Moscow.

Approximately sixty German writers were organized in national "sections" within the local Writers' Unions, and forty additional writers and journalists may be added who publish in German from time to time. In their age distribution there is a great resemblance between the Jewish and German writers. Few in either group were born after 1930; this means that the continuity of both literatures depends mainly on the appearance of a new generation of writers. In this respect, the chances for the continuity of German culture are better than those of the Jews. Today, in addition to *Neues Leben*, a German daily newspaper, *Freundschaft*, is published in Tselinograd in Kazakhstan, with a circulation of approximately 25,000, and a weekly newspaper *Rote Fahne* in Slavgorod in Siberia, with a circulation of approximately 8,000. Since 1981 a literary-social yearly alamanac, *Heimatliche Weiten*, has also appeared in Moscow. The number of published books and newspapers is greater for the Germans than for the Jews: in the years 1967–80 approximately 200 German books were published.[26] They have a substantive as well as a quantitative advantage—their chances for continuity are greater due to the expanding study of the German language and the emergence of a new generation of publicists and journalists. It is more difficult to compare the situation of the Germans and Jews regarding the impact of the national literature and press on their national self-identity. It seems, though, that in both cases the impact is limited.

In 1956, after a break of a few years, amateur Yiddish drama groups resumed their activities. In the years 1956–57 twenty groups were established, ten of which were more or less professional, including in 1967 the Birobidzhan Drama Theater. Some of the groups survived for only a short period. A theater of special importance is the Jewish Chamber Music Theater in Birobidzhan, established in November 1978 under the management of Iurii Sherling, with the participation of forty-five actors. The first German group was established only in 1969 in Kustanai (Kazakhstan). The first professional group "Freundschaft" was established in Karaganda in 1968, and the first professional German theater was established in 1981 in the town of Termitau, also in Kazakhstan.

In the realm of art we find a great resemblance in the conditions of the Jews and Germans. Both try to take advantage of relatively favorable circumstances, yet face many difficulties, since they lack a territorial basis and are, furthermore, in the midst of a progressive process of assimilation. The latter applies to the Jews more than to the Germans: in the 1979 census, 57 percent of the latter declared that German was their mother tongue, whereas only 14.2 percent of the Jews regarded a Jewish language as such.

In the field of radio broadcasting, a major difference exists between Germans and Jews. The Jews have not enjoyed the reappearance of Yiddish-language broadcasts (outside of Birobidzhan), which were active until 1949, while the Germans have had their own divisions at "Radio Moscow" since 1956, "Radio Alma-Ata" since 1957, "Radio Frunze" since 1962, and "Radio Slavgorod" since 1974.

In the field of historical, demographic, and economic research, there is a greater resemblance between the Germans and the Jews. National research institutions such as those that existed in the twenties and thirties have not been reestablished and research has been carried out on an individual basis through the initiative of a few scientists working within the framework of general universities and institutes.

Possible Solutions for the Exterritorial National Minorities

In the post-Stalin period no consistent or clear policy has been adopted toward solving the problem of the exterritorial nations. The Soviet authorities continue their efforts but still resort to ad hoc solutions to specific issues.

Four possible solutions should be considered, concerning the problem of the exterritorial minorities.

1. Assimilation The trend of the Soviet authorities since the 1930s has been to bring about the assimilation of the exterritorial minorities, the "weak link," or the "fluid nations," as Stalin defined them. In reality, however, this most desirable solution, from the regime's point of view, can be only partially implemented. On the one hand, the regime actually creates obstacles to assimilation through the registration of nationality in internal passports or identity cards. On the other hand, the strengthening of nationalism among Russians and other nationalities in the Soviet Union creates an environment hostile toward Jews and Germans which likewise prevents their assimilation, or at the very least hinders it.

2. The Territorial Solution At the other end of the radical solutions to the national problem of the exterritorial minorities is the possibility of granting them a federative territorial unit. The last two attempts to revive the territorial solution with respect to Soviet Jews were launched in the years 1944–48, namely the suggestion to establish a Jewish republic in the Crimea and the reinvigoration of the idea of Birobidzhan by augmenting migration to that area. Both attempts failed and since then, in spite of rumors that arise from time to time, the Soviet authorities have not returned to these plans. Moreover, no such demand (for concentration within the Soviet Union) exists among the Jewish population or its national movement.

As for the Germans, during the years 1964–67 they demanded a territorial solution through the rehabilitation of the Autonomous German Republic of the Volga and the concentration of the Germans there. However, their demands were totally rejected by the Soviet regime which claimed that the wheels of history cannot be reversed, that the Germans were well absorbed in their new residential areas, and were needed there. Moreover, it was impossible to find an uninhabited area for the purpose of establishing a German republic. In the years 1972–74, a proposal was made by Germans to enable Germans who wished to do so to concentrate in the Kaliningrad area (previously East Prussia). This proposal got no reaction from the authorities. According to reports that reached the West, in June 1979 a secret meeting was held in the Presidium of the Supreme Soviet of Kazakhstan, to discuss the possible establishment of an autonomous German republic with its center in the Termitau *oblast*. It was also reported that in reaction to this meeting Kazakh students launched angry demonstrations, calling for a "single undivided Kazakhstan." The "representative" of the Germans in the USSR Supreme Soviet, Lidiia Kritz, came out against "imperialist circles" who spread rumors alleging that the Germans aspired to establish their own German republic, whereas in fact they were perfectly happy in their present residential areas.[27]

3. The Exterritorial National Solution: A National-Cultural Autonomy According to this solution, the Jews and Germans would remain in their places of residence and would be granted all the necessary tools to maintain their national identities. In fact, the solution which was adopted in the second half of the fifties toward the Germans, and in a minor way toward the Jews, is the exterritorial one. This solution is the result of a compromise between the aspirations of the Soviet regime to totally abolish the nationality of the Germans and the Jews, and its practical needs, which are affected by both internal and external pressures. This is also the most acceptable solution at this stage from the point of view of the exterritorial national minorities. If they want to survive they have no choice but to conduct a constant struggle for the existence of their national culture.

Among the Jews, the national-communist group has been drastically weakened, and can no longer withstand the tide. The question is thus whether the Jewish-Zionist national movement, which exerts an influence over part of the Jewish population in the Soviet Union, will adopt this plan as an intermediate solution and will be willing to fight for its implementation.

Among the Germans, the situation is different: a larger national-communist group exists which exerts a wider influence on the German population. Certainly, the significant emigrant movement which broke away from the national-communists in the early 1970s because of their frustration at their repeated failure to achieve a national solution within the Soviet Union will clearly not support national-cultural autonomy.

4. The Emigration Solution The emigration solution, which was hardly implemented until the end of the 1960s, has now become one of the most acceptable solutions for an important part of both the Jewish and German populations in the Soviet Union.[28] Indeed, during the years 1971–84, 258,000 Jews and 85,000 Germans emigrated from the Soviet Union. The emigration potential is estimated at approximately 400,000 Jews and 300,000 Germans, comprising 15–20 percent of these populations. In both cases a drastic decline in the emigration rate took place in the early and mid-1980s. For the six years 1981–86, some 16,400 Jews and 9,500 Germans left the Soviet Union. As of 1987 the numbers rose again: in that year just over 8,000 Jews and nearly 14,500 Germans emigrated, and in 1988 approximately 22,400 Jews and 47,700 Germans left the country.

In conclusion, it can be said that despite the inconsistencies in Soviet nationalities policy in general which are the outcome of the basic clash between the short- and long-term solution of the nationality problem, an evident continuity is discernible in the discriminatory policy toward the exterritorial national minorities throughout the post-Stalin period. The Soviet leadership has shown itself manifestly unwilling to revise their situation by either transforming them into territorial nationalities or enabling them to develop their national cultures as was the practice in the 1920s. As for the exterritorial national minorities themselves, differences do exist, deriving from distinct historical constellations and the specific national problems of each of them.

Notes

1. See, for example, M. Decter, "The Germans and Jews: A Study in Contrast," *Congress Bi-Weekly—A Journal of Opinion and Jewish Affairs*, 1966, vol. 33, no. 16, pp. 27–37.
2. See R. Karklins, "The Interrelationship of Soviet Foreign and Nationality Policies. The Case of the Foreign Minorities of the USSR," Ph.D. dissertation, Chicago, 1975; J. A. Armstrong. "Mobilized and Proletarian Diasporas," *American Political Science Review*, 1976, no. 70, pp. 393–400; J. A. Armstrong, "The Ethnic Scene in the Soviet Union: The View of the Dictatorship," in E. Goldhagen, ed., *Ethnic Minorities in the Soviet Union* (New York: Praeger, 1968), pp. 3–49.
3. For a broader discussion of this point, see B. Pinkus, *The Soviet Government and the Jews 1948–1967: A Documented Study* (Cambridge: Cambridge University Press, 1984), pp. 1–48.
4. For religion among the Germans, see Benjamin Pinkus and Ingeborg Fleischhauer, *Die Deutschen in der Sowjetunion* (Baden-Baden: Nemos, 1987), pp. 337–48 and 464–69.
5. For the deportations, see A. Nekrich, *The Punished Peoples* (New York: W. W. Norton, 1978); R. Conquest, *The Nation Killer* (New York: Macmillan, 1970); A. Sheehy, *The Crimean Tatars, Volga Germans and Meskhetians: Soviet Treatment of Some National Minorities* (London: Minority Rights Group, 1973); A. Fisher, *Crimean Tatars* (Standford: Hoover Institution Press, 1978).
6. *Vedomosti Verkhovnogo Soveta SSSR*, 1955, nos. 17 and 19; *Sbornik zakonov SSSR 1938–1967* (Moscow: AN SSSR, 1968), vol. 2, pp. 165 and 629–31; *Khronika zashchiti prav v SSSR* (New York: Khronika, 1975), no. 12, pp. 50–51; *Neues Leben*, January 20, 1965.
7. E. Schwabenland-Haynes, "The Restoration of the Volga German Republic," *American Historical Society of Germans from Russia*, 1973, no. 12, p. 12; A. Sheehy, ibid., 1976, no. 13, p. 5, and no. 22, p. 1; B. Lewitskyj, *Politische Opposition in der Sowjetunion, 1960–1972* (Munich: DTV, 1972), pp. 231–35.
8. S. Tokarev, "Problemy etnicheskikh obshchnostei," *Voprosy filosofii*, 1964, no. 11, p. 51.
9. I. Tsamerian, "Aktualnye voprosy marksistsko-leninskoi teorii natsii," *Voprosy istorii*, 1967, no. 6, p. 109; V. Kozlov, "Etnos i ekonomika—etnicheskaia i ekonomicheskaia obshchnost'," *Sovetskaia etnografiia*, 1970, no. 2, p. 48; V.

Kozlov, "O poniati etnicheskoi obshchnosti," ibid., 1967, no. 2, pp. 110–11; and V. Kozlov, "Sovremennye etnicheskie protsessy," ibid., 1969, no. 2, p. 72.
10. I. Tsamerian, *Natsii i natsional'nye otnosheniia v razvitom sotsialisticheskom obshchestve* (Moscow: Nauka, 1979), pp. 52–57.
11. Iu. Bromlei, "Opyt tipologizatsii etnicheskikh obshchnostei," *Sovetskaia etnografiia*, 1972, no. 5, pp. 61–80.
12. For the image of the Soviet Germans in post–World War II Soviet literature, see Pinkus and Fleischhauer, *Die Deutschen in der Sowjetunionen*, chapter 6; for that of the Jews, see J. Vogt, "When Natisizim Became Zionisim—An Analysis of Political Cartoons," in S. Ettinger, ed., *Antisemitism in the Soviet Union, Its Roots and Consequences* (Jerusalem: The Hebrew University, 1983), vol. 3, pp. 159–94.
13. *Freundschaft*, August 12, 1984.
14. "KPSS v tsifrakh," *Partiinaia zhizn'*, 1976, no. 10, p. 16.
15. The calculations concerning deputies to the USSR Supreme Soviet are based on *Deputaty Verkhovnogo Soveta SSSR* (Moscow: Izvestiia Sovetov deputator trudiashchikhsia SSSR, 1962–1974), and the Soviet press (in Russian and German).
16. *Sostav deputatov Verkhovnykh Sovetov respublik i mestnykh sovetov* (Moscow: n.p., 1959); *Itogi vyborov i sostav deputatov Verkhovnykh Sovetov respublik i autonomnykh respublik* (Moscow: n.p., 1971, 1973, 1975).
17. Hélène Carrère d'Encausse, *L'empire éclaté. La révolte des nations en URSS* (Paris: Flammarion, 1978), pp. 99–121.
18. L. Malinowski in *Neues Leben*, July 2–16, 1969.
19. Data on Jews in the educational system are taken from M. Altshuler, *Hakibbutz hayehudi bivrit hamoatzoat beyamenu* (Heb.); (Jerusalem: Magnes, 1979), pp. 125–64; Pinkus, *The Soviet Government and the Jews*, pp. 29–33; Z. Halevy, *Jewish University Students and Professionals in Tsarist and Soviet Russia* (Tel Aviv: Diaspora Institute, 1976), pp. 195–243; *Moskva v tsifrakh* (Moscow: Statistika, 1979).
20. *Les Réalités*, 1957, no. 136, pp. 64–67 and 101–4; *National Guardian*, June 25 and September 3, 1956.
21. See W. Korey, "International Law and the Right to Study Hebrew in the USSR," *Soviet Jewish Affairs*, vol. 11, no. 1, 1981, pp. 3–18.
22. See the testimony of Mark Drachinsky and Vera Yedidya in her chapter "The Struggle for the Study of Hebrew" in this volume.
23. *Sbornik prikazov i instruktsii Ministerstva prosveshcheniia RSFSR*, 1957, no. 26, quoted in *Heimatbuch der Deutschen aus Russland* (Stuttgart: Landsmannschaft der Deutschen aus Russland, 1965), pp. 5–6.
24. *Politicheskii dnevnik* (Amsterdam: Fond imeni Gertsena, 1972), pp. 102–5.
25. *Pechat' v SSSR* (Moscow: Statistika, 1959–82). For the print run of *Sovetish heymland*, see Ch. Shmeruk, "Twenty-Five Years of Sovetish heymland: Impressions and Criticism" in this volume.
26. *Neues Leben*, February 25, 1981.

27. See *Der Spiegel*, October 15, 1979; *Sowjetunion heute*, 1979, no. 8; *Kulturpolitische Korrespondenz*, 1979, no. 382, pp. 15–16.
28. For the emigration of Soviet national minorities, see B. Pinkus, "The Emigration of National Minorities from the USSR in the Post–Stalin Era," *Soviet Jewish Affairs*, vol. 13, no. 1, 1983, pp. 3–36.

18

The Soviet Regime and Anti-Zionism: An Analysis

Jonathan Frankel

On the face of it, Soviet anti-Zionism would seem to be a rather barren subject of enquiry. The Bolshevik and Russian Communist movements have always been hostile to Zionist ideology and this hostility has been reinforced in recent decades by the revival of overt anti-Semitism in the USSR on the one hand, and by the strongly anti-Israel orientation of Soviet Middle Eastern policy, on the other. Many dozens of books and thousands of articles on Zionism (or, rather, against it) have been published in the Soviet Union; and most of this material is extremely repetitious and of little intrinsic interest.

But while such an estimate is accurate so far as it goes, it is nonetheless highly misleading, for Soviet anti-Zionism, although an ideological constant, has varied enormously both in the forms and in the intensity of its expression. Indeed, it will be argued here that there are four different phenomena which fall under the one general heading of anti-Zionism, each with its own history and its own political logic. But, of course, these categories, however distinct in origin and essence, still overlap and interact in reality, thus complicating still further the analysis of a subject which superficially looks so monotonous.

First, Zionism has throughout been refuted by the vast majority of Russian Marxists as an attempt to divert energies from the socialist cause in Russia and into utopian, bourgeois channels. From this point of view, it is perceived as a domestic, internal, political issue. But second, as against this, it has also been denounced as an instrument of imperialism in the struggle against the movements of national liberation. And it is thereby categorized as an obstacle to the worldwide advance of communism.

Third, anti-Zionism has come to serve as the primary euphemism for governmental Judeophobia, making it possible in extreme cases for the Soviet media to reproduce the most violent attacks on Jewry—reminiscent and even imitative of Black Hundred literature—while in the same breath denouncing "anti-Semitism."

Finally, anti-Zionism has also become a factor in the triangular relationship between the USSR, Israel, and the Arab world and as such is to a large extent treated pragmatically according to the changing exigencies of Soviet foreign policy in the Middle East at any given moment.

These four types of anti-Zionism emerged as clearly recognizable, well-defined, and readily imitable "models" at different periods of time. Thus, while the first two categories were developed in the first decades of Bolshevik history—in the period of Lenin—the latter two took firm shape only after World War II, in the last years of Stalin's rule. Yet although each "model" was first formed in its own specific period, today they are all in play, interacting and intertwining.

The first concerted campaign conducted by revolutionary Marxism against Zionism was the work not of the Bolsheviks or Mensheviks, but of the Jewish Bund (the General Jewish Labor Union in Lithuania, Russia, and Poland). In the Zionist movement led by Theodor Herzl, the Bund saw a potential rival threatening its campaign to recruit support from both the Jewish proletariat and the intelligentsia. It was therefore particularly hostile to the labor and socialist Zionist groups which organized in the years 1900–1906 and it accused them of acting objectively—if not always consciously—in the interests of the bourgeoisie. The primary contention of the Bundists was that Zionism was a utopian fantasy which could not possibly lead to any significant amelioration in the dire situation of East European Jewry. In short, like religion, it acted as a political opiate diverting energies from the struggle for revolution and socialism which alone could put an end to anti-Semitism and discrimination. A resolution of the fourth congress of the Bund in 1901 stated bluntly that "under no circumstances should Zionists be allowed into either our economic [trade-union] or our political organizations."[1]

In contrast, the Bolsheviks and Mensheviks paid almost no attention in those years to Zionism, which they clearly regarded as a marginal, albeit utopian—and hence negative—phenomenon. Ironically, when it came to Jewish issues, Lenin, Martov, and their party comrades directed their heavy guns entirely against the Bund which, as they saw it, threatened to undermine the organizational and ideological centralization of the Russian Social Democratic Labor party. The Bund as a constituent body within that party represented a direct threat, while the Zionist movement was simply too remote to attract their fire. However, their overall hostility to both Bundism and Zionism in the years 1900–1906 was neatly summed up by Georgii Plekhanov in the interview which he granted Vladimir Jabotinsky in 1905. He there declared that the Bundists were simply "Zionists afraid of seasickness."[2] At the same time, he was ready to pay the Zionist socialist party, Poale Zion, a dubious, back-handed compliment, stating that they were "far more consistent than the Bund."[3]

If the first "model" of anti-Zionism was thus developed in the period 1900–1906, the second resulted from the new emphasis that Lenin and the Soviet leadership came to assign to the colonial world in the 1920s following the failure of the Communist Revolution to sweep over Europe during the period of the Civil War. Lenin argued increasingly that imperialism as a worldwide system could perhaps be undermined by revolutions in Asia and Africa. National liberation movements, even though bourgeois or petty-bourgeois in character, could decisively reinforce the revolutionary cause of the world proletariat.

Given the fact that the Zionist settlers in Palestine came overwhelmingly from Europe and that the Balfour Declaration could be regarded as an integral part of British imperial policy, it was in no way surprising that the Comintern now chose to condemn Zionism as a colonialist enterprise. Not the Jews but the Arabs, according to this scheme of things, were called upon to wage the war of national liberation. The Second Congress of the Comintern, held in August 1920, adopted an explicitly anti-Zionist clause:

A glaring example of the deception practiced on the working-classes of an oppressed nation by the combined efforts of Entente imperialism and the bourgeoisie of that same nation is offered by the Zionists' Palestine venture (and by Zionism as a whole, which, under the pretence of creating a Jewish State in Palestine in fact surrenders the Arab working people of Palestine, where the Jewish workers form only a small minority, to exploitation by England).[4]

During the 1920s, both these types of anti-Zionism enjoyed official standing in Soviet ideology and policy. At home, the Zionist organizations were gradually placed beyond the law and forced by arrests, imprisonment, and penal exile to disband. Hebrew, as a modern language to be used in education, literature, and the arts, shared a similar fate. The Jewish Section of the Soviet Communist party (the *Evsektsiia*)—which was led primarily by former members of the Bund, the Poale Zion, and the other Jewish socialist parties who had gone over to communism in the years 1918–21—exerted great efforts to combat popular support for Zionism and to eliminate the movement as an organized force.[5]

At the same time, the Comintern constantly urged the need for the conversion of the Palestine Communist party from a party primarily made up of Jews to one which would be predominantly Arab. Following the widespread Arab riots of 1929 in which many traditional Jews (most notably in Hebron) were massacred, the Comintern redoubled its demand for the "Arabization" of the PCP. The resolution of the Executive Committee of the Comintern on the riots reads, in part, as follows:

> Thus, notwithstanding the fact that the insurrectionary movement was a response to an Anglo-Zionist provocation, to which Arab reactionaries (feudalists and priesthood) tried to answer with a pogrom . . . it was still a national liberation movement, an anti-imperialist all-Arab movement.[6]

Nonetheless, it would be wrong to give the impression that the war on Zionism was a central concern of the Soviet regime, in general. The contrary was the case. For the Communist leadership, as opposed to the *Evsektsiia* (which here was largely following in the ideological tradition of the Bund), Zionism remained very much a peripheral issue, albeit not as marginal as in the period prior to 1917.

Thus, it is a remarkable fact that a number of Zionist organizations were permitted to survive in Soviet Russia far longer than almost any other noncommunist political groupings. While the Bund, for example, was forceably disbanded in 1921, the Poale Zion (in one of its left-wing incarnations) retained its legal and public existence until 1928.[7] Again, the Zionist pioneer youth movement, Hehaluts, was able to survive and even to run its own training groups until 1926–27.[8] The famous Hebrew repertory company, Habima, likewise maintained its own theater in Moscow until 1926.[9]

Even more noteworthy, perhaps, was the fact that both Poale Zion and Hehaluts were permitted to bring out their own journals in the USSR. The Poale Zion publication, *Evreiskaia proletarskaia mysl'*, persistently argued against the official Comintern line with regard to Palestine. It maintained that the Communists, instead of relying primarily on the Arab national and peasant movements, should aim for the establishment of proletarian "hegemony" in Palestine. In this strategy (which clearly drew inspiration from Trotsky's ideology) a central role was assigned to the organized Jewish proletariat, however numerically small, as a revolutionary vanguard. In other words, there was here a clear attempt to demonstrate that Zionism (albeit in its most left-wing form) could serve the interests of the world Communist movement.[10] Similar ideas (sometimes coined "Yishuv-ism") were long advocated by members of the Palestine Communist party, and had been argued as early as 1920 by a delegate from Palestine to the Second Congress of the Comintern.[11]

Another feature of this period worthy of remark was the fact that young Zionist activists condemned to prison and penal exile in Siberia were frequently given the opportunity to renounce Soviet citizenship and emigrate to Palestine instead of serving out their sentences. Many hundreds of pioneers thus reached Palestine from the USSR during the 1920s.

Perhaps of no less importance was the desire on the part of the Soviet authorities during the New Economic Policy (NEP) period to receive aid from such American Jewish organizations as the Joint Distribution Committee and Ort. Even though the funds were earmarked for various Jewish farming, educational, and welfare projects in the USSR, they still represented a significant source of foreign currency. And this aid was given much more readily in the knowledge that Jewish life in the USSR was not monolithically communist.

Finally, it should be noted that during the 1920s, the central authorities devoted more of their information efforts to combating anti-Semitism than Zionism. And the thinking behind this order of priorities was understandable enough. The regime was still seen as politically insecure and it could not be forgotten that during the Civil War anti-Semitism had been exploited with extraordinary effect by the White Armies to stir up public hostility against the Bolsheviks. Anti-Semitism was perceived as a real threat; Zionism as a side issue both at home and abroad.

However, in the years 1947–53, this pattern was totally reversed. Zionism in various—and indeed contradictory—ways, was now treated as an issue of truly central importance; while anti-Semitism increasingly (albeit unavowedly) was employed as a major weapon in the politics and the information policy of the USSR and the Soviet bloc. While both these developments took place in this one short period, and fast became almost indistinguishable, nonetheless, each had its own history and (initially, at least) its own separate logic.

By now, much has been written on the dramatic reversal in Soviet Middle East policy which led to the decision of October 1947 to support the partition of Palestine and the creation in that country of a Jewish state. And it is not the purpose of this chapter to go over this by now familiar ground once again. But there are certain features of that reversal which are of particular significance for an overall analysis of Soviet anti-Zionism.

As Yaacov Ro'i has demonstrated convincingly, the volte-face was not the result of a sudden impulse.[12] The first indications that the USSR might be reconsidering its attitude to the Jewish people (the Yishuv) in Palestine can be traced back to the early 1940s, and by the autumn of 1943 these signs were becoming much less tentative, more frequent, and stronger. In part, the readiness to open up contacts (economic, cultural, and political) was simply part of the total campaign to mobilize every possible source of support for the Soviet war effort. Thus, in 1942, the USSR established the Jewish Anti-Fascist Committee as a vehicle designed above all to influence American Jewry.[13] It was clearly hoped that the Jews in the United States would, in turn, bring pressure to bear in favor of the early establishment of the second front in Western Europe. As part of this appeal to world Jewry, it was only natural likewise to establish a good working relationship with the Yishuv, which enjoyed great prestige among the American Jews and was itself completely involved in the anti-Nazi war effort.

Again, during the years 1943–45, the USSR saw the opening to the Yishuv—and even a measure of support for it—as a logical consequence of the alliance with the West and as a possible way to ensure Soviet participation in the postwar settlement in the Middle East.

But once victory was at hand, the USSR entered a two-year period in which its prevailing policy was designed to leave the basic options open. And one such option remained a return to a single-minded, pro-Arab stance reinforced by the classic opposition to Zionism. Thus, in a work on *The Palestine Problem*, published in Moscow in 1946, V. Lutskii, a recognized authority on the Middle East, could state bluntly that Palestine was "an Arab country" and deliver a violent attack on Zionism.

The Zionists call themselves the representatives of the Jewish people. But, in practice, their ideology, political aspirations, and methods are profoundly antidemocratic, are alien and inimical to the Jewish masses . . . the propaganda of racist exclusivity and of racial superiority, totalitarianism, and the use of terror, together with social demagoguery—such is the political arsenal of Zionism.[14]

During the session of the UN General Assembly in May 1947, Gromyko was still hedging his bets, calling for "an independent, dual, democratic, homogeneous Arab-Jewish state" in Palestine.[15]

It was only in October that the USSR finally announced its decision to vote for partition: the establishment of two states in Palestine, one Jewish and the other Arab. At one level, this was an extraordinary development. Without the unwavering support of the USSR, the State of Israel could not have been created nor could it have survived in the years 1947–48. Through its part in the decisive General Assembly vote of 29 November 1947 and subsequent UN confrontations; in the Czechoslovak armaments agreement and airlift of arms; and in the encouragement of Jewish refugees to make their way from Eastern to Western Europe (a movement much swollen by the repatriation of some 200,000 Jews from the USSR to Poland)—the Soviet Union made possible the fulfillment of the Zionist dream.

However, this turn of events, remarkable though it was, can perhaps be best understood not as an ideological reversal, but as the development of a new dimension—the third "model" in the Soviet attitude to Zionism. For, even during the honeymoon period in Soviet-Yishuv relations—from the autumn of 1947 until the summer of 1948—the USSR studiously avoided explicit expression of approval in any shape or form for Zionism per se as an ideology. True, certain statements could be understood, perhaps, to endorse implicitly fundamental tenets of the Zionist creed, as most notably when Gromyko stated at the UN that: "As we know, the aspirations of a considerable part of the Jewish people are linked with the problem of Palestine and of its future administration. This fact scarcely requires proof."[16]

However, throughout, Gromyko and Semen Tsarapkin—as in this quotation—chose to speak of the "Jewish people," the "Jewish population," and the "Jews," but not of Zionism or Zionists. In this way, nothing was done to remove the strictly negative connotation which these latter terms carried in the Soviet political lexicon. This was by no means simply an issue of semantics. Even at the height of cooperation with the USSR, in their contacts with representatives of the USSR, the leaders, spokesmen, diplomats, and go-betweens of the Yishuv (and subsequently of the new State of

Israel) never, for example, dared raise the general issues of Soviet Jewry, still less of Jewish emigration from the Soviet Union.[17]

What the Stalin regime had done, therefore, was to make a radical distinction between Zionism as an ideology and a world movement, on the one hand, and the Yishuv as a nationality already established in Palestine, on the other. The Soviet spokesmen ignored the entire question of what they saw as the illegitimate origins and dubious paternity of Jewish settlement, preferring to treat it strictly ad hoc, on merit.

And in the given context, of course, the Yishuv was from the Soviet point of view playing a decisively "progressive" role. In its determined opposition to British rule and hegemony in Palestine—up to and including armed resistance and terror—it was acting in every way as an ideal national liberation movement. Its struggle and victories dealt decisive blows at British power in the Middle East and, hence, according to the Communist concept, to world imperialism.

Moreover, during the short period of total support for the Yishuv— approximately from March 1948 when the first arms arrived from Czechoslovakia for the Hagana (the Jewish defence force) until July, when the second cease-fire was proclaimed—there seems to have been an implicit decision to subordinate domestic strategy to foreign policy tactics. So, for example, the public campaign against Jewish nationalism in contemporary Yiddish literature which had begun in 1947 was not maintained during these crucial months.[18] The famous Yiddish actor and manager, Shlomo Mikhoels, was murdered in Minsk in January 1948 by members of the Soviet security forces, but this fateful crime was not immediately followed up by the arrest or assassination of any of the other writers or artists active in the various fields of Yiddish culture. And when the State of Israel was proclaimed in May 1948, both the Jewish Anti-Fascist Committee and the Jewish community of Moscow sent messages of congratulations to Chaim Weizmann as the first president of the new country.[19]

But this overriding emphasis on the achievement of tactical advantage in the Middle East proved to be very short-lived. Once the British had left Palestine and the survival of the new state was more or less assured, the Soviet regime opened a second front (without immediately abandoning the first). It now once again, as in the past, began to treat Zionism as largely a domestic issue. Support for Israel was gradually reduced and, by 1949, the abundant supply of both armaments (from Czechoslovakia) and of Jewish emigrants (from Eastern Europe generally)—which had proved of such decisive importance in 1948—had been cut off.

From the late summer of 1948, hostile references to "Zionism" and "Zionists" began to reappear in the Soviet press. In September of that year, Ilya Ehrenburg published a full-scale article in *Pravda* explaining that the new State of Israel belonged to the world of capitalism and could have no attraction for anybody living in the USSR:

> The working people in Israel—enjoy the sympathy not only of the Soviet Jews but of all Soviet people—there are no supporters of Glubb Pasha among us. . . . But the citizen of a socialist society cannot find anything attractive in the fate of a people weighted down by the yoke of capitalist exploitation. . . . I think that the working people of the State of Israel, who are far removed from the mysticism of the Zionists, . . . are now looking to the North, to the Soviet Union.[20]

Izrail Genin's book, *Palestinskaia problema* (The Palestine Problem), which was highly critical of Zionism, was published a few months later, in December.[21]

In retrospect, it is clear that a new, and totally unprecedented, policy toward the Jews of the USSR and the Communist bloc was launched late in 1948. At first, this policy found different expressions in public (in the press and propaganda campaigns) and in secret (in the seven circles of the hell run by the security services). But as the series of political trials gained momentum in the years 1949–53, so the macabre inventions of the security forces were brought out into the open and became the stuff of mass publicity. And one of the major strands running through this development was the increasing emphasis put on anti-Zionism—a trend which culminated in the Prague trial of November 1952 and the "Doctors' Plot" of January 1953.

However, common to all aspects of the new policy, whether hidden away in the cellars of the secret police or displayed for all to see in the newspapers, was its brutal Judeophobia. The Jews living under Soviet rule now stood in danger of being damned not just as Zionists, but also—or variously —as "bourgeois nationalists" and "cosmopolitans."

Thus, the Yiddish press, publishing houses, and theaters were closed down totally in the winter of 1948–49 and many of the leading figures who had been active therein were arrested. They were accused primarily of Jewish, "bourgeois" nationalism and, secondarily, of "Zionism." This act of liquidation, which culminated in August 1952 in the execution of some two dozen leading writers, was not publicized. But in this same period, a public campaign was launched against many Jews prominent as writers and critics in the Russian, Ukrainian, and other Soviet languages (Yiddish apart) who were now condemned as "cosmopolitans."[22]

It is only possible to speculate on the motives underlying this many-pronged attack on Jewish institutions and public figures, and, by implication, on the Jews en masse, in the Soviet Union and in the Communist bloc. But there can be hardly any doubt that it was ultimately inspired, and perhaps even directed, by Stalin personally. Certainly, the campaign in the Soviet Union itself was halted almost immediately after his death on 5 March 1953 (although it dragged on longer in some of the satellite countries).[23] Moreover, it can also be asserted with a high degree of confidence, that a desire to placate Arab opinion and to put Soviet influence in the Middle East on a broader base was not a major consideration. The assault on Jewish institutions and on Jews as individuals predated the initially tentative overtures made to the Arab world, while relatively cordial relations with Israel were maintained at least until 1950 (and in diminishing degree until 1952).

There appear to have been two primary factors at work here. First, there was the desire to seal off the Jews inside the Soviet bloc hermetically, thus cutting their every link with world Jewry and with Israel. In the period 1948–53, Zhdanov's "two-camp" theory became the dominant ideological line in Soviet international relations,[24] and the Jews were clearly suspect because of the close familial and emotional ties linking them both to the Jewish communities in the Western world, particularly in the United States (now regarded as the main bastion of imperialism) and likewise to the new State of Israel. The triple assault on Jewish "bourgeois nationalism," cosmopolitanism, and Zionism was designed respectively, and cumulatively, to isolate the Jews in the USSR and in the bloc from each other, from the West, and from Israel. In sum, they fell victim to what came to be termed in popular parlance "the cold war" and its most visible form of expression, "the iron curtain."

Yet, at the same time, this was clearly not the only type of motivation. The great publicity extended first to anticosmopolitanism and then to anti-Zionism was bound (and must have been designed) to encourage the open expression of popular Judeophobia. Given the extraordinary problems facing the Stalinist system in postwar Europe—problems much aggravated by the crucial decision to reject Marshall aid in 1947—there was an obvious temptation to use the Jews in their traditional role of scapegoat.

What made it possible for the Communist movement to yield to this temptation was partly Stalin's own personal hostility, constantly growing in his last years, toward the Jewish people. Fed by a paranoia ever more pathological, his hostility evidently developed into outright hatred.[25] But to an important extent, Stalin's personal inclinations were probably shared not only by large sections of the population (which, never friendly to the Jews, had been exposed for years to the direct influence of Nazi propaganda), but also by many within the party *apparat* and the government hierarchy.[26]

The pattern which had emerged gradually in the USSR since the 1920s was now repeated in highly accelerated form in—and to a large extent simply exported to—the new Communist states of the Soviet bloc. In the early stages of the new regimes, Jews were permitted, and even encouraged, to play an important role in the upper echelons of the Party, the state, the security forces, and the army. But as the Communist system consolidated itself, the tendency was to replace them by members of the major (territorially based) nationalities. In this way, Stalin's postwar regime attained a double purpose. It first used Jewish Communists, relying on them as strict "internationalists" to maintain a high degree of loyalty to Moscow. And then it rounded on them, purged them, and foisted on them the blame for the terrible socioeconomic conditions then prevailing.

Of course, it would be totally erroneous to suggest that the Jews were the only victims of the purges. Initially, at least in the years 1949–51, those Communists suspected of nationalist deviation (Gomulka, Rajk, Kostov, Patrascanu) were in the greatest danger and, throughout, "Titoism" remained a major form of anathema held in readiness to fall almost at random on the leaders of the bloc countries. But even in 1949 at the public trials of Kostov in Bulgaria and of Rajk in Hungary the theme of "Zionist" agents was introduced (even though neither of the two was a Jew).

By the time of the Slansky trial in November 1952, themes of worldwide Jewish and Zionist conspiracy had been elevated to a central place (although espionage on behalf of "imperialism," Titoism, and Trotskyism remained among the wide range of charges). Eleven of the fourteen accused at the Prague trial and six of the nine doctors publicly accused in *Pravda* on 13 January 1953 of plotting to murder the Soviet leadership were Jews.[27] (A natural side effect of this policy was the angry break in diplomatic relations with Israel in February 1953.)

No opportunity was lost to emphasize the "Jewish origin" of the accused. In both the Slansky case and the "Doctors' Plot," a terrible picture was built up of a vast octopus-like espionage network, centered on Washington but employing a great variety of agencies and instrumentalities in order to plant spies and saboteurs in every nook and cranny of the Communist world. In the case as presented by the prosecution, a key role was assigned to Israel, to the World Zionist Organization, and to the Joint Distribution Committee. The underlying theme was that Slansky and the other ten Jewish defendants had used their communism strictly as a cover to cloak their true role as members of a worldwide anticommunist, imperialist, and Zionist, conspiracy.[28] The image created could have been taken straight from *The Protocols of the Elders of Zion,* except for the one important difference that those held responsible were accused not as Jews but as Zionists—a grotesque caricature when applied to Communists known in the main for their extreme devotion to Marxist internationalism and profound detestation for Zionism as the most important form of Jewish nationalism.

This reluctance to describe Jews and world Jewry directly as a diabolical force is what has made it possible for observers to term this phenomenon "anti-Semitism without anti-Semites." But, of course, only the most ideologically iron-clad Communists could fail to see that the term "Zionists" was being used as a euphemism for "Jews" or "Semites," and that the Soviet regime of Stalin's last years was moving toward a policy of Judeophobia so extreme as to arouse not wholly unjustified fears of a second—Communist—Holocaust. Indeed, there is much evidence to suggest that on the eve of his death, Stalin was planning the mass exile of Soviet Jewry to labor camps (meaning, to a large extent, death camps). Thus, in sum, the fourth "model" of Soviet anti-Zionism, first developed in the years 1949–53, was synonymous with an anti-Semitism reminiscent of czarist Russia at its worst, or even—in its view of world Jewry as one vast, satanic, conspiracy—of Nazi Germany.

Stalin died on 5 March 1953 and over the next eleven years (until Khrushchev's overthrow in October 1964) the Soviet leadership took steps to dissociate itself publicly from the extraordinary, mass brutality for which the regime of the dead leader had been responsible. At the Twentieth and Twenty-Second Party Congresses, held in 1956 and 1961, respectively, Khrushchev demonstrated exceptional boldness in his attempts to expose to a significant extent the vast dimensions attained by the official terror, to shatter the cult of Stalin, and thus to ground his own leadership on new foundations.

However, even during the years of Khrushchev's ascendancy, it was noted by many observers that his power to introduce radical change appeared to be much limited by internal opposition from within the upper echelons of the Party and the government. And these speculations received dramatic confirmation when Khrushchev was suddenly forced out of office by a well-planned maneuver in October 1964. The new leadership, headed by Brezhnev and Kosygin, lost little time in bringing the official anti-Stalin campaign to a halt. But at the same time, this campaign was never formally repudiated and Stalin's reputation has been rehabilitated only in part (primarily in relation to his role as a wartime leader) and only piecemeal. Nevertheless, from time to time—most notably, perhaps, in 1966, prior to the Twenty-Third Party Congress—it was rumored that Stalin's memory was once again to be officially restored to its former glory. And these rumors in turn triggered off opposition, some of it quite open, in the form of petitions, but much of it (one can safely assume) conducted behind the scenes.

The inconclusive nature of this struggle over Stalin's posthumous reputation can be seen as symptomatic of the dilemmas and inner divisions which have characterized Soviet government over the last thirty years. On the one hand, there are clearly forces at work urging consistent measures of internal liberalization—in the sense not of a multiparty or parliamentary system, but, rather, of a political regime approximating that of Lenin's last years, 1922–24. The fact that Janos Kadar has been able to implement a gradualist policy of economic and even political relaxation in Hungary over a period of many years always demonstrated that such a reversal was possible. And it is just such a volte-face which is now being witnessed in the Soviet Union with the ascendancy of Mikhail Gorbachev.

But, as against this, there are powerful groups within the Soviet leadership that advocate a return if not to full-fledged Stalinism, then at least to a much more authoritarian system of government (which would, inter alia, put Stalin back on the pedestal from which he was removed so unceremoniously in 1956). Such a neo-Stalinist regime, it can be assumed with some confidence, would combine stricter measures of repression and intimidation with chauvinist and xenophobic appeals to popular sentiment. The fact that Pamiat, an organization representing extreme Russian nationalism and often openly anti-Semitic, is allowed to function openly in the present-day Soviet Union suggests that even now neo-Stalinist forces retain considerable strength within the Communist party.

Given this constant and unresolved tug-of-war, it is not surprising that in the post-Stalin era, anti-Zionism has recurred in all four of its varieties and that, in certain periods, it has been possible to find—side by side and in the most extreme forms—directly contradictory approaches to this same issue. As in the late czarist era, the Jewish question has become endowed with a symbolic significance, far beyond anything that can be explained by its strictly empirical dimensions. Whether or not to exploit popular anti-Semitism (only thinly disguised as anti-Zionism); whether or not to allow the development of some Jewish culture (primarily today Hebrew or Russian rather than Yiddish in form); and whether or not to allow Jewish emigration—are issues which have taken on major significance because of the great weight with which Russian history (both czarist and Soviet) has endowed them.

The outside observer can rarely make out through the obfuscating fog which surrounds the politics of the Kremlin who exactly belongs to which faction, but it is possible to learn from the study of the press, publication patterns, and other overt policies what issues are at stake and which school of thought appears to be in the ascendant at any given moment. The frequency with which the Zionist issue is, or is not, raised in the Soviet media—as well as the weight assigned it and the way it is described—tend to fluctuate violently. To follow these fluctuations is as though to read a barometer reflecting the various trends of thought on the Jewish question within the Soviet leadership and also the reactions of that leadership to the Jewish nationality within the USSR, to the State of Israel, to world Jewry, and to the interrelationship between them.

During the period 1953-64, a conscious effort was made, most obviously, perhaps, by Khrushchev himself, to replace Stalinist by Leninist norms in both domestic and foreign policy. In practice, this reversal fell far short of its professed goals, as was probably inevitable given the fact that almost all the Soviet leaders had risen to the top during the Stalin period and as a direct result of the purges; there was no small measure of unconscious caricature in Khrushchev's would-be Leninism.

Nonetheless, during the decade which followed Stalin's death, official policies toward the Jewish question changed beyond all recognition. In April 1953, the "Doctors' Plot" was publicly declared null and void,[29] the result of false evidence, and in July diplomatic relations with Israel were restored.[30]

These reversals were dramatic in themselves, but they were given minimal publicity in the Soviet media. By and large, the tendency now prevailing was to treat Jewish issues as marginal and, if anything, to give them even less weight than the minuscule percentage constituted by the Jews in the total population (approximately 1 percent). The assumption now seems to have been that if left undisturbed and to its own devices, the Jewish population could be expected to undergo a process of rapid assimilation. It was to describe the situation prevailing in this period that the term "the Jews of silence" was coined by Western observers.

Strictly speaking, there was an element of exaggeration in this description. Contacts with the West at many levels—from the summit meetings down to the encouragement of tourism (albeit within strict limits)—made it impossible to impose a policy of total neglect and indifference. Various gestures, albeit more of symbolic than of substantive importance, were made, such as the republication in a limited edition of the peace prayer book *(Siddur)* in 1956; the reopening of a (very small) *yeshiva* in Moscow in 1957;[31] and the establishment of a Yiddish journal, *Sovetish heymland,* in 1961.[32]

Moreover, a number of campaigns launched by the Khrushchev regime, and in accord with his personal style of "mobilization" politics, brought with them (whether originally so intended or not) a number of side effects which had every appearance of being anti-Semitic. An extraordinarily high percentage of the defendants condemned to death in the years 1961–64 for economic crimes were Jews[33] And the antireligious campaign of 1959–64 threw up a large number of crass and crude attacks on Judaism of which T. Kychko's *Iudaizm bez prykras* (Judaism Unembellished. Ukr.) was only the most extreme example.[34]

Yet the overall strategy of conscious neglect—much less than benign, but also not harshly malign—was unmistakable. Thus Khrushchev, in his famous speech at the Twentieth Party Congress, devoted some time to exposing the mechanics and meaning of the "Doctors' Plot," but chose to ignore its Jewish aspect entirely. Jews no longer had to fear wholesale dismissal from their jobs, still less arbitrary arrest, as under Stalin, but no attempt was made to restore to them equal access—on merit—to the more prestigious institutions of higher learning or to the more conspicuous and sought-after areas of employment (the higher ranks of the army; the diplomatic service; the upper levels of government and party).

It is in this context that the new attitude to Zionism can best be understood. Insofar as the Khrushchev regime sought to reduce the Jewish question at home to an inconspicuous marginality, it logically chose to avoid almost entirely the issue of Zionism as a public issue. Given the highly emotive overtones that (thanks to the late Stalin years) the term itself carried with it, its very use was now largely dropped from the official vocabulary. This decision was presumably reinforced by the strategy of "peaceful coexistence," openings to the West which dictated (in Soviet eyes, at least) attempts to reduce unnecessary points of friction with world, particularly American, Jewry.

Paradoxically, however, the policy of the new regime toward Israel was potentially far more dangerous than that pursued even during the late Stalin period. The fortress mentality which had accompanied the "two-camp" strategy had discouraged attempts to form alliances with noncommunist and nonaligned countries. In contrast, the quasi-Leninist line of the successor leadership involved a relatively forward strategy based on active support for "national liberation movements." The Czechoslovak arms agreement concluded with the Nasser regime in Egypt in 1955 was symptomatic of the active attempts now made to woo anti-Western (or anti-imperialist) forces within the Arab world.[35]

But this pro-Arab and anti-Israel policy was pursued—like the pro-Yishuv policies of 1947–48—without reference to Zionism per se. Israel was almost exclusively treated in ad hoc terms as a Middle Eastern state to be condemned for its pro-imperialism, not because of its illegitimate ideological origins and not because of its sinister ties to world Jewry.

Thus, for example, during the Suez crisis, Premier Bulganin could write bluntly to Ben-Gurion that the latter's policies, by "sowing hatred for the State of Israel among the peoples of the East such as cannot but make itself felt with regard to the future of Israel . . . puts in jeopardy the very existence of Israel as a state."[36] But in the Soviet pronouncements, Israel was in most cases not only linked to Britain and France; but also described as merely a junior partner of the imperialist powers.

Interestingly enough, one of the rare references at that time to "Zionism" appeared in a statement issued on November 6 by a group of prominent Soviet Jews (among them A. M. Deborin, D. Zaslavskii, I. I. Mints, Natan

Rybak, and General Y. G. Kreizer). They declared that Israel had been brought to "the edge of catastrophe by the reactionary Zionists"; praised "the progressive people" in Israel itself who opposed the war; and called on "the working people in all the countries of the world, including the Jews among them, to raise their voice in strong protest against the criminal adventure of Anglo-French imperialism and its Israeli hangers-on."[37] The fact that this rare reference to "Zionism" appeared in a document signed by Soviet Jews and addressed primarily to left-wing Jewish circles in the West (as well as to their conationals in the USSR), lends weight to the hypothesis that it was considered too provocative a term to be employed on a casual basis by the Soviet media at large.

During the period 1960–64, for which a detailed survey has been made (see table 18.1) there were almost no articles at all on Zionism per se in the Soviet press. (In contrast, there were a not insignificant number of articles against Judaism as a religion.) The Soviet regime was, of course, aware of the interest in Israel—as a Jewish country and even, perhaps, as a future home—felt by a high percentage of Soviet Jewry. But it chose to neutralize these sentiments by a series of low-key measures. A trickle of articles was published describing living conditions in Israel and the absorption of new immigrants in the bleakest possible terms. An approximately similar number of articles appeared attacking Israeli diplomats accredited to the USSR for seeking to contact and entice Soviet Jews. Without any publicity, Jews guilty of Zionist activities (such as attending discussion meetings or distributing leaflets) were arrested, tried, and imprisoned. On the other hand, the occasional expulsion of Israeli diplomats was publicized (in order, presumably, to deter Soviet citizens from contacting the Israeli embassy).[38]

Finally, Jewish emigration from the USSR to Israel was kept at a very low rate (even though it was significantly higher than the all but zero level prevailing in the years 1948–53). The considerable fluctuations even within this limited framework suggest that the grant of emigration permits was being used to send political signals to the Israeli, and possibly also to the Arab or American, governments. Certainly, the drastic drop which occurred in the period 1957–79 has to be read as retaliation for the Suez campaign.[39] But here, again, such maneuvers were concealed from the public at large, both within the USSR and abroad.

The sudden expulsion of Khrushchev from office in October 1964 did not lead to any abrupt or major change in Soviet domestic or foreign policy. And yet, it can be argued that even in the relatively short period of less than three years leading up to the June war of 1967, a new pattern of government (which, inter alia, began to influence official attitudes toward the Jewish question and Zionism) was beginning to emerge.

It is almost beyond doubt that Khrushchev's downfall was engineered because of his persistent attempts to challenge entrenched bureaucracies and sectional privilege. The successor—the "collective leadership" eventually dominated by Leonid Brezhnev—naturally enough refrained studiously from policies of radical organizational reform and proved extremely wary in the removal of powerful officials. As an inevitable result, monolithic control (never as complete as theories of totalitarianism imply) was now increasingly negated by centrifugal forces. The separate branches of government —the industrial ministries, the armed forces, the security agencies, the party and Central Committee apparatus, or even subgroups within these vast bureaucracies—became increasingly free to assert their separate and often conflicting interests and opinions.[40] Brezhnev himself is reported to have told Bohumil Simon in November 1968, "Not even I can do what I like; I can only achieve about a third of what I would like to do."[41]

In practice, this meant that policies toward the interrelated issues of Zionism, Israel, and Jewry (in the USSR, the bloc, and the West) now often revealed inner contradictions. What is more, it seems probable that this confusion on the Soviet side was compounded by the conflicting signals coming from Israel, where David Ben-Gurion, who had kept a firm hand on the reins of government, had been replaced as prime minister by Levi Eshkol, whose more relaxed style frequently suggested a desire to have one's cake and to eat it, too.

On the one hand, the new Soviet leadership took a number of steps which, by stripping Khrushchev's quasi-Leninism of its crudities and discriminatory bias, seemed designed to make possible a rapprochement with the Jewish people at home and abroad. The academic years 1965–66 and 1966–67 both saw a very significant rise in the number of Jews admitted to higher education. The drop in the number of open attacks on Judaism likewise suggested a clear-cut repudiation of previous policy. The executions for economic crime came to a halt. And in September 1965, *Pravda* reminded its readers that "Lenin demanded that a constant 'struggle be conducted against anti-Semitism—this foul inflation of racial discrimination and national animosity.' "[42]

Again, the more than threefold increase in the grant of visas for emigration to Israel (from 388 in 1963 to 1,444 in 1965) was presumably intended as a gesture of goodwill toward Israel. And, remarkably, in December 1966 Kosygin declared at a press conference in Paris—and his words were published in the Soviet press—apropos of the reunification of Jewish families, that if there are some "who want to leave the Soviet Union, the gates are open to them. This does not raise any fundamental question."[43] Moreover, the years 1965–66 witnessed an unprecedented number of cultural exchanges between Israel and the USSR, including the dispatch of an agricultural exhibit to the Soviet Union, a tour of the USSR by the popular singer Geula Gil, and a visit to Israel by the writer Konstantin Simonov.[44]

But this was by no means the entire picture. In this same period, a mounting (but uneven) acquiescence in—and even adoption of—the use by Arab leaders of the term "Zionism" as a term of violent political abuse became visible. This phenomenon was not altogether new, but, nonetheless, observers had noted, for example, that Khrushchev, during his visit to Egypt in May 1964, had demonstratively refused to follow Nasser's public attack on "Zionist nazism." As against this, in October 1965, it was a Soviet delegation which at an important UN committee introduced a resolution bracketing "Zionism" for condemnation, together with "anti-Semitism" and "nazism."[45]

Moreover, the USSR demonstrated a mounting irritation with the tentative moves of the Eshkol government to turn the plight of Soviet Jewry (particularly the all but total elimination of its own cultural and educational facilities) into an issue of public agitation. Eshkol's speech of January 1966 in the Knesset evoked sharp remonstrances from the Soviet government. (Eshkol had expressed his hope that "the pressures imposed by the Jewish people and enlightened public opinion will alter their [the Soviet] position on the Jewish problem.")[46]

However, it was apparently the decision of the USSR to give full backing to the new left-wing Ba'th regime (installed in Damascus by a coup in February 1966) which produced a clear-cut deterioration in the relations between the two countries. In its anxiety to demonstrate its solidarity with the Syrian regime, the USSR now showed itself ready, in a way unknown since 1953, to exploit publicly its ideological hostility to Zionism. Most notably, the joint Soviet-Syrian communiqué of April 1966 expressed the "solidarity" of the two countries with "the Palestinian Arabs" and "support for their [the Palestinians'] lawful rights in the just struggle against Zionism."[47] A significant side effect of this new trend was the gradual, but definite, transfer of Soviet support from the more moderate branch of the Israeli Communist movement (Maki) to the more radical Rakah.

However, it is important to note that this more pro-Arab and anti-Israel line did not bring in its wake an anti-Zionist campaign in the Soviet media. Indeed, it is a notable fact that only one such article appeared in the Soviet press throughout 1966. Anti-Zionism, per se, was treated at this stage as simply a minor aspect of the Arab-Israeli dispute, an incidental part of the price worth paying for Syrian goodwill.

It was the June war that brought with it a major break in the pattern of development which had prevailed basically unchanged since 1953. During the period 1967-71, the attempt to maintain the marginality of the Jewish question in general, and of Zionism in particular, was progressively abandoned. Every year saw this Pandora's box forced open wider and wider.

The defeat of Egypt during the Suez campaign of 1956—a potential blow to Soviet prestige—had apparently not produced any long-term political repercussions in the USSR or the bloc, which were shaken at this time by the Polish October and the invasion of Hungary. But the June war clearly acted as a destabilizing force.

It was followed at once by significant changes in the Soviet leadership. The months of June and July 1967 saw the removal of Vladimir Semichastnyi as head of the KGB; of Aleksandr Shelepin from the Central Committee Secretariat; and of Nikolai Egorychev from his post as first secretary of the Moscow party organization. Rumors in Moscow had it that these dismissals nipped in the bud attempts to use the Middle East debacle as a weapon in the power struggle against the Brezhnev-Kosygin leadership.[48]

In Poland, there was open exultation in military circles at the proxy defeat of Soviet arms and a number of high officers (including General Czeslaw Mankiewicz, the chief of air defense) were dismissed.[49] And in Czechoslovakia, the mounting campaign against the Novotny regime increasingly took up the cause of Israel.[50] There, the opposition publicly questioned the decision of the government to join the USSR and the other bloc countries (apart from Romania) in severing diplomatic relations with Israel following the war (again in contrast to the milder steps taken in 1956). The well-known writer Ladislaw Mnacko even went to Israel in 1967 on a prolonged visit in order to demonstrate his solidarity with that country, for which he was deprived of his citizenship. Following the replacement of Novotny by Dubcek in January 1968, however, his citizenship was restored and he returned home in triumph in May of that year. A month later, a mass petition on the Israeli issue was organized by students at the Charles University in Prague; it stated inter alia that diplomatic relations had been severed "at a time when some spokesmen of the Arab states were proclaiming genocide [and so] we consider this step to have been not only politically but also morally wrong."[51]

Nonetheless, despite the violent verbal attacks launched by the USSR (and by a number of bloc countries) against Israel, no immediate decision was taken to play the anti-Zionist card in order, variously or jointly, to appease the Arab world; to divert opposition from the government onto a scapegoat; or to intimidate the Jews at home lest they swell the dissident ranks or, alternatively, demand the right to emigrate. The latter half of 1967 did see a sudden rise in the number of articles in the Soviet press devoted to anti-Zionism (see chart 18.1), from none in the first six months to a total of eighteen in the latter half of the year, but this figure—however significant, because unprecedented since Stalin's death—did not constitute a campaign. What is more, the total for the entire year of 1968 came to hardly more, nineteen in all.

It was in Poland and Czechoslovakia, both torn in 1968 by devastating political crises, that anti-Zionism now really came into its own. In the struggle for survival, various forces within the Communist leadership and *apparat* proved ready to unleash the anti-Semitic furies (albeit veiled as "anti-Zionist"). It thus became fully apparent, for the first time, that Stalin's public resort to this tactic in the period 1952–53 (so totally opposed to Lenin's credo) had been no mere personal madness, but was considered legitimate and logical by important groups within the Communist movement in the Soviet bloc.

From March 1968 and through the summer of that year, a massive campaign against Zionism was launched in Poland. The Polish public found itself presented once again (as in 1952–53) with an image of the world as largely dominated by the octopus of Zionist control. In the words of *Prawo i Zycie* in March, it was "a conspiratorial group connected with the Zionist Center"[52] which was now trying to overthrow communism in Poland. Inspired originally, it seems, by the so-called "Partisan" group led by General Moczar (head of the security forces), this campaign was quickly preempted by Gomulka himself, who in the struggle for power was granted the backing of Moscow.

Day after day, mass meetings and rallies were held to condemn the Zionist enemy (now often depicted in cartoons and on posters as a long-nosed creature of subhuman mien). As the result of this campaign, the majority of the some twenty-five thousand Jews still remaining in Poland were forced to leave the country. It was doubly ironical that many of those Jews who were driven out had been committed Communists (and thus ideologically hostile to Zionism) and again, that it was arranged for them to leave on Israeli visas.

The invasion of August 1968 set in motion essentially the same mechanism in Czechoslovakia. A systematic attempt was made—by those ready to support the Soviet action—to depict the invasion as an emergency measure required to prevent the country from being taken over by the Zionist conspiracy. The few Jews prominent in public life, Frantisek Kriegel, Edouard Goldstuecker, and Ota Sik, were constantly depicted as the prime movers in this allegedly planned coup. That this line did not develop still further was due to the fact that the openly pro-Soviet faction, led by Vasil Bilak and Alois Indra, proved too isolated even after the invasion to take power. There is some evidence that the Soviet security forces hoped that an anti-Zionist show trial with Kriegel and Goldstuecker as the primary defendants would be staged, but here again the stubborn rearguard action staged by Dubcek, Smrkovsky, and the mass of the Czech people made such plans unrealistic.[53]

The Soviet press assigned a prominent place in its coverage of the events in Poland and Czechoslovakia to the anti-Zionist theme. But, as already noted above, no overall campaign of public agitation (involving full-scale articles, books, meetings, and rallies) was organized at this stage. The complete text of Gomulka's speech, delivered on 19 March 1968, was published in the USSR,[54] but its main demand (that Jews with Zionist leanings be encouraged to leave the country) had the presumably unplanned effect of reinforcing the hopes of many Soviet Jews eager to emigrate to Israel or the West.[55]

Indeed, what, from the year 1969 onward, appears to have turned anti-Zionism into a constant theme of Soviet propaganda—and, on occasion, into the object of massive, ad hoc campaigns—was the determination of the Soviet regime (or of dominant groups within it) to react dramatically against the Jewish emigration movement. That the years 1968–70 witnessed a striking upsurge in the strength and boldness of that movement is beyond question. A number of factors were at work here.

During the years 1964–68, expectations of a liberalizing evolution within the Soviet system had been on the rise, particularly among the intelligentsia (in which the Jews were highly represented). This entire conception, already challenged by the Sinyavsky-Daniel trial of February 1966, was now shattered by the invasion of Czechoslovakia. And thoughts of reform gave way to those of escape.

Nonetheless (paradoxically, perhaps), it was considered with some justice that to organize openly dissentient activity under Brezhnev was considerably less dangerous than it had been under Khrushchev. Arrest and imprisonment were used more sparingly as weapons against political deviation. This fact now encouraged, for example, the widespread development of samizdat and it also made possible the public reemergence — for the first time since the late 1920s — of a movement (or, at least, of interlocking groups) which openly declared themselves Zionist.[56]

Finally, here too, the June war played its part. The extraordinary military victory undoubtedly served to inspire many Soviet Jews with a new national pride and courage. And, at the same time, Israel was now at least partially released — with the break in diplomatic relations — from the constraints hitherto imposed on its policy toward Soviet Jewry by the fear of reprisals by the USSR.

Throughout 1969 a slight rise in the number of anti-Zionist articles made itself felt, primarily because at the beginning of the year Iurii Ivanov published his book, "Beware of Zionism!" This work was reviewed in a considerable number of Soviet journals, and it went far to make Zionism once again an acceptable object of ideological attack as it always had been (except during 1947–48) up until 1953. The first edition of Ivanov's work, which proved to be only one of many such anti-Zionist books (and booklets) published in subsequent years, was perceptively less violent in tone than the second, which came out over a year later, in 1970.[57] The difference between the two editions is indicative of the radical effect of the massive anti-Zionist campaign which built up through the winter of 1969–70, reaching a crescendo in the month of March.

The opening salvo in this campaign was published in *Pravda* on 30 November 1969. Entitled "Disaster for the Simple Man,"[58] the article was written by the Georgian correspondent of the paper, and it was presumably intended to serve as an oblique response to the decision of the Israeli government to publish a letter addressed by eighteen Georgian Jewish families to the United Nations Commission on Human Rights.[59] No direct mention of this letter ever seems to have been made in the Soviet press, but its publication—together with Golda Meir's demand made in the Knesset on November 19 that all Soviet Jews who so wished be allowed to emigrate to Israel[60]—was no doubt seen by the USSR as a provocative change in the rules of the game as played theretofore. In its introduction to the article, *Pravda* stated that "international Zionist circles and the right-wing Israeli leadership have recently launched a stormy propaganda campaign in support of the Jews who ostensibly want to go to Israel."[61]

In its scale, the mass public agitation against Zionism and Israel that now developed, hesitantly at first and then as a tidal wave, was without precedent and has gone unmatched since. Nontheless, it proved to be the first in an entire series of similar (albeit much less extensive) campaigns which were launched throughout the seventies. They can be seen to have followed something of a set pattern; and, at the same time, to have revealed the profound inner contradictions which have come to characterize Soviet policy toward the Jewish question since 1967.

That they were designed primarily to persuade, cajole, and intimidate the Jews within the USSR is almost beyond doubt. They were frequently timed, as in the winter of 1969–70, in specific response to initiatives taken by Israel or by Jewish organizations in the West on behalf of Soviet Jewry and the right of free emigration. The goal was to suggest that these overtures were disreputable or even criminal. And the attacks were often oblique (in order, presumably, to avoid inflating information best kept in obscurity). Thus, in January 1971 a rash of attacks on the extremist Jewish Defense League (JDL) was published to coincide with the first Leningrad trial, and a month later the first Brussels Conference on Soviet Jewry was matched by a spate of articles against Zionism. The second such conference, held five years later, saw the repetition of this phenomenon on a still larger scale.[62] Again, during the summer months of 1971, a large batch of articles on the JDL and Zionism came out, to coincide, it would seem, with the trials of Zionist activists then being held in Leiningrad, Riga, and Kishinev. The actual trials received only limited local coverage.[63] And the very high peak which was reached in early 1972 turns out on examination to have followed immediately on the Twenty-Eighth Zionist Congress held in Jerusalem from January 18.

One of the most noteworthy features of the agitation in early 1970 was the fact that Soviet Jews, both as individuals and in groups, were called upon to play a highly conspicuous role in the campaigns. Early in March, prominent Jews gave press conferences in Moscow, Riga, Kishinev, and Tbilisi.

Hundreds of letters from Soviet Jews were now published in the press. Special statements were issued by six hundred party activists in Birobidzhan; by groups of Jewish workers in Moscow, the Moscow region, and Odessa; by Jewish writers in the Ukraine (including L. Pervomaiskii and N. Rybak); by the Moscow rabbi, L. I. Levin, and other leading Jewish figures; by a group of "believing Jews" in Kiev; and by fifty-two well-known Jews (among them, Arkadii Raikin; General David Dragunskii; and M. M. Plisetskaia). The policy of neglect had thus given way to a policy of ideological activization, a concerted attempt to consolidate Soviet Jewry in a united front against Zionism. As an exercise in mobilization, there had been nothing remotely like this since the Jewish Anti-Fascist Committee had sought to maximalize the anti-Nazi war effort. In its depiction of the anti-Zionist struggle as the cause of the progressive forces within the Jewish people, it seemed to be harking back to the 1920s.

However, even the most cursory glance at the actual content of what was published in March 1970—and, indeed, in the subsequent agitations throughout the decade—reveals a fundamental conflict of purpose. The polarization between what can be termed quasi-Leninism and neo-Stalinism was startling. That division which had been so noticeable in Eastern Europe during the year of 1968, setting off Hungary, Yugoslavia, and Romania against Poland, East Germany, and the anti-Dubcek forces in Czechoslovakia, now became a—perhaps the—basic characteristic of Soviet agitation and propaganda in relation to the Jewish question.

What, after all, was the message which this enormous volume of agitational material was meant to convey to Soviet Jewry? On the one hand, many of the articles and statements issued throughout the 1970s obviously sought to assure the Jews that they were equal citizens of the USSR; that they were wanted in Soviet society; and that they had no rational reason to leave the socialist motherland in order to suffer the hardships facing the new immigrant in Israel.

Statistics relative to Soviet Jewry, which had hitherto been kept in obscurity (or publicized solely for foreign consumption), were now widely published in the Soviet press. During the Second World War, 114 (or 117, according to another source) Jews had received the highest military award, Hero of the Soviet Union, and 160, 722 had been awarded medals. "Jews, who constitute slightly more than 1 percent of the population of the country, stand in third place after the Russians and Ukrainians so far as students in institutions of higher education are concerned. . . . Of every hundred people of Jewish nationality, twenty have higher education."[64] "In the USSR Academy of Sciences, fifty-seven academicians and corresponding members are of Jewish nationality. Ninety-six Jews have been awarded the Lenin Prize; fifty-five . . . the title, Hero of Soviet Labour."[65]

Again, it was declared, anti-Semitism is illegal in the USSR. "It is, of course, essential to wage a decisive struggle against anti-Semitism as against Zionism. That is what the great Lenin taught."[66] Or, as was pointed out in another article, Lenin had written that "those who sow hatred against the Jews must be held in utter contempt."[67] In the USSR, stated *Komsomol'-skaia pravda* in March 1970, "anti-Semitism is banned by law. Why do not the Zionists apply their energies to having such a law adopted in the United States?"[68]

As against such appeals for trust, there was the contradictory line that sought to formulate the anti-Zionist case in the terms which had been abandoned on 5 March 1953, the day that Stalin died. A veritable phantasmagoria was conjured up before the eyes of the reader. Once again, the Joint Distribution Committee, the B'nai B'rith, and the other major American Jewish organizations were described as links in the espionage network controlled by the "Zionist Center." Once again, "Zionists" (a term used frequently as more or less synonymous with Western Jewry) were depicted as in control of almost unlimited wealth, power, and influence.

"The Joint," we read in *Pravda Ukrainy* of January 28, 1970, was "founded by the American bankers, F. Warburg, J. Schiff and others—theoretically to help their poor brethren, but in fact to finance subversion in the socialist countries."[69] Or, again: "In the events of 1968 in Czechoslovakia . . . the Zionist Concern was assigned . . . the task of seizing the press organs and other means of mass communication."[70] As V. Bol'shakov put it: "A person who adopts the Zionist faith automatically becomes an agent of the international Zionist Concern and consequently an enemy of the Soviet people."[71]

It was, however, the persistent attempt made to link Zionism to Nazism —or even to equate the two—which lent much of the material a peculiarly alarming tone. Time and time again it was implied that Jews shared with Germans the responsibility for the Holocaust. "The Zionists," wrote E. Evseev, "should put up a memorial to Hitler. After all, it was the raving Führer in his *Mein Kampf* who asserted the basic dogma of Zionism—the existence of 'a worldwide Jewish people' and of 'the Jewish race.'"[72]

"Among those besmirched by the filthy alliance with the Hitlerites," (here Bol'shakov again), "were the agents of the Zionist Concern who were active during the war years in . . . Europe."[73] Even in the statement signed by fifty prominent Ukrainian Jews we read that, "The tragedy of Babii Iar remains eternally characterized not only by the cannibalism of the Hitlerites but also by the indelible disgrace brought upon themselves by their accomplices and disciples—the Zionists."[74]

The constant publication of variations on this theme could only serve to negate the efforts being made to reassure the Jews that they could feel secure in the USSR. Fear and alienation were bound to be the reaction of a large proportion of the Jews faced with this material. The echoes of Poland in 1968 and of the Stalinist system in 1952–53 were strong enough to conjure up images of mass deportations, arrests, trials, expulsions, or worse, which, judging by recent experiences, threatened all Jews—Zionists, non-Zionists, and anti-Zionists alike.

Even at the time, in 1970, it seemed implausible that this extreme polarity could have resulted from the guidance of one hidden hand. To provoke and simultaneously condemn anti-Semitism is a typical example of Stalinist "dialectics." But it is also characteristic of this tactic that both the true purpose and its diversionary negation be made equally plain for all to understand, brutally obvious. In contrast, the contradictions, and consequent confusion, now gave every indication of being genuine.

It would certainly be erroneous to suggest in any way that the two lines, the quasi-Leninist and neo-Stalinist, represented two organized camps within the Soviet Communist movement. The two approaches could be found side by side in the same paper, in different works by the same author, or even in one article. Nonetheless, they did represent two opposed philosophies of communism, the one seeking some kind of rough-and-ready internationalism which would guarantee a secure place for the members of every nationality (albeit not an equal opportunity for each individual, still less for every nationality), the other seeking a monolithic unity of the majority forged by a common hatred for selected "enemies," both internal and external (very much as depicted by George Orwell in *Animal Farm* and *1984*, which were both inspired, after all, by his contemporary observation of Stalin's system at work).

During the year 1970 (see table 18.1 and chart 18.1) almost two hundred articles were published attacking Zionism, while another one hundred and fifteen took as their theme the equality enjoyed (in various fields) by the

Jews in the USSR. But this ratio of approximately two to one cannot be seen as an accurate reflection of the division between the neo-Stalinist and quasi-Leninist trends. Of the anti-Zionist articles, slightly over half fell into the latter category, depicting Zionism (variously or jointly) as allied to Hitlerism during the war, brutally racialist, Nazi in spirit, a vast network of espionage and subversion. The other half followed the classic pattern, established in the 1920s, describing Zionism as an instrument of the Jewish bourgeoisie to be employed in the class struggle and (or) of Western imperialism in its conflict with national liberation movements.

When the observer goes beyond the year 1970 to examine the statistical trends over the next decade, a number of facts stand out clearly. First, no campaign comparable to that of March 1970 was launched again. Even in 1976, an unusually active year, the number of articles devoted to anti-Zionism was only a little above one-quarter of the total reached in 1970. Nevertheless, there was no return to the pattern characteristic of the period 1954–67. Anti-Zionism was now established as a permanent feature in the repertoire of official agitation and propaganda; and the total number of articles on aspects of the Jewish question was now far higher than prior to 1967. Third, the number of articles dealing with the theme of equal rights was usually but not always—1974 was an exception—much lower than that devoted to attacks on Zionism as well as than that providing descriptions of Israel as a form of hell for the new immigrant. This ratio marked a total inversion of the pre-1967 trends (although during the Khrushchev period, attacks on Judaism as a religion had often been more numerous than articles on the theme of equality) (see table 18.1). Whether these fluctuations were politically significant remains unclear. Certainly, they do not appear to have coincided with the concurrently fluctuating rates of Jewish emigration or, alternatively, with the ups and downs of Soviet involvement in the Israel-Arab conflict. On the other hand, it would, perhaps, be possible to argue for a correlation between this pattern and the ebb and flow of Soviet-American relations (détente; the Soviet reaction to President Carter's emphasis on the civil rights issue).

A relatively new development starting in the late 1970s has been the translation of anti-Zionist material into non-Soviet languages. The very decision to propose it is a departure from the policy prevailing prior to 1964 —and, to all intents and purposes, prior to 1967. If this phenomenon signifies a concerted attempt to win friends and influence people in the Third World through the dissemination of anti-Zionist propaganda it would, surely, have to be seen as a gain for the neo-Stalinist line and as an attempt to repeat on a global scale the agitation employed in the bloc during the period 1951–53. After all, in 1975, the USSR had taken the lead at the United Nations in having Zionism condemned as "racism" by a coalition of communist and third world countries. However, in order to estimate the importance of this trend, it would be necessary to undertake a far-reaching analysis similar to that applied here to the Soviet press and this is a study which has still to be attempted.[75]

Since the mid-1970s there has accumulated direct evidence to confirm the fact that the contradictions in the Soviet treatment of the Jewish question and Zionism do reflect fundamental differences of opinion within the Soviet regime. Thus, for example, the protocols of a conference on Zionism held in Moscow at the Institute of Oriental Studies in February 1976 (first published in samizdat and later in the West), in which a number of institutes of the Academy of Sciences were represented, became extremely stormy and the more controversial speakers found it hard to make themselves heard.

Representing what has been termed the quasi-Leninist position at the conference were, most notably, A. Kislov (of the USA and Canadian Institute), L. I. Dadiani (of the Institute of the International Labor Movement), I. A. Kryvelev (of the Institute of Ethnography), and M. N. Kovostovtsev (an Academician); while the neo-Stalinist case was put by E. Evseev, by E. D. Mordzhinskaia (of the Institute of Philosophy), and by L. Ia. Modzhoian. Many others adopted intermediate positions, some tilting to the one pole, some to the other.

It was Kislov and those who followed in his footsteps who were obviously on the offensive in this particular forum. Their primary argument was that anti-Zionism, as presented by Evseev and his school, provided the basis for "the myth of Soviet anti-Semitism." Kovostovtsev made no bones about it and attacked "the cheap journalistic anti-Semitism" peddled by that school. The view of Zionism as "a monolith"; the use of such terms as "Zionist capital" or "Jewish capital"; the constant resort to such concepts as "the worldwide Zionist conspiracy," "Zionism is fascism," or "Zionism is the offspring of Judaism" were nothing less than disastrous. This entire approach antagonized fraternal Communist movements abroad and the Jewish population at home.

It was essential, argued Kislov, to take into account that the Zionist movement had "a complex structure" and was characterized by "contradictions." Clear distinctions had to be made between the various categories: "ultra-Zionists," on the one hand, and mere "pro-Zionists," on the other; or "clericals" as against "anticlericals." "One must," he concluded, "write accurately without errors, maintaining a balance—and in particular, not launch noisy propaganda campaigns on the occasion of this or that anti-Soviet action by the Zionists." A similar point was made, interestingly enough, by V. I. Kiselev who in general sought the middle ground and himself made a number of outrageous statements worthy of an Evseev or a Bol'shakov. "It is necessary," he concluded, "to institute centralization in the publication process of 'anti-Zionist literature,' to use actively the 'right of veto' when it comes to 'erroneous manuscripts' . . . regardless of who it is that is seeking to publish them and of why or of where he is trying to do so."

From the other side, the cry went up that there was no room in this struggle for such excessive sophistication. "Zionism," declared a member of the African Institute, "is 'our enemy in the Third World.' . . . There is no point trying to make 'differentiations' regarding the Zionist movement which constitutes an opponent united to an unusual degree and it is pointless to stand on ceremony with it. *A la guerre comme à la guerre.*" A number of speakers, worried by the tone of the meeting, jumped to the defence of V. Begun and Evseev, noting that they had received various forms of official recognition. ("Who can say anything bad about Evseev?" asked Mordzhinskaia. "If there is any such person, let him get up on the platform and speak out. We in the Institute of Philosophy have faith in him.")

Evseev himself, although obviously uncomfortable (he asked to have the attacks on him removed from the protocol), did not pull his punches. Zionism, he declared, was "the storm-trooper of imperialism." It was an "extreme expression of anticommunism, anti-Sovietism, cosmopolitanism, and racism." The Zionists, for their own ends, "exaggerate the extent and danger of anti-Semitism" (to conjure up such a "phantom" was essential from their point of view), but "in the class struggle of the proletariat, Zionism is a greater enemy than anti-Semitism."[76]

Another unusual piece of evidence which again throws light on these fundamental inner divisions was the review article—published in *Sovetish heymland* in March 1980—of V. Begun's book, *Vtorzhenie bez oruzh'iia* (An Invasion Without Arms). In this review, the authors insisted that the book (a second edition) contained "serious faults" and that the publishers should never have brought it out again, because "important defects had been discovered [in the earlier version] which were exploited by hostile—anti-Soviet—propaganda." What the authors did not point out—but probably had very much in mind—was that the reprint of Begun's book was by no means an isolated or exceptional incident. On the contrary, the years 1979–81 even surpassed the level of the early 1970s when it came to the publication of books and booklets devoted to attacks (often in the most violent terms) on Zionism (see chart 18.2).

Three major points were made by the article. First, it was absurd to argue (as Begun did) that the non-Jews who supported Zionism were either "politically naive" or had been "bought." Could this be said, for example, of all the U.S. presidents from Truman to Carter? The truth was that the Zionist enterprise had proved to be useful to the global interests of capitalism. But "according to Begun it emerges that it is not Zionism which plays the role of auxiliary to world imperialism, but rather world imperialism which is a mere handmaiden of Zionism."

Second, Begun was in profound error when he argued here and elsewhere that anti-Semitism was to be seen primarily not as an instrument of counterrevolution but as a reaction of the lower classes against (what he termed) "the mass invasion of the most important spheres of society by the Jewish bourgeoisie"; as (again in his words) "the elemental [*stikhish*] answer of the enslaved strata of the toiling people against barbaric exploitation by the Jewish bourgeoisie." And he had erred no less when he concluded that it has been a major mistake on the part of the Soviet regime in the 1920s to spend so little time attacking Zionism and so much agitating against anti-Semitism "which was illegal and did not exist." This entire trend of thought, argued the review, was at utter variance with communist teaching. "Why has Begun taken on himself the thankless task of revising the clear and forceful standpoint of V. I. Lenin and of the Communist party on . . . anti-Semitism?"

Finally, they made the point that the anti-Zionist struggle "divides the heart of many people" and that "our ideological opponents make sure to exploit every inaccurate phrase in our publications . . . on anti-Zionism. Therefore the errors relating to the issues discussed here are absolutely impermissible."[77]

In 1982, another remarkable article appeared (this time in the journal *USA—Economics, Politics, Ideology*) which, again, totally rejected the neo-Stalinist approach to anti-Zionism. Here, the approach taken was oblique. By marshaling an impressive array of statistics, culled from the research of

Western social scientists, the monstrous apparition of Zionism as a, or the, dominant force in American politics was deflated like a pricked balloon. Insofar as there is (or was) a Jewish voting bloc it had formed in support of Roosevelt's "reformist line" and not in support of Zionism. The idea of all the Jews "voting in one way on orders from the Zionist lobbyists is a myth totally unrelated to reality." In the 1980 elections, the Jewish vote (divided between Carter, Anderson, and Reagan) "had put an end to its own existence." As for the notorious Israeli lobby, estimates suggested that its influence extended to no more than "half a million voters of Jewish origin" and that the hard-core "Zionist nucleus" did not number more than 10 percent of that total.

Moreover, pro-Israeli sentiment did not guarantee automatic support for the policies of any given Israeli government and polls showed that by a clear margin (49 percent as against 36 percent) the majority of American Jewry was ready to accept a Palestinian state. Again, of the 1,748 daily newspapers published in the United States, only 3 percent "belong to the bourgeoisie of Jewish origin." And, although some of the most influential newspapers such as the *New York Times* do belong to "the bourgeois nationalistic elite of Jewish society," they often take strong issue with Israel.[78] In sum, here was a relatively sophisticated exercise in the "differentiation" which had so occupied the conference at the Institute of Oriental Studies in 1976.

The profoundly contradictory nature of anti-Zionist propaganda in the years since 1967 has to be seen, in all probability, as reflecting the lack of agreement—and outright conflict—characteristic of Soviet policy toward the Jewish question in general during this same period. The massive campaign of March 1970, designed as part of an attempt to suppress the Zionist upsurge in the USSR, was followed within a year by the decision to permit large-scale emigration to Israel. Thereafter, throughout the decade, emigration rates fluctuated sharply, with a minimal total of some thirteen thousand in 1975 and a maximal figure of over fifty-one thousand in 1979. In the years 1980–86, the emigration dropped to levels reminiscent of those prevailing in the 1960s; since then, they have risen sharply but have not returned to the levels of the 1970s.

It is possible to interpret these figures as simply a function of East-West relations, and the fate of Jewish emigration as totally dependent on the fortunes of détente. The fact that the emigration of the Soviet Germans has closely paralleled that of the Jews[79] reinforces this theory.[80] However, it seems more probable, in the light of such studies as this undertaken here, that domestic factors have also played a significant role. The need to maintain internal security can be used as an argument both in favor of large-scale emigration (an easy method to rid the USSR of malcontented elements) and against it (an incentive to other minorities to make particularist demands). Or, again, the economy requires skilled manpower; but privileged places in the universities, in research, and in production are subject to ever-greater competition as the various "underrepresented" and powerful nationalities clamor for their "fair share" of the cake.

In sum, it can be assumed that there are those in the Soviet regime who would like to see the Jews of the USSR, like the Jews of Poland in 1968, simply expelled. There are others who seek to have them fully integrated through a system of equal opportunities in many educational and economic spheres. And the government since 1967 has been steering now closer to Scylla, now to Charybdis.

Conclusion

It is the contention of this chapter that the policies of the Stalin regime in the period 1947–53 toward the Jewish question—both at home and abroad —brought with them a fundamental change in Soviet attitudes to Zionism. Until then, Zionism had been opposed domestically as a bourgeois ideology and abroad as an instrument of Western imperialism in the Middle East. As such, it was a subject that received little attention from the Soviet authorities in general, and the struggle against it was considered to be the concern primarily of the "Yiddish-speaking" Communists (the *Evsektsiia* and other such official Jewish organizations).

But Stalin initiated two entirely different, and contradictory, strategies in relation to the Zionist issue. One was the policy of silence applied to Zionism as an ideology when, for pure *raison d'état*, he decided to support the establishment of Israel. The other was the use of anti-Zionism as a cover under which to introduce the crudest forms of governmental anti-Semitism.

The effect of this last maneuver has been that ever since Stalin's death in 1953, the very term "Zionism" has remained potentially controversial, and, indeed, highly problematic, from the point of view of the Soviet leadership. This complication has been compounded by the increasing effort of forces within the Arab world to rally world opinion against "Zionism"— using that term as an emotive epithet embodying all that is evil. During the immediate post-Stalin and Khrushchev periods (1953–64), the tendency was, therefore, to reduce anti-Zionism to a strictly marginal role in Soviet agitation and propaganda, while, nonetheless, implementing actively pro-Arab and anti-imperialist (meaning anti-Israeli) policies in the Middle East.

Finally, since the period 1967–70, Zionism has been restored to the lexicon of—and, in certain limited periods has even been assigned a central place in—the Soviet media. But this reversal has brought with it radical divisions of opinion in the Soviet regime with a quasi-Leninist school at one pole; neo-Stalinists at the other; and a large formless mass at the center pulled in both directions. The contradictions revealed in this one specific field beyond doubt reflect similar conflicts within the regime regarding the Jewish question as a whole and, indeed, the very nature of the Soviet future.

With the rise of Gorbachev, neo-Leninism has come to enjoy a remarkable resurgence. And one of the side effects of this development has been that overall—and for the time being at least—official anti-Zionist propaganda has become less massive in output, less violent in tone, and less entangled with anti-Semitism.

Tables 18.1 and 18.2 are based on an analysis of the articles reproduced from the Soviet press in *Evrei i evreiskii narod* (Excerpts from the Soviet Press) (The Center for Research and Documentation of East European Jewry, The Hebrew University of Jerusalem, 1960–80), specifically the sections: (1) Jewish religion; (2) Jews in History and Culture; (3) Jews and Jewish History in Russia and the USSR; (4) Soviet Jews and the State of Israel; (5) World Jewry and the State of Israel.

It should be noted that the number of newspapers and journals surveyed by *Evrei i evreiskii narod* has not been constant. However, with the exception of the first year of the present survey, 1960, these variations have not, in our view, been significant. In most years, over 150 newspapers and journals were examined and the few additions or reductions involved marginal and specialized publications which rarely dealt with Zionism. Finally, it should be pointed out that the decision to assign the various articles to the different categories was based on the general assessment of my research assistant (Mordechai Zeldon) and not on a system of word counts.

Table 18.1
Soviet Articles on Jewish Themes (1960–1980)

	1960	1961	1962	1963	1964	1965	1966	1967	1968
Anti-Zionism as reaction	0	1	0	2	0	3	1	12	14
Anti-Zionism as racism (Nazi equation)	0	1	1	0	0	0	0	6	5
Jewish religion and/or history as reaction	13	34	35	25	16	5	14	19	7
Jewish religion and/or history as racism	1	1	0	0	0	0	0	1	3
Israel in crisis, *olim* disappointed	9	11	12	9	8	11	12	15	1
Diplomats, tourists packages as interference	7	5	2	5	23	7	6	0	0
Diplomats, tourists etc. as subversion	0	0	6	0	0	0	2	2	14
Anti-Soviet provocation abroad (JDL)	0	0	0	0	0	0	1	0	1
Equal rights of Jews in USSR	2	3	17	25	39	16	32	55	7
Aliya activists	0	0	0	1	0	1	0	0	2
Total	32	56	73	67	86	43	68	110	54

1969	1970	1971	1972	1973	1974	1975	1976	1977	1978	1979	1980
31	90	30	138	40	2	30	27	16	30	51	36
12	96	15	31	18	6	8	24	18	6	11	12
16	3	3	16	14	16	7	3	6	6	5	5
0	0	0	1	0	0	0	2	2	0	0	0
1	10	31	40	52	52	65	56	45	22	62	59
1	6	4	16	2	5	6	10	16	8	20	13
0	1	1	0	1	0	0	5	6	0	0	0
1	11	36	5	5	3	13	29	7	3	0	3
44	115	29	21	14	29	16	30	25	23	25	15
0	0	5	5	11	3	6	13	13	19	11	10
106	332	154	273	157	116	151	199	154	117	185	153

Table 18.2
Articles on Jewish Themes by Selected Newspapers

	1970							1976							1980						
	P	LG	KZ	PU	PV	ZV	SL	P	LG	KZ	PU	PV	ZV	SL	P	LG	KZ	PU	PV	ZV	SL
Anti-Zionism as reaction	2	1	4	4		2	4	5	1		1					1					
Anti-Zionism as racism (Nazi comparison)	11	2	2		1		1	1	1	1				1		3	1				
Jewish religion and/or history as reaction																					1
Jewish religion and/or history as racism																					

	P	LG	KZ	PU	PV	ZV	SL
Israel in crisis; Disappointed *olim* and other emigrants		1		2	3	1	1
						1	5
						1	1
Diplomats, tourists, packages as interference	3						
Diplomats, tourists, packages as international subversion			1				
Anti-Soviet provocation abroad (JDL, etc.)	1	1	1	1	8	1	
Equal rights of Jews in USSR				1	1	1	2	1	1
Aliya activists	9	2	5	3	10	1	1

Key: P = *Pravda* LG = *Literaturnaia gazeta* KZ = *Krasnaia zvezda* PU = *Pravda Ukrainy* PV = *Pravda Vostoka* ZV = *Zaria Vostoka* SL = *Sovetskaia Litva*

Chart 18.1

ARTICLES ON ZIONISM AS RELATED TO TOTAL NUMBER OF ARTICLES ON JEWISH THEMES (1962-1978)

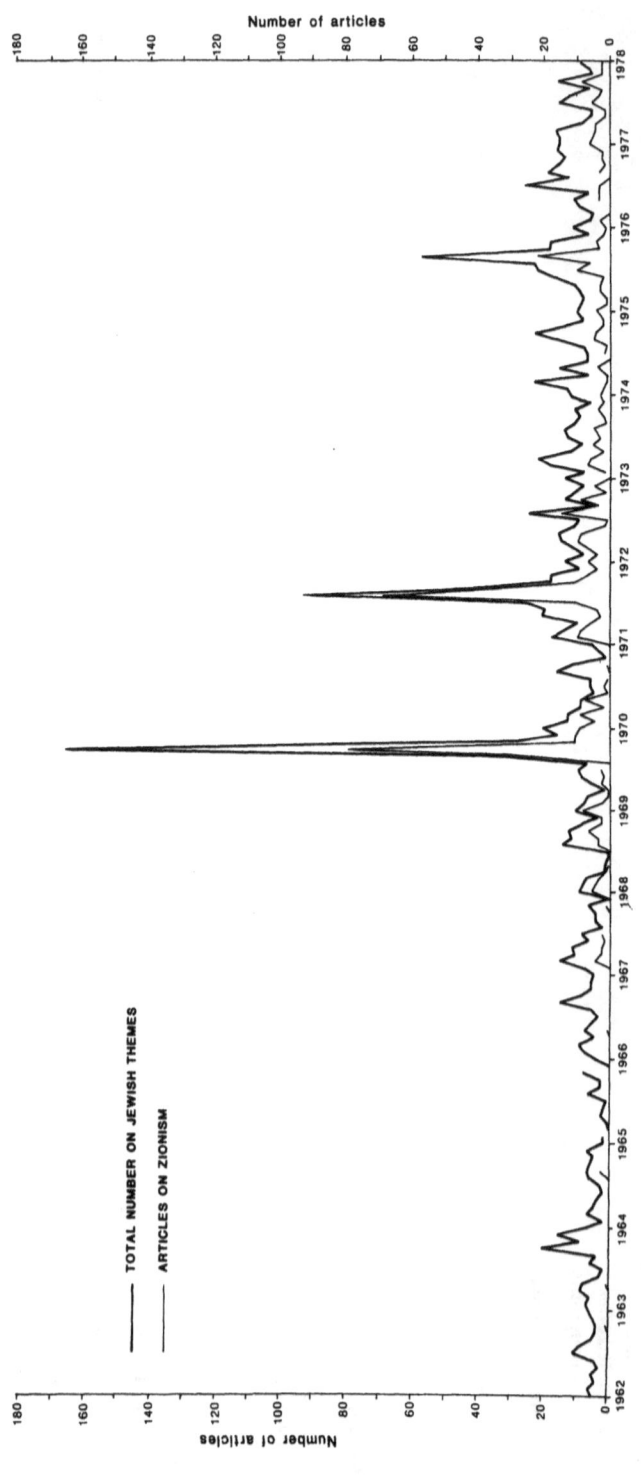

Chart 18.2

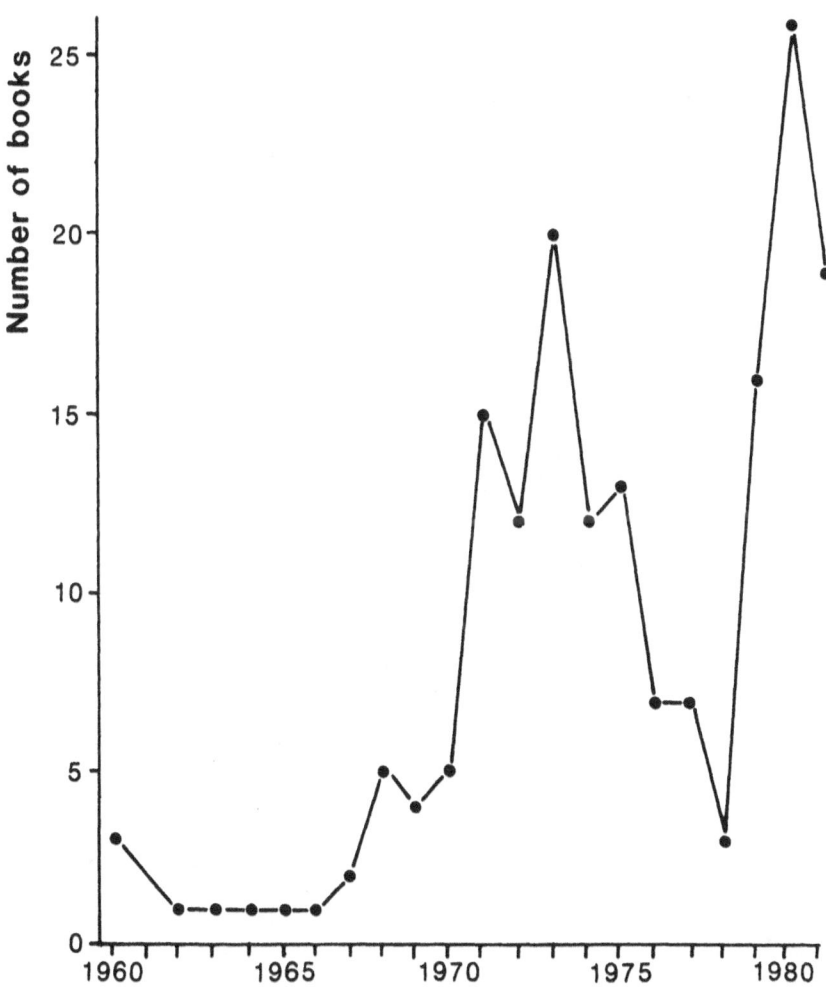

Notes

This chapter appeared as Research Paper No. 55 of the Soviet and East European Research Center, the Hebrew University of Jerusalem. The author is profoundly grateful to Mordechai Zeldon, a research assistant at the Hebrew University, who undertook the massive and trying analysis which appears in the tables and charts. Without his assistance and advice this project could not have been brought to a successful conclusion.

1. "Der ferter kongres fun algemaynem yidishn arbeter bund in rusland un polyn," *Der yidisher arbeter*, no. 12 (1901), p. 101.
2. V. Jabotinsky, "Nabroski bez zaglavikh: beseda s G.V. Plekhanovym," *Khronika evreiskoi zhizni*, nos. 41–42 (October 28, 1905), p. 30.
3. Ibid., p. 31.
4. J. Degras (ed.), *The Communist International 1919–1943*, vol. 1 (London, 1956), p. 144.
5. On the *Evsektsiia*, see Z. Y. Gitelman, *Jewish Nationality and Soviet Politics: The Jewish Sections of the CPSU 1917–1930* (Princeton, 1972); and M. Altshuler, *Hayevsektsiah bivrit hamoazot (1918–1930); bein leumiut lekomunizm* (Tel Aviv, 1980).
6. J. Degras (ed.), *The Communist International 1919–1943*, vol. 3 (London, 1965), p. 80.
7. See, e.g., B. Gurevitz, "Un cas de communisme national en Union soviétique: le Poale Zion 1918–1928,: *Cahiers du monde russe et soviétique* 15 (1974), pp. 333–71.
8. On Hehaluts in Soviet Russia, see D. Pines, *Hehalutz bekur hamahapekha: korot hahistadrut huhaluts berusiya* (Tel Aviv, 1938); and B. Vest [West], *Naftelei dor: korot tnuat haavodah hatsiyonit tseirei tsiyon-hitahdut berusiya sovietit* (Tel Aviv, 1947).
9. E.g., R. Ben-Ari, *Habima* (New York, n.d.), p. 253.
10. E.g., Z. Greiter, "Klassovye i natsionalnye otnosheniia i kommunisticheskaia taktika v Pelestine," *Evreiskaia proletarskaia mysl'*, nos. 40–42 (1926), pp. 19–23.
11. For this speech, see [The Communist International], *Berichte zum zweiten Kongress der Kommunistischen Internationale* (Hamburg, 1921), pp. 184–87. (The delegate from Palestine represented the emergent Communist party, then still the Socialist Labour party of Palestine and often known by its Hebrew acronym, Mo.P.S.—Mifleget hapoalim hasotsialistit.)
12. Y. Ro'i, *Soviet Decision Making in Practice: The USSR and Israel 1947–1954* (New Brunswick, N.J., 1980), pp. 13–106.
13. See S. Redlich, *Propaganda and Nationalism in Wartime Russia: The Jewish Anti-Fascist Committee in the USSR 1941–1948*, East European Monographs, no. 108 (n.p., 1982), pp. 1–72.
14. V. B. Lutskii, *Palestinskaia problema* (Moscow, 1946), p. 13.
15. *United Nations: Official Records of the First Special Session of the General Assembly, vol. 1 (Verbatim Record 28 April–15 May, 1947)*, p. 134.
16. Ibid., p. 131.
17. Y. Ro'i, *Soviet Decision Making*, pp. 205–6.
18. On this campaign see, for example, Benjamin Pinkus, *The Soviet Government and the Jews 1948–1967: A Documented Study* (Cambridge, 1984), pp. 147–50.
19. Y. Ro'i, *Soviet Decision Making*, pp. 187, 307.
20. I. E[h]renburg, "Po povodu odnogo pisma," *Pravda*, September 21, 1948.
21. I. Genin, *Palestinskaia problema* (Moscow, 1948).
22. On the anticosmopolitan campaign, see, for example, B. Pinkus, *The Soviet*

Government and the Jews, pp. 151–64. For an overall account of the policy toward the Jews in the late Stalin period: Y. A. Gilboa, *The Black Years of Soviet Jewry, 1939–1953* (Boston, 1971).

23. On postwar developments in the emergent Soviet bloc: Peter Meyer et al., *The Jews in the Soviet Satellites* (Syracuse, N.Y., 1953).
24. For the text of the declaration issued by the founding conference of the Cominform (September 1947), see *Documents on International Affairs 1947–1948* (The Royal Institute of International Affairs, London, 1952), pp. 122–25.
25. On Stalin's anti-Semitic comments and outbursts, see particularly S. Allilueva, *Only One Year* (New York, 1969), pp. 152–55; and M. Djilas, *Conversations with Stalin* (New York, 1962), pp. 154, 170–71.
26. On anti-Semitism in the USSR, see W. Korey, *The Soviet Cage: Anti-Semitism in Russia* (New York, 1973); S. Ettinger et al. (eds.), *Anti-Semitism in the USSR; Its Roots and Consequences,* 3 vols. (Jerusalem, 1978–83); and B. Weinryb, "Antisemitism in Soviet Russia," in L. Kochan (ed.), *The Jews in Soviet Russia* (London, 1972), pp. 288–320.
27. On the Prague trial see, for example, J. Pelikan (ed.), *The Czechoslovak Political Trials 1950–1954* (London, 1970); E. Loebl. *Sentenced and Tried: The Stalinist Purges in Czechoslovakia* (London, 1969); and Josefa Slanska, *Report on My Husband* (London, 1969).
28. For the transcript of the Prague trial: *Procès des dirigeants du centre de conspiration contre l'Etat dirigé par Rudolf Slansky* (Prague, 1953).
29. "Soobshchenie Ministerstva vnutrennikh del SSSR," *Pravda,* April 4, 1953.
30. Y. Ro'i, *Soviet Decision Making,* pp. 469–78.
31. On the status of Judaism as an official religion in the USSR, see J. Rothenberg, *The Jewish Religion in the Soviet Union* (New York, 1971).
32. On this journal see A. Brumberg, " 'Sovyetish Heymland' and the Dilemmas of Jewish Life in the USSR," *Soviet Jewish Affairs,* no. 3 (1972), pp. 27–41; also Ch. Shmeruk, "Twenty-Five Years of *Sovetish heymland:* Impressions and Criticism," in this volume.
33. On the economic trials, see Evgeniia Evelson, *Sudebnye protsessy po ekonomicheskim delam v SSSR (v 60ye gody).* (London, 1986); and B. Pinkus, *The Soviet Government and the Jews,* pp. 201–7.
34. T. Kychko, *Iudaizm bez prykras* (Kiev, 1963).
35. On the post-Stalin metamorphosis in policy toward the third world, and specifically the Middle East see, for example, O. M. Smolansky, *The Soviet Union and the Arab East Under Khrushchev* (Lewisburg, 1974).
36. *Documents on International Affairs 1956* (London, 1959), p. 292.
37. "Po povodu agressii Izrailia, Anglii i Frantsii protiv Egipta," *Pravda,* November 6, 1956.
38. E.g., the expulsion of Eliyahu Hazan, attacked by D. Zaslavskii, "Diplomat s ulitsy Lilienblum," *Pravda,* September 22, 1957.
39. On the role of Jewish emigration from the USSR as a factor in Soviet foreign policy, see Y. Ro'i, "Jewish Emigration and Soviet-Arab Relations, 1954–67,"

in Elie Kedourie and Sylvia G. Haim (eds.), *Zionism and Arabism in Palestine and Israel* (London, 1982), pp. 210–27.
40. E.g., J. F. Hough and M. Fainsod, *How the Soviet Union is Governed* (Cambridge, Mass., 1979), pp. 518–55.
41. Z. Mlynar, *Night Frost in Prague: The End of Humane Socialism* (London, 1980), p. 163.
42. "Leninskaia druzhba narodov," *Pravda*, September 5, 1965.
43. "Zhit' v mire, razvivat' sotrudnichestvo," *Pravda*, December 5, 1966.
44. On Israeli-Soviet relations in the 1960s, see, for example, Y. Govrin, *Israel-Soviet Relations 1964–66* (The Hebrew University: Soviet and East European Research Center, paper no. 29, 1978).
45. UN General Assembly, Third Committee, Document A/6181, October 20, 1965 (as quoted in Y. Govrin, *Israel-Soviet Relations*, p. 87).
46. Quoted in Govrin, *Israel-Soviet Relations*, p. 90.
47. "V interesakh ukrepleniia mira vzaimnogo sotrudnichestva," *Pravda*, April 26, 1966.
48. E.g., Hough and Fainsod, *How the Soviet Union is Governed*, p. 258.
49. On the purge of the Polish armed forces, see M. Checinski, *Poland: Communism, Nationalism, Anti-Semitism* (New York, 1982), pp. 205–6.
50. See, for example, H. Gordon Skilling, *Czechoslovakia's Interrupted Revolution* (Princeton, 1976), pp. 633–34; and Galia Golan, *The Czechoslovak Reform Movement* (Cambridge, 1971), pp. 236–39.
51. *Student*, May 29, 1968, as quoted by P. Lendvai, *Anti-Semitism Without Jews* (New York, 1971), p. 267.
52. March 24, 1968 (as quoted in Lendvai, *Anti-Semitism Without Jews*, p. 89). On the anti-"Zionist" campaign in Poland and the expulsion of the Jews: Checinski, *Poland*, pp. 208–55.
53. Lendvai, *Anti-Semitism Without Jews*, p. 280.
54. "Vystuplenie tovarishcha V. Gomulki na vstreche s partiinym aktivom Varshavy," *Pravda*, March 22, 1968.
55. M. Gelfond, "Illegal Zionist Activity in the Soviet Union in the 1950s–1960s," in D. Prital (ed.), *In Search of Self: the Soviet Jewish Intelligentsia and the Exodus* (Jerusalem, 1982), p. 40.
56. For example, ibid.
57. Iurii Ivanov, *Ostorozhno Sionizm!: Ocherki po ideologii, organizatsii i praktike Sionizma* (Moscow, 1969). The second edition, 1970, is considerably enlarged (208 pp. as against 176).
58. G. Lebanidze, "Prostomu cheloveku zdes gibel'," *Pravda*, November 30, 1969.
59. On the campaign of 1970, see Z. Ben-Shlomo, "The Current Anti-Zionist Campaign in the USSR," *Bulletin on Soviet and East European Jewish Affairs*, no. 5 (May 1970), pp. 1–13; and J. Frankel, "The Anti-Zionist Press Campaigns in the USSR 1969–1971: An Internal Dialogue?" *Soviet Jewish Affairs*, no. 3 (May 1972), pp. 3–26. (For a reservation about a key argument in this latter article: A. Z. Rubinstein, *Red Star on the Nile: The Soviet-Egyptian Influence Relationship Since the June War* (Princeton, 1977), pp. 112–13, note).

60. *Haaretz*, November 20, 1969.
61. *Pravda*, November 30, 1969.
62. In the light of these findings, it was possible to predict with a measure of confidence that the third world conference on Soviet Jewry (held in Jerusalem in March 1983) would be followed by a sharp rise in the level of anti-Zionist propaganda. This proved to be the case. (On the Anti-Zionist Committee of the Soviet Public, announced on April 1, 1983, see The Institute of Jewish Affairs, *Research Report* no. 6 (London, 1983); and T. Friedgut, *Soviet Anti-Zionism and Anti-Semitism: Another Cycle* (The Hebrew University: Soviet and East European Research Center, paper no. 54, 1984.)
63. See J. Frankel, "The Anti-Zionist Press Campaigns," pp. 9–10.
64. S. Borisovskii, "Kleveta i pravda," *Trud*, February 26, 1970.
65. "Tsifry i fakty," ibid.
66. L. Berenshtein and M. Fridel, "Pod chyu didku plyashut sionisty," *Izvestiia*, December 14, 1969.
67. Quoted in G. Plotkin, "Masko i litso Sionizma," *Pravda*, December 12, 1969.
68. "Ul'tra na sluzhbe sionizma," *Komsomol'skaia pravda*, March 21, 1970.
69. V. Gol'dshtein and D. Kogan, "Blagodeteli iz firmy Dinermani Ko," *Pravda Ukrainy*, January 28, 1971.
70. V. Bol'shakov, "Anti-semitizm—professiia sionistov," *Pravda*, February 19, 1971.
71. Ibid.
72. E. Evseev, "Fashizm pod goluboi zvezdoi," *Komsomol'skaia pravda*, May 17, 1970.
73. Bol'shakov in *Pravda*, February 19, 1971.
74. "Obuzdat agressorov, presech zlodeianiia sionistov," *Pravda Ukrainy*, March 13, 1970.
75. It should, nonetheless, be noted that of the many dozen books cited in the lists compiled by N. Bibichkova (see chart 18.1) there are only three in English (Iu. Kolesnikov, *The Promised Land: A Novel; The White Book: Evidence, Facts, Documents;* and L. Dadiani (ed.), *Zionism: Enemy of Peace and Social Progress*). All three were published in the years 1980–81. One book (by L. Berenshtein) in French (published in 1979) and one in Spanish by V. Bol'shakov, (1971) are also listed. It is thus apparently premature to talk of a general trend in this direction. In order to obtain a fuller picture it would be necessary, first, to compile a more complete list of foreign-language publications and, second, to examine Soviet broadcasts to the third and Western worlds.

Yet another area where great caution would seem to be called for is in any attempt to discern statistically significant variations between one newspaper and another in their treatment of Jewish issues (see table 8.2).

76. E. L. Smolar, "Protokoly antisionistskikh mudretsov," *Evreiskii samizdat*, vol. 16 (Jerusalem, 1978), pp. 131–37. (The words are those of A. Kislov.)
77. R. Brodsky and Yu. Shulmayster, "Tsi iz dos an oysgebeserte oyflage," *Sovetish heymland* (March 1980), pp. 139–42. (V. Begun's book is *Vtorzhenie bez oruzhiia* [Moscow 1979]. This is a second, revised edition.)

78. N. V. Osipova and S. M. Rogov, "SShA: blizhnevostochnyi uzel: vnutripoliticheskie aspekty," *SShA—ekonomika, politika, ideologiia*, no. 4 (April 1982), pp. 20–25.
79. On the comparative emigration rates of the various nationalities, see B. Pinkus, "The Emigration of National Minorities From the USSR in the Post-Stalin Era," *Soviet Jewish Affairs*, no. 1 (1983), pp. 3–36; also B. Pinkus, "Soviet Government Policy Toward the Extraterritorial National Minorities: Comparison Between the Jews and the Germans," in this volume.
80. Yaacov Ro'i has suggested (in a written comment on this chapter) that in his view, on the contrary, "the close parallels of Jewish and German emigration point to the dominance of domestic considerations." His argument is that the USSR does not regulate its relations with the Federal German Republic in strict accord with Soviet-U.S. relationships. Thus, if external factors were primary, there should logically be significant variations in the emigration rates of the two nationalities.

19

The Right to Jewish Culture in the Soviet Union

Stephen J. Roth

In the discussion of Jewish culture in the Soviet Union and the demand to be able to maintain and foster Jewish culture there, it is of paramount importance to realize that this demand is not for a privilege or a luxury but for an elementary human right, recognized by international as well as Soviet domestic law.

At the same time the right to culture in general poses a number of basic questions, all of which are of direct relevance to Jewish culture rights in the Soviet Union. The first such question arises from the fact that, while certain cultural activities are typically individual, others can be exercised only by a group, or by members of a group in community with other members of the same group. Who are, then, the bearers of the human right to such collective cultural activities—the individuals or the group? The answer might probably vary according to the type of activity, but the international community has found a solution by according so-called "group rights" not to the group as such but to "persons" belonging to the group.[1] International law thus avoided—for legal, historical, and political reasons—giving groups an international personality. This solution brought into the gambit of cultural rights an entirely different one: the right of assembly. For practical purposes, it will therefore be appropriate in this chapter to distinguish between the cultural rights of individuals without reference to a group (which we shall call with legal imprecision "individual rights") and the cultural rights of a member of a minority group to be exercised collectively (which we shall call "collective rights").

The second question relates to the content of cultural rights, which in turn depends on the definition of culture. This term lends itself to the widest interpretation; to attempt to give it a precise meaning would be an unproductive exercise. An extensive understanding of culture would include mores, life-style, social habits, values, preferences, and even prejudices. Clearly, in a determination of the right to culture such a wide definition would prove impracticable—although very often it is in the broader, general areas that distinctive characteristics are retained by Jews even when they are completely divorced from Jewish culture in the narrow sense, and this is true for Soviet Jews as well. But while it may be difficult to devise legal norms for such a wide definition of culture, present international law treats culture very restrictively. It only provides for the right to education, the right to participate in cultural life, freedom of scientific research and cultural activity, and the right to intellectual property, with special assurances to minorities to enjoy their own culture.[2]

This classification is, however, too narrow for a discussion of the rights of Soviet Jewry, because it includes neither the right to one's language (which international law regards as a distinct "linguistic right"), nor the right to one's religious heritage, which has deep cultural significance (but would normally be treated under "freedom of religion"). In the case of Soviet Jews language and religious heritage are definitely of primary cultural concern. We therefore include these categories in our analysis of the right to Jewish culture in the USSR.

In the discussion of internationally protected rights, the provisions of the Helsinki Final Act and the Concluding Document of the Madrid CSCE Meeting will also be taken into account, even though they are legally not binding and therefore, strictly speaking, do not constitute international law. They are, however, politically binding accords with legal implications. Moreover, the Ten Principles of the Helsinki Final Act, including Principle VII on Human Rights, are incorporated in the USSR Constitution of 1977 as its Article 29. Lately, the status of the Final Act has been increased by the International Court of Justice which stated that the provisions of the Act indicate the legal opinion of the participating states that they have to observe the rules the Act contains.[3] However, regional law, like the European, American, and African human rights charters, will be ignored since they have no relevance to the USSR. (The Soviet Union is not a party to the European Convention on Human Rights.)

In each of the various categories the rights derived from Soviet domestic legislation will also be touched upon, although only in a rudimentary way.

Individual Cultural Rights

Individual cultural rights are those which belong to every person irrespective of whether he does or does not belong to a special group, such as a religious or national minority. (A person may have group rights as well, but they are separate from, and additional to, his individual rights.)

The Right to Education The Universal Declaration of Human Rights (hereinafter UDHR), Article 20, stipulates that everybody has the right to education, which shall be directed to the full development of the human personality and the strengthening of respect for human rights, and shall promote understanding, tolerance, and friendship among all nations, racial and religious groups, and shall further the activities of the United Nations for the maintenance of peace. This provision is repeated in a slightly expanded form in the International Covenant on Economic, Social, and Cultural Rights (hereinafter ICESC); one of its additions is that "education shall enable all persons to participate effectively in a free society."

There are special provisions in international law regarding parents' rights in the field of education. According to UDHR, Article 26(3), they "have a prior right to choose the kind of education that shall be given to their children." The same right (called "liberty") of parents is proclaimed in ICESC, Article 13(3), in the International Covenant on Civil and Political Rights (hereinafter ICCPR), Article 18(4), and in the UNESCO Convention Against Discrimination in Education (hereinafter UNESCO Convention), Article 5(b); the latter two instruments specify that parents have a right to ensure the religious and moral education of their children "in conformity with their own convictions." It is important to realize that all these international treaties and agreements have been adhered to by the USSR and, according to the Soviet legal system, have greater force than domestic law (Article 65 of the Fundamentals of Legislation of the USSR and the Union Republics on Education—hereinafter Fundamentals of Education).

Overriding all these rights to education (as indeed all other rights) is the fundamental principle that their implementation must be free from discrimination on grounds of race, color, ethnic origin, or religion (as well as other grounds less relevant to this paper). This is of special significance to Soviet Jews, because in latter years there has been considerable discrimination in the admission of Jews to institutions of higher learning, either by way of denial of admission or by admission to inferior institutions only. This fact emerges from the statistics of the Soviet student population and from various studies conducted, including those by Soviet mathematicians B. I. Kanevskii and V. A. Sendero, by Naum Meiman and Grigorii Freiman, and other anonymous studies.[4] It is, however, fair to state that in the 1980s this discrimination has considerably diminished.

An even more pernicious interference with the right to education is the almost regular removal from universities or other institutions of higher learning of applicants for emigration, or their children, both from teaching positions or as students. This is one of the forms of harassment applicants have to suffer and it is a violation both of the right to leave and the right to education.

There is no specific provision in international law about the right of parents to arrange for private tuition. This omission is of some consequence to Soviet Jews. In the absence of Jewish schools or extracurricular religious classes, it is only in the home that Jewish children can obtain tuition in Jewish subjects. Indeed, the Soviet authorities constantly refer to the right of parents to teach their children, in answer to charges regarding the absence of organized religious teaching. However, a solution to the problem of Jewish education through parental tuition is wholly inadequate. Given the paucity of Jewish cultural and religious life and facilities in the USSR, most parents lack the necessary knowledge to give their children a Jewish education of any kind. It is therefore essential that parents have the right to engage teachers for home tuition. This would not mean creating private schools (which are not permitted in the USSR,) not even when several children in a large family might be taught together.

There arises an additional difficulty in the implementation in the Soviet Union of the international legal provisions regarding parents' rights to ensure the religious and moral education of their children "in comformity with their own convictions." Article 66 of the Soviet Constitution makes it an obligation for parents "to concern themselves with the upbringing of children" but adds that parents "are obliged to raise them as worthy members of socialist society"; Article 36 speaks generally of educating citizens "in the spirit of . . . socialist internationalism"; while Article 57 of the Fundamentals of Education formulates this even more clearly: parents are "obliged to bring up children in the spirit of lofty communist morality." Thus, Soviet law replaces parents' "own convictions" as the guiding principle in international law for parental education, with the convictions of the state and party.[5]

The right of education means not just the right to receive education but also the right to educate. In this respect some interesting developments have taken place very recently through the introduction of "individual enterprises" in the Soviet economic and social system. The Law on Individual Enterprise (or Individual Labor Activity), adopted on 19 November 1986,[6] allows individual enterprise "in the provision of paid services" and mentions particularly services in "cultural areas." Although teaching is not included in the illustrative enumeration of such services in Article 18 of the law (only "tutorship" in support of existing school or academic courses is mentioned), the Article contains a "catch-all" phrase: "Other types of social and cultural services shall be allowed, unless prohibited by the legislation of the Union of Soviet Socialist Republics and Union Republics." However, Article 19 lists among the outlawed areas: "Instruction in subjects and courses outside the curricula of the schools of general education, vocational schools, specialized secondary and higher educational institutions of the USSR." This excludes religious teaching from the realm of the "private enterprise" system since religion is not part of any of the educational institutions mentioned. (Religious seminaries are not "institutions of the USSR.")

This prohibition does not, however, exclude the teaching of Hebrew, which is taught at several higher educational state institutions. But there are other provisions in the Law which make it very difficult for Soviet Jews to engage in Hebrew teaching as an individual enterprise. Article 17 demands from the individual "proper experience" and—in activities regulated by law—"proper training." Since those wishing to engage in individual enterprise require a special permit, the authorities issuing such permits may well question the qualifications of the would-be Hebrew teachers. Refuseniks who have lost their jobs also face an additional hurdle: according to Article 3, individual enterprise shall be allowed to citizens who "participate in social production (when they are free from their main job), to housewives, invalids, pensioners and university, institute, and school students." "Other citizens not involved in social production" can engage in individual enterprise only according to "the needs of society" as envisaged by Soviet legislation. Refuseniks out of work are not engaged in social production and the teaching of Hebrew would hardly be classified as a "need of society." In fact, a case is known where a permit given to one refusenik to teach Hebrew was withdrawn because he had no regular job.

Finally, one has to consider the issue of self-education, alone or in community with others. Article 45 of the USSR Constitution of 1977 assures students "the provision of facilities for self-education." The self-education of citizens is also extolled in Article 12 of the Fundamentals of Education. But self-education does not necessarily mean learning alone; the normal meaning of the term covers any educational effort outside of school. It would apply to self-education in private groups of like-minded students, whether called seminars or discussion groups. Yet these are prohibited, or at best meet with great difficulties.

Language Tuition A special aspect of the right to education is the right to teach or study a foreign language—any language, whether English, Dutch, Chinese, or, if you will, Hebrew. (This is quite separate from the right to use Hebrew as a "Jewish language" which will be discussed under the collective minority rights.) This right is so self-evident that the drafters of the international legal instruments did not even think of the possibility that it would be questioned and therefore needed to be stipulated. But the Helsinki Final Act specifically lists, in its chapter on "Co-operation in the Field of Education," the intention of the participating states

> to encourage the study of foreign languages . . . as an important means of expanding communication among people for their better acquaintance with the culture of each country as well as for the strengthening of international co-operation; to this end to stimulate . . . the further development and improvement of foreign language teaching and the diversification of choice of languages taught at various levels, paying due attention to less widely spread and studied languages.

Surely, if the diversification is to encourage the study of Faeroese, Celtic, or Rhaetic, one must at least tolerate the learning of Hebrew, the vehicle of transmission of the Bible, perhaps the greatest cultural treasure of European civilization. Nevertheless, the Soviets have systematically suppressed the study of Hebrew.

Soviet domestic law *does not* deal with the question of language tuition. Article 36 of the USSR Constitution guarantees to all citizens "the possibility to use their native language," but this deals only with "use" not "teaching" and would help few Jews in regard to Hebrew, as only in the rarest cases, if any, would Hebrew be their mother tongue. The "use" of Yiddish is, indeed, not questioned—but its teaching is not facilitated by this clause.

The private teaching of language as an "individual enterprise" has been discussed above under "The Right of Education." The study of Hebrew in groups, like private *ulpanim* or other forms of group activities such as have developed in the Soviet Union in recent years, raises the question of the freedom of assembly (the same problem applies to private "cultural seminars"). In international law this freedom is well established—in the UDHR (Article 20[1]) and in the ICCPR (Article 21). Some restrictions on the exercise of the right of "peaceful assembly" are permissible in international law, but according to the ICCPR they must be established by law and must be "necessary in a democratic society in the interests of national security, of public safety, public order *(ordre publique)*, the protection of public health or morals, or the protection of the rights and freedoms of others." None of these permissible restrictions, not even the vague term *"ordre publique,"* could conceivably apply to a peaceful meeting for the study of Hebrew. After all, the Soviet Constitution also guarantees to all citizens the freedom of assembly, even if restricted to assemblies held "in the interests of the people and in order to strengthen and develop the socialist system" (Article 50); the only other known restriction is laid down in law in Article 190-3 of the RSFSR Criminal Code which prohibits "the organization of, and likewise, the active participation in group activities which violate public order in a coarse manner or which are attended by clear disobedience of the legal demands of representatives of authority."[7] The criterion of crude violation of public order certainly does not apply to the Hebrew study circles and, as to the point of disobedience of the legal demands of authority, the crux is how far these demands are "legal." However, the Soviet practice is different. "An assembly or meeting can be held only if it is organized by the State." To organize a gathering, even in a private apartment, is considered "an unusual thing" and "holding an assembly or a meeting without following the established custom of gathering only under proper supervision is regarded as an attempt to escape ideological leadership and the control of the authorities"—to quote the Soviet human rights expert, Valerii Chalidze.[8]

The Right to One's Religious Heritage The spiritual expression par excellence of religion cannot be separated from culture, certainly not in the case of Jews. Freedom of religion comprises the rights to manifest one's religion in practice, worship, observance, and teaching (UDHR, Article 18 and ICCPR, Article 18[1]). The first three will not be discussed in this analysis as they belong to a treatment of freedom of religion. However, the fourth—the right to teach religion—is in the case of Jews very relevant to culture.

The teaching of religion among Soviet Jews gains special importance if one considers that, according to Soviet data, the number of religious Jews in the country was approximately only 60,000 in 1980.[9] In reality the correct number is most probably higher, but it is still a small percentage of the two million Jews in the population. The exercise of the right to teach religion meets with exactly the same difficulties as Jewish education in general (outlined above).

A recent development under the aegis of *perestroika* indicates a slight change. Konstantin Kharchev, chairman of the Council for Religious Affairs of the USSR Council of Ministers, in an article written on the seventieth Anniversary of Lenin's decree "On the Separation of Church from State and School from Church" of 20 January 1918, argued that this decree "was not designed to 'destroy' or 'ban' the church or religion" and pointed out that "the decree allowed the possibility of private religious study and instruction. Religious instruction could be given in special educational institutions and parents themselves would determine whether or not to give their children religious instruction in the family and whether or not to use ministers of religion for that purpose." Needless to say, Kharchev regards Lenin's principles as the "correct course" to pursue, admits that "the practical application of the principles and provisions of the [Leninist] decree and the norms based on it still needs to be improved in many respects," and hints at new legislation in this direction.[10] This sounds hopeful. But there is already a follow-up which reminds one of another Leninist principle: one step forward, two steps back. A few weeks later an article in the paper of the Moscow Regional Committee of the Soviet Communist party, *Moskovskaia pravda*, criticized the Marina Roshcha Synagogue in Moscow for teaching Jewish children along religious-nationalist lines, whereupon the Torah class in the synagogue was banned.[11]

The Right to Participate in Cultural Life The right of Soviet Jews to participate freely in cultural life, to enjoy the arts and share in scientific advancement and its benefits, as proclaimed in Article 27(1) of the UDHR and Article 15(1) (a)–(b) of the ICESC (the latter does not mention the arts) is, in normal circumstances, not interfered with if it means participation in Soviet culture. The right is, in fact, ensured by Article 34 of the USSR Constitution which guarantees equality of citizens in cultural life. Indeed, Soviet Jews have made many notable contributions to art, science, and culture in the widest sense.[12] But the right is completely denied to those who apply for permission to leave the country for the purpose of family reunion. In addition to the restrictions suffered in the field of education, including the dismissal from teaching positions, such applicants are stripped of their academic degrees; excluded from academic associations; their works are withdrawn from circulation; they cannot have new works published in the USSR or sent abroad for publication; and their names are removed from new publications which they coauthored or from references relating to their earlier works. This amounts to an attempt to make such would-be emigrants nonpersons in the scientific, literary, artistic, and general cultural world. The great human problems created by Soviet policies toward Jewish scientists are fully described in one of the Jewish presentations to delegates attending the CSCE Human Rights Experts' Meeting in Ottawa in 1985.[13] This treatment violates Article 34 of the USSR Constitution which forbids discrimination on grounds of "status."

The right to participate in cultural life means participation not only nationally but also on an international scale. It is true that Article 27(1) of the UDHR speaks of participating "in the cultural life of the community" —without defining whether community is a restriction to national boundaries or not—but the ICESC, Article 15(1), drops reference to "the community" which, as Yoram Dinstein justifiably argues, indicates that "the right to take part in cultural life pertains to culture everywhere."[14]

Participation in cultural life can be broken down into various component parts, such as access to facilities, creation, dissemination, and contacts and cooperation. The Helsinki Final Act devotes a special section of its chapter on "Co-operation and Exchanges in the Field of Culture" to the need for promoting "fuller mutual *access* by all to the achievements—works, experiences and performing arts—in the various fields of culture"; the chapter on education lays down the aim "to improve *access* . . . for students, teachers and scholars of the participating States of each other's educational, cultural and scientific institutions." The right to "broad *access* to the cultural treasures of their own land and of the world" is also upheld by Article 46 of the Soviet Constitution but the "cultural treasures" are qualified by the addition "that are preserved in state and other public collections," which means both a restriction of the right and a control of the cultural content.

Similarly, in the field of *creation*, the Helsinki Final Act lists the facilities to be provided for cultural workers. In regard to *dissemination* the Act specifically mentions "the dissemination of books and artistic works," "dissemination of scientific information and documentation," promotion of travel and meetings for cultural activities, exchange of scholars, teachers and students, and so forth.

In all these areas, Jews in the Soviet Union do not enjoy the facilities to which they are entitled. They have no access to Jewish books—if sent from abroad, they are usually confiscated. They have no outlet for their creations—there are no Jewish publishing houses, Jewish literary or scholarly magazines in Russian, the language of most Soviet Jews (with the exception of *Sovetish heymland*'s Russian annual *God za godom*, published since 1985), no Jewish galleries or exhibition halls, and only limited opportunities for actors. Jews, therefore, cannot disseminate their work and, if they have applied for emigration, even their authorship of their past work is "eliminated."

The most serious problem in the participation in cultural life arises for Soviet Jews in the field of *contacts and cooperation*. Once again, international law is on their side. In Article 15(4) of the ICESC, the parties to the Covenant "recognise the benefits to be derived from the encouragement and development of international contacts and co-operation in the scientific and cultural fields." The Helsinki Final Act contains numerous provisions regarding direct international contacts, conferences, seminars, travel to such conferences and meetings, or exchanges in cultural matters. Yet to Jews in the Soviet Union such contacts and direct cooperation are denied in Jewish cultural matters, and to refusenik scientists and scholars even on general cultural or scientific issues. Refuseniks are mostly not allowed to attend conferences even within the USSR. Jewish scholars or cultural workers from abroad are mostly impeded in trying to establish contact with their Jewish peers in the Soviet Union.

Even the Soviet Constitution, in Article 46, refers to "cultural exchanges with other countries" as one of the "cultural benefits" to which citizens are entitled. But in Soviet practice this means exchanges arranged and controlled by the state.

Freedom of Scientific Research and Cultural Activity The ICESC, Article 15(3), contains the important undertaking by the parties to the Covenant "to respect the freedom indispensable for scientific research and creative activity." Freer flow of information and ideas, aimed at by the provisions of the Helsinki Final Act, may be regarded an essential accompaniment to the freedom of cultural creation. The Soviet Constitution, in Article 47 guarantees "freedom of scientific, technical, and artistic work" and declares that "the state provides . . . support for voluntary societies . . . in the arts." But like many other rights and freedoms guaranteed by the Constitution, this one too is qualified by the words "in accordance with the aims of building communism." This has been interpreted as a blanket authorization to restrict the freedom of creative activity to the point where it becomes virtually nonexistent (though *glasnost'* has somewhat eased the situation). The restriction has affected all cultural workers, but is particularly strongly felt by Jews, if they wish to create works of Jewish content.

No wonder that under these circumstances "Jewish studies" were practically nonexistent in the Soviet Union for many years. However, there are some recent positive developments. A number of young scholars work on Jewish subjects in the field of linguistics, Jewish history, and ethnography —as reported by Igor Krupnik, a research fellow of the Institute of Ethnography of the USSR Academy of Sciences.[15] At a meeting of the Lithuanian Cultural Fund in January 1988 the creation of a few positions for Judaic scholars at the Lithuanian Academy of Sciences was demanded. And *Sovetish heymland* announced that as of July 1988 it would have a special section devoted to the history of the Jewish people; although the July 1988 issue, which—like the July 1986 and July 1987 issues—was a collection of the works of young writers, had a "historical notes" section, it was only in January 1989 that the journal began having a historical section.

The Right to Intellectual Property The right to one's intellectual property is established in Article 27(2) of the UDHR and in Article 15(1)(c) of the ICESC. They provide that "everyone has the right to the protection of the moral and material interests resulting from any scientific, literary or artistic production of which he is the author." The Soviet Constitution, in its Article 47, states that "the rights of authors, inventors, and innovators are protected by the state." Nevertheless, as has been explained earlier, scientists and cultural workers who have applied to emigrate are subject to a number of restrictions in regard to their past and future productions. For instance, removal of the names of refuseniks from publications which they coauthored or coedited may affect their material interests in terms of royalties and so forth; the same applies to their exclusion from similar future assignments; and what is even more painful, their virtual elimination from the scholarly or artistic community does serious damage to their morale, reputation, and career. A similar violation can be seen in the fact that, on emigration, scientists and cultural workers are often not allowed to take with them the manuscripts of yet unpublished works.

Collective Cultural Rights

The rights due to Soviet Jews as a collectivity are particularly meaningful from a Jewish point of view and at the same time these rights suffer the greatest abridgments. The collective rights follow from the double status of Soviet Jewry as a national minority and as a religious group. The rights are expressed in the following wording of Article 27 of the ICCPR:

> In those States in which ethnic, religious or linguistic minorities exist, persons belonging to such minorities shall not be denied the rights, in community with the other members of their group, to enjoy their own culture, to profess and practice their own religion, or to use their language.

Although the rights recognized in this provision are attached to "persons," they may be said to constitute collective rights, firstly because they derive from the persons belonging to a collectivity and secondly because their exercise is protected "in community with the other members of their group."

The text of the provision speaks of three types of minorities: ethnic, religious, and linguistic. The three categories may, and in the majority of cases, do overlap. Soviet Jewry is a typical illustration of this. Jews are recognized in the USSR as a Soviet nationality; *ipso facto* they are also recognized as a linguistic minority, or at least Yiddish is accepted as a "language of a Soviet people," that is, the Jews. Lastly, they are recognized as a religious community. They therefore enjoy minority protection under all the three headings of the above paragraph.

Different types of minorities have different interests: the ethnic minority

THE RIGHT TO JEWISH CULTURE 367

is primarily concerned with the enjoyment of its culture: a religious minority wants to profess and practice its religion; and a linguistic minority needs to be able to use its language. But the text does not limit any group to the protection of its particular interest and in any event the differentiation becomes meaningless in the case of overlap, as for Soviet Jews.

National (Ethnic) Minority Rights What is the content of a national minority right? The object of the right was explained by the Permanent Court of International Justice (PCIJ) in its advisory opinion in the *Minority Schools in Albania* case. Based on the minority treaties concluded after the First World War, the Court found the underlying idea of national minority rights to be "preserving the characteristics which distinguish them [the members of the minority] from the majority and satisfying the ensuing special needs." These needs were described as being, first, to ensure equality of members of the minority with other nationals of the state, and, secondly, "to ensure for the minority elements suitable means for the preservation of their racial peculiarities, their traditions and their national characteristics." To this end, the Court found that minorities must be able to have their own charitable, religious, and social institutions, schools, and other educational establishments.[16] The first of these two objectives— equality before the law—is a political, rather than a cultural right, and is therefore not discussed here;[17] the second can be expressed briefly as protection against cultural assimilation. This indeed is the essence of the content of national minority rights.

The Helsinki Final Act adds further provisions to minority protection. In Principle VII, the participating states undertake in regard to national minorities, to

afford them the full opportunity for the actual enjoyment of human rights and fundamental freedoms and . . . in this manner, protect their legitimate interests in this sphere.

This comprehensive declaration is strengthened by further statements in the section "Culture and Education of the Final Act":

The participating States, recognizing the contribution that national minorities or regional cultures can make to co-operation among them in various fields of culture, intend, when such minorities or cultures exist within their territory, to facilitate this contribution, taking into account the legitimate interest of their members.

The Concluding Document of the CSCE Follow-Up Meeting in Madrid underlines the need for dynamism in minority protection. Paragraph 11 of the "Principles" in the chapter "Questions Relating to Security in Europe" provides:

[The participating states] stress also the importance of *constant progress* in ensuring the respect for and actual enjoyment of the rights of persons belonging to national minorities as well as protecting their legitimate interests as provided for in the Final Act. (Emphasis added)

The term "legitimate interests" is undefined but it would not be wrong to say that they are well expressed in the above-quoted Advisory Opinion of the Permanent Court of International Justice. The Helsinki provisions, however, added a new aspect to minority rights: cooperation among them, which the participating states are supposed to facilitate. (Actually, they undertake to facilitate the "contribution" to culture made by minorities through such cooperation, but one cannot facilitate the end without facilitating the means which produce it.) The Helsinki text is, however, somewhat unclear in this instance. What does "cooperation among" national minorities mean? It could mean cooperation within the same country between different national minorities, with different traditions and speaking different languages, as existed in the 1920s, in the period of the minority treaties. But surely, a sensible interpretation must also indicate that members of the same national minority—say, Jews or Germans—in different countries, are allowed to cooperate with each other across frontiers.

According to the above-quoted texts, national minority rights can be broken down into the following elements: right to education in their own culture; right to their own institutions; and right to international cooperation.

Education. In the specific area of education, national minority rights find expression in the UNESDO Convention, which stipulates in Article 5(1)(c) that:

It is essential to recognise the right of members of national minorities to carry on their own educational activities, including the maintenance of schools and, depending on the educational policy of each State, the use or the teaching of their own language.

It will be noted that the clause lists four rights: to carry on their own educational activities, the maintenance of schools, the use of their own language in education, and the teaching of their own language. The last two can apply only to national minorities which are also linguistic minorities and will therefore be discussed under that heading. The first two rights, however, lead to two highly interesting conclusions. The first is that, contrary to the general belief, minority education or schools need not be in a minority language. As Yoram Dinstein rightly says: "When an ethnic minority is involved, the central issue is not the use or the teaching of a language, but the cultural content and substance of education." Based on the experience of Soviet Jewry, he adds: "What really counts is not whether members of an ethnic minority can obtain education in their own language but whether they can study their cultural heritage in any language."[18] The second conclusion is that minority education need not be limited to schools; they are only one form of minority education.

If language is not essential, what is the essence of minority education? Again, we are aided by the Permanent Court of International Justice which defined it as "ensuring the instruction and upbringing of their [the minority members'] children in accordance with the spirit and traditions" of the group.[19]

Article 5(c) of the UNESCO Convention makes a few qualifications: the exercise of the right must not prevent the members of the minority from understanding the culture and language of the community as a whole or from participating in its activities; it must not prejudice national sovereignty; the standard of education in minority schools must not be lower than the general standard laid down by the authorities; and the attendance at minority schools must be optional. These are reasonable qualifications which do not undermine the right to minority schools.

This right to minority schools or extramural minority education is blatantly violated in regard to Soviet Jewry. There is no Jewish school in the USSR, not even in the Jewish Autonomous *oblast* of Birobidzhan. Some Jewish subjects may appear in a restricted manner in academic institutions. But there are no extramural seminars, courses, or other facilities for learning a Jewish cultural subject—Jewish history, law, ethics, literature, art, sociology—anywhere in the Soviet Union.

Minority Institutions. It has been shown above that the right of a national minority to establish and maintain its own institutions—whether cultural, social, or philanthropic—is an essential element in its ability to survive as a specific entity and that, in particular, the right to cultural institutions is part and parcel of the right "to enjoy (its) own culture." Such cultural institutions (using the term in its broadest sense) would be publications devoted to the culture of the minority, publishing houses, libraries, museums, exhibition halls and art galleries, theater companies, choirs and orchestras, clubs, and reading rooms. To all of these, minorities are entitled by international law.

Yet the reality shows that, for two million Soviet Jews, there are only two Jewish periodicals in Yiddish, one public library in Birobidzhan (and a general library in Moscow with a Jewish section), the Sholem Aleichem Museum in Pereiaslav Khmel'nitskii in the Ukraine, two professional theater companies without premises, giving only a small number of performances a year, some amateur companies, and a few occasional concerts. Above all, the most essential institutions, without which it is difficult to conceive of the creation or maintenance of the other institutions, namely some central communal body of the Jewish communities scattered over the Soviet Union, is nonexistent.

Only lately, since Gorbachev came to power, have there been some moves for improvement: the opening of a Chagall Museum in his birthplace Vitebsk is under consideration and in Vilnius the reopening of the museum closed in 1949 is being demanded. The opening of a private library and an exhibition of Judaica in a private apartment, both in Moscow, have been "tolerated" by the authorities, as have private concerts in Leningrad which were given a municipal hall for future performances.

International Cooperation. In the section of this chapter on individual cultural rights, we have already referred to the provisions of the Helsinki Final Act regarding cultural cooperation at large. The various means of cooperation encouraged and facilitated for individuals must apply *a fortiori* to national minorities, since the Helsinki Final Act specifically recognizes the value of their international cooperation.

In spite of these provisions, cooperation of the Jewish national minority in the USSR with Jews in other countries is practically prohibited—except in a very weak and occasional form with Jews in the other socialist countries in Eastern Europe on a purely religious basis. Soviet Jewry cannot belong to any international Jewish body, so that Soviet Jewish representatives are not permitted to participate in international Jewish conferences devoted to culture, religion, education, Jewish studies, and the like.

There is an interesting question relating to this right to international cooperation. According to the wording of the Helsinki Final Act, it is established as cooperation between national minorities. Does this limit Soviet Jewry to cooperation with other Jewish minorities in the Diaspora, and does it exclude cooperation with the Jewish community of Israel which is not a minority? A strict interpretation of the letter of the Helsinki Final Act would produce this result; but by the spirit of the Act, which clearly aims at an improvement of the minority culture through cooperation, it would be nonsensical to conclude that cooperation with a majority community of the same culture, which could invariably offer the greatest inspiration and assistance, is not permitted. One cannot, however, overlook the political implications of cooperation with the dominant population of a foreign state; in this instance, even more than in other cases, the cooperation, in order to stand a chance of being tolerated, would have to be patently and visibly cultural, avoiding the slightest suspicion of containing political elements.

Religious Minority Rights   The rights of religious minorities are defined in Article 27 of the ICCPR as professing and practicing their religion. The same rights are repeated in Principle VII of the Helsinki Final Act.

The Final Act contains also another important provision which appears in the subsection "Travel" of the "Human Contacts" chapter. It reads:

> The [participating states] confirm that religious faiths, institutions and organizations, practicing within the constitutional framework of the participating States, and their representatives can, in the field of their activities, have contacts and meetings among themselves and exchange information.

This clause was specifically re-affirmed in the Madrid Concluding Document.

Wherever there exists a personal identity among members of a religious and a national (cultural) minority, as in the case of Jews, the religious group facilities—or their absence—have a direct impact on the cultural life of that group. Indeed, in the case of Jews much of the religious tradition and literature is an inseparable part of the Jewish cultural heritage. However, beyond dealing with these cultural implications, the subject of religious group rights is not explored here as it belongs more properly to a study of the religious rights of Soviet Jewry.

Linguistic Minority Rights The language rights of linguistic minorities go much further than the individual's right to learn any language he chooses. Minority groups are entitled to use their own language in community with other members of their group. ICCPR Article 27, which establishes the right, does not indicate what is meant by "use." The minority treaties concluded after the First World War specified that linguistic minorities could establish their own schools and institutions and use their own language for publications at public meetings, and in their relations with courts of law and other authorities. In districts with a large minority population they were ensured instruction in primary schools in their own language and an equitable share of public funds allocated to educational, religious, and charitable purposes.[20]

The linguistic rights of minorities in the field of education are spelled out in Article 5c of the UNESCO Convention which recognizes the teaching of the minorities' language and its use in education (although they are made dependent on the educational policy of each state and are subject to the qualifications regarding understanding the majority culture and language, standards of education, and optional attendance mentioned earlier). The difference between the two rights is clear. The "use of language" means that in minority schools any subject—history, geography, mathematics—can be taught in the minority language, and that other educational activities—school assemblies, ceremonial and other public occasions—can be conducted in that language. The teaching *of* their language means language tuition, whether in schools or in extramural courses. Both activities are recognized as a right.

Article 36 of the Soviet Constitution also guarantees Soviet citizens of different nationalities "the possibility to use their native language." The 1986 Program of the Communist Party of the Soviet Union also pledges "The equal right of all citizens of the USSR to use their native language and the free development of the language will be ensured in the future as well."

Two points must be specially emphasized. The first is that the use or teaching of the minority language need not be restricted to schools. The rights apply to all educational activities of the minority. This is of paramount importance to Soviet Jews, as the demand for separate Jewish schools abated a long time ago. But the demand for informal Jewish educational activities—courses, seminars, and so on—is all the stronger.

The second point is that linguistic rights are not restricted to linguistic minorities. On the contrary; Article 5c of the UNESCO Convention accords them specifically to national minorities. It does not matter, therefore, whether today Soviet Jewry is still a linguistic minority. The statistics in this respect are that, in the 1979 census 14.24 percent of Soviet Jews claimed a Jewish language as their mother tongue and an additional 5.35 percent claimed one as their second language. It follows from these figures that one-fifth of Soviet Jewry knows a national language. The number of those interested in learning such a language is, however, by all available information, considerably higher.

In connection with the linguistic rights of Soviet Jewry, the question needs to be discussed as to what is Soviet Jewry's "own language" or, more precisely, what do the Soviet authorities regard as the language of Soviet Jews? In fact, several languages are recognized as Jewish languages. The principle one is Yiddish, recognized as the language of the Jewish minority in the 1920s largely due to the efforts of the *Evsektsiia*. The languages of the Oriental Jewish communities—Georgian Jews, Bukharan Jews, Mountain Jews, Krymchaks—are also recognized, although lately there is a conscious policy to let them "wither away."[21]

Hebrew appears in encyclopaedias and other reference books as a Jewish language and its link with contemporary Jewry is increasingly recognized. This, however, is not the same as being a "language of Soviet Jews" or "the language of a Soviet people"—and only these categories count in the linguistic rights of a minority in the USSR. Consequently, Hebrew does not enjoy the protection afforded to minority languages.

Not only do the Soviet authorities recognize Jewish minority languages but they often take the view that Jewish culture is, or must be, culture in a Jewish language—for all practical purposes in Yiddish. "Official" Jewish cultural activities, that is, those assisted or approved by the state, are all in Yiddish. Whether identifying Jewish culture with Yiddish is a deliberate device or a misconception on the part of the authorities is not easy to tell. It could well be the second, for good reasons. First, it corresponds to what Jewish culture was in the main in the first three decades of the Soviet experience, up to its institutional suppression in 1948. Second, it fits in with the Soviet concept of nationalities which are all seen as (and, in fact, mostly are) linguistic minorities as well as ethnic ones.

However, it is exactly in regard to the linguistic aspect of national cultures that considerable changes have been taking place during recent years, partly because members of nationalities are increasingly dispersed outside their national republic or territory, but mainly because of the open, although not admitted, policy of "Russification." More and more works which, by all criteria other than the linguistic, can be regarded as "nationality culture" appear in Russian. At a conference on "International Ties and the Interaction of Nationality Cultures in the USSR," held from 30 November to 3 December 1976, it was emphasized partly as a defence against the charge of "Russification" that ethnic coloration is by no means determined by language alone but also by the contents of art-culture and its nonlinguistic forms of expression and is related to the social psychology of separate ethnic groups.[22]

Consequently, there is no justification, in terms of Soviet nationality policy, in restricting Jewish culture to Yiddish. A new generation of Soviet Jews has grown up since 1948 who no longer speak Yiddish and demand the expression of their Jewish culture in Russian. To say this is not to suggest that Soviet Jews should give up the linguistic rights due to them. It is merely demanding that these linguistic rights not become a straitjacket for Jewish cultural expression.

The use and teaching of Hebrew could probably not be ensured under the linguistic rights of minorities, since it is unlikely that the Soviet authorities could be made to recognize Hebrew as "the language of a Soviet people." The issue may have to be tackled in the two ways discussed earlier: partly as an *individual* right to the use, teaching, and learning of any language, and partly as the collective right of national minorities to their own educational activities, which international law does not restrict to performance in the language of the minority. The combination of these two sets of rights gives full protection both to Hebrew teaching and to seminars, and so forth, conducted in Hebrew.

Misconceptions and Policies

One should not conclude this analysis of the cultural rights of Soviet Jewry without taking note of certain misconceptions in Soviet thinking regarding the nature of Jewish culture, because these misconceptions must necessarily distort the application of the provisions protecting Jewish culture, even if they were applied in full. These misconceptions (or perhaps just convenient excuses) surface from time to time. We have already mentioned one such misconception: the belief that Jewish culture has to be in Yiddish or is equivalent to Yiddish culture. Other such distortions are that Hebrew as the holy language and the language of the State of Israel is ideologically and politically loaded; that Jewish culture is the same as the contribution of Jews to Soviet culture: that Jewish culture in the Soviet Union can exist without reference to and contact with world Jewish culture; and that Jewish culture can be satisfied through the Jewish religious structure (the existing synagogues). There are also more general misconceptions in regard to culture which affect Jews as well: the identification of unofficial cultural activities with dissidence and even anti-Soviet attitudes; and the theory that Jewish culture ought to be based on the national territory (hence one theater company operating in Moscow is formally Birobidzhan-based, and books for teaching of Yiddish are published in Birobidzhan and only distributed there). As Gitelman points out, the Soviet concept of the national question, ever since 1913, is cultural autonomy for compactly settled ethnic groups; "It discriminates against territorially scattered nationalities or ethnic groups and even against members of a territorially compact nationality who happen to live outside the national region."[23]

Lastly, we would be discussing Soviet rights in a vacuum if we were not to take note of the fact that in the Soviet system all rights are subject in their implementation to extralegal social and political policies. In the case of minority rights, the policies in question are those relating to nationalities. The respective importance of the "merger" or "drawing together" of nationalities, or the creation of "a new historical community of the Soviet people" on the one hand, and the recognition of the legitimacy or the maintenance of separate nationality characteristics on the other, vary in these policies from one period to another. This affects all nationality cultures, including that of the Jewish minority. Yet the 1986 CPSU Program does not depart substantially from the 1961 Program on this issue: the thrust is toward creating "a unified culture of the Soviet people," but "the multi-national character of the Soviet people is recognized.[24]

It follows from the above that it is not enough to invoke well-entrenched international or domestic rights regarding Jewish culture in the Soviet Union. These misconceptions will have to be removed and the policies must move in the right direction in order to have the rights implemented in practice. But first and foremost, there must be a will to let Soviet Jews enjoy the rights to which they are entitled by both Soviet and international law.

Notes

1. The position is the same in regard to the right to religion. Religious activities, too, can be strictly individual or can require the community of members of the same faith. The right is therefore accorded in international law to "persons" and not to religious denominations as such, but it includes the right of persons to communal activities.
2. An excellent analysis is presented by Yoram Dinstein, "Cultural Rights," in *Israel Yearbook on Human Rights,* vol. 9, 1979, pp. 58–81.
3. Judgment of the International Court of Justice of June 27, 1986, in the case concerning military and paramilitary activities in and against Nicaragua *(Nicaragua v. United States of America),* paragraph 189.
4. See Lukasz Hirszowicz, "Anti-Jewish Discrimination in Education and Employment," in *Proceedings of the Experts' Conference on Soviet Jewry Today* of the Institute of Jewish Affairs (IJA), London and the Israel-Diaspora Institute, Tel Aviv, held in London, January 4–6, 1983 (London; IJA, 1985), pp. 25–30.
5. In the West European human rights system, governed by the European Convention on Human Rights, to which, as already stated, the USSR is not a party, the European Court of Human Rights clearly restricted the right to indoctrinate children by making it incumbent on the state, in its educational function, to "take care that information or knowledge included in the curriculum is conveyed in an objective, critical and pluralistic manner." Case of Kjeldsen et al., 23 *Judgements and Decisions of the European Court of Human Rights* 26.
6. *Pravda,* November 21, 1986.
7. William B. Simons (ed.), *The Soviet Codes of Law* (Alphen aan den Rijn: Sijthoff & Noordhoff, 1980), p. 127.
8. Valerii Chalidze, *To Defend These Rights: Human Rights and the Soviet Union* (New York: Random House, 1974), pp. 73–74.
9. Iosif M. Shapiro, "Judaism in the USSR," *Nauka i religiia,* no. 3, 1980, pp. 38–39.
10. *Izvestiia,* January 27, 1988.
11. *Jewish Chronicle,* April 15, 1988.
12. See J. Miller (ed.), *Jews of Soviet Culture* (Transaction Books for the Institute of Jewish Affairs: New Brunswick, N.J. and London, 1984).
13. "The Position of Soviet Jewry. Human Rights and the Helsinki Accords," prepared for the CSCE Meeting of Experts on Human Rights and Fundamental Freedoms in Ottawa, May 7 to June 17, 1985, published by the Institute of Jewish Affairs, London, on behalf of the International Council of the World Conference on Soviet Jewry, 1985, pp. 49–51.

14. See Dinstein, op. cit., p. 77.
15. Igor Krupnik, "The Contribution of the Younger Generation of Soviet Scholars to Jewish Studies in the USSR," *Soviet Jewish Affairs*, vol. 17, no. 2, Summer-Autumn 1987, pp. 35–48.
16. Advisory Opinion of April 6, 1985, PCIJ 1935, Sec. A/B, No. 64.
17. It is protected, inter alia, by ICCPR Article 2(1).
18. Dinstein, op. cit., pp. 70–71.
19. Advisory Opinion of the Permanent Court of International Justice in the *Greco-Bulgarian "Communities"* case of July 31, 1930, PCIJ 1930, Sec. B, No. 17.
20. According to Article 9 of the Minority Treaty between the Allied and Associate Powers and Poland, concluded in Versailles on June 28, 1919, (which served as a model for all other minority treaties), the exact definition is:

    In towns and districts where there is a considerable proportion of Polish nationals belonging to racial, religious or linguistic minorities.

21. For the non-Ashkenazi communities and their languages, see Michael Zand, "Notes on the Culture of the Non-Ashkenazi Jewish Communities Under Soviet Rule" in this volume.
22. *Sovetskaia Estoniia*, December 2, 1976.
23. Zvi Gitelman, "What Future for Jewish Culture in the Soviet Union?" *Soviet Jewish Affairs*, vol. 9, no. 1, 1979, pp. 24–28.
24. Lukasz Hirszowicz, "The 27th Soviet Party Congress," *Soviet Jewish Affairs*, vol. 16, no. 2, 1986, pp. 10–11.

20

Notes on the Culture of the Non-Ashkenazi Jewish Communities Under Soviet Rule

Michael Zand

To the memory of
Jean-Jacques Newman,
alias Ya'akov ha-Cohen Neeman,
alias reb Yankev Noyman
alias Kuba,
alias the Colonel with the Trucks,
alsia Zhenya
        —a legend untold

I

There are in the USSR several non-Ashkenazi Jewish communities. In geographical sequence from west to east they are as follows:

1. The Krymchaks, the indigenous Jewish community of the Crimean peninsula whose native tongue, Judeo-Crimean Tatar, or, simply, Krymchak, is the Jewish ethnolect of Crimean Tatar.[1] Of the estimated 8,000 Krymchaks on the eve on the Soviet-German war of 1941-45, at least 70 percent were exterminated by the Nazis. Most of the survivors still live in the Crimea, but the overwhelming majority of them have not retained the community's native tongue and use Russian instead;[2]
2. Georgian Jews who inhabit the Georgian SSR (Soviet Socialist Republic) on the western side of the Caucasus and whose native tongue is Georgian; Jews speak three dialects of this language to which they add a

restricted number of specifically Jewish lexicalisms (including Hebraisms) predominantly common for all three dialects;[3]

3. The Mountain Jews of the Caucasus who inhabit the Dagestan ASSR (Autonomous Soviet Socialist Republic) and the Azerbaidzhan SSR on the eastern side of the Caucasus and whose native tongue, Judeo-Tat, is the Jewish ethnolect of Tat. This ethnolect is historically divided into four dialects (one of them being now almost extinct);[4]

4. The Bukharan Jews who inhabit the Uzbek and Tadzhik SSRs in Central Asia and whose native tongue, Judeo-Tadzhik, or, in other terminology, Bukharan Jewish, is the Jewish ethnolect of Tadzhik.[5]

There are also in the Soviet Union two small groups of later non-Ashkenazi Jewish arrivals:

1. The so-called Lakhlukhs, an offspring of the Persian (Iranian) Azerbaidzhan subgroup of the Kurdistani Jews. They began to settle in the Caucasus, chiefly in the area of Tbilisi, the capital of Georgia, in about the nineteenth century, but their main influx occurred toward the end of World War I. Since most of those who came with the World War I wave retained their Persian citizenship, they were approached in the late 1930s by the Soviet authorities with the alternative of becoming Soviet subjects or going back to Iran, and a considerable number chose the latter. Their native tongue is a dialect of the Jewish ethnolect of Neo-Aramaic;[6]

2. The remnants of the Jadid al-Islam group, the crypto-Jews of Mashad, Iran. These Jews, who had outmigrated from Mashad to Central Asia in the immediate aftermath of the forced Islamization of all Mashadi Jews in 1839, gradually merged into the Bukharan Jewish community. However, the second wave of outmigrants who came to Central Asia after its annexation by Russia, mainly in the 1880s and 1890s, and settled predominantly in Askhabad (now Ashkhabad, capital of the Turkmen SSR) and Merv (now Maryi, in the same republic) continued to be a branch of their mother crypto-Jewish community and retained their Persian citizenship. Many returned to Iran in the 1920s, and others did so in the late 1930s, when placed by the Soviet authorities in the same dilemma as the Lakhlukhs. However, some remained, mainly in the towns of Maryi, Bairam-Ali, and Iolotan in the Turkmen SSR.

There are also in the USSR Karaites concentrated mainly in the Crimea (in the towns of Bakhchisarai and Evpatoriia), in the Lithuanian

SSR (in Vilnius, Trakai, and Ponevezhis) and in the Ukrainian towns of Lutsk and Galich. Historically Jewish (though nonrabbinic) they nevertheless have long defined themselves—in Eastern Europe—first as a separate religious and then as a separate ethnoreligious group, and in the Soviet period as a separate *natsional'nost'* (ethnic group).[7]

This chapter will attempt to survey briefly and hence at times unavoidably sketchily the history of the culture of the Krymchaks and the Mountain and Bukharan Jews in the Soviet period. The survey of the culture of the Georgian Jews, now at the final stage of preparation, will be published separately. The survey will deal only with the verbal expression of this culture. For the purpose of this chapter we define as culture the sum total of the folklore, and the educational, theatrical, and literary activities of these communities in their native tongues. The Lakhlukhs and the Central Asian Mashadi Jews are not included in this survey since there are no data of such cultural creativity among them in the period under discussion. As to the Karaites, their excitingly interesting cultural renaissance of the 1920s and 1930s took place in pre-World War II Poland (to which their towns of residence, currently in the Lithuanian and Ukrainian SSRs, then belonged), and thus is beyond the framework of our discussion.[8] Since the cultural activities of the Krymchaks and the Bukharan Jews were terminated in the Soviet Union in the late 1930s and in 1940, respectively, their cultural activities will be surveyed first, and the survey of Mountain Jewish cultural activity which still pertains, though, as we shall see, in a very limited scope, will close the chapter.

II

It seems worthwhile to preface the survey itself by some notes on the similarities and differences in the cultural typology of the communities under discussion prior to the Soviet period. To make the picture more complete, this part comprises the Georgian Jewish community too.

The first common trait of these communities vis-à-vis the main corps of Soviet Jewry is that they are non-Ashkenazi. In more precise terminology they can be defined as belonging to that part of world Jewry which is known in its aggregate as Oriental Jewry, although their origins differ: the Krymchaks are historically, in the main, lingually Turkified Romaniots (the Greek-speaking Jews of the Byzantine Empire) who were joined by Italian

THE NON-ASHKENAZI JEWISH COMMUNITIES 381

(through the Genoese Black Sea colonies), Spanish (via Italy and the Ottoman Empire), Georgian, and Ukrainian Ashkenazi Jews, while the Bukharan and Mountain Jews are historically part of the Jewry of the so-called Greater Iranian Area, and the Georgian community has its beginnings in outmigrants from that same area amalgamated afterward by waves of outmigrants from Byzantium and, possibly, Armenia.

Regarding the religious ritual on the eve of Sovietization, all of them used the so-called Sephardi (Spanish) rite accepted by them at different times. The first to accept it were, evidently, the Mountain Jews who commenced using the Sephardi rite not later than the end of the sixteenth to the beginning of the seventeenth century. It is reasonable to suppose that at approximately the same time Italian prayer books, and accordingly the Sephardi rite, found their way into the Georgian Jewish community, too. No data are available about the rites used by these two communities before this time. The Spanish rite was introduced to the Bukharan Jews at the end of the eighteenth century by the reformer of their religious life Rabbi Yosef Maman Ma'aravi (1752–1823), a Moroccan Jew by origin who reached the community as a fund-raiser from the Holy Land, but decided to remain in Bukhara in order to improve the deteriorated religious situation there.[9] Before this they used the so-called Khorasani rite (evidently this is the rite of the unique prayer book manuscript found in the late nineteenth century in Bukhara and usually defined as a "Persian rite" prayer book.[10]

As to the Krymchaks, the Spanish rite was introduced among them only in the late nineteenth century by the Jerusalem-born and educated Rabbi Hayyim Hizkiyahu Medini (1832–1904) who was rabbi of the town of Karasubazar (now Belogorsk), then the Krymchaks' main center, in the years 1867–99.[11] Here the Sephardi rite replaced the specifically Krymchak Kaffa rite introduced at the beginning of the sixteenth century in Kaffa (now Feodosiia), then the main Jewish center in the Crimea, by Rabbi Moshe ben Ya'akov ha-Gole, alias Moshe mi-Kiev the Second (1448–ca. 1520) and based mainly on the Romania (Romaniot) rite. Apparently the Kaffa rite continued to be used partially or for special occasions by some Krymchaks even after the introduction of the Spanish rite.[12] All four communities inhabited non-Slavic areas which became parts of the Russian Empire at a relatively late stage—the end of the eighteenth (the Crimea) and nineteenth centuries (Georgia, Azerbaidzhan and Dagestan, and Central Asia). Three of these areas, namely the Crimea, Azerbaidzhan and Dagestan, and Central Asia were Muslim, and Jewish life there was regulated by a set of rules known in their aggregate as "the Umar conditions" which granted Jews a kind of intracommunal autonomy on certain discriminating and humiliating terms. For about one-half of the Bukharan Jewish community "the Umar conditions" continued to prevail even after Central Asia had become a part of the Russian Empire since they remained subjects of the emir of Bukhara, who, though fully controlled by the Russians, governed his puppet country according to Muslim tradition. In Christian Georgia, Jews were serfs for about half a millennium, at least from the end of the fourteenth century up to the 1860s and even the beginning of the 1870s.

All four communities differed in their language behavior vis-à-vis the host population of their respective areas of domicile. The main difference in this respect was between the Georgian Jewish community and the three other communities under discussion. Since the Georgian Jews shared their language with the host population in almost all places, they had no need of any other language in their relations with it. Even more, since the three dialects of Georgian the Jews spoke were dialects they shared with the host population of the three regions of Georgia most of them inhabited, the Jews had no need of any other dialect of Georgian beyond that of their respective regions. Hence the Georgian Jews were monolingual and in all the above three regions—monodialectal. The two places of exception were the town of Tskhinvali situated in a region with a substantial Ossetian population and the town of Akhaltsikhi with a substantial Muslim Turkish-speaking population. In these two places many Jews were bilingual, using Ossetian or Turkish in their contacts with those who spoke these languages. However, only the males were bilinguals; practically all domains of language behavior of the Jewish female were within the Jewish community. Apart from these two places, the Georgian Jewish community was the only one among those surveyed here in which both sexes were monolingual. For the situation of intracommunal interlocution in the undesirable presence of non-Jewish speakers of Georgian there existed a secret lect, *givruli* (lit. "Hebrew"), Georgian phonetically, morphologically, and syntactically, and mixed Georgian-Hebrew lexically.

A clear-cut female monolingualism/monodialectalism (for the reason indicated above) which stood in sharp contrast to a variety of male language behaviors where more than one dialect/language were involved, was a feature common to all of three other communities. Therefore, in the following survey of the language behavior of these communities vis-à-vis the host population, male language bahavior only will be discussed.

On the eve of the Sovietization of their respective areas both the Krymchaks and the Bukharan Jews can be defined as bidialectal and bilingual. The Krymchaks used their ethnolect of Crimean Tatar in the intracommunal domains of language behavior and Crimean Tatar proper in the domains where the interlocutors were Crimean Tatars (and/or local Karaites). However, already prior to Sovietization the Crimea was a multiethnic area where the Crimean Tatars, the main indigenous ethnic group, constituted only about one-quarter of the population, the majority being Russians.[13] As the majority language, Russian was the *lingua franca* for the other ethnic groups of the peninsula. Thus not only the Krymchaks, but the whole non-Russian population of the Crimea were practically bilingual and members of all ethnic groups would use either their own languages or Russian, as appropriate. In such places inhabited by Krymchaks as the Crimea's main town, Simferopol, the resort town of Feodosiia, and the big industrial town of Kerch, where the Russians formed the overwhelming majority and the rest of the population also belonged mostly to those who did not speak Crimean Tatar, Russian was the Krymchaks' only instrument of communication in their extracommunal contacts. Thus the Krymchaks on the eve of Sovietization can be defined from the sociolinguistic point of view as bidialectal (Judeo-Crimean Tatar–Crimean Tatar) and bilingual (Crimean Tatar–Russian).

In 1911 a semisecular "Crimean Jewish Talmud Torah" was established in Karasubazar with Russian as the language of instruction of general disciplines.[14] In the 1910s a number of Krymchak children (including girls) began to go to Ashkenazi professional schools in Simferopol, Feodosiia, and Kerch where the language of instruction was Russian and to Russian schools in Karasubazar and Simferopol.[15] Since the girls' knowledge of Russian upon their entering Russian schools was nil, preparatory preschool Russian courses were set up for them in Simferopol.[16] Thus by the time of Sovietization a tiny, but culturally influential, stratum of Krymchaks had emerged, which could be defined not only as Judeo-Crimean Tatar–Russian bilinguals, but as Judeo-Crimean Tatar–Russian equibilinguals.[17] One may suppose even that a certain preference for Russian as the language of a higher status already began to develop within this stratum. The small group of Krymchaks who outmigrated in the late nineteenth to early twentieth century from the Crimea to the town of Novorossiisk on the Caucasian shore of the Black Sea were monodialectal and bilingual (Judeo-Crimean Tatar–Russian). Among them the processes of equibilingualism and preference for Russian were evidently developing even more rapidly.

The Bukharan Jews, too, used their ethnolect of Tadzhik in the intracommunal domains of language behavior. Yet most of the Muslim population in the main area of Bukharan Jewish domicile (the towns of Bukhara and Samarkand and some smaller adjacent towns and townships) were Tadzhik–Uzbek equibilinguals or nearly equal bilinguals. And in verbal contacts with these interlocutors the Bukharan Jews used the respective local dialect or subdialect of Tadzhik proper. However, Uzbek was used by them too—in cases where the interlocutors were Uzbek monolinguals from rural areas or from small Uzbek monolingual, or nearly monolingual, urban enclaves. Hence in the main area of their domicile the Bukharan Jews were bidialectal (Judeo-Tadzhik–Tadzhik) and bilingual (Tadzhik–Uzbek). In two areas inhabited by Bukharan Jews their language behavior differed. In the town of Dushanbe and its environs in the Gissar Valley (now the capital of the Tadzhik SSR) they were bidialectical only, using their ethnolect intracommunally and some sort of Bukharan subdialect of Tadzhik with elements of its local dialect in their contacts with the local Tadzhik monolingual population. In the towns of their domicile in the Fergana Valley (today's Andizhan, Namangan, and Fergana *oblasts*, Uzbek SSR) they used their ethnodialect intracommunally and Uzbek in their contacts with the local monolingual or nearly monolingual Uzbek population.

The language situation of the Mountain Jews was the most complicated. The main center of the community was the town of Derbent (in the southern part of today's Dagestan ASSR). There existed a clear and generally accepted hierarchy of "correctness" among the dialects of Judeo-Tat, the Derbent (central) dialect being regarded as "the most correct." Accordingly, the speakers of this dialect were monodialectal, using their own dialect even in their contacts with speakers of other dialects. The speakers of the now almost extinct Vartashen (historically Shirvan) dialect (the lowest in the hierarchy of "correctness") were also practically monodialectal since, because of their relative geographical remoteness from the speakers of other dialects of Judeo-Tat, their contacts with the latter were scarce. The speakers of two other dialects, the so-called Qaytaqi (Northern Dagestani) dialect and the dialect of Kuba, were bidialectal, using their own dialects in their respective dialectal areas and the Derbent dialect (or their own dialects "Derbentified") in interdialectal contacts. Because of the remoteness of the Jewish speakers from other, Muslim and Christian, speakers of the language there was as a rule no outcommunal bidialectism. The speakers of the dialects of Derbent, Kuba, and Vartashen were for all practical purposes Judeo-Tat–Azerbaidzhani equibilinguals, the speakers of the Qaytaqi dialect were either Judeo-Tat–Qumiq (the main indigenous Turkic language of Dagestan) bilinguals—in their original area of domicile, or—in Groznyi (now the capital of the Chechen-Ingush ASSR) and Nalchik (now the capital of the Kabardino-Balkar ASSR) where groups of them settled in the late nineteenth century—Judeo-Tat–Chechen and Judeo-Tat–Kabardino-Cherkassian bilinguals, respectively. Most of the speakers of the Vartashen, Derbent, and Qaytaqi dialects were tri- and even quadrilinguals and in the last case—even pentalingual. Such multilingualism meant for the speakers of the Vartashen dialect: Judeo-Tat–Azerbaidzhani–Armenian– and (the Vartashen dialect of) Udin; for the speakers of the Derbent dialect: Judeo-Tat–Azerbaidzhani–Lezgi–Tabasarani; and for the speakers of the Qaytaqi dialect (in their main area of residence only): Judeo-Tat–Qumiq–Avar–Dargwa (Dargin)–Tabasarani.

The Georgian, Mountain, and Bukharan Jewish communities were still far less exposed to Russian than were the Krymchaks. Russians were present in large numbers in some places of Jewish domicile, especially Tiflis, Georgia's main town (now Tbilisi, the capital of the Georgian SSR); in the areas inhabited by the Mountain Jews, Baku, the main town of Azerbaidzhan (now the capital of the Azerbaidzhani SSR), Port-Petrovsk (now Makhachkala, capital of the Dagestan ASSR), Groznyi, and Nalchik: and in the areas inhabited by the Bukharan Jews, Tashkent, the main town of the Turkestanskii krai, the Central Asian territories under direct czarist administration (now capital of the Uzbek SSR), Samarkand, and Skobelev (now Fergana). As a rule their knowledge of local languages was nil and thus they had to be contacted in Russian. In the first decade and a half of the twentieth century, some semisecular schools for Mountain and Bukharan Jewish children began to function, where the general disciplines, as in the case of Karasubazar's "Crimean Jewish Talmud-Torah," were taught in Russian. A few children went to Russian schools.[18] However, only very few members of the Georgian, Mountain, and Bukharan communities had a good mastery of the language, although we know of a few Mountain and Bukharan Jews who could be defined as equibilinguals (respectively Judeo-Tat–Russian and Judeo-Tadzhik–Russian).[19] The rest of the members of all three communities who had been exposed to Russian usually just managed to make themselves understood in an elementary, often subnormative Russian. Russian was also the standard means of outcommunal intra-Jewish contact, usually contacts between members of one of the communities under discussion and Ashkenazim of the Russian Empire.

Finally, the place of Hebrew in the language behavior of the non-Ashkenazi communities should be discussed. It was learned predominantly as the sacred language and most of the males had an understanding of it, limited by the framework of the prayer book and the yearly cycle of the Torah reading. However, in one place in Georgia, at least, namely Tskhinvali, it had also a certain standing as a spoken language, at first as the only means of communication between the town's chief rabbi since the late 1890s, an Ashkenazi from Lithuania, Avraham Khvoles (1857–1931), and his flock and since 1906 as the language of instruction in the local Talmud-Torah patterned on the type introduced in the Ashkenazi Russian community by moderate religious modernists.[20] In 1902 a semisecular Georgian Jewish school was founded in Tiflis where Hebrew was taught (by Ashkenazi teachers from Vilna) according to the "Hebrew through Hebrew" method.[21] Its history lacks documentation, but possibly the Tiflis five-form Georgian Jewish school founded during Georgia's short-lived independence (1918–21) can be seen as its continuation. In this school, too, the "Hebrew through Hebrew" method was applied and Hebrew was, apparently, the only language of instruction. The school's headmaster was Natan Eliashvili.[22]

In 1898 a semisecular school where the language of instruction was Hebrew was founded in Samarkand by a rich businessman Hizqiyo Yissakharov (1861–1912). The main teacher in the school was a Jerusalem-born and -educated rabbi of Sephardi origin, Shlomo Tajer (1866–1936), who afterward became the chief rabbi of the Bukharan Jews of the Turkestanskii krai.[23] A number of other Palestinian-born Sephardim, such as Avraham Pinto, David-Hayy Adra'i, Aharon ben Shim'on, Yisrael Turjeman, and Avraham Safan (Tsafan) Mizrahi[24] were also engaged in teaching Hebrew to Bukharan Jewish children in the Turkestanskii krai, formally as private tutors in rich families but actually as teachers in a kind of nonformal, semisecular school functioning in private homes: a pattern resembling the same kind of schools operated by the local Muslim modernists, the socalled *jadids*. As for the Mountain Jewish community, Hebrew was the language of instruction parallel to Russian in its above-mentioned semisecular schools.[25]

To sum up our survey of the cultural typology of the communities under discussion prior to the Soviet period, one has, it seems, to regard their language behavior as a multimember polysystem[26] in which a clearly defined function and value was ascribed to each language and dialect. The simplest, two-member polysystem was that of the majority of Georgian Jews: high, sacred language (Hebrew)–low, everyday secular language (Georgian). The most complicated, seven-member polysystem was that of the speakers of the Qaytaqi dialect of Judeo-Tat: high, sacred language (Hebrew)—high intracommunal dialect (the Derbent dialect)—plus all five commonly spoken languages as listed above, namely low intracommunal dialect (the Qaytaqi dialect), high outcommunal language (Qumiq), the second-in-value outcommunal language (Avar), the third-in-value outcommunal language (Dargwa), and the lowest-value outcommunal language (Tabasarani). Were a speaker of that dialect to master Russian, then for him the polysystem would be eight-membered, with Russian having the highest value in the outcommunal language hierarchy. Were he also to master Hebrew not only as the sacred language, but also as a spoken language and/or language of writing, then it would be given double-high value as the secular intra-Jewish language.

All four communities were deeply influenced by the cultures of the host population. The Krymchaks and the Georgian and Bukharan Jews shared a substantial part of their verbal folklore with the host population, while among the Mountain Jews, professional Jewish performers performed Azerbaidzhani poetical folklore alongside their own folklore in Azerbaidzhan and Southern Dagestan, and Qumiq poetical folklore in Northern Dagestan.[27] Some specimens of the folklore of Bukharan and Mountain Jews bear witness to an impact of classical Persian literature.[28]

Three of the communities under discussion, namely the Krymchaks, the Mountain, and the Bukharan Jews, used their native tongues also as their literary languages written in Hebrew characters with some diacritics. However, the extent of the tradition of writing differed greatly. The oldest-known document and the oldest-known inscriptions in Persian (and Tadzhik is one of the continuations of classical, i.e., early medieval, Persian) in Hebrew characters (Judeo-Persian) are from the eighth century and both are from the larger Central Asian area (the document from Dandan-Uiliq,

Eastern Turkestan, i.e., the Xianjiang province of today's China; the inscriptions from the Tang-i Axao Valley of today's northern Afghanistan).[29] The tradition of Judeo-Persian Bible translations dates back apparently to the twelfth century,[30] and the oldest Judeo-Persian poetical texts are from the fourteenth century.[31] In the sixteenth to eighteenth centuries a number of poetical works in Judeo-Persian flavored with Tadzhikisms were composed in Central Asia, mainly in Bukhara.[32]

The first poem in Judeo-Tadzhik proper, *Ba yodi Khuydodcha* (To the memory of little Khuydod) was written in 1809 by Ibrohim (Avraham) ben Abulkhayr.[33] The first printed book in which Judeo-Tadzhik was used— the Book of Psalms in Hebrew with a parallel Judeo-Tadzhik translation— appeared in 1883 (in Vienna).[34] Since then Hebrew–Judeo-Tadzhik or just Judeo-Tadzhik books appeared regularly and up to the beginning of World War I about 120 of them had been published. Almost all of them were printed in Jerusalem, where a group of Bukharan Jewish authors emerged headed by Shim'on Hakham (1843–1910). Their predominant literary creativity was not the writing of original works, but the translation of works they evidently regarded as the most suitable for dissemination within their community. The main source of translations was the traditional nexus of religious texts. However, next in importance in their eyes were the oeuvres of East European Enlightenment *(Haskala)* Hebrew authors. The most popular of these translations became Shim'on Hakham's rendering (1908; reprint 1913) of the first modern Hebrew novel, *Ahavat Tsiyon* (Love of Zion) by Avraham Mapu (1808–1867). Shakespeare's *Comedy of Errors,* too, was translated (in 1911) from its Hebrew adaptation by David Kuilakov.[35] The first newspaper in Judeo-Tadzhik, *Rahamim,* was launched in 1910 (in Skobelev, now Fergana; discontinued in 1914).

A document in Hebrew dated 1865 speaks about an already existing tradition of writing in Judeo-Tat,[36] but there are no data revealing when this tradition emerged. The first book in which Judeo-Tat was used—a Judeo-Tat–Hebrew dictionary—was composed in the 1870s to the 1880s by the chief rabbi of southern Dagestan, Yanghil Itskhakovich (Ya'akov Yitshaki [b. 1848, d. 1917 in Palestine]).[37] The first printed book in Judeo-Tat, *Matlab Siyuniho* (The Goal of the Zionists; translation of Y. Sapir's Russian *Sionizm*) appeared in 1908 (in Vilna). However, only one more Judeo-Tat book was published prior to World War I—a prayer book in Hebrew with a parallel Judeo-Tat translation (Vilna, 1909). Both translations were done by an early Mountain Jewish Zionist Asaf Pinhosov (executed by the Soviets in 1920).

By the early twentieth century an amateur theatrical circle was operating in Derbent. Its repertoire was based on the Bible, and the plays were, apparently, of semi-improvisational character.[38] Supposedly some theatrical activities of the same sort existed also in Baku in the second decade of the century.[39] A Judeo-Tat newspaper whose Russian title only, *Ekho gor* (The echo of the mountains), is known to the present author was launched in 1915 (in Baku), but only three issues appeared.[40] The main means of the Mountain Jews' literary creativeness, however, remained verbal folklore, although a genre existed which can be defined as a transitional stage from the anonymous folklore to authored literature. This was the authored song, *ma'ni*, which, first sung by its creator, *ma'nikhu* (poet-cum-singer) was then performed by others mentioning the author's name.[41]

The earliest-known document in Judeo-Crimean Tatar (the introductory lines of which are in Hebrew) is a letter from the head and six notables of the Jewish community of Kaffa to the community of Karasubazar. The letter was apparently written in the very late sixteenth century when the leading role passed from the Kaffan community to the community of Karasubazar, or shortly afterward. Unfortunately its main Judeo-Crimean Tatar part, too, was published only in Hebrew rendering.[42] The first text with exact dating whose main part is in Judeo-Crimean Tatar is a species of proceedings of the Karasubazaran *bet-din* (rabbinic court of law) for the years 1703–17. Most of its halakhic decisions are in Judeo-Crimean Tatar. Only a brief survey of it was published with but one sentence on its main, Judeo-Crimean Tatar, part.[43] The second text with exact dating in this ethnolect is the *pinkas* (record book) of Karasubazar for the years 1785–97. Of its thirty records, twenty-eight are in Judeo-Crimean Tatar and only two in Hebrew.[44] The present whereabouts of all these texts are unknown. The only early document in Judeo-Crimean Tatar published in the original is a letter in the name of the Krymchaks of Karasubazar to Czar Aleksandr I (1801–1825), dated 12 May 1818.[45] The first printed book in which this ethnolect was used was a collection of religious hymns in Hebrew with a parallel Judeo-Crimean Tatar translation published in 1902 (in Jerusalem). Seven more books in which Judeo-Crimean Tatar was used appeared in the period 1903–6, after which publication of Krymchak books was discontinued for reasons not yet established. All books were of a religious character and consisted predominantly of ritual texts in Hebrew with parallel translations.[46] The dominant means of the Krymchaks' literary self-expression was still verbal folklore. It was habitual to assemble verbal folklore works in handwritten anthological collections (*jonkler*). At times an anthology was assembled by several generations of a family. Big anthologies were highly reputed and known by the names of their collector-owners.[47] Thus, though the works anthologized remained anonymous, the anthologies were, in a way, authored.

A unique book in which part of the text was in Georgian in Hebrew characters—a Hebrew-Georgian phrase book, *Sefer hinukh hane'arim* (Book for the education of adolescents) by Siman Rizhinashvili, was published in 1892 (in Jerusalem).

In the mid-1910s a series of polemical articles by Georgian Jews on Jewish problems was published in general Georgian newspapers. Typologically, these articles were identical with Jewish publicistic activity in any non-Jewish language. The difference was that usually such activity had its own organs and platforms, and in this case the general rostra played host in the absence of any Jewish ones. One of the principal themes of these articles was essentially identical with the theme which had preoccupied Jewish newspapers in non-Jewish languages in other areas some decades earlier, namely the theme of enlightenment and the relationship between it and religion. However, it had one distinctive trait of its own. Georgian Jewish enlightenment came into existence in the age of Zionism, and the two formed in their mainstream one integral whole. The main and most bitter opponent of this enlightenment-cum-Zionism was the traditional religious leadership. The latter was backed since 1916 by a new factor, the Habad wing of Hasidism which began to set up circles among the Georgian Jews. The second principal theme was more specific. In 1916 a group of young Georgian Jewish assimilationists headed by two students, the brothers Yoseb and Mikhail Khananashvili, put forward the thesis that the Georgian Jews were ethnic Georgians and "Israelites by religion." At the center of both discussions stood Rabbi David Baazov (1883–1947) whose *Weltanschauung* was an amalgam of moderate orthodox religiosity, enlightenment, and Zionism. The assimilationists were actively backed by some influential Georgian intellectuals, and gradually the general Georgian press stopped providing facilities for their opponents.[48] This became one of the main incentives for the enlightenment-Zionist group to launch in March 1918 in Kutais (now Kutaisi) the first specifically Jewish periodical in the

Georgian language, *Khma ebraelisa* (The Jewish Voice). Its publication was discontinued some time in 1919.[49]

III

The cultural history of the Krymchaks during the Soviet period has not yet been researched. Hence this chapter is but a first attempt at summarizing the scarce data the writer has succeeded in accumulating.

The Crimea became Soviet only at the very end of 1920. In 1921 it was proclaimed a Soviet Autonomous Republic within the Russian Soviet Federative Republic, and Crimean Tatar, alongside Russian, was made one of its two official languages. Though closely related to Crimean Tatar and being, as stated above, its Jewish ethnolect, Judeo-Crimean Tatar (Krymchak) was recognized as a lingual entity of its own.[50] Two reasons at least caused this recognition. The first was one of principle: according to the Soviet language building *(iazykovoe stroitel'stvo)* policy of the 1920s to early 1930s, the language of every ethnolinguistic group, regardless of its numerical strength, had to be granted the officially equal status of a language of writing and school instruction.[51] The second reason was pragmatic. As everywhere, the Russian Communist party (of Bolsheviks) saw in religion its main ideological rival. However, since the Crimea was regarded as an "Oriental" area, the Soviets behaved here in conformity with the so-called "Eastern policy of the Communist party" which stressed the necessity to "exercise particular caution and be particularly heedful of the survivals of national sentiments among the labouring masses of the oppressed or unequal nations"[52] and to replace "the direct way of combating the religious prejudices . . . by indirect and more cautious ways."[53] Thus the authorities refrained until 1928–29 from a frontal attack on the religion of the "Orientals." Until then the Communist party established a network of secular schools, communist in spirit, in which tuition was conducted in local languages, which were regarded as the best instrument for getting the upper hand over religion.

Since the Krymchaks were seen as a part of the indigenous "Oriental" population, the "Eastern policy" had to be applied to them, too. However, they had to be provided with an educational network of their own, separate from that of the Crimean Tatars and of the Ashkenazim (the 1926 census showed about 34,000 Ashkenazi Jews in the Crimea as compared with

6,000 Krymchaks).[54] Though the Krymchaks shared their spoken language with the Crimean Tatars (despite some dialectal distinctions), until 1928 their writing systems were completely different: whereas that of Crimean Tatar was based on the Arabic alphabet, that of Judeo-Crimean Tatar was based on the Hebrew alphabet. In 1928 both Crimean Tatar and Judeo-Crimean Tatar orthography were converted into the so-called Latinized (i.e., Latin) alphabet, though the inventory of characters was slightly different (Karaitic Crimean Tatar, almost identical with Crimean Tatar, was given the same inventory of characters as Judeo-Crimean Tatar.)[55] But even then the authorities refrained from fusing the educational network of the Krymchaks with that of the Crimean Tatars. They evidently appreciated that, despite all the slogans of peoples' friendship, the near-identity of the new writing systems of the Crimean Tatar language and its Jewish ethnolect was not an instrument capable of bridging over the tremendous difference of the two ethnic self-identities, especially given the centuries-long Crimean Tatar tradition of holding the Jews in utmost scorn. As for the Crimea's Ashkenazim, though both groups identified themselvs as Jews, their communal identity and language differed. Besides, the "Eastern policy" did not apply to Ashkenazim, so that the attack on the position of religion among them in the Crimea in the early 1920s was as brutal as in the Slavic heartland, despite the fact that they had become far more secularized than the Krymchaks already prior to the Revolution. Among the latter, as evidenced by a letter from the Soviet Union published in Agudat Israel's *Haderekh* in 1925, the traditional religious education of children was still conducted in a very active and, apparently, quite legal way in the mid-1920s.[56]

Already in the very early 1920s a process began of outmigration of Krymchaks from Karasubazar, the center of their predominant concentration prior to Sovietization, to larger and, therefore, more attractive towns in the Crimea. By 1926 only 16.3 percent of the members of the community dwelt in Karasubazar.[57] The former Karasubazarans settled chiefly in Simferopol, and to an extent also in Kerch. By 1926 Simferopol became the main Krymchak center with 23.5 percent of the members of the community concentrated there.[58] In the late 1920s and the very beginning of the 1930s outmigrants from Karasubazar established two Krymchak *kolkhozy* (collective farms)—*Krymchakh* (the Krymchak) and *Yengi Krymchakh* (The New Krymchak).[59] In the early 1930s a wave of outmigration of Krymchaks began from the Crimea, this time mainly from Feodosiia and Kerch, to such towns as Novorossiisk, which, as we have seen, already had a Krymchak community, and Sukhum (now Sukhumi).[60]

Evidently, in all places of Krymchak domicile in the Crimea, secular schools, communist in spirit, were established, with Judeo-Crimean Tatar as the language of instruction. In all likelihood, the first of these was the Karasubazar school, opened in 1921 on the basis of the semisecular "Crimean Jewish Talmud-Torah" established there in 1911.[61] Despite the evergrowing outmigration from the town, the school seems to have had a sizable attendance throughout the 1920s. One can deduce this from the fact that in 1930 the Commission for the Rural Placement of Jewish Toilers attached to the Presidium of Soviet Nationalities, Komzet, announced the construction there of a new school building.[62] Apparently all Krymchak schools, except one, were of the elementary type (grades 1 through 4). The sole exception was the Simferopol school, which was of the "incomplete secondary school" type (*nepolnaia sredniaia shkola*, grades 1 through 7) which were quite widespread at the time in the Soviet school system. In this school Judeo-Crimean Tatar and Russian were languages of instruction. The precise distribution of functions between the two languages of instruction in the school's curriculum is uncertain. It can be surmised that Russian was used in teaching either the sciences or all disciplines at the secondary school level (grades 5 through 7).[63] A network of literacy courses (*likbez*) for adults was also initiated.[64]

The leading Krymchak educationalist of the 1920s to 1930s was Saq-Yuda (Yizhaq Yehuda) Kaya (known also under the Russianized form of his name as Isaak Samuilovich Kaya; 1887–1956), the first Krymchak to graduate (in 1909) from the well-known Jewish modernist educational institution—the Vilna Teachers' Institute—and the founder and headmaster of the Karasubazaran "Crimean Jewish Talmud-Torah".[65] Kaya was the author of the textbook of the community's mother tongue used in the Krymchak schools and, evidently, the most experienced pedagogue in the field of humanities in the whole Krymchak educational network. In 1925 he also wrote, together with the Crimean-Tatar educationalist A. Odabash, a manual of Crimean-Tatar. In 1926 Kaya published in three issues of the Crimean-Tatar teachers' journal *Oquy ishleri* (Study Topics) a lengthy article in which he surveyed *in extenso* the situation and problems of Krymchak education. Another well-known Krymchak educationalist of those years was Aia (Haya, Khaya Isaakovna) Trevgoda, the headmistress of the Simferopol seven-form school.[66]

Not later than 1923 a Krymchak club was established in Simferopol at which an amateur theatrical group performed. In late 1927 or early 1928 a "Jewish dramatic circle" was also founded in Kerch under the aegis of the board of the local section of Ozet, the Association for the Rural Placement of Jewish Toilers subordinate to the Evsektsiia and the party. It seems quite probable that Krymchak clubs also functioned in such places of Krymchak concentration as Karasubazar, Feodosiia, and the Krymchak *kolkhozy*, though no data are available.[67]

Parallel to housing amateur theatrical activities the clubs usually had at least two more functions, which are relevant to the terms of reference of the present chapter: to stimulate the interest of their members and visitors in the printed word (i.e., to have reading room and/or book-lending facilities) and to regularly host lectures for mass audiences, mainly on political and ideological topics. The former function and to a lesser extent the latter would be fulfilled also by two other components of "the political-educational network"—the "red corner" (a reading room offering mainly news-related political literature and periodicals) and the *bazovaia izba-chital'-nia*,[68] the latter being intended mainly for the countryside. A report in *Tribuna* states the establishing of *bazovye izby-chital'ni* and red corners in the Crimea by Ozet in 1930, but with no reference to the Krymchak settlements.[69] It seems, however, highly probable that red corners must have been set up in the Krymchak areas of Feodosiia and Karasubazar and that the *bazovye izby-chital'ni*, being a must for every *kolkhoz*, were absolutely unavoidable for the Krymchak *kolkhozy*, too.[70]

However, the functions under discussion could not be fulfilled using Judeo-Crimean Tatar only, in which there were only a negligible number of publications restricted mainly to elementary school textbooks. Hence the Krymchak "political-educational" institutions also had to have in stock and to provide the Krymchak reader with publications not in his mother tongue. Since on the eve of the Soviet period almost all male members of the community knew Russian, and a number of the community's male and female youngsters went to schools where Russian was a, or the, language of instruction, the bulk of the printed material provided to the Krymchak reader by Krymchak "political-educational" institutions was in Russian.[71]

It seems very doubtful, too, that the lecturers could be solely speakers of Judeo-Crimean Tatar. Political-educational activity, both among the Ashkenazi settlers in the Crimea, where Pale *shtetl* Jews were being "productivized" through settlement on the land as collective farmers[72] and among the

Krymchaks, was under the aegis of the *Evsektsiia* (until its disbandment in 1930). Thus the topics not covered by lecturers in Judeo-Crimean Tatar were in all likelihood covered in Russian (and Yiddish) by Ashkenazi lecturers. Except in the two Krymchak *kolkhozy* and possibly in some Karasubazar cooperative workshops, Krymchaks had now to work everywhere in ethnically heterogeneous collectives where Russian was the only means of verbal communication. In this way increasing numbers of Krymchaks were being exposed to Russian on levels more sophisticated than the previous level of intercommunal communication that had been restricted normally to more or less simple interlocutions on daily living needs, and this exposure became a standard facet of their language behavior.

Accordingly, ever-growing numbers of Krymchaks were becoming not just Judeo-Crimean Tatar–Russian bilinguals, but Judeo-Crimean Tatar–Russian equibilinguals. Accordingly, too, the preference for Russian as the language of a higher status, which apparently had already existed in the equibilingual stratum of the Krymchaks in the pre-Soviet period, must have gained more and more adherents. Since typologically the outcome of such a preference is, as a rule, a language shift, that is, the abandonment of the low–preference tongue of the equibilingual in favor of his high–preference tongue, increasing numbers of Krymchaks will have abandoned Judeo-Crimean Tatar in favor of Russian. Already in the 1926 census 25.9 percent of Krymchaks did not declare the language of their community as their own language—a percentage exceeding by far that registered among any other Oriental Jewish community of the USSR (cf. 0.4 percent among the Georgian Jews, 3 percent among the Mountain Jews, and 6.2 percent among the Bukharan Jews) and comparable with the all–Soviet percent of Ashkenazi Jews (28.1).[73] Almost all of the 25.9 percent shifted to Russian (24.5 percent as against 1.4 percent to "other languages").[74] Though no numerical data on the ratio of Judeo-Crimean Tatar and Russian among the Krymchaks are available for the rest of the 1920s, the 1930s, and up to the extermination of most of the community by the Nazis, there can hardly be any doubt that the process of the language shift from the former to the latter gathered momentum in these years.

The only Krymchak poet of the period known to us by name, Yakov Chapichev (1909–1945) wrote his verse in Russian. Born in Novorossiisk, he spent most of his life in Dzhankoi, the Crimea. In 1934 he enlisted in the army, where he soon became an officer, but in 1938 he was expelled from the party and discharged from the army for expressing doubts about the arrest of the commanding officer of his unit as "an enemy of the people." He made a living first as a bootblack and then as an engine stoker, his job when the only collection of his poetry was published in 1939 in Simferopol. In the same year the purges died down and he was reinstated in the party. He was preparing a second collection when the armored division, on whose newspaper he was a literary worker, was sent to the front. He died in action and was posthumously decorated a Hero of the Soviet Union. Chapichev's poetry, like that of many Ashkenazi Russian-language poets of this period, is devoid of any ethnic marker, its main motifs being typical of contemporary Soviet epic poetry.[75]

In the late 1930s most of the languages of the USSR which had had their alphabets "Latinized" in the late 1920s to early 1930s were converted to Cyrillic-based alphabets. However, some of them did not undergo this conversion and in this fashion got "demoted" to the lowest rank in the Soviet sociolinguistic hierarchy—the rank of the unwritten language *(bespis'mennyi iazyk)*, that is a language of oral communication only. The overwhelming majority of "nonconverted" languages were languages of small ethnolinguistic groups within the orbit, and under a strong lingual and cultural impact of big ethnolinguistic groups. Many of them were within the orbit of Russian. These included (of the Turkic group of languages) Karaitic Crimean Tatar, Urum, and (the language of the so-called Mariupol Greeks) Shor; (of the Finno-Ugrian group of languages) Veps, Izhor, and Saam; (of the Tungus-Manchurian group of languages) Ude; (of the Chukotkan-Kamchatkan group of languages) Itelmen; and (of the Paleoasian group of languages) Ket. Their "demotion" to the rank of unwritten language meant that all their functions as written languages *(pis'mennyi iazyk)*, that is, publication, school instruction, and "political-educational network" activities, would from now on be taken over by Russians. Judeo-Crimean Tatar, too, became one of these "nonconverted" languages.[76] Thus publicational activities in this language, negligible as they had been, were condemned to total discontinuation, as was its use as a language of instruction and of "dramatic circle" performances.

One more Jewish language of the USSR shared the same fate—Judeo-Tadzhik—the language of the Bukharan Jewish community. However, there had been a difference in the status of the two languages in terms of the Soviet sociolinguistic hierarchy prior to their "demotion": whereas Judeo-Crimean Tatar was just a "written language," Judeo-Tadzhik could be defined as having had the highest ranking—that of literary language *(liter-*

aturnyi iazyk)—judging by its far broader functioning as the language of all verbal forms of the community's culture, including mass media, school instruction, regular book publishing and professionalized stagecraft (see below). There was also a difference in the position of both languages vis-à-vis the Russian language. Judeo-Crimean Tartar was within the orbit of Russian as the main language of the area of domicile of its speakers. As stated above, already in 1926 about one-quarter of all Krymchaks had abandoned the community's language in favor of Russian and the process of this language shift for the rest of the 1920s and the 1930s must have gathered momentum very rapidly. In the case of speakers of Judeo-Tadzhik, on the other hand, not Russian, but Uzbek and Tadzhik were the main languages of the area of domicile. In 1926 not more than about 6 percent of the speakers of Judeo-Tadzhik had shifted to Russian (see the data quoted above). Though the shift to Russian could not but gather momentum among the Bukharan Jews, especially in towns with a predominantly Russian or largely Russian population, such as Tashkent, Stalinabad (now Dushanbe), and Samarkand, the ratio of Russian and Judeo-Crimean Tatar among them was nothing like the ratio of Russian and Judeo-Crimean Tatar among the Krymchaks. However, the decision-making authorities evidently saw both communities as convenient objects for accelerated lingual Russification through "degradation" of their languages to the "nonwritten rank, the first as one of many mini-enclaves (parallel with the speakers of other "small languages" within the continuum of Russian), and the second as a small Jewish drop in the Muslim ocean, a drop which would prefer to shift to the imperial tongue, as the tongue of higher status, rather than to the main local languages.

From the above one can conclude that Krymchak verbal culture was still constrained to find its main expression in folklore. Of the few specimens of verbal folklore oeuvres in Judeo-Crimean Tatar recorded in the Soviet period, it seems that only three can be chronologized with certainty as having been actually composed during this period. One of these is a thirty-two-verse poem about the 1921–22 famine in the Crimea, which resulted in the loss of many lives among the poorer strata of the population, including about 10 percent of the members of the Krymchak community who were predominantly craftsmen. Prosodically very characteristic of Turkic folklore in general (syllabic meter, rhyming by means of repetition, with some lines left unrhymed), the poem describes eloquently the disasters of the famine and exposes the rich (seemingly of the community) and the

Tatars as the villains. Interesting is the mention of what seems to be the specifically Krymchak habit of kindling lights in the synagogue after burial.[77]

Two others are Holocaust poems. As already stated, not less than 70 percent of the community were exterminated by the Nazis. The extermination of most of the Krymchaks took place between 11 December 1941, when the Krymchaks of Simferopol were shot near the village of Mazanki in the vicinity of the town, and 18 January 1942, when the Krymchaks of Karasubazar were gassed in the so-called *dushequbkas* (hermetically closed vans filled by the exhaust gas of the motor).[78] The last to die were the Krymchaks of Sevastopol: the town was seized by the Germans on 4 July 1942, and its Jews were murdered on the 12th of the month.[79]

The shorter of the two Judeo-Crimean Tatar Holocaust poems seems to have been written by a Sevastopol survivor. Composed according to the Turkic folklore patterns described above, the poem condenses in its twenty-two short lines the horrors of life in the besieged fortress-town—named throughout the poem not by its official name, but by its slightly changed pre-Russian name Akhyar (originally Akhtyar) according to the habit of using pre-Russian toponyms known also among the Crimean Tatars—and all the despair of a S[y]real (Jew), whose people are being killed "from the front of Kerch up to Akhyar . . . like sheep."[80]

The other poem[81] is connected with the extermination of the Krymchaks of Simferopol (named, accordingly, Aq-mechid). Unlike the two other poems this one has a distinctive stanza composition. The main vehicle for conveying the poem's tenor is the contraposition of "we" ("On these Crimean fields/ /We have been victimized": "We were taken out from Aq-Mechit"; "We know already/ /Where we are going"; "Dig deeper the grave for us"; "Do not forget us, my people") and "the soldiers," that is, the Einsatzgruppe Germans who performed the mass execution ("Vicious soldier, lead us//Do not squeeze our arms"; "The soldiers killing us"; "Do not forget our people turned ill-fated/ /By the hands of soldiers"). In its "death of my people" and "do not forget" leitmotifs the poem strikingly resembles what is perhaps the greatest of the Holocaust's literary testimonies. "Song of the Murdered Jewish People" by Yitzhak Katznelson (1886–1944). It is to be regretted that the anonymous Krymchak analogue to Yitzhak Katznelson's poem has not yet found its way into Holocaust anthologies and remains under the category of philological esoterica.

In 1955 a group of Krymchaks approached the Soviet authorities with a request to regard the Krymchaks not as Jews, but as a separate *natsional'-nost'*.[82] The "scholarly" level of the argumentation in favor of this secession can be seen from its summary in Peisakh's entry on the Krymchaks in the third edition of the Great Soviet Encyclopaedia: "The ethnogenesis of the Krymchaks has not yet been established definitely. As it seems, the basis for their formation was the ancient local population (which accepted the Judaic religion) with a later admixture of Jewish, Turkic and, possibly, Italian (Genoese) elements."[83] Although contradicting such sound historical data as may be available, this argumentation was, apparently, enough for the authorities (if they needed any at all), and the request was fulfilled.

Today, over thirty years after the Krymchaks' official secession from Jewish peoplehood, nearly all members of this group (with the exception of a very few who succumbed neither to the temptation to escape discriminatory limitations by being registered as non-Jews nor to the pressure of those who were regarded as standing at the top of the intracommunal hierarchy) are stated in the *natsional'nost'* paragraph of their identity cards not as Jews, but as Krymchaks. Given the almost complete shift from the community's mother tongue to Russian, the complete Russian acculturation of practically all Krymchaks (except, perhaps, a very tiny and rapidly disappearing stratum of females in the over-seventy age group), the almost nil involvement in the *aliya* movement, and the ever-growing, indeed very fast process of outcommunal marriages with non-Jews (mainly with Russians), the Krymchaks are a Jewish group on the verge of complete disappearance through assimilation within the surrounding (predominantly Russian) population.

The sole bond which still keeps the community together is the residual collective memory, which finds its main manifest expression in the memory of the Holocaust. The memorializing of the Holocaust has distinctive folklore features. It is distinctively Jewish, too, despite the official non-Jewishness of the Krymchaks. Holocaust Memorial Day is commemorated every year (since the very late 1950s to early 1960s) on December 11 by a massive gathering of Krymchaks from all over the USSR in Simferopol and a visit to the site where the extermination was carried out. Though commemorated according to the lay calendar, Holocaust Day bears a name strongly associated with Jewish religious tradition—*T[u]qun* in Hebrew *tiqqun*; this is shortened from *tiqqun yom hazzikkaron*, lit. "institution of the day of commemoration," or from *tiqqun haneshama*, lit. "institution of [prayer for] the soul"), the Judeo-Crimean Tatar equivalent of the Yiddish *yortsayt* (*jahrzeit* in the accepted English spelling), commemoration of the deceased. Heads are covered, traditional Krymchak—and kosher-style—food is partaken, folklore songs in Judeo-Crimean Tatar are sung, though most of the participants have a very vague, if any, knowledge of the language, and *Kaddish* (the prayer for the deceased) is recited—usually by one of the Ashkenazi invitees known to have an expertise in Jewish religious tradition and/or Hebrew.[84] At least in this respect the behest "Do not forget us!" is still fulfilled.

IV

On 1 May 1918 Turkestanskii krai was proclaimed the Soviet Republic of Turkestan. In 1920 the Red Army put an end to the existence of the Bukharan emirate which became the Soviet People's Republic of Bukhara. In 1924 both republics ceased to exist and the Uzbek Soviet Socialist Republic was proclaimed with Tadzhikistan forming an autonomy within it until in 1929 it, too, became a Soviet Socialist Republic. As soon as the Turkestan branch of the *Evsektsiia* got established (evidently very soon after the *Evsektsiia* was officially founded in October 1918) it was invested with control over the Bukharan Jewish community of the Republic of Turkestan,[85] although it consisted almost entirely of Ashkenazim with little, if any, knowledge of Bukharan Jews.[86] Not later than early 1919 the "Native Jewish National Central Bureau" of the People's Commissariat of Education was founded.[87] One of its main tasks was setting up a network of Soviet schools. Apparently, the first Soviet school for Bukharan Jewish children began to operate in the same year in Samarkand where most of the Bukharan Jews of Turkestanskii krai lived. The first teachers who worked in it were Ashkenazim who did not know Judeo-Tadzhik. One of them, Y. Z. Amitin-Shapiro, succeeded in publishing a Hebrew-language geography course, which seems to have been the last textbook in Hebrew published under Soviet rule;[88] another, Sh. Edel'man, prepared a textbook in Hebrew on the natural sciences, but it was never published.[89] The only means of communication between teachers and pupils was Hebrew. By the end of 1922 ten Soviet schools for Bukharan Jewish children were functioning in the Republic of Turkestan.[90]

In 1920, upon the establishment of the Bukharan People's Soviet Republic, two Soviet Jewish schools with Hebrew as the language of instruction were also set up in the town of Bukhara. One was named after A. Mapu, evidently because of the enormous popularity of Shim'on Hakham's Judeo-

Tadzhik translation of his *Ahavat Tsiyon,* and the second after H. N. Bialik.[91] Notwithstanding the *Evsektsiia*'s bitter opposition to Hebrew, a conference of Bukharan Jewish communists held at the end of June to the beginning of July, 1921, maintained that "Hebrew is to be seen as the language of instruction and culture."[92] However, in late 1921 the Turkestani People's Commissariat of Education ordered that instruction in Bukharan Jewish schools be conducted in Judeo-Tadzhik and not in Hebrew.[93] It is not clear when the change of the language of instruction actually took place. However, since the order was issued in late 1921 one must deduce that it could not have taken place earlier than the 1922–23 school year.

The first people able to teach in Judeo-Tadzhik were apparently the graduates of the three-month teachers' courses in Tashkent and the yearly teachers' courses in Samarkand, both initiated in 1919. However, the bulk of the teachers of the Bukharan Jewish educational network throughout the whole period of its existence came from the Tashkent Bukharan Jewish teachers' seminary (until 1930 officially named the Institute of People's Education) founded in 1920.[94] The first head of the seminary was Yitshak Ben-Simon of Jerusalem, in all likelihood one of the Sephardi teachers who taught Hebrew to Bukharan Jewish children in the pre-Soviet period.[95] In 1923 all its teachers were still Ashkenazim.[96] In the beginning some of the courses here too were taught in Hebrew, others in Russian,[97] although by 1923 all the courses were taught in Russian,[98] Hebrew, however, remaining one of the disciplines until 1924.[99] The seminary was under tight supervision by the *Evsektsiia.* At least since 1923 membership in the Communist Youth League *(Komsomol)* was a sine qua non for acceptance to the seminary.[100] Nevertheless, in accordance with the "Eastern policy" of the Communist party, students were served kosher food.[101] In essence the seminary was an educational institution of the secondary school type with pedagogical specialization. In accordance with the Soviet rubrication of institutions of this type in 1930 it was classified as a *tekhnikum* (Soviet term for specialized secondary schools). In the same year it was transferred to Kokand;[102] the reason given was the shortage of living space in Tashkent.[103] The total number of the seminary's graduates from its establishment and up to late 1935–early 1936 was about 200.[104]

In 1930 there were in Uzbekistan alone 30 Bukharan Jewish schools with 3,000 pupils and 120 teachers. In 1934 the number of pupils in these schools reached 4,000 and the number of teachers 170.[105] In 1935 the number of Bukharan Jewish schools in the republic was 35.[106] However, the 1938 data show a sharp decrease in both the number of Bukharan Jewish schools and of pupils in these schools: the number of Bukharan Jewish schools in this year was only 15 and 2,420 pupils attended them—only 50.5 percent of the total number of schoolchildren among "local Jews."[107] As we shall see below, the decision to discontinue cultural and educational activities in Judeo-Tadzhik was already made in 1938 and hence the stage-by-stage closure of schools where it was the language of instruction was but a method of implementing this decision. No data are available for the distribution of the nearly half of the total number of Bukharan Jewish children who were pupils of non-Bukharan Jewish schools between schools in local languages (i.e., in Uzbekistan predominantly in Uzbek, but in Samarkand and Bukhara also in Tadzhik) and in Russian. However, empirical observations must bring one to the conclusion that the preference was already then given to Russian schools, that is, to acculturation in the imperial, Russian culture.[108]

In 1934 there were in Uzbekistan fifteen Bukharan Jewish clubs and twenty-eight Bukharan Jewish red *chaikhanas* (teahouses; the Central Asian version of red corners).[109] In 1931 a Bukharan Jewish historical and ethnographic museum was officially opened in Samarkand (on the basis of an amateurish nucleus set up as early as 1922).[110]

As everywhere in the USSR, one of the main functions of the clubs was to host amateur drama groups, whose existence dates back to the early 1920s. To function they needed repertoire, so that their existence was an incentive for literary creativity.

An amateur drama group functioned as a part of the extracurricular activities of the students of the Tashkent Bukharan Jewish teachers' seminary. One of its plays was based on the biblical story of Joseph, another was a kind of *Purimspiel*. At least one play bore no relation to Jewish traditions, namely a musical comedy by the Azerbaidzhani composer and playwright Uzeyr Hadzhibekov (1885–1948), *Arshin mal alan* (One who measures cloth by the arshin; a nickname for peddlers of cloth) (1913), that was highly popular throughout the Russian/Soviet Muslim periphery.[111] Apparently the same Joseph play was performed by an amateur group in Samarkand which also performed a dramatization of the Judeo-Tadzhik translation by Shim'on Hakham of Mapu's *Ahavat Tsiyon*. The play's name was *Amnun va Tomor* (Amnon and Tamar) after the names of the novel's main heroes.[112] This may have been the same group which at the beginning of the 1920s staged in Judeo-Tadzhik translation a Hebrew play *Haavot vehabanim* (Fathers and Sons) by Sh. Edel'man. The topic of the play was the generation gap and the conflict between generations in the community caused by the new Soviet reality. The play was also performed in the same translation by an amateur group in Bukharan,[113] probably the same drama group of pupils of the Jewish schools of Bukhara that in 1922 performed what was evidently the identical dramatization of Hakham's translation of *Ahavat Tsiyon*. This group, too, performed a Joseph play, apparently the same as staged by the drama groups of Tashkent and Samarkand.[114] An amateur drama group existed also in Kokand in the first years of Soviet rule. The group was linked with the Kokand section of *Tarbut*, a cultural-educational society of Zionist orientation which apparently began to function in Central Asia in 1918, was subjected to vicious persecutions at least as of 1921, and was finally banned in 1922. It seems that the Kokand group performed both in Hebrew and Judeo-Tadzhik.[115]

The activities of the amateur groups occupied an important place in the cultural life of the Bukharan Jewish community, and works of drama constituted a relatively large proportion of the general literary output. One of these was the five-act play *Hukumati padar dar dukhtar* (A Father's Power Over His Daughter), by P. Pardozov and M. Borukhov,[116] published in Tashkent in 1921, which was the progenitor of a large number of works of drama, prose, and poetry on the theme of women's rights.

Toward the end of the decade the activities of the amateur theatrical group in Kokand were revived; a circle of amateur playwrights regularly provided the group with a topical repertoire.[117]

The most outstanding poet of the twenties was Yahiel Oqilov (1900–72), whose earliest poetry, written during the Soviet period, dates from 1918. In 1927 he published in Tashkent a collection of poems. *Dadi u* (Her Father), which was the first collection of poems in Judeo-Tadzhik to be published in the Soviet period.[118] A. Yusupov, Y. Hakhamov, and Muhib (poetical pen name of Mordkhay Bachaev, b. 1911; in Israel since 1973) also began to publish poetry. There was virtually no belletristic prose during this period.

On 16 November 1925 the first issue of the weekly *Rushnoi* (Light) was published in Samarkand. It was renamed *Bayroqi mihnat* (Banner of Labor) in April 1930 and transferred in October of that year to Tashkent. In 1933 it became a daily.[119]

The conversion of Judeo-Tadzhik from the Hebrew to the Latin script was initiated in 1929, but the process was completed only in 1931–32.[120] Possession of books in Hebrew and/or Judeo-Tadzhik published in the pre-

Soviet period was regarded as seditious, and most of them were destroyed or buried in these years (1929–30), as were books in the Arabic script among the indigenous Muslim population.[121]

The period of transition to the Latin script coincided with the transfer of the center of newspaper and book publishing from Samarkand to Tashkent, the capital of the Uzbek SSR, although Samarkand remained the area with the largest concentration of Bukharan Jews. The last book in which Samarkand, together with Tashkent, is indicated as the place of publication —Menashe Aminov's play *Zulmi boyon* (Oppression by the Rich)—is dated 1930. Since that time and until Bukharan Jewish publications ceased to appear in the USSR, all books in the Bukharan Jewish dialect were published in Tashkent. The literary and sociopolitical bimonthly journal *Hayoti mihnati* (Toiling Life), later *Adabiyoti soveti* (Soviet Literature), was published as of 1931 in Tashkent[122] and became, together with the "literary page" in *Bayroqi mihnat*, the most important publishing platform of Bukharan Jewish literature.

In 1932 the section of Bukharan Jewish (or, to use the official terminology of the time, "indigenous Jewish") writers was formed in Tashkent attached to the *Orqkomitet* (Organizing Committee) of Soviet writers of Uzbekistan.[123]

Drama continued to be the most important literary genre in the 1930s. This was perhaps due less to a desire to satisfy readers' requirements than to the necessity to ensure a regular supply of new plays for the amateur theatrical groups and the first professional Bukharan Jewish troupe established in Samarkand in 1932 from among the amateur groups.[124] This professional company staged both dramas and musicals.

The musical dramas were frequently based on plays translated from Uzbek, for example *Halima* by Ghulam Zarifi and *Farhad and Shirin* by Khurshid. Toward the end of his life, one of the leading Tadzhik poets of the 1920s to early 1930s, Payrav Sulaymoni (1899–1933), who was of *chala* origin (i.e., Jews forcibly converted to Islam in the nineteenth century), collaborated with the Samarkand Bukharan Jewish theater.[125]

A basic theme of Bukharan Jewish drama in the thirties was women's rights. This was also a principal theme in the literatures of the Central Asian peoples in whose midst the Bukharan Jews lived. Although a Bukharan Jewish play on the struggle for women's rights had, as we have seen, been published as early as 1921, plays on this theme during the thirties bear clear traces of the influence of Uzbek drama on women's rights in the traditional Muslim milieu. This literary borrowing resulted in works in which the Bukharan Jewish woman, who enjoyed far more personal freedom than her Uzbek counterpart living in a polygamous household, spoke and behaved in a manner dictated not by real life but by the author's dependence on existing Uzbek patterns. Paradoxically, this subject, which played a central role in all Central Asian and, indeed, all Muslim literature in the USSR, was entwined with another subject—the settling of the Jews on the land—which greatly preoccupied contemporary Soviet Yiddish literature. This latter theme was predominant in another play by Menashe Aminov, *Hayoti haqiqi* (True Life: 1931), and in Y. Haimov's play *Nojot* (Deliverance; 1938) the theme of the struggle for women's rights was presented as secondary to the main theme, that of class stratification and class struggle. The latter theme was dramatized by a somewhat banal device characteristic of Soviet literature in this period: the members of one family (in this case brother and sister) were portrayed as opposite poles of a class conflict. The same theme was put forward, in terms of a *Kulturkampf*, in *Dushmanoni frunti madani* (Enemies on the Cultural Front), by L. Mordekhaev and P. Abramov (1934).

Bukharan Jewish drama of the 1930s suffered serious aesthetic weaknesses: melodrama, a pathos often identical in tone and vocabulary with "leading articles" in the Soviet press, and a naïveté of dramatic devices and plot.

In the realm of prose, the highest stage of development was reached by the short story. Here too, there was much on the artistic and aesthetic level which likened it to its counterpart in contemporary Uzbek and Tadzhik prose such as the preponderance of description over action, the high degree of predictability of the plot development, patchy characterization, and the rigid psychology of the characters. Nonetheless, the Bukharan Jewish short story is, in terms of literary technique, of far higher quality than the drama, for example several of the short stories in Y. Haimov's *Zindaqoniyi nav* (New Life; 1935), and his collection for children *Roh ba zindaqoni* (The Way of Life; 1940), *Posboni Vatan* (Guardian of the Motherland; 1939) by Nison Fuzaylov, and *Javoniyi usto Sholum* (The Youth of Shalom the Craftsman; 1940) by B. Qalandarov (b. 1911, died in action 1943).

Mushe Yahudaev's (d. 1965) *Tuhmat* (The Blood Libel; 1935), Gavriel Samandarov's (b. 1910) *Khomloyi kuhna* (Old School; 1934), and Menashe Ishoqboev's *Pisari 'Alisho* (Elisha's Son; 1939) whose plot takes place during World War I, are the only works of Bukharan Jewish prose of the 1930s which deal with the life of the community before the establishment of Soviet rule in Central Asia. The predominant theme of the Bukharan Jewish short story is the participation of Bukharan Jews in the Revolution and in Soviet life. G. Samandarov's *Bobojon* (1933) is devoted to the struggle to establish Soviet rule in Central Asia, in which the hero, a Bukharan Jew, is an active fighter for Soviet power. Ishoqbaev's *Fabriki bereshum* (The Silk-Weaving Mill; 1934) deals with socialist construction and production. The heroes are young workers in a silk-weaving mill where most of the employees are Jews. Aminov's *Piri bedin* (The Old Atheist; 1934) focuses on new features in the way of life, as does Haimov's *Yatimchaho* (The Little Orphans; 1934), which describes the sufferings of two brothers orphaned by the murder of their parents by the Basmachis (Muslim guerrilla fighters against the Soviets) and how one of them finds happiness in a children's home and the other in a factory school of industrial apprentices.

The documentary feature story (a genre characteristic of Soviet prose in general and known by its Russian term as *ocherk*) was developed in this period. It was characterized by an extremely high degree of ideological involvement, which was sometimes expressed in overt sloganizing and the saturation both of the author's text and the dialog of the characters with ready-made newspaper clichés. These stories include Aharun Saidov's *Az mahalla ba kolkhuz* (From the Jewish Quarter to the Kolkhoz; 1934); Ishhoqboev's *Tuyi Zaevu Adino* (The Wedding of Zeev and Adina; 1934), a sketch from the life of the Jewish collective farm in which the hero and heroine are, naturally, shock-workers (workers who surpass the norm) in the socialist fields; and Yahudaev's *Kolkhuzi namuna* (The Model Kolkhoz; 1934).

The versification of official ideology, notably of those aspects which were at a given time supposed to be "instilled," "achieved," "converted into reality," and so forth occupies an extremely important place in Bukharan Jewish poetry in the 1930s. Perhaps one of the most striking examples of the versification of the official prescriptions is Pinhos Abramov's poem *Shish sharti rafiq Stalin* (The Six Conditions of Comrade Stalin; 1934). This was given a subtitle which described the author's specific purpose without ambiguity—*Mukhtasar ba tariqi she'rquyi* (Summary in Verse). Indeed, Abramov's poem is nothing other than a synopsis in verse form of Stalin's ideas of 1931 on "the success of the construction of the Soviet socialist economy," known in contemporary Soviet jargon as "The Six Historic Conditions of Comrade Stalin."

THE NON-ASHKENAZI JEWISH COMMUNITIES 407

In its formal aspects Bukharan Jewish poetry during these years was in many respects almost identical to poetry in Tadzhik. Like its Tadzhik counterpart, Bukharan Jewish poetry continued to remain on the whole true to the traditional quantitative meters. The most notable poets of this period were Korgar (poetical pen name of Yunoton Kuraev; 1908–85) who published the collections of poetry *Mevayi inqilob* (Fruit of the Revolution; 1932) and *Bayroqi zafar* (The Banner of Victory; 1935), and the long poems *Dah sol* (Ten Years; 1935) and *Deputat* (Deputy; 1940);[126] and Muhib-Bachaev, author of three books of poems *Bahori surkh* (Red Spring: 1931), *Quvati kolektivi* (The Collective Strength; 1931), and *Sadoyi mihnat* (The Voice of Labor; 1932). The latter poet combined a mastery of the Persian and Judeo-Persian classical tradition with experiments in the application of Russian poetical forms. Among others he sometimes published poems about nature, which were fairly unusual for the poetry of those years. Other poets, H. Kaykov, Y. Hakhamov, and K. Yusupov, also published works in this period.

The years of the "Great Terror" did not spare Bukharan Jewish culture. Most of the arrests in Central Asia and therefore in the Bukharan Jewish community were in 1938. Writers, journalists, and teachers, many of whom constituted the elite and major driving force of Bukharan Jewish culture, were arrested, imprisoned, and sent to camps. Among the arrested were the poets Y. 'Oqilov and Muhib-Bachaev, the playwright M. Aminov, the editor in chief of *Bayroqi mihnat*, A. Saidov, the paper's administrative manager, Haim Kabontarov, the linguist Yaquv Kalontarov (1903–87), and the head of the Bukharan Jewish department of the Uzbek State Publishing House, Rahamim Badalov.[127] 'Oqilov and Y. Kalontarov were released within a relatively short time in the course of the Stalin-Beria campaign of demonstratively freeing a small number of "guiltlessly calumniated." Aminov was imprisoned for several years,[128] while Muhib-Bachaev spent sixteen years in jail, camps, and exile, and Saidov, H. Kalontarov, and Badalov died behind bars.

The arrests were undertaken against the background, and possibly as a part, of the closing down of all Bukharan Jewish cultural activities. In 1938, too, the publication of *Bayroqi mihnat* and *Adabiyoti soveti* was discontinued and the Jewish theater and museum in Samarkand were closed.[129] According to a decision of the Central Committee of the Communist Party of Uzbekistan read out to the last editor in chief of *Bayroqi mihnat*, Y. Kuraev, (but never made public), the newspaper was closed down since it had fully completed its revolutionary duty and the cultural and political level of Bukharan Jewish toilers had become high enough.[130] Evidently about the same time, in 1938–39, the Bukharan Jewish clubs were closed too. With the beginning of the conversion of Central Asian languages from the Latin to the Cyrillic alphabet, Judeo-Tadzhik was left unconverted. This meant that it was doomed to disappear as a language of publishing and instruction. As a reason for the discontinuation of its functioning as such it was stated—orally, but again never made public—that, according to the scholarly opinion the authorities asked for, the language of the Bukharan Jews was not a language of its own, but a dialect of Tadzhik.[131] In 1940, publications and instruction in Judeo-Tadzhik were halted and thus the demolition of Bukharan Jewish culture activities became complete.

Now almost half a century after this demolition one can only wonder what real meaning and real use, if any, the recently publicized decision about establishing a council for Bukharan Jewish literature in the Uzbekistan Writers' Union can have.[132] To try to play on the fashionable terminology of today, this reconstruction *(perestroika)* looks more like a case of mere *glasnost'* (in its original meaning—proclaiming in public). Practically speaking there is no way to reestablish the Bukharan Jewish culture *ex nihilo*.

V

It was only in 1920 that the Bolsheviks established themselves relatively firmly in the main areas inhabited by the Mountain Jews, Dagestan and Azerbaidzhan. In the Mountain Jewish community, as among the Krymchaks and the Bukharan Jews, several amateur theatrical companies were founded by Mountain Jews who supported Soviet power at a very early stage of Bolshevik rule. At least two of these companies were founded by groups which combined pro-Soviet sympathies with some sort of Zionist aspirations. One of them, established in Baku in 1922, functioned at a club named after the leader and ideologue of Marxist Zionism, Ber Borokhov (1881–1917).[133] The club operated under the auspices of the Caucasus Regional Committee of the EKP (Russian acronym for Jewish Communist party), *Poale Zion*. The head of the theatrical company was Herzl Ravvinovich-Gorskii (b. 1904 or 1906, executed 1937), son of the Baku Mountain Jewish chief rabbi, Efraim Ravvinovich.[134] Ravvinovich was also the editor of the newspaper *Korsokh* (The Toiler), the organ of the Caucasus Regional

Committee of the EKP and its Youth League which was launched on 5 February 1922, with its premises at the Borokhov club.

Another theatrical company, that in Derbent, was a natural continuation of the theatrical activities which had begun there at the beginning of the century. On the eve of the Soviet takeover and subsequently, it was headed by Manashir Sholumov.[135] In its early Soviet stage its repertoire included plays on both Soviet and Bible-related themes.[136] It is quite possible that the Derbent company, like its Baku counterpart, had links with EKP *Poale Zion*. By analogy with the situation in Central Asia, it is also likely that the company had links with *Tarbut*, the Zionist-oriented cultural organization which operated in the early years of Soviet rule. In 1922 the local Soviet authorities appointed Yuno Semenov (1899–1961) to take charge of the company's activities. Indeed, Semenov has been officially (or almost officially) acknowledged as the "founder of the Tat theater."[137] Not later than early 1924 the company was renamed GEM, a Russian acronym for *Gorsko-evreiskaia molodezh'* (Mountain Jewish Youth).[138] In 1920 amateur theatrical companies are said to have been established in Kuba and Port-Petrovsk (renamed Makhachkala in 1922).[139]

Members of these amateur companies were the authors of the first Mountain Jewish plays. It seems certain that the scripts provided considerable possibilities for improvisation. Some were apparently naive attempts to create a revolutionary drama. This was the case, for example, with the play *Podshoh, rabi va 'oshir* (The Tsar, the Rabbi, and the Wealthy Man) which was performed in Kuba in 1920; its author, Ya'ghu Aharunov, was thirteen years old at the time. To judge from its name, a similar case was that of P. Sharbatov's *Kuk savdogar—revolyutsioner* (A Merchant's Son—a Revolutionary), performed the same year in Port-Petrovsk.[140]

Issues which reflected the oncoming crisis of the community's traditional inner structure provided the major theme of many plays. Thus Herzl Ravvinovich-Gorskii's play. *Bahar das baba-daday* (The Fruits of the Parents' Deeds), performed in 1922 by the Borokhov club company, tells the tragedy of two young lovers who perish on account of their parents' attachment to traditional customs.[141] Another play, *Khublari* (The Dowry; 1929) by Y. Ben-'Ammi (pseudonym of Yasha'yo Binyaminov), attacks the custom of paying a dowry for the bride. The plays of Ya'ghu Birorov (fell in World War II), Natan Salomonov and Nikolai (Noftoli) Anisimov (d. around 1966) dealt with similar issues.[142]

Undoubtedly, the most remarkable playwright of this period was Semenov, who also wrote poetry and short stories. Semenov's most popular plays in the 1920s were *'Amaldana ilchi* (The Clever Matchmaker; 1924), *Du alatfurukhho* (Two Sellers of Second-hand Goods; 1924), and *Mahsum* (1927), which was especially popular and performed until the late 1930s.[143] It dealt with the topical issue of the right of young people to decide their own future, without being subject to the authority of the head of the family. The actual plot was taken from a folk tale about the tragic love of the princess Afris for the handsome youth Mahsum.

Only one play on a Bible-related theme is known to us by name. This is *Amnun va Tomor* (Amnon and Tamar), a Judeo-tat dramatization of Mapu's *Ahavat Tsiyon*.[144] The identity of the author of the Judeo-Tat stage version of Mapu's novel, which was performed in Derbent under the Soviets not later than 1922, is unknown. There are also no data of any Judeo-Tat translation of Mapu's novel that might have preceded its appearance on the stage.

Mountain-Jewish drama of the 1920s was strongly influenced by contemporary Azerbaidzhani drama. Each play was characterized by simplicity of plot, an unidimensionality of characters, and an abundance of couplets not necessarily connected with the plot.

If for the Mountain Jewish playwright of the 1920s the stage was virtually the only vehicle through which he could communicate with his public, the major vehicle for poets and story writers was unquestionably the press. The history of the Soviet Mountain Jewish press begins in 1924: the first organ appeared in Nalchik, the capital of Kabardo-Balkaria, where a relatively small number of Jews lived, concentrated in a ghettolike quarter. The newspaper was an organ of the local party committee and the Soviet administrative authority. Apparently in March 1924 the paper began to appear in four languages—Russian, Kabardino-Cherkassian, Qarachay-Balkarian, and Judeo-Tat. Its title was the *Krasnaia Kabarda* (Red Kabarda); in May 1924 it became the *Kabardino-Balkarskaia bednota* (The Kabardino-Balkar Poor) and in April 1931 it was replaced by three separate monolingual newspapers, Judeo-Tat being dropped.[145]

Another paper which contained texts in Judeo-Tat was *Serlo* (Light),[146] the organ of the city and regional party committees and city and regional soviets in Groznyi, the capital of the Chechen Autonomous Region, where a group of Mountain Jewish cultural activists emerged led by Zakoi Khudainatov, author of a children's Judeo-Tat primer *Avali abat* (The First Step; 1928).[147] Here too the Jewish population was relatively small and the

Judeo-Tat material was allotted a much smaller place (a few columns) in *Serlo* than in *Kabardino-Balkarskaia bednota*. This Judeo-Tat "corner" was probably launched early in 1929,[148] and could not have long survived the ending of the Judeo-Tat page in the Nalchik paper.

A separate Mountain Jewish newspaper, the weekly *Zahmatkash* (The Toiler), was started in Derbent on 3 June 1928. It appeared under this title until November 1938, and later as *Ghirmizina astara* (Red Star); it ceased publication a month after the German invasion of the USSR (the last registered issue is of 23 July 1941).[149] The Soviet authorities refused a request on the part of Mountain Jewish cultural activists shortly after the paper began appearing to convert it into a daily and publish a monthly literary magazine as a supplement.[150] *Zahmatkash* played an important role in Judeo-Tat literary life in the years 1928–41. Its first editor was 'Asoil (Asael) Binaev (1882–1958), a *maskil* rabbi (i.e., a rabbi who had had secular education) who became a communist at an early stage of Soviet rule in Derbent. A literary circle which included most of the Mountain Jewish litterateurs of the time emerged around the paper.

The Mountain Jewish poets of the 1920s—Yahiil Matatov (1888–1943), Rahamim Rubinov (1893–1955), Yishogh Hanukhov (1903–71), Yuno Semenov, Ya'ghu Aharunov, Boris Gavrilov (b. 1908), Natan Salomonov, and Zavulun Nabinovich—dealt mainly with topical social and political themes. Since the newspaper was virtually the only literary outlet, poetry increasingly reflected current affairs.

As in Bukharan Jewish drama, the theme of women's emancipation took pride of place in Mountain Jewish poetry of the time. The theme was expressed mainly through contrasting Soviet declarations on the "liberation of women from bondage" with the lot of the Mountain Jewish woman in pre-Soviet times. (In reality, their position in the late 1920s did not differ from that of earlier times.) This theme appears in Y. Aharunov's *Dukhdar doghi* (The Mountain Maiden; 1928), Y. Hunukhov's *Ay, zan mizrah* (Oh, Oriental Woman; 1928), and poems by Y. Matatov, B. Gavrilov, and others. Y. Hanukhov's *Jofokasha daday* (The Toiling Mother: 1928), in which the tough domestic chores of a Mountain Jewish mother are portrayed realistically and with emotion, appears to be the only poem of this type not characterized by a monotonous declaratory style.

Prose works in Judeo-Tat began to be published only in the late 1920s. One of the first prose writers was Y. Semenov. His best story, *Oshnahoy an rabi Hasdil* (The Mistresses of Rabbi Hasdil; 1928–29) focused on the (fairly successful) caricature of the principal hero—a hypocrite rabbi, crook, drunkard, and lecher. Despite the negative character of the rabbi the story is not basically antireligious. It is unclear whether this was deliberate, in accordance with the tactic of attacking religion indirectly,[151] or whether it reflected the author's instinctive attitudes.

Literary criticism in Judeo-Tat also dates from the late 1920s. Like general Soviet criticism of the period, it was dogmatic and unsophisticated. Aharunov was the main representative of this genre. The following two articles by him are typical of both author and period: *Nuvus dagor hoymu va Leninizm-bolshevizm* (Our Writers and Leninism-Bolshevism) and *Revolutsiyay kulturi va jofokashhoy juhurun doghi* (The Cultural Revolution and the Toiling Mountain Jews), articles whose titles reflect their content. In 1928 the decision was finally taken to convert the Judeo-Tat writing system into the so-called "Latinized" (i.e., the Latin) alphabet.[152] In April 1929 a "Mountain Jewish alphabet conference" was held in Baku, the capital of Azerbaidzhan.[153] The conversion process continued throughout 1929 and in 1930 practically everything published in Judeo-Tat was printed in the new alphabet.

At the beginning of the 1930s, a literary circle of Mountain Jews was established in Moscow. The circle ran parallel to that of Derbent, which remained the principal centre of Mountain Jewish literature. The Moscow circle was linked to the Tat section of Tsentroizdat (the central publishing house for minority languages) that existed from February 1931 to mid-1934. Major figures in the Moscow circle were Y. Ben-'Ammi (Binyaminov), who headed the section, and N. Anisimov. Its few members were mostly students in higher educational institutions and when most of them graduated in the mid-1930s the circle ceased to exist. The most prominent of them were: the poet, playwright, and prose writer Mishi (Moshe) Bakhshiev (1910–1972); the poet Manuvah (Manoah) Dadashev (1913–43); the poet Daniil Atnilov (1915–68), and the first professional translator from Russian into Judeo-Tat, Zavulun Bakhshiev.

In 1934 a third Mountain Jewish literary circle emerged—in Baku. This resulted from a decision adopted on 17 June 1934 by the Central Committee of the Communist Party of Azerbaidzhan to launch a Judeo-Tat newspaper, *Kommunist,* and a Mountain Jewish section in the Azerbaidzhan Gosizdat (State Publishing House) which was intended to replace the Moscow Judeo-Tat publishing operations. Y. Aharunov was appointed to head both.[154] *Kommunist* was first published in September 1934.[155] Aharunov's deputy in the publishing establishment was Y. Semenov, who moved from Derbent to Baku in late 1934. These two became the leading figures in the literary circle. Other important participants were the poet Divyo (Tuvya) Bakhshiev (b. 1914), the brother of Mishi Bakhshiev, and the folklorist and lexicographer 'Avadyo 'Avadiaev. In May 1938 *Kommunist*'s publication was discontinued. Evidently about the same time the regional newspaper of the town of Kuba (Azerbaidzhan) with a substantial Mountain Jewish population, *Gyzyl Guba* (Red Kuba), dropped its Judeo-Tat section. On an unknown date in late 1937 the Mountain Jewish section of the Azerbaidzhani SSR *Gosizdat*, was also closed.[156] In this way the Baku circle virtually ceased to exist, as did all public activity and all publishing in Judeo-Tat in Azerbaidzhan. As far as we know, the reasons for this were never made public.

The main genre of Mountain Jewish literature in the 1930s was poetry. The poets who began writing in the 1920s continued to publish. The most prolific of them was Y. Semenov, whose works continued to center on the struggle against religion. A clear example of this subject is his poem *Ari sifirtura vosdora* (To Buy a Tora Scroll). Another major theme of his poetry in this period was the solidarity of the workers of the world, for example in *Ari bikorhoy Germaniya* (To Germany's Unemployed). By the early 1930s a young generation of poets who had grown up and been educated in the Soviet period had begun to occupy a leading position in Judeo-Tat poetry. In 1932 M. Bakhshiev published his first collection of poems, *Komsomol*. M. Bakhshiev's poetry, like that of many poets of "the Soviet East" of that period, praised dedication to socialism (*Zarblu jofo* ["Shock" Work]; 1936) and the friendship of Soviet nationalities (the poem *Kosta*, 1936, devoted to the leading Ossetian poet, Kosta Khetagurov). The crisis of the traditional structure of Mountain Jewish life occupies a special place in the poems of M. Bakhshiev wrote in the 1930s. This subject is tackled for the most part by a blissful description of how the Mountain Jews were becoming rooted in Soviet reality. The best of his poems on this subject is *Muhbat* (Love), a dialogue between a mother who attempts to persuade her daughter to agree to an arranged marriage and the daughter who rejects this idea.

In his *Zanho a kolkhoz* (Women in the *Kolkhoz*; 1933) D. Bakhshiev deals simultaneously with the "woman problem" and the establishment of collective farms. The main theme of the poem is the refusal of the men to accept women as equal members in the *kolkhoz*.

M. Dadashev is particularly successful in tackling the issue of women.

His poem on this theme *Du koqhoz* (Two Letters; 1934) is possibly the best Mountain Jewish poem of the 1930s. It is written in the form of a correspondence between the lovers Pisah and Mozol. Although it is not lacking in ideological slogans and clichés, it is far superior to most Mountain Jewish poetry in its compact and balanced structure, lyrical qualities, and profound analysis of the characters of the heroes.

The major characteristics of Judeo-Tat poetry of the 1930s are its increasing remoteness from traditional folkloristic prosody and the transition to the syllabotonic prosody and rhyming patterns of Russian poetry. Poems written in the folkloristic prosody are normally called *ma'ni*, in line with the traditional terminology, while those written in the Russian prosody are known by the Russian terms *stikhotvorenie* or *stikhi*.

Y. Semenov played the most prominent role in Mountain Jewish dramaturgy of the early 1930s just as he had in the previous decade. The theme of one of his best-known plays *Du biror* (The Two Brothers; the early 1930s) was the establishment of *kolkhozy* among the Mountain Jews. A sharp confrontation takes place between two brothers: one, Dovid, is a former Red partisan; the other, Noftoli, is a weakling who is influenced by his father-in-law, a *kulak*, who sabotages efforts to establish the *kolkhoz*. Y. Semenov's other well-known drama of this period is *Zanbaba* (The Stepmother) whose theme is mixed marriages. While this problem first became topical in the community during this period, in the play it is projected onto a dramatic situation at the beginning of the century, when the problem was virtually nonexistent. The heroes—the Mountain Jew Binami (Binyamin) and his Lezgi[157] sweetheart Zibo—are finally compelled because of their love to leave their native village.

In the second half of the 1930s the primacy in Mountain Jewish dramaturgy passed from Y. Semenov to Mishi Bakhshiev. His *Basghuni iqidho* (Victory of the Heroes; 1936), which deals with the Civil War in Dagestan, is the first heroic drama in Judeo-Tat. In 1940, M. Bakhshiev was awarded a prize as a prominent playwright of Dagestan for his play *Khori* (The Soil; 1939), whose theme was the struggle of "retrograde and harmful elements" against the "internationalization" of Mountain Jewish *kolkhozy*, that is, their unification with non-Jewish collective farms. This policy was intended by the authorities among other things, to detach the Jews from their traditions by abolishing the ethnically homogeneous framework of their way of life.

Drama in this period was artistically superior to that written in the

1920s and early 1930s. The plots had more turning points, dramatic tension was greater, and the dialogue was written more professionally. Even so, the heroes of these plays often spoke in slogans.

Mountain Jewish prose developed rather more slowly. The first novella in Judeo-Tat, M. Bakhshiev's *A pushorahi toza zindaguni* (Towards the New Life) appeared in 1932. The plot of the novella unfolds against the background of events during the prerevolutionary years and the first years of the Revolution. The heroine, Liyo (Lea), experiences several serious personal crises, including two unsuccessful marriages. Her luck finally turns— thanks to the assistance of the *Komsomol*. Although Bakhshiev wrote this novella in Moscow, it was constructed according to Azerbaidzhani models of the 1920s (simple plot and revolutionary pathos combined with melodramatic sentimentality). His second novella *Vataghachiho* (The Fisherman; 1933) is set among the Jewish fishermen of Derbent. Here, too, the story is simple and straightforward, even monotonous. Bakhshiev must, however, be given full credit for his skillful portrayal of the heroes in both of his early novellas.

Shorter prose genres are represented in this period mainly by the stories of Semenov. Artistically the most accomplished of these are *Abasi* (Twenty Copeck Coin), on the antireligious theme characteristic of his work, and *'Uzat jofora* (Honor to Labor), on life in a *kolkhoz*.

In the late 1930s documentary feature stories and feuilletons by Hizghil (Yehezqel) Avshalumov (Ovsholumov, b. 1913) began to appear in *Zahmatkash*. His first big prose work in Judeo-Tat—the novella *Basghuni jovonho* (The Victory of the Young)—was published in 1940.

The works of Hizghiyo Dadashev (b. 1854 or 1860), d. 1944) occupy a special place in Judeo-Tat prose of the 1930s. Dadashev was a professional storyteller before the Revolution and in the 1920s and 1930s. He became literate only in his final days. Many traditional stories and tales told by him were recorded in the late 1930s. Dadashev also composed tales on topical Soviet subjects, combining folkloristic motifs with Soviet slogans and clichés.

The "Great Terror" of 1936–38 struck a heavy blow at the culture, in particular the literature, of the Mountain Jews. H. Ravvinovich-Gorskii, Y. Matatov, Y. Ben-'Ammi (Binyaminov, A. Binaev, and A. 'Avadiaev were arrested, for the most part in late 1937 to early 1938. With the exception of Binaev, all of them perished in Soviet jails and forced labor camps. By the end of the 1930s Y. Aharunov and D. Bakhshiev had permanently abandoned Judeo-Tat literary work of any kind; Aharunov became a prominent party *apparatchik* in Azerbaidzhan, Bakhshiev a lecturer on party history in higher education establishments in Moscow and, from the late 1940s, a prolific author of popular books on this subject. Nothing is known of what befell Z. Khudainatov, S. Rubinov, A. Badalov, N. Salomonov, Z. Nabinovich, and Z. Bakhshiev since the late 1930s. Their names do not appear in any later publications. Thus, by the end of the 1930s the literature of the Mountain Jews had lost about half of its authors. The only Mountain Jewish literary circle which remained in existence was that of Derbent that became the Derbent-Makhachkala circle, because a number of leading Mountain Jewish writers came to live in the Dagestan capital. In 1938 Judeo-Tat was converted from the Latin to the Cyrillic alphabet. The main, and after 1941, the sole publisher in Judeo-Tat was the Dagestan *Gosizdat*, with its poor polygraphic facilities.

As we have noted above, one month after the beginning of the Soviet-German war the last Judeo-Tat newspaper ceased to appear. Several Mountain Jewish writers were conscripted, of whom M. Dadashev and Y. Birorov fell at the front. No publications in Judeo-Tat appeared in 1942–45.

Publishing was resumed in late 1946, when two tiny brochures appeared concerning the elections to the Supreme Soviet of the Dagestan ASSR and the RSFSR. On 21 July 1947 a newspaper in Judeo-Tat, *Ghirmizina 'alam* (The Red Banner), was started in Derbent. But on 25 April 1952 it was closed down, without, as far as we know, any reason being given.[158]

In 1947 two original books appeared—a collection of poems by various poets edited by Daniil Atnilov, the most active Mountain Jewish litterateur of the early postwar years, and a collection of Dadashev's tales—as well as two political brochures translated from Russian. In 1948 only one book—a collection of poems and stories by Atnilov—appeared. In 1949 nothing written originally in Judeo-Tat was published, but two small collections (69 and 34 pages, respectively) of Pushkin's works translated by Atnilov appeared. In 1950 the first postwar book by M. Bakhshiev (then still on active service), *Odomihoy yaki* (Kith and Kin), a collection of poems, stories, and plays, appeared, as did seven topical political brochures, while Sergei Izgiiaev (Siyun Hizghiyoyev, 1922–72) published the first postwar collection of works by Mountain Jewish authors. Nothing was published in 1951, and the 1952 output consisted of only one book, an 86-page collection of poems by Izgiiaev.

The closure of the 'Tat' theater in Derbent in 1946, on the pretext that it attracted only a small audience,[159] was a heavy blow to Judeo-Tat culture.

The closure of this last functioning Mountain Jewish theater put an end to Judeo-Tat dramaturgy. Like all the indigenous languages of Dagestan, Judeo-Tat had been used since 1938 as a medium of instruction for all disciplines only at the elementary school level (grades 1 through 4).[160] Apparently in the late 1940s (the exact date is unclear), however, Judeo-Tat as a medium of instruction was abolished completely and instruction at all levels was henceforth in Russian only. As of this time the Jews thus had no schools of their own. Several years later it was said in justification of this step that the authorities had complied with the desire of the Mountain Jewish population for Russian culture.[161]

It therefore seems that the anti-Semitism of the so-called "Black Years of Soviet Jewry"—the post–World War II period which reached its apogee in 1948–53—affected Mountain Jewish culture as well. By the late 1930s, the language of the community, which was usually described in Russian publications as "Tat (Mountain Jewish)," was sometimes labeled "Tat" only; in the post–World War II period this became the rule. (Judeo)-Tat continued to be one of the nine official languages of the Dagestan ASSR,[162] although as of the late 1940s it was no longer used in the schools (unlike other ethnic groups who as of 1954 were likewise deprived of the right to use their language in education, but whose languages ceased being called official languages), and as of 1952 it became the only official indigenous language of Dagestan without its own newspaper.[163] Periodicals were launched in all the indigenous "official" languages, except Judeo-Tat.[164] Furthermore, not one Mountain Jewish writer appeared either in the "Evenings of Dagestan Culture and Literature" arranged in Moscow in 1950, or in literary evenings and meetings with readers which were regularly held in the towns and villages of Dagestan in these years.[165] "The chronicle of the literary life of Dagestan" does not indicate whether the Mountain Jewish section of the Writers' Union of Dagestan operated during these years and whether the issue of its activity or otherwise ever appeared on the union's official agenda.[166]

In the mid-1950s M. Bakhshiev and H. Avshalumov returned to Dagestan after prolonged military service (twelve and fourteen years, respectively). Their return significantly strengthened the ranks of the Mountain Jewish writers but had little impact on the frequency and quantity of the printed output in Judeo-Tat; they themselves wrote during these years in Russian as well as in their mother tongue. The only book in Judeo-Tat published in 1953 (after Stalin's death) was a collection of poems by Atnilov. In 1954 the total published output in Judeo-Tat was two political brochures translated from Russian. In 1955 a limit of two original *belletristic* publications per year appears to have been established. In 1959 one of the two volumes published was *Nuvusdagorhoy tati* (Tat Writers), an almanac intended as an annual; since 1960 it has been entitled *Vatan sovetimu* (Our Soviet Homeland). It did not appear in 1961, 1967, 1969, 1972, and 1980; in the last of these years an anthology of Mountain Jewish poetry also entitled *Vatan sovetimu* was evidently a substitute for it.

After the elimination of Judeo-Tat as the language of instruction in schools, a growing number of Mountain Jews had difficulties in reading in the mother tongue and knew it only as a second language if at all, their main language being Russian. One result of the decline of Judeo-Tat is that a number of Mountain Jewish writers use Russian and not Judeo-Tat, their knowledge of which is either inadequate or nonexistent. The most prominent of these are the poet Lazar Amirov, the prosaist Feliks Bakhshiev (the son of M. Bakhshiev), the playwright Maia Nakhshunova (Nahshunova), the critic and prosaist Manashir (Menashshe) Azizov, the critic Manashir Iakubov (Ya'ghubov), the critic and literary historian Galina Musakhanova, whose principal concern is Qumyq literature, and the antireligious publicist Liudmila Avshalumova (the daughter of H. Avshalumov). These writers occasionally touch upon Mountain Jewish or general Jewish themes, or introduce Jewish themes into their other writings and their works appear in translation in *Vatan sovetimu*. The sole exception is Liudmila Avshalumova, whose theme, the Jewish religion, is explicitly Jewish. However, they are essentially writers with no ethnic affiliation, something that is unusual in Dagestan, the multiethnic character of which exists alongside strong feelings of ethnic self-identification. The presence in this group of the daughter of H. Avshalumov and the son of M. Bakhshiev is characteristic of the second generation of the Soviet Mountain Jewish cultural elite who—like the second generation of the Soviet Yiddish-language cultural elite—have abandoned their mother tongue, at least as a means of literary self-expression, in favor of Russian.

Notwithstanding the above, an open letter in 1961 to an American newspaper, signed by five prominent Mountain Jews, including H. Avshalumov and M. Bakhshiev, claimed that the Mountain Jews "enjoy broad opportunities for developing our language and our culture."[167]

Unlike in the 1920s, when dramaturgy was the leading genre of Judeo-Tat literature, and the 1930s, when poetry occupied this position, since the

1950s prose has been at the forefront. M. Bakhshiev and H. Avshalumov are the central figures in prose. In the years immediately following his return to Dagestan, Bakhshiev published several collections of works in Russian: *Rasskazy o moikh zemliakakh* (Tales About My Countrymen; 1956); a collection of short stories, *Prostye liudi* (Common Folk; 1958); and a collection of documentary feature stories about collective farmers, *Zashumiat sady* (The Gardens Will Rustle; 1962). A characteristic feature of these works is the author's insistence on appearing primarily not as a Mountain Jewish but as an all-Dagestani writer. Only a few of the works in these collections deal with subjects derived from the life of the Mountain Jews. The best among them is the documentary story *Gyul'boor* (published also in Judeo-Tat in M. Bakhshiev, *Odomihoy vatanma, Vikhda omora nuvusda chiho* (People of My Homeland, Selected Works; 1960). This story concerns the life of Gulbohor Davydova (Dovidova), a collective farmer from Derbent who was awarded the title of Hero of Socialist Labor for her achievements in viticulture. The majority of characters in Bakhshiev's Russian-language works are not Mountain Jews but members of other Dagestani ethnic groups.

Bakhshiev's greatest achievement in prose is the first Judeo-Tat multi-plotted novel, *Khushahoy ongur* (Bunches of Grapes; 1963). Its main plot is typical of the so-called *"kolkhoz* novel," a genre which was widespread in Soviet literature in the 1950s and 1960s, and it focused on a clash between an innovator in viticulture and those favoring old-fashioned methods. But this plot is interwoven with several others—a family saga, a war theme, a picaresque theme, and the life story of the writer 'Asoil Binayev which is told mainly by means of a flashback device. This last theme contains criticism of aspects of life under Stalin which Bakhshiev develops in a rather hesitant way, indicating self-censorship. Though hesitant and inconsistent, Bakshiev was, in fact, the only Mountain Jewish writer to attempt to "square accounts" with the Stalin era.

Avshalumov writes less on the war than Bakhshiev. Three stories by him on this theme appeared in *Dusdi* (Friendship; 1956), the first collection he published following his demobilization. He subsequently dealt with this subject surprisingly rarely. In Avshalumov's prose, all-Dagestani themes too are less pronounced than in that of Bakhshiev, though their number is substantial. Thus, many of Avshalumov's humorous and satirical writings of the late 1950s and early 1960s deal with the Dagestani Muslim environment. In the short story *Vokhurdai an sar bilogh* (Encounter at the Spring), he portrays humorously but in a positive light the men from a Dagestani Muslim village who, contrary to traditions, help their wives to bring water from the spring. In the short story *Mughoray Soymishiho* (The Lovers' Cave) the abduction of the bride, a deeply rooted tradition among the Muslims of the Caucasus, is reduced to a mere farce. The short story *Dardhoy pira Hasan* (The Sufferings of Old Hasan) depicts the feelings of an old Muslim about pig-breeding in his *kolkhoz*. The best work by Avshalumov on a general Dagestani theme is his Russian-language novella *Tolmach imama* (The Interpreter of the Imam; 1967). The hero is a Russian soldier captured by Muslim insurgents who befriends his captors, marries a local girl, and becomes the interpreter of the *imam* Shamil, the leader of the anti-Russian struggle of the Caucasian Mountain Muslims in 1834–59.

Many of Avshalumov's stories portray the present-day life of the Mountain Jews of Dagestan. Two of his documentary stories are about the Mountain Jewish Heroes of Socialist Labor, the viticulturalists Gulbohor Davydova (mentioned above) and Shalmu (Shlomo) Rabaev. He describes with gentle irony the everyday life of the Jewish village in the short stories '*Ajal zanho* (Women's Death), *Shuvar an du hovu* (The Husband of Two Wives), *Maslahat na hunghar* (Edifying Talk and Hunghar—A Popular Dish), all written in the mid-1950s to early 1960s. Avshalumov's principal interest is the traditional way of life of the Mountain Jews. The novella *Zanbirar* (The Sister-in-Law; 1971) deals with the life of the social elite of the Mountain Jews in Derbent at the time of the Revolution. While his portrait of this circle of wealthy Mountain Jews is distinctly critical, his detailed reconstruction of the traditional way of life betrays his interest in it.

The time span of the novella *Kuk qudil* (The Jester's Son; 1974) is the years 1908–17.[168] In this novella, too, the author describes the traditional Mountain Jewish way of life on the verge of its disappearance. The portrayal of many of the characters—their dress, living quarters, and leisure pursuits—is effected with almost sculptural detail and an ethnographer's precision. By this means, a vibrant picture of the life of the Mountain Jewish village immediately prior to the Soviet period is conveyed. There is a deep inner contradiction in this novella. On one hand, the way in which Avshalumov describes the traditional Mountain Jewish way of life obviously expresses his nostalgia for its lost integrality; on the other hand, his ideological aim is to create, on the model of the Russian revolutionary epic, a Mountain Jewish epic canvas of the Revolution, which led to this loss.[169]

Avshalumov's story *Dovid—vazir Khon an Tabasaru* (Dovid, Vizir of Tabasaran's Kban; mid-1950s) is an adaptation of a Mountain Jewish legend concerning the establishment of the village Nugdi (Mushgur). According to the legend, the Jewish founders of the village fled from Tabasaran on learning that the ruler was contemplating converting them to Islam. The idea of the Jews' readiness to abandon a place they had inhabited for hundreds of years solely in order not to betray their religion is unacceptable to Avshalumov. In his adaptation, therefore, the Jews escape from Tabarasan because the ruler wishes to avail himself of the *ius primae noctis*, a right nonexistent among the Muslims, including those of Dagestan. Another addition to the legend is the "friendship of the peoples" theme—a must for a Soviet writer, in particular a non-Russian one. Avshalumov, however, pays much attention to preserving the characteristic style of the Mountain Jewish legends and his story therefore appears fairly authentic. He also portrays lovingly the personality of the titular hero of the legend, David the Wise, a character who has parallels in the folklore of many Jewish communities. Avshalumov also drew on Mountain Jewish folklore for his series of humorous short stories based on the folklore figure of Shimi Darbandi.

The short stories by Amladan Kukullu which appear in the collection *Sinamishi* (The Test; 1968), intended for primary school children, have a didactic purpose. But this feature is discreetly interwoven with a simple but tasteful plot, descriptions of Dagestani landscapes, and the relations between the young heroes and their parents, which are conveyed lyrically. The fact that Kukullu's works are intended for Mountain Jewish schoolchildren is ironical since the children now learn Russian at school and hence read Russian and not Judeo-Tat, the teaching of which, as we have seen, was abolished about two decades before the appearance of this small volume.

The novella *Birorho* (Brothers) by Mikhoil Dadashev merits attention as a quasi-artistic response to the recent emigration movement among the Mountain Jews. Though published in 1980 it was written (or completed) in 1977, during the high tide of the Mountain Jews' emigration to Israel, in Derbent, where, at that time, almost every Jewish family was influenced by the spirit of *aliya* (emigration to Israel). *Brothers* is a biography of sorts set against the background of the history of Derbent in the Soviet period. Fourteen of its sixteen chapters are devoted to the period up to 1922, while the remaining chapters hastily summarize the period since then. At the beginning and throughout the main part of the story, the hero Oshir is a poor young Mountain Jew (the author prefers the designation "Tat") from Derbent who joins the Bolsheviks and fights heroically against their enemies, of whom the Zionists are presented as the most insidious. At the end of the story, Oshir is a retired colonel and director of a large factory. Oshir's brother Shanda leaves his native land at an early stage only to undergo trials and tribulations in the United States and, especially, in Israel. He eventually dies from a heart attack brought on by his joy when, after several refusals, the Tel Aviv authorities permit him to return to Derbent. In this way, a Soviet phenomenon—the denial of the right to leave—is projected by the author onto Israel.

Post-Stalin Mountain Jewish poetry remained for the most part on the same artistic level as that of the 1930s. Thus one of Semenov's last poems *Ma shohidum* (I Am a Witness) is a song of praise to the Soviet system absolutely indistinguishable from its kind in the 1930s, except that Stalin is not mentioned, Bakhshiev, too, published poetry from time to time. His preferred theme remains the emancipation of the woman. He deals with this theme in the same way as he did in the poems he wrote in the 1930s, although the situation of the Mountain Jewish woman had changed considerably in the meantime. In his long poem *Agronom* Bakhshiev praises a young Mountain Jewess who has acquired a new, "male," profession. In another long poem, *Igid jofo* (The Hero of Labor), he once again praises the viticulturist Gulbohor Davydova.[170] Bakhshiev's sole innovation in relation to his poetry of the 1930s is a shift from Mountain Jewish to general Dagestani subjects, similar to the shift in some of his prose works. Thus in his poem *Zanhoy doghi* (The Women Mountaineers), each four-line stanza praises a woman who belongs to one of the ethnic groups of Dagestan in the following order: a Lezgi, a Dargwa (Dargin), an Avar, a Mountain Jewess (designated a "Tat"), a Qumyq, and a Lakk.

The meter and rhyme in all these poems are in accordance with Russian prosody models. However, his *Nanni nanam* (Lullaby) imitates the intonation and style of the Mountain Jewish folkloristic lullaby. The poem exudes the warmth of a lullaby, notwithstanding the last stanza in which the motif of comparing the bad old days with the good new ones is repeated for the umpteenth time. In his poem *Chastushkahoy kolkhozi* (Kolkhoz Chastushkas), Bakhshiev adapts a Russian folkloristic genre, (a *chastushka* is a four-line song of humorous or satirical content.)

The most remarkable poet of these years is D. Atnilov. During the period under discussion Atnilov lived permanently in Moscow, where he was isolated from everyday Judeo-Tat speech. This was, evidently, the reason for his acute sensitivity for the language; indeed, his Judeo-Tat is much purer and his loans from Russian fewer than is the case with poets who lived within the Judeo-Tat-speaking community. Intent on demonstrating the richness of his mother tongue, Atnilov uses words which are archaic in everyday speech, including Hebrew words displaced by Russian and Azerbaidzhani borrowings. His poetry also shows the influence of his Moscow circle of Russian poets, who in the late 1950s were intensively seeking new forms and means of poetic expression. The posthumous collection of poems, *Gulhoy insoni* (The Flowers of Mankind; 1971), which sums up Atnilov's poetry in the 1950s and 1960s, includes poems with a free meter, a varying number of lines per stanza, and rhymes intentionally lacking in precision characteristic of the innovative Russian poets of the time.

Atnilov wrote only a few poems on specific Mountain Jewish themes, possibly on account of his isolation from the Mountain Jewish milieu. His major subjects are either all-Soviet or all-Dagestani. Examples of the former are two of his large poems, *Zoia,* about the renowned partisan Zoia Kosmodemianskaia, and *Valentina Tereshkova,* about the Soviet woman cosmonaut (this was his last big work). Examples of his all-Dagestani themes are *Zavod Dagogni* (The Plant "Lights of Dagestan"), *Ghalay Darband* (The Fortress of Derbent), *Kholi 'Asanat* (Asanat's Carpet; about a Tabasarani carpet weaver), and *'Aziza Dagestan* (Dear Dagestan). The use of the Russian "Dagestan" instead of the Judeo-Tat "Doghistu" in this last poem stresses the poem's all-Dagestani character, since Russian is the common language of all ethnic groups of Dagestan.

Another outstanding poet of the period—and a prolific one—is Izgiiaev. Many of his poems contain reminiscences of the war, in which he was an active participant; there is much pathos and rhetoric, as in so much Soviet war poetry, but also sincerity. The poem *Usdo* (The Master) depicts his meeting as a youth with the old *ma'nikhu* (poet-cum-singer) Shoul Simandu. The *ma'nikhu* here symbolizes the tradition of Mountain Jewish poetry, and the poem may be seen as a declaration by the poet that his work is a continuation of a revered tradition.

Topical themes occupy considerable place in the poems of Shimshun Safonov, as in the works of most Mountain Jewish poets. Their quality differs little from other works of this genre, although many of his poems about Dagestani landscapes are distinguished by sincerity and refinement of description. This is the case with some of the poems in his collection *Parza ma'ni ma* (Fly, My Song; 1968), and several others which appeared in *Vatan sovetimu*. Zoia Semendueva (Simanduyeva) began to publish poetry in the 1960s. Her collections *Voygay dul* (The Heart's Desire; 1967), *Komuna* (The Rainbow; 1974), and *Uchitel'* (The Teacher; 1981) are intended for schoolchildren and generally deal with topical subjects, but her unremitting search for new poetic forms must be held to her credit. In the late 1970s, anti-Zionist poems were published parallel with the Jewish emigration of the period. An example of this genre is B. Gavrilov's *Pashmuni* (Repentance) which is written in the form of a statement in rhyme by Mountain Jewish emigrants to Israel.

There were few works of drama in Judeo-Tat in the post-Stalin period. As with poetry these works were not superior to the average artistic level of the Mountain Jewish dramaturgy of the 1930s. There seems to be a direct correlation between this fact and the diminishing role of the Mountain Jewish theater. When the authorities closed down the last professional Mountain Jewish theater in 1946, and its actors dispersed in various directions, two of them took up employment in Mountain Jewish *kolkhozy* as instructors of amateur theatrical circles.[171] In the early 1960s a wider framework for amateur theatrical activity was reestablished on the basis of these two existing dramatic circles. At first called the "Inter-*Kolkhoz* Tat Theater" of Derbent, it was renamed the "Tat People's Theater" in 1966.[172] One play of above-average quality is M. Bakhshiev's *Du daday* (Two Mothers; 1965), which centers on a confrontation between a natural and an adoptive mother. The play by Semen (Shim'un) Yusufov (now in Israel), *Jufda parusdakho* (A Pair of Swallows; 1966–68), which deals with contemporary Mountain Jewish life, as well as H. Avshalumov's comedy *Domor na 'arus* (Bridegroom and Bride; 1960) and his stage adaptation of his *Dovid— vazir Khon an Tabasaru* (named *Toza maskan,* The New Dwelling Place) also merit a mention.

One thesis that has become more and more manifest in the Mountain Jewish publications of the post-Stalin period deserves special attention. It is the thesis that the Mountain Jews are not a part of the Jewish people but comprise a *sui generis* ethnic entity, namely "Tats." This thesis was apparently first advanced by N. Anisimov in 1932 in a book which was the first and, alas, the only Judeo-Tat grammar in Judeo-Tat.[173] At that time the thesis was so alien to the community that it was stillborn. Atnilov revived it in the late 1950s. In 1960 he published a poem under the title *Khalgh tati*

(The Tat People) in which he describes "the Tat people" as one of the forty-plus peoples of Dagestan and a "tiny people" of Iranian origin.[174] In an undated poem in praise of his mother tongue, A *zuhun tati* (*In the Tat Language*), published posthumously, Atnilov refers to "my Tat people."[175] The theme was put forward once more in the mid-1970s in Mountain Jewish publications, when an acute feeling of Jewishness was inclining thousands of Mountain Jews toward emigrating to Israel. The main exponent of the thesis was L. Avshalumova.[176] In the same period M. Dadashev had the principal positive non-Jewish character in his novella *Brothers* declare almost as a self-evident truth that "The Tats are not Jews."[177]

In 1979 the proponents of the thesis somehow succeeded in getting a supportive decision of the scholarly council of the Institute of Ethnography of the USSR Academy of Sciences,[178] although the thesis itself had no sound basis even in terms of the Soviet theory of ethnicity. Its lack of foundation was demonstrated by V. Chernin in his response in *Sovetish heymland*[179] to an article one of the most ardent "Tatists" of the 1980s, M. Matatov, had published in the leading Soviet journal in the field of social and cultural anthropology (in Soviet terminology—ethnography), *Sovetskaia etnografiia*.[180] In 1981 Matatov's article was republished in *Vatan sovetimu*, prefaced by the announcement of the decision of the scholarly council of the Institute of Ethnography.

However, Tatism was not just a theoretical position adopted by a number of Mountain Jewish *hommes de plume*, frustrated because of their Jewishness; it was apparently the official policy of de-Judaizing the Mountain Jews propagated with the backing of the authorities and, perhaps, on their initiative. On 20 May 1979, an announcement was published in *Dagestauskaia provda* notifying Mountain Jewish citizens that they could change the *natsional'nost'* registration in their identity cards to "Tat," and police registration departments began to conduct this re-registration. This was done— as was noted in a Jewish samizdat travelogue, "without asking the holder of the identity card, without his consent and even in the face of his non-agreement."[181] In 1986, Matatov in coauthorship with Zh. Golotvin published a further article advocating Tatism. Although this article, too, was devoid of any solid argumentation and showed the author's ignorance of the basic relevant literature (or, at best, a very defective acquaintance with a few of the publications quoted in it), it appeared in a leading Soviet historiographic journal *Voprosy istorii* and in 1987 was republished in the main Dagestani literary and political magazine *Sovetskii Dagestan*.[182] Also in 1986

H. Avshalumov, who in the past had on several occasions publicly defined himself as a Mountain Jew (including in the aforementioned open letter of 1961), published in the official CPSU organ *Sovetskaia Rossiia* an article in which he defined himself and his fellow Mountain Jews as Tats falsely described as Jews by Zionists.[183] Despite the large-scale emigration of Mountain Jews to Israel in the 1970s and its partial renewal in the very year that Avshalumov published his article when the Gorbachev leadership decided to reopen the gates, even if on a small scale, the Tatist trend put forward by the upper stratum of the community and especially its active application by the authorities cannot be ignored.

VI

The above discussion seems to lead us to some general conclusions. In order for the picture to be more complete in drawing these conclusions the author will also take into consideration his observations on the culture of the Georgian Jewish community under Soviet rule, although the Georgian findings have not been reflected in these notes.

The Sovietization of the areas inhabited by the communities under discussion found them in the process of cultural modernization. The incentives to modernization differed in each community. Yet it meant essentially the same for them all: exposure to secular studies; to secularized Hebrew and secularized Hebrew culture, predominantly that of the East European *Haskala* or Enlightenment and of the *Hibat Tsiyon* (Love of Zion, the pre-Zionist East European philo-Palestinian movement) and the early Zionist type; and to Russian and Russian culture, including the Russian-language secularized culture of the Ashkenazim of the Russian Empire (for the Georgian Jewish community the exposure to tendencies in and contacts with some rostra of contemporary Georgian culture must be added which found its expression both in the trend of the "ethnic Georgians of Israelite faith" and in the Jewish polemic on Jewish topics in the all-Georgian press). The process of modernization differed from one community to another— both horizontally (the percentage of those undergoing modernization in relation to the general size of the community) and vertically (the total sum of the social strata involved). Nevertheless, on the whole one can see it as a process in which mainly the upper strata of the various communities were involved (this postulate was less valid for the Krymchak community with its very vague social stratification; however, here modernization was restricted to the elementary education level).

Since the very beginning of Soviet rule a definite isomorphism can be observed in its behavior toward the cultural life of all four communities. In the early 1920s, in accordance with its so-called "Eastern policy," the Russian Communist party (of Bolsheviks) behaved toward these communities along the lines of the tactics it used toward all other "indigenous" ethnic groups in Russia's so-called Oriental periphery (which were predominantly Muslim, save for Armenia, Georgia, and the major part of Ossetia). A Soviet-controlled educational network was regarded as the most effective means for channeling Communist doctrine to the younger generation—the generation of the would-be "builders of socialism." Red corners (or red *chaikhanas* for Central Asian sedentary ethnic groups, including the Bukharan Jews), clubs, and amateur theatrical companies were considered the most effective tools for propagating this doctrine among the people at large. For this purpose the Communist party was ready for a time to display a permissive attitude toward the Jewish religion (for example, there was a flourishing of religious education among the Krymchaks, and kosher food was provided in the *Evsektsiia*-supervised Bukharan Jewish teachers' seminary) to the same extent as it was regarding the Georgian Orthodox church and Islam in the Crimea, Dagestan, Azerbaidzhan, and Central Asia. The Communist party was similarly prepared to make concessions to the Zionist-spirited modernist intellectuals of the communities under discussion in order to draw them into cooperation in the educational network, club, and amateur theatrical activities (through education in Hebrew in Soviet Jewish schools in Georgia and Central Asia, and plays on "nationalist" topics in clubs and amateur theatrical companies of all the communities), not unlike those it countenanced in its interaction with the Muslim reformist *jadids* (literally the new ones or innovators) in Central Asia and the Muslim modernist Left of various ilks in Dagestan and Azerbaidzhan.

The conversion of the writing systems of the Krymchaks, the Mountain Jews, and the Bukharan Jews from the Hebrew into the Roman alphabet coincided with the conversion of the writing systems of the USSR's Muslims from Arabic into various types of Roman-based alphabets and was actually planned as a part of the latter development. The "Latinizatsiia" ("Latinization," as the conversion was called) had, in addition to its declared and undoubtedly true purpose—to elevate the level of literacy—at least two further undeclared yet nonetheless true ones. The first was to tear asunder the chain of tradition, to restrict the access of the new "Latinized" generations to their cultural heritage recorded in the pre-Latinized writing system and thus to get complete control of this heritage which would either be forgotten or at best after selection and censorship only that which could be regarded and interpreted as matching the new ideology would be published in the new script. The second purpose was to divorce the indigenous population of the Soviet "East" from the broader civilization to which they belonged: the Muslim civilization, whose alphabet was Arabic, and the Jewish civilization, whose alphabet was Hebrew.

By the end of the 1930s the Soviets stopped experimentation in constructing specific Krymchak and Bukharan Jewish segments of the new Soviet civilization. Simultaneously, the specifically Jewish culture in the Georgian language, which began to emerge in the late 1920s to early 1930s and whose emergence had a striking typological resemblance to that of the Russian-language Jewish culture of the late nineteenth century, was eliminated as well, though its last vestige, the Georgian Jewish museum in Tbilisi, survived until the end of the 1940s or very early 1950s. Cultural activity in Judeo-Tat was stopped at this time in Azerbaidzhan where about half of the Mountain Jewish community resided. Absurd as it may sound when discussing the reality of the period of the Great Terror, the reason for the noncancellation of cultural activities in Judeo-Tat in Dagestan was a constitutional one. The time for abolishing not only constitutionally granted activities but even the constitutionally granted autonomies of the various ethnic groups had not yet come, and [Judeo-] Tat was constitutionally one of the official languages of the Dagestan Autonomous Republic. However, ten or so years later an essential part of cultural activity in this language—namely educational activity—was discontinued in Dagestan. Thus, although the Mountain Jews still express themselves—in a very limited way—in their own language, the community's younger generations, who have been devoid of education in this language for about forty years, prefer to express themselves in Russian. The example of the Krymchaks and the Mountain Jews shows that under circumstances of discrimination Jewish cultural elites, whose omni-Jewish identity has been weakened by the long-enforced divorce from general Jewish civilization, can endeavor to seek new, fictitious "ethnic" identifies as the only escape from being frustrated by their Jewishness.

Notes

An early version of the fourth part and a slightly different version of the fifth part of this chapter were published respectively in *Soviet Jewish Affairs*, vol. 9 (1979), no. 2, pp. 15–23 and vols. 15 (1985), no. 2, pp. 3–22 and 16 (1986), no. 1, pp. 35–52. For technical reasons the diacritics have been omitted here in transliterating from the USSR's eastern languages.

1. The term "Jewish ethnolect" is used as the adaptation on the level of sociodialectology of the definition of Jewish language proposed by me in 1979, namely: "Jewish language is a language serving in a certain area in its spoken or written form or both of these only by the Jewish population of this area"; see "Bimat hokrim. Habalshanut hayehudit—hameshutaf, hameyuhad vehabe'ayati," *Pe'amim*, 1 (1979), p. 55.
2. For a general history of the Krymchaks, see Y. Keren, *Yahadut Krim mikadmutah ve'ad hashoah* (Jerusalem: Reuven, Mass., 1981), pp. 11–53, 316–19; V. Moskovich, B. Tukan, "Adat hakrimchakim—toldotehem, tarbutam uleshonam," *Pe'amim*, 14 (1982), pp. 5–14. On Judeo-Crimean Tatar, see V. Filonenko, "Krymchakskie etuidy," *Rocznik orientalistychny*, vol. 35 (1972), no. 1, pp. 7–10; V. Moskovich, B. Tukan, op. cit., pp. 19–26; V. Chernin, "Der inhalt fun di terminen 'krimchak' un 'krimchakishe shprakh,' " *Sovetish heymland* (1983), no. 11, pp. 153–57 (Russian version—different in details: "O poiavlenii etnonima 'krymchak' i poniatiia 'krymchakskii iazyk,' " in I. Krupnik (ed.), *Geografiia i kul'tura etnograficheskikh grupp tatar v SSSR* (Moscow: Moskovskii filial geofrachicheskogo obshchestva SSSR, 1983), pp. 97–102. On the destruction of the community and its post–World War II situation. see R. Loeventhal, "The Extinction of the Krimchaks in World War II," *The American Slavic and East European Review*, vol. 10(1951), esp. pp. 135–36; Y. Ben-Tsvi (I. Ben-Zvi), *Nidhey Yisrael*, 2nd ed. (Jerusalem: Yad Yitshak Ben-Tsvi, 1967), pp. 208–11; Filonenko, op. cit., pp. 10–11; Chernin, op. cit., p. 157 (Russian version, p. 102). For relative statistical data, see M. Kupovetskii, "Dinamika chislennosti i rasseleniia karaimov i krymchakov za poslednie dvesti let," in Krupnik, op. cit., pp. 85–87.
3. For a general survey of the history of the community, see A. Ben-Meir (Kriheli [Krikheli]) and M. Neyshtat, "Gruziya," in Y. Tsur (ed.), *Hatfutsa: Mizrah-Eropa* (Jerusalem: Keter, 1976), pp. 121–42; [M. Zand], "Gruzinskie evrei," *Kratkaia evreiskaia entsiklopediia*, vol. 2 (Jeruslaem: The Society for Research on Jewish Communities, 1982 [vol. 1 was published by Keter, 1976]) henceforth cited as *KEE*, clmns. 236–45; G. Ben-Oren and V. Moskovich, "Meafyeney leshon hadibur shel yehudey Gruziya," *Pe'amim*, 31(1987), pp. 116–17. It seems, however, that their instructive analysis of the specifics of Georgian as used by Jews does not prove this thesis or, at any rate, does not meet the criteria of the definition referred to in note 1.
4. For a general survey of the history of the community, see [M. Zand], "Gorskie evrei," *KEE*, vol. 2, clmns. 182–91. The best description of Judeo-Tat is still

N. Anisimov, *Grammatik zuhun tati* (Moscow: Tsentroizdat, 1932), pp. 64–182; see also relative paragraphs in A. Griunberg and L. Davydova, "Tatskii iazyk," in V. Rastorgueva (ed.), *Osnovy iranskogo iazykoznaniia. Novoiranskie iazyki. Zapadnaia gruppa, prikaspiiskie iazyki* (Moscow: Nauka, 1982), pp. 231–85; [M. Zand]," Evreisko-tatskii iazyk," *KEE*, vol. 2, clmns. 459–62.

5. For a general survey of the history of the community, see M. Zand, "Bukhara," *Encyclopaedia Judaica Year Book, 1975–76*. (Jerusalem: Keter, 1976), pp. 183–92; M. Har-El (Babayof), *Nahalat Ya'akov* (Tel Aviv: "published by the family" [1983]), pp. 92–101. The best description of Judeo-Tat is still I. Zarubin "Ocherk razgovornogo iazyka samarkandskikh evreev (Opyt kharakteristiki. Materialy)," *Iran*, [vol.] 2 (Leningrad: Izdatel'stvo AN SSSR, 1927), pp. 95–125; see also D. Niiazov, "O iazyke sredneaziatskikh evreev," *Voprosy vostokovedeniia. Sbornik statei* (Tashkent: Izdatel'stvo AN Uzbekskoi SSR, 1979), pp. 92–100; [M. Zand], "Evreiski-tadzhikskii iazyk," *KEE*, vol. 2, clmns. 453–55.

6. Publications on this community and its branch inside the Soviet Union have so far been very scarce. See, on the latter, P. Kalika and Y. Iushvayev, "Yidnameyer," *Sovetish heymland* (1983), no. 5, pp. 166–70; E. Grossman, "Aramaic Jews: A Special Identity," *Jerusalem Post*, February 10, 1987; I. I. Krupnik and M. S. Kupovetskii, " 'Lakhlukhi'—kurdistanskie evrei v SSSR," *Sovetskaia etnografiia*, 1988, no. 2, pp. 102–10.

7. On the demographic situation of the Karaites during the Soviet period, see Kupovetskii, op. cit., pp.79–82; on their present sociolinguistic situation, see K. Musaev, *Grammatika karaimskogo iazyka. Fonetika i morfologiia* (Moscow: Nauka, 1964), pp. 6–9; V. Moskovich and B. Tukan, " 'Leshon Kedar.' Netunim leshoniim 'al motsa hakaraim utoldotehem beKrim uvMizrah Eropa," *Pe'amim*, 6, (1980), pp. 79–80.

8. See A. Zaiaczkowski, "Die karaimische Literatur," *Filologiae Turcicae Fundamenta*, vol. 2 (Wiesbaden: Otto Harrassowitz, 1964), pp. 799–800; R. Kaplanov, "K istorii karaimskogo literaturnogo iazyka," in I. Krupnik (ed.), *Malye i dispersnye etnicheskie gruppy v evropeiskoi chasti SSSR* (Moscow: Moskovskii filial geograficheskogo obshchestva SSSR, 1985), pp. 102–3.

9. See A. Ya'ari, *Sifrey yehudey Bukhara. Bibliyografya [. . .] 'im mavo* (Jerusalem: [special reprint with separate pagination from vols. 18 (1941) and 19 (1942) of *Qiryat Sefer*], 1942), pp. 2–7; W. Fischel, "The Leaders of the Jews of Bokhara," in L. Jung (ed.), *Jewish Leaders, 1750–1940* (New York: Bloch, 1953), pp. 538–42; M. Eshel, *Gallerya. Dmuyot shel rashey yahadut Bukhara* (Jaffa: Bet hatarbut lihudey Bukhara beYisrael, [1965 or 1966]), pp. 17–29; N. Tajer, *Toldot yehudey Bukhara beBukhara uvYisrael*. Two parts in one book (Tel Aviv: published by the author, 1971 [predominantly a collection of biographies; text partially in Judeo-Tadzhik]), part 1, pp. 52–63.

10. See the photoreproduction of this manuscript with introduction and commentaries in Sh. Tal (ed.), *Nosah hatfila shel yehudey Paras* (Jerusalem: Mehkon Ben-Tsvi, 1980).

11. On his Crimean period, see M. Benayahu, "Rabi Hayyim Hizkiyahu Medini (Prakim mitoldotav)," *Hemed Yisrael* (Jerusalem: Misgav ladakh, 1947), pp. 87–91.
12. On the Kaffa rite, see Y. Markon, "Maamar 'al odot mahazor minhag Kafa," in *Zikaron leAvraham Eliyahu* [Harkavi] (St. Petersburg: 1909), pp. 449–469; Sh. Bernshtayn, "Hamahazor keminhag Kafa. Toldotav vehitpathuto," in Sh. Bernshtayn and G. Hungin (eds.), *Sefer yovel likhvod Shmuel Kalman Mirski* (New York: n.p., 1958).
13. See relative statistical data based on the 1897 census in A. Bennigsen, "The Turks under Tsarist and Soviet Rule," in G. Hambly (ed.), *Central Asia* (London: Weidenfeld and Nicolson, 1969), p. 195; on the multiethnicity of the Crimea in the 1910s, see K. Iu. Bumberg (ed.), *Krym. Putevoditel'* (Simferopol: Krymskoe obshchestvo estesvoispytatelei i liubitelei prirody, [1914], pp. 284–317.
14. See I. Kaya, "Narodnoe obrazovanie u 'krymchakov'," *Vestnik evreiskogo prosveshcheniia* (March 1914), no. 29, pp. 78–79. Apparently the Simferopol "Talmud-Torah for the Children of the Krymchak Jews" founded in 1902 was its less successful predecessor.
15. See Kaya, op. cit., p. 79.
16. Ibid.
17. On this term, see J. Morrison, "Equibilingualism: Some Psychological Aspects," *The Advancement of Science*, vol. 14 (1958), no. 56, pp. 287–90; cf. also the discussion on the meaning of the concept of ambilingualism (= equibilingualism) in P. Christophersen, *Second-language Learning. Myth and Reality* (Harmondsworth, Middlesex: Penguin Books, 1973), pp. 67–68.
18. The first Mountain Jew to get a formal Russian education, a son of the chief rabbi of Sharbat Nissim-oghly in North Dagestan, was Il'ia Anisimov (1862–1920s?), who in the 1880s studied at the Moscow higher technical school. He was, undoubtedly, a very rare exception. See on him, M. Altshuler, "Eliyahu Anisimov hoker, 'adat hayehudim haharariim," *Sefunot*, new series, vol. 1 (1980), pp. 287–310.
19. I. Anisimov began to publish in Russian at the age of nineteen; see I. Anisimov, "Kavkazkie evrei-gortsy," *Rassvet* (1881), no. 18, clmns. 710–13; no. 24, pp. 948–52.
20. See Y. Ammi-Hay and A. Topchiashvili, "Yehudey Gruziya vehatarbut ha'ivrit), in B. Vest (ed.), *Naftuley dor. Korot tnu'at ha'avoda hatsionit Tse'irey Tsiyon —Hitahdut berusiya hasovietit. Leyovel 25 shana latnu'a. 1920–1945* (Tel Aviv: Mishlahat huts laarets shel Tse'irey-Tsiyon-Hitahdut berusiya, 1945), p. 308; N. Eliashvili, *Hayehudim hagruzim bigruziya uveretz-Yisrael*, edited by G. Kressel (Tel Aviv: Tcherikover, 1975), pp. 56–58. Natan Eliashvili (b. 1893, d. in Palestine 1929) was A. Khvoles's pupil and a leading Georgian Jewish Zionist; on A. Khvoles, see also G. Ben–Oren, "Harav Avraham Halevi Hvoles," in M. Cohen (ed.), *Prakim betoldot yehudey hamizrah. Homer 'ezer le'iyyun banose*, vol. 5 (Jerusalem: Ministry of Education and Culture, 1981), pp. 269–70.

21. See M. Altshuler, "Hape'ilut hatarbutit hasovietit bekerev yehudey Gruziya," *Behinot*, 6 (1975), p. 105 and note 10 there. On the educational activities of the initiator of this school, Dr. Lang, see also "Za nedeliu," *Voskhod* (1902), no. 3, clmn. 7.
22. See N. Eliashvili, op. cit., pp. 64–65.
23. See Eshel, op. cit., p. 106; Tajer, op. cit., part 2, p. 20; S. H. Asherov, *Misamarkand 'ad Petah-Tikva. Zikhronot ma'apil bukhari* (Tel Aviv: Brit yotsei Bukhara beyisrael, 1977), p. 390.
24. On all of them save Avraham Safan Mizrahi, see Ya'ari, op. cit., p. 39.
25. Zionist circles just emerging in the community can be seen as another possible source for the secularized use of Hebrew. Indirect proof of this can be seen in the fact that a, or the, Derbent delegate to the 1901 Tiflis Congress of the Zionists of the Caucasus addressed the congress in Hebrew (see the untitled and unsigned republication of the *Tiflisskii listok*, a report on the congress, in *Voskhod* [1901], no. 50, clmn. 18).
26. The use of the concept "polysystem" here in regard to the language behavior of the communities under discussion is inspired by its use in literary studies by Prof. Itamar Even-Zohar (Tel Aviv University) who was also, if I am not mistaken, the first to propose it.
27. See M. Zand, "Sifrut yehudey hahar shel Kavkaz," *Pe'amim*, 13 (1982), p. 53.
28. The only attempt known to me to investigate this impact on Mountain Jewish folklore is N. Avshalumova, "Poemay romantikai Firdousi 'Bizhan va Manizha' va ovosunay khalghi tati 'Bazhon va Manazhon'," *Vatan sovetimu* (henceforth cited as VS; see on this yearbook section 5 of this article), 1986, pp. 68–76. Avshalumova's article is to be praised for its pioneering spirit. A considerable part of a recent collection of proverbs and adages in use in the Bukharan Jewish community (I. Mahvashev, *Fol'klor va yoddoshtho* [Tel Aviv: published by the family, 1985], pp. 10–52; for the author, see the fourth part of this article) is in fact a collection of quotations from Persian classical poetry, at times changed to an extent by oral transmission through the generations.
29. See on the document D. Margoliouth, with an Introductory Note by M. A. Stein and Communications from W. Bacher, A. Cowley, and J. Wiesner, "An Early Judeo-Persian Document from Khotan, in the Stein Collection, with Other Early Persian Documents," *Journal of the Royal Asiatic Society* (1903), pp. 735–61; B. Utas, "The Jewish-Persian Fragment from Dandan-Uiliq," *Orientalia Suecana*, 17 (1968), pp. 123–26; on the inscriptions, W. Henning, "Inscriptions of Tang-i Azao," *Bulletin of the School of Oriental and African Studies*, 20(1957), pp. 335–42.
30. See G. Lazard, "La Dialectologie du judéo-persan," *Studies in Bibliography and Booklore*, vol. 8 (1968), nos. 2–4, p. 87.
31. See [M. Zand], "Evreisko-persidskaia literatura," *KEE*, vol. 2, clmn. 445.
32. See ibid., clmn. 446; [idem], Evreisko-tadzhikskaia literatura," ibid., clmn. 450.
33. Published by C. Salemann as "Chudaidat. Ein judisch-bucharisches Gedicht,"

Mémoires de l'Académie Impériale des Sciences de St.-Pétersbourg, 7th series, vol. 42(1897), no. 14 (Judeo-Persica nach St.-Petesburger Handschriften.1).
34. See Ya'ari, op. cit., p. 29.
35. The most complete list of these books is given by Ya'ari, op. cit., pp. 7–63.
36. Letter (in Hebrew) of Rabbi Yitshak Mizrahi (1795–1877) to the heads of the police of Derbent, Dagestan, as quoted in Y.-Y. Charnyi, *Sefer masa'ot beerets Kavkaz uvmedinot asher me'ever lekavkaz* (St. Petersburg; n.p. 1884), p. 48.
37. Prepared for publication by the present author. Will be published by the Ben-Zvi Institute, Jerusalem.
38. See G. Safronov (misprint for Safanov), "O teatre gorskikh evreev (vospominaniia aktera derbentskogo gosteatra gorskikh evreev)," *Krug* (1978), no. 49, p. 26; see also a letter of his quoted in N. Ilishaev, "Ostorozhno—nasil'stvennaia assimiliatisiia!" in N. Ilishaev, *S Kavkaza v Ierusalim* (Tel Aviv: S. Segal, 1981), p. 114.
39. In 1913 a preparatory school was opened there with Judeo-Tat as the language of instruction; see F. Shapiro, "Gorskie evrei (evrei-taty)," in *Feliks L'vovich Shapiro" sbornik statei i materialov* (Jerusalem: Evreiskoe agentstvo [Sokhnut], 1983), p. 74.
40. See Shapiro, op. cit., p. 75.
41. See Zand, "Sifrut Yehudey hahar," pp. 23–24, 48.
42. E. Deinard, *Masa Krim* (Warsaw: Y. Goldman, 1878), pp. 122–24.
43. See F. Perel'man, "Po povodu odnoi krymchatskoi rukopisi," *Voskhod* (1902), no. 15, clmns. 41–44.
44. See I. Kaya, "Po povodu odnoi krymchakskoi rukopisi," *Izvestiia tavricheskogo obshchestva istorii, arkheologii i etnografii*, 1 (1927), pp. 3–6.
45. See Filonenko, op. cit., pp. 11–13.
46. See Y. Ben-Tsvi (I. Ben-Zvi), "Sifrutam shel yehudey Krim," *Qiryat Sefer*, 28 (1952–53), pp. 251–54; V. Moskovich and B. Tukan. "Adat hakrimchakim," pp. 28–29.
47. See Filonenko, op. cit., p. 15; Y. Peysakh, "Krimchakes" [part 2], *Sovetish heymland* (1974), no. 7, p. 141.
48. The main writer on D. Baazov and the main collector of his works was his daughter Fanny (in Georgian pronunciation Pani, in Russianized form Faina) Baazova (1912–1980). See [F. Baazova], "Baazov David," *KEE*, vol 1, clmns. 269–70.
49. The second issue of *Khma ebraelisa* is dated 25 March (Julian calendar), 1918 (see P. Baazori (ed.), *David da Gertsel Baazoebi. Krebuli*, (Jerusalem: the Hebrew University and Tel Aviv University, 1976), p. 94. Ammi-Hay and Topchiashvili (op. cit., p. 309) and Eliashvili (op. cit., p. 65) call this organ "a weekly," and the latter maintains that it "existed approximately eight months." However, its sixth-seventh issue is dated 8 December 1918 (see the photo of a part of its front page in Baazova, op. cit., p. 138); also G. Ben-Oren. "Hasifrut hayafa shel sofrim yehudim bemea ha'esrim begruziya," in

Y. Betsalel (ed.), *Kitvey sofrim yehudim sfardim umizrahiim bilshonot yehudiyot vezarot. Seker bibliografi shel hasifrut hayafa bamea ha'esrim*, vol. 1 (Tel Aviv: Tel Aviv University, 1982), p. 207. This shows that *Khma ebraelisa* was published over a period of at least ten months, but, on the other hand, did not appear every week. A. Refaeli (Tsentsiper), *Bemaavak lageula* (Tel Aviv: Davar and 'Ayanot, 1956), p. 55, and following him M. Altshuler ("Hape'ilut," p. 105, note 9) contend that fifteen issues of *Khma ebraelisa* were published in 1919; Ben-Oren informed me that he, too, found references to issues of 1919.

50. An expression of this recognition is the presence of the Krymchaks in a list of 132 *natsional'nosti* (ethnic groups; in fact 131 are listed) in whose languages *Tsentroizdat* (the Central Publishing House of the Peoples of the USSR attached to the Central Executive Committee of the USSR) and publishing houses of the non-Russian periphery under its aegis published (127 of the languages on the list) or intended to publish. See K. Rykhlevskii, "Natsional'-naia v SSSR za 15 let," *Revoliutsiia i natsional'nosti* (1932), nos. 10–11, p. 84. See also the listing there—for the same reason—of Bukharan Jews (named "Bukharans") and of Mountain Jews (named "Tats").

51. The literature on this—both Soviet and Western—is plentiful. The ideologists of this policy saw, or at any rate put forward, as its starting point the slogan of "providing the population with schools with instruction in all local languages spelled out in an article by Lenin written in 1914 whose main theme was the denial of Russian as the obligatory state language. See V. Lenin, "Nuzhen li obiazatel'nyi gosudarstvennyi iazyk?" in V. Lenin, *Sochineniia*, 4th ed., vol. 20 (Moscow: Gosudarstvennoe izdatel'stvo politicheskoi literatury, 1948), p. 56.

52. The 1919 "Programme of the Russian Communist Party," as quoted in J. Stalin, "The Policy of the Soviet Government on the National Question in Russia" [1920], in J. Stalin, *Works*, vol. 4 (Moscow: Foreign Languages Publishing House, 1953), p. 374.

53. Ibid., p. 375 (J. Stalin's commentary on the above formula).

54. The total number of Jews in the Crimea according to this census was 39,921 (see Y. S[lutsky], "Crimea," *Encyclopaedia Judaica*, vol 5 (Jerusalem: Keter, 1971), clmn. 1107; the total number of Krymchaks in the USSR according to the census was 6,383 (F. Lorimer, *The Population of the Soviet Union: History and Prospects* (Geneva: League of Nations, 1946), p. 55; Kupovetskii, op. cit.), i.e. only 6 percent of the members of the community dwelt outside the Crimea.

55. See E. Allworth, *Nationalities of the Soviet East; Publications and Writing Systems. A Bibliographical Directory and Transliteration Tables for Iranian—and Turkic—Language Publications, 1818–1945, Located in U.S. Libraries* (New York: Columbia University Press, 1971), p. 323. See also B. Grands, "Opyt klassifikatsii novogo alfavita s tochki zreniia unifikatsii," in D. Korkmasov (ed.), *Pis'mennost' i revoliutsiia*, 1st collection (Moscow—Leningrad: VTsK N[ovogo] A[lfavita], 1933), pp. 130, 132.

56. Quoted in A. Yodfat, "Letoldot hadat hayehudit bivrit hamo'atsot," *Behinot*, 6 (1975), p. 46, note 11.
57. Ibid.
58. See Peysakh, op. cit., [part 1]. *Sovetish heymland*, 1974, no. 7, p. 177; Kupovetskii, op. cit., p. 85.
59. See Kupovetskii, op. cit., p. 85.
60. Ibid.
61. According to E. Peysakh (op. cit., [part 1], p. 175) and the anonymous author of "Kaya, Isak" (*Sovetish heymland* (1983), no. 1, p. 169 [section "Materialn far a leksikon fun der yidisher sovetisher literatur"]) I. Kaya headed the Karasubazar modernist Talmud-Torah (see the second part of this article; both call it a secular school) until 1921. Both confine themselves to a short and rather evasive indication of this fact without mentioning any reason for the termination of Kaya's headmastership. As stated, 1921 was the year the Sovietization of the Crimea began. Wherever possible the Soviets transformed the already existing schools into Soviet ones, so it stands to reason that this happened in this case too and someone else was found by the new authorities who was more suitable for heading a Soviet school.
62. See "Kul'tobsluzhivanie evreiskikh pereselentsev v Krymu," *Tribuna* (1930), no. 13, p. 18. All measures mentioned in this report are discussed with bureaucratic pedantry only at the *raion* (district) level and therefore the town of Karasubazar is not named as the place where one of the announced "16 new school buildings" will be built, but the Karasubazar *raion*.
63. On the Simferopol school, see Peysakh, op. cit., [part 1], p. 177. As to teaching in Russian, both probabilities are in accordance with the proposals of Soviet experts on the ethnic minorities' schools. On the former, see A. Chekhov, "Russkii iazyk v shkolakh natsional'nykh men'shinstv," *Prosveshchenie natsional'nostei* (1929), no. 1, p. 89 (subtype 2 of "the type normal for the national minorities' schools of the RSFSR [Russian Soviet Federative Socialist Republic]: partial instruction in Russian "because of the absence of teachers able to teach these disciplines in the mother tongue"); on the latter, see I. Davydov, "O probleme iazykov v prosvetitel'noi rabote sredi natsional'-nostei," *Prosveschenie natsional'nostei* (1929), no. 1, p. 19 (schools for the "group B" ethnic minorities—small or medium ones whose "language is poor, of local importance"; elementary school—"in the national language" (i.e. in the ethnic minority's language); secondary school—"in the language of the republic whose territory the given *natsional'nost'* inhabits, or in Russian."
64. See Peysakh, op. cit., [part 1], p. 177. Indicative of the beginning of the emergence of this trend is, e.g., the chapter on the usage of the mother tongue by B. Rodnovich, "Natsionalizatsiia (korenizatsiia) apparata," in N. Nurmakov (ed.), *Natsional'noe stroitel'stvo v RSFSR k XV godovshchine Oktiarkria* (Moscow: Izdatel'stvo 'Vlast' sovetov' pri Prezidiume VTsIK, 1933) pp. 14ff.
65. See Peysakh, op. cit. [part 1], pp. 175–76; "Kaya, Isak"; both articles avoid

mentioning that Saq-Yuda Kaya belonged to the hereditary elite of the community as evidenced by his very family name which means "manager, headman." A certain Coia, filius Adolkarem is mentioned as early as 1455 among the signatories to a petition (in the Genoese dialect of Italian) from the Jews of Kaffa to the heads of the Genoese St. George Bank (see G. Khoker, "Evrei v genuezskoi Kafe v 1455 g.," *Evreiskaia starina*, 5 (1912), p. 68. The first to publish the correct etymology of the name Kaya as having the above meaning only was I. Kotler ("Familii krymchakov kak istochnik ikh etnicheskoi istorii," in I. Krupnik (ed.), *Malye i dispersnye*, p. 87; cf. the wrong additional etymologization as "rock" on the basis of modern [Judeo-]Crimean Tatar in S. Vaisenberg, "Familii karaimov i krymchakov," *Evreiskaia starina*, 6 (1913), p. 398).

66. See Peysakh, op. cit. [part 1], p. 177.
67. Ibid., p. 176, and "Dramksuzhok Ozeta v Kerchi," *Tribuna* (1928), no. 6, p. 20.
68. Literally, "basic peasant house-reading room," i.e., a peasant house housing a reading room which serves as the basis for political educational activity.
69. See "Kul'tobsluzhivanie."
70. Accordingly, a certain part of Ozet approbations for obtaining literature must have been allotted also to *bazovye izby-chital'ni* of the Krymchak *kolkhozy*. See on this kind of approbation B. Lobovskii, "Shefiacheiki na pomosch' kollektivizatsii (pis'mo iz Kryma)," *Tribuna* (1930), no. 8, p. 18.
71. The fact that a certain Piastro (a family name specific in the USSR only for the Krymchaks) is included among the reader-reporters (the so-called local reporters *[korrespondenty s mest]* or worker-peasant reporters *[raboche-krest'ianskie korrespondenty]* of *Tribuna evreiskoi sovetskoi obshchestvennosti* proves the exposure of Krymchaks to Russian language political-educational printed material. See his letter (signed as all other letters of this kind by the family name only) in "Iz korrespondentsii OZET-korov," *Tribuna* (1931), no. 9, p. 14.
72. For the resettlement of former Pale Jews in the Crimea, see Y. Keren, *Hahaityashvut hahaklait hayehudit bahatsi hai Krim (1922–1947)* (Jerusalem: S. Zak, 1973); Y. Golde, *Di yidishe erd-arbeter in Krim* (Moscow: Emes, 1932); Russian version: *Evrei-zemledel'ts v Krymu* (Moscow: Emes, 1932); I. Sudarski, *Di yidishe ibervanderung in Krim* (Kharkov-Kiev: Ukrmelukhenatsmindfarlag, 1932); E. Morrissey, *Jewish Workers and Farmers in the Crimea and Ukraine* (New York: n.p., 1937).
73. See Lorimer, op. cit.
74. See Kupovetskii, op. cit., p. 84.
75. My main sources for Chapichev's biography are E. Feigin, "Mal'chik pliashet pod dozhdem," in E. Feigin, *Tvoi sinov'ia* (Tbilisi: Literatura da khelovneba, 1967), pp. 5–339 and S. Borzunov, "Nedopetaia pesnia," in S. Borzunov, *S perom i automatom* (Moscow: Voennoe izdatel'stvo, 1974), pp. 81–186. See also A. Priblude, "A held a krimchak—Yakov Chapichev," *Sovetish heymland* (1976), no. 1, pp. 143–44; "Geroi Sovetskogo Soiuza maior Chapichev Iakov Iudovich," in Ia. Ingerman (ed.), *Evreiskii samizdat* (Jerusalem: CRD, 1978),

vol. 14, pp. 301–6; and S. Borzunov, "Khrabromu suzhdeno bessmostie," *Kniga v geroiakh*, no. 3 (Moscow: Voenizdat, 1968).

76. Shor, Veps, Izhor, Saam Ude, and Itelmen are listed among the "small ethnic groups *[narodnosti]* of the USSR that have lost *[sic]* the written idiom *[pis'mennost']* in the mother tongue" in A. Baziev and M. Isaev, *Iazyk i natsiia* (Moscow: Nauka, 1973), p. 121; on Karaitic Crimean Tatar as a written language, see above.

77. Recorded by V. Filonenko in 1928 in Simferopol from a girl-student, Z. Zengrin (see Filonenko, op. cit., p. 16) and published in Baziev and Isaev, op. cit., pp. 21–22; Russian translation and a short commentary, ibid., pp. 22–23.

78. A. Klevan, "Hakrimchakim—mikehilot Yisrael sheharvu bashoa," *Bama'arakha* (May 1984), no. 283, p. 7.

79. Y. Keren, *Yahadut Krim*, pp. 317–18.

80. Sent from the USSR by Ra'ya Bekman to her niece Lea (Liza) Velvelsky in Israel (undated). First published in Hebrew transcription (at times with mistakes) from the original Cyrillic transcription, with a Hebrew translation (at times erroneous too) from L. Velvelski's oral Russian translation in Keren, *Yahadut Krim*, pp. 317–18.

81. Recorded by I. Kaya in 1947 in Novorossiisk from Moisei (Moshe) Purim (see Filonenko, op. cit., p. 16), published in Filonenko, op. cit., pp. 31–32, Russian translation and a short commentary in ibid., pp. 32–34.

82. Private information. The appeal was pioneered, reportedly, by Y. Peysakh.

83. "Krymchaki," *Bol'shaia sovetskaia entsiklopediia*, vol. 13 (Moscow: Sovetskaia entsiklopediia, 1973), clmn. 1540. The entry is unsigned. On Y. Peysakh's authorship of it, see K. Beyder, (untitled introduction to Peysakh, op. cit. [part 1], p. 170).

84. For what is evidently the first mention and definition of t[u]qun (transcribed as *tkun*) in print, see Chernin, op. cit., p. 157 (omitted in the Russian version of the article). For the first published description of it (transcribed as *thum*), see "Path of the Wanderer" [on Prof. A. Khazanov], *Scopus*, 36 (1986), p. 41.

85. See A. A. Gershuni, *Yehudim veyahadut bevrit hamo'atsot* (Jerusalem: Feldheim, 1970), p. 266; Y. Pinhasi, "Yehudey Bukhara," in M. Altshuler, Y. Pinhasi, and M. Zand, *Yehudey Bukhara vehayehudim hahararim: shney kibutsim bidrom Brit hamo'atsot* (Jerusalem: hamakhon leyahadut zmanenu, hauniversita haivrit, 1973), pp. 16–17.

86. Mahvashev (op. cit., Hebrew part, p. 13) says about one of the heads (according to him *the* head) of the Turkestan branch of the *Evsektsiia*, A. Bogod: "He did not know anything about Bukharan Jews. He thought that only Askenazi Jews exist. Despite this he conducted all educational affairs related to Jews." During the first years of the Sovietization of Central Asia, Bogod headed the national minorities department of the People's Commissariat of Education of the Soviet Republic of Turkestan (see Z. Amitin-Shapiro, *Ocherki sotsialisticheskogo stroitel'stva sredi sredneaziatskikh evreev* (Tashkent: Gosizdat UzSSR,

1933), p. 14. As a student of the Tashkent Bukharan Jewish teachers' seminary (see below), I[shoq] Mahvashev (b. 1905–d. in Israel 1978) must have known Bogod personally.
87. See S. Urazaev, *Turkestanskaia ASSR i ee gosudarstvenno-pravovye osobennosti* (Tashkent: Gosizdat Uzbekskoi SSR, 1958), p. 1125; *Kul'turnoe stroitel'stvo v Turkestanskoi ASSR (1917–1924 gg.). Sbornik dokumentov*, vol. 1: *Kul'turnoe stroitel'stvo v Turkestanskoi ASSR v period ustanovleniia sovetskoi vlasti i grazhdanskoi voiny (1917–1920 gg.).* (Tashkent: Izdatel'stvo "Uzbekistan," 1973), p. 386.
88. See Y. Amitin-Shapira, *Geografya klalit. Yedi'ot elementariyot mehageografya hafisit haklalit 'al yesod yedi'at erets Turkistan 'im metodika ktsara lehoraat hageografya* (Tashkent: hakomisariat lehaskala, 1920).
89. I saw the manuscript on frequent visits to S. (Solomon Bentsionovich) Edel'man from the late 1940s and up to my departure from the USSR in 1971. Like his colleague Amitin-Shapiro, but before him, Edel'man left Uzbekistan for Moscow and became a Soviet authority on the economics of public food catering.
90. A Bogod, "Prosvetitel'naia rabota sredi natsional'nykh men'shinstv," *Nauka i prosveshchenie* [Tashkent] (1922), p. 67, as quoted in Amitin-Shapiro, op. cit., p. 67.
91. Shulamit Tilayof, *Shirat Shulamit* (Tel Aviv: published by the author, 1981), p. 25.
92. Report on the conference published in *Rosta* (Tashkent), July 3, 1921, as quoted in Amitin-Shapiro, *Ocherki*, p. 69.
93. See ibid.
94. For the teachers' courses, see Amitin-Shapiro, op. cit., p. 68; for the date of the foundation of the seminary, see ibid., p. 74; M. Ben'iaminov, *Bukharskie evrei* (New York: published by the author, 1983), p. 41 (Ben'iaminov himself had in the 1920s been a student of the Tashkent seminary; in general the book written "for a certainly family date . . . by memory only" (p. 188) is but a bunch of subjective stray notes).
95. See Mahvashev, op. cit., Hebrew part, p. 13.
96. Ibid., p. 12 (1923 was the year of Mahvashev's acceptance to the seminary).
97. Amitin-Shapiro, *Ocherki*, p. 75.
98. Mahvashev, op. cit., Hebrew part, p. 12.
99. Amitin-Shapiro, *Ocherki*, p. 75.
100. Mahvashev, op. cit., Hebrew part, pp. 12–13. According to Mahvashev, before he was sent from Samarkand to the seminary he was "hastily given a *Komsomol* membership card."
101. Amitin-Shapiro, *Ocherki*, p. 75; Y. Ben-Tsvi [I. Ben-Zvi], op. cit., p. 177; Mahvashev, op. cit., Hebrew part, p. 13.
102. Amitin-Shapiro, *Ocherki*, p. 77; Ben'iaminov, op. cit., p. 41.
103. Amitin-Shapiro, *Ocherki*, p. 77.
104. See A. Miral, "Vozrozhdenie evreev Uzbekistana," *Tribuna* (1936), no. 24, p. 28.
105. "Uzbekistan (Mitl-Azie)," in S. Dimanshteyn (ed.), *Yidn in FSSR. Zamlbukh*

(Moscow: Mezhdunarodnaia kniga un Emes, 1935), p. 232; Amitin-Shapiro (*Ocherki*, p. 71) gives a sum total for the 1930–31 school year of 6,978 pupils in elementary and secondary schools (including the so-called "schools for the adolescent" and for the *"kolkhoz* youth," that is for youngsters studying at elementary level). However, his data apparently incorporate all the Jewish pupils of Uzbekistan, inclusive of Bukharan Jews in non-Bukharan Jewish schools and Ashkenazim.

106. See Miral, op. cit., p. 28.
107. S. Radzhabov, *Iz istorii stroitel'stva sovetskoi shkoly v Uzbekistane* (Tashkent: Gosizdat Uzbekskoi SSR, 1957), p. 60 and table 7 there.
108. I have been unable to find any data about Bukharan Jewish schools in towns of Tadzhikistan, Kazakhstan, Kirgiziia, and Turkmenistan with relatively large Bukharan Jewish populations. However, the existence of such schools at least in some of these republics is known and it can hardly be doubted that there, too, the process of decline and subsequent disappearance of these schools and the transfer to Russian schools was identical.
109. See "Uzbekistan (Mitl-Azie)," b. 232.
110. See Amitin-Shapiro, *Ocherki*, pp. 123–26; M. Bachaev [Muhib], *Dar "juvoli sangin." Yoddoshtho*, vol. 1 (Jerusalem: haigud ha'olami shel yehudey Asiya hamerkazit, brit yotsey Bukhara, 1988; henceforth cited as Bachaev, *Memoirs*) pp. 151–52.
111. For the dramatization of the story of Joseph, see Bachaev, *Memoirs*, pp. 110–13; for the two other plays, see Ben'iaminov, op. cit., pp. 74–75.
112. See Ben'iaminov, op. cit., p. 73.
113. I was told this by Sh. Edel'man. Neither the original Hebrew text of the play nor its Judeo-Tadzhik version was ever published. The original Hebrew text of the first act was given me by Sh. Edel'man in 1969.
114. See S. Tilayof, op. cit., pp. 25–28, 269–72.
115. On *Tarbut* in Central Asia, the Kokand group, and its performances in Hebrew, see Y. Ben-Tsvi [I. Ben-Zvi], op. cit., pp. 175–77. On Bukharan Jewish amateur drama groups "at the dawn of the cultural revolution in Central Asia" (i.e., in the 1920s), see also Ben'iaminov, op. cit., p. 73.
116. Here and henceforth, when the first name of an author remains unknown to me, only the initial is given, according to Soviet publishing practice.
117. See B. Pestovskii, "Le théâtre des juifs boukhariens," *Bulletin d'information. Organ de la Société pour relations culturelles entre l'URSS et l'étrangère* (1928), nos. 7–8, p. 16.
118. See N. Mallaev, "Muboriz shoir," in Y. Oqilov, *Qumri* (Tashkent: Ghafur Ghulom nomidagi Adabiyot va san'at nashriyoti, 1983), p. 7. (The book—62 pages in small pocket format—is a posthumous edition of Oqilov's twenty-six selected poems in Uzbek translation. The author of its preface, a Bukharan Jew, is known as a student of Uzbek literature.)
119. See *Gazety SSR. 1917–1960. Bibliograficheskii spravochnik*, vol. 1 (Moscow: Vsesoiuznaia knizhnaia palata, 1970), p. 196; see also [A.] Saidov, "Desiatiletie 'Bairaki mikhnat'," *Tribuna* (1935), no. 14, p. 22.

120. See [A.] Jabbori, "Ba munosibati qabul kardani alifboyi navi yahudi va tojiki," *Ovozi tojik*, March 11, 1928; P. Abramuf [Abramov], "Hamzabononi tojikon niz alifboyi navro qabul kardand," *Rahbari donish* (1928), nos. 4-5, p. 17; Y. Kalontarov, *Proekti orfografiyai navi zaboni yahudihoyi mahali. Az tarafi orgbyuro asosan tasdiq karda shudaqi hast* (Tashkent: "Bayroqi mihnat", 1934). The name of the first author was scraped off with a razor blade (as that of a nonperson) from my copy of this brochure which I got some time between 1951 and 1953; Ia. Kalontarov, "Voprosy orfografii mestnoevreiskogo iazyka," in *Problemy iazyka. Sbornik uzbekskogo nauchno-issledovatel'skogo instituta iazyka i literatury*, no. 1 (Tashkent: 1934), pp. 53-60.
121. See Gershuni, op. cit., p. 267, who refers, however, to the 1937-40 period.
122. See Saidov, op. cit., p. 35; and cf. Bachaev, *Memoirs*, pp. 245-56, where the date given is early 1932.
123. See A. Sayiduf [Saidov], P. Abromuf [Abramov], and M. Aminuf [Aminov], "Sari sukhari," in A. Sayiduf, P. Abromuf, and M. Aminuf (eds.), *Almanakhi adabiyoti nafisi yahudihoyi mahali* (Tashkent: Nashriyoti davlatii UzSSR, 1934), pp. 12-13.
124. See "Uzbekistan (Mitl-Azie)," p. 232; Bachaev, *Memoirs*, pp. 286-89.
125. References to Payrav Sulaymoni's *chala* origin (common knowledge in Tadzhik literary circles) and his collaboration with the Samarkand Jewish theater disappeared from Tadzhik literary publications in the post-World War II period. They are absent also in the most detailed research on the poet: S. Tabarov, *Payrav Sulaymoni* (Dushanbe: Nashriyoti davlatii Tojikiston, 1962).
126. For Y. Korgar-Kuraev's biography, see N. Mallaev, *Shoir-grazhdanin*, in Y. Korga, *Ozod vatanim bor* (Tashkent: Ghafur Ghulom nomidagi Adabiyot va san'at nashriyoti, 1978), pp. 5-7 [preface to a selection of twenty-eight of Y. Korgar-Kuraev's poems in Uzbek translation]; "Shoir Yunoton Kruaev vafot kard," *Umed. Hatikva* (Bulletin of Haigud ha'olami shel yehudey Asiya hamerkazit, the World Association of Central Asian Jews; Tel Aviv), (September 1985), nos. 17-18, [p. 7; not paginated]; [M. Abramov,] "Shoir Korgar," *Oinai jahon, Rei ha'olam* (Tel Aviv) (1986), no. 5, [p. 18; not paginated].
127. See Bachaev, *Memoirs*, pp. 464-67; the same source also provides names of others who were arrested.
128. See [M. Abramov], "Menashe Aminov va *pisarash* Yosef," *Oinai jahon. Rei ha'olam* (Tel Aviv) (1986), no. 6, p. 12.
129. The last registered issue of *Bayroqi mihnat* is that of May 27, 1938 (see *Gazety*, vol. 1 [Moscow: Knizhnaia palata SSSR, 1970], p. 197). The exact dates of the closure of *Adabiyoti soveti* and the theater are not clear. The museum was closed in April 1938 (see Bachaev, *Memoirs*, pp. 476-77).
130. This formula was transmitted by Kuraev to Bachaev [Muhib] "as if he was reading from the text" (Bachaev, *Memoirs*, pp. 471-72). The same reason was given for the closure of the Uighur newspaper published in Uzbekistan (see Bachaev, *Memoirs*, pp. 476-77).
131. This statement was made to Y. Kalontarov, the leading Bukharan Jewish

linguist of that time, who recounted it to me in 1957. The Iranologist Anna Rozenfel'd (of Leningrad) was named as the authority whose opinion was asked for and given.

132. See "V tvorcheskikh soiuzakh," *Pravda vostoka*, May 1, 1988; also *Birobidzhaner shtern*, June 5, 1988. My thanks are due to Dr. H. Spier (London) and Dr. A. Beker (Jerusalem) for drawing my attention to the latter. For a recent attempt to establish a Cultural Asian Jewish Commission under the aegis of the Tadzhik SSSR Cultural Foundation, see O. Panfilov, "Istoriia naroda—ne anekdot," *Komsomolets Tadzhikistana*, January 22, 1989.

133. I. Braginskii, "Iz biografii vtorogo pokoleniia sovetskikh vostokovedov," *Narody Azii i Afriki* (1967), no. 5, pp. 247, 249, describes this club as "the club of working youth." He also maintains that it was established by "a group of Tat members of the *Komsomol*."

134. I. Braginskii, op. cit., passim, gives the name of the head of the company as Girsil Gorskii, noting (p. 250) that Gorskii was a pseudonym. As his closest school friend (p. 246), Braginskii must have known his real surname, the identity of his father, and the fact that he was named after Herzl, the founder of political Zionism.

135. G. Musakhanova, "A kin pursush hasul omorai literaturay tati," VS (1978), pp. 59–61 (henceforth cited as "A kin"), mentions as two separate circles the "theatrical circle" which was closed down in 1919 and the "cultural-educational circle" formed in the early 1920s. However, it appears that the leading members of both circles were identical and that part of the repertoire of each circle was the same and identical to that of the 1904 company. See also (and especially on N. Sholumov): Y. Yagudayev (Yahudoyev), "Yorovurdiho az zindaguni teatr tati," part 1, VS (1978), p. 72.

136. See Musakhanova, "A kin," p. 59, on the "1918–19 circle." However, this could hardly have been the case in 1918–19, when Derbent was in the hands of forces violently opposed to the Bolsheviks.

137. See M. Khanukayev (Hanukayev), "Az gunjondogor," in Yuno Semyonov, *Vikhda omora proizvedeniyaho* (Makhachkala: Dagestanskoe knizhnoe izdatel'stvo, 1964), p. 5; G. Musakhanova, "Yuno Semyonov," in F. Nazarevich and P. Yusufov (eds.), *Istoriia dagestanskoi sovetskoi literatury* (henceforth "Hist. Dag. Lit."), vol. 2 (Makhachkala: Izdatel'stvo Dagestanskogo filiala AN SSSR, 1967), p. 417. Semenov's appointment must be seen in connection with an order of the local *Revkom* several months before, instructing all theaters in Dagestan to perform "in accordance with the spirit of the time"—see "Hist. Dag. Lit.," vol. 1, p. 351.

138. See *Krasnyi Dagestan*, February 29 and March 9, 1924, as quoted in Musakhanova, "A kin," pp. 61–62.

139. For the Kuba theatrical company, see the testimony of one of its founders, Y. Agarunov (Aharunov), "Chutar yaratmish biriga literaturay tati," part 1, VS (1974), pp. 66–67; for the Port-Petrovsk company, see Musakhanova, "A kin," p. 61. Her information on this company is derived from one of its founders, P. Shcherbatov (Sharbatov).

140. On the first play, see its author's testimony—Agarunov, op. cit., part 1, pp. 66–67. On both plays, see Musakhanova, "A kin," p. 61.
141. Not preserved. For a summary of the play's plot and details of its first performance, see Braginskii, op. cit., pp. 250–51.
142. On Birorov's plays, see B. Miller, "O kubinskom govore tatskogo narechiia gorskikh evreev Kavkaza," in *Zapiski Instituta vostokovedeniia AN SSSR*, 1 (1932), p. 70.
143. Y. Yagudayev, op. cit., part 2, VS (1979), p. 75, mentions performances in Derbent and Baku; Agarunov, op. cit., part 1, p. 76, mentions performances in Baku.
144. M. Dadashev, *Birorho* (Makhachkala: Dagestanskoe knizhnoe izdatel'stvo, 1980), pp. 128–31, claims that the play, the name of which he gives incorrectly as *Odom va Tomor*, was an isolated and unsuccessful attempt (see on this M. Dadashev's novella below). According to Musakhanova, "A kin," p. 59, a number of plays on themes "taken from the Torah," were staged.
145. *Gazety*, vol. 3 (1978), pp. 22–23.
146. See D. Shaulov and R. Razilov, "Gorskie evrei i latinskii alfavit," in *Revoliutsiia i gorets* (1929), no. 5 (7), p. 61.
147. For Khudainatov, see also Agarunov, op. cit., part 1, VS, 1974, p. 72, and part 2, VS, 1976, p. 65 (on his attempt to do away with Russian loanwords in Judeo-Tat); Shaulov and Razilov, op. cit., pp. 60–61 (on his championing the conversion of Judeo-Tat writing into the Latin alphabet).
148. The Judeo-Tat corner in *Serlo* could have been launched only after the Third Plenum of the All-Union Central Committee for the New Turkic Alphabet. See Shaulov and Razilov, op. cit., p. 61. The plenum took place in Kazan on December 18–23, 1928 (see *Kul'tura i pismennost' Vostoka*, vol. 4 (1929), p. 158).
149. *Gazety*, vol. 3 (1978), p. 216. The reference to the transfer of *Zahmatkash* to Makhachkala and its alleged consequences, in B. Manoakh, *Plenniki Salmana sara (iz istorii evreev Vostochnogo Kavkaza* (Jerusalem: published by the author, 1984), p. 99, is incorrect.
150. See D. Shaulov, "Gorskie evrei na putiakh kul'turnoi revoliutsii (Pis'mo iz Groznogo)," *Revoliutsiia i gorets* (1929), no. 10 (12), p. 57.
151. Direct attacks on religion in Dagestan were considered counterproductive by an important local communist leader, N. Samurskii-Efendiev (executed 1938) —see Samurskii (Efendiev), *Dagestan* (Moscow-Leningrad: n.p., 1925), p. 132.
152. See "Novaia orfografiia gorskikh evreev," *Tribuna* (1928), no. 15, p. 22.
153. See Miller, op. cit., p. 27, note 4.
154. See Agarunov, op. cit., part 1, pp. 75–76; and Dadashev, op. cit., pp. 128–31. The Azerbaidzhan State Publishing House was established in 1924.
155. *Gazety*, vol. 1 (1970), p. 117; the first listed issue is no. 2 of September 30, 1934.
156. The final issue of *Kommunist* appeared on May 22, 1938—see *Gazety*, ibid. On *Gyzyl Guba*, see *Gazety*, vol. 3 (1978), p. 223. It seems from Agarunov, op.

cit., part 1, pp. 75–76, that the Judeo-Tat section of the Azerbaidzhani *Gosizdat* operated for three years, i.e., until autumn 1937.
157. A Dagestani ethnic group, neighbors of the Mountain Jews.
158. See *Gazety*, vol. 3, p. 246.
159. According to Yagudayev, op. cit. part 2, p. 76, "People did not come to the performances. . . . This compelled the authorities to close down our theater in 1946."
160. See G. Daniialov, "Ot narodnosti k natsii," in M. Vagabov (ed.), *Oktiabrskaia revoliutsiia i reshenie natsional'nogo voprosa v Dagestane* (Makhachkala: Dagestanskoe knizhnoe izdatel'stvo, 1967), p. 301. On instruction of Judeo-Tat "before the Great Patriotic War," see M. Ikhilov, "Gorskie evrei," in M. O. Kosvena, I. Lavrova, et al. (eds.), *Narody Kavkaza*, vol. 1 (Moscow: Izdatel'stvo AN SSSR, 1960), p. 561.
161. Ikhilov vaguely refers to "after the war" as the time when Judeo-Tat was abolished as a medium of instruction, op. cit., 561. In 1955, however, he still maintained that "instruction in the lower grades is given in the mother Tat tongue, in the higher grades—in Russian;" see M. Ikhilov, "Gorskie evrei," in M. Kosven and K. M. Khashaev (eds.), *Narody Dagestana* (Moscow: Izdatel'stvo AN SSSR, 1955), p. 240. In this paper he also stated that the *Ghirmizina 'alam* was still appearing, although its publication had been discontinued three years earlier.
162. See *Konstitutsiia (Osnovnoi zakon) Dagestanskoi Avtonomnoi Sovetskoi Sotsialisticheskoi Respubliki (s izmeneniiami i dopolneniiami, priniatymi na I sessii Verkhovnogo Soveta Dagestanskoi ASSR tret'ego sozyva)* articles 24, 78, 111, 112, in *Konstitutsiia (Osnovnoi zakon) RSFSR. Konstitutsii (Osnovnye zakony) avtonomnykh sovetskikh sotsialisticheskikh respublik vkhodyashchikh v sostav RSFSR* (Moscow: Gospolitizdat, 1952), pp. 94, 103–4, 110–11.
163. For newspapers of that time in other indigenous official languages, see *Gazety*, vol. 3 (1978), p. 254—Avar; vol. 2, p. 161, vol. 3, pp. 109, 112—Dargwa (Dargin); vol. 3, p. 592—Lakk; vol. 3, pp. 166, 571, 587, vol. 4, p. 161—Lezgi; vol. 3, p. 406—Qumyq; vol. 3, p. 70—Tabasarani. For all-Dagestani Avar, Dargwa, Lezgi, and Qumyq newspapers of the period under discussion, see also I. Pashaev, "Osobennosti massovo-politicheskoi raboty KPSS v usloviiakh mnogonatsional'noi respubliki," in *Torzhestvo leninskoi nationsional'noi politiki KPSS* (Makhachkala: Dagestanskoe knizhnoe izdatel'stvo, 1968), p. 136.
164. See "Hist. Dag. Lit.," vol. 1, pp. 392–94 (quarterlies in Avar, Dargwa, Lakk, Lezgi, and Qumyq, and an annual almanac in Tabasarani).
165. Ibid., pp. 381, 393.
166. Ibid.
167. *Morgn frayheyt*, January 22, 1961, as quoted in B. Pinkus, *The Soviet Government and the Jews, 1948–1967. A Documented Study* (Cambridge: Cambridge University Press, 1984), p. 464 (document 170).
168. See H. Avshalumov, *Kuk qudil* (Makhachkala: Dagestanskoi khizhnoe izdatel'stvo, 1974), pp. 48, 91, 148, 171, 185.

169. This did not go unnoticed by a Soviet reviewer of the last print of the Russian version of the novella—Kh. Avshalumov, *Vozmezdie. Povest'. Rasskazy* (Moscow: n.p., 1978), pp. 3–186)—although it is expressed rather evasively: "the social emphasis *[zaostrennost]* of the novella, correct though it is in itself, is at times excessively straightforward"; see S. Akhmedov, "Povest' i rasskazy," *Sovetskii Dagestan* (1979), no. 1 (81), p. 73.
170. On the image of Gulbohor Davydova in Mountain Jewish literature, see G. Musakhanova, *"Chihrat zanho a literaturay tati"*, VS (1979), p. 71.
171. See Yagudayev, op. cit., part 2, p. 76.
172. On the establishment of the "inter-*kolkhoz* theater," see ibid. According to Daniialov, *Istoriia Dagestana*, vol. 4 (Moscow: Nauka, 1968), p. 239, this theater had been established by 1960. However, it is not mentioned in the list of Dagestani theaters in 1967 given in Daniialov, op. cit., pp. 333, 335. On the change of name, see Almoni, "Hayehudim hahararim," in David Prital (ed.), *Haintelligentsiya hayehudit bivrit hamo'atsot*, vol. 3 (Jerusalem: hamo'atsa hatsiburit lema'an yehudey brit hamo'atsot, 1979), p. 51. Here the theater is said to have been formed out of three amateur circles. The information given by Yagudayev, however, would seem to be more reliable, as it was provided by someone who participated in the events themselves.
173. See N. Anisimov, *Grammati zuhun tati* (Moscow: Tsentroizdat, 1932), pp. 21–26.
174. See D. Atnilov, "Khalgh tati," VS (1960), p. 31.
175. Idem, *Gulhoy insoni* (Makhachkala: Dagestanskoe knizhnoe izdatel'stvo, 1971), p. 38.
176. See L. Avshalumova, "Iudaizm hisdi din-do'ot an mohlugh juhure az da khalghhoygay 'ulom dur, jayla sokhdai," VS (1976), pp. 68–78; see also the chapter "Sionizm i tak nazyvaemyi 'tatskii vopros'," (pp. 123–61) in her book *Kritika iudaizma i sionizma* (Makhachkala: Dagestanskoe knizhnoe izdatel'stvo, 1986).
177. M. Dadashev, op. cit. p. 163.
178. See M. Matatov, "Durgunihoy sionisti va haghi 'ilmi," VS (1981), p. 50.
179. See V. Chernin, "Tsu neytikn zikh hipotezes in a visnshaftlekher argumentatsiye? Vegn M. Matatovs artikl 'Tsu der frege vegn dem tatishn etnos'," *Sovetish heymland* (1982), no. 10, pp. 132–38.
180. See M. Matatov, "K voprosu o tatskom etnose," *Sovetskaia etnografiia* (1981), no. 5, pp. 109–12.
181. I. Taiar (S. Iantovskii), *Sinagoga-razgromlennaia, no nepokorennaia* (Jerusalem: Biblioteka Aliia, 1987), p. 67.
182. See Zh. Golotvin and M. Matatov, "Taty," *Voprosy istorii* (1986), no. 11, pp. 185–88; republished in *Sovetskii Dagestan* (1987), no. 2, pp. 76–79.
183. See Kh. Avshalumov, "Yadovitii grib na sviatoi zemle," *Sovetskaia Rossiia*, September 4, 1986.

21

Superpower Relations and Jewish Identity in the Soviet Union

Avi Beker

In many ways the level of Jewish emigration from the Soviet Union has become a barometer of Soviet-American relations. For the last two decades Jewish emigration seems to have risen and fallen, not predictably like the tides, but in a consistent and discernible pattern which followed superpower relations. The conspicuous ups and downs in Jewish emigration underscore a very clear linkage, notwithstanding Soviet assertions to the contrary, to the state of relations between the United States and the Soviet Union.

The peak periods of Jewish emigration, 1971–73 and 1978–79, and the year of renewed emigration and the release of all Prisoners of Zion, 1987, have some common characteristics. In these three periods American and Soviet leaders met in summit meetings. In each period a major arms control agreement was signed. In addition, in all three instances a Soviet desire for Western economic benefits can be easily discerned.

The record high figure of Jewish emigration in 1979 (51,320) was clearly orchestrated as a background setting for the June 1979 Vienna summit between President Jimmy Carter and Soviet leader Leonid Brezhnev, when the two leaders signed the SALT II treaty and discussed a nuclear test ban. Similarly, the Soviets were encouraged by growing sentiment in Congress to waive the $300 million limitation on grants to the USSR (the Stevenson amendment) as well as to lift the Jackson-Vanik amendment.[1] Also, early in spring 1979 the U.S. Commerce Department permitted a computer sale that had been canceled in 1978, while the appointment of the former IBM chairman Thomas Watson, himself an advocate of increased trade with the

Soviets, rather than a professional diplomat, to serve as American ambassador to Moscow seemed to signal that Carter was genuinely in favor of increasing trade relations.[2]

The deterioration in U.S.-USSR relations following the Soviet invasion of Afghanistan in 1979 brought an immediate slump in Jewish emigration to 21,471 in 1980 and 9,447 in 1981.

Along similar lines it can be argued that the Nixon-Kissinger policy of détente was responsible for the sharp increase in Jewish emigration figures in the early 1970s from 1,044 in 1970 to 13,022 in 1971, 31,681 in 1972 (when Nixon and Brezhnev signed the ABM and SALT I agreements), and 34,733 in 1973 (summits in Washington and San Clemente). Perhaps the Jackson-Vanik amendment to the Trade Reform Act of 1974 caused the drop to barely 13,221 in 1975, though détente relations between the superpowers continued.

The year 1987, too, which brought at its end the signing of the INF treaty at the Washington summit (December 7), was the highest year of Jewish emigration since 1981 (8,155)—a ninefold increase over the previous year. During this year all Prisoners of Zion were released and some of the best-known refuseniks were granted exit visas.

Under Republican administrations there have been far more summits than under Democratic presidents; three with Eisenhower, three with Nixon (and one more with Ford who replaced him), and five with Reagan, while only one with each Democratic president: Kennedy, Johnson, and Carter. Moreover, only under Republican administrations have effective arms control agreements been signed and later ratified by the Senate (ABM, SALT I, Vladivostok, and INF).

Generally, summit meetings as such did not bring immediate and concrete results for the Jews. Summits are an important symbol and technique in superpower relations, but sometimes they arouse misleading expectations and cause policy miscalculations. In most cases the summit provides personal contact between the leaders, forces them to concentrate on the issues on the agenda, and helps to revive compromises frozen by bureaucratic infighting. The record shows that, given the nature of superpower relations which since World War II have been overshadowed by nuclear deterrence, summit meetings and their agreements virtually always focus exclusively on measures of nuclear arms control and military conflicts. The other aspects of superpower relations are of secondary significance (trade) or even of marginal importance (human rights). Only in 1987 did Jewish issues enter the official summit agenda. Nevertheless, though not usually on the summit agenda, the Jews have clearly benefited from the process of give-and-take which precedes and follows summits. Apparently the Soviets regard the Jewish issue as an important factor in American public awareness, with special significance for their image in the West. For instance, in 1979 the Soviets continued to allow Jewish emigration in record numbers as they hoped for ratification of SALT II. Jewish emigration, without being a prerequisite for the holding of summits, has become an integral part of the summit process. It can be assumed that if summits become more frequent and deal more meaningfully with economic issues (under *perestroika*) there will be more likelihood that the Jewish issue, and other human rights matters, are included.

With all these ups and downs in Jewish emigration which are closely related to superpower relations, Jewish cultural activities in the Soviet Union remained insignificant and virtually nonexistent. The record demonstrates that dramatic increases in Jewish emigration were not coupled with measures to improve the status of Judaism and Jewish culture in the USSR. On the contrary, a reverse correlation can be shown between emigration and the policy of the Soviet regime toward Jewish dissidents and their struggle for Jewish cultural rights and the means to give expression to their national identity.

The Soviet leadership clearly separated the emigration issue from that of the dissidents and their rights, and continued its crackdown against them while emigration increased. Moreover, emigration was accompanied by a rising tide of anti-Semitism in various forms. For the purposes of improving their image in the context of détente and the relaxation of international tensions the Kremlin was ready to export Jews, but continued to resist importing the spirit of détente into Soviet society.

Before the days of emigration, gestures on Jewish culture were used as a ploy to please Western public opinion. The measures were mostly insignificant, cosmetic, and propagandistic and were juxtaposed with a continuing vicious anti-Semitic campaign inside the Soviet Union. As Soviet Minister of Culture Ekatarina Furtseva bluntly put it in 1961: "If the USSR did anything at all for Yiddish culture, it would not be for domestic reasons, but to please our friends abroad."[3]

Soviet Jewry on the Summit Agenda

The Reykjavik summit of October 1986, though disruptive in its atmosphere, was an important landmark from a Jewish point of view. As indicated by the *New York Times,* the Reykjavik summit was a major change from previous Soviet-American summit meetings in the sense that the human rights issue was included in the agenda officially and in a publicized manner. As reported in the press, "the status of Soviet Jews has emerged in advance as a central topic at the Reagan-Gorbachev meeting."[4] President Reagan and his aides made public statements arguing that the political climate in the United States would not tolerate a Gorbachev visit to America without a significant relaxation in Soviet emigration policies. This development made an arms control-human rights/Jewish emigration linkage a fact of life in superpower negotiations. At the next Reagan-Gorbachev summit (Washington, December 1987) another step forward was made when, for the first time in the history of Soviet-American relations, the issue of human rights was explicitly included in a *joint* Soviet-American announcement of a summit agenda. As David Shipler wrote in the *New York Times:*

Rarely has there been as much harmony between an administration and an interest group as there is now between the Reagan Administration and the organizations campaigning on behalf of Soviet Jewry.

The movement for Soviet Jewry was, indeed, satisfied with the policy of President Reagan and Secretary of State Shultz, thus "leading to a remarkable accord between the lobbyist and the lobbied."[5]

Perhaps the failure to reach any understanding at Reykjavik was also conducive to creating more awareness and a greater sense of urgency on both sides and led to the well-prepared and successful summit in Washington a year later. In the year following Reykjavik, the Soviets gave up on their demand to link SDI with any arms control agreement and at the same time allowed an impressive emigration, though far below the 1979 record. Slow progress was also made on the question of Soviet-Israeli diplomatic relations which had been severed by the Soviets in 1967. A Soviet delegation arrived in Israel in July 1987 to deal with consular matters, and an Israeli delegation arrived in Moscow in July 1988.

The policy of *glasnost'* has aroused new hopes for the possibility of a more positive link between emigration and domestic openness to cultural rights.

Indeed, the increase in emigration in 1987 was not coupled with a crackdown on Jewish activists or with a wave of official anti-Semitism or anti-Zionism. In 1987 the Kremlin, albeit to a very small degree, showed a certain readiness to discuss its position on Jewish life within the Soviet Union and made some gestures, such as the opening of a kosher kitchen in the Moscow synagogue, the training of a few new rabbis in the United States, and the study of Hebrew, again under the auspices of the synagogue. These gestures were discussed in Moscow in March 1987 in meetings between Soviet officials and Edgar Bronfman, president of the World Jewish Congress, and Morris B. Abram, chairman of the Conference of Presidents of Major American Jewish Organizations. At these meetings the Soviet side made promises on Jewish emigration and the release of Prisoners of Zion, as well as on the aforementioned cultural-religious gestures.[6]

As indicated later in this chapter, religious and cultural measures have little effect or significance on daily Jewish life in the Soviet Union and testify to the difficulties of developing Jewish life in that country. These difficulties have been brought to the fore since *glasnost'* has also led to the surfacing of the Russian ultranationalistic, anti-Semitic organization *Pamiat'* (Memory). Since the origins of *Pamiat'* lie in the cultural aspects of nationalism, its existence will remain a pending threat to any form of Jewish culture and religion. True, in the Soviet official press one can find criticism of anti-Semitism and directly of *Pamiat'*,[7] yet it is clear that if they do not actually orchestrate the activities of *Pamiat'* the authorities use them as a safety valve in order to pursue broader reforms in other fields. Thus, even in the context of "democratization," the Jews are an easy scapegoat, left to experience a "street" anti-Semitism instead of a governmental one.

Glasnost', Arms Control, and Human Rights

The 1987 U.S.-Soviet treaty on elimination of intermediate-range nuclear missiles (INF), which was signed at the December summit in Washington D.C., contained some new elements that went beyond a strict bookkeeping of missiles and silos. First of all the treaty implied an actual destruction of nuclear weapons by both parties. However, the treaty has the most detailed and far-ranging verification of any disarmament pact in history. The verification procedure, at least historically and conceptually, marks a departure in the Soviet attitude to the interdependence of foreign and domestic policy in the age of nuclear technology. The question is to what extent this new "openness" in the field of arms control implies domestic reforms in cultural rights for ethnic minorities in the Soviet Union.

As indicated by Jonathan Schell, a close observer of the nuclear arms race, the verification procedures of the INF treaty tower over every other accomplishment. "It is so important that the agreement might well be renamed the On-Site Inspection Agreement."[8] The Soviet acceptance, for the first time in the nuclear age, of the principle of on-site inspection, is perhaps the most striking fruit of *glasnost'*, tying together the Soviet domestic situation with Moscow's foreign policy.

From the beginning of the nuclear age, the Soviet Union made no secret of its complete rejection of any form of control authority and outside inspection of its nuclear facilities. When, on 14 June 1946, the Americans introduced the Baruch Plan at the newly established United Nations Atomic Energy Commission, the basic idea was that a supranational International Atomic Development Authority would begin inspection and verification before actual disarmament took place. The Soviets rejected the American plan and reversed the priorities: first disarmament and then control.[9] In a speech to the Security Council in March 1947, Soviet representative Andrei Gromyko indicated in clear terms Soviet fears of political and ideological contamination. The idea of control was regarded by the Soviets as "thoroughly vicious and unacceptable" and completely alien to the notion of sovereignty. His remarks on the effects of control on domestic affairs were explicit and forceful:

Unlimited control would mean an unlimited interference in the economic life of the countries on whose territories the control would be carried out and interference in their internal affairs. The Soviet Union and probably not only the Soviet Union cannot allow the fate of its national economy to be turned over to this organ.[10]

The Baruch Plan reflected the intellectual strains in American thinking in the aftermath of Hiroshima and Nagasaki. It was assumed by American scientists that openness, friendliness, and cooperation with the Soviets were essential.[11] The American secretary of war, Henry Stimson, wrote to President Truman on 25 April 1945 that the control of nuclear weapons would be revolutionary and "would involve such thorough-going rights of inspection and internal controls as we have never heretofore contemplated."[12] Similarly, on 1 June 1946 Edward Teller, one of the leading American nuclear scientists, made a sweeping proposal for an open society with free communications jointly guaranteed by the United States and the Soviet Union.[13]

It is evident that in the days of Stalin, the link between disarmament and the human rights of the individual was salient. At the time the Soviets were rejecting the Baruch Plan at the United Nations, they also refused to allow a handful of Soviet women married to Britons and Americans during the war to leave the Soviet Union. As one commentator has pointed out: "If what these few women could tell about life in Russia was considered to be a danger justifying this extraordinary inhumanity and pettiness, what of inspection of bomb installation and research facilities?"[14]

Against this background it is quite understandable why the INF treaty with its verification measures is regarded as a major turning point. The question is whether these Soviet concessions entail any significance for the Soviet domestic scene. While there is no doubt that Gorbachev's *glasnost'* includes a great amount of public relations hype, it is widely agreed that he is also striving for domestic changes implying a new approach to human rights as well. In the Moscow peace forum, for instance, addressing an audience of nearly 1,000 artists, intellectuals, businessmen, and political figures from eighty countries, Gorbachev called for the "broad democratization" of Soviet society, which he declared "irreversible."[15]

Glasnost' and *perestroika* have created both expectations and confusion among Western observers, who find it difficult to separate between the style and substance of Gorbachev's policies. On the one hand, there is a widespread feeling that Gorbachev's reforms are, indeed, irreversible; on the other hand, some experts question the possibility of their application in Soviet conditions.[16]

It is generally agreed that, given the picture of a debilitated Soviet economy, Gorbachev is under constant pressure to cut military spending, move able-bodied men out of the military into the civilian economy, and create an atmosphere in East-West relations which will allow him to get cash and credits, as well as technology, from the West.

It is beyond the scope of this chapter and this volume as a whole to evaluate the overall subject of the Gorbachev reforms and the significance of *glasnost'* and *perestroika*. However, for the purposes of our discussion, namely the future of Jewish identity and culture in the Soviet Union, some aspects are worth further consideration.

It is still unclear to what extent, if at all, the Soviet Union's willingness and efforts in the field of arms control and international security will affect the domestic arena, including human rights. Michael Howard, a leading expert on military strategy and international security, draws a clear distinction between Moscow's arms control goals and its human rights policy. Indeed, says Howard, there is in Gorbachev's Soviet Union a fundamental questioning of the implicit Marxist notion of the inevitability of a happy ending for mankind—the triumph of socialism. Instead, Gorbachev recognizes the nuclear threat as imposing a catastrophic threat to mankind and, thus, the urgent need to avert it. Nevertheless, Howard emphasizes, the debate in the Soviet Union is only about means and not about the final goal: the achievement of world socialism. "The debate is not about political liberalization or human rights . . . there is no indication in any of this debate that human rights will be respected in the Soviet Union any more than they are at present, except in so far as that is helpful to the improvement of the socialist economy."[17] In other words, even the breakthrough in verification inside the USSR achieved in the INF treaty is a far cry from the notion of an open society with free communications envisioned by American nuclear scientists in the days of the Baruch Plan.

The failure of the Helsinki agreements to advance human rights in the Soviet Union is also a failure of expectations that goes back to the early days of the cold war. To this very day there is a major discrepancy between Western and Eastern conceptions of human rights; it is doubtful, as recently observed, "whether those rights which we [in the West] consider inalienable and take for granted as central to our way of life are similarly misunderstood . . . by most East Europeans [who] accord primacy to collective rather than individual and socio-economic rather than political rights."[18]

The nationalist unrest in both the Asian and European parts of the Soviet Union has dramatized the problems Moscow is facing in granting religious and cultural rights to ethnic and national minorities. Traditionally, the study of Soviet foreign policy motivation and behavior has paid little attention to the nationality factor. The Soviets, for their part, both in official statements and through their commentators, have, however, indicated that the nationality issue is of major significance in their foreign relations and that they react very sensitively to external criticism of their nationalities policy.[19] Waves of protest, accompanied by calls for autonomy and even independence, periodically sweep the three Baltic republics annexed by the Soviet Union in 1940. But of greater concern are almost fifty million Muslims, representing a fast-growing demographic threat to the dwindling ethnic Russian minority. In a polyglot nation of more than one hundred recognized nationalities, religious and cultural freedom may well be costly. In 1987 the Russians constituted 51.5 percent of the total Soviet population, while the other 48.5 percent belong to various non-Russian minorities of different ethnic, religious, and cultural backgrounds. By the year 2000, according to projections by the United States Census Bureau, the Russians will become a minority of 49 percent.[20] It is hard to picture Gorbachev, while pursuing some of his economic reforms, as having the will and the political backing to chart a dramatic policy in order to placate the non-Russian 50 percent of the population. As long as he does not do this, it is inconceivable that he will make a dramatic departure in granting new cultural rights to Soviet Jews.

Human Rights Linkages

The debate on the linkage between arms control and human rights precedes, accompanies, and follows any negotiation and agreement between the superpowers on arms control. The Reagan administration has gone further than any previous administration in linking these issues, and in particular the question of Jewish emigration, within the framework of superpower high-politics. As we have noted, the Reykjavik summit of October 1986 was a major landmark in this regard. A speech by Secretary of State George Shultz in Los Angeles on 31 October 1986, in which he alluded again to this linkage (mentioning Jewish emigration specifically) aroused the usual concern from different circles. A *New York Times* editorial, entitled "The Right Priority for Human Rights," concluded with the following observation: "Human Rights and arms control are fundamental concerns of the American people. Holding one hostage to the other does a disservice to both."[21] Thus, from a tactical point of view, the Soviet Jewry movement faces a problem in linking any issue of human rights with questions on which the survival of the planet may depend.

On the other hand, people like former Prisoner of Zion Natan Shcharansky insist that human rights and arms talks must be linked without, at the same time, letting the Soviet Union use Jews as currency in arms negotiations. The principle of free emigration for all Soviet Jews who desire it must, according to Shcharansky, be part and parcel of superpower strategic negotiations.[22]

Instead of using the term linkage it may be preferable, for practical reasons, to find a formula that would encompass what was said both by

Secretary of State Shultz and Natan Shcharansky. Shultz explained at the meeting in Los Angeles that there is "a very great limitation on the kind of progress that we can make in establishing a more stable and more workable situation between our countries as long as the human rights situation remains what it is." Shcharansky for his part noted that human rights must be viewed as a major factor in lessening mutual suspicion between the superpowers and creating an atmosphere of trust and goodwill, which is critical for arms control. In sum, without using the term linkage, one can allude to the problem of Soviet Jewry as an important factor for the removal of distrust between the superpowers, a process which is crucial for mutual understanding and agreements between states.

In the winter 1986 issue of *Foreign Affairs*, Robert Collen, *Newsweek*'s diplomatic correspondent, presented a thorough analysis of the problem of Soviet Jewry and suggested a few strategies for the campaign. Collen clearly opposed the arms control option:

> The history of the past 15 years suggests that there are two carrots to which the Soviets will respond: trade and arms control. Clearly, arms control policy, which so directly affects American national security, cannot be determined on the basis of what is likely to aid Soviet Jews. But trade is another matter. The trick is to devise a set of trade incentives—to be extended one at a time depending on Soviet behavior—that serves both American interests and those of Soviet Jews.[23]

Collen's assertion that arms control cannot be determined by the condition of Soviet Jewry does not deny the fact that a linkage exists in the background that becomes more critical during the painstaking process of arms control negotiations. In such a process, which can never be isolated from the international environment, factors such as public relations, the international image of the participants, and good intentions play an important role. Thus, without placing the Jewish issue as a quid pro quo to be traded with cuts in nuclear missiles and warheads, the linkage remains, if the American side raises it, as an effective instrument in the negotiating process.

Neshira, Aliya, and Jewish Culture

Professor Herman Baranover, a former refusenik who lives in Israel, contends that the difference between dropouts and *olim* is self-evident: "those who have a strong Jewish identity come to Israel; those who completely lack this identity have no reason to come, and don't come."[24]

The drop-out phenomenon which started in the early 1970s on a small scale and gradually increased, overtaking *aliya* by 2:1 in 1979–80 and 3:1 in 1987, has transformed Soviet Jewish *aliya* into another movement of emigration. The drop-out rates dealt a major blow to the idealistic Zionist struggle for Soviet Jewry and created tremendous embarrassment and confusion among its activists. It has become apparent that the Soviet Jewry movement cannot blame the Soviets for everything and just shrug its shoulders by saying that Gorbachev succeeded in lulling the West into inaction on the Jewish question.

Facing the strong trend of Soviet Jews' assimilation and de-Judaization in America (where it is both faster and easier than in the USSR), the Zionist establishment confronts a terrible dilemma. If the end result of the campaign for Soviet Jewry is the emigration of the overwhelming majority from one exile to another with a faster rate of assimilation, is it worthwhile? The hasty and abortive attempt of the Israeli government to convince the United States to stop giving special refugee status to Jews emigrating from the Soviet Union only dramatized the confusion and lack of long-term policy planning on the Soviet Jewry question. The idea was rejected by the American Congress, the administration, and Jewish organizations.[25] Instead of blaming U.S. policy and the community aid which is given to the *noshrim* (drop-outs) in the United States, the Zionist establishment must check its own house first, look into absorption problems in Israel, and intensify its efforts to raise Jewish identity and motivation within the Soviet Union.

The interesting phenomenon today is that there is no longer a discernible split in the Soviet Jewry movement on the issue of Jewish culture. The clear dichotomy of the past, between those who asked to concentrate on reviving Jewish culture and those who regarded it as a betrayal of the Zionist idea, no longer exists. Nobody expects a significant development in Jewish culture within the Soviet Union in proportions known in Western societies. On the contrary, the fear is that under *glasnost* the majority of the Jews who lack any formal Jewish education and background would prefer the path of complete assimilation and become acculturated in Soviet society. Sometimes, though, as we have seen, the "democratization" process in the fields of the economy and culture may give rise to anti-Semitic undercurrents and, thus, in a negative way, will once again give rise to a renewed

Jewish awareness and identity. For instance, it is reported that democratization in employment procedures has already undermined the job prospects of Jewish students graduating from universities. Previously, the monolithic Soviet state guaranteed them jobs in their specialty, at least to some extent: "Now the state no longer compels employers to take people they don't want. So one hears about recent Jewish graduates who have been directly told in job interviews, 'We don't want your sort here.' "[26]

Both in the movement for Soviet Jews and among the activists in the Soviet Union, Jewish culture and religion are regarded as an important instrument, though limited in its potential, for enhancing the struggle for *aliya*. Unlike the 1970s when Jewish activists were often not ready even to listen to the notion of introducing Jewish culture to the USSR, today both activists and the Jewish establishment in the West consider ways and means to strengthen Jewish culture and identity in the Soviet Union.

Outspoken supporters of the struggle for *aliya,* including those who tried to pressure the United States to stop giving special refugee status to Soviet emigrants, are more open today to the necessity of more Judaism in the Soviet Union. The Israeli minister of absorption, Ya'acov Tsur, a secular Kibbutz member, surprised an Orthodox journalist when he admitted that "teaching Jewish values, including the teaching of Judaism, Hebrew and observance of *mitzvot* [religious precepts] are the major instruments in the struggle against *neshira*. . . . Without placing Jewish education as the first priority there will not be *aliya* from the Soviet Union."[27]

As a matter of fact, the approach of the Zionist establishment to the issue of Jewish culture in the Soviet Union has not been without vicissitudes. From an emphasis in the 1950s and 1960s on the demand "let the Jews live as Jews," including retaining their culture, in the 1970s the movement, as well as the activists in the Soviet Union, rejected efforts toward enhancing Jewish culture, focusing exclusively on emigration. Today, there is a consensus among former and current activists who are still in the Soviet Union that there is no future for Judaism in the Soviet Union. On the one hand, all of them would agree with Mark Azbel's personal account of his life as a refusenik that "the situation of Jews in Russia is, in fact, insoluble, given the culture and mentality of the population."[28] On the other hand, more and more activists are adopting a more instrumental approach to Jewish culture and religion as a tool to enhance *aliya*.[29]

It is understood that in the large-scale emigration of some 300,000 as of 1968, most of the motivated Jews, those who concluded that in the USSR they could not live as Jews, have left the Soviet Union. For the remaining Jews, most of whom are without any positive motivation (only negative, as a result of anti-Semitism), the revival of Jewish culture is critical for them to develop a sense of Jewish identity.

In dealing with Jewish culture and identity in today's Soviet Union one must take into consideration the dramatic changes that have overtaken the Jewish activist movement there in recent years. A new generation of religiously observant activists has grown up, comprising today the major component of the movement, replacing the former group of secular Zionist realists, as well as the groups of scientists and Hebrew teachers. Jewish culture in today's Soviet Union is more religion-oriented, reflecting similar trends within Soviet society as a whole. Though the numbers are still in the hundreds, the religiously observant activists provide the core of the leadership of the movement. Virtually all of them are recent *hozrim bitshuva*, who have come to religion in the past five years or so. In Moscow, for instance, the majority of young Hebrew teachers are religious. Within the religious group one can find leanings toward a variety of trends in Orthodox Judaism: Habad and other Hasidim and national-religious and even anti-Zionist groups. Some thought should perhaps be given to ways and means of unifying the groups in order to set a common campaign for religious and cultural rights.

Conclusion

The major thrust of this chapter has been to emphasize the extent to which the fate of the Jews in the Soviet Union depends on the relations between the superpowers. As shown, the emigration figures can serve as a barometer of Soviet-American relations. Jewish culture, however, is a different case. It seems still very unlikely that the issues of culture and religion could become part and parcel of superpower negotiations. As Dimitri K. Simes puts it:

Détente should not preclude human rights diplomacy. It is, however, incompatible with political crusades against Moscow under the banner of human rights."[30]

Nevertheless, at the same time, Dimitri Simes adds, the Soviets are well aware that private organizations do have a bearing on official United States policy and that their pressure is legitimate. This method provides the

American administration with the teeth for quiet diplomacy and creates an implicit linkage between human rights and other dimensions of superpower relations.

Pressure on human rights and cultural rights is especially related to long and continuous processes where economic leverage is also significant. Measures such as the Jackson-Vanik and the Stevenson amendments can continue to be linked to demands on human and cultural rights.

As put by Edgar Bronfman, the chairman of the Seagram Company and president of the World Jewish Congress (WJC): "while the Soviets claim there is no connection between human rights and the furtherance of Soviet-American trade—there most assuredly is such a link. American businessmen will remain reluctant to expose themselves to risk in other markets by trading with a country that is perceived to be persecuting Jews and other minorities."[31]

The history of both Russia and the Soviet Union is intertwined with cycles of reform and counterreform, of liberation and repression as well as periods of cultural stagnation. The ultimate extent of the Gorbachev reforms and their impact on Jewish culture in the Soviet Union remain to be seen. The year of writing, 1988, has witnessed signs of a national Jewish awakening in the Soviet Union with a clear tendency among the Jews to regularize Jewish life. This trend has developed along two main paths:

1. Jewish cultural projects under the aegis of the establishment and with the cooperation of world Jewry including Israel.
2. Independent, extra-establishment cultural endeavors, though with the complete knowledge and acquiescence of the authorities.

The establishment has officially recognized the existence of Jewish cultural associations in various communities and sometimes, as in the Baltic republics, has actually welcomed their appearance. These associations sometimes emphasize Yiddish culture and loyalty to the regime; in many cases they retain the desire to emigrate and even emphasize Jewish-Zionist culture with the ultimate intention of making *aliya*. Outside the establishment, the authorities have also allowed the formation of three Jewish bodies: the Soviet-Israel Friendship Society (a declared Zionist and pro-Israel organization founded in May 1988, with a couple of hundred members and branches in several cities), the Jewish Cultural Association, in Moscow (also founded in May 1988) and the Union of Hebrew Teachers in the USSR (founded in September 1988, with one hundred registered teachers from all over the country).

At the beginning of November 1988, Bronfman went to Moscow at the head of a delegation which included, for the first time ever, leaders of the Jewish Agency: the chairman, Simcha Dinitz, who is also the chairman of the World Zionist Organization, and Mendel Kaplan, the chairman of the Agency's board of governors. The delegation held talks with Soviet officials and reported that the Soviet Union expressed a clear willingness to be more direct in dealing with the issue of Jewish culture, and to allow Israeli institutions, such as the Jewish Agency, to have a role in providing materials and teachers and in shaping the programs.[32]

It became evident that the Soviet Union of Mikhail Gorbachev regards its policy toward its Jews, particularly the strengthening of their ties with world Jewry, as an important element of its new global posture. The International Council of the World Conference on Soviet Jewry, the body which coordinates international efforts on behalf of Soviet Jewry, responded in resolutions which perhaps mark a departure from the previous confrontation line toward the Soviet Union. At its meeting in Jerusalem in December 1988, the Council decided to move toward a major emphasis on developing Jewish culture, on a long-term basis, in the Soviet Union. Simcha Dinitz, who also serves as the head of the World Conference on Soviet Jewry, said that the movement would have to learn to combine its advocacy role with cultural work inside the Soviet Union. Dinitz said that the movement's cultural projects would be planned and implemented together with Soviet Jews. "They no longer have to act as an 'underground,' and we should not relate to them any more as 'refuseniks' or 'activists,' but as local Jewish leaders."

Bronfman, in his remarks to the Conference, said that world Jewry would have to think about how to acknowledge significant changes in Soviet Jewish life, on the assumption that the promises given by the Soviets would materialize. World Jewry would have to reconsider how to change its strategy and tactics; instead of demonstrating in front of embassies, it should engage in cultural work, sending rabbis, teachers, artists, and others to build up Jewish life in the Soviet Union.[33]

The struggle to revive Jewish culture and Judaism has become an important instrument of the Soviet Jewry movement. As shown in this volume, Jewish cultural and religious activities have been virtually nonexistent in the Soviet Union. Those that are maintained by the establishment are basically symbolic, while those that have resulted from initiatives of individual Jews or small groups are often short-lived, as a result of constraints imposed by the authorities. The variety of activities in the religious and cultural fields which have been recorded here are in the final event marginal in terms of the size and educational level of the Jewish population. Their very existence, mostly without official approval and sometimes actually underground, is just another living testimony to the saga of the Jewish struggle for national identity in the Soviet Union.

Notes

1. *New York Times* editorial, April 6, 1979. In December 1974 Congress adopted an amendment to the Export-Import Ban Bill introduced by Senator Adlai Stevenson III limiting U.S. credits to the Soviet Union to $300 million; credits above that sum were to depend on Soviet mitigation of restrictions on emigration, as well as a responsible approach to arms control, the force-reduction talks and the Middle East. In the same month, the Senate passed Senator Henry Jackson's amendment to the Export Administration Act (a parallel amendment introduced by Representative Charles Vanik had been passed by the House in December 1973); this amendment prevented the Administration from granting Most Favored Nation (MFN) status to countries which imposed restrictions on emigration.
2. Robert Freedman adds the improvement of Sino-American relations as another variable influencing Soviet Jewish emigration. See Robert O. Freedman (ed.), *Soviet Jewry in the Decisive Decade, 1971–1980* (Durham, N.C.: Duke University Press, 1984), pp. 47–48.
3. *Jerusalem Post*, February 3, 1961. Cited in William Korey, *The Soviet Cage* (New York: Viking Press, 1973), p. 35. This is not convincing, since the so-called Chinese card was part and parcel of détente and arms control talks between the superpowers. Simultaneously with the American entry into strategic negotiations with the Soviets, the Americans tried to enhance their relationship with China. Robert O. Freedman, "Soviet Jewry and Soviet-American Relations: A Historical Analysis," in Freedman (ed.), *Soviet Jewry*, pp. 38–67.
4. "Soviet Jewish Emigration Gains in the Agenda," *New York Times*, October 11, 1986.
5. "Pre-Summit Push on Emigration," *New York Times*, November 10, 1987.
6. *New York Times*, April 1, 1987.
7. For a background on *Pamiat'*, see Howard Spier, "Soviet Antisemitism Unchained: The Rise of the Historical and Patriotic Association 'Pamyat'," Research Report no. 13, July 1987, Institute of Jewish Affairs London; William Korey, "The Pamyat Phenomenon," *Present Tense*, January–February 1988, pp. 36–40.

8. "A Modest Treaty but a Step Toward Realism," *International Herald Tribune*, December 1, 1987.
9. Avi Beker, *Disarmament Without Order: The Politics of Disarmament at the United Nations* (Westport, Conn.: Greenwood Press, 1985), pp. 14–22.
10. United Nations, Security Council, Official Records, Second Year (22), March 5, 1947.
11. Stanley A. Blumberg and Gwin Owens, *Energy and Conflict: The Life and Times of Edward Teller* (New York: G. P. Putnam's Sons, 1976), p. 339.
12. Henry L. Stimson and McGeorge Bundy, *On Active Service in Peace and War* (New York: Octagon, 1974), pp. 35–36.
13. Edward Teller, "A Suggested Amendment to the Acheson Report," *Bulletin of the Atomic Scientists*, 1, no. 12 (June 1, 1946): 5.
14. Adam B. Ulam, *The Rivals: America and Russia Since World War II* (New York: Penguin Books, 1977), p. 37.
15. *Time Magazine*, March 2, 1987, p. 7.
16. See "Gorbachev or Not, Reform Will Stay," *New York Times*, July 10, 1987; "Gorbachev Calls for Fresh View of Marx," *Christian Science Monitor*, February 19, 1988.
17. Michael Howard, "Russia Rethinks the Revolution," *The World Today*, November 1987, p. 185.
18. See Vojtech Mastny, *Helsinki, Human Rights and European Security: Analysis and Documentation* (Durham, N.C.: Duke University Press, 1986), p. 145.
19. Rasma Karklins, "The Nationality Factor in Soviet Foreign Policy," in Roger E. Kanet (ed.), *Soviet Foreign Policy* (New York: Praeger, 1982) pp. 58– 59.
20. "Gorbachev is Feeling the Heat From the South," *New York Times*, March 6, 1988.
21. *New York Times*, November 13, 1986.
22. Natan Shcharansky, "Human Rights, Arms Talks Must be Linked," *Wall Street Journal*, November 4, 1986.
23. Robert Collen, *Foreign Affairs*, Winter 1986, p. 262.
24. Herman Baranover, "Stemming the Drop-Out Rate," *Jerusalem Post*, August 27, 1987.
25. "Let Soviet Jews Decide," *New York Times* editorial, March 8, 1987.
26. "Culture in the USSR: The View from Goskomizdat," *Wall Street Journal*, February 2, 1988.
27. *Erev Shabbat* (a Hebrew ultra-Orthodox weekly), October 30, 1987. For a similar statement by Uri Gordon of the Labor party and head of the Jewish Agency *aliya* department, see *Yom hashishi*, March 25, 1988.
28. Mark Azbel, *Refusenik* (New York: Paragon House, 1981).
29. *Jerusalem Post*, February 14, 1988.
30. Dimitri K. Simes, "Human Rights and Detente," in Grayson Kirk and Nils H. Wersell (eds.), *The Soviet Threat: Myths and Realities* (New York: Proceedings of the Academy of Political Science, 1978), p. 147.
31. "Gorbachev's Visit: Will Trade Follow the Summit Talks?" *New York Times* (Business Section), December 6, 1987.

32. The talks on the cultural center in Moscow were conducted with the head of the Council for Religious Affairs, Konstantin Kharchev. Dinitz and Kaplan also met briefly with Foreign Minister Eduard Shevardnadze, after the latter finished a lengthy discussion with Bronfman; see "Jewish Culture and Comfort in the Soviet Union," *Jerusalem Post*, November 10, 1988.
33. Bronfman also said that world Jewry should establish a "Jewish Peace Corps" that would mobilize manpower to revive Jewish life in the Soviet Union. Jewish communities in Israel and the Diaspora, he said, would now be able to make "twinning" arrangements to support Jewish cultural centers in as many as two hundred localities. He said that these efforts would be funded and carried out through the WJC and the Jewish Agency; see *Jerusalem Post*, December 2, 1988. On February 12, 1989, Bronfman participated at the opening of the first Jewish community center in Moscow at the Solomon Mikhoels Cultural Center. Among the Jewish leaders who attended the ceremony was Elie Wiesel, the Nobel Peace laureate, author of *The Jews of Silence*. Commending Soviet Jews for having protected their heritage, Wiesel said, "What a statement of faith you have made." "Lasting Faith of Soviet Jews Moves Wiesel," *New York Times*, February 13, 1989.

Index

A pushorahi toza zindaguni (Towards the New Life), 415
A zuhun tati (In the Tat Language), 425
Abasi (Twenty Copeck Coin), 415
Abkhaz ASSR. *See* Sukhumi
ABM agreement, 446
"About One Letter," 218
Abram, Morris B., 449
Abramis, Izrail, 177
Abramov, Pinhos, 405–6
Abramovich, Pavel, 138, 154
Abramzon, Ikhiel, 142, 153, 160 n.10
Acculturation, 14, 399, 455. *See also* Assimilation
Activism, Jewish, 9–10, 12, 29–41 passim, 88, 91, 95–96, 100, 127, 148, 156, 181, 262–65, 286, 288–89, 456. *See also* Prisoners of Zion; Refuseniks; Zionism; Zionist youth groups
Adabiyoti soveti, 407, 440 n.127
Adenauer, Konrad, 302
Adra'i, David-Hayy, 386
Afghanistan, 446
Agronom, 442
Agronov, Abraham, 149
Agudat, Israel, 392
Agurskii, Mikhail, 164 n.57, 258
Aharon, Ben Shim'on, 386
Aharunov, Ya'ghu, 409, 411–12, 415–16
Ahavat Tsiyon (Love of Zion), 388, 400–403, 410
Aikhenvald, Aleksandra, 18, 285
Aikhenvald, Iulii Isaevich, 285
Aizenshtat, Esfir, 153
'Ajal zanho (Women's Death), 420
Akhaltsikhi, 382

Akhmatova, Anna, 209–10
Aleichem, Sholem, 170, 172, 175, 193, 200, 203, 270
Aleksandr I, Czar, 389
Aleksandrovich, Michail, 176
Aleksandrovich, Rivka, 155
Aliger, Margarita, 74–86 passim, 90
Aliya, 8, 14–15, 20, 29, 33–34, 38 n.22, 39 n.32, n.33, n.34, 42, 47, 50, 52–53, 55–57, 59, 62–63, 65, 88, 91, 96–101, 103, 106, 126, 139, 157, 169, 179–80, 182, 184, 194, 196, 248–49, 252, 257, 262, 326, 328, 333, 341, 421, 455–58
All Union Coordinating Committee, 96
All Union *Znanie* (Knowledge) Society, 282
Alma-Ata, 78
Al'shanskii, Naum, 156
"Alte layt", 207 n.44
'Amaldana ilchi (The Clever Matchmaker), 410
Aminov, Menashe, 404–5, 407
Amirov, Lazar, 418
Amitin-Shapiro, Z., 400
Amusin, Iosif, 284
Andizhan, 171
Andreev (Fain), German, 256
Animal Farm, 36
Anisimov, Il'ia, 431 n.18
Anisimov, Nikolai (Noftoli), 409, 412
Anti-cosmopolitan campaign, 318–20
Anti-Semitism, 5, 7, 12, 31, 39 n.33, 42, 44–50, 52–56, 58–59, 66–67, 69 n.2, 74, 78–79, 90, 96, 103, 113, 117, 213, 216–17, 222, 225–30, 257, 260, 269–70, 310–11, 321, 324, 327–28, 330, 335, 338–40, 357, 417, 447, 449, 455–57

463

Anti-Sovietism, 44, 47, 50, 94, 127, 145, 147, 225
Anti-Zionism, 14, 16, 59, 139, 193, 310–54 passim, 424, 449, 457
Antilov, Daniil, 412, 416, 417
Antokolsky, Mark, 276
Antwerp, 173
Apelbaum, Moyshe (Mikhail), 170
Aq-mechid, 398
Arab-Israeli conflict, 327–29, 337. *See also* Israeli War of Independence; Six Day War; Suez crisis
Arab World, 311, 319, 325–26, 328–30, 342. *See also* Soviet policy toward Middle East
Arabic script, 404, 427
Arbeit, 303
Ardamatskii, Vasilii, 217
Ari bikorhoy Germaniya (To Germany's Unemployed), 413
Ari sifirtura vosdora (To Buy a Tora Scroll), 413
Armenian SSR, 56, 172, 229, 381
Aronas, Eines Feivel, 178
Arshin mal alan, 402
Art, Applied, 276–77
Ashkhabad (Askhabad), 379
Assimilation, 4–5, 9–10, 14, 23 n.14, 45, 50, 53, 64, 106, 140, 151, 211, 223, 264, 269, 276, 304, 455
Autonomous German Republic of the Volga, 291, 294, 298, 305
'Avadiaev, A., 415
Avali abat (The First Steps), 410
Avars, 282, 385, 387
Avidar, Yosef, 120
Avigur, Shaul, 164 n.58
Avshalumov (Ovshalumov), Hizghil (Yehezqel), 415, 417–19, 424, 426
Avshalumova, Liudmila, 418
Avshalumova, N., 432 n.28
Ay,zan mizrah (Oh, Oriental Woman,) 411
Az mahalla ba kolkhuz (From the Jewish Quarter to the Kolkhoz), 406
Azbel' Mark, 258, 456
Azerbaidzhan SSR, 379, 381, 385, 387, 408, 410, 413, 427–28. *See also* Baku; Kuba
Azhaev, Vasilii, 214

Aziia i Afrika segodnia, 210
'Aziza Dagestan (Dear Dagestan), 423
Azizov, Manashir (Menashshe), 418

Ba yodi Khuydodcha (To the Memory of Little Khuydod), 388
Baazov, David, 390
Baazov, Meir, 140
Babel, Isak, 202, 223–24
Babii Iar, 98, 336
Babii Iar (poem), 224
Babii Iar (novel), 225
Bachaev, Mordkhay, 403
Badalov, A., 416
Bagritskii, Eduard, 202, 209
Bahori surkh (Red Spring), 407
Bairam-Ali, 379
Baital'skii (Domal'skii, I.) Mikhail, 104, 258
Bakhchisarai, 379
Bakhshiev, Divyo (Tuvya), 413, 415–16
Bakhshiev, Feliks, 418
Bakhshiev, Mishi (Moshe), 412–13, 416–19, 422, 424
Bakhshiev, Zavulun, 412, 416
Baku, 259, 358, 408, 412
Balasnaia, Riva (Rivka), 176
Balfour Declaration, 312
Balkars, 293
Baltic republics, 14, 16–17, 19, 47, 109 n.10, 113, 134 n.67, 140, 168–69, 183, 247–48, 254 n.2, 259, 452, 458. *See* Estonian, SSR; Latvian SSR; Lithuanian SSR
"Bar Kokhba," 170
Bar Mitzvah, 128
"The Barber of Seville," 170
Bardonoshvili, Iosif, 278
Baruch Plan, 450–52
Basghuni igidho (Victory of the Heroes), 414
Basghuni jovonho (The Victory of the Young), 415
Bashkir ASSR, 281
Basmachi, 405
Ba'th regime (Syria), 328
Bayroqi mihnat (Banner of Labor), [*Rushnoi (Light)*], 403, 404, 407, 440 n.129
Bayroqi zafar (The Banner of Victory), 407
Begun, Barukh, 266–67

INDEX 465

Begun, Iosif, 153–54, 253, 258, 267
Begun, V., 339–40
Belaia kniga iskhoda, 100–101
Belogorsk (Karasubazar), 381
Belorussian SSR, 13, 31, 113, 171, 302. See also Bobruisk; Gomel; Minsk
Ben-'Ammi, Y. (Yesha'yo Binyaminov), 409, 412, 415
Ben-Gurion, David, 325, 327
Ben-Horin, 143
Ben Sever, Mordekhai, 164 n.57
Ben-Simon, Yitshak, 401
Ben-Zvi, Yitzhak, 120
Benovolenskii, V. V., 23
Bergelson, Dovid, 171, 191
Bessarabia, 254 n.2, 259
Between Hammer and Sickle, 118
"Beware of Zionism!" 332
Bialik, Haim Nahman, 90, 92, 141, 143, 153, 175, 177, 203, 247, 401
Bibliotek (Library), 192
Bilak, Vasil, 331
Binaev, 'Asoil (Asael), 411, 415, 419
Birobidzhan, 11, 19, 144, 173, 193, 196, 200, 203, 273–74, 278, 280, 283, 286, 291–92, 302, 305, 334, 369–70, 375
Birobidzhan Drama Theater, 303
Birobidzhaner shtern, 144, 193, 202, 274, 280–81, 302
Birorho (Brothers), 421, 425
Birorov, Ya'ghu, 409, 416
Black Book, The, 224, 231 n.16
Black Hundreds, 225, 227, 231 n.17, 311
"Black Years," 114, 117, 139, 222, 229, 284, 417
Blank, Aleksandr, 152, 180
Blum, Mark, 178
B'nai B'rith, 123, 335
Bobojon, 406
Bobruisk, 45
Bogaroz, Larissa, 21, 103
Bogod, A., 437 n.86
Boiarskaia, Riva, 179
Bol'shakov, V., 335–36, 339
Bolsheviks, 9–10, 311–12, 314, 408, 427
Borisov, Vladimir, 37 n.17
Borokhov, Ber, 408
Borshchagovskii, Aleksandr, 207 n.44
Borukhov, M., 403

Brailovskii, Viktor, 258
Branover, German, 142–43, 454–55
Braudo, Mark, 169–70
Brezhnev, Leonid, 4, 22 n.2, 64, 160, 297, 322, 327, 329, 332, 445–46
Briskman, Chaim, 264
Brit Ivrit Olamit (World Association for Hebrew Language and Culture), 138, 160 n.11
Britain, 312, 325
Broadcasts: Israeli, 32–33, 39 n.34, 56, 99, 116, 138–40, 146, 151, 158, 160 n.14, 164 n.57, 166 n.76, 251, 269. See also *Kol Tsion Lagola*, Voice of Israel; Soviet, 304. See also Radio Moscow
Brodetskaia, Tina, 95–96, 146, 163 n.43
Bromlei, Iu., 295
Bronfman, Edgar, 449, 458–59, 462 n.33
Brushtein, Aleksandra Iakovlevna, 216
Brussels, 173
Brussels Conference on Soviet Jewry, 333
Bubennov, Mikhail, 216–17, 230 n.7
Budalov, Rahamim, 407
Budapest Jewish Theological Seminary, 19
Bukhara, 277, 382, 384, 388, 400, 402–3
Bukharan Jewish Community, 47, 109 n.10, 140, 149, 171, 181, 259, 275, 373, 379–88, 395–97, 400–8, 427–28, 437 n.86, 439 n.108
Bukharan People's Soviet Republic, 400
Bukhbinder, Nokhem, 197
Bukhina, Evgeniia, 155–56, 165 n.69
Bulganin, Nikolai, 325
Bund, 9–10, 311–13
Buria, (The Storm), 214, 221
Butman, Gil'ia, 147, 151–52, 163 n.49, 164 n.57
Bylenki, Moyshe, 202
Byzantine Empire, 380–81

Carter, James, 337, 445–46
Caucasus, 21, 209, 293, 379. See also Armenian SSR; Azerbaidzhan SSR; Georgian SSR; Mountain Jews
Central Asia, 21, 131, 150, 183, 209, 379, 381–82, 387, 403, 405, 427. See also Kirgiz SSR, Tadzhik SSR, Turkmen SSR, Uzbek SSR
Chagall, Mark, 276; Museum, 286, 370

Chaikov, Iosif, 276
Chalidze, Valerii, 361
Chapichev, Yakov, 395–96
Charles University (Prague), 330
Chastushkahoy kolkhozi (Kolkhoz Chastushkas), 422
Chechen-Ingush ASSR, 410. *See also* Groznyi
Chechens, 293
Chego zhe ty khochesh' (What Do You Want?), 226
Cherkassian language, 385
Chernikhovsk, 171
Chernikhovsky, Shaul, 247
Chernin, Velvl (Vladimir), 199–200, 202–3, 285, 425
Chernoglaz, David, 152
Chernovtsy, 146, 172, 174, 177, 278
Chesnokov, D. I., 227, 231 n.18
Chlenov, Mikhail, 267–68
Chobruitskii, Samuil', 114
Choral Synagogue (Moscow), 113–15, 120–22, 126, 130 n.16, 264, 287, 449
Christianity, 57, 60, 63, 67, 71 n.13, 427
Chukotkan-Kamchatkan Languages, 396
Churchill, Winston S., 94
Chuvashes, 281–82
Collectives, professional, 45
Collen, Robert, 454
Comedy of Errors, 388
Comintern, 312–13
Commissariat for Jewish Affairs (Evkom), 10
Commission for the Rural Placement of Jewish Toilers (Komzet), 393–94
Communist Party of Azerbadzhan, 412
Communist Party of Belorussia, 127
Communist Party of Lithuania, 169
Communist Party of Uzbekistan, 407
Conference of Presidents of Major Jewish Organizations, 449
Council for Religious Affairs, 19, 120, 287, 362, 462 n.32
CPSU (Communist Party of the Soviet Union), 10, 34, 41 n.52, 168, 372. *See also* Bolsheviks; Communist Party of Azerbadzhan; Communist Party of Belorussia; Communist Party of Lithuania; Communist Party of Uzbekistan; *Evsektsiia*; Ideology; Komsomol; Twentieth Party Congress
CPSU (Central Committee Secretariat and Apparatus), 210, 327, 329
Crimea, ASSR, 11, 293, 305, 378–79, 381, 383–84, 391–94, 427, 434 n.54. *See also* Bakhchisarai; Belogorsk; Crimean Tatars; Evpatoriia; Feodosiia; Karaites; Karasubazar; Kerch; Mazanki; Sevastopol; Simferopol
Crimean Tatars, 293–94, 378, 383, 391–92
CSCE (Conference for Security and Cooperation in Europe), Concluding Document of Madrid Meeting, 356, 368, 371; Human Rights Experts' Meeting, 363. *See also* Helsinki Final Act and Accords
Cuba, 196
Culture, Jewish officials, 17–19, 194, 373
Czechoslovakia, 6, 16, 260, 279, 316–17, 325, 329–32, 334–35

Dadashev, Hizghiyo, 415
Dadashev, Manuvah (Manoah), 412–13, 416
Dadashev, Mikhail, 421, 425
Dadi u (Her Father), 403
Dadiani, L.I., 23 n.19, 338
Dagestan ASSR, 131 n.25, 149, 379, 381, 387, 408, 423, 427, 428. *See also* Derbent; Makhachkala; Mountain Jews; Qaytaqi
Dagestanskaia pravda, 425
Dah sol (Ten Years), 407
Daleko ot Moskvy (Far From Moscow), 214
Damskii portnoi (The Women's Tailor), 206 n.39, 207 n.44
Dance, Israeli, 180, 187 n.24
Daniel, Iulii. *See* Sinyavsky-Daniel trial
Dar, David, 83
Dardhoy pira Has (The Sufferings of Old Hasan), 420
Dargin (Dargwa), 385, 387
Daudet, Alphonse, 284
Daugavpils (Dvinsk), 170
Davidovich, Efim, 156
Davydova, Gulbahor, 419
Day Is Still Long, The, 193
Dead Sea Scrolls, 283
Deborin, A. M., 325

Decade of Euphoria, A: Western Literature in Post-Stalin Russia, 228
"Decades of National Art," 230 n.2
Degen, Iona, 48, 70 n.4
Dekatov, Anatoli, 138, 160 n.10
Dektor, Feliks, 260–61
Demography, Jewish, 274–75, 292, 296, 298–300, 434 n.54
Den' poezii, 212
Deportation of Ethnic Minorities, 293–94
Deputat (The Deputy), 407
Der blutiker shpas (The Bloody Joke), 280
Derbent, 149, 384–85, 387, 389, 409–10, 416
Derbent-Makhachkala Circle, 416
De-Stalinization, 15, 90, 117, 120, 169, 191, 218–21, 228, 230, 321–22
Détente, 27, 325, 337, 341, 447
Deviatyi val (The Ninth Wave), 214, 221
Di tsayt (Time), 280
"Dialogues on Jewish Culture in the Soviet Union," 200
Dimarov, Anatolii, 227
Dinitz, Simcha, 459, 462 n.32
Dinstein, Yoram, 363, 369
Dnepropetrovsk, 274
Dnevnik Marietty Shaginian (The Diary of Marietta Shagnian), 219
Doctors' Plot, 55, 117, 119, 214, 217, 222, 225, 318, 320–21, 323–24
Dol'nik, Solomon, 150
Dolzhanskaia, Tamar, 77
Domal'skii, I. *See* Baitalskii, Mikhail
Domor na'arus (Bridegroom and Bride), 424
Donat, Alexander, 77, 81, 83
Doroga ukhodit v dal' (The Road Slips Away into the Distance), 216
Dos oyigerikhe folk (The Restored People), 285
Dostoevsky, Feodor, 103
Dovid—vazir Khon an Tabasaru (Dovid, Vizir of Tabarasaran's Khan), 421, 424
Doytsh (Deich), Lev, 197
Drabkin, David, 36 n.6, 138
Dragunskii, David, 334
Draznin, Meir, 150, 156, 165 n.69
Drezner, Solomon, 147, 152–53
Driz, Shayke, 179, 283
Drobizheva, L. M., 4, 7, 15

Druskenniki, 170
Druzhba narodov, 226
Du alatfurukhho (Two Sellers of Second-hand Goods), 410
Du biror (Two Brothers), 414
Du daday (Two Mothers), 424
Du koghoz (Two Letters), 414
Dubcek, Alexander, 330–31, 334
Dubnow, Simon, 90
Dusdi (Friendship), 419
Dushanbe (Stalinabad), 171, 173, 384, 397
Dushmanoni fronti madani (Enemies on the Cultural Front), 405
Dvasun, 50
Dzintari, 170

Economic trials, 324, 327
Edel'man, Hava, 153, 174
Edel'man, Sh., 400
Edelshtein, Iulii, 253
Education. *See* Fundamentals of Legislation of the USSR and the Union of Republics on Education; Soviet policy toward language
Egorychev, Nikolai, 329
Egypt, 325, 328, 329. *See also* Suez crisis
Ehrenburg, Il'ia, 84–85, 214, 218, 220–24, 318
Einstein, Albert, 76, 80
Eisenhower, Dwight, 446
Ekho gor (The Echo of the Mountains), 389
Ekonomicheskie problemy sotsializma v SSSR (The Economic Problems of Socialism in the USSR), 220
Elef Millim (One Thousand Words), 145, 147, 149, 152–54, 156, 249, 252
Eliashvili, Natan, 386
Eliav, Aryeh L., 118
Emigration, Jewish, 8, 14–18, 20, 24–25, 28, 29, 32, 54, 58–59, 65, 69, 95, 98, 101, 106, 122, 126, 151, 227, 256, 263, 276, 296, 306, 317, 331, 341–42, 354 n.80, 358, 424, 445–49, 453, 455, 460 n.1, n.2. *See also* Aliya; Soviet policy toward emigration
Emil'ianov, Valerii, 103
Erikson, Erik, 22
Eshkol, Levi, 327–28
Essas, Il'ia, 260

Estonian SSR, 171, 197, 247, 281. *See also* Tallinn; Tartu
Europe, 210, 224
European Convention on Human Rights, 356, 376 n.5
Eve, The, 193
Evpatoriia, 379
Evrei v SSSR, 102–5, 107–8, 257–61
Evreiskaia proletarskaia mysl', 313–14
Evreiskii samizdat (Jewish Samizdat) 1, 73, 258
Evseev, E., 335, 338–39
Evsektsiia (Jewish Section of CPSU), 10, 12, 17, 158, 247, 342, 373, 394–95, 400–401, 408–9, 427
Evtushenko, Evgenii, 70 n.4, 224–25, 269
Exodus, 39 n.35, 89–92, 107, 255
Export Administration Act, 460 n.1
Export-Import Ban Bill, 460 n.1
Eynikeyt, 50

Fabriki bereshum (The Weaving Mill), 406
Fadeev, Aleksandr, 84
Fain, Veniamin (Benjamin), 105, 107, 242–45, 257, 261
Falik, Pinhas, 177
Farhad and Shirin, 404
Fast, Howard, 90, 92, 107
Federovich, Balis, 170
Fedorovna, Vera, 83
Fefer, Itzik, 171, 191
Feigin, Grisha, 36 n.12, 141–42, 149
Feldman, Jacques, 144
Feodosiia (Kaffa), 381, 383, 389, 392, 394
Fergana, 171, 385
Fergana Valley, 384
Feuchtwanger, Lion, 227, 228
Feuilletons, 92–94, 105, 107
Fichman, Yaacov, 177
Finn, Shmeul Yosef, 287
Finn-Ugrian languages. *See* Izhor; Saam; Veps
Flier, Iakov, 176
Folks-shtime, 202, 279
Ford, Gerald, 446
France, 325
Freiman, Grigorii, 358
Freundschaft, 303
Freylakhs, 278

Friedberg, Maurice, 227–28
Friedgut, Theodore, 21
Frug, Shimon, 90
Frunze, 177
Fundamentals of Legislation of the USSR and the Union of Republics on Education, 357–58, 360
Furtseva, Ekaterina, 154, 447
Fuzaylov, Nison, 405

Galich, 380
Galkin, Milia, 276
Gal'perin, Aleksandr, 156
Gaon's Synagogue (Vilnius), 28
Garber, David, 148, 178
Garber, Miriam, 178
Gavrilov, Boris, 411
Gelfond, Meir, 143–44, 255
Gelman, Emanuil, 59–60
GEM (*Gorskoevreiskaia molodezh'*—Mountain Jewish Youth), 409
Gendlin, Zhenia, 58
Genin, Izrail, 318
Genoese Black Sea colonies, 381
Georgian Jewish Museum, 428
Georgian SSR, 18, 48, 109 n.10, 116, 131 n.23, 25, 140, 149, 172, 181, 259, 275, 279, 332, 373, 378, 381–82, 385–87, 390, 395, 426–28. *See also* Akhaltsikhi; Kutaisi; Sukhumi; Tbilisi; Tskhinvali
Gerenrot, Anatolii, 155, 165 n.69
German Democratic Republic, 279, 334, 354 n.80
Germans (Soviet), 290–309 passim, 354 n.80, 341
Gershenzon, Mikhail, 223
Gessen, Iulii, 197
Ghalay Darband (The Fortress of Derbent), 423
Ghirmizina 'alam (The Red Banner), 416
Ghirmizina astara (Red Star), 411
Gil, Geula, 328
Gil, Pinkhas, 59
Gindelshtein-Sevella, Iuliia, 47
Ginzburg, Iosif, 140, 161 n.23
Gissar Valley, 384
Giterman, Moshe, 81–82, 258
Glasnost', 70 n.4, 276, 279, 284, 288, 365, 448–51, 455

Gluskina, Gita, 284
Gnesin, Mikhail, 175
God za godom (Year after Year, 201, 364
Gogol, Nikolai, 103
Goldberg, Ben-Zion, 114
Golden, Max, 285
Goldstuecker, Edouard, 331
Golotvin, Zh. 425
Gomel, 274
Gomulka, Wladyslaw, 330–31
Gorbachev, Mikhail, 6, 70 n.4, 159 n.3, 322, 343, 370, 426, 448, 451, 458–59. *See also Glasnost'; Perestroika*
Gorbunov, Timofei, 172
Gordonov, Eliezer, 174
Gorelik, Shmaryahu, 156
Gorkii, 151
Gorky, Maksim, 18, 177; Literary Institute, 195, 199, 216, 283
Goset (Yiddish State Theater), 169–71, 185 n.3
Gosizdat, 413, 414
Grande, B. M., 148
Granovskii, Iasha, 141, 161 n.23
Great Russians, 6–7, 247, 291, 383, 385, 453
Great Soviet Encyclopedia, 399
Great Synagogue (Tel Aviv), 115
Greater Iranian Area, 381
Greeks, 293. *See also* Mariupol Greeks
Gribachev, Nikolai, 82–83
Grimberg, Fayina, 198–200
Gromyko, Andrei, 316, 450
Grossman, Vasilii, 217, 224, 229–30, 230 n.7
Groznyi, 385, 410
Gruzberg, Semen, 276
Gubenko, Yakov, 206 n.39
Gulhoy insoni (The Flowers of Mankind), 423
Gurvich, Emil, 172
Gurvich, Iakov, 148
Gurvits, Samuil, 138
Gutin, Izrail', 143, 162 n.34
Gyul'boor, 419
Gyzyl Guba (Red Kuba), 413

Haavot vehabanim (Fathers and Sons), 402–3
Habad. *See* Hasidim of Habad
Habima, 313

Hadassah Magazine, 126
Haderekh, 392
Hadzhibekov, Uzeyr, 402
Hagana, 317
ha-Gole, Moshe ben Ya'akov, 381
Haimov, Y., 405
Hakham, Shim'on, 388, 400, 401, 403
Hakhamov, Y., 403, 407
Halevy, Yehuda, 283
Halima, 404
Halkin, Shmuel, 170–71, 174, 176
Hanukov, Yishogh, 411
Hasafa haivrit, 154, 164 n.57, n.58
Hasidim of Habad, 124, 129 n.2, 133 n.53, 140, 161 n.18, 390, 457
Hatekufa, 145
Hayit, Yitzhak, 144
Hayoti haqiqi (True Life), 405
Hayoti mihnati (Toiling Life), 404
Hazan, Eliyahu, 182
Hebrew (language), 11, 16–18, 20, 22, 37 n.17, 38 n.22, 40, 56–58, 89, 93, 105, 127, 136–67 passim, 175–78, 182, 186 n.12, 197–98, 203, 246–54, 257, 263, 268–69, 273, 275, 283–84, 300–302, 313, 359–61, 373, 375, 386–91, 400–401, 403, 427–28, 432 n.25, 457. *See also Brit Ivrit Olamit; Elef millim; Hasafa haivrit; Mori; Ulpanim*
Hehaluts, 313
Heimatliche Weiten, 303
Heine, Heinrich, 76
Helsinki Final Act and Accords, 106, 356, 363, 365, 367–68, 370–71, 452
Herzl, Theodor, 90, 311
Herzog, Isaac, 114
Hitler, Adolph, 224, 229, 335–37. *See also* Holocaust; Nazi Germany and Nazism
Hofshteyn, Dovid, 174, 191
Hofshteyn, Feige, 176
Holidays, Jewish, 29, 33, 37 n.15, 112; Hanukkah, 114–15; High Holy Days, 113–15; Passover, 97, 112, 115, 118, 128, 135 n.68, 178; Pentecost, 115; Purim, 97, 279; Sabbath, 112, 119, 129 n.2; Simhat Torah, 37 n.15, 99, 118–19, 125, 264; Yom Kippur, 113, 116, 128, 130 n.16
Hollander, David, 121

Holocaust, 30, 35, 37 n.18, 40 n.39, 48–50, 66, 74, 79, 89, 96, 113–14, 174, 196, 207 n.44, 212, 224–25, 228–30, 259, 276–77, 288, 335–36, 398–400
Howard, Michael, 452
Hukumati padar dar dukhtar (*A Father's Power Over His Daughter*), 403
Hungarians (Soviet), 301
Hungary, 322, 329, 334

Iakerson, Shimon, 18, 185
Iakobson, Anatolii, 58
Iakubov (Ya'ghubov) Manashir, 418
Iantovskii, Semen, 264, 286
Iaunzem, Irma, 171
Ideology, 51–52, 310–11, 336–37, 343. *See also* Anti-Zionism; Marxism; Marxism-Leninism; Zionism
Igid jofo (*The Hero of Labor*), 422
Ilishaev, Nisim, 149
"In the Brief Moment Between Today and Tomorrow," 196
Indra, Alois, 331
Inger, Gersh, 276
Ingush, 293
INF Treaty, 446, 449, 450–52
Institute of Ethnography (USSR Academy of Sciences), 365, 425
Institute for Foreign Languages, 146
Institute of Oriental Studies (Georgian SSR Academy of Sciences), 137
Institute of Oriental Studies (USSR Academy of Sciences), 137, 285, 338, 341
Institute of the Peoples of Asia and Africa, 211
Intelligentsia, Jewish, 44, 46–47, 49, 60, 62–63, 65, 68, 90, 104, 128, 220, 263, 332
Intelligentsia, Russian (pre-1917), 44, 93
Intelligentsia (general), 60–61, 104, 226, 332
International Council of the World Conference on Soviet Jewry, 459
International Covenant of Civil and Political Rights (ICCPR), 357, 361–62, 365, 371–72
International Covenant on Economic, Social and Cultural Rights (ICESCR), 357, 362, 364–65

International Red Cross, 178
"International Ties and the Interaction of Nationality Cultures in the USSR," 374
Iolotan, 379
Iosipovich, Elazar, 270
Iran (Persia), 379. *See also* Greater Iranian Area; Jadid al-Islam; Kurdistani Jews; Lakhlukhs
Ishoqboev, Menashe, 405
Iskhod, 98–100
Islam, 379, 381–82, 384, 427–28, 452
Israel, 17, 40 n.40, 46, 49, 50–60, 64–67, 101, 151, 179, 249, 252–53, 261, 455; delegations to USSR, 31, 32, 38 n.23, 37 n.16, n.17, 39 n.33, 96, 97, 118, 151, 164 n.55, 145, 180, 187 n.36; diplomatic representation in USSR, 114–16, 118–20, 122, 132 n.32, 135, 139, 144, 147, 149, 151, 155, 175, 177–79, 181–83, 187 n.37, 326, 448; establishment of, 14, 30, 90, 114, 147, 218, 248, 259, 312–17; image of, 269. *See also* Jerusalem
Israeli Communist Party, 142, 162 n.28, 329. *See also* Palestine Communist Party
Israeli War of Independence, 30
Istoriia moei zhizni (*History of My Life*), 215–16
Italy, 380–81
Iton, 96–98, 256
Itskhakovich, Yanghil (Ya'akov Yitzhaki), 388
Iudaizm bez prykas (*Judaism Unembellished*), 324
Iunost', 24
Ivan Denisovich, One Day in the Life of, 224
Ivanov, Iurii, 332
Izgiiaev, Sergei (Siyun Hizghiyoyev), 416, 423
Izhor (language), 396

Jabotinsky, Vladimir, 90, 92–94, 105, 107, 312
Jackson, Henry, 460 n.1
Jackson-Vanik amendment, 445–46, 458
Jadid al-Islam, 379, 386, 427
Javits, Jacob, 122
Javoniyi usto Sholum (*The Youth of Shalom the Craftsman*), 405
Jephthas Tochter (*Jephtha's Daughter*), 227

Jew in Post-Stalin Soviet Literature, The, 227
Jewish Agency, 459, 462 n.33
Jewish Anti-Fascist Committee, 114, 222, 315, 317, 334
Jewish Autonomous Region. *See* Birobidzhan
Jewish Chamber Music Theater, 278
Jewish Cultural Association, 458
Jewish Defense League, 333
Jewish Drama Studio Theater (Moscow Jewish Dramatic Ensemble), 200, 278
Jewish identity, 5–9, 13–15, 23 n.14, 44, 46–47, 48, 53, 55–56, 59–60, 64, 102–4, 112, 125, 128, 151, 182, 222, 269, 455, 457
Jewish religion, 18–21, 29, 35, 36 n.12, 46, 60, 71 n.13, 103, 112–35 passim, 136, 140, 252, 263–65, 275–76, 287, 362, 371, 375, 449, 452; see Holidays, Jewish
Jews of Silence, 119
Jofokasha daday (The Toiling Mother), 411
Johnson, Lyndon, 446
Joint Distribution Committee, 314, 321, 335
Judaica, 18–20, 197
Judaism. *See* Jewish religion
Judeo-Crimean Tatar (Krymchak) (language), 378, 383–84, 389, 391–400
Judeo-Tadzhik (language), 379, 384, 388, 396–97, 400–403, 408
Judeo-Tat (language), 379, 384–85, 387, 389, 410–16 passim, 428, 443 n.161
Jufda Parusdakho (A Pair of Swallows), 424

Kabardinians, 282
Kabardino-Balkar ASSR, 385, 410
Kabardino-Balkarskaia bednota (The Kabardino-Balkar Poor) [Krasnaia kabarda (Red Kabarda)], 410–11
Kabardino-Cherkassian, 410
Kadar, Janos, 322
Kaddish (Ravel) 177, 181
Kagan, Lev, 176
Kaganovich, Lazar, 230 n.10
Kaliningrad, 171, 173, 305
Kalinovskaia, Dina, 201–2, 207 n.44
Kalmyk ASSR, 209
Kalmyks, 293

Kalontarov, Haim, 407
Kalontarov, Yaquv, 407
Kaminka, Emanuel, 172
Kandel', Feliks, 258
Kanevskii, B. I., 358
Kanovich, Grigorii, 201–3
Kanson, Izrail', 129 n.2
Kantor, Fira, 58
Kaplan, Anatolii (Tanhum), 276
Kaplan, Mendel, 459, 462 n.32
Karaganda, 178
Karaites, 379–80
Karaitic Crimean Tatar (language), 396
Karasubazar, 383, 389, 392–95, 398
Karlin, Sasha Yitzhak ben Avraham, 270
Katz, Label, 123
Katznelson, Yitzhak, 398
Kaunas, 19, 155, 157, 168–70, 177, 278, 287–88
Kaya, Saq-Yuda (Yizhaq Yehuda), 393, 436 n.66
Kaykov, H., 407
Kazakh SSR, 294, 298, 300–301, 303, 305
Kazakov, Yasha, 36 n.5, 37 n.15, 125
Kazan', 141
Kenan, Amos, 97
Kennedy, John F., 446
Kerch, 383, 392
Kerler, Yosef, 176, 180
Ket (language), 396
KGB, 34, 41 n.47, 82, 106, 146, 154, 176, 183, 182 n.24, 186 n.18, 187 n.37, 229, 250, 263–64, 266–67, 279, 329. *See also* MGB; NKVD
Khabarovsk, 142, 173, 283
Khabarovsk Book Publishers, 283
Khaiatovskii, Veniamin, 170, 176
Khaimov, Iakov, 270
Khakimov, Kamran, 269–70
Khalgh tati (The Tat People), 424–25
Khananashvili, Mikhail, 390
Khananashvili, Yoseb, 390
Khanin, Mikhail, 264
Kharchev, Konstantin, 19, 120, 287, 362, 462 n.32
Kharkov, 78, 89, 157, 172, 259, 274
Khavkin, David, 49, 53–54, 96, 153
Khazanov, Boris, 104
Kheifets, Mikhail, 68

Khma ebraelisa (The Jewish Voice), 390–91, 433 n.49
Kholi 'Asanat (Asanat's Carpet), 423
Khomloyi kuhna (Old School), 405
Khorasani rite, 381
Khori (The Soil), 414
"*Khoziain*" ("The Boss"), 228–29
Khrushchev, Nikita, 62, 64, 90, 117, 192, 219, 230 n.10, 293, 300, 302, 321–28, 332, 337, 343. *See also* Secret Speech
Khublari (The Dowry), 409
Khudainatov, Z., 416
Khurshid, 404
Khushahoy ongur (Bunches of Grapes), 419
Khvoles, Avraham, 386
Kid for Two Zuzim, A, 202
Kiev, 37 n.15, 50, 59, 71 n.12, 78, 122, 125, 143, 155, 157, 172–73, 176, 179, 186 n.22, 215, 259, 274, 276, 278–79, 334
Kiev University, 81
Kirgiz SSR, 177, 294, 299, 301. *See also* Frunze
Kirzhnits, Avrom, 197
Kiselev, Vl., 339
Kishinev, 78, 81, 89, 155, 174, 177, 182, 213, 231 n.18, 274, 278, 287, 333–34
Kishinev trial, 94
Kislov, A., 338–39
Kissinger, Henry, 446
Klainbart, Mikhail, 167 n.98
Klaipeda (Memel), 170
Kliachkin, Mikhail, 104
Kochetov, Vsevolod, 226
Kochin, Samuil', 143
Kogan, Isak, 140
Kogan, Pavel, 48
Kokand, 171, 401, 403
Kol Ha'am, 162 n.28
Kol Tsion Lagola (The Voice of Zion to the Diaspora), 139, 160 n.14. *See also* Voice of Israel
Kol Yaacov Yeshiva, 125, 301, 324
Kolkhozy: Krymchak 392, 394; Mountain Jewish, 414, 424
Kolkhuzi namuna (The Model Kolkhoz), 406
Kol'tsov, Mikhail, 223, 231 n.15
Komi ASSR. *See* Vorkuta
Kommunist, 412–13
Komsomol (Communist Youth League), 34, 81, 123, 168, 196, 401
Komsomol (novel), 413
Komsomol'skaia pravda, 335
Komuna (The Rainbow), 424
Komzet (Commission for the Rural Placement of Jewish Toilers), 393
Koreans (Soviet), 282, 293
Korgar (Yunoton Kuraev), 407
Korsokh (The Toiler), 408
Kosloff, Irving, 122
Kosta, 413
Kostomarov, Nikolai, 231 n.18
Kosygin, Aleksei, 322, 328–29
Kotlyar, Yosef, 176
Kovno. *See* Kaunas
Kovostovtsev, M. N., 338
Kozlov, V., 295
Kozlovskii, Sergei, 176
Krantz, Moisei, 144–45
Kravtsov, Gershon, 276
Krechmar, Boris, 149
Kreizer, Y. G., 326
Kriegel, Frantisek, 331
Krikunsov, Petr, 59–60
Kritz, Lidiia, 305
Krivorutskii, Peisakh, 276
Krupnik, Igor, 197, 285, 365
Krushevan, Pavolakii, 231 n.18
Krymchak Kaffa rite, 381
Krymchaks, 275, 373, 378, 380, 383, 385, 387–90, 391–400, 426–28, 434 n.50, n.54
Kryvelev, I. A., 338
Kuba, 149, 384–85, 409, 413
Kudaba, Ceslava, 288
Kuibyshev, 141
Kuilakov, David, 388
Kuk gudil (The Jester's Son), 420
Kuk savdogar-revolyutsioner (A Merchant's Son—A Revolutionary), 409
Kukullu, Amladan, 421
Kuniaev, Stanislav, 68, 70 n.4, 72 n.17
Kurdistani Jews, 379. *See also* Lakhlukhs
Kurgantsev, Mikhail, 210–11
Kutaisi (Kutais), 390
Kuznetsov, Anatolii, 225
Kuznetsov, Eduard, 88
Kvitko, Leyb, 174, 177, 191, 283

INDEX   473

Kychko, T., 324

Lakhlukhs, 379
Language, 12–13, 18–19, 29, 93, 105, 136–67 passim, 198–99, 203, 206 n.39, 378–444 passim. *See also* Soviet policy toward
Languages, Jewish, 158 n.1, 254, 275, 429 n.1, 378–444 passim. *See also* Hebrew; Judeo-Crimean Tatar (Krymchak); Judeo-Tadzhik; Judeo-Tat; Karaitic Crimean Tatar; Yiddish
Last of the Just, The, 255
Latvian SSR, 53, 141, 148, 170–71, 178, 197, 246–48. *See also* Daugavpils; Dzintari; Riga; Rumboli
Law on Individual Enterprise (Individual Labor Activity), 358
Lazaris, Vladimir, 258
Lenin, Vladimir, 6, 9, 295, 312, 322–23, 335, 362, 434 n.51
Lenin Library, 148, 162 n.28
Leninabad, 209
Leningrad, 28, 36 n.8, 37 n.15, 78, 80, 83, 89, 96, 119, 121–27, 141, 143, 146, 152, 156, 161 n.27, 170–71, 173, 177, 248, 259, 264, 268, 274, 276, 278–79, 284–85, 301, 333, 370
Leningrad Polytechnical Institute, 142–43
Leningrad State Museum of History and Religion, 286
Leningrad Synagogue, 119, 147
Leningrad trial, 16, 249, 255–56
Leninism. *See* Ideology; Marxism-Leninism
Leninskoe znamia, 208, 210
Lerner, Aleksandr, 107–8
Levin, Hanokh, 260
Levin, Judah Leib, 125–27, 134 n.56, 334
Levitan, Isak Ilich, 276
Levitin, Lev, 56
Levitin, Vladimir, 144, 162 n.36
Lezgi, 388
Library of Foreign Literature, 148
Lifshitz, Mikhail, 219–21
Lifshitz, Nehama, 168–88 passim
Lifshitz, Yehuda Hirsh, 176
Lipkin, Semen, 209–12
Lipkovskii, Leonid, 153
Lipsky, Yosef, 195

Lissitzky, L., 276
Literature, Israeli, 90, 175, 186 n.14, 269–70
Literature, Jewish, 18, 47, 56, 60, 66, 113, 280–84, 364. *See also* Bukharan Jewish Community; *Khma ebraelisa*; Krymchaks; Mountain Jews; *Samizdat*
Literature, Russian, 208–31 passim, 270, 272. *See also Den' poezii*; *Iunost'*; *Literaturnaia Armeniia*; *Literaturnaia gazeta*; *Molodaia gvardiia*; *Novyi mir*; *Ogonek*; *Oktiabr'*
Literature, Yiddish, 170, 176–77, 191–207 passim, 280–84, 302, 317, 370, 405. *See also Sovetish heymland*
Literaturnaia Armeniia, 229
Literaturnaia gazeta, 220, 225
Lithuanian (language), 170–72, 177, 227
Lithuanian Academy of Sciences, 365
Lithuanian Cultural Fund, 365
Lithuanian SSR, 143, 148, 169–71, 178, 183, 200, 247–48, 288, 379–80. *See also* Druskenniki; Kaunas; Klaipeda; Ponevezhis; Trakai; Vilnius
Lithuanian SSR Philharmonic Society, 169–70
Liubarsky, Lazar, 37 n.17
Liuboshits, Emil, 47
Liudi, gody, zhizn' (People, Years, Life), 218, 222, 224
Lomovskaia, Ester, 53–54, 79–81, 89, 109, 165 n.74
Lomovskii, Volt, 47, 89, 109, 165 n.74
London, Jack, 284
Lukacs, Georg, 219
Lukianovskaia, 50
"Lullaby to Babii Iar," 179
Lunts, Aleksandr, 258
Lur'e, Liia, 147, 163 n.49, 164 n.57
Lurie, Jessie Zel, 126
Lutsk, 380
Lutsker, Mark, 59
Lutskii, V., 315
Lvov, 50, 150, 183, 277

Ma shohidum (I am a Witness), 422
Ma'aravi, Yosef Maman, 381
Maccabees, 48, 92–93, 97
Magarik, Aleksei, 246, 252–53, 254 n.1
Mahsum, 410

Maiakovskii, Vladimir, 179, 226
Makhachkala (Port-Petrovsk), 149, 385, 409
Maki. See Israeli Communist Party
Maksimov, Vladimir, 226
Malkin, Aleksandr, 148
Malkin, Karl, 148, 153, 164 n.58
Mandelshtam, Osip, 60, 104
Manger, Itzik, 177
Mankiewicz, Czeslaw, 329
Mapu, Avraham, 388, 400, 402
Marchenko, Anatolii, 21
Marina Roshcha Synagogue, 362
Mariupol Greeks, 396
Markish, David, 211
Markish, Perets, 171, 174, 191, 222–23
Marks i Engel's ob iskusstve (Marx and Engels on Art), 219
Marshak, Samuil, 202, 224
Marshall, S. L., 94, 97
Marshall Plan, 320
Marx, Karl, 76, 80
Marxism, 51–52, 219–20, 310–11, 321, 408, 452
Marxism-Leninism, 44, 51, 292, 323
Mary (Merv), 379
Mashad, 379–80
Maslahat na hunghar (Edifying Talk and Hunghar—A Popular Dish), 420
Matatov, M., 425
Matatov, Yahil, 411, 415
Matlab Siyuniho (The Goal of Zionists), 388
Mazanki, 398
Media, Soviet, 59, 120, 184, 191, 324, 326, 329–31, 333–37, 343–49, 449. See also *Leninskoe znamia; Moskovskaia pravda; Neues Leben; Pravda; Pravda Ukrainy; Sovetskaia Rossiia; Voprosy istorii*
Medini, Hayyim Hizkiyahu, 381
Meiman, Naum, 358
Meir, Golda, 30, 49, 98, 114–15, 332
Mekhlis, Lev, 230 n.10
Men, Aleksandr, 103
Mendelevich, Yosef, 110 n.31, 129 n.2, 256
Mendele Moikher Setorim. See Setorim, Mendele Moikher
Mensheviks, 311–12
Meras, Itshak, 227
Meskhetians, 293–94

Mevayi inquilob (Fruit of the Revolution), 407
MGB (Ministry of Internal Security), 115
Mikhailov, Nikolai, 172
Mikhoels, Solomon (Shlomo), 171, 176, 222–23, 317; Cultural Center, 462 n.33
Mikoian, Anastas, 294
Miller, Abraham, 287
Miller, Israel, 122
Mil'man, Vitalii, 258
Ministry of Culture, USSR, 169
Ministry of Education (RSFSR), 301
Minorities, Ethnic, 290–309, passim, 367–71. See also Avars; Balkars; Chechens; Chuvashes; Crimean Tatars; Germans; Greeks; Hungarians; Ingush; Kabardinians; Kalmyks; Koreans; Krymchaks; Meskhetians; Ossetians; Poles
Minority Schools in Albania, 367
Minsk, 41 n.44, 53, 89, 96, 113, 156–57, 172, 259, 274, 276, 278–79, 287, 317
Mints, I. I., 325
Mintz, Izrail', 145, 148, 153
Mizrahi, Avraham Safan (Tsafan), 386
Mnacko, Ladislaw, 94, 329
Moczar, Mieczyslaw, 330
Modigliani, Amedeo, 223
Modzhoian, L. Ia., 338
Mogilev-Podolsk, 48
Mogilever, Vladimir, 152
Moldavian SSR, 56, 213. See also Bessarabia; Kishinev
Molodaia gvardiia, 226
Mordekhaev, L., 405
Mordovian ASSR, 178
Mordzhinskaia, E. D., 338–39
Moredin, Nahman, 155
Mori, 148, 154–56
Moscow, 19–20, 28, 31, 36 n.8, 37 n.15, 49, 56, 58, 60–61, 69 n.1, 78, 89, 96, 98, 105, 113, 115–16, 118, 120, 122–36, 138, 140, 145, 151–54, 156, 171–73, 175–77, 181–82, 187 n.24, 200, 257, 259–60, 263–64, 266, 268–70, 274, 276, 284–87, 329, 334, 370, 459, 462 n.32
Moscow Cultural Symposium. See Symposium on Jewish Culture
Moscow Jewish Religious Society. See Choral Synagogue
Moscow Medical Institute, 49

INDEX   475

Moscow *obkom* (regional party committee), 208
Moscow *oblast' ispolkom* (executive committee), 208
Moscow Physics Institute, 183
Moscow State University, 56, 60, 140, 199, 300
Moskovskaia pravda, 362
Moskva, 209–10
Mountain Jews, 47, 109 n.10, 149, 259, 275, 281, 373, 379–81, 384–87, 395, 408–28 passim
Mughoray Soymishiho (The Lovers' Cave), 419
Muhbat (Love), 413
Muhib (Bachaev, Mordkhay), 403, 407
Mukachevo (Muncacz), 155
Murmansk, 173
Musakhanova, Galina, 418
My Glorious Brothers, 90, 92, 107

Nabinovich, Zavulun, 411, 415
Nakhshunova (Nahshunova), Maia, 418
Nalchik, 385, 410
Namangan, 170
Namir, Mordecai, 114
Nanni nanam (Lullaby), 422
Nasser, Gamal Abdul, 325, 328
National liberation movements, 311–12, 317, 337
Native Jewish National Central Bureau, 400
Navusdagorhoymu va Leninizm-bolshevizm (Our writers and Leninism-Bolshevism), 412
Nazi Germany and nazism, 7, 14, 139, 247–48, 277, 287, 328, 335, 337, 378, 395, 398. See also Hitler, Adolph; Holocaust
Neiborgen, Arnold, 92
Neiburger, Pinhas, 141, 161 n.23
Neizvestnyi, Ernst, 61
Nekrasov, Viktor, 225
Neo-Stalinism, 322, 336
Neshira, 455–57
Neues Leben, 303
New Economic Policy (NEP), 11, 314
New York Board of Rabbis, 122
New York Times, 341
Night in Babii Iar. See *Damskii Portnoi*

Nister, Der, 171
Nixon, Richard, 100, 446
NKVD, 293
Nojot (Deliverance), 405
Non-Ashkenazi Jewish Communities, 378–444 passim. See also Bukharan Jewish Community; Georgian SSR; Mountain Jews
North America, 17, 280. See also United States of America
Nosovskii, Mikhail, 154
Novorossiisk, 48, 384, 393
Novosibirsk, 78, 151, 165 n.74, 299
Novotny, Anotonin, 329–30
Novyi mir, 215, 219–21
Nudel'man, Rafael, 258, 260

"O Subbota," 207 n.44
"Ob iskrennosti v literature" (About Sincerity in Literature), 219
October Revolution, 193
Odabash, A., 393
Odessa, 44–45, 78, 89, 122, 125, 155, 173, 182, 209, 264, 274, 277, 334
Odomihoy vatanma, vikhda omora nuvusda chico (People of my Homeland, Selected Works), 419
Odomihoy yaki (Kith and Kin), 416
Ogonek, 226
Oktiabr', 226
Ontman, Liliia, 146, 148, 164 n.57
Oqilov, Yahiel, 403, 407
Oquy ishleri (Study Topics), 393
Orlov, Boris, 258
Ort, 314
Orwell, George, 336
Osherovich, Mendel, 176
Oshnahoy an rabi Hasdil (The Mistresses of Rabbi Hasdil, 410–11
Osipov, Vladimir, 63
Ossetians, 282
Otten, Nikolai, 217
Ottepel' (The Thaw), 220–21
Ottoman Empire, 381
Ovsishcher, Lev, 156

Pale of Settlement, 216, 224, 247
Paleoasian languages. See Ket

Palestine (pre-1948), 49–50, 113–14, 169, 312, 314–16
Palestine Communist Party, 313–14
The Palestine Problem (Genin), 318
The Palestine Problem (Lutskii), 315–16
Palestinian Arabs, 312–14, 328
Palhan, Moshe (Trakhtman), 248
Pamiat' (Memory), 322–23, 449. *See also* Anti-Semitism
Panerai, 287
Pardozov, P., 403
Paris, 173, 328
Parza ma'ni ma (Fly, My Song), 424
Pashmuni (Repentance), 424
Pasternak, Boris, 53
Paustovskii, Konstantin, 215, 224
Peace prayer book, 324
Pecherskii, Gennadii (Gedalia), 119–21, 147
Peerce, Jan, 186 n. 13
Peisakh, Y., 399
Pen, Alexander, 175, 177
Perakh, Mark, 44
Pereiaslav Khmel'nitskii, 286, 370
Perestroika, 447, 451
Perets, Y. L., 203
Permanent Court of International Justice (PCIJ), 367–89
Persia. *See* Iran
Persov, Shmuel, 191
Pervomaiskii, L., 334
Pinhosov, Asaf, 389
"Pinia from Zhmerinka," 217
Pinkas, Julius (Pascin), 223
Pinskii, Yisrael, 129 n.2, 161 n.18
Pinto, Avraham, 386
Piri bedin (The Old Atheist), 406
Pisari 'Alisho (Elisha's Son), 405
Pischal'nik, Igor', 161 n.23
Plekhanov, Georgii, 312
Plis, Vladimir (Ze'ev), 287
Plisetskaia, M. M., 334
Plotkin, Zvi, 140
Poale Zion (Zionist Socialist Party), 312–13, 408–9. *See also Evreiskaia proletarskaia mysl'*
Podol'skii, Boris, 175, 163 n.43
Podol'skii, Semen, 150
Podriadchick, Eliezer, 176, 178

Podshoh, rabi va 'oshir (The Tsar, the Rabbi and the Wealthy Man), 409
Pokras, Dmitrii, 170, 185 n.6
Poland, 6, 16, 20, 97, 142, 150, 176, 260, 280, 288, 329–31, 336, 342
Polarevich, Yehezkel, 182
Poles (Soviet), 282, 301
Polianskii, Dmitrii, 225
Polishchuk, Aleksandr, 210–11
Politics, Soviet, 43–44, 51, 62, 68, 297, 327
Pol'skii, Viktor, 138
Pol'tinnikov, Natan, 165 n.74
Pomerants, Grigorii, 63, 71 n.13
Pomerantsev, Vladimir, 219
Ponevezhis, 380
Posboni Vatan, 405
Povest' o zhizni (The Story of My Life), 215, 224
Prague trial. *See* Slansky
Pravda, 217–18, 225, 230 n.7, 320, 327, 332–33
Pravda Ukrainy, 335
Prawo i Zycie, 330
Pregerzon, Zvi, 140, 143, 150, 283
Prestin, Vladimir, 138, 153–54
Prisoners of Zion, 246, 253, 267, 445–46, 449
Prisons, 143–45, 147, 150, 158, 178, 191. *See also* Gomel; Karaganda; Lukianovskaia; Mordovia; Prisoners of Zion; Refuseniks; Siberia; Vorkuta
Prokof'ev, Dmitrii, 268–69
Prostye liudi (Common Folk), 419
Pulver, Lev, 170, 176
Pushkin, Alexander, 177, 416
Puteshestvie po Sovetskoi Armenii (Journey through Soviet Armenia), 219

Qalandarov, B., 405
Qarachay-Balkarian, 410
Qaytaqi, 384–85, 387
Qumiq, 385, 387, 418
Quvatti kolektivi (The Collective Strength), 407

Rabbinical Council of America, 121–22
Rabinovich, K., 37 n.16
Radio Moscow (in Hebrew), 269

INDEX   477

Radovskii, Aleksandr, 258
Rafes, Moishe, 197
Rahamim, 388
Rahel (Rahel Bluwstein), 175, 177
Raikin, Arkadii, 334
Ram, Bella, 258
Rasskazy o moikh zemliakakh (Tales About My Countrymen), 419
Ravel, Maurice, 177, 178
Ravinov, Len, 171
Ravvinovich, Efraim, 408
Ravvinovich-Gorskii, Herzl, 408–9, 415, 441 n.134
Reagan, Ronald, 446, 448
Refuseniks, 100, 196, 249, 252, 258, 263, 267, 359–60, 364, 366, 446, 456. See *also* Prisoners of Zion
Regelson, Lev, 57
Remenik, Hirsh, 156
Remenik, Ita, 156
Remeniuk, Elia, 276
"The Return of Breathing Consciousness," 214
Revolutsiyay kulturi va jofokashhoy juhuran doghi (The Cultural Revolution and the Toiling Mountain Jews), 412
Reykjavik. See Soviet-U.S. summits
Riga, 28, 36 n.26, 37 n.15, 78, 81, 89, 92, 96, 118, 124–26, 142, 149, 155, 161 n.17, 170, 176–78, 181–82, 247–48, 259, 264, 274, 277–78, 333–34
Rimsky-Korsakov, Nikolai, 170
Rishal', Vol'f, 145, 162 n.39
"*Risunok na dne*," 207 n.44
Rizhinashvili, Siman, 390
Robeson, Paul, 172
Roginskii, Vladimir, 154, 166 n.90
Roh ba zindagoni (The Way of Life), 405
Ro'i, Yaacov, 315, 354 n.80
Roitkop, Dina, 178
Rol'nikaite, Mariia, 227
Romania, 16, 334
Romania (Romaniot) rite, 381
Romano, Emmanuele, 223
Rosinas, Samuelis, 276
Rostov, 151
Rostropovich, Mstislav, 176
Rote Fahne, 303
Roth, Joseph, 223

Royzn, Berl, 202
RSFSR, 141, 171, 210, 274, 282, 301–2. See *also* Bashkir ASSR; Chernikhovsk; Dagestan ASSR; Gorkii; Kabardino-Balkar ASSR; Kaliningrad; Kalmyk ASSR; Kazan'; Khabarovsk; Komi SSR; Kuibyshev; Leningrad; Mordovian ASSR; Murmansk; Novorossiisk; Saratov; Siberia; Smolensk; Sovetsk; Stalingrad; Sverdlovsk; Tomsk; Ul'ianovsk
Rubin, Anatolii, 96, 146, 150
Rubin, Il'ia, 258
Rubin, Vitalii, 38 n.28, 44, 69 n.1
Rubinov, Rahamim, 411, 416
Rubinshtain, Abram, 137
Rubinshtein, Nataliia, 80–81
Rudin, Elisha, 283
Rumboli, 277
Russian culture, 12–13, 93, 213
Russian Empire, 318–82, 426
Russian language, 12–13, 18–19, 45, 78, 89, 93, 105, 170, 172, 176–77, 198–201, 203, 206 n.39, 207 n.44, 250–51, 261, 275, 374, 378, 383–86, 393–95, 397, 399, 401, 410, 417–18, 421, 426–27 n.51
Russian Social Democratic Labor Party, 312
Russkaia mysl'l, 256
Rutshtain, Leonid, 141, 163 n.46, 248–49
Rybak, Natan, 326, 334
Rybakov, Anatolii, 201–2, 282

Saam (language), 396
Sadoyi mihnat (The Voice of Labor), 407
Safanov, Shimshun, 423
Saidov, Aharun, 406–7
Sakharov, Andrei, 255
Salomonov, Natan, 409, 411, 416
SALT II, 445, 447
Saltykov-Shchedrin Library, 142, 146
Samandarov, Gavriel, 405–6
Samarkand, 89, 124, 170, 286, 385, 397, 401–4
Samizdat (unofficial literature), 32–33, 39 n.35, 41 n.45, 52, 55, 62, 68, 73–111 passim, 194, 200, 229, 255–61 passim, 276, 332, 338. See *also Evrei v SSSR; Evreiskii samizdat; Iskhod; Iton; Tarbut*
Sandler, Boris, 196

Saratov, 116, 141
Schell, Jonathan, 450
Schiff, J., 335
Schwartz-Bart, André, 90, 255
Secret Speech, 192, 221
Sefer hinukh hane'arim (Book for the Education of Adolescents), 390
Seforim, Mendele Moikher, 113, 203, 247
Segal, Dmitrii, 258
Segal, Shmuel, 164 n.57
SEM (Union of Jewish Youth), 50
Semendueva (Simanduyeva), Zoia, 424
Semenov, Yuno, 409–11, 413
Semichastnyi, Vladimir, 329
Senderei, Samuil' (Shaul), 170
Sendero, V. A., 358
Sephardi (Spanish) rite, 381
Serlo (Light), 410–11, 422 n.148
Sevastopol, 398
Sevella, Efraim, 45
Shaevich, Adolf, 287
Shaginian, Marietta, 217, 219
Shakespeare, William, 388
Shakhnovskii, Vladimir, 153–54
Shamiakin, Ivan, 210
Shapiro, Feliks,137, 147–48, 284
Shapiro, Sara, 258
Sharbatov, P., 409
Shcharansky, Natan, 268, 453–54
Shchliakhami zhittia (In the Path of Life), 227
Shekhtman, Eli, 193, 204 n.7
Shelepin, Aleksandr, 329
Shepshelovits, Mikhail, 36 n.6
Sherenshtein, Luiza, 276
Shevardnadze, Eduard, 6, 462 n.32
Shevtsov, Ivan, 225
Shifrin, Avram, 79, 150
Shimanov, Gennadii, 103
Shinkar', Mordekhai, 150
Shipler, David, 448
"Shir hashirim," 170
Shish sharti rafiq Stalin (The Six Conditions of Comrade Stalin), 406
Shlifer, Shlomo, 114–15, 121, 133 n.56
Shlonsky, Avraham, 177
Shmerler, Esfir, 149, 165 n.74
Shmukler, Iuliia, 56, 258
Shnaider, Iosif, 53–54, 178

Shneur, Zalman, 175
Sholem Aleichem. *See* Aleichem, Sholem
Sholumov, Manashir, 409
Shor (language), 396
Shperber, Efim, 141–42, 161 n.23
Shrofter, Ben-Zion, 155
Shturman, Dora, 53
Shubin, Moshe, 149
"*Shulamith*," 170
Shul'ner, Efim, 141–42
Shultz, George, 448–49, 454
Shuvar an du hovu (The Husband of Two Wives), 420
Shvartsblat, Izrail, 287
Siberia, 81, 144, 258, 300. *See also* Novosibirsk; Tomsk; Vladivostok
Siddur. *See* Peace prayer book
Sik, Ota, 331
Silver, Ditza, 269
Silver, Valerii, 269
Simes, Dmitri K., 457–58
Simferopol, 383, 384, 392, 398–99
Simon, Bohumul, 327
Simonov, Konstantin, 220, 328
Sinai War, 31, 38 n.24
Sinamishi (The Test), 421
Sino-American relations 460 n.2
Sinyavsky-Daniel trial, 332
Six Day War, 16, 30, 32, 35, 37 n.22, 38 n.25, 41 n.43, 58–59, 89, 94, 107, 149, 210–11, 249, 259–60, 262, 329, 332
Sixth World Festival of Youth and Students, 38 n.23, 145, 187 n.24
Slansky-Gemeinder trial, 214, 318, 320–21
Slavs, 6. *See also* Great Russians
Slepak, Vladimir, 99
Slovin, Boris, 81, 92
Slovin, Leah (Lidiia), 91, 94, 178
Slutskii, Boris, 86 n.6, 228–29
Smirnov, A. A., 154
Smirnov, Vasilii, 226
Smolensk, 172
Smrkovsky, Josef, 331
Snieckus, Antanas, 169, 185 n.5
Sofronov, Anatolii, 217
Soiuz, 208–12
Solzhenitsyn, Aleksandr, 63, 71 n.15, 214, 224–25, 255

"Song of the Murdered Jewish People," 398
Songs, Israeli, 38 n.22, 40 n.40, 126, 145–46, 158, 175
Songs, Jewish, 18, 20, 56, 126, 170, 173, 176, 184, 187 n.24, 277–78, 370. *See also* Lifshitz, Nehama; Songs, Yiddish
Songs, Yiddish, 20, 169, 171, 173–74, 176–77, 181. *See also* Lifshitz, Nehama
Sotnikova, Emma, 258
Sovetish heymland, 15, 18, 106, 191–207 passim, 277, 279–80, 282–83, 285, 302, 324, 339–40, 364–65, 425. *See also* Bibliotek
Sovetsk, 171
Sovetskaia etnografiia, 425
Sovetskaia Rossiia, 210, 426
Soviet Hungarians, 301
Soviet-Israeli Friendship Society, 458
Soviet Jewry: attitude toward USSR, 45, 47, 50, 52–55, 57–59, 72 n.17, 298; and economic status, 31, 34; and education of, 7–8, 15, 22, 42, 45, 65, 274, 299, 357–58; and Jewish education of, 12, 15, 37 n.15, 44, 62, 65, 144–45, 149, 247, 258, 262, 264, 276, 287, 300, 358, 369, 372–73, 392–93, 400–402, 435 n.63, 456; and national movement of, 34, 42–72 passim, 73, 78, 80–81, 86, 88, 91–92, 106–7, 125, 127–28, 146, 150, 169, 173, 182, 184, 208–31 passim, 248, 257, 458; and youth, 43–44, 46, 49–56, 58, 117–18, 147; *See also* Anti-Semitism; Intelligentsia, Jewish; Jewish religion
Soviet policy, toward: emigration, 16–17, 54, 57, 65, 95, 183, 247–48, 252, 263, 314, 317–18, 323, 326–27, 331, 341, 363, 365, 445–49, 453, 460 n.1, n.2; extraterritorial national minorities, 6, 290–309 passim; human rights, 452–53, 457–58; inernal passports, 5–7, 10, 293, 425; Israel, 16–17, 139, 147, 246, 248, 280, 302, 310–54 passim; Jewish activism, 34, 52–53, 106, 114–15, 139–40, 147, 150, 262, 314, 326, 333; Jewish culture, 11, 171–72, 184, 262, 273, 277, 281, 284, 300, 318–19, 407–8, 411, 414, 424, 427, Jewish publications, 89; Jewish religion, 19, 116, 137, 371, 392, 427, 449; language, 136–67 passim, 177, 246, 253, 275, 358, 360–61, 372–74, 391, 396, 401, 434 n.51, 449; Middle East, 310, 315, 319, 325, 328, 337, 342–43; nationalities, 44, 292, 425; religion, 63, 275, 292, 359, 361–62, 371, 391, 427; Soviet bloc, 329–31, 334; Soviet Jewry, 42, 49, 54–55, 107, 168, 247, 262, 366, 370, 407, 445–62; Third World, 338; United States, 27, 445–62 passim
Soviet-U.S. summits: 446; Reykjavik (1986), 448–49; San Clemente (1973), 446; Vienna (1979), 445; Washington (1987), 446, 449
Soviet Writers' Union, 191, 220, 302
Sovetskii Dagestan, 425
Sovremennyi iazyk ivrit, 285
Spain, 381
Stalin, Joseph, 9, 209, 213, 217, 219–20, 226, 248, 262, 275, 292, 295, 304, 319–23, 336, 342, 406, 419, 451
Stalin Prize, 214, 219
Stalingrad, 82, 141
Stalinism 7, 9, 11, 13, 36 n.5, 66, 85, 114, 119, 137, 143, 192, 214, 217, 219, 225, 247, 322, 330, 334, 336–38, 340–43. *See also* De-Stalinization
Starkova, Klavdiia, 147
Staskaviciute, Aleksandra, 171
Stevenson, Adlai, 460 n.1
Stevenson, Robert Louis, 284
Stevenson amendment, 445, 458
Stimson, Henry, 450
Strategic Defense Initiative (SDI), 448
Suez crisis (1956), 325–26, 329. *See also* Sinai War
Sukhumi, 89, 393
Sukonik, Aleksandr, 68
Sulaymoni, Payrav, 404
Surov, Aleksei, 216, 230 n.7
Svechinskii, Vitalii, 49–51
Sverdlovsk, 89, 141–42, 155
Svetlov, Mikhail, 83
Svirskii, Aleksei, 215–16
Svirskii, Grigorii, 227
Swift Sword, 94, 97
Symposium on Jewish Culture (Moscow, 1976), 105–8, 238–45, 262–63
Synagogues, 18–19, 34, 37 n.15, 49, 112–35 passim 145, 155. *See also* Choral Syn-

Synagogues (*continued*)
  agogue; Gaon's Synagogue; Jewish religion; Leningrad Synagogue; Marina Roshcha Synagogue
Syria, 328–29

Tabasarani, 385, 387
Tadzhik SSR, 209, 379, 387–88, 397, 400. *See also* Dushanbe; Gissar Valley; Leninabad
Tajer, Shlomo, 386
Tal, Siddi, 177
Tallinn, 171, 177, 213, 278
Tarbut, 102, 105, 108, 261, 403, 409
Tartu, 171
Tashkent, 48, 124, 157, 170, 274, 385, 397, 410, 403–4
Tat People's Theater (Inter-*Kolkhoz* Tat Theater), 424, 444 n.172
Tatar (language), 209
Tbilisi (Tiflis), 116, 137, 149, 157, 268, 284, 301, 334, 379, 385–86
Tblisi State University, 137
Teller, Edward, 450–51
Temkin, Aleksandr, 258
Tevia the Milkman, 270
Theater, Israeli, 269
Theater, Jewish, 18–19, 113, 174–75, 277–80, 370. *See also* Habima; Jewish Chamber Music Theater; Jewish Drama Studio Theater; Tat People's Theater
Theater, Yiddish, 168–69, 177, 269, 303. *See also* Birobidzhan Drama Theater; Goset
Third World, 312, 337
Tiazhelyi pesok (*Heavy Sands*), 201, 282
Tiflis Congress of the Zionists of the Caucasus, 432 n.25
Tito, Josip Broz, 320
Tlia (*The Louse*), 225
Tokarev, S., 295
Tolkachev, Zinovii, 276
Tolmach imama (*The Interpreter of the Imam*), 420
Tolstoy, Leo, 177, 199
Tomsk, 78, 81
Topper, Ino, 176
Tourists, in USSR, 120, 122, 139, 149, 155–56, 253, 284, 324

Toza maskan (*The New Dwelling Place*), 424
Trade Reform Act. *See* Jackson-Vanik amendment
Trakai, 380
Trakhtman, Mikhail. *See* Palhan, Moshe
Treplekh aroyf tsu a nes (*Stairs to a Miracle*), 196
Trevgoda, Aia (Khaya Isaackovna Haya), 393
Trotsky, Leon, 314, 320
Truman, Harry, 450
Tsadikov, Aleksandr, 147, 163 n.48
Tsamerian, I., 295
Tsarapkin, Semen, 316
Tsentroizdat, 412
Tsetlin, Mikhail ("Amari"), 223
Tshernin, Velvl (Vladimir), *See* Chernin, Velvl
Tsinberg (Zinberg), Yisroel, 197
Tsirul'nikov, Natan, 146–47
Tsitsuashvili, Gershon, 149
Tsitsuashvili, Mikhail, 149
Tskhinvali, 382, 386
Tsur, Ya'acov, 456
Tuhmat (*The Blood Libel*), 405
Tungus-Manchurian languages. *See* Ude
Turjeman, Yisrael, 386
Turkestan (Turkestanskii krai), 385–86, 400
Turkic languages. *See* Karaitic Crimean Tatar; Urum; Shor
Turkmen SSR, 379. *See also* Ashkhabad; Bairani-Ali; Iolantan; Maryi
Tuwim, Julian, 223
Tuyi Zaevu Adino (*The Wedding of Zeev and Adina*), 406
Tvardovskii, Aleksandr, 220
Twentieth Party Congress, 54, 302, 321, 324. *See also* Secret Speech.
Twenty-Eighth Zionist Congress, 333
Tyshler, Aleksandr, 223, 276

Uchitel' (*The Teacher*), 424
Ude (language), 396
Udin (language), 385
Ukrainian SSR, 13, 31, 56, 109 n.10, 113, 116, 171–73, 215, 269, 278, 293, 298, 302, 334, 336, 380–81. *See also* Chernov-

tsy; Dnepropetrovsk; Galich; Kharkov; Kiev; Lutsk; Lvov; Mogilev-Podolsk; Mukachevo; Odessa; Pereiaslav Khmel'nitskii; Vinnitsa; Zhmerinka
Ulanovskaia, Maia, 53, 58
Ul'ianovsk, 141
Ul'ianovskii, Lev, 154
Ulpanim, 139, 147, 150–53, 155–57, 167 n.97, n.98, 175, 250–51, 361. *See also* Hebrew
"Umar Conditions," 382
Undzer shtetl brent (Our Small Town is Burning, 181
Union of Hebrew Teachers in the USSR, 458
Union of Writers of the USSR, 177, 269
United Nations, 248, 278, 316, 328, 332, 338, 357
U.N. Atomic Energy Commission, 450
UNESCO, 153; Convention Against Discrimination in Education, 357, 368–69, 372–73
United States of America, 19, 22, 196, 210, 315, 335, 337, 341, 354 n.80, 455, 460 n.3; and relations with USSR, 27, 445–62 passim. *See also* Détente; Soviet-U.S. summits
U.S.A.-Economics, Politics, Ideology, 340–41
U.S. Commerce Department, 445
U.S. Congress, 445, 455
Universal Declaration of Human Rights (UDHR), 357, 361, 362, 365
Ural Polytechnical Institute, 55–56
Uris, Leon, 39 n.35, 89–92
Urum (language), 396
Usdo (The Master), 423
USSR Academy of Sciences, 211. *See also* Institute of Ethnography; Institute of Oriental Studies; Institute of the Peoples of Asia and Africa
USSR Constitution (1977), 136, 184, 356, 360, 363, 365
Utkin, Iosif, 83
'Uzat jofora (Honor to Labor), 415
Uzbek SSR, 168, 170, 209, 270, 379, 400, 401, 404–5. *See also* Andizhan; Bukhara; Fergana; Fergana Valley; Kokand; Namangan; Samarkand; Tashkent; Turkestan

V nachale zhizni (At the Beginning of Life), 224
Vaisblit, Petr, 155
Vaisman, Barukh, 150, 165 n.67
Valentina Tershkova, 423
Valk, Eli, 148, 164 n.55
Vanik, Charles, 460 n.1
Vartashen (Shirvan, dialect), 384–85
Vasilevskii, Pavel, 56–57
Vataghachiho (The Fisherman), 414
Vatan sovetimu (Our Soviet Homeland) [Nuvusdagorhoy tati (Tat Writers)], 281, 418, 424–25
Veps (language), 396
Verdi, Giuseppe, 170
Vergelis, Aron, 106, 192, 195–97, 202, 206 n.33, 280, 286
Vienna, 173, 445
Vilna Teachers Institute, 393
Vilnius, 19, 36n.6, 89, 95, 140, 142, 155, 170, 172, 176–79, 182, 200, 264, 274, 278, 287–88, 380
Vilnius Jewish Museum, 287–88
Vilnius Music Academy, 169
Vilsker, Leyb, 197, 205 n.13, 284
Vinaver, Iakov, 59
Viner, Iuliia, 255
Vinnikov, Isak, 137
Vinnitsa, 143, 172
"Violetta," 170
Vladimirova, Liia, 258
Vladivostok, 142
Vladivostok agreement, 40
Vo imia ottsa i syna (In the Name of the Father and the Son), 225
Voice of Israel *(Kol Israel)*, 116, 148, 151, 164 n.57, 166 n.76, 269
Voitovetskii, Froim, 55
Voitovetskii, Il'ia, 55–56
Vokhurdai an sar bilogh (Encounter at the Spring), 419–20
Vol'f, Efraim, 50
Volin, A., 258
Voloshin, Arkadii, 156
Volvovskii, Ari, 253
Voprosy istorii, 425
Vorkuta, 143, 150
Voronel, Aleksandr, 15, 52, 88, 104
Voronel', Nina, 258

Voygay dul (The Heart's Desire), 424
Vtorzhenie bez oruzh'iia (An Invasion Without Arms), 339–40

War and Peace, 199
Warburg, F., 335
"Warm Lands," 170
Warsaw ghetto, 97
Watson, Thomas, 445–46
"We the Polish Jews," 223
Weizmann, Chaim, 317
"Western Territories" (annexed during and after World War II), 14, 16, 31, 47, 139, 150, 254, 259
"What is the People I," 210–11
Wiesel, Elie, 99, 118–19, 181, 462 n.33
World Jewish Congress, 449, 458, 462 n.33
World War II, 14, 47–49, 74, 121, 209, 315, 334
World Zionist Organization, 321. *See also* Twenty-Eighth Zionist Congress
Writers' Union. *See* Union of Writers of the USSR

Yahudaev, Mushe, 405–6
Yatimchaho (The Little Orphans), 405
Yeshiva, 124 (Habad). *See also* Kol Yaacov Yeshiva
Yeshiva University, 287
Yiddish culture, 13–15, 18–19, 154, 191, 273–89 passim, 300, 302, 318–19, 373–75, 458. *See also* Literature, Yiddish; Songs, Yiddish; Theater, Yiddish; Yiddish (language)
Yiddish (language), 10–13, 16–17, 19, 37 n.17, 45, 55–56, 89, 105–6, 136, 160 n.14, 176–78, 182, 194, 196, 198–201, 203, 206 n.39, 207 n.44, 246, 273, 275, 278, 361, 366, 373–75
Yiddish State Theater. *See* Goset
Yishuv (Jewish settlement in Palestine before 1948), 312, 314, 316–17
Yissakharov, Hizquiyo, 386
Yom Kippur War, 40 n.42
"Your Victory", 74–86 passim, 90
Youth Festival (1957). *See* Sixth World Festival of Youth and Students
Yugoslavia, 334

Yusufov, Semen (Shim'un), 424
Yusupov, A., 403
Yusupov, K., 407

Za pravoe delo (For the Right Cause), 217
Zabara, Natan, 193
Zahmatkash (The Toiler), 411, 415
Zalozhniki, 227
Zanbaba (The Stepmother), 414
Zanbirar (The Sister-in-Law), 420
Zand, Michael, 36 n.12, 88, 137, 153, 164 n.55, 211
Zanho o kolkhoz (Women in the Kolkhoz), 413
Zanhoy doghi (The Women Mountaineers), 122
Zarblu jofo ("Shock" Work), 413
Zaretskii, Isak, 140
Zaretskii, Vladimir, 140, 164 n.57
Zarifi, Gulam, 404
Zashumiat sady (The Gardens Will Rustle), 419
Zaslavskii, David (Dovid), 197, 327
Zavod Dagogni (The Plant "Lights of Dagestan"), 423
Zelichonok, Ruald, 253
Zhdanov, Andrei, 319
Zhizn' i sud'ba (Life and Fate), 229
Zhmerinka, 49–50
Zil'berman, David, 178
Zil'berman, Grigorii, 145–46, 163 n.43
Zindagoniyi nav (New Life), 405
Zinger, Lev, 285
Zingeris, Emmanuelis, 18, 288
Zionism, 8, 16–18, 21, 39, 47, 49–50, 53–55, 64–66, 81, 90–91, 96, 116, 127, 137–38, 141, 144–45, 156–57, 161 n.17, 178–83, 210–11, 224, 247, 302, 306, 310–54 passim, 390, 408–9, 426, 432 n.25, 455, 458
Zionist youth groups, 49, 56, 113. *See also* Dvasun; Eynikeyt; Hehaluts; SEM
Znamia, 74, 78
Zoia, 423
Zubin, M., 107
Zulmi boyon (Oppression by the Rich), 404
Zuskin, Binyomin, 171
Zusman-Epshtain, Shoshana, 146, 163 n.49